**THE ANATOMY
OF PROGRAMMING LANGUAGES**

THE ANATOMY
OF PROGRAMMING
LANGUAGES

Alice E. Fischer

University of New Haven

Frances S. Grodzinsky

Sacred Heart University

Prentice Hall, Englewood Cliffs, New Jersey 07632

Library of Congress Cataloging-in-Publication Data

FISCHER, ALICE E.
   The anatomy of programming languages / Alice E. Fischer, Frances
S. Grodzinsky.
     p.   cm.
   Includes index.
   ISBN 0-13-035155-5
   1. Programming languages (Electronic computers) I. Grodzinsky,
Frances Schlamowitz. II. Title.
   QA76.7.F57 1993
   005.13–dc20
                                                          92-16937
                                                          CIP

Acquisitions Editor: Bill Zobrist
Supplements Editor: Alice Dworkin
Prepress Buyer: Linda Behrens
Manufacturing Buyer: Dave Dickey
Copy Editor: Nikki Herbst
Cover Design: Bruce Kenselaar
Cover Art: Uniphoto
Editorial Assistant: Danielle Robinson

 ©1993 by Prentice-Hall, Inc.
A Paramount Communications Company
Englewood Cliffs, New Jersey 07632

The author and publisher of this book have used their best efforts in preparing
this book. These efforts include the development, research, and testing of the
theories and programs to determine their effectiveness. The author and
publisher make no warranty of any kind, expressed or implied, with regard to
these programs or the documentation contained in this book. The author and
publisher shall not be liable in any event for incidental or consequential
damages in connection with, or arising out of, the furnishing, performance, or
use of these programs.

Printed in the United States of America

10 9 8 7 6 5 4 3 2

ISBN 0-13-035155-5

PRENTICE-HALL INTERNATIONAL (UK) LIMITED, *London*
PRENTICE-HALL OF AUSTRALIA PTY. LIMITED, *Sydney*
PRENTICE-HALL CANADA, INC., *Toronto*
PRENTICE-HALL HISPANOAMERICANA, S.A., *Mexico*
PRENTICE-HALL OF INDIA PRIVATE LIMITED, *New Delhi*
PRENTICE-HALL OF JAPAN, INC., *Tokyo*
SIMON & SCHUSTER ASIA PTE. LTD., *Singapore*
EDITORA PRENTICE-HALL DO BRASIL, LTDA., *Rio de Janeiro*

We dedicate this work to our bridge partners

We dedicate this work to our fellow partners

Contents

Exhibits Listed by Topic

0.1.1 LANGUAGES

Ada

FORTH

FORTRAN

LISP

Miranda

Pascal

Scheme

Prolog

Other Languages

0.1.2   CONCEPTS

Language Design and Specification

Lambda Calculus

Control structures

Types

Application Modeling, Generics, and Polymorphic Domains

History

Preface

This text is intended for a course in advanced programming languages or the structure of programming language and should be appropriate for students at the junior, senior, or master's level. It should help the student understand the principles that underlie all languages and all language implementations.

This is a comprehensive text which attempts to dissect language and explain how a language is really built. The first eleven chapters cover the core material: language specification, objects, expressions, control, and types. The more concrete aspects of each topic are presented first, followed by a discussion of implementation strategies and the related semantic issues. Later chapters cover current topics, including modules, object-oriented programming, functional languages, and concurrency constructs.

The emphasis throughout the text is on semantics and abstraction; the syntax and historical development of languages are discussed in light of the underlying semantical concepts. Fundamental principles of computation, communication, and good design are stated and are used to evaluate various language constructs and to demonstrate that language designs are improving as these principles become widely understood.

Examples are cited from many languages including Pascal, C , C++, FORTH, BASIC, LISP, FORTRAN, Ada, COBOL, APL, Prolog, Turing, Miranda, and Haskell. All examples are annotated so that a student who is unfamiliar with the language used can understand the meaning of the code and see how it illustrates the principle.

It is the belief of the authors that the student who has a good grasp of the structure of computer languages will have the tools to master new languages easily.

The specific goals of this book are

- To reason clearly about programming languages.

- To develop principles of communication so that we can evaluate the wisdom and utility of the decisions made in the process of language design.

- To break down language into its major components, and each into small pieces so that we can focus on competing alternatives.

- To define a consistent and general set of terms for the components out of which programming languages are built, and the concepts on which they are based.

- To use these terms to describe existing languages, and in so doing clarify the conflicting terminology used by the language designers and untangle the complexities inherent in so many languages.

- To see below the surface appearance of a language to its actual structure and descriptive power.

- To understand that many language features that commonly occur together are, in fact, independent and separable. To appreciate the advantages and disadvantages of each feature. To suggest ways in which these basic building blocks can be recombined in new languages with more desirable properties and fewer faults.

- To see the similarities and differences that exist among familiar languages and to learn new ones.

- To use the understanding so gained to suggest future trends in language design.

ACKNOWLEDGMENTS

The authors are indebted to several people for their help and support during the years we have worked on this project. First, we wish to thank our families for their uncomplaining patience and understanding.

We thank Michael J. Fischer for his help in developing the sections on lambda calculus, functional languages and logic, and for working out several sophisticated code examples. In addition, his assistance as software and hardware systems expert and TeX guru made this work possible.

Several reviewers read this work in detail and offered invaluable suggestions and corrections. We thank these people for their help: Dirk Grunwald, *University of Colorado*; Karl Abrahamson, *Washington State University*; James F. Peters, III, *University of Arkansas*; V. S. Sunderam, *Emory University*. Special thanks go to Robert Fischer and Roland Lieger for reading beyond the call of duty and to Gary Walters for his advice and for the material he has contributed.

Finally, we thank our students and colleagues at the University of New Haven and at Sacred Heart University for their feedback on the many versions of this book.

Parts of this manuscript were developed under a grant from Sacred Heart University.

THE ANATOMY
OF PROGRAMMING LANGUAGES

PART

1

ABOUT LANGUAGE

1

The Nature of Language

───── **Overview** ───────────────────────────────────

      This chapter introduces the concept of the nature of language. The purpose of language is communication. A set of symbols, understood by both sender and receiver, is combined according to a set of rules, its grammar or syntax. The semantics of the language defines how each grammatically correct sentence is to be interpreted. Using English as a model, language structures are studied and compared. The issue of standardization of programming languages is examined. Nonstandard compilers are examples of the use of deviations from an accepted standard.

This is a book about the structure of programming languages. (For simplicity, we shall use the term "language" to mean "programming language".) We will try to look beneath the individual quirks of familiar languages and examine the essential properties of language itself. Several aspects of language will be considered, including vocabulary, syntax rules, meaning (semantics), implementation problems, and extensibility. We will consider several programming languages, examining the choices made by language designers that resulted in the strengths, weaknesses, and particular character of each language. When possible, we will draw parallels between programming languages and natural languages.

      Different languages are like tools in a toolbox: although each language is capable of expressing most algorithms, some are obviously more appropriate for certain applications than others. (You can use a chisel to turn a screw, but it is not a good idea.) For example, it is commonly understood that COBOL is "good for" business applications. This is true because COBOL provides a large variety of symbols for controlling input and output formats, so that business reports may easily be made to fit printed forms. LISP is "good for" artificial intelligence applications because it supports dynamically growing and shrinking data. We will consider how well each language models the objects, actions, and relationships inherent in various classes of applications.

Rather than accept languages as whole packages, we will be asking:

- What design decisions make each language different from the others?
- Are the differences a result of minor syntactic rules, or is there an important underlying semantic issue?
- Is a controversial design decision necessary to make the language appropriate for its intended use, or was the decision an accident of history?
- Could different design decisions result in a language with more strengths and fewer weaknesses?
- Are the good parts of different languages mutually exclusive, or could they be effectively combined?
- Can a language be extended to compensate for its weaknesses?

1.1 COMMUNICATION

A natural language is a symbolic communication system that is commonly understood among a group of people. Each language has a set of symbols that stand for objects, properties, actions, abstractions, relations, and the like. A language must also have rules for combining these symbols. A speaker can communicate an idea to a listener if and only if they have a common understanding of enough symbols and rules. Communication is impaired when speaker and listener interpret a symbol differently. In this case, either speaker and/or listener must use feedback to modify his or her understanding of the symbols until commonality is actually achieved. This happens when we learn a new word or a new meaning for an old word, or correct an error in our idea of the meaning of a word.

English is for communication among people. Programs are written for both computers and people to understand. Using a programming language requires a mutual understanding between a person and a machine. This can be more difficult to achieve than understanding between people because machines are so much more literal than human beings.

The meaning of symbols in natural language is usually defined by custom and learned by experience and feedback. In contrast, programming languages are generally defined by an authority, either an individual language designer or a committee. For a computer to "understand" a human language, we must devise a method for translating both the syntax and semantics of the language into machine code. Language designers build languages that they know how to translate, or that they believe they can figure out how to translate.

On the other hand, if computers were the only audience for our programs we might be writing code in a language that was trivially easy to transform into machine code. But a programmer must be able to understand what he or she is writing, and a human cannot easily work at the level of detail that machine language represents. So we use computer languages that are a compromise between the needs of the speaker (programmer) and listener (computer). Declarations, types, symbolic names, and the like are all concessions to a human's need to understand what someone has written. The concession we make for computers is that we write programs in languages that can be translated with relative ease into machine language. These languages have limited vocabulary and limited syntax. Most belong to a class called *context-free languages*, which can be parsed easily using a stack. Happily, as our skill at translation has increased, the variety and power of symbols in our programming languages have also increased.

The language designer must define sets of rules and symbols that will be commonly understood among both human and electronic users of the language. The *meaning* of these symbols is generally conveyed to people by the combination of a formal semantic description, analogy with other languages, and examples. The meaning of symbols is conveyed to a computer by writing small modules of machine code that define the action to be taken for each symbol. The rules of syntax are conveyed to a computer by writing a compiler or interpreter.

To learn to use a new computer language effectively, a user must learn exactly what combinations of symbols will be accepted by a compiler and what actions will be invoked for each symbol in the language. This knowledge is the required common understanding. When the human communicates with a machine, he must modify *his own* understanding until it matches the understanding of the machine, which is embodied in the language translator. Occasionally the translator fails to "understand" a phrase correctly, as specified by the official language definition. This happens when there is an error in the translator. In this case the "understanding" of the translator must be corrected by the language implementor.

1.2 SYNTAX AND SEMANTICS

The *syntax of a language* is a set of rules stating how language elements may be grammatically combined. Syntax specifies how individual words may be written and the order in which words may be placed within a sentence.

The semantics of a language define how each grammatically correct sentence is to be interpreted. In a given language, the *meaning* of a sentence in a compiled language is the object code compiled for that sentence. In an interpreted language, it is the internal representation of the program, which is then evaluated. *Semantic rules* specify the meaning attached to each placement of a word in a sentence, the meaning of omitting a sentence element, and the meaning of each individual word. A speaker (or programmer) has an idea that he or she wishes to communicate. This idea is the speaker's *semantic intent*. The programmer must choose words that have the correct semantics so that the listener (computer) can correctly interpret the speaker's semantic intent.

All languages have syntax and semantics. Chapter 4 discusses formal mechanisms for expressing the syntax of a language. The rest of this book is primarily concerned with semantics, the semantics of particular languages, and the semantic issues involved in programming.

1.3 NATURAL LANGUAGES AND PROGRAMMING LANGUAGES

We will often use comparisons with English to encourage you to examine language structures intuitively, without preconceived ideas about what programming languages can or cannot do. The objects and functions of a program correspond to the nouns and verbs of natural language. (We will use the word "functions" to apply to functions, procedures, operators, and some commands. Objects include variables, constants, records, and so on.)

There are a number of language traits that determine the character of a language. In this section we compare the ways in which these traits are embodied in a natural language (English) and in various programming languages. The differences between English and programming languages are real, but not as great as they might at first seem. The differences are less extreme now than they were ten years ago and will decrease as programming languages continue to evolve. Current programming language research is directed toward:

- Easing the constraints on the order in which statements must be given.
- Increasing the uses of symbols with multiple definitions.
- Permitting the programmer to talk about and use an object without knowing details of its representation.
- Facilitating the construction of libraries, thus increasing the number of words that can be understood "implicitly."
- Increasing the ability of the language to express varied properties of the problem situation, especially relationships among classes of objects.

1.3.1 Structure

Programs must conform to very strict structural rules. These govern the order of statements and sections of code, and particular ways to begin, punctuate, and end every program. No deviation from these rules is permitted by the language definition, and this is enforced by a compiler.

The structure of English is more flexible and more varied, but rules about the structure of sentences and of larger units do exist. The overall structure of a textbook or a novel is tightly controlled. Indeed, each kind of written material has some structure it must follow. In any situation where the order of events is crucial, such as in a recipe, English sentences must be placed in the "correct" sequence, just like the lines in a program.

Deviation from the rules of structure is permitted in informal speech, and understanding can usually still be achieved. A human listener usually attempts to correct a speaker's obvious errors. For example, scrambled words can often be put in the right order. We can correct and understand the sentence: "I yesterday finished the assignment." Spoonerisms (exchanging the first letters of nearby words, often humorously) can usually be understood. For example, "I kee my sids" was obviously intended to mean "I see my kids". A human uses common sense, context, and poorly defined heuristics to identify and correct such errors.

Most programming language translators are notable for their intolerance of a programmer's omissions and errors. A compiler will identify an error when the input text fails to correspond to the syntactic rules of the language (a "syntax error") or when an object is used in the wrong context (a "type error"). Most translators make some guesses about what the programmer really meant, and try to continue with the translation, so that the programmer gets maximum feedback from each attempt to compile the program. However, compilers can rarely correct anything more than a trivial punctuation error. They commonly make faulty guesses which cause the generation of heaps of irrelevant and confusing error comments.

Some compilers actually do attempt to correct the programmer's errors by adding, changing, respelling, or ignoring symbols so that the erroneous statement is made syntactically legal. If the attempted correction causes trouble later, the compiler may return to the line with the error and try a different correction. This effort has had some success. Errors such as misspellings and errors close to the end of the code can often be corrected and enable a successful translation. Techniques have been developed since the mid-1970s and are still being improved. Such error-correcting compilers are uncommon because of the relatively great cost for added time and extra memory needed. Some people feel that the added costs exceed the added utility.

1.3.2 Redundancy

The syntactic structure of English is highly redundant. The same information is often conveyed by several words or word endings in a sentence. If required redundancy is absent, as in the sentence "I finishes the assignment tomorrow", we can identify that errors have occurred. The lack of agreement between "I" and "finishes" is a syntactic error, and the disagreement of the verb tense (present) with the meaning of "tomorrow" is a semantic error. [Exhibit 1.1]

Exhibit 1.1.   Redundancy in English.

The subject and verb of a sentence must "agree" in number. Either both must be singular or both plural:

Correct:	Mark likes the cake.	Singular subject, singular verb.
Wrong:	Mark like the cake.	Singular subject, plural verb.

The verb tense must agree with any time words in the sentence:

Correct:	I finished the work yesterday.	Past tense, past time.
Wrong:	I finish the work yesterday.	Present tense, past time.

Where categories are mentioned, words belonging to the correct categories must be used.

Correct:	The color of my coat is black.	Black is a color.
Wrong:	The color of my coat is back.	Back is not a color.

Sentences must supply consistent information throughout a paragraph. Pronouns refer to the preceding noun. A pronoun must not suddenly be used to refer to a different noun.

Correct:	The goalie is my son. He is the best. His name is Al.
Wrong:	The goalie is my son. He is the best. He is my father.

These errors in English have analogs in programming languages. The first error above is analogous to using a nonarray variable with a subscript. The second and third errors are similar to type errors in programming languages. The last error is analogous to faulty use of a pointer.

A human uses the redundancy in the larger context to correct errors. For example, most people would be able to understand that a single letter was omitted in the sentence "The color of my coat is back". Similarly, if a listener fails to comprehend a single word, she or he can usually use the redundancy in the surrounding sentences to understand the message. If a speaker omits a word, the listener can often supply it by using context.

Programming languages are also partly redundant, and the required redundancy serves as a way to identify errors. For example, the first C declaration in Exhibit 1.2 contains two indications of the intended data type of the variable named price: the type name, int, and the actual type, float, of the initial value. These two indicators conflict, and a compiler can identify this as an error. The second line contains an initializer whose length is longer than the declared size of the array named table. This lack of agreement in number is an identifiable error.

Exhibit 1.2.   Violations of redundancy rules in ANSI C.

```
int price = 20.98;                 /* Declare and initialize variable. */
int table[3] = {11, 12, 13, 14}; /* Declare and initialize an array. */
```

1.3.3   Using Partial Information: Ambiguity and Abstraction

English permits *ambiguity*, that is, words and phrases that have dual meanings. The listener must *disambiguate* the sentence, using context, and determine the actual meaning (or meanings) of the speaker.[1]

To a very limited extent, programming languages also permit ambiguity. Operators such as + have two definitions in many languages, *integer + integer* and *real + real*. Object-oriented languages permit programmer-defined procedure names with more than one meaning. Many languages are *block-structured*. They permit the user to define contexts of limited scope, called *blocks*. The same symbol can be given different meanings in different blocks. Context is used, as it is in English, to disambiguate the meaning of the name.

The primary differences here are that "context" is defined very exactly in each programming language and quite loosely in English, and that most programming languages permit only limited ambiguity.

English supports *abstraction*, that is, the description of a quality apart from an instance. For example, the word "chair" can be defined as "a piece of furniture consisting of a seat, legs, and back, and often arms, designed to accommodate one person."[2] This definition applies to many kinds of chairs and conveys some but not all of a particular chair's properties. Older programming languages do not support this kind of abstraction. They require that all an object's properties be specified when the name for that object is defined.

Some current languages support very limited forms of abstraction. For example, Ada permits names to be defined for *generic objects*, some of whose properties are left

---

[1] A pun is a statement with two meanings, both intended by the speaker, where one meaning is usually funny.

[2] Cf. Morris [1969].

temporarily undefined. Later, the generic definition must be *instantiated* by supplying actual definitions for those properties. The instantiation process produces fully specified code with no remaining abstractions which can then be compiled in the normal way.

Smalltalk and C++ are current languages whose primary design goal was support for abstraction. A Smalltalk declaration for a class "chair" would be parallel to the English definition. Languages of the future will have more extensive ability to define and use partially specified objects.

1.3.4   Implicit Communication

English permits some things to be understood even if they are left unsaid. When we "read between the lines" in an English paragraph, we are interpreting both explicit and implicit messages. Understanding of the explicit message is derived from the words of the sentence. The implicit message is understood from the common experience of speaker and listener. People from different cultures have trouble with implicit communication because they have inadequate common understanding.

Some things may be left implicit in programming languages also. Variable types in FORTRAN and the type of the result of a function in the original Kernighan and Ritchie C may or may not be defined explicitly. In these cases, as in English, the full meaning of such constructs is defined by having a mutual understanding, between speaker and listener, about the meaning of things left unspecified. A programmer learning a new language must learn its implicit assumptions, more commonly called *defaults*.

Unfortunately, when a programmer relies on defaults to convey meaning, the compiler cannot tell the difference between the purposeful use of a default and an accidental omission of an important declaration. Many experienced programmers use explicit declarations rather than rely on defaults. Stating information explicitly is less error prone and enables a compiler to give more helpful error comments.

1.3.5   Flexibility and Nuance

English is very *flexible*: there are often many ways to say something. Programming languages have this same flexibility, as is demonstrated by the tremendous variety in the solutions handed in for one student programming problem. As another example, APL provides at least three ways to express the same simple conditional branch.

Alternate ways of saying something in English usually have slightly different meanings, and subtlety and nuance are important. When different statement sequences in a programming language express the same algorithm, we can say that they have the same meaning. However, they might still differ in subtle ways, such as in the time and amount of memory required to execute the algorithm. We can call such differences *nuances*.

The nuances of meaning in a program are of both theoretical and practical importance. We are content when the work of a beginning programmer has the correct result (a way of measuring its meaning). As programmers become more experienced, however, they become aware of the subtle implications of alternative ways of saying the same thing. They will be able to produce a program with the same meaning as the beginner's program, but with superior clarity, efficiency, and compactness.

1.3.6   Ability to Change and Evolve

Expressing an idea in any language, natural or artificial, can sometimes be difficult and awkward. A person can become "speechless" when speaking English. Words can fail to express the strength or complexity of the speaker's feelings. Sometimes a large number of English words are required to explain a new concept. Later, when the concept becomes well understood, a word or a few words suffice.

English is constantly evolving. Old words become obsolete and new words and phrases are added. Programming languages, happily, also evolve. Consider FOR-TRAN for example. The original FORTRAN was a very limited language. For example, it did not support parameters and did not have an IF. . . THEN. . . ELSE statement. Programmers who needed these things surely found themselves "speechless", and they had to express their logic in a wordy and awkward fashion. Useful constructs were added to FORTRAN because of popular demand. As this happened, some of the old FORTRAN words and methods became obsolete. While they have not been dropped from the language yet, that may happen someday.

As applications of computers change, languages are extended to include words and concepts appropriate for the new applications. An example is the introduction of words for sound generation and graphics into Commodore BASIC when the Commodore 64 was introduced with sound and graphics hardware.

One of the languages that evolves easily and constantly is FORTH. There are several public domain implementations, or dialects, used by many people and often modified to fit a user's hardware and application area. The modified dialect is then passed on to others. This process works like the process for adding new meanings to English. New words are introduced and become "common knowledge" gradually as an increasing number of people learn and use them.

Translators for many dialects of BASIC, LISP, and FORTH are in common use. These languages are not fully *standardized*. Many dialects of the original language emerge because implementors are inspired to add or redesign language features. Programs written in one dialect must be modified to be used by people whose computer "understands" a different dialect. When this happens we say that a program is *nonportable*. The cost of rewriting programs makes nonstandardized programming languages unattractive to commercial users of computers. Lack of standardization can also cause severe difficulties for programmers and publishers: the language specifications and reference material must be relearned and rewritten for each new dialect.

1.4 THE STANDARDIZATION PROCESS

Once a language is in widespread use, it becomes very important to have a complete and precise definition of the language so that compatible implementations may be produced for a variety of hardware and system environments. The standardization process was developed in response to this need. A language standard is a formal definition of the syntax and semantics of a language. It must be a complete, unambiguous statement of both. Language aspects that are defined must be defined clearly, while aspects that go beyond the limits of the standard must be designated clearly as "undefined". A language translator that implements the standard must produce code that conforms to all defined aspects of the standard, but for an undefined aspect, it is permitted to produce any convenient translation.

The authority to define an unstandardized language or to change a language definition may belong to the individual language designer, to the agency that sponsored the language design, or to a committee of the American National Standards Institute (ANSI) or the International Standards Organization (ISO). The FORTRAN standard was originated by ANSI, the Pascal standard by ISO. The definition of Ada is controlled by the U.S. Department of Defense, which paid for the design of Ada. New or experimental languages are usually controlled by their designers.

When a standards organization decides to sponsor a new standard for a language, it convenes a committee of people from industry and academia who have a strong interest in and extensive experience with that language. The standardization process is not easy or smooth. The committee must decide which dialect, or combination of ideas from different dialects, will become the standard. Committee members come to this task with different notions of what is good or bad and different priorities. Agreement at the outset is rare. The process may drag on for years as one or two committee members fight for their pet features. This happened with the original ISO Pascal standard, the ANSI C standard, and the new FORTRAN-90 standard.

After a standard is adopted by one standards organization (ISO or ANSI), the definition is considered by the other. In the best of all worlds, the new standard would be accepted by the second organization. For example, ANSI adopted the ISO standard for Pascal nearly unchanged. However, smooth sailing is not always the rule. The new ANSI C standard is not acceptable to some ISO committee members, and when ISO decides on a C standard, it may be substantially different from ANSI C.

The first standard for a language often clears up ambiguities, fixes some obvious defects, and defines a better and more portable language. The ANSI C and ANSI LISP standards do all of these things. Programmers writing new translators for this language must then conform to the common standard, as far as it goes. Implementations may also include words and structures, called *extensions*, that go beyond anything specified in the standard.

1.4.1   Language Growth and Divergence

After a number of years, language extensions accumulate and actual implementations diverge so much that programs again become nonportable. This has happened now with Pascal. The standard language is only minimally adequate for modern applications. For instance, it contains no support for string processing or graphics. Further, it has design faults, such as an inadequate case statement, and design shortcomings, such as a lack of static variables, initialized variables, and support for modular compilation. Virtually all implementations of Pascal for personal computers extend the language. These extensions are similar in intent and function but differ in detail. A program that uses the extensions is nonportable. One that doesn't use extensions is severely limited. We all need a new Pascal standard.

When a standardized language has several divergent extensions in common use, the sponsoring standards agency may convene a new committee to reexamine and restandardize the language. The committee will consider the collection of extensions from various implementations and decide upon a new standard, which usually includes all of the old standard as a subset.

Thus there is a constant tension between standardization and diversification. As our range of applications and our knowledge of language and translation techniques increase, there is pressure to extend our languages. Then the dialects in common use become diversified. When the diversity becomes too costly, the language will be restandardized.

1.5 NONSTANDARD COMPILERS

It is common for compilers to deviate from the language standard. There are three major kinds of deviations: extensions, intentional changes, and compiler bugs. The list of differences in Exhibit 1.3 was taken from the Introduction to the *Turbo Pascal Reference Manual, Version 2.0*. With each new version of Turbo, this list has grown in size and complexity. Turbo Pascal version 5 is a very different and much more extensive language than Standard Pascal.

An *extension* is a feature added to the standard, as string operations and graphics primitives are often added to Pascal. Items marked with a "+" in Exhibit 1.3 are true extensions: they provide processing capabilities for things that are not covered by the standard but do not change the basic nature of the language.

Exhibit 1.3.   Summary of Turbo Pascal deviations from the standard.

Syntactic Extensions	Semantic Extensions	Semantic Changes	
		!	Absolute address variables
		!	Bit/byte manipulation
		!	Direct access to CPU memory and data ports
	+		Dynamic strings
*			Free ordering of sections within declaration part
	+		Full support of operating system facilities
*			In-line machine code generation
*			Include files
		!	Logical operations on integers
*			Program chaining with common variables
	+		Random access data files
	+		Structured constants
	+		Type conversion functions (to be used explicitly)

Sometimes compiler writers believe that a language, as it is officially defined, is defective; that is, some part of the design is too restrictive or too clumsy to use in a practical application environment. In these cases the implementor often redefines the language, making it nonstandard and incompatible with other translators. This is an *intentional change*. Items marked with a "!" in Exhibit 1.3 change the semantics of the language by circumventing semantic protection mechanisms that are part of the standard. Items marked by a "*" are extensions and changes to the syntax of the language that do not change the semantics but, if used, do make Turbo programs incompatible with the standard.

A *compiler bug* occurs where, unknown to the compiler writer, the compiler implements different semantics than those prescribed by the language standard. Examples of compiler bugs abound. One Pascal compiler for the Commodore 64 required a semicolon after every statement. In contrast, the Pascal standard requires semicolons only as separators between statements and *forbids* a semicolon before an ELSE. A program written for this nonstandard compiler cannot be compiled by a standard compiler and vice versa.

An example of a common "bug" is implementation of the mod operator. The easy way to compute i mod j is to take the remainder after using integer division to calculate i/j. According to the Pascal standard, quoted in Exhibit 1.4,[3] this computation method is correct if both i and j are positive integers. If i is negative, though, the result must be adjusted by adding in the modulus, j. The standard considers the operation to be an error if j is negative. Note that mod is only the same as the mathematical remainder function if $i >= 0$ and $j > 0$.

Exhibit 1.4.   The definition of mod in Standard Pascal.

- The value of i mod j is the value of $i-(k*j)$ for an integer value k, such that $0 <= (i \text{ mod } j) < j$. (That is, the value is always between 0 and j.)
- The expression i mod j is an error if j is zero or negative.

Many compilers ignore this complexity, as shown in Exhibits 1.5 and 1.6. They simply perform an integer division operation and return the result, regardless of the signs of i and j. For example, in OSS Pascal for the Atari ST, the mod operator is defined in the usual nonstandard way. The OSS Pascal reference manual (pages 6-26) describes mod as follows:

The modulus is the remainder left over after integer division.

Compiling and testing a few simple expressions [Exhibit 1.5] substantiates this and shows how OSS Pascal differs from the standard. Expression 2 gives a nonstandard answer. Expressions (3) through (6) compile and run, but shouldn't. They are designated as errors in the standard, which requires the modulus to be greater than 0. These errors are not detected by the OSS Pascal compiler or run-time system, nor does the OSS Pascal reference manual state that they will not be detected, as required by the standard.

---

[3]Cooper [1983], page 3-1.

Exhibit 1.5.   The definition of mod in OSS Pascal for the Atari ST.

	Expression	OSS Result	Answer According to Pascal Standard
1.	5 mod 2	1	Correct.
2.	-5 mod 2	-1	Should be 1 (between 0 and the modulus -1).
3.	5 mod -2	1	Should be detected as an error.
4.	-5 mod -2	-1	Should be detected as an error.
5.	5 mod 0	0	Should be detected as an error.
6.	-5 mod 0	-1	Should be detected as an error.

Exhibit 1.6.   The definition of mod in Turbo Pascal for the IBM PC.

	Expression	Turbo Result	Answer According to Pascal Standard
1.	5 mod 2	1	Correct.
2.	-5 mod 2	-1	Should be -1 + 2 = 1.
3.	5 mod -2	1	Should be an error.
4.	-5 mod -2	-1	Should be an error.
5.	5 mod 0	Run-time error	Correct.
6.	-5 mod 0	Run-time error	Correct.

In defense of this nonstandard implementation, one must note that this particular deviation is common and the function it computes is probably more useful than the standard definition for mod.

The implementation of mod in Turbo Pascal is different, but also nonstandard, and may have been an unintentional deviation. It was not included in the list of nonstandard language features [Exhibit 1.3]. The author of this manual seems to have been unaware of this nonstandard nature of mod and did not even describe it adequately. The partial information given in the Turbo reference manual (pages 51–52) is as follows:

- mod is only defined for integers
- its result is an integer
- $12 \bmod 5 = 2$

The reference manual for Turbo Pascal version 4.0 still does not include mod on the list of nonstandard features. However, it does give an adequate definition (p. 240) of the function it actually computes for mod:

- "the mod operator returns the remainder from dividing the operands:
- $i \bmod j = i - (i/j) * j$.

The sign of the result is the sign of i. An error occurs if $j = 0$."

Compiling and testing a few simple expressions [Exhibit 1.6] substantiates this definition. Expression 2 gives a nonstandard answer. Expressions (3) and (4) are designated as errors in the standard, which requires the modulus to be greater than 0. These errors are not detected by the Turbo compiler. Furthermore, its reference manual does not state that they will not be detected, as required by the standard.

While Turbo Pascal will not compile a `div` or `mod` operation with 0 as a constant divisor, the result of "i mod 0" can be tested by setting a variable, j, to zero, then printing the results of i mod j. This gives the results on lines (5) and (6).

Occasionally, deviations from the standard occur because an implementor believes that the standard, although unambiguous, defined an item "wrong"; that is, some other definition would have been more efficient or more useful. The version incorporated into the compiler is intended as an *improvement* over the standard. Again, the implementation of `mod` provides an example here. In many cases, the programmer who uses `mod` really wants the arithmetic remainder, and it seems foolish for the compiler to insert extra lines of code in order to compute the unwanted standard Pascal function. At least one Pascal compiler (for the Apollo workstation) provides a switch that can be set either to compile the standard meaning of `mod` or to compile the easy and efficient meaning. The person who wrote this compiler clearly believed that the standard was "wrong" to include the version it did rather than the integer remainder function.

The implementation of input and output operations in Turbo Pascal version 2.0 provides another example of a compiler writer who declined to implement the standard language because he believed his own version was clearly superior. He explains this decision as follows:[4]

> The standard procedures GET and PUT are not implemented. Instead, the READ and WRITE procedures have been extended to handle all I/O needs. The reason for this is threefold: Firstly, READ and WRITE give much faster I/O, secondly variable space overhead is reduced, as file buffer variables are not required, and thirdly the READ and WRITE procedures are far more versatile and easier to understand than GET and PUT.

The actual Turbo implementation of READ did not even measure up to the standard in a minimal way, as it did not permit the programmer to read a line of input from the keyboard one character at a time. (It is surely inefficient to do so but essential in some applications.) Someone who did not know that this deviation was made on purpose would think that it was simply a compiler bug. This situation provides an excellent example of the dangers of "taking the law into your own hands".

Whether or not we agree with the requirements of a language standard, we must think carefully before using nonstandard features. Every time we use a nonstandard feature or one that depends on the particular bit-level implementation of the language, it makes a program harder to port from one system to another and decreases its potential usefulness and potential lifetime. Programmers who use nonstandard "features" in their code should segregate the nonstandard segments and thoroughly document them.

---

[4]Borland [1984], Appendix F.

EXERCISES

1. Define natural language. Define programming language. How are they different?
2. How are languages used to establish communication?
3. What is the syntax of a language? What are the semantics?
4. What are the traits that determine the character of a language?
5. How do these traits appear in programming languages?
6. What need led to standardization?
7. What is a "standard" for a language?
8. What does it mean when a language standard defines something to be "undefined"?
9. How does standardization lead to portability?
10. What three kinds of deviations are common in nonstandard compilers?
11. What are the advantages and disadvantages of using nonstandard language features?

2

Representation and Abstraction

_____ **Overview** _____

This chapter presents the concept of how real-world objects, actions, and changes in the state of a process are represented through a programming language on a computer. Programs can be viewed as either a set of instructions for the computer to execute or as a model of some real-world process. Languages designed to support these views will exhibit different properties. The language designer must establish a set of goals for the language and then examine them for consistency, importance, and restrictions. Principles for evaluating language design are presented. Classification of languages into groups is by no means an easy task. Categories for classifying languages are discussed.

2.1 WHAT IS A PROGRAM?

We can view a program two ways.

1. *A program is a description of a set of actions that we want a computer to carry out.* The actions are the primitive operations of some real or abstract machine, and they are performed using the primitive parts of a machine. Primitive actions include such things as copying data from one machine register or a memory location to another, applying an operation to a register, or activating an input or output device.

2. *A program is a model of some process in the real or mathematical world.* The programmer must set up a correspondence between symbols in the program and real-world objects, and between program functions and real-world processes. Executing a function represents a change in the state of the world or finding a solution to a set of specifications about elements of that world.

These two world-views are analogous to the way a builder and an architect view a house. The builder is concerned with the method for achieving a finished house. It should be built efficiently and the result should be structurally sound. The architect is concerned with the overall function and form of the house. It should carry out the architect's concepts and meet the client's needs.

The two world-views lead to very different conclusions about the properties that a programming language should have. A language supporting world-view (1) provides ready access to every part of the computer so that the programmer can prescribe in detail *how* the computer should go about solving a given problem. The language of a builder contains words for each material and construction method used. Similarly, a program construction language allows one to talk directly about hardware registers, memory, data movement, I/O devices, and so forth. The distinction isn't simply whether the language is "low-level" or "high-level", for assembly language and C are both designed with the builder in mind. Assembly language is, by definition, low-level, and C is not, since it includes control structures, type definitions, support for modules, and the like. However, C permits (and forces) a programmer to work with and be aware of the raw elements of the host computer.

A language supporting world-view (2) must be able to deal with abstractions and provide a means for expressing a model of the real-world objects and processes. An architect deals with abstract concepts such as space, form, light, and functionality, and with more concrete units such as walls and windows. Blueprints, drawn using a formal symbolic language, are used to represent and communicate the plan. The builder understands the language of blueprints and chooses appropriate methods to implement them.

The languages Smalltalk and Prolog were designed to permit the programmer to represent and communicate a world-model easily. They free the programmer of concerns about the machine and let him or her deal instead with abstract concepts. In Smalltalk the programmer defines classes of objects and the processes relevant to these classes. If an abstract process is relevant to several classes, the programmer can define how it is to be accomplished for each. In Prolog the programmer represents the world using formulas of mathematical logic. In other languages, the programmer may use procedures, type declarations, structured loops, and block structure to represent and describe the application. Writing a program becomes a process of representing objects, actions, and changes in the state of the process being modeled [Exhibit 2.1].

The advantage of a "builder's" language is that it permits the construction of efficient software that makes effective use of the computer on which it runs. A disadvantage is that programs tailored to a particular machine cannot be expected to be well suited to another machine and hence they are not particularly portable.

Moreover, a programmer using such a language is forced to organize ideas at a burdensome level of detail. Just as a builder must be concerned with numerous details such as building codes, lumber dimensions, proper nailing patterns, and so forth, the program builder likewise deals with storage allocation, byte alignment, calling sequences, word sizes, and other details which, while important to the finished product, are largely unrelated to its form and function.

By way of contrast, an "architect's" language frees one from concern about the underlying machine and allows one to describe a process at a greater level of abstraction, omitting the minute details. A great deal of discretion is left to the compiler designer in choosing methods to carry out the specified actions. Two compilers for the same architect's language often produce compiled code of widely differing efficiency and storage requirements.

Exhibit 2.1.   Modeling a charge account and relevant processes.

Objects: A program that does the accounting for a company's charge accounts must contain representations for several kinds of real-world objects: accounts, payments, the current balance, items charged, items returned, interest.

Actions: Each action to be represented involves objects from a specified class or classes. The actions to be represented here include the following:

- Credit a payment to an account.
- Send a bill to the account owner.
- Debit a purchase to an account.
- Credit a return to an account.
- Compute and debit the monthly interest due.

Changes of state: The current balance of an account, today's date, and the monthly payment date for that account encode the *state* of the account. The balance may be positive, negative, or zero, and a positive balance may be either ok or overdue. Purchases, returns, payments, and monthly due dates and interest dates all cause a change in the state of the account.

In fact, there is no necessary reason why there must be a compiler at all. One could use the architect's language to specify the form and function of the finished program and then turn the job over to a program builder. However, the computer *can* do a fairly good job of automatically producing a program for such languages, and the ability to have it do so gives the program architect a powerful tool not available to the construction architect—the ability to rapidly prototype designs. This is the power of the computer, and one of the aspects that makes the study of programming language so fascinating!

2.2   REPRESENTATION

A *representation of an object* is a list of the relevant facts about that object in some language [Exhibit 2.2]. A *computer representation of an object* is a mapping of the relevant facts about that object, through a computer language, onto the parts of the machine.

Some languages support *high-level* or *abstract* representations, which specify the functional properties of an object or the symbolic names and data types of the fields of the representation [Exhibit 2.3]. A high-level representation will be mapped onto computer memory by a translator. The actual number and order of bytes of storage that will be used to represent the object may vary from translator to translator. In contrast, a computer representation is *low level* if it describes a particular implementation of the object, such as the amount of storage that will be used, and the position of each field in that storage area [Exhibit 2.4].

Exhibit 2.2.   Representations of a date in English.

Dates are abstract real-world objects. We represent them in English by specifying an era, year, month, and day of the month. The era is usually omitted and the year is often omitted in representations of dates, because they can be deduced from context. The month is often encoded as an integer between 1 and 12.

Full, explicit representation: January 2, 1986 AD
Common representations: January 2, 1986
                                   Jan. 2, '86
                                   Jan. 2
                                   1-2-86
                                   2 Jan 86
                                   86-1-2

Exhibit 2.3.   High-level computer representations of a date.

An encoding of the last representation in Exhibit 2.2 is often used in programs. In a high-level language, the programmer might specify that a date will be represented by three integers, as in this Pascal example:

```
TYPE date = RECORD year, month, day:  integer END;
VAR BirthDate:  date;
```

The programmer may now refer to this object and its components as:

```
BirthDate  or
BirthDate.year  or  BirthDate.month  or  BirthDate.day
```

Exhibit 2.4.   A low-level computer representation of a date.

In a low-level language such as assembler or FORTH, the programmer specifies the exact number of bytes of storage that must be allocated (or ALLOTted) to represent the date. In the FORTH declaration below, the keyword VARIABLE causes 2 bytes to be allocated, and 4 more are explicitly allocated using ALLOT. Then the programmer must manually define selection functions that access the fields of the object by adding an appropriate offset to the base address.

```
VARIABLE birth_date 4 ALLOT
: year 0 + ;         ( Year is first -- offset is zero bytes. )
: month 2 + ;        ( Month starts two bytes from the beginning. )
: day 4 + ;          ( Day is the fifth and sixth bytes. )
```

The variable named birth_date and its component fields can now be accessed by writing:

```
birth_date  or
birth_date year  or  birth_date month  or  birth_date day
```

A *computer representation of a process* is a sequence of program definitions, specifications, or statements that can be performed on representations of objects from specified sets. We say that the representation of a process is *valid*, or correct, if the transformed object representation still corresponds to the transformed object in the real world.

We will consider three aspects of the quality of a representation: semantic intent, explicitness, and coherence. Abstract representations have these qualities to a high degree; low-level representations often lack them.

2.2.1   Semantic Intent

A data object (variable, record, array, etc.) in a program has some intended meaning that is known to the programmer but cannot be deduced with certainty from the data representation itself. This intended meaning is the programmer's *semantic intent*. For example, three 2-digit integers can represent a woman's measurements in inches or a date. We can only know the intended meaning of a set of data if the programmer communicates, or declares, the context in which it should be interpreted.

A program has *semantic validity* if it faithfully carries out the programmer's explicitly declared semantic intent. We will be examining mechanisms in various languages for expressing semantic intent and ensuring that it is carried out. Most programming languages use a data type to encode part of the semantic intent of an object. Before applying a function to a data object, the language translator tests whether the function is defined for that object and, therefore, is meaningful in its context. An attempt to apply a function to a data object of the wrong type is identified as a semantic error. A type-checking mechanism can thus help a programmer write semantically valid (meaningful) programs.

2.2.2   Explicit versus Implicit Representation

The structure of a data object can be reflected *implicitly* in a program by the way the statements are arranged [Exhibit 2.5], or it can be declared *explicitly* [Exhibit 2.6]. A language that can declare more kinds of things explicitly is more *expressive*.

Exhibit 2.5.   The structure of a table expressed implicitly.

Pascal permits the construction and use of sorted tables, but the fact that the table is sorted cannot be explicitly declared. We can deduce that the table is sorted by noting that a sort algorithm is invoked, that a binary search algorithm is used, or that a sequential search algorithm is used that can terminate a search unsuccessfully before reaching the end of the table.

The order of entries (whether ascending or descending) can be deduced by careful analysis of the following three items:

- The comparison operator used in a search ($<$ or $>$)
- The order of operands in relation to this operator
- The result (true or false) that causes the search to terminate

Deductions of this sort are beyond the realistic present and future abilities of language translators.

Exhibit 2.6.   COBOL:The structure of a table expressed explicitly.

COBOL allows explicit declaration of sorted tables. The key field(s) and the order of entries may be declared, as in the following example. This table is intended to store the names of the fifty states of the United States and their two-letter abbreviations. It is to be stored so that the abbreviations are in alphabetical order.

```
01  state-table.
    02  state-entry
        OCCURS 50 TIMES
        ASCENDING KEY state-abbrev
        INDEXED BY state-index.
        03  state-abbrev      PICTURE XX.
        03  state-name        PICTURE X(20).
```

This table can be searched for a state abbreviation using the binary-search utility. A possible call is:

```
SEARCH ALL state-entry
    AT END PERFORM failed-search-process
    WHEN st-abbrev (state-index) = search-key PERFORM found-process.
```

COBOL also permits the programmer to declare Pascal-like tables for which the sorting order and key field are not explicitly declared. The SEARCH ALL command cannot be used to search such a table; the programmer can only use the less efficient sequential search command.

Information expressed explicitly in a program may be used by the language translator. For example, if the COBOL programmer supplies a KEY clause, the processor will permit the programmer to use the efficient built-in binary search command, because the KEY clause specifies that the file is sorted in order by that field. The less-efficient sequential search command must be used to search any table that does not have a KEY clause.

A language that permits explicit communication of information must have a translator that can identify, store, organize, and utilize that information. For example, if a language permits programmers to define their own types, the translator needs to implement type tables (where type descriptions are stored), new allocation methods that use these programmer-defined descriptions, and more elaborate rules for type checking and type errors.

These translator mechanisms to identify, store, and interpret the programmer's declarations form the *semantic basis* of a language. Other mechanisms that are part of the semantic basis are those which implement binding (Chapters 6 and 9), type checking and automatic type conversion (Chapter 14), and module protection (Chapter 15).

2.2.3 *Coherent versus Diffuse Representation*

A representation is *coherent* if an external entity (object, idea, or process) is represented by a single symbol in the program (a name or a pointer) so that it may be referenced and manipulated as a unit [Exhibit 2.7]. A representation is *diffuse* if various parts of the representation are known by different names, and no one name or symbol applies to the whole [Exhibits 2.8 and 2.9].

Exhibit 2.7.   A stack represented coherently in Pascal.

A stack can be represented by an array and an integer index for the number of items currently in the array. We can represent a stack coherently by grouping the two parts together into a record. One parameter then suffices to pass this stack to a function.

```
TYPE stack = RECORD
                 store:  ARRAY [1..max_stack] of stack_type;
                 top:  0..max_stack
             END;
```

Exhibit 2.8.   A stack represented diffusely in FORTRAN and Pascal.

A stack can be represented diffusely as an array of items and a separate index (an integer in the range 0 to the size of the array).

FORTRAN: A diffuse representation is the only representation of a stack that is possible in FORTRAN because the language does not support heterogeneous records. These declarations create two objects which, taken together, comprise a stack of 100 real numbers:

```
REAL    STSTORE( 100 )
INTEGER STTOP
```

Pascal: A stack can be represented diffusely in Pascal. This code allocates the same amount of storage as the coherent version in Exhibit 2.7, but two parameters are required to pass this stack to a procedure.

```
TYPE stack_store = ARRAY [1..max_stack] of stack_type;
     stack_top = 0..max_stack;
```

Exhibit 2.9.   Addition represented diffusely or coherently.

FORTH: The operation of addition is represented diffusely because addition of single-length integers, double-length integers, and mixed-length integers are named by three different symbols (+, D+, and M+), and no way is provided to refer to the general operation of "integer +".

C: The operation of addition is represented coherently. Addition of single-length integers, double-length integers, and mixed-length integers are all named "+". The programmer may refer to "+" for addition, without concern for the length of the integer operands.

A representation is coherent if all the parts of the represented object can be named by one symbol. This certainly does not imply that all the parts must be stored in consecutive (or contiguous) memory locations. Thus an object whose parts are connected by links or pointers can still be coherent [Exhibit 2.10].

Exhibit 2.10.   A coherently but not contiguously represented object.

LISP: A linked tree structure or a LISP list is a coherent object because a single pointer to the head of the list allows the entire list to be manipulated. A tree or a list is generally implemented by using pointers to link storage cells at many memory locations.

C: A sentence may be represented as an array of words. One common representation is a contiguous array of pointers, each of which points to a variable-length string of characters. These strings are normally allocated separately and are not contiguous.

The older languages (FORTRAN, APL) support coherent representation of complex data objects only if the object can be represented by a homogeneous array of items of the same data type.[1] Where an object has components represented by different types, separate variable names must be used. COBOL and all the newer languages support coherent heterogeneous groupings of data. These are called "records" in COBOL and Pascal, and "structures" in C.

The FORTRAN programmer can use a method called *parallel arrays* to model an array of heterogeneous records. The programmer declares one array for each field of the record, then uses a single index variable to refer to corresponding elements of the set of arrays. This diffuse representation accomplishes the same goal as a Pascal array of records. However, an array of records represents the problem more clearly and explicitly and is easier to use. For example, Pascal permits an array of records to be passed as a single parameter to a function, whereas a set of parallel arrays in FORTRAN would have to be passed as several parameters.

Some of the newest languages support coherence further by permitting a set of data representations to be grouped together with the functions that operate on them. Such a coherent grouping is called a "module" in Modula-2, a "cluster" in CLU, a "class" in Smalltalk, and a "package" in Ada.

2.3 LANGUAGE DESIGN

In this section we consider reasons why a language designer might choose to create an "architect's language" with a high degree of support for abstraction, or a "builder's language" with extensive control over low-level aspects of representation.

2.3.1 Competing Design Goals

Programming languages have evolved greatly since the late 1950s, when the first high-level languages, FORTRAN and COBOL, were implemented. Much of this evolution has been made possible by the improvements in computer hardware: today's machines are inconceivably cheap, fast, and large (in memory capacity) compared to the machines available in 1960. Although those old machines were physically bulky and tremendously expensive, they were hardly more powerful than machines that today are considered to be toys.

---

[1]The EQUIVALENCE statement can be used to circumvent this weakness by defining the name of the coherent object as an overlay on the storage occupied by the parts. This does not constitute adequate support for compound heterogeneous objects.

Along with changes in hardware technology came improvements in language translation techniques. Both syntax and semantics of the early languages were ad hoc and clumsy to translate. Formal language theory and formal semantics affected language design in revolutionary ways and have resulted in better languages with cleaner semantics and a more easily translatable syntax.

There are many aspects of a language that the user cannot modify or extend, such as the data structuring facilities and the control structures. Unless a language system supports a preprocessor, the language syntax, also, is fixed. If control structures and data definition facilities are not built in, they are not available. Decisions to include or exclude such features must, therefore, be made carefully. A language designer must consider several aspects of a potential feature to decide whether it supports or conflicts with the design goals.

During these thirty years of language development, a consensus has emerged about the importance of some language features, for example, type checking and structured conditionals. Most new languages include these. On other issues, there has been and remains fundamental disagreement, for instance, over the question of whether procedural or functional languages are "better". No single set of value judgments has yet emerged, because different languages have different goals and different intended uses. The following are some potential language design goals:

- Utility. Is a feature often useful? Can it do important things that cannot be done using other features of the language?
- Convenience. Does this feature help avoid excessive writing? Does this feature add or eliminate clutter in the code?
- Efficiency. Is it easy or difficult to translate this feature? Is it possible to translate this feature into efficient code? Will its use improve or degrade the performance of programs?
- Portability. Will this feature be implementable on any machine?
- Readability. Does this form of this feature make a program more readable? Will a programmer other than the designer understand the intent easily? Or is it cryptic?
- Modeling ability. Does this feature help make the meaning of a program clear? Will this feature help the programmer model a problem more fully, more precisely, or more easily?
- Simplicity. Is the language design as a whole simple, unified, and general, or is it full of dozens of special-purpose features?
- Semantic clarity. Does every legal program and expression have one defined, unambiguous, meaning? Is the meaning constant during the course of program execution?

These goals are all obviously desirable, but they conflict with each other. For example, a simple language cannot possibly include all useful features, and the more features included, the more complicated the language is to learn, use, and implement. Ada illustrates this conflict. Ada was designed for the Department of Defense as a language for embedded systems, to be used in all systems development projects, on diverse kinds of hardware. Thus it necessarily reflects a high value placed on items at the beginning and middle of the preceding list of design goals. The result is a very large language with a long list of useful special features.

Some language researchers have taken as goals the fundamental properties of language shown at the end of the list of design goals. Outstanding examples include

Smalltalk, a superior language for modeling objects and processes, and Miranda, which is a list-oriented functional language that achieves both great simplicity and semantic clarity.

2.3.2 The Power of Restrictions

Every language imposes restrictions on the user, both by what it explicitly prohibits and by what it simply doesn't provide. Whenever the underlying machine provides instructions or capabilities that cannot be used in a user program, the programming language is imposing a restriction on the user. For example, Pascal does not support the type "bit string" and does not have "bit string" operators [Exhibit 2.11]. Thus Pascal restricts access to the bit-level implementations of objects.

Exhibit 2.11.   A basic type not supported by Pascal.

Basic type implemented by most hardware: bit strings
Common lengths: 8, 16, and 32 bits (1, 2, and 4 bytes)

Operations Built into Most Hardware	Symbol in C
a right shift n places	a >> n
a left shift n places	a << n
a and b	a & b
a or b	a | b
a exclusive or b	a ^ b
complement a	~ a

The reader must not confuse logical operators with bitwise operators. Pascal supports the logical (Boolean) data type and *logical operators and*, *or*, and *not*. Note that there is a difference between these and the *bitwise operators* [Exhibit 2.12]. Bitwise operators apply the operation between every corresponding pair of bits in the operands. Logical operators apply the operation to the operands as a whole, with 00000000 normally being interpreted as False and anything else as True.

Exhibit 2.12.   Bitwise and logical operations.

The difference between bitwise and logical operations can be seen by comparing the input and output from these operations in C:

Operation	Operands as Bit Strings	Result	Explanation
bitwise and	10111101 & 01000010	00000000	no bit pairs match
logical and	10111101 && 01000010	00000001	both operands represent True
complement	~ 01000010	10111101	each bit is flipped
logical not	! 01000010	00000000	operand is True

In general, restrictions might prevent writing the following two sorts of sentences:

1. Useless or meaningless sentences such as "3 := 72.9 + $'a'$ ".
2. Sentences useful for modeling some problem, that could be written efficiently in assembly code but are prohibited.

A good example of a useful facility that some languages prohibit is explicit address manipulation. This is supported in C [Exhibit 2.13]. The notation for pointer manipulation is convenient and is generally used in preference to subscripting when the programmer wishes to process an array sequentially.

Exhibit 2.13.   Useful pointer operations supported in C.

In the C expressions below, p is a pointer used as an index for the array named "ages". Initially, p will store the machine address of the beginning of ages. To make p index the next element, p will be incremented by the number of bytes in one element of ages. The array element is accessed by dereferencing the pointer.

This code contains an error in logic, which is pointed out in the comments. It demonstrates one semantic problem that Pascal's restrictions were designed to prevent. The loop will be executed too many times, and this run-time error will not be detected. Compare this to the similar Pascal loop in Exhibit 2.14.

```
int ages[10];            /* Array "ages" has subscripts 0..9.  */
...
p = ages;                /* Make p point at ages[0].  */
end = &ages[10];         /* Compute address of eleventh array element. */
while (p <= end){        /* Loop through eleventh array address. */
  printf("%d \n", *p);   /* Print array element in decimal integer format. */
  p++;                   /* Increment p to point at next element of ages.  */
}
```

In contrast, manipulation of addresses is restricted in Pascal to prevent the occurrence of meaningless and potentially dangerous dangling pointers (see Chapter 6). Address manipulation is prohibited and address arithmetic is undefined in Pascal. Nothing comparable to the C code in Exhibit 2.13 can be written in Pascal. A pointer can't be set to point at an array element, and it cannot be incremented to index through an array.

This is a significant loss in Pascal because using a subscript involves a lot of computation: the subscript must be checked against the minimum and maximum legal values, multiplied by the size of an array element, and added to the base address of the array. Checking whether a pointer has crossed an array boundary and using it to access an element could be done significantly faster.

Let us define *flexibility* to mean the absence of a restriction, and call a restriction *good* if it prevents the writing of nonsense, and *bad* if it prevents writing useful things. Some restrictions might have both good and bad aspects. A *powerful* language must have the flexibility to express a wide variety of actions—preferably a variety that approaches the power of the underlying machine.

But power is not a synonym for flexibility. The most flexible of all languages is assembly language, but assemblers lack the power to express a problem solution succinctly and clearly. A second kind of power is provided by sophisticated mechanisms in the semantic basis of a language that let the programmer express a lot by saying a little. The type definition and type checking facility in any modern language is a good example of a powerful mechanism.

A third kind of power can come from "good" restrictions that narrow the variety of things that can be written. If a restriction can eliminate troublesome or meaningless sentences automatically, then programmers will not have to check, explicitly, whether such meaningless sections occur in their programs. Pascal programs rarely run wild and destroy memory. But C and FORTH programs, with unrestricted pointers and no subscript bounds checking, often do so. A language should have enough good restrictions so that the programmer and translator can easily distinguish between a meaningful statement and nonsense.

For example, an attempt to access an element of an array with a subscript greater than the largest array subscript is obviously meaningless in any language. The underlying machine hardware permits one to FETCH and STORE information beyond the end of an array, but this can have no possible useful meaning and is likely to foul up the further operation of the program. The semantics of standard Pascal prescribe that the actual value of each subscript expression should be checked at run time. An error comment is generated if the value is not within the declared array bounds. Thus all subscripting in Pascal is "safe" and cannot lead to destruction of other information [Exhibit 2.14].

Exhibit 2.14.   A meaningless operation prohibited in Pascal but not in C.

Subscripts are checked at run time in Pascal. Every subscript that is used must be within the declared bounds.

```
VAR ages:  array[0..9] of integer;
    p:  integer;
...
p := 0;
while p <= 10 do begin        { Loop through last array subscript.  }
    writeln( ages[p] );       { Print the array element.  }
    p:=p+1                    { Make p point at next element of array.  }
end;
```

The last time around this loop the subscript, p, has a value that is out of range. This will be detected, and a run-time error comment will be generated. The analogous C code in Exhibit 2.13 will run and print garbage on the last iteration. The logical error will not be detected, and no error comment will be produced.

No such array bounds check is done in C. Compare Exhibits 2.13 and 2.14. These two code fragments do analogous things, but the logical error inherent in both will be trapped by Pascal and ignored by C. In C, a FETCH operation with too large a subscript can supply nonsensical information, and a STORE can destroy vital, unrelated information belonging to variables allocated before or after the array. This situation was exploited to create the computer network "worm" that invaded hundreds of computer systems in November 1988. It disabled these systems by flooding their processing queues with duplicates of itself, preventing the processing of normal programs. This escapade resulted in the arrest and conviction of the programmer.

Often, as seen in Exhibit 2.13, a single feature is both useful and dangerous. In that case, a language designer has to make a value judgment about the relative importance of the feature and the danger in that feature. If the designer considers the danger to outweigh the importance, the restriction will be included, as Wirth included the pointer restrictions in Pascal. If the need outweighs the danger, the restriction will not be included. In designing C, Kernighan and Ritchie clearly felt that address manipulation was vital, and decided that the dangers of dangling pointers would have to be avoided by careful programming, not by imposing general restrictions on pointers.

2.3.3 Principles for Evaluating a Design

In the remaining chapters of this book we will sometimes make value judgments about the particular features that a language includes or excludes. These judgments will be based on a small set of principles.

Principle of Frequency

The more frequently a language feature will be used, the more convenient its use should be, and the more lucid its syntax should be. An infrequently used feature can be omitted from the core of the language and/or be given a long name and less convenient syntax.

C provides us with examples of good and poor application of this principle. The core of the C language does not include a lot of features that are found in the cores of many other languages. For example, input/output routines and mathematical functions for scientific computation are not part of the standard language. These are relegated to libraries, which can be searched if these features are needed. There are two C libraries which are now well standardized, the "math library" and the "C library" (which includes the I/O functions).

The omission of mathematical functions from C makes good sense because the intended use of C was for systems programming, not scientific computation. Putting these functions in the math library makes them available but less convenient. To use the math library, the loader must have the library on its search path and the user must include a header file in the program which contains type declarations for the math functions.

On the other hand, most application programs use the input-output functions, so they should be maximally convenient. In C they aren't; in order to use them a programmer must include the appropriate header file containing I/O function and macro declarations, and other essential things. Thus nearly every C application program starts with the instruction "#include ⟨stdio.h⟩". This could be considered to be a poor design element, as it would cost relatively little to build these definitions into the translator.

Principle of Locality

A good language design enables and encourages, perhaps even enforces, locality of effects. The further the effects of an action reach in time (elapsed during execution) or in space (measured in pages of code), the more complex and harder it is to debug a program. The further an action has influence, the harder it is to remember relevant details, and the more subtle errors seem to creep into the code.

To achieve locality, the use of global variables should be minimized or eliminated and all transfers of control should be short-range. A concise restatement of this principle, in practical terms is:

Keep the effects of everything confined to as local an area of the code as possible.

Here are some corollaries of the general principle, applied to lexical organization of a program that will be debugged on-line, using an ordinary nonhierarchical text editor:

- A control structure that won't fit on one screen is too long; shorten it by defining one or more scopes as subroutines.
- All variables should be defined within one screen of their use. This applies whether the user's screen is large or small—the important thing is to be able to see an entire unit at one time.
- If your subroutine won't fit on two screens, it is too long. Break it up.

Global Variables.

Global variables provide a far more important example of the cost of nonlocality. A global variable can be changed or read anywhere within a program. Specifically, it can be changed accidentally (because of a typographical error or a programmer's absentmindedness) in a part of the program that is far removed from the section in which it is (purposely) used.

This kind of error is hard to find. The apparent fault is in the section that is supposed to use the variable, but if that section is examined in isolation, it will work properly. To find the cause of the error, a programmer must trace the operation of the entire program. This is a tedious job. The use of unnecessary global variables is, therefore, dangerous.

If the program were rewritten to declare this variable locally within the scope in which it is used, the distant reference would promptly be identified as an error or as a reference to a semantically distinct variable that happens to have the same name.

Among existing languages are those that provide only global variables, provide globals but encourage use of locals and parameters, and provide only parameters.

Unrestricted use of global variables.   A BASIC programmer cannot restrict a variable to a local scope. This is part of the reason that BASIC is not used for large systems programs.

Use of global variables permitted but use of locals encouraged.   Pascal and C are block structured languages that make it easy to declare variables in the procedure in which they are used.[2] Their default method of parameter passing is call-by-value. Changing a local variable or value parameter has only local effects. Programmers are encouraged to use local declarations, but they can use global variables in place of both local variables and parameters.

---

[2]Local declarations are explained fully in Chapter 6; parameters are discussed in Chapter 9, Section 9.2.

Use of global variables prohibited.   In the modern *functional languages* there are no global variables. Actually, there are no variables at all, and parameter binding takes the place of assignment to variables. Assignment was excluded from this class of languages because it can have nonlocal effects. The result is languages with elegant, clean semantics.

Principle of Lexical Coherence

Sections of code that logically belong together should be physically adjacent in the program. Sections of code that are not related should not be interleaved. It should be easy to tell where one logical part of the program ends and another starts. A language design is good to the extent that it permits, requires, or encourages lexical coherence.

This principle concerns only the surface syntax of the language and is, therefore, not as important as the other principles, which concern semantic power. Nonetheless, good human engineering is important in a language, and lexical coherence is important to make a language usable and readable.

Poor lexical coherence can be seen in many languages. In Pascal the declarations of local variables for the main program must be near the top of the program module, and the code for main must be at the bottom [Exhibit 2.15]. All the function and procedure definitions intervene. In a program of ordinary size, several pages of code come between the use of a variable in main and its definition.

Recently, hierarchical editors have been developed for Pascal. They allow the programmer to "hide" a function definition "under" the function header. A program is thus divided into levels, with the main program at the top level and its subroutines one level lower. If the subroutines have subroutines, they are at level three, and so on. When the main program is on the screen, only the top level code appears, and each function definition is replaced by a simple function header. This brings the main program's body back into the lexical vicinity of its declarations. When the programmer wishes to look at the function definition, simple editor commands will allow him to descend to that level and return.

Exhibit 2.15.   Poor lexical coherence for declarations and code in Pascal.

The parts of a Pascal program are arranged in the order required to permit one-pass compilation:

- Constant declarations
- Type declarations
- Variable declarations
- Procedure and Function declarations
- Code

Good programming style demands that most of the work of the program be done in subroutines, and the part of the program devoted to subroutine definitions is often many pages long. The variable declarations and code for the main program are, therefore, widely separated, producing poor lexical coherence.

A similar lack of coherence can be seen in early versions of LISP.[3] LISP permits a programmer to write a function call as a literal function, called a *lambda expression*, followed by its actual arguments, as shown at the top of Exhibit 2.16. The dummy parameter names are separated from the matching parameter values by an arbitrarily long function body.

Exhibit 2.16.   Syntax for lambda expressions in LISP.

The order of elements in the primitive syntax is:

```
((lambda
     ( ⟨list of dummy parameter names⟩ )
     ( ⟨body of the function⟩ ))
⟨list of actual parameter values⟩)
```

The order of elements in the extended syntax is:

```
(let
     ( ⟨list of dummy name - actual value pairs⟩ )
     ( ⟨body of the function⟩ ))
```

This lack of lexical coherence makes it awkward and error prone for a human to match up the names with the values, as shown in Exhibit 2.17. The eye swims when interpreting this function call, even though it is simple and the code section is short.

Exhibit 2.17.   A LISP function call with poor coherence.

The following literal function is written in the primitive LISP syntax. It takes two parameters, x, and y. It returns their product plus their difference. It is being called with the arguments 3.5 and $a + 2$. Note that the parameter declarations and matching arguments are widely separated.

```
((lambda ( x y )
           (+ (* x y)
              (- x y) ))
    3.5 (+ a 2) )
```

Newer versions of LISP, for example Common LISP,[4] offer an improved syntax with the same semantics but better lexical coherence. Using the let syntax, dummy parameter names and actual values are written in pairs at the top, followed by the code. This syntax is shown at the bottom of Exhibit 2.16, and an example of its use is shown in Exhibit 2.18.

---

[3]McCarthy et al. [1962].
[4]Kessler [1988], p. 59.

Exhibit 2.18.   A LISP function call with good coherence.

The following function call is written in LISP using the extended "let" syntax. It is semantically equivalent to the call in Exhibit 2.17.

```
(let ((x 3.5) (y (+ a 2) ))
     ((+  (* x y)
          (- x y)) ))
```

Compare the ease of matching up parameter names and corresponding arguments here, with the difficulty in Exhibit 2.17. The lexically coherent syntax is clearly better.

A third, and extreme, example of poor lexical coherence is provided by the syntax for function definitions in SNOBOL. A SNOBOL IV function is defined by a function header of the following form:

$$(\text{'}\langle\text{name}\rangle \ (\langle\text{parameter list}\rangle) \ \langle\text{local variable name list}\rangle\text{'}, \text{'}\langle\text{entry label}\rangle\text{'})$$

The code that defines the action of the subroutine can be anywhere within the program module, and it starts at the line labeled ⟨entry label⟩. It does not even need to be all in the same place, since each of its lines may be attached to the next by a GOTO.

Thus a main program and several subroutines could be interleaved. (We do admit that a sane programmer would never do such a thing.) Exhibit 2.19 shows a SNOBOL program, with subroutine, that translates an English sentence into Pig Latin. The line numbers are not part of the program but are used to key it to the program notes that follow.

Principle of Distinct Representation

Each separate semantic object should be represented by a separate syntactic item. Where a single syntactic item in the program is used for multiple semantic purposes, conflicts are bound to occur, and one or both sets of semantics will be compromised. The line numbers in a BASIC program provide a good example.

BASIC was the very first interactive programming language. It combined an on-line editor, a file system, and an interpreter to make a language in which simple problems could be programmed quickly. The inclusion of an editor posed a new problem: how could the programmer modify the program and insert and delete lines? The answer chosen was to have the programmer number every line, and have the editor arrange the lines in order by increasing line number.

BASIC was developed in the context of FORTRAN, which uses numeric line numbers as statement labels. It was, therefore, natural for BASIC to merge the two ideas and use one mechanism, the monotonically increasing line number, to serve purposes (1) and (2) below. When the language was extended to include subroutines, symbolic names for them were not defined either. Rather, the same line numbers were given a third use. Line numbers in BASIC are, therefore, multipurpose:

1. They define the correct order of lines in a program.
2. They are the targets of GOTOs and IFs.
3. They define the entry points of subroutines (the targets of GOSUB).

Exhibit 2.19.   Poor lexical coherence in SNOBOL.

SNOBOL has such poor lexical coherence that semantically unrelated lines can be interleaved, and no clear indication exists of the beginning or end of any program segment. This program converts English to Pig Latin. It is annotated below.

```
1.          DEFINE('PIG(X) Y,Z','PIG1')   :(MAIN)
2. PROC     OUTPUT = PIG(IN)
3. MAIN     IN = INPUT                     :F(END) S(PROC)
4. PIG1     PIG = NULL
5.          X SPAN('')=                     :F(RETURN)
6. LOOP     X BREAK('').Y SPAN('')=         :F(RETURN)
7.          Y LEN(1).Z =
8.          PIG = PIG Y Z 'AY'              :(LOOP)
9. END      OUTPUT = '.'
```

Program Notes.

The main program begins on line 1, with the declaration of a header for a subroutine named PIG. Line 1 directs that execution is to continue on the line named MAIN. The subroutine declaration says that the subroutine PIG has one parameter, X, and two local variables, Y and Z. The subroutine code starts on the line with the label "PIG1".

Lines 2, 3, and 9 belong to the main program. They read a series of messages, translate each to Pig Latin, write them out, and quit when a zero-length string is entered.

Lines 4 through 8 belong to the subroutine PIG. Line 4 initializes the answer to the null string. Line 5 strips leading blanks off the parameter, X. Line 6 isolates the next word in X (if any), and line 7 isolates its first letter. Finally, line 8 glues this word onto the output string with its letters in a different order and loops back to line 6.

A conflict happens because inserting code into the program requires that line numbers change, and GOTO requires that they stay constant. Because of this, adding lines to a program can be a complicated process. Normally, BASIC programmers leave regular gaps in the line numbers to allow for inserting a few lines. However, if the gap in numbering between two successive lines is smaller than the number of lines to be inserted, something will have to be renumbered. But since the targets of GOTOs are not marked in any special way, renumbering implies searching the entire program for GOTOs and GOSUBs that refer to any of the lines whose numbers have been changed. When found, these numbers must be updated [Exhibit 2.20]. Some BASIC systems provide a renumbering utility, others don't. In contrast, lines can be added almost anywhere in a C program with minimal local adjustments.

Principle of Too Much Flexibility

A language feature is bad to the extent that it provides flexibility that is not useful to the programmer, but that is likely to cause syntactic or semantic errors.

For example, any line in a BASIC program can be the target of a GOTO or a GOSUB statement. An explicit label declaration is not needed—the programmer simply refers to the line numbers used to enter and edit the program. A careless or typographical error in a GOTO line number will not be identified as a syntactic error.

Exhibit 2.20.   BASIC: GOTOs and statement ordering both use line numbers.

Line numbers in BASIC are used as targets of GOTO and also to define the proper sequence of the statements; the editor accepts lines in any order and arranges them by line number. Thus the user could type the following lines in any order and they would appear as follows:

```
2  SUM = SUM + A
4  PRINT SUM
6  IF A < 10 GO TO 2
8  STOP
```

Noticing that some statements have been left out, the programmer sees that three new lines must be inserted. The shortsighted programmer has only left room to insert one line between each pair, which is inadequate here, so he or she renumbers the old line 2 as 3 to make space for the insertion. The result is:

```
1  LET SUM = 0
2  LET A = 1
3  SUM = SUM + A
4  PRINT SUM
5  LET A = A + 1
6  IF A < 10 GO TO 2
8  STOP
```

Notice that the loop formed by line 6 now returns to the wrong line, making an infinite loop. Languages with separate line numbers and statement labels do not have this problem.

Every programmer knows which lines are supposed to be the targets of GOTOs, and she or he could easily identify or label them. But BASIC supplies no way to restrict GOTOs to the lines that the programmer knows should be their targets. Thus the translator cannot help the programmer ensure valid use of labels.

We would say that the ability to GOTO or GOSUB to any line in the program without writing an explicit label declaration is excessively flexible: it saves the programmer the minor trouble of declaring labels, but it leads to errors. If there were some way to restrict the set of target lines, BASIC would be a better and more powerful language. Power comes from a translator's ability to identify and eliminate meaningless commands, as well as from a language's ability to express aspects of a model.

Another example of useless flexibility can be seen in the way APL handles GOTO and statement labels. APL provides only three control structures: the function call, sequential execution, and a GOTO statement. A GOTO can only transfer control locally, within the current function definition. All other control structures, including ordinary conditionals and loops, must be defined in terms of the conditional GOTO.

As in BASIC, numeric line numbers are used both to determine the order of lines in a program and as targets of the GOTO. But the problems in BASIC with insertions and renumbering are avoided because, unlike BASIC, symbolic labels are supported. A programmer may write a symbolic label on a line and refer to it in a GOTO, and this will have the correct semantics even if lines are inserted and renumbering happens.

During compilation of a function definition (the process that happens when you leave the editor), the lines are renumbered. Each label is bound to a constant integer value: the number of the line on which it is defined. References to the label in the code are replaced by that constant, which from then on has exactly the same semantics as an integer. (Curiously, constants are not otherwise supported by the language.)

Semantic problems arise because the labels are translated into integer constants and may be operated on using integer operations such as multiplication and division! Further, the APL GOTO is completely unrestricted; it can name either a symbolic label or an integer line number, whether or not that line number is defined in that subroutine. Use of an undefined line number is equivalent to a function return. These semantics have been defined so that some interpretation is given no matter what the result of the expression is [Exhibit 2.21].

Exhibit 2.21. Strange but legal GOTOs in APL.

The GOTO is written with a right-pointing arrow, and its target may be any expression. The statements below are all legal in APL.

$\rightarrow (x + 2) - 6$	Legal so long as the result is an integer.
$\rightarrow 3\ 4\ 7$	An array of line numbers is given; control will be transferred to the first.
$\rightarrow \iota\ 0$	ι N returns a vector of N numbers, ranging from 1 to N. Thus, ι 0 returns a vector of length 0, which is the null object. A branch to the null object is equivalent to a no-op.

Because the target of a GOTO may be computed and may depend on variables, any line of the subroutine might potentially be its target. It is impossible at compile time to eliminate any line from the list of potential targets. Thus, at compile time, the behavior of a piece of code may be totally unpredictable.

APL aficionados love the flexibility of this GOTO. All sorts of permutations and selection may be done on an array of labels to implement every conceivable variety of conditional branch. Dozens of useful idioms, or phrases, such as the one in Exhibit 2.22, have been developed using this GOTO and published for other APL programmers to use.

Exhibit 2.22. A computed GOTO idiom in APL.

$$\rightarrow (\text{NEG, EQ, POS}) [\ 2 + \times \text{N}\ ]$$

This is a three-way branch very similar to the previous example and analogous to the FORTRAN `arithmetic` IF. The signum function, $\times$, returns -1 if N is negative, $+1$ if N is positive, and 0 otherwise. Two is added to the result of signum, and the answer is used to subscript a vector of labels. One of the three branches is always taken.

It is actually fun to work on and develop a new control structure idiom. Many language designers, though, question the utility and wisdom of permitting and relying on such idiomatic control structures. They must be deciphered to be understood, and the result of a mistake in definition or use is a totally wrong and unpredictable branch. Even a simple conditional branch to the top of a loop can be written with four different idioms, all in common use. This makes it difficult to learn to read someone else's code. Proofs of correctness are practically impossible.

We have shown that APL's totally unrestricted GOTO has the meaningless and useless flexibility to branch to any line of the program, and that the lack of any other control structure necessitates the use of cryptic idioms and produces programs with unpredictable behavior. These are severe semantic defects! By the principle of *Too Much Flexibility*, this unrestricted GOTO is bad, and APL would be a more powerful language with some form of restriction on the GOTO.

The Principle of Semantic Power

A programming language is powerful (for some application area) to the extent that it permits the programmer to write a program easily that expresses the *model*, the *whole model*, and *nothing but the model*. Thus a powerful language must support explicit communication of the model, possibly by defining a general object and then specifying restrictions on it. A restriction imposed by the language can support power at the price of flexibility that might be necessary for some applications. On the other hand, a restriction imposed by the user expresses only the semantics that the user wants to achieve and does not limit him or her in ways that obstruct programming.

The programmer should be able to specify a program that computes the "correct" results and then be able to verify that it does so. All programs should terminate properly, not "crash". Faulty results from correct data should be provably impossible.

Part of a model is a description of the data that is expected. A powerful language should let the programmer write data specifications in enough detail so that "garbage in" is detected and does not cause "garbage out".

The Principle of Portability

A *portable program* is one that can be compiled by many different compilers and run on different hardware, and that will work correctly on all of them. If a program is portable, it will be more useful to more people for more years. We live in times of constant change: we cannot expect to have the same hardware or operating system available in different places or different years.

But portability limits flexibility. A portable program, by definition, cannot exploit the special features of some hardware. It cannot rely on any particular bit-level representation of any object or function; therefore, it cannot manipulate such things. One might want to do so to achieve efficiency or to write low-level system programs.

Languages such as Standard Pascal that restrict access to pointers and to the bit-representations of objects force the programmer to write portable code but may prohibit her or him from writing efficient code for some applications.

Sometimes features are included in a language for historical reasons, even though the language supports a different and better way to write the same thing. As languages develop, new features are added that improve on old features. However, the old ones are seldom eliminated because *upward compatibility* is important. We want to be able to recompile old programs on new versions of the translator. Old languages such as COBOL and FORTRAN have been through the process of change and restandardization several times. Some features in these languages are completely archaic, and programmers should be taught not to use them [Exhibit 2.23]. Many of these features have elements that are inherently error prone, such as reliance on GOTOs. Moreover, they will eventually be dropped from the language standard. At that point, any programs that use the archaic features will require extensive modernization before they can be modified in any way.

Exhibit 2.23. An archaic language feature in FORTRAN.

The `arithmetic IF` statement was the only conditional statement in the original version of FORTRAN. It is a three-way conditional GOTO based directly on the conditional jump instruction of the IBM 704. An example of this statement is:

```
IF (J-1) 21, 76, 76
```

The expression in parentheses is evaluated first. If the result is negative, control goes to the first label on the list (21). For a zero value, control goes to the second label (76), and for a positive value, to the third (76). More often than not, in practical use, two of the labels are the same.

The `arithmetic IF` has been superseded by the modern `block IF` statement. Assume that ⟨block 1⟩ contains the statements that followed label 21 above, and ⟨block 2⟩ contains the statements following statement 76. Then the following `block IF` statement is equivalent to the `arithmetic IF` above:

```
IF J-1 .LT. O THEN
    ⟨block 1⟩
ELSE
    ⟨block 2⟩
ENDIF
```

Our answer to redundant and archaic language features is simple: don't use them. Find out what constitutes modern style in a language and use it consistently. Clean programming habits and consistent programming style produce error-free programs faster.

Another kind of redundancy is seen in Pascal, which provides two ways to delimit comments: (* This is a comment. *) and { This is a comment. } The former way was provided, as part of the standard, for systems that did not support the full ASCII character set. It will work in all Pascal implementations and is thus more portable. The latter way, however, is considered more modern and preferred by many authors. Some programmers use both: one form for comments, the other to "comment out" blocks of code.

The language allows both kinds of comment delimiters to be used in a program. However, mixing the delimiters is a likely source of errors because they are not interchangeable. A comment must begin and end with the same kind of delimiter. Thus whatever conventions a programmer chooses should be used consistently. The programmer must choose either the more portable way or the more modern way, a true dilemma.

2.4 CLASSIFYING LANGUAGES

It is tempting to classify languages according to the most prominent feature of the language and to believe that these features make each language group fundamentally different from other groups. Such categorizations are always misleading because:

- Languages in different categories are fundamentally more alike than they are different. Believing that surface differences are important gets in the way of communication among groups of language users.
- We tend to associate things that occur together in some early example of a language category. We tend to believe that these things must always come together. This impedes progress in language design.
- Category names are used loosely. Nobody is completely sure what these names mean, and which languages are or are not in any category.
- Languages frequently belong to more than one category. Sorting them into disjoint classes disguises real similarities among languages with different surface syntax.

2.4.1 Language Families

Students do need to understand commonly used terminology, and it is sometimes useful to discuss a group of languages having some common property. With this in mind, let us look at some of the "language families" that people talk about and try to give brief descriptions of the properties that characterize each family. As you read this section, remember that these are not absolute, mutually exclusive categories: categorizations are approximate and families overlap heavily. Examples are listed for each group, and some languages are named several times.

Interactive Languages.

An interactive language is enmeshed in a system that permits easy alternation between program entry, translation, and execution of code. We say that it operates using a REW cycle: the system Reads an expression, Evaluates it, and Writes the result on the terminal, then waits for another input.

Programs in interactive languages are generally structured as a series of fairly short function and object definitions. Translation happens when the end of a definition is typed in. Programs are usually translated into some intermediate form, not into native machine code. This intermediate form is then interpreted. Many interactive languages, such as FORTH and Miranda, use the term "compile" to denote the translation of source code into the internal form.

Examples: APL, BASIC, FORTH, LISP, T, Scheme, dBASE, Miranda.

Structured Languages.

Control structures are provided that allow one to write programs without using GOTO. Procedures with call-by-value parameters[5] are supported. Note that we call

---

[5]See Chapter 9.

Pascal a structured language even though it contains a GOTO, because it is not necessary to use that GOTO to write programs.

Examples: Pascal, C, FORTH, LISP, T, Scheme.

Strongly Typed Languages.

Objects are named, and each name has a type. Every object belongs to exactly one type (types are disjoint). The types of actual function arguments are compared to the declared types of the dummy parameters during compilation. A mismatch in types or in number of parameters will produce an error comment. Many strongly typed languages, including Pascal, Ada, and ANSI C, include an "escape hatch"—that is, some mechanism by which the normal type-checking process can be evaded.

Examples: FORTRAN 77, Pascal, Ada, ANSI C (but not the original C), ML, Miranda.

Object-oriented Languages.

These are extensions or generalizations of the typed languages. Objects are typed and carry their type identity with them at all times. Any given function may have several definitions, which we will call *methods*.[6] Each method operates on a different type of parameter and is associated with the type of its first parameter. The translator must *dispatch* each function call by deciding which defining method to invoke for it. The method associated with the type of the first parameter will be used, if it exists.

Object-oriented languages have nondisjoint types and function inheritance. The concept of *function inheritance* was introduced by Simula and popularized by Smalltalk, the first language to be called "object-oriented". A type may be a subset of another type. The function dispatcher will use this subset relationship in the dispatching process. It will select a function belonging to the supertype when none is defined for the subtype.

Actually, many of these characteristics also apply to APL, an old language. It has objects that carry type tags and functions with multiple definitions and automatic dispatching. It is not a full object-oriented language because it lacks definable class hierarchies.

Examples: Simula, Smalltalk, T, C++. APL is object-oriented in a restricted sense.

Procedural Languages.

A program is an ordered sequence of statements and procedure calls that will be evaluated sequentially. Statements interact and communicate with each other through variables. Storing a value in a variable destroys the value that was previously stored there. (This is called destructive assignment.) Exhibit 2.24 is a diagram of the history of this language family. Modern procedural languages also contain extensive functional elements.[7]

Examples: Pascal, C, Ada, FORTRAN, BASIC, COBOL.

---

[6]This is the term used in Smalltalk.
[7]See Chapter 8.

Exhibit 2.24.   The development of procedural languages.

Concepts and areas of concern are listed on the left. Single arrows show how these influenced language design and how some languages influenced others. Dotted double arrows indicate that a designer was strongly influenced by the bad features of an earlier language.

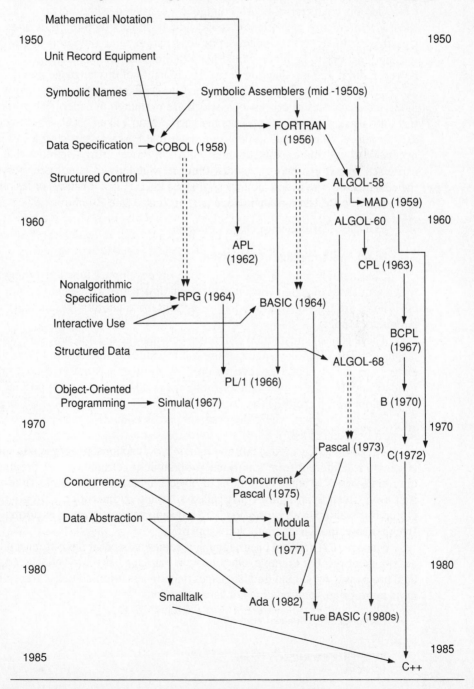

Functional Languages, Old Style.

A program is a nested set of expressions and function calls. Call-by-value parameter binding, not assignment, is the primary mechanism used to give names to variables. Functions interact and communicate with each other through the parameter stack.

Certain characteristics are commonly associated with functional languages. Most are interactive and oriented toward the list data structure. Functions are objects that can be freely manipulated, passed as parameters, composed, and so on. Permitting functions to be manipulated like other objects gives a language tremendous power. Exhibit 2.25 is a diagram of the development of this language family.

LISP and its modern lexically scoped descendants support destructive assignment and sequences of expressions, which are evaluated in order. When these features are used, these languages become "procedural", like Pascal. These languages are, therefore, "functional" in the same sense that Pascal is "structured". It is never necessary to use the semantically messy GOTO in Pascal. Any semantics that can be expressed with it can be expressed without it. Similarly, it is not necessary to use the semantically messy destructive assignment in LISP, but it is used occasionally, to achieve efficiency, when changing one part of a large data structure.

Examples: LISP, Common LISP, T, Scheme.

Functional Languages, New Style.

Considerable work is now being done on developing functional languages in which sequences of statements, variables, and destructive assignment do not exist at all. Values are passed from one part of a program to another by function calls and parameter binding.

There is one fundamental difference between the old and new style functional languages. The LISP-like languages use call-by-value parameters, and these new languages use call-by-need (lazy evaluation).[8] A parameter is not evaluated until it is needed, and its value is then kept for future use. Call-by-need is an important semantic development, permitting the use of "infinite lists", which are objects that are part data and part program, where the program part is evaluated, as needed, to produce the next item on the list.

The terminology used to talk about these new functional programming languages is sometimes different from traditional programming terminology. A program is an unordered series of static definitions of objects, types, and functions. In Miranda it isn't even called a "program", it is called a "script". "Executing a program" is replaced by "evaluating an expression" or "reducing an expression to its normal form." In either case, though, computation happens.

Since pure functional programming is somewhat new, it has not reached its full development yet. For example, efficient array handling has yet to be included. As the field progresses, we should find languages that are less oriented to list processing and more appropriate for modeling nonlist applications.

Examples: ML, Miranda, Haskell.

---

[8]Parameter passing is explained fully in Chapter 9.

Exhibit 2.25.   The development of functional languages.

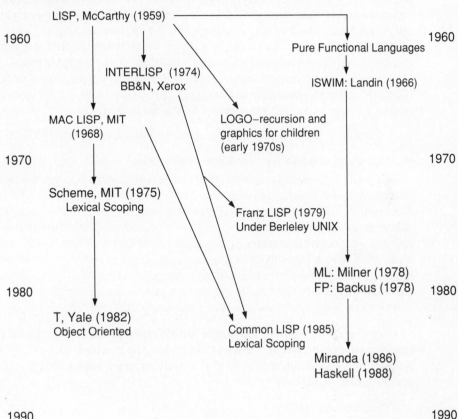

Parallel Languages.

These contain multitasking primitives that permit a program to fork into two or more asynchronous, communicating tasks that execute some series of computations in parallel. This class of languages is becoming increasingly important as highly parallel hardware develops.

Parallel languages are being developed as extensions of other kinds of languages. One of the intended uses for them is to program highly parallel machines such as the HyperCube. There is a great deal of interest in using such machines for massive numeric applications like weather prediction and image processing. It is not surprising, therefore, that the language developed for the HyperCube resembled a merger of the established number-oriented languages, FORTRAN and APL.

There is also strong interest in parallel languages in the artificial intelligence community, where many researchers are working on neural networks. Using parallelism is natural in such disciplines. In many situations, a programmer wishes to evaluate several possible courses of action and choose the first one to reach a goal. Some of the computations may be very long and others short, and one can't predict which are which. One cannot, therefore, specify an optimal order in which to evaluate the possibilities. The best way to express this is as a parallel computation: "Evaluate all these computations in parallel, and report to me when the first one terminates". List-oriented parallel languages will surely develop for these applications.

Finally, the clean semantics of the assignment-free functional languages are significantly easier to generalize to parallel execution, and new parallel languages will certainly be developed as extensions of functional languages.

Examples: Co-Pascal, in a restricted sense. LINDA, OCCAM, FORTRAN-90.

Languages Specialized for Some Application.

These languages all contain a complete general-purpose programming language as their basis and, in addition, contain a set of specialized primitives designed to make it convenient to process some particular data structure or problem area. Most contain some sophisticated and powerful higher-level commands that would require great skill and long labor to program in an unspecialized language like Pascal. An example is dBASE III which contains a full programming language similar to BASIC and, in addition, powerful screen handling and file management routines. The former expedites entry and display of information, the latter supports a complex indexed file structure in which key fields can be used to relate records in different files.

Systems programming languages must contain primitives that let the programmer manipulate the bits and bytes of the underlying machine and should be heavily standardized and widely available so that systems, once implemented, can be easily ported to other machines.

Examples: C, FORTH.

Business data processing languages must contain primitives that give fine and easy control over details of input, output, file handling, and precision of numbers. The standard floating-point representations are not adequate to provide this control, and some form of fixed-point numeric representation must be provided. The kind of printer or screen output formatting provided in FORTRAN, C, and Pascal is too clumsy and does not provide enough flexibility. A better syntax and more options must be provided. Similarly, a modern language for business data processing must have a good facility for defining screens for interactive input. A major proportion of these languages is devoted to I/O.

Higher-level commands should be included for common tasks such as table handling and sorting. Finally, the language should provide good support for file handling, including primitives for handling sequential, indexed, and random access files.

Examples: RPG (limited to sequential files), COBOL, Ada.

Data base languages contain extensive subsystems for handling *internal* files, and relationships among files. Note that this is quite independent of a good subsystem for screen and printer I/O.

Examples: dBASE, Framework, Structured Query Language (SQL).

List processing languages contain primitive definitions for a linked list data type and the important basic operations on lists. This structure has proven to be useful for artificial intelligence programming.

Implementations must contain powerful operations for direct input and output of lists, routines for allocation of dynamic heap storage, and a *garbage collection* routine for recovery of dynamically allocated storage that is no longer accessible.

Examples: LISP, T, Scheme, Miranda.

Logic languages are interactive languages that use symbolic logic and set theory to model computation. Prolog was the first logic language and is still the best known. Its dominant characteristics define the language class. A Prolog "program" is a series of statements about logical relations that are used to establish a data base, interspersed with statements that query this data base. To evaluate a query, Prolog searches that data base for any entries that satisfy all the constraints in the query. To do this, the translator invokes an elaborate expression evaluator which performs an exhaustive search of the data base, with backtracking. Rules of logical deduction are built into the evaluator.

Thus we can classify a logic language as an interactive data base language where both operations and the data base itself are highly specialized for dealing with the language of symbolic logic and set theory. Prolog is of particular interest in the artificial intelligence community, where deductive reasoning on the basis of a set of known facts is basic to many undertakings.

Examples: HASL, FUNLOG, Templog (for temporal logic), Uniform (unifies LISP and Prolog), Fresh (combines the functional language approach with logic programming).

Array processing languages contain primitives for constructing and manipulating arrays and matrices. Sophisticated control structures are built in for mapping simple operations onto arrays, for composing and decomposing arrays, and for operating on whole arrays.

Examples: APL, APL-2, VisiCalc, and Lotus.

String processing languages contain primitives for input, output, and processing of character strings. Operations include searching for and extracting substrings specified by complex patterns involving string functions. Pattern matching is a powerful higher-level operation that may involve exhaustive search by backtracking. The well-known string processing languages are SNOBOL and its modern descendant, ICON.

Typesetting languages were developed because computer typesetting is becoming an economically important task. Technical papers, books, and drawings are, increasingly, prepared for print using a computer language. A document prepared in such a language is an unreadable mixture of commands and ordinary text. The commands handle files, set type fonts, position material, and control indexing, footnotes, and glossaries. Drawings are specified in a language of their own, then integrated with text. The entire finished product is output in a language that a laser printer can handle. This book was prepared using the languages mentioned below, and a drafting package named Easydraw whose output was converted to Postscript.

Examples: Postscript, TeX, LaTeX.

Command languages are little languages frequently created by extending a system's user interface. First simple commands are provided; these are extended by permitting arguments and variations. More useful commands are added. In many cases these command interfaces develop their own syntax (usually ad hoc and fairly primitive) and truly extensive capabilities. For example, entire books have been written about UNIX shell programming. Every UNIX system includes one or several "shells" which accept, parse, and interpret commands. From these shells, the user may call system utilities and other small systems such as grep, make, and flex. Each one has its own syntax, switches, semantics, and defaults.

Command languages tend to be arcane. In many cases, little design effort goes into them because their creators view them as simple interfaces, not as languages.

Fourth-generation languages evolved with the development of personal computers. This curious name was applied to diverse systems developed in the mid-1980s. Their common property was that they all contained some powerful new control structures, statements, or functions by which you could invoke in a few words some useful action that would take many lines to program in a language like Pascal. These languages were considered, therefore, to be especially easy to learn and "user friendly", and the natural accompaniments to "fourth-generation hardware", or personal computers.

Lotus 1-2-3 and SuperCalc are good examples of fourth-generation languages. They contain a long list of commands that are very useful for creating, editing, printing, and extracting information from a two-dimensional data base called a *spreadsheet*, and subsystems for creating several kinds of graphs from that data.

HyperCard is a data base system in which it is said that you can write complex applications without writing a line of code. You construct the application with the mouse, not with the keyboard.

The designers of many fourth-generation languages viewed them as *replacements* for programming languages, not as *new* programming languages. The result is that their designs did not really profit as much as they could have from thirty years of experience in language design. Like COBOL and FORTRAN, these languages are ad hoc collections of useful operations.

The data base languages such as dBASE are also called "fourth-generation languages", and again their designers thought of them as replacements for computer languages. Unfortunately, these languages do not eliminate the need for programming. Even with lots of special report-generating features built in, users often want something a little different from the features provided. This implies a need for a general-purpose language within the fourth-generation system in which users can define their own routines. The general-purpose language included in dBASE is primitive and lacks important control structures. Until the newest version, dBASE4, procedures did not even have parameters, and when they were finally added, the implementation was unusual and clumsy.

The moral is that there is no free lunch. An adaptable system must contain a general-purpose language to cover applications not supported by predefined features. The whole system will be better if this general-purpose language is carefully designed.

2.4.2 Languages Are More Alike than Different

Viewing languages as belonging to "language families" tends to make us forget how similar all languages are. This basic similarity happens because the purpose of all languages is to communicate models from human to machine. All languages are influenced by the innate abilities and weaknesses of human beings and are constrained by the computer's inability to handle irreducible ambiguity. Most of the differences among languages arise from the specialized nature of the objects and tasks to be communicated using a given language.

This book is not about any particular family of languages. It is primarily about the concepts and mechanisms that underlie the design and implementation of all languages, and only secondarily about the features that distinguish one family from another. Most of all, it is not about the myriad variations in syntax used to represent the same semantics in different languages. The reader is asked to try to forget syntax and focus on the underlying elements.

EXERCISES

1. What are the two ways to view a program?
2. How will languages supporting these views differ?
3. What is a computer representation of an object? A process?
4. Define semantic intent. Define semantic validity. What is their importance?
5. What is the difference between explicit and implicit representation? What are the implications of each?
6. What is the difference between coherent and diffuse representation?
7. What are the advantages of coherent representation?
8. How can language design goals conflict? How can the designer resolve this problem?
9. How can restrictions imposed by the language designer both aid and hamper the programmer?
10. Why is the concept of locality of effect so important in programming language design?
11. What are the dangers involved when using global variables?
12. What is lexical coherence? Give an example of poor lexical coherence.
13. What is portability? Why does it limit flexibility?
14. Why is it difficult to classify languages according to their most salient characteristics?
15. What is a structured language? Strongly typed language? Object-oriented language? Parallel language? Fourth-generation language?
16. Why are most languages more similar than they are different? From what causes do language differences arise?

17. Discuss two aspects of a language design that make it hard to read, write, or use. Give an example of each, drawn from a language with which you are familiar.

18. Choose three languages from the following list: Smalltalk, BASIC, APL, LISP, C, Pascal, Ada. Describe one feature of each that causes some people to defend it as the "best" language for some application. Choose features that are unusual and do not occur in many languages.

3

Elements of Language

—— Overview ————————————————————

This chapter presents elements of language, drawing correlations between English parts of speech and words in programming languages. Metalanguages allow languages to describe themselves. Basic structural units, words, sentences, paragraphs, and references, are analogous to the lexical tokens, statements, scope, and comments of programming languages.

Languages are made of words with their definitions, rules for combining the words into meaningful larger units, and metawords (words for referring to parts of the language). In this section we examine how this is true both of English and of a variety of programming languages.

3.1 THE PARTS OF SPEECH

3.1.1 Nouns

In natural languages nouns give us the ability to refer to objects. People invent names for objects so that they may catalog them and communicate information about them. Likewise, names are used for these purposes in programming languages, where they are given to program objects (functions, memory locations, etc.). A *variable declaration* is a directive to a translator to set aside storage to represent some real-world object, then give a name to that storage so that it may be accessed. Names can also be given to constants, functions, and types in most languages.

First-Class Objects

One of the major trends throughout the thirty-five years of language design has been to strengthen and broaden the concept of "object". In the beginning, programmers

47

dealt directly with machine locations. Symbolic assemblers introduced the idea that these locations represented real-world data, and could be named. Originally, each object had a name and corresponded to one storage location. When arrays were introduced in FORTRAN and records in COBOL, these aggregates were viewed as collections of objects, not as objects themselves.

Several years and several languages later, arrays and records began to achieve the status of *first-class objects* that could be manipulated and processed as whole units. Languages from the early seventies, such as Pascal and C, waffled on this point, permitting some whole-object operations on aggregate objects but prohibiting others. Modern languages support aggregate-objects and permit them to be constructed, initialized, assigned to, compared, passed as arguments, and returned as results with the same ease as simple objects.

More recently, the functional object, that is, an executable piece of code, has begun to achieve first-class status in some languages, which are known as "functional languages". The type object has been the last kind of object to achieve first-class status. A type object describes the type of other objects and is essential in a language that supports generic code.

Naming Objects

One of the complex aspects of programming languages that we will study in Chapter 6 involves the correspondence of names to objects. There is considerable variation among languages in the ways that names are used. In various languages a name can:

- Exist without being attached, or *bound*, to an object (LISP).
- Be bound simultaneously to different objects in different scopes (ALGOL, Pascal).
- Be bound to different types of objects at different times (APL, LISP).
- Be bound, through a pointer, to an object that no longer exists (C).

Conversely, in most languages, a single object can be bound to more than one name at a time, producing an *alias*. This occurs when a formal parameter name is bound to an actual parameter during a function call.

Finally, in many languages, the storage allocated for different objects and bound to different names can overlap. Two different list heads may share the same tail section [Exhibit 3.1].

Exhibit 3.1.   Two overlapping objects (linked lists).

List 1: → The → Only → Direction → From → Here → Is → Up.

List 2: → Your → Time

3.1.2 Pronouns: Pointers

Pronouns in natural languages correspond roughly to pointers in programming languages. Both are used to refer to different objects (nouns) at different times, and both must be *bound to* (defined to refer to) some object before becoming meaningful. The most important use of pointers in programming languages is to label objects that are dynamically created. Because the number of these objects is not known to the programmer before execution time, he cannot provide names for them all, and pointers become the only way to reference them.

When a pointer is bound to an object, the address of that object is stored in space allocated for the pointer, and the pointer refers indirectly to that object. This leads to the possibility that the pointer might refer to an object that has *died*, or ceased to exist. Such a pointer is called a "dangling reference". Using a dangling reference is a programming error and must be guarded against in some languages (e.g., C). In other languages (e.g., Pascal) this problem is minimized by imposing severe restrictions on the use of pointers. (Dangling references are covered in Section 6.3.2.)

3.1.3 Adjectives: Data Types

In English, adjectives describe the size, shape, and general character of objects. They correspond, in a programming language, to the many data type attributes that can be associated with an object by a declaration or by a default. In some languages, a single attribute is declared that embodies a set of properties including specifications for size, structure, and encoding [Exhibit 3.2]. In other languages, these properties are independent and are listed separately, either in variable declarations (as in COBOL) or in type declarations, as in Ada [Exhibit 3.3].

Exhibit 3.2.   Size and encoding bundled in C.

The line below declares a number that will be represented in the computer using floating-point encoding. The actual number of bytes allocated is usually four, and the precision is approximately seven digits. This declaration is the closest parallel in C to the Ada declaration in Exhibit 3.3.

```
float price;
```

Exhibit 3.3.   Size and encoding specified separately in Ada.

- The Ada declarations below create a new type named REAL and a REAL object, price.
- The use of the keyword digits indicates that this type is to be derived from some predefined type with floating-point encoding.
- The number seven indicates that the resulting type must have at least seven decimal digits of precision.

```
type REAL is digits 7;
price:  REAL;
```

Some of the newer languages permit the programmer to define types that are related hierarchically in a tree structure. Each class of objects in the tree has well-defined properties. Each subclass has properties of its own and also inherits all the properties of the classes above it in the hierarchy. Exhibit 3.4 gives an example of such a type hierarchy in English. The root of this hierarchy is the class "vertebrate," which is characterized by having a backbone. All subclasses "inherit" this property. At the next level are birds, which have feathers, and mammals, which have hair. We can, therefore, conclude that robins and chickens are feathered creatures, and that human beings are hairy. Going down the tree, we see that roosters and hens inherit all properties of chickens, including being good to eat. According to the tree, adults and children are both human (although members of each subclass sometimes dispute this). Finally, at the leaf level, both male and female subclasses exist, which inherit the properties of either adults or children.

Exhibit 3.4.   A type hierarchy with inheritance in English.

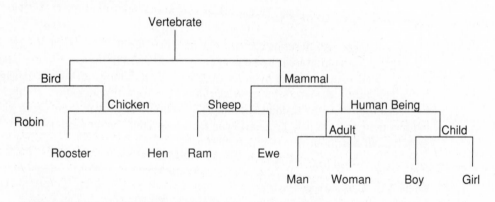

"Inheritance" means that any function defined for a superclass also applies to all subclasses. Thus if we know that constitutional rights are guaranteed for human beings, we can conclude that girls have these rights.

Using an object-oriented language such as Smalltalk a programmer can implement types (classes) with exactly this kind of hierarchical *inheritance* of type properties. (Chapter 16 deals with this topic more fully.)

3.1.4 Verbs

In English, verbs are words for actions or states of being. Similarly, in programming languages, we see action words such as RETURN, BREAK, STOP, GOTO, and :=. Procedure calls, function calls, and arithmetic operators all direct that some action should happen, and are like action verbs. Relational operators (=, >, etc.) denote states of being—they ask questions about the state of some program object or objects.

In semistandard terminology, a function is a program object that receives information through a list of arguments, performs a prescribed computation on that information, calculates some "answer," and returns that value to the calling program. In most languages function calls can be embedded within the argument lists of other function calls, and within arithmetic expressions. Function calls are usually denoted by writing the function name followed by an appropriate series of arguments enclosed in parentheses. Expressions often contain more than one function call. In this case each language defines (or explicitly leaves undefined) the order in which the calls will be executed.[1]

A procedure is just like a function except that it does not return a value. Because no value results from executing the procedure, the procedure call constitutes an entire program statement and cannot be embedded in an expression or in the argument list of another call.

An operator is a predefined function whose name is often a special symbol such as "+". Most operators require either one or two arguments, which are called *operands*. Many languages support infix notation for operators, in which the operator symbol is written between its two operands or before or after its single operand. Rules of precedence and associativity [Chapter 8, Section 8.3.2] govern the way that infix expressions are parsed, and parentheses are used, when necessary, to modify the action of these rules.

We will use the word "function" as a generic word to refer to functions, operators, and procedures when the distinctions among them are not important.

Some languages (e.g., FORTRAN, Pascal, and Ada) provide three different syntactic forms for operators, functions, and procedures [Exhibit 3.5]. Other languages (e.g., LISP and APL) provide only one [Exhibits 3.6 and 3.7]. To a great extent, this makes languages *appear* to be more different in structure than they are. The first impression of a programmer upon seeing his or her first LISP program is that LISP is full of parentheses, is cryptic, and has little in common with other languages. Actually, various "front ends", or preprocessors, have been written for LISP that permit the programmer to write using a syntax that resembles ALGOL or Pascal. This kind of preprocessor changes only cosmetic aspects of the language syntax. It does not add power or supply kinds of statements that do not already exist. The LISP preprocessors do demonstrate that LISP and ALGOL have very similar semantic capabilities.

The Domain of a Verb

The definition of a verb in English always includes an indication of the domain of the verb, that is, the nouns with which that verb can meaningfully be used. A dictionary provides this information, either implicitly or explicitly, as part of the definition of each verb [Exhibit 3.8].

Similarly, the domain of a programming language verb is normally specified when it is defined. This specification is part of the program in some languages, part of the documentation in others. The *domain of a function* is defined in most languages by a function header, which is part of the function definition. A header specifies the number of the objects required for the function to operate and the formal names by which those parameters will be known. Languages that implement strong typing also require the types of the parameters to be specified in the header. This information is used to ensure that the function is applied meaningfully, to objects of the correct types [Exhibit 3.9].

---

[1] This issue is discussed in Chapter 8.

The *range of a function* is the set of objects that may be the result of that function. This must also be specified in the function header (as in Pascal) or by default (as in C) in languages that implement type checking.

Exhibit 3.5.   Syntax for verbs in Pascal and Ada.

These languages, like most ALGOL-like languages, have three kinds of verbs, with distinct ways of invoking each.

> Functions: The function name is written followed by parentheses enclosing the list of arguments. Arguments may themselves be function calls. The call must be embedded in some larger statement, such as an assignment statement or procedure call. This is a call to a function named "push" with an embedded call on the "sin" function.

> ```
> Success := push(rs, sin(x));
> ```

> Procedures: A procedure call constitutes an entire program statement. The procedure name is written followed by parentheses enclosing the list of arguments, which may be function calls. This is a call on Pascal's output procedure, with an embedded function call:

> ```
> Writeln (Success, sin(x));
> ```

> Operators: An operator is written between its operands, and several operators may be combined to form an expression. Operator-expressions are legal in any context in which function calls are legal.

> ```
> Success := push(rs, (x+y)/(x-y));
> ```

Exhibit 3.6.   Syntax for verbs in LISP.

LISP has only one class of verb: functions. There *are* no procedures in LISP, as all functions return a value. In a function call, the function name and the arguments are enclosed in parentheses (first line below). Arithmetic operators are also written as function calls (second line).

> ```
> (myfun arg1 arg2 arg3)
> (+ B 1)
> ```

Exhibit 3.7.   Syntax for verbs in APL.

APL provides a syntax for applying operators but not for function calls or procedure calls. Operators come in three varieties: dyadic (having two arguments), monadic (having one argument), and niladic (having no arguments).

- Dyadic operators are written between their operands. Line [1] below shows "+" being used to add the vector (5 3) to B and add that result to A. (APL expressions are evaluated right-to-left.) Variables A and B might be scalars or length two vectors. The result is a length two vector.

- Monadic operators are written to the left of their operands. Line [2] shows the monadic operator "|", or absolute value.

- Line [3] shows a call on a *niladic operator*, the read-input operator, "□ ". The value read is stored in A.

```
[1] A + 5 3 + B
[2] |A
[3] A← □
```

The programmer may define new functions but may not use more than two arguments for those functions. Function calls are written using the syntax for operators. Thus a dyadic programmer-defined function named "FUN" would be called by writing:

```
A FUN B
```

When a function requires more than two arguments, they must be packed or encoded into two bunches, sent to the function, then unpacked or decoded within the function. This is awkward and not very elegant.

Exhibit 3.8.   The domain of a verb in English.

Verb: Cry

Definition for the verb cry, paraphrased from the dictionary.[2]

1. To make inarticulate sobbing sounds expressing grief, sorrow, or pain.
2. To weep, or shed tears.
3. To shout, or shout out.
4. To utter a characteristic sound or call (used of an animal).

The domain is defined in definitions (1) through (3) by stating that the object/creature that cries must be able to sob, express feelings, weep, or shout. Definition (4) explicitly states that the domain is an animal. Thus all of the following things can "cry": human beings (by definitions 1, 2, 3), geese (4), and baby dolls (2).

Exhibit 3.9.   The domains of some Pascal functions.

Predefined functions	Domains
chr	An integer between 0 and 127.
ord	Any object of an enumerated type.
trunc	A real number.

A user-defined function header: FUNCTION search (N:name; L:list): list;

The domain of "search" is pairs of objects, one of type "name", the other of type "list". The result of "search" is a "list"; its range is, therefore, the type "list".

---

[2]Morris [1969], p. 319.

3.1.5   Prepositions and Conjunctions

In English we distinguish among the parts of speech used to denote time, position, conditionals, and the relationship of phrases in a sentence. Each programming language contains a small number of such words, used analogously to delimit phrases and denote choices and repetition (WHILE, ELSE, BY, CASE, etc.). The exact words differ from language to language. Grammatical rules state how these words may be combined with phrases and statements to form meaningful units. By themselves these words have little meaning, and we will deal with them in Chapter 10, where we examine control structures.

3.2   THE METALANGUAGE

A language needs ways to denote its structural units and to refer to its own parts. English has sentences, paragraphs, essays, and the like, each with lexical conventions that identify the unit and mark its beginning and end. Natural languages are also able to refer to these units and to the words that comprise the language, as in phrases such as "the paragraph below", and "USA is an abbreviation for the United States of America". These parts of a language that permit it to talk about itself are called a *metalanguage*. The metalanguage that accompanies most programming languages consists of an assortment of syntactic delimiters, metawords, and ways to refer to structural units. We consider definitions of the basic structural units to be part of the metalanguage also.

3.2.1   Words: Lexical Tokens

The smallest unit of any written language is the *lexical token*—the mark or series of marks that denote one symbol or word in the language. To understand a communication, first the tokens must be identified, then each one and their overall arrangement must be interpreted to arrive at the meaning of the communication. Analogously, one must separate the sounds of a spoken sentence into tokens before it can be comprehended. Sometimes it is a nontrivial task to separate the string of written marks or spoken sounds into tokens, as anyone knows who has spent a day in a foreign country.

This same process must be applied to computer programs. A human reader or a compiler must first perform a *lexical analysis* of the code before beginning to understand the meaning. The portion of the compiler that does this task is called the *lexer*.

In some languages lexical analysis is trivially simple. This is true in FORTH, which requires every lexical token to be *delimited* (separated from every other token) by one or more spaces. Assembly languages frequently define fixed columns for operation codes and require operands to be separated by commas. Operating system command shells usually call for the use of spaces and a half dozen punctuation marks which are tokens themselves and also delimit other tokens. Such simple languages are easy to lexically analyze, or *lex*. Not all programming languages are so simple, though, and we will examine the common lexical conventions and their effects on language.

The lexical rules of most languages define the lexical forms for a variety of token types:

- Names (predefined and user-defined)
- Special symbols
- Numeric literals
- Single-character literals
- Multiple-character string literals

These rules are stated as part of the formal definition of every programming language. A lexer for a language is commonly produced by feeding these rules to a program called a *lexer generator*, whose output is a program (the lexer) that can perform lexical analysis on a source text string according to the given rules. The lexer is the first phase of a compiler. Its role in the compiling process is illustrated in Exhibit 4.3.

Much of the feeling and appearance of a language is a side effect of the rules for forming tokens. The most common rules for delimiting tokens are stated below. They reflect the rules of Pascal, C, and Ada.

- Special symbols are characters or character strings that are nonalphabetic and nonnumeric. Examples are ";", "+", and ":=". They are all predefined by the language syntax. No new special symbols may be defined by the programmer.
- Names must start with an alphabetic character and must not contain anything except letters, digits, and (sometimes) the "_" symbol.
- Everything that starts with a letter is a name.
- Names end with a space or a special symbol.
- Special symbols generally alternate with names and literals. Where two special symbols or two names are adjacent, they must be separated by a space.
- Numeric literals start with a digit, a "+", or a "−". They may contain digits, ".", and "E" (for exponent). Any other character ends the literal.
- Single-character literals and multiple-character strings are enclosed in matching single or double quotes. If, as in C, a single character has different semantics from a string of length 1, then single quotes may be used to delimit one and double quotes used for the other.

Note that spaces are used to delimit some but not all tokens. This permits the programmer to write arithmetic expressions such as "a*(b+c)/d" the way a mathematician would write them. If we insisted on a delimiter (such as a space) after every token, the expression would have to be written "a * (b + c) / d ", which most programmers would consider to be onerous and unnatural.

Spaces *are* required to delimit arithmetic operators in COBOL. The above expression in COBOL would be written "a * (b + c) / d". This awkwardness is one of the reasons that programmers are uncomfortable using COBOL for numeric applications. The reason for this requirement is that the "−" character is ambiguous: COBOL's lexical rules permit "−" to be used as a hyphen in variable names, for example, "hourly-rate-in". Long, descriptive variable names greatly enhance the readability of programs.

Hyphenated variable names have existed in COBOL from the beginning. When COBOL was extended at a later date to permit the use of arithmetic expressions, an ambiguity arose: the hyphen character and the subtraction operator were the same character. One way to avoid this problem is to use different characters for the two purposes. Modern languages use the "−" for subtraction and the underbar, "_", *which has no other function in the language*, to achieve readability.

As you can see, the rules for delimiting tokens can be complex, and they do have varied repercussions. The three important issues here are:

- Code should be readable.
- The language must be translatable and, preferably, easy to lex.
- It is preferable to use the same conventions as are used in English and/or mathematical notation.

The examples given show that a familiar, readable language may contain an ambiguous use of symbols. A few language designers have chosen to sacrifice familiarity and readability altogether in order to achieve lexical simplicity. LISP, APL, and FORTH all have simpler lexical and syntactic rules, and all are considered unreadable by some programmers because of the conflict between their prior experience and the lexical and syntactic forms of the language.

Let us examine the simple lexical rule in FORTH and its effects. In other languages the decision was made to permit arithmetic expressions to be written without delimiters between the variable names and the operators. A direct consequence is that special symbols (nonalphabetic, nonnumeric, and nonunderbar) must be prohibited in variable names. It may seem natural to prohibit the use of characters like "+" and "(" in a name, but it is not at all necessary.

FORTH requires one or more space characters or carriage returns between every pair of tokens, and because of this rule, it can permit special characters to be used in identifiers. It makes no distinction between user-defined names and predefined tokens: either may contain any character that can be typed and displayed. The string "#$%" could be used as a variable or function name if the programmer so desired. The token "ab*" could never be confused with an arithmetic problem because the corresponding arithmetic problem, "a b *", contains three tokens separated by spaces. Thus the programmer, having a much larger alphabet to use, is far freer to invent brief, meaningful names. For example, one might use "a+" to name a function that increments its argument (a variable) by the value of a.

Lexical analysis is trivially easy in FORTH. Since its lexical rules treat all printing characters the same way and do not distinguish between alphabetic characters and punctuation marks, FORTH needs only three classes of lexical tokens:

- Names (predefined or user-defined).
- Numeric literals.
- String literals. These can appear only after the string output command, which is ". "" (pronounced "dot-quote"). A string literal is terminated by the next """ (pronounced "quote").

These three token types correspond to semantically distinct classes of objects that the interpreter handles in distinct ways. Names are to be looked up in the dictionary and executed. Numeric literals are to be converted to binary and put on the stack. String literals are to be copied to the output stream. The lexical rules of the language thus correspond directly to its semantics, and the interpreter is very short and simple.

The effect of these lexical rules on people should also be noted. Although the rules are simple and easy to learn, a programmer accustomed to the conventions in other languages has a hard time learning to treat the space character as important.

3.2.2 Sentences: Statements

The earliest high-level languages reflected the linguistic idea of sentences: a FORTRAN or COBOL program is a series of sentencelike statements.[3] COBOL statements even end in periods. Most statements, like sentences, specify an action to perform and some object or objects on which to perform the action. A language is called "procedural", if a program is a sequence of statements, grouped into procedures, to be carried out using the objects specified.

In the late 1950s, when FORTRAN and COBOL were developed, the punched card was the dominant medium for communication from human to computer. Programs, commands to the operating system, and data were all punched on cards. To compile and (one hoped) run a program, the programmer constructed a "deck" usually consisting of:

- An ID control card, specifying time limits for the compilation and run.[4]
- A control card requesting compilation, an object program listing, an error listing, and a memory map.[5]
- A series of cards containing the program.
- A control card requesting loading and linking of the object program.
- A control card requesting a run and a core dump[6] of the executable program.
- A control card marking the beginning of the data.
- A series of cards containing the data.
- A JOB END control card marking the end of the deck.

Control cards had a special character in column 1 by which they could be recognized. Because a deck of cards could easily become disordered by being dropped, columns 73 through 80 were conventionally reserved for identification and sequence

---

[3]Caution: In a discussion of formal grammars and parsing, the term "sentence" is often used to mean the entire program, not just one statement.

[4]Historical note: Some of the items on the control cards are hard to understand in today's environment. Limiting the time that a job would be allowed to run (using a job time limit) was important then because computer time was very costly. In 1962, time on the IBM 704 (a machine comparable in power to a Commodore 64) cost $600 per hour at the University of Michigan. For comparison, Porterhouse steak cost about $1 per pound. Short time limits were specified so that infinite loops would be terminated by the system as soon as possible.

[5]The memory map listed all variable names and their memory addresses. The map, object listing, and core (memory) dump together were indispensable aides to debugging. They permitted the programmer to reconstruct the execution of the program manually.

[6]Most debugging was done in those days by carefully analyzing the contents of a core (memory) dump. The kind of trial and error debugging that we use today was impractical because turnaround time for a trial run was rarely less than a few hours and sometimes was measured in days. In order to glean as much information as possible from each run, the programmer would analyze the core dump using the memory maps produced by the compiler and linker. The programmer would trace execution of the program step by step and compare the actual contents of each memory location to what was supposed to be there. Needless to say, this was slow, difficult, and beyond the capabilities of many people. Modern advances have made computing much more accessible.

numbers. The JOB END card had a different special mark. This made it easy for the operating system to abort remaining segments of a job after a fatal error was discovered during compilation or linking.

Because punched cards were used for programs as well as data, the physical characteristics of the card strongly influenced certain aspects of the early languages. The program statement, which was the natural program unit, became tightly associated with the 80-column card, which was the natural media unit. Many programmers wrote their code on printed coding forms, which looked like graph paper with darker lines marking the fields. This helped keypunch operators type things in the correct columns.

The designers of the FORTRAN language felt that most FORTRAN statements would fit on one line and so chose to require that each statement be on a separate card. The occasional statement that was too long to fit could be continued on another card by placing a character in column six of the second card. Exhibit 3.10 lists the fields that were defined for a FORTRAN card.

Exhibit 3.10.   Field definitions in FORTRAN.

Columns	Use in a FORTRAN program
1	A "C" or a "*" here indicates a comment line.
1–5	Statement labels
6	Statement continuation mark
7–72	The statement itself
73–80	Programmer ID and sequence numbers.

End of statement. At end of line, unless column 6 on the *next* card is punched to indicate a continuation of the statement.

Indenting convention. Start every statement in column 7. (Indenting is not generally used.)

COBOL was also an early fixed-format language, with similar but different fixed fields. Due to the much longer variable names permitted in COBOL, and the wordier and more complex syntax, many statements would not fit on one line. A convention that imitated English was introduced: the end of each statement was marked by a period. A group of statements that would be executed sequentially was called a "paragraph", and each paragraph was given an alphanumeric label. Within columns 13–72, indenting was commonly used to clarify the meaning of the statements.

Two inventions in the late 1960s combined to make the use of punched cards for programs obsolete. The remote-access terminal and the on-line, disk-based file system made it both unnecessary and impractical to use punched cards. Languages that were designed after this I/O revolution reflect the changes in the equipment used. Fixed fields disappeared, the use of indentation to clarify program structure became universal, and a character such as ";" was used to separate statements or terminate each statement.[7]

3.2.3 Larger Program Units: Scope

English prepositions and conjunctions commonly control a single phrase or clause. When a larger scope of influence is needed in English, we indicate that the word pertains to a paragraph. In programming languages, units that correspond to such paragraphs are called *scopes* and are commonly marked by a pair of matched opening and closing marks. Exhibits 3.11, 3.13, and 3.15 show the tremendous variety of indicators used to mark the beginning and end of a scope.

In FORTRAN the concept of "scope" was not well abstracted, and scopes were indicated in a variety of ways, depending on the context. As new statement types were added to the language over the years, new ways were introduced to indicate their scopes. FORTRAN uses five distinct ways to delimit the scopes of the DATA statement, DO loop, implied DO loop, logical IF (true action only), and block IF (true and false actions) [Exhibit 3.11]. This nonuniformity of syntax does not occur in the newer languages.

Two different kinds of ways to end scopes are shown in Exhibit 3.11. The labeled statement at the end of a DO scope ends a specific DO. Each DO statement specifies the statement label of the line which terminates its scope. (Two DOs are allowed to name the same label, but that is not relevant here.) We say that DO has a *labeled scope*. In contrast, all block IF statements are ended by identical ENDIF lines. Thus an ENDIF could end any block IF statement. We say that block IF statements have *unlabeled scopes*.

The rules of FORTRAN do not permit either DO scopes or block IF scopes to overlap partially. That is, if the beginning of one of these scopes, say B, comes between the beginning and end of another scope, say A, then the end of scope B must come before the end of scope A. Legal and illegal nestings of labeled scopes are shown in Exhibit 3.12.

All languages designed since 1965 embody the abstraction "scope". That is, the language supplies a single way to delimit a paragraph, and that way is used uniformly wherever a scope is needed in the syntax, for example, with THEN, ELSE, WHILE, DO, and so on. For many languages, this is accomplished by having a single pair of symbols for begin-scope and end-scope, which are used to delimit any kind of scope [Exhibit 3.13]. In these languages it is not possible to nest scopes improperly because the compiler will always interpret the nesting in the legal way. A compiler will match each end-scope to the nearest unmatched begin-scope. This design is attractive because it produces a language that is simpler to learn and simpler to translate.

---

[7]Most languages did not use the "." as a statement-mark because periods are used for several other purposes (decimal points and record part selection), and any syntax becomes hard to translate when symbols become heavily ambiguous.

Exhibit 3.11. Scope delimiters in FORTRAN.

The following program contains an example of each linguistic unit that has an associated scope. The line numbers at the left key the statements to the descriptions, in the table that follows, of the scope indicators used.

```
1       INTEGER A, B, C(20), I
2       DATA A, B /31, 42/
3       READ* A, B, ( C(I), I=1,10)
4       DO 80 I= 1, 10
5       IF (C(I) .LT. 0) C(I+10)=0
6       IF (C(I) .LT. 100) THEN
7       C(I+10) = 2 * C(I)
8       ELSE
9       C(I+10) = C(I)/2
10      ENDIF
11 80   CONTINUE
12      END
```

Scope of	Begins at	Ends at	Line #s
Dimension list	"(" after array name	The next ")"	1
DATA values	First "/"	Second "/"	2
Implied DO	"(" in I/O list	I/O loop control	3
Subscript list	"(" after array name	Matching ")"	3
DO loop	Line following DO	Statement with DO label	5 - 11
Logical IF	After (⟨condition⟩)	End of line	5
Block IF (true)	After THEN	ELSE, ELSEIF, or ENDIF	7
Block IF (false)	After ELSEIF or ELSE	ELSE, ELSEIF, or ENDIF	9

Exhibit 3.12. Labeled scopes.

Correct Nesting: Faulty Nesting:

Begin Scope A
  Begin Scope B

  End Scope B
End Scope A

Begin Scope A
  Begin Scope B

End Scope A
  End Scope B

Exhibit 3.13.   Tokens used to delimit program scopes.

Language	Beginning of scope	End of scope
C	{	}
LISP	(	)
Pascal	BEGIN	END
	RECORD	END
	CASE	END
PL/1	DO;	END;
	DO ⟨loop control⟩;	END;

If an end-scope is omitted, the next one will be used to terminate the open scope regardless of the programmer's intent [Exhibit 3.14]. Thus an end-scope that was intended to terminate an IF may instead be used to terminate a loop or a subprogram. A compiler error comment may appear on the next line because the program element written there is in an illegal context, or error comments may not appear until the translator reaches the end of the program and finds that the wrong number of end-scopes was included. If an extra end-scope appears somewhere else, improper nesting might not be detected at all.

Exhibit 3.14.   Nested unlabeled scopes in Pascal.

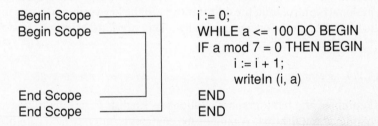

Using one uniform end-scope indicator has the severe disadvantage that a nesting error may not be identified as a syntactic error, but become a logical error which is harder to identify and correct. The programmer has one fewer tool for communicating semantics to the compiler, and the compiler has one fewer way to help the programmer achieve semantic validity. Many experienced programmers use comments to indicate which end-scope belongs to each begin-scope. This practice makes programs more readable and therefore easier to debug, but of course does not help the compiler.

A third, intermediate way to handle scope delimiters occurs in Ada. Unlike Pascal, each kind of scope has a distinct end-scope marker. Procedures and blocks and labeled loops have fully labeled end-scopes. Unlike FORTRAN, a uniform syntax was introduced for delimiting and labeling scopes. An end-scope marker is the word "end" followed by the word and label, if any, associated with the beginning of the scope [Exhibit 3.15].

Exhibit 3.15. Lexical scope delimiters in Ada.

Begin-scope markers	End-scope markers
⟨block_name⟩: ⟨declarations⟩ BEGIN	END ⟨block_name⟩
PROCEDURE ⟨proc_name⟩	END ⟨proc_name⟩;
LOOP	END LOOP;
⟨label⟩:LOOP	END LOOP ⟨label⟩;
CASE	END CASE
IF ⟨condition⟩ THEN or	
ELSIF ⟨condition⟩ THEN	ELSIF, ELSE, or END IF
ELSE	END IF

It is possible, in Ada, for the compiler to detect many (but not all) improperly nested scopes and often to correctly deduce where an end-scope has been omitted. This is important, since a misplaced or forgotten end-scope is one of the most common kinds of compile-time errors.

A good technique for avoiding errors with paired delimiters is to type the END marker when the BEGIN is typed, and position the cursor between them. This is the idea behind the *structured editors*. When the programmer types the beginning of a multipart control unit, the editor inserts all the keywords and scope markers necessary to complete that unit meaningfully. This prevents beginners and forgetful experts from creating malformed scopes.

3.2.4 Comments

Footnotes and bibliographic citations in English permit us to convey general information about the text. Analogously, comments, interspersed with program words, let us provide information about a program that is not part of the program. With comments, as with statements, we have the problem of identifying both the beginning and end of the unit. Older languages (COBOL, FORTRAN) generally restrict comments to separate lines, begun by a specific comment mark in a fixed position on the line [Exhibit 3.16]. This convention was natural when programs were typed on punch cards. At the same time it is a severe restriction because it prohibits the use of brief comments placed out of the way visually. It therefore limits the usefulness of comments to explain obscure items that are embedded in the code.

The newer languages permit comments and code to be interspersed more freely. In these languages, statements can be broken onto multiple lines and combined freely with short comments in order to do a superior job of clarifying the intent of the programmer. Both the beginning and end of a comment are marked [Exhibit 3.17]. Comments are permitted to appear anywhere within a program, even in the middle of a statement.

Exhibit 3.16.   Comment lines in older languages.

In these languages comments must be placed on a separate line, below or above the code to which they apply.

Language	Comment line is marked by
FORTRAN	A "C" in column 1
COBOL	A "*" in column 7
original APL	The "lamp" symbol: ⍝ at the beginning of a line
BASIC	REM at the beginning of a line

Exhibit 3.17.   Comment beginning and end delimiters.

These languages permit a comment and program code to be placed on the same line. Both the beginning and end of the comment is marked.

Language	Comments are delimited by
C	/* ... */
PL/1	/* ... */
Pascal	(* ... *) or { ... }
FORTH	(...)

A nearly universal convention is to place the code on the left part of the page and comments on the right. Comments are used to document the semantic intent of variables, parameters, and unusual program actions, and to clarify which end-scope marker is supposed to match each begin-scope marker. Whole-line comments are used to mark and document the beginning of each program module, greatly assisting the programmer's eye in finding his or her way through the pages of code. Some comments span several lines, in which case only the beginning of the first line and end of the last line need begin- and end-comment marks. In spite of this, many programmers mark the beginning and end of every line because it is aesthetically nicer and sets the comment apart from code.

With all the advantages of these partial-line comments, one real disadvantage was introduced by permitting begin-comment and end-comment marks to appear anywhere within the code. It is not unusual for an end-comment mark to be omitted or typed incorrectly [Exhibit 3.18]. In this case all the program statements up to the end of the next comment are taken to be part of the nonterminated comment and are simply "swallowed up" by the comment.

Exhibit 3.18. An incomplete comment swallowing an instruction.

The following Pascal code appears to be ok at first glance, but because of the mistyped end-comment mark, the computation for `tot_age` will be omitted. The result will be a list of family members with the wrong average age!

A "person_list" is an array of person cells, each containing a name and an age.

```
PROCEDURE average_age(p:  person_list);
VAR famsize, tot_age, k:integer;
BEGIN
    readln(famsize); (* Get the number of family members to process.*)
    tot_age := 0;
    FOR k := 1 TO famsize DO BEGIN
        writeln( p[k].name ); (* Start with oldest family member.  * )
        tot_age := tot_age + p[k].age; (* Sum ages for average.  *)
    END;
    writeln('Average age of family = ', tot_age/famsize)
END;
```

The translator may not ever detect this violation of the programmer's intent. If the next comment is relatively near, and no end-scope markers are swallowed up by the comment, the program may compile with no errors but run strangely. This can be a very difficult error to debug, since the program looks correct but its behavior is inconsistent with its appearance! Eventually the programmer will decide that he or she has clearly written a correct instruction that the compiler seems to have ignored. Since compilers do not just ignore code, this does not make sense. Finally the programmer notices that the end-comment mark that should be at the end of some prior line is missing.

This problem is an example of the cost of over-generality. Limiting comments to separate lines was too restrictive, that is, not general enough. Permitting them to begin and end anywhere on a line, though, is more general than is needed or desired. Even in languages that permit this, comments usually occupy either a full line or the right end of a line. A more desirable implementation of comments would match the comment-scope and comment placement rules with the actual conventions that most programmers use, which are:

- whole-line comments
- partial-line comments placed on the right side of the page
- multiple-line comments

Thus comments should be permitted to occur on the right end of any line, but they might as well be terminated by the end of the line. Permitting multiple-line comments to be written is important, but it is not a big burden to mark the beginning of every comment line, as many programmers do anyway to improve the appearance of their programs. The payoff for accepting this small restriction is that the end-of-line mark can be used as a comment-end mark. Since programmers do not forget to put carriage returns in their programs, comments can no longer swallow up entire chunks of code. Some languages that have adopted this convention are listed in Exhibit 3.19.

Exhibit 3.19.   Comments terminating at the end of a line.

These languages permit comments to occupy entire lines or the right end of any line. Comments start with the comment-begin mark listed and extend to the carriage return on the right end of the line. (TeX is a text processing language for typesetting mathematical text and formulas. It was used to produce this book.)

Language	Comment-begin mark
Ada	--
LISP	; (This varies among implementations.)
TeX	%
UNIX command shell	#
C++	//

Some languages support two kinds of comment delimiters. This permits the programmer to use the partial-line variety to delimit explanatory comments. The second kind of delimiter (with matched begin-comment and end-comment symbols) is reserved for use during debugging, when the programmer often wants to "comment out", temporarily, large sections of code.

3.2.5   Naming Parts of a Program

In order to refer to the parts of a program, we need metawords for those parts and for whatever actions are permitted. For example, C permits parts of a program to be stored in separate files and brought into the compiler together by using "#include ⟨file_name⟩". The file name is a metaword denoting a section of the program, and "#include" is a metaword for the action of combining it with another section.

Most procedural languages provide a GOTO instruction which transfers control to a specific labeled statement somewhere in the program. The statement label, whether symbolic or numeric, is thus a metaword that refers to a part of the program. Since the role of statement labels cannot be fully understood apart from the control structures that use them, labels are discussed with the GOTO command in Section 11.1.

3.2.6   Metawords that Let the Programmer Extend the Language

There are several levels on which a language may be extended. One might extend:

- The list of defined words (nouns, verbs, adjectives).
- The syntax but not the semantics, thus providing alternative ways of writing the same meanings one could write without the extension.
- The actual semantics of the language, with a corresponding extension either of the syntax or of the list of defined words recognized by the compiler.

Languages that permit the third kind of extension are rare because extending the semantics requires changing the translator to handle a new category of objects. Semantic extension is discussed in the next chapter.

Extending the Vocabulary

Every declaration extends the language in the sense that it permits a compiler to "understand" new words. Normally we are only permitted to declare a few kinds of things: nouns (variables, constants, file names), verbs (functions and procedures), and sometimes adjectives (type names) and metawords (labels). We cannot normally declare new syntactic words or new words such as "array". The compiler maintains one combined list or several separate lists of these definitions. This list is usually called the "symbol table", but it is actually called the "dictionary" in FORTH. New symbols added to this list always belong to some previously defined syntactic category with semantics defined by the compiler.

Each category of symbol that can be declared must have its own keyword or syntactic marker by which the compiler can recognize that a definition of a new symbol follows. Words such as TYPE, CONST, and PROCEDURE in Pascal and INTEGER and FUNCTION in FORTRAN are metawords that mean, in part, "extend the language by putting the symbols that follow into the symbol table."

As compiler technology has developed and languages have become bigger and more sophisticated, more kinds of declarable symbols have been added to languages. The original BASIC permitted no declarations: all two-letter variable names could be used without declaration, and no other symbols, even subroutine names, could be defined. The newest versions of BASIC permit use of longer variable names, names for subroutines, and symbolic labels. FORTRAN, developed in 1954–1958, permitted declaration of names for variables and functions. FORTRAN 77 also permits declaration of names for constants and COMMON blocks. ALGOL-68 supported type declarations as a separate abstraction, not as part of some data object. Pascal, published in 1971, brought type declarations into widespread use. Modula, a newer language devised by the author of Pascal, permits declaration and naming of semantically separate modules. Ada, one of the newest languages in commercial use, permits declaration of several things missing in Pascal, including the range and precision of real variables, support for concurrent tasks, and program modules called "generic packages" which contain data and function declarations with type parameters.

Syntactic Extension without Semantic Extension

Some languages contain a macro facility (in C, it is part of the preprocessor).[8] This permits the programmer to define short names for frequently used expressions. A macro definition consists of a name and a string of characters that becomes the meaning of the name [Exhibit 3.20]. To use a macro, the programmer writes its name, like a shorthand notation, in the program wherever that string of characters is to be inserted [Exhibit 3.21].

---

[8]The C preprocessor supports various compiler directives as well as a general macro facility.

Exhibit 3.20.   Definition of a simple macro in C.

In C, macro definitions start with the word #define, followed by the macro name. The string to the right of the macro name defines the meaning of the name.

The #define statements below make the apparent syntax of C more like Pascal. They permit the faithful Pascal programmer to use the familiar scoping words BEGIN and END in a C program. (These words are not normally part of the C language.) During preprocessing, BEGIN will be replaced by "{" and END will be replaced by "}".

```
#define BEGIN {
#define END }
```

Exhibit 3.21.   Use of a simple macro in C.

Macro Calls.   The simple macros defined in Exhibit 3.20 are called in the following code fragment. Unfortunately, the new scope symbols, BEGIN and END, and the old ones, "{" and "}", are now interchangeable. Our programmer can write the following code, defining two well-nested scopes. It would work, but it isn't "pretty" or clear.

```
BEGIN  x = y+2;
       if (x < 100) { x += k; y = 0; END
       else x = 0; }
```

Macro Expansion.   During macro expansion the macro call is replaced by the defining string. The C translator never sees the word BEGIN.

```
{  x = y+2;
   if (x < 100) { x += k; y = 0; }
   else x = 0; }
```

A preprocessor scans the source program, searching for macro names, before the program is parsed. These macro names are replaced by the defining strings. The expanded program is then parsed and compiled. Thus the preprocessor commands and macro calls form a separate, primitive, language. They are identified, expanded, and eliminated before the parser for the main language even begins its work.

The syntax for a macro language, even one with macro parameters, is always simple. However, piggy-backing a macro language on top of a general programming language causes some complications. The source code will be processed by two translators, and their relationship must be made clear. Issues such as the relationship of macro calls to comments or quoted strings must be settled.

In C, preprocessor commands and macro definitions start with a "#"in column 1.[9] This distinguishes them from source code intended for the compiler. Custom

---

[9]Newer C translators permit the "#"to be anywhere on the line as long as it is the first nonblank character.

(but not compiler rules) dictates that macro names be typed in uppercase characters and program identifiers in lowercase. Case does not matter to the translator, but this custom helps the programmer read the code.

Macro *calls* are harder to identify than macro *definitions*, since they may be embedded anywhere in the code, including within a macro definition. Macro names, like program identifiers, are variable-length strings that need to be identified and separated from other symbols. Lexical analysis must, therefore, be done before macro expansion. Since the result of expansion is a source string, lexical analysis must be done again after expansion. Since macro definitions may contain macro calls, the result of macro expansion must be rescanned for more macro calls. Control must thus pass back and forth between the lexer and the macro facility. The lexical rules for the preprocessor language are necessarily the same as the rules for the main language.

In the original definition of C, the relationship among the lexer, preprocessor, and parser was not completely defined. Existing C translators thus do different things with macros, and all are "correct" by the language definition. Some C translators simply insert the expanded macro text back into the source text without inserting any blanks or delimiters. The effect is that characters outside a macro can become adjacent to characters produced by the macro expansion. The program line containing the expanded macro is then sent back to the lexer. When the lexer processes this, it forms a single symbol from the two character strings. This "gluing" action can produce strange and unexpected results.

The ANSI standard for C has clarified this situation. It states that no symbol can bridge a macro boundary. Lexical analysis on the original source string is done, and symbols are identified, before macro expansion. The source string that defines the macro can also be lexed before expansion, since characters in it can never be joined with characters outside it. These rules "clean up" a messy situation. The result of expanding a macro still must be rescanned for more macro calls, but it does not need to be re-lexed. The definition and call of a macro within a macro are illustrated in Exhibits 3.22 and 3.23.

Exhibit 3.22.   A nest of macros in C.

The macros defined here are named PI and PRINTX. PRINTX expands into a call on the library function that does formatted output, printf. The first parameter for printf must be a format string, the other parameters are expressions denoting items to be printed. Within the format, a % field defines the type and field width for each item on the I/O list. The "\t" prints out a tab character.

```
#define PI        3.1415927
#define PRINTX    printf("Pi times x = %8.5f\t", PI * x)
```

A general macro facility also permits the use of parameters in macro definitions [Exhibit 3.24]. In a call, macro arguments are easily parsed, since they are enclosed in parentheses and follow the macro name [Exhibit 3.25]. To expand a macro, formal parameter names must be identified in the definition of the macro. To do this, the tokens in the macro definition must first be identified. Any token that matches a parameter name is replaced by the corresponding argument string. Finally, the entire string of characters, with parameter substitutions, replaces the macro call.

Exhibit 3.23.   Use of the simple PRINTX macro.

The macro named PRINTX is used below in a for loop.

```
for (x=1; x<=3; x++) PRINTX;
```

Before compilation begins, the macro name is replaced by the string printf("Pi times x = %8.5f\t", PI * x), giving a string that still contains a macro call:

```
for (x=1; x<=3; x++) printf("Pi times x = %8.5f\t", PI * x);
```

This string is rescanned, and the call on the macro PI is expanded, producing macro-free source code. The compiler then compiles the statement:

```
for (x=1; x<=3; x++) printf("Pi times x = %8.5f\t", 3.1415927 * x);
```

At run time, this code causes x to be initialized to 1 before the loop is executed. On each iteration of the loop, the value of x is compared to 3. If x does not exceed 3, the words "Pi times x = " are printed, followed by the value of 3.1415927 * x as a floating-point number with five decimal places (%8.5f), followed by a tab character (\t). The counter x is then incremented. The loop is terminated when x exceeds 3. Thus a line with three fields is printed, as follows:

```
Pi times x = 3.14159    Pi times x = 6.28319    Pi times x = 9.42477
```

Exhibit 3.24.   A macro with parameters in C.

The macro defined here is named PRINT. It is similar to the PRINTX macro in Exhibit 3.22, but it has a parameter.

```
#define PRINT(yy) printf(#yy " = %d\t", yy)
```

The definition for PRINT is written in ANSI C. References to macro parameters that occur within quoted strings are not recognized by the preprocessor. However, the "#" symbol in a macro definition causes the parameter following it to be converted to a quoted string. Adjacent strings are concatenated by the translator. Using both these facts, we are able to insert a parameter value into a quoted format string.

The original definition of C did not clearly define whether tokens were identified before or after macro parameters were processed. This is important because a comment or a quoted string looks like many words but forms a single program token. If a preprocessor searches for parameter names before identifying tokens, quoted strings will be searched and parameter substitution will happen within them. Many C translators work this way; others identify tokens first. The ANSI C standard clarifies this situation. It decrees that tokenization will be done uniformly before parameter substitution.

Exhibit 3.25.   Use of the print macro with parameters.

The macro named PRINT is used here, with different variables supplied as parameters each time.

```
PRINT(x); PRINT(y); PRINT(z);
```

These macro calls will be expanded and produce the following compilable code:

```
printf("x = %d\t", x);
printf("y = %d\t", y);
printf("z = %d\t", z);
```

Assume that at run time the variables x, y, and z contain the values 1, 3, and 10, respectively. Then executing this code will cause one line to be printed, as follows:

```
x = 1     y = 3     z = 10
```

Macro names are syntactic extensions. They are words that may be written in the program and will be recognized by the compiler. Unlike variable declarations they may stand for arbitrarily complex items, and they may expand into strings that are not even syntactically legal units when used alone. Macros can be used to shorten code with repetitive elements, to redefine the compiler words such as BEGIN, or to give symbolic names to constants. What they *do not* do is extend the semantics of the language. Since all macro calls must be expanded into compilable code, anything written with a macro call could also be written without it. No "power" is added to the language by a macro facility.

EXERCISES

1. Why are function calls considered verbs?
2. What is the domain of a verb? Define the domain and range of a function.
3. What is a data type? Inheritance?
4. What is a metalanguage?
5. What is a lexical token? How are lexical tokens formed? Use a language with which you are familiar as an example. What are delimiters?
6. How are programming language statements analogous to sentences?
7. What is the scope of a programming language unit? How is it usually denoted?
8. How is it possible to improperly nest scopes? How can this be avoided by designers of programming languages?
9. What is the purpose of a comment? How are comments traditionally handled within programs? What is the advantage of using a carriage return as a comment delimiter?
10. The language C++ is an extension of C which supports generic functions and type checking. For the most part, C++ is C with additions to implement things that the C++ designers believed are important and missing from C. One of the additions is a second way

to denote a comment. In C, a comment can be placed almost anywhere in the code and is delimited at both ends. In this program fragment, two comments and an assignment statement are intermingled:

```
x=y*z  /* Add the product of y and z */+x;  /* to x.  */
```

C++ supports this form but also a new form which must be placed on the right end of the line and is only delimited at the beginning by "//":

```
x=y*z + x // Add the product of y and z to x.
```

Briefly explain why the original comment syntax was so inadequate that a new form was needed.

11. How can we extend a language through its vocabulary? Its syntax?

12. What is a macro? How is it used within a program?

4

Formal Description of Language

The syntax of a language is its grammatical rules. These are usually defined through EBNF (Extended Backus-Naur Form) and/or syntax diagrams, both discussed in this chapter. The meaning of a program is represented by p-code (portable code) or by a computation tree. The language syntax defines the computation tree that corresponds to each legal source program.

Semantics are the rules for interpreting the meaning of programming language statements. The semantic specification of a language defines how each computation tree is to be implemented on a machine so that it retains its meaning. Being always concerned with the portability of code, we define the semantics of a language in terms of an implementation-independent model. One such model, the abstract machine, is composed of a program environment, shared environment, stack, and streams. The semantic basis of a language means the specific version of the machine that defines the language, together with the internal data structures and interpretation procedures that implement the abstract semantics. Lambda calculus is an example of a minimal semantic basis.

A language may be extended primarily through its vocabulary and occasionally through its syntax, as in EL/1, or through its semantics, as in FORTH.

4.1 FOUNDATIONS OF PROGRAMMING LANGUAGES

Formal methods have played a critical role in the development of modern programming languages. Formal methods were not available in the mid-1950s when the first higher-level programming languages were being created. The most notable of these efforts was FORTRAN, which survives (in greatly expanded form) to this day. Even though the syntax and semantics of the early FORTRAN were primitive by today's standards, the complexity of the language was at the limit of what could be handled by the methods then available. It was quickly realized that ad hoc methods are severely limited in what they can achieve, and a more systematic approach would be needed to handle languages of greater expressive power and correspondingly greater complexity.

Contemporaneously with the implementation of the FORTRAN language and compiler, a new language, ALGOL, was being defined using a new formal approach for the specification of syntax and semantics. Even though it required several more years of research before people learned how to compile ALGOL efficiently, the language itself had tremendous influence on the design of subsequent programming languages. Concepts such as block structure (cf. Chapter 7) and delayed evaluation of function parameters (cf. Chapter 8), introduced in ALGOL, have reappeared in many subsequent modern programming languages.

ALGOL was the first programming language whose syntax was formally described. A notation called BNF, for Backus-Naur Form, was invented for the purpose. BNF turned out to be equivalent in expressive power to context-free grammars, developed by the linguist Noam Chomsky for describing natural language, but the BNF notation turned out to be easier for people, so variations on it are still used in describing most programming languages. An attempt was made to give a rigorous English-language specification of the semantics of ALGOL. Nevertheless, the underlying model was not well understood at the time, and ALGOL appeared at first to be difficult or impossible to implement efficiently.

Syntax and semantic interpretations were specified informally for early languages. Then, motivated by the new need to describe programming languages, formal language theory flourished. Some of the major developments in the foundations of computer science are shown in Exhibit 4.1. Formal syntax and parsing methods grew from work on automata theory and linguistics [Exhibit 4.1]. Formal methods of semantic specification [Exhibit 4.2] grew from early work on logic and computability and were especially influenced by Church's work on the lambda calculus. In this chapter, we give a brief introduction to some of the formal tools that have been important to the development of modern-day programming languages.

4.2 SYNTAX

The rules for constructing a well-formed sentence (statement) out of words, a paragraph (module) out of sentences, and an essay (program) out of paragraphs are the syntax of the language. The syntax definitions for most programming languages take several pages of text. A few are very short, a few very long. There is at least one language (ALGOL-68) in which the syntax rules that determine whether or not a statement should compile are so complicated that only an expert can understand them.

It is usual to define the syntax of a programming language in a *formal language*. A variety of formalisms have been introduced over the years for this purpose. We present two of the most common here: Extended Backus-Naur Form (EBNF) and syntax diagrams.

Exhibit 4.1.   Foundations of computer science.

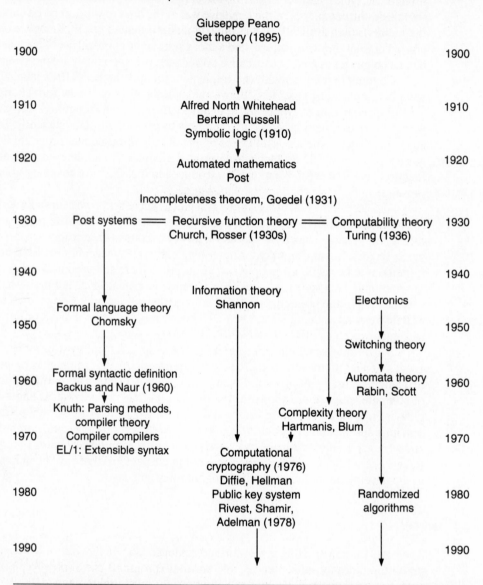

An EBNF language definition can be translated by a program called a *parser generator*[1] into a program called a *parser* [Exhibit 4.3].[2] A parser reads the user's source

---

[1]The old term was "compiler compiler". This led to the name of the UNIX parser generator, yacc, which stands for "yet another compiler compiler".

[2]A parser generator can only handle grammars for "context-free" languages. Defining this language class is beyond the scope of this book. Note, though, that the grammars published for most programming languages are context free.

Exhibit 4.2. Formal semantic specification.

1930   Post systems ——— Recursive function theory ——— Computability theory   1930
                         Church, Rosser (1930s)   Turing (1936)

                                    ↓

1940   Lambda calculus   1940
                              Church (1941)

1950   1950

                                    ↓

                          Program correctness
                          and verification (1960s)

1960   Referential transparency, Strachey   1960
                  Formal semantic definition
                  SECD machine, Landin (1964)

                  Vienna definition of PL/1 (1967)
                                    ▼
                  Denotational semantics (1971)
                          Scott, Strachey   1970
1970   Concurrency, Dijkstra (1968)
                                    ↓   ↓
                  Milner: Type theory (1978)   Hoare: CSP (1978)
                                                    Distributed computing (1978)
                                    | Lamport
1980   ↓   ↓   1980
                  Functional languages:
                          ML   Collaborative computing
                       Miranda   1988
                       Haskell   ↓
1990   ▼   1990

code programs and determines the *syntactic category* (part of speech) of every source symbol and combination of symbols. Its output is the list of the symbols defined in the program and a *parse tree*, which specifies the role that each source symbol is serving, much like a sentence diagram of an English sentence. The parser forms the heart of any compiler or interpreter for the language.

The study of formal language theory and parsing has strongly affected language design. Older languages were not devised with modern parsing methods in mind. Their syntax was usually developed ad hoc. Consequently, a syntax definition for such a language, for example FORTRAN, is lengthy and full of special cases. By today's standards these languages are also relatively slow and difficult to parse.

Exhibit 4.3. The compiler is produced from the language definition.

In the following diagram, programs are represented by rectangles and data by circles. The lexer and parser can be automatically generated from the lexical specifications and syntax of a context-free language by a parser generator and its companion lexer generator. This is represented by the vertical arrows in the diagram. The lexer and parser are the output data of these generation steps.

A code generator requires more hand work: the compiler writer must construct an assembly code translation, for every syntax rule in the grammar, which encodes the semantics of that rule in the target machine language.

The lexer, parser, and code generator are programs that together comprise the compiler. The compilation process is represented by the horizontal chain in the diagram.

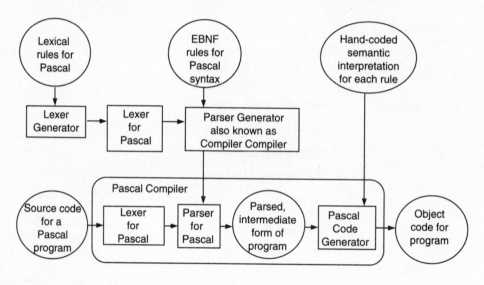

Newer languages are designed to be parsed easily by efficient algorithms. The syntax for Pascal is brief and elegant. Pascal compilers are small, as compilers go, and can be implemented on personal computers. The standard LISP translator[3] is only fifteen pages long!

4.2.1   Extended BNF

"Backus-Naur Form", or *BNF*, is a formal language developed by Backus and Naur for describing programming language syntax. It gained widespread influence when it was used to define ALGOL in the early 1960s. The original BNF formalism has since been extended and streamlined; a generally accepted version, named "Extended BNF", is presented here.

---

[3]Griss and Hearn [1981].

Take one!
192.168.0.2 Mac
192.168.0.1 XP
3 2K
1W3099423
COMPUSA
TECHNICAL SERVICES
We Make Technology Work.

When you need technical service, call CompUSA. We can send technical engineers to your home or office. Whether you're facing the challenges of staffing a new project, dealing with business expansion or just need to repair your system, CompUSA can fulfill your technical service needs.

Some of the skilled professionals who are part of the CompUSA IT support family include:

Technology Consultants

Web Designers

Unix Administrators

Java Developers

Customer Support Engineers

A+ Certified Technicians

In addition to IT staffing support and technical services such as repairs or upgrades, we provide 24 hour over-the-phone technical support and flexible service programs. Call CompUSA today and find out how our expert services and technical staffing can bring new value to your business.

1-877-593-3494

26946

An EBNF grammar consists of:

- A starting symbol.
- A set of terminal symbols, which are the keywords and syntactic markers of the language being defined.
- A set of nonterminal symbols, which correspond to the syntactic categories and kinds of statements of the language.
- A series of rules, called productions, that specify how each nonterminal symbol may be expanded into a phrase containing terminals and nonterminals. Every nonterminal has one production rule, which may contain alternatives.

The Syntax of EBNF

The syntax for EBNF itself is not altogether standardized; several minor variations exist. We define a commonly used version here.

- **The starting symbol** must be defined. One nonterminal is designated as the starting symbol.
- **Terminal symbols** will be written in **boldface** and enclosed in 'single quotes'.
- **Nonterminal symbols** will be written in regular type and enclosed in ⟨angle brackets⟩.
- **Production rules.** The nonterminal being defined is written at the left, followed by a "::=" sign (which we will pronounce as "goes to"). After this is the string, with options, which defines the nonterminal. The definition extends up to but does not include the "." that marks the end of the production. When a nonterminal is *expanded* it is replaced by this defining phrase. Blank spaces between the "::=" and the "." are ignored.
- **Alternatives** are separated by vertical bars. Parentheses may be used to indicate grouping. For example, the rule

$$s ::= (a \mid bc) d .$$

indicates that an 's' may be replaced by an 'ad' or a 'bcd'.
- **An optional syntactic element** is a something-or-nothing alternative—it may be included or not included as needs demand. This is indicated by enclosing the optional element in square brackets, as follows:

$$s ::= [a] d .$$

This formula indicates that an 's' may be replaced by an 'ad' or simply by a 'd'.
- **An unspecified number of repetitions** (zero or more) of a syntactic unit is indicated by enclosing the unit in curly brackets. For example, the rule

$$s ::= \{a\}d .$$

indicates that an 's' may be replaced by a 'd', an 'ad', an 'aad', or a string of any number of 'a's followed by a single 'd'. A frequently occurring pattern is the following:

$$s ::= t\{t\}$$

This means that 's' may be replaced by *one or more* copies of 't'.

Recursive rules.

Recursive production rules are permitted. For example, this rule is directly recursive because its right side contains a reference to itself:

$$s ::= asz \mid w .$$

This expands into a single 'w', surrounded on the left and right by any number of matched pairs of 'a' and 'z': awz, aawzz, aaawzzz, etc.

Tail recursion is a special kind of recursion in which the recursive reference is the last symbol in the string. Tail recursion has the same effect as a loop. This production is tail recursive:

$$s ::= as \mid b \ .$$

This expands into a string of any number of 'a's followed by a 'b'.

Mutually recursive rules are also permitted. For example, this pair of rules is mutually recursive because each rule refers to the other:

$$s ::= at \mid b \ .$$
$$t ::= bs \mid a \ .$$

A single 's' could expand into any of the following: b, aa, abb, abaa, ababb, ababaa, etc.

Combinations of alternatives, optional elements, recursions, and repetitions often occur in a production, as follows:

$$s ::= \{a \mid b\} \, [c] \, d \ .$$

This rule indicates that an 's' may be replaced by any of the following: d, ad, bd, cd, acd, bcd, aad, abd, aacd, abcd, bd, bad, bbd, bcd, bacd, bbcd, and many more.

Using EBNF

To illustrate the EBNF rules, we give part of the syntax for Pascal, taken from the ISO standard [Exhibit 4.4]. The first few rules of the grammar are given, followed by several rules from the middle of the grammar which define what a "statement" is. The complete set of EBNF grammar rules cannot be given here because it is too long.[4] Following are brief explanations of the meaning of these rules.

- The production for the starting symbol states that a `program` consists of a heading, a semicolon, a block, and a period. The semicolon and period are terminal symbols and will form part of the finished program. The symbols "program-heading" and "program-block" are nonterminals and need further expansion.
- The program-heading starts with the terminal symbol "program", which is followed by the name of the program and an optional, parenthesized list of parameters, used for file names.
- The program parameters, if they are used, are just a list of identifiers, that is, a series of one or more identifiers separated by commas.
- The program block consists of a series of declarations followed by a single compound statement.
- The production for "compound statement" forms an indirectly recursive cycle with the rules for statement sequence, and statement. That is, a statement can be a structured statement, which can be a compound statement, which contains a statement-sequence, which contains a statement, completing the cycle.
- The rule for "statement" contains an optional label field and the choice between "simple-statement" and "structured-statement".

---

[4]It occupies nearly six pages in Cooper [1983].

● The rules for simple-statement and structured-statement define all of Pascal's control structures.

Generating a Program.

To *generate* a program (or part of a program) using a grammar, one starts with the specified starting symbol and expands it according to its production rule. The starting symbol is replaced by the string of symbols from the right side of its production rule. If the rule contains alternatives, one may use whichever option seems appropriate. The resulting expansion will contain other nonterminal symbols which then must be expanded also. When all the nonterminals have been expanded, the result is a grammatically correct program.

We illustrate this derivation process by using the EBNF grammar for ISO Standard Pascal to generate a ridiculously simple program named "little". Parts, but not all, of this grammar are given in Exhibit 4.4.[5]

Exhibit 4.4.   EBNF production rules for parts of Pascal.

```
program ::= ⟨program-heading⟩ ';' ⟨program-block⟩ '.'  .
program-heading ::= 'program' ⟨identifier⟩ [ '(' ⟨program-parameters⟩ ')' ].
program-parameters ::= ⟨identifier-list⟩ .
identifier-list ::= ⟨identifier⟩ { ',' ⟨identifier⟩ } .
program-block ::= ⟨block⟩ .
block ::= ⟨label-declaration-part⟩ ⟨constant-declaration-part⟩
        ⟨type-declaration-part⟩ ⟨variable-declaration-part⟩
        ⟨procedure-and-function-declaration-part⟩ ⟨statement-part⟩ .
variable-declaration-part ::= [ 'var' ⟨variable-declaration⟩ ';' {⟨variable-declaration⟩ ';' } ] .
variable-declaration ::= ⟨identifier-list⟩ ';' ⟨type-denoter⟩.
statement-part ::= compound statement .
compound-statement ::= 'begin' ⟨statement-sequence⟩ 'end' .
statement-sequence ::= ⟨statement⟩ { ';'⟨statement⟩ } .
statement ::= [ ⟨label⟩ ':' ] ( ⟨simple-statement⟩ | ⟨structured-statement⟩ ).
simple-statement ::= ⟨empty-statement⟩ | ⟨assignment-statement⟩ |
                     ⟨procedure-statement⟩ | ⟨goto-statement⟩ .
structured-statement ::= ⟨compound-statement⟩ | ⟨conditional-statement⟩ |
                     ⟨repetitive-statement⟩ | ⟨with-statement⟩ .
```

The starting symbol is ⟨program⟩. Wherever possible, more than one nonterminal symbol is reduced on each line, in order to shorten the derivation.

```
⟨program⟩
⟨program-heading⟩ ; ⟨program-block⟩ .
program ⟨identifier⟩ ; ⟨block⟩ .
program little ; ⟨label-declaration-part⟩ ⟨constant-declaration-part⟩
        ⟨variable-declaration-part⟩ ⟨procedure-and-function-declaration-part⟩
        ⟨statement-part⟩ .
```

---

[5]The complete grammar can be found in Cooper [1983], pp 153–58.

program little ; var ⟨variable-declaration⟩ ; ⟨compound-statement⟩ .

program little ; var⟨identifier-list⟩ : ⟨type-denoter⟩ ;
   begin ⟨statement-sequence⟩ end .

program little ; var ⟨identifier⟩ : ⟨type-denoter⟩ ;
   begin ⟨statement⟩ ; ⟨statement⟩ end .

program little ; var x : integer ;
   begin ⟨simple-statement⟩ ; ⟨simple-statement⟩ end .

program little ; var x : integer ;
   begin ⟨assignment-statement⟩ ; ⟨procedure-statement⟩ end .

program little ; var x : integer ;
   begin ⟨variable-access⟩ := ⟨expression⟩ ;
   ⟨procedure-identifier⟩ (⟨writeln-parameter-list⟩) end .

program little ; var x : integer ;
   begin ⟨entire-variable⟩ := ⟨simple-expression⟩ ;
   writeln (⟨write-parameter⟩) end .

program little ; var x : integer ; begin ⟨variable-identifier⟩:= ⟨term⟩ ;
   writeln (⟨expression⟩) end .

program little ; var x : integer ; begin ⟨identifier⟩ := ⟨factor⟩ ;
   writeln (⟨simple-expression⟩) end .

program little ; var x : integer ; begin x := ⟨unsigned-constant⟩ ;
   writeln (⟨term⟩) end .

program little ; var x : integer ; begin x := ⟨unsigned-number⟩ ;
   writeln (⟨factor⟩) end .

program little ; var x : integer ; begin x := ⟨unsigned-integer⟩ ;
   writeln (⟨variable-access⟩) end .

program little ; var x : integer ; begin x := 17 ;
   writeln (⟨entire-variable⟩ end .

program little ; var x : integer ; begin x := 17 ;
   writeln (⟨variable-identifier⟩) end .

program little ; var x : integer ; begin x := 17 ; writeln (⟨identifier⟩) end .

program little ; var x : integer ; begin x := 17 ; writeln (x) end .

Parsing a Program.

The process of *syntactic analysis* is the inverse of this generation process. Syntactic analysis starts with source code. The parsing routines of a compiler determine how the source code corresponds to the grammar. The output from the parse is a tree-representation of the grammatical structure of the code called a *parse tree*.

There are several methods of syntactic analysis, which are usually studied in a compiler course and are beyond the scope of this book. The two broad categories of parsing algorithms are called "bottom-up" and "top-down". In top-down parsing, the parser starts with the grammar's starting symbol and tries, at each step, to generate the next part of the source code string. A brief description of a "bottom-up" method should serve to illustrate the parsing process. In a "bottom-up" parse, the parser searches the source code for a string which occurs as one alternative on the right side of some production rule. Ambiguity is resolved by looking ahead k input symbols. The matching string is replaced by the nonterminal on the left of that rule. By repeating this process, the program is eventually reduced, phrase by phrase, back to the starting symbol. Exhibit 4.5 illustrates the steps in forming a parse tree for the body of the program named "little".

All syntactically correct programs can be reduced in this manner. If a compiler cannot do the reduction successfully, there is some error in the source code and the compiler produces an error comment containing some guess about what kind of syntactic error was made. These guesses are usually close to being correct when the error is discovered near where it was made. Their usefulness decreases rapidly as the compiler works on and on through the source code without discovering the error, as often happens.

4.2.2 Syntax Diagrams

Syntax diagrams were developed by Niklaus Wirth to define the syntax of Pascal. They are also called "railroad diagrams", because of their curving, branching shapes. This is the form in which Pascal syntax is usually presented in textbooks. Syntax diagrams and EBNF can express exactly the same class of languages, but they are used for different purposes. Syntax diagrams provide a graphic, two-dimensional way to communicate a grammar, so they are used to make grammatical relationships easier for human beings to grasp.

EBNF is used to write a grammar that will be the input to a parser generator. Corresponding to each production is code for the semantic action that the compiler should take when that production is parsed. The rules of an EBNF syntax are often more broken up than seems necessary, in order to provide "hooks" for all the semantic actions that a compiler must perform. When a grammar for the same language is presented as syntax diagrams, several EBNF productions are often condensed into one diagram, making the entire grammar shorter, less roundabout, and easier to comprehend.

A Wirth syntax diagram definition has the same elements as an EBNF grammar, as follows:

- A starting symbol.
- Terminal symbols, written in **boldface** but without quotes, sometimes also enclosed in round or oval boxes.
- Nonterminal symbols, written in regular type.
- Production rules are written using arrows (as in a flow chart) to indicate alternatives, options, and indefinite repetition. Each rule starts with a nonterminal symbol written at the left and ends where the arrow ends on the right.

Nonterminal symbols are like subroutine calls. To expand one, you go to the correct diagram, follow the arrows through the diagram until it ends, and return to the calling point to finish the calling production. Branch points correspond to alternatives and indicate that any appropriate choice can be made. Repetition is encoded by backward-pointing arrows which form explicit loops. Direct and indirect recursion are both allowed.

Syntax diagrams are given in Exhibits 4.6 and 4.7, which correspond exactly to the EBNF grammar fragments in Exhibit 4.4.

Exhibit 4.5.   Parsing a simple Pascal program.

   We perform a bottom-up parse of part of the program named "little", using standard Pascal syntax, part of which is shown in Exhibit 4.4. Starting with the expression at the top, we identify a single token or a consecutive series of tokens that correspond to the right side of a syntactic rule. This series is then "reduced", or replaced by the left side of that rule. The final reduction is shown at the bottom of the diagram.

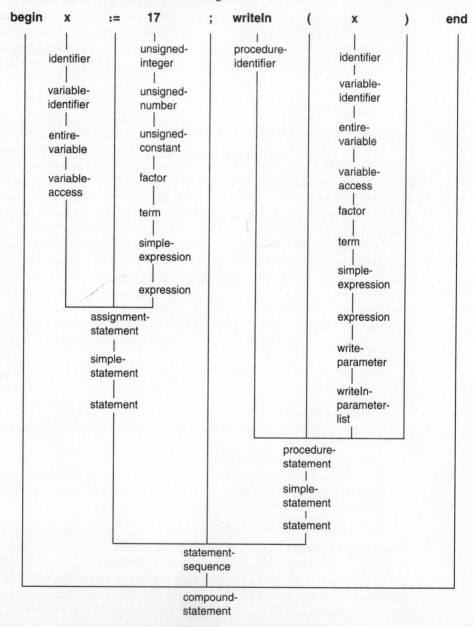

Exhibit 4.6.   Syntax diagram for "program".

This diagram corresponds to the EBNF productions for program, program-heading, program-parameters, and identifier list. The starting symbol is "program" .

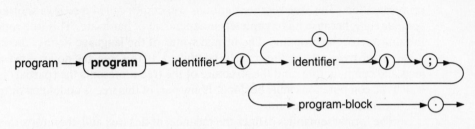

Exhibit 4.7.   Syntax diagrams for "statement".

These diagrams correspond to the EBNF productions for statement, simple-statement, structured-statement, compound-statement, and statement-sequence.

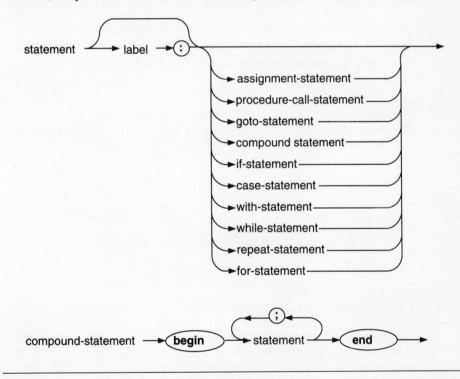

In spite of the simplicity and visual appeal of syntax diagrams, though, the official definition of Pascal grammar is written in EBNF, not syntax diagrams. EBNF is a better input language for a parser generator and provides a clearer basis for a formal definition of the semantics of the language.

4.3 SEMANTICS

4.3.1 The Meaning of a Program

A modern language translator converts a program from its source form into a tree representation. This tree representation is sometimes called *p-code*, a shortening of *portable code*, because it is completely independent of hardware. This tree represents the *structure* of the program. The formal syntax of the language defines the kinds of nodes in the tree and how they may be combined. In this tree, the nodes represent objects and computations, and the structure of the tree represents the (partial) order in which the computations must be done. If any part of this tree is undefined or missing, the tree may have no meaning.

The formal semantics defines the meaning of this tree and, therefore, the *meaning* of the program. A language implementor must determine how to convert this tree to machine code for a specific machine so that his or her translation will have the same meaning as that defined by the formal semantics. This two-step approach is used because the conversion from source text to tree form can be the same for all implementations of a language. Only the second step, code generation, is hardware-dependent [Exhibit 4.8].

Exhibit 4.8.   Translation: From source to machine code.

The object code was generated by OSS Pascal for the Atari ST.

Source code: **P-code tree:**

```
begin
x := 17;
y:= x+1
end
```

Object code:

```
moveq #17,d0
move d0,x
addq #1,d0
move d0,y
```

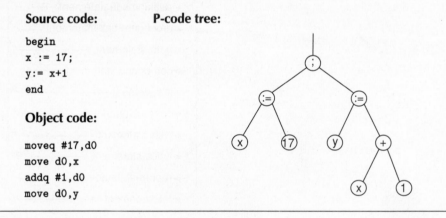

4.3.2 Definition of Language Semantics

The rules for interpreting the meaning of statements in a language are the semantics of the language. In order for a language to be meaningful and useful, the language designers, compiler writers, and programmers must share a common understanding of those semantics. If no single semantic standard exists, or no common understanding of the standard exists, various compiler writers will implement the language differently, and a programmer's knowledge of the language will not be transferable from one implementation to another. This is indeed the situation with both BASIC and LISP; many incompatible versions exist.

Knowing the full syntax of a programming language is enough to permit an experienced person to make a guess about the semantics, but such a guess is at best rough, and it is likely to be wrong in many details and in some major ways. This is because highly similar syntactic forms in similar languages often have different semantics.

The syntax of a programming language needs only to describe all strings of symbols that comprise legal programs. To define the semantics, one must either define the results of some real or abstract computer executing the program, or write a complete set of mathematical formulas that axiomatize the operation of the program and the expected results. Either way, the definition must be complete, precise, correct, and nonambiguous. Neither kind of definition is easy to make.

The semantics of a language must thus define a highly varied set of things, including but not limited to:

- What is the "correct" interpretation of every statement type?
- What do you mean when you write a name?
- What happens during a function call?
- In what order are computations done?
- Are there syntactically legal expressions that are not meaningful?
- In what ways does a compiler writer have freedom?
- To what extent must all compilers produce code that computes the same answers?

In general, answering such questions takes many more pages than defining the syntax of a language. For example, syntax diagrams for Pascal can be printed in eight pages, three of which also contain extensive semantic information.[6] In contrast, a complete semantic description of Pascal, at a level that can be understood by a well-educated person, takes 142 pages.[7] Part of the reason for this difference is the dissimilarity between the metalanguages in which syntax and semantics are defined.

The semantics of natural languages are communicated to learners by a combination of examples and attempts to describe the meaning. The examples are required because an English description of semantics will lack precision and be as ambiguous as English. Similarly, English alone is not adequate to define the semantics of a programming language because it is too vague and too ambiguous to define highly complex things in such a way that no doubt remains about their meaning.

Just as it is possible to create a formal system such as EBNF to define language syntax, it is possible to create a formal system to define programming language semantics.[8] There is a major difference, though. The languages used to express syntax are relatively easy to learn and can be mastered by any student with a little effort. The languages used to express semantics are very difficult to read and extremely difficult to write.

The primary use for a formal semantic definition is to establish a single, unambiguous standard for the semantics of the language, to which all other semantic

---

[6]Dale and Lilly [1985], pp. A1–A8.

[7]Cooper [1983].

[8]Historical note: The "Vienna Definition of PL/1" defined a new language for expressing semantics and defined the semantics of PL/1 in it. ALGOL-68 also had its own, impenetrable, formal language that tried to eliminate most of the need for a semantic definition by including semantics in the syntax. The result was a book-length syntax.

descriptions must conform. It defines all details of the meaning of the language being described and provides a precise answer to any question about details of the language, even details that were never considered by the language designer or semantics writer. Precision and completeness are more important for this purpose than readability, and formal semantic definitions are not easy to read.

A definition which only experts can read can serve as a standard to determine whether a compiler implements the standard language, but it is not really adequate for general use. Someone must study the definition and provide additional explanatory material so that educated nonexperts can understand it. Following is a quote from Cooper's Preface[9] which colorfully expresses the role of his book in providing a usable definition of Pascal semantics:

> The purpose of this manual is to provide a correct, comprehensive, and comprehensible reference for Pascal. Although the official Standard promulgated by the International Standards Organization (ISO) is 'correct' by definition, the precision and terseness required by a formal standard makes it quite difficult to understand. This book is aimed at students and implementors with merely human powers of understanding, and only a modest capacity for fasting and prayer in the search for the syntax or semantics of a *domain-type* or *variant selector*.

Cooper's book includes the definitions from the ISO standard and provides added explanatory material and examples. Compiler writers and textbook authors, in turn, can (but too many do not) use books such as *Standard Pascal* to ensure that their translations, explanations, and examples are correct.

4.3.3 The Abstract Machine

In order to make language definitions portable and not dependent on the properties of any particular hardware, the semantics of a computation tree must be defined in terms of an abstract model of a computer, rather than some specific hardware. Such a model has elements that represent the computer hardware, plus a facility for defining and using symbols. It forms a bridge between the needs of the human and computer. On one hand, it can represent symbolic computation, and on the other hand, the elements of the model are chosen so that they can be easily implemented on real hardware.

We describe an *abstract machine* here which we will use to discuss the semantics of many languages. It has five elements: the program environment, the stack, streams, the shared environment, and the control.

This abstract machine resembles both the abstract machine underlying FORTH[10] and the SECD machine that Landin used to formalize the semantics of LISP.[11] Landin's SECD machine also has a stack and a control. Its environment component is our program environment, and our streams replace Landin's dump.

The FORTH model contains a dictionary which implements our program environment. FORTH has two stacks (for parameters and return addresses) which together implement our stack, except that no facility is provided for parameter names or

---

[9]Cooper [1983], p. ix.
[10]Brodie [1987], Chapter 9.
[11]Landin [1964].

local names.[12] The FORTH system defines input and output from files (our streams) and how a stream may be attached to a program. Finally, FORTH has an interpreter and a compiler which together define our control element.

Our abstract machine has one element, the shared environment, not present in either the FORTH model or the SECD machine, as those models did not directly support multitasking.

Program Environment.

This environment is the context internal to the program. It includes global definitions and dynamically allocated storage that can be reached through global objects. It is the part of the abstract machine that supports communication between any non-hierarchically nested modules in a single program. Each function, F, exists in some symbolic context. Names are defined outside of F for objects and other functions. If these names are in F's program environment, they are known to F and permit F to refer to those objects and call those functions.

The program environment is implemented by a symbol table ("oblist" in LISP, "dictionary" in FORTH). When a symbol is defined, its name is placed in the symbol table, which connects each name to its meaning. Predefined symbols are also part of the environment. The meaning of a name is stored in some memory location, either when the name is defined or later. Either this space itself (as in FORTH) or a pointer to it (as in LISP) is kept adjacent to the name in the symbol table. Depending on the language, the meaning may be stored into the space by binding and initialization and/or it may be changed by assignment.

Shared Environment.

This is the context provided by the operating system or program development "shell". It is the part of the abstract machine that supports communication between a program and the outside world. A model for a language that supports multitasking must include this element to enable communication between tasks. Shared objects are in the environment of two or more tasks but do not "belong" to any of them.

Objects that can be directly accessed by the separate, asynchronous tasks that form a job are part of the shared environment. Intertask messages are examples.

The Stack.

The stack is the part of the computation model that supports communication between the enclosing and enclosed function calls that form an expression. It is a segmented structure of theoretically unlimited size. The top stack segment, or frame, provides a local environment and temporary objects for the currently active function. This local environment consists of local names for objects outside the function (parameters) and for objects inside the function (local variables). Local environments for several functions can exist simultaneously and will not interfere with each other. Suspension of one function in order to execute another is possible, with later reactivation of the first in the same state as when it was suspended.

---

[12]The dictionary in FORTH 83 is structured as a list of independent vocabularies, giving some support for local names.

The stack is implemented by a stack. A stack pointer is used to point at the stack frame (local environment) for the current function, which points back to a prior frame. A frame for a function F is created above the prior frame upon entry to F, and is destroyed when F exits. Storage for function parameters and a function return address are allocated in this frame and initialized (and possibly later removed) by the calling program.

Upon entry to F, the names of its parameters are added to the local environment by binding them to the stack locations that were set up by the calling program. The local symbols defined in F are also added to the environment and bound to additional locations allocated in F's stack frame. The symbol table is managed in such a way as to permit these names to be removed from the environment upon function exit.

Streams.

Streams are one medium of communication between different tasks that are parts of a job. A program exists in the larger context of a computer system and its files. The abstract machine, therefore, must reflect mass storage and ways of achieving data input and output. A *stream* is a model of a sequential file, as seen by a program. It is a sequence, in time, of data objects, which can be either read or written. Symbolic names for streams and for the files to which they are bound must be part of the program environment.

The concept of a stream is actually more general than the concept of a sequential file. Suppose two tasks are running concurrently on a computer system, and the output stream of one becomes the input stream of the other. A small buffer to hold the output until it is reprocessed can be enough to implement both streams.

Control.

The control section of the abstract model implements the semantic rules of the language that define the order in which the pieces of the abstract computation tree will be evaluated. It defines how execution of statements and functions is to begin, proceed, and end, including the details of sequencing, conditional execution, repetition, and function evaluation. (Chapter 8 deals with expressions and function evaluation, and Chapter 10 deals with control statements.)

Three kinds of control patterns exist: functional, sequential, and asynchronous.[13] These patterns are supported in various combinations in different languages. Each kind of control pattern is associated with its own form of communication, as diagrammed in Exhibit 4.9.

Functional control elements communicate with each other by putting parameters on the stack and leaving results in a return register. In the diagram, functions F1, F2, and F3 are all part of Process_1 and have associated stack frames on the stack for Process_1. When F3 is entered, its stack frame is created. Then when F3 calls F2 and F2 calls F1, frames for F2 and F1 are created on the stack. The frame for F1, indicated by a "<", is the "current" frame. Parameters are initialized during the function-calling process. When F1 returns it will return a 6 to F2.

---

[13]Developed fully in Chapter 8.

Exhibit 4.9.   Communication between modules.

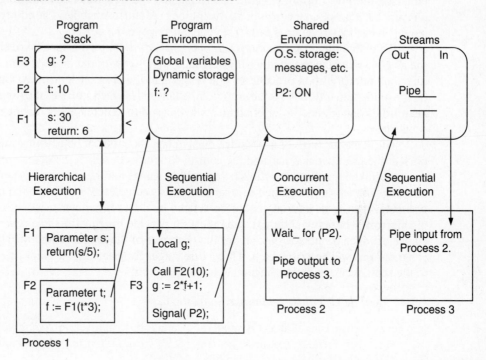

Functions within the same process share access to global variables in the program environment for that process. Sequential constructs in these functions communicate by assigning values to these variables. Function F2 communicates with F3, and sequential statements in F3 communicate with each other through the global variable named "f" in the program environment. F1 will return the value 6 to F2, which will assign it to a global variable, f. This variable is accessible to F3, which will use its value to compute g.

Concurrent tasks communicate through the shared environment. Process_1 and Process_2 share asynchronous, concurrent execution and synchronize their operations through signals left in the shared environment.

Sequential tasks communicate through streams. The output from Process_2 becomes the input for Process_3. To implement this, the operating system has connected their output and input streams through an operating system "pipe". This pipe could be implemented either by conveying the data values to Process_3 as soon as they are produced by Process_2 or by storing the output in a buffer or a file, then reading it back when the stream is closed.

A Semantic Basis.

The formal semantic definition of a language must include specific definitions of the details of the abstract machine that implements its semantics. Different language models include and exclude different elements of our abstract machine. Many languages do not support a shared environment. The new functional languages do not support a program environment, except for predefined symbols. The control elements, in particular, differ greatly from one language to the next.

We define the term *semantic basis of a language* to mean the specific version of the abstract machine that defines the language, together with the internal data structures and interpretation procedures that implement the abstract semantics. Layered on top of the semantic basis is the syntax of the language, which specifies the particular keywords, symbols, and order of elements to be used to denote each semantic unit it supports.

The semantic basis of a language must define the kinds of objects that are supported, the primitive actions, and the control structures by which the objects and actions are linked together, and the ways that the language may be extended by new definitions. The features included in a semantic basis completely determine the power of a language; items left out cannot be defined by the programmer or added by using macros. Where two different semantic units provide roughly the same power, the choice of which to include determines the character of the language and the style of programs that will be written in it. Thus a wise language designer gives careful thought to the semantic basis before beginning to define syntax.

4.3.4 Lambda Calculus: A Minimal Semantic Basis

It is perhaps surprising that a very small set of semantic primitives, *excluding goto and assignment*, can form an adequate semantic basis for a language. This was proven theoretically by Church's work on lambda calculus.[14]

Lambda calculus is not a programming language and is not directly concerned with computers. It has no programs or objects or execution as we understand them. It is a symbolic, logical system in which formulas are written as strings of symbols and manipulated according to logical rules.

We need to be knowledgeable about lambda calculus for three reasons. First, it is a *complete* system: Church has shown that it is capable of representing any computable function. Thus any language that can implement or emulate lambda calculus is also complete.

Second, lambda calculus gives us a starting point by defining a minimal semantic basis for computation that is mathematically clean. As we examine real computer languages we want to distinguish between necessary features, nice features (extras), nonfeatures (things that the language would be better off without), and missing features which limit the power of the language. The lambda calculus gives us a starting point for deciding which features are necessary or missing.

Finally, an extended version of lambda calculus forms the semantic basis for the modern functional languages. The Miranda compiler translates Miranda code into tree structures which can then be interpreted by an augmented lambda calculus interpreter. Lambda calculus has taken on new importance because of the recent research on functional languages. These languages come exceedingly close to capturing the essence of lambda calculus in a real, translatable, executable computer language. Un-

---

[14]Church [1941].

derstanding the original formal system gives us some grasp of how these languages differ from C, Pascal, and LISP, and supplies some reason for the aspects of functional languages that seem strange at first.

Symbols, Functions, and Formulas

There are two kinds of symbols in lambda calculus:

- A single-character symbol, such as y, used to name a parameter and called a *variable*.
- Punctuation symbols '(', ')', '.', and 'λ'.

These symbols can be combined into strings to form *formulas* according to three simple rules which follow. The parenthesis are optional.

1. A variable is a formula.
2. If y is a variable and F is a formula, then $(\lambda y.F)$ is a formula, which is called a *lambda expression*; y is said to be the *parameter* of the lambda expression, and F is its *body*.
3. If F and G are formulas, then (FG) is a formula, which is called an *application*.

Thus every lambda calculus formula is of one of three types: a variable, a lambda expression, or an application. Examples of formulas are given in Exhibit 4.10.

Exhibit 4.10.   Lambda calculus formulas.

Formulas	Comments
x	Any variable is a formula.
$(\lambda x.((yy)x))$	Lambda expressions are formulas.
$(\lambda z.(y(\lambda z.z)))$	The body of this lambda expression is an application.
$((\lambda z.(zy))x)$	Why is this formula an application?

Lambda calculus differs from programming languages in that its programs and its semantic domain are the same. Formulas can be thought of as programs or as the data upon which programs operate. A lambda expression is like a function: it specifies a parameter name and has a body that usually refers to that parameter.[15] An application whose first formula is a lambda expression is like a function call— the function represented by the lambda expression is called with the second formula as an argument. Thus $((\lambda x.F)G)$ intuitively means to call the function $(\lambda x.F)$ with argument G. However, not all formulas can be interpreted as programs. Formulas such as (xx) or $(y(\lambda x.z))$ do not specify a computation; they can be thought of as data.

In order to talk about lambda formulas, we will often give them symbolic names. To avoid confusing our names, which we use to talk *about* formulas, with variables,

---

[15]The syntax defined here supports only one-argument functions. There is a common variant which permits multiargument functions. This form can be mechanically converted to the single-argument syntax.

which *are* formulas, we use uppercase letters when naming formulas. As a short-hand for the statement, "let F be the formula $(\lambda x.(yx))$", we will write simply $F = (\lambda x.(yx))$. If we then write a phrase like, "the formula (Fz) is an application", the formula we are talking about is $((\lambda x.(yx))z)$. In general, wherever F appears, it should be replaced by its definition. Since names are just a shorthand for formulas, a circular "definition" such as $F = (\lambda x.(yF))$ is meaningless. Examples of symbols and definitions are shown in Exhibit 4.11.

Exhibit 4.11.   Lambda calculus names and symbols.

Formulas	Comments
x, y, z, etc.	Single lowercase letters are variables.
$G = (\lambda x.(y(yx)))$	A symbolic name may be defined to stand for a formula.
$H = (GG)$	Previously defined names may be used in describing formulas.

As another shorthand, when talking about formulas, we may omit unnecessary parentheses. Thus we may write $\lambda x.y$ instead of $(\lambda x.y)$. In general, there may be more than one way to insert parentheses to make a meaningful formula. For example, $\lambda x.yx$ might mean either $(\lambda x.(yx))$ or $((\lambda x.y)x)$. We use the rules that the body of a lambda expression extends as far to the right as possible, and sequences associate to the left. Thus, in the above example, the body of the lambda expression is yx, so the fully parenthesized form is $(\lambda x.(yx))$. Examples of these rules are given in Exhibit 4.12.

Exhibit 4.12.   Omitting parentheses when writing lambda calculus formulas.

Shorthand	Meaning
fxy	$((fx)y)$
$\lambda x.\lambda y.x$	$(\lambda x.(\lambda y.x))$
$\lambda x.x\lambda y.y$	$(\lambda x.(x(\lambda y.y)))$
$(\lambda x.(xx))(zw)$	$((\lambda x.(xx))(zw))$
$\lambda x.\lambda y.yzw$	$(\lambda x.(\lambda y.((yz)w)))$

Free and Bound Variables.

A parameter name is a purely local name. It *binds* all occurrences of that name on the right side of the lambda expression. A symbol on the right side of a lambda expression is *bound* if it occurs as a parameter, immediately following the symbol λ, on the left side of the same expression or of an enclosing expression. The scope of a binding is the entire right side of the expression. In Exhibit 4.14, the λx defines a local name and binds all occurrences of x in the expression. We say that each bound occurrence of x refers to the particular λx that binds it.

An occurrence of a variable x in F is *free* if x is not bound. Thus the occurrence of p in $(\lambda y.py)$ is free, but the occurrence of y in that same formula is bound (to λy). In the formula $(x(\lambda x.((\lambda x.x)x)))$, the variable x occurs five times. The second and third occurrences are bindings; the other three occurrences are uses. The first occurrence is free, since it does not lie within the scope of any λx-expression. The fourth occurrence is bound to the third occurrence, and the fifth occurrence is bound to the second occurrence.

These binding rules are the familiar scoping rules of block-structured programming languages such as Pascal. The operator λx declares a new instance of x. All occurrences of x within its scope refer to that instance, unless x is redeclared by a nested λx. In other words, an occurrence of a variable is always bound to the innermost enclosing block in which x is declared.

Representing Computation

Church invented a way to use lambda formulas to represent computation. He assigned interpretations to certain formulas, making them represent the basic elements of computation. (Some, but not all, lambda expressions have useful interpretations.) The formulas shown in this chapter are some of the most basic in Church's system, including formulas that represent truth values [Exhibit 4.13], the integers [Exhibit 4.15], and simple computations on them [Exhibit 4.16]. More advanced formulas are able to represent recursion. As you work through these examples the purpose and mechanics of these basic definitions should become clearer.

Exhibit 4.13.   Lambda expressions for TRUE and FALSE.

Expressions	Comments
$T = \lambda x.\lambda y.x$	The symbol "T" represents the logical value TRUE. You should read the definition of T as follows: T is a function of parameters x and y. Its body ignores y and returns x. (We say the argument y is "dropped".)
$F = \lambda x.\lambda y.y$	"F" names the lambda expression which represents FALSE.

Now that we know what lambda calculus formulas are, we need to talk about what they do. Evaluation rules allow one formula to be transformed to another. A formula which cannot be transformed further is said to be in *normal form*. The meaning of a formula is its normal form, if it has one; otherwise, the formula is undefined. An undefined formula corresponds to a nonterminating computation. Exhibit 4.14 dissects an expression and looks at its parts.

Reduction.

Consider a lambda expression which represents a function. At the abstract level, the meaning, or semantics, of the expression is the mathematical function that it com-

---

Exhibit 4.14. Dissection of a lambda expression.

A lambda expression, with name:

$2 = \lambda x.\lambda y.x(xy)$

Useful interpretation:

the number two

Breakdown of elements

$2 =$	Declares the symbol "2" to be a name for the following expression.
$\lambda x.$	The function header names the parameter, "x". Everything that follows this "." is the expression body.
$\lambda y.x(xy)$	The body of the original expression is another expression with a parameter named "y". Parameter names are purely arbitrary; this expression would still have the same meaning if it were rewritten with a different parameter name, as in: $\lambda q.x(xq)$.
$x(xy)$	This is the body of the inner expression. It contains a reference to the parameter "y" and also references to the parameter "x" from the enclosing expression.

---

putes when applied to an argument. Intuitively, we want to be able to freely replace an expression by a simpler expression that has the same meaning. The rules for beta and eta reduction permit us to do so.

The main evaluation rule for lambda calculus is called *beta reduction* and it corresponds to the action of calling a function on its argument. A *beta reducible expression* is an application whose left part is a lambda expression. We also use the term *beta redex* as a shortening of "reducible expression". When a lambda expression is applied to an argument, the argument formula is substituted for the bound variable in the body of the expression. The result is a new formula.

A second reduction rule is called *eta reduction*. Eta reduction lets us eliminate one level of binding in an expression of the form $\lambda x.f(x)$. In words, this is a special case in which the lambda argument is used only once, at the end of the body of the expression, and the rest of the body is a lambda expression applied to this parameter. If we apply such an expression to an argument, one beta reduction step will result in the simpler form $f(x)$. Eta reduction lets us make this transformation *without supplying an argument*. Specifically, eta reduction permits us to replace any expression of the form $\lambda x.f(x)$, where f represents a function, by the single symbol f.

After a reduction step, the new formula may still contain a redex. In that case, a second reduction step may be done. When the result does not contain a beta-redex or eta-redex, the reduction process is complete. We say such a formula is in *normal form*.

Many lambda expressions contain nested expressions. When such an expression is fully parenthesized it is clear which arguments belong to which function. When parentheses are omitted, remember that *function application associates to the left*; that is, the leftmost argument is substituted first for the parameter in the outermost expression.

We now describe in more detail how reduction works. When we reduce a formula (or subformula) of the form $H = ((\lambda x.F)G)$, we replace H by the formula F', where F' is obtained from F by substituting G for each reference to x in F. Note that if F contains another binding λx, the references to *that* binding are not replaced. For example, $((\lambda x.xy)(zw))$ reduces to $((zw)y)$ and $((\lambda x.x(\lambda x.(xy)))(zz))$ reduces to $(zz)(\lambda x.(xy))$.

When an expression containing an unbound symbol is used as an argument to another lambda expression, special care must be taken. Any occurrence of a variable in the argument that was free before the substitution must remain free after the substitution. It is not permitted for a variable to be "captured" by an unrelated λ during substitution. For example, it is *not* permitted to apply the reduction rule to the formula $((\lambda x.(\lambda y.x))(zy))$, since y is free in (zy), but after substitution, that occurrence of y would not be free in $(\lambda y.(zy))$. To avoid this problem, the parameter must be renamed, and all of its bound occurrences must be changed to the new name. Thus $((\lambda x.(\lambda y.x))(zy))$ could be rewritten as $((\lambda x.(\lambda w.x))(zy))$, after which the reduction step would be legal.

Examples of Formulas and Their Reductions

The formulas T and F in Exhibit 4.13 accomplish the equivalent of branching by manipulating their parameters. They take the place of the conditional statement in a programming language. T (true) returns its first argument and discards the second. Thus it corresponds to the IF..THEN statement which evaluates the THEN clause when the condition is true. Similarly, the formula F (false) corresponds to the IF..ELSE clause. It returns its second parameter just as an IF statement evaluates the second, or ELSE clause, when the condition is false.

Exhibit 4.15.   Lambda calculus formulas that represent numbers.

$$
\begin{aligned}
0 &= \ \lambda x.\lambda y.\, y \\
1 &= \ \lambda x.\lambda y.\, xy \\
2 &= \ \lambda x.\lambda y.\, x(xy)
\end{aligned}
$$

The formula for zero has no occurrences of its first parameter in its body. Note that it is the same as the formula for F. Zero and False are also represented identically in many programming languages.

The formula for the integer one has a single x in its body, followed by a y. The formula for two has two x's. The number n will be represented by a formula in which the first parameter occurs n times in succession.

The *successor function*, S, applied to any integer, gives us the next integer. Exhibit 4.16 shows the lambda formula that computes this function. Given any formula for a number n, it returns the formula for $n + 1$. The function *ZeroP* (zero predicate) tests whether its argument is equal to the formula for zero. If so, the result is T, if not,

F. Exhibit 4.17 shows how we would call *S* and *ZeroP*. The process of carrying out these computations will be explained later.

Exhibit 4.16.   Basic arithmetic functions.

The successor function for integers.

Given the formula for any integer, n, this function adds one x and returns the formula for the next larger integer.

$$S = \lambda n.(\lambda x.\lambda y.nx(xy))$$

Zero predicate.

This function returns *T* if the argument = 0 and *F* otherwise.

$$ZeroP = \lambda n.n(\lambda x.F)T$$

Exhibit 4.17.   Some lambda applications.

An application consists of a function followed by an argument. The first three applications listed here use the number symbols defined in Exhibit 4.15 and the function symbols defined in Exhibit 4.16. These three applications are evaluated step-by-step in Exhibits 4.18, 4.19, and 4.20.

$(S \quad 1)$	Apply the successor function to the function *1*.
$(ZeroP \quad 0)$	Apply *ZeroP* to *0* (Does *0* = zero?)
$(ZeroP \quad 1)$	Does *1* = zero?
$((GH) \quad x)$	Apply formula *G* to formula *H*, and apply the result to x.

The last application has the same meaning when written without the parentheses: "*GHx*".

Church was able to show that lambda calculus can represent all computation, by representing numbers, conditional evaluation, and recursion. Crucial to the power of his system is that there is no distinction between objects and functions. In fact, "objects", in the sense of data objects, were not defined at all. Expressions called "normal forms" take their place as concrete things that exist and can be tested for identity. A formula is in normal form if it contains no redexes. Not all formulas have a normal form; some may be reduced infinitely many times. These formulas, therefore, do not represent objects. They are the analog of infinite recursions in computer languages.

For example, let us define the symbol "*twin*" to be a lambda expression that duplicates its parameter:

$$twin = \lambda x.xx$$

The function "*twin*" can be applied to itself as an argument. The application looks like this:

$$(twin \quad twin)$$

The preceding line shows this application symbolically. Now we rewrite this formula with the name of the function replaced by its definition. Parentheses are used, for clarity, to separate expressions:

$$((\lambda x.xx)(twin))$$

This formula contains a redex and so it is not in normal form. When we apply the reduction rule, the function, $\lambda x.xx$, makes two copies of its parameter, giving:

$$(twin \quad twin)$$

Thus the result of reduction is the same as the formula we started with! Clearly, a normal form can never be reached.

Higher-Order Functions

If lambda calculus were a programming language, we would say that it treats functions as *first-class objects* and supports *higher-order functions*. This means that functions may take functions as parameters and return functions as results. With this potential we can do some highly powerful things.

We can define a lambda expression, F, to be the *composition* of two other expressions, say G and H. (This means that F is the expression produced by applying G to the result of H.) This cannot be done in most programming languages. C, for example, permits you to *execute* a function G on the result of *executing* H. But C does not let you write a function that takes two functional parameters, G and H, and returns a function, F, that will later accept some argument and apply first H to it and then apply G to the result.

A formula that implements recursion can be defined as the composition of two higher-order functions. Thus lambda calculus does not need to have recursion "built in"; it can be defined within the system. In contrast, recursion is, and must be, "built into" C and Pascal.

A language with higher-order functions also permits one to *curry* a function. G is a *currying* of F if G has one fewer parameter than F and computes its result by calling F with a constant in place of the omitted parameter. Currying, combined with generic dispatching,[16] is one way to implement functions with optional arguments.

Evaluation / Reduction

Any model of computation must represent action as well as objects. Actions are represented in the lambda calculus by applying the *reduction rule*, which requires applying the renaming and substitution rules.

To reduce a formula, F, one finds a subformula, S, anywhere within F, that is reducible. To be reducible, S must consist of a lambda expression, L, followed by an argument, A. The reduction process then consists of two steps: renaming and substitution.

Renaming.

Renaming is required only if unbound symbols occur in A. They must not have the same name as L's parameter. If such a name conflict occurs, the parameter in L must be renamed so that the unbound symbol will not be "captured" by L's parameter. The new name may be any symbol whatsoever. The formula for L is simply rewritten with the new symbol in place of the old one.

---

[16]See Chapter 18.

Substitution.

After renaming, each parameter reference on the right side of L is replaced by a copy of the entire argument-expression, and the resulting string replaces the subexpression S. The λ, the dummy parameter, and the "." are dropped.

Exhibits 4.18, 4.19, and 4.20 illustrate the reduction process. Three simple formulas are given and reduced until they are in normal form. The comments on the left in these exhibits document each choice of redex and the corresponding substitution process. The following explanations are given so that you may develop some intuition about how these functions work.

Exhibit 4.18.   Reducing $(S \quad 1)$.

Compute the Successor of 1. The answer should be 2. For clarity, the formula for one has been written using p and q instead of x and y. (This is, of course, permitted. The symbols that are used for *bound* variables may be renamed any time.)

Write out S.	$(\lambda n.(\lambda x.\lambda y.nx(xy))\, 1)$
Substitute 1 for n, reduce.	$(\lambda x.\lambda y.1\, x\, (xy)\,)$
Write out the definition of 1.	$(\lambda x.\lambda y.(\lambda p.\lambda q.pq)\, x\, (xy))$
Substitute x for p, and reduce.	$(\lambda x.\lambda y.\, (\lambda q.xq)\, (xy))$
Substitute (xy) for q, reduce.	$(\lambda x.\lambda y.x(xy))$

The answer is the formula for 2, which is, indeed, the successor of 1.

Exhibit 4.19.   Reducing $(ZeroP \quad 0)$.

Apply *ZeroP* to 0, that is, determine whether 0 equals zero. The answer should be T.

Write out *ZeroP* followed by *0*.	$((\lambda n.n(\lambda x.F)\, T)\, 0\,)$
Substitute 0 for n in the body of *ZeroP* and reduce.	$(\, 0\, (\lambda x.F)\, T\,)$
Write out the formula for zero.	$(\, (\lambda x.\lambda y.y)\, (\lambda x.F)\, T)$
Substitute $(\lambda x.F)$ for x, and reduce.	$((\lambda y.y)\, T)$
Substitute T for y, reduce.	T

So 0 does equal 0. Note that the argument, $(\lambda x.F)$, was dropped in the fourth step because the parameter, x, was not referenced in the body of the function.

Exhibit 4.20.   Reducing $(ZeroP \quad 1)$.

Write out *ZeroP* followed by 1.	$((\lambda n.n(\lambda x.F)\, T)\, 1\,)$
Substitute 1 for n, reduce.	$(\, 1\, (\lambda x.F)\, T)$
Write out the formula for 1.	$(\, (\lambda x.\lambda y.xy)\, (\lambda x.F)\, T)$
Substitute $(\lambda x.F)$ for x, reduce.	$(\, (\lambda y.(\lambda x.F)\, y)\, T)$
Substitute T for y, reduce.	$((\lambda x.F)\, T)$
Substitute T for x and reduce.	F

On the last line, the parameter x does not appear in the body of the function, so the argument, T, is simply dropped. So *1* does not equal *0*.

Applying *ZeroP* to any nonzero number would give the same result, but involve one more reduction step for each x in the formula.

Successor.   Intuitively, the successor function must take a numeric argument (a nest of two lambda expressions) and insert an additional copy of the outermost parameter into the middle of the formula. This is accomplished as follows:

- On the first reduction step, the formula for S embeds its argument, n, in the middle of a nested lambda expression. The symbols x and y in the formula for S are bound by the lambdas at the left. We rename the bound variables in the formula for n to avoid confusion; during the reduction process, this p and q will be eliminated.

- The formula for n now forms a redex with the x in the tail end of the formula for S. Reducing this puts as many copies of x into the result as there were copies of p in n. Remember, we want to end up with exactly one additional copy of x.

- This added x comes from the (xy) at the right of the formula for S. The result of the preceding reduction forms a redex with this (xy). When we reduce, this final x is sandwiched between the other x's and the y, as desired.

Essentially, the y in a number is a "growth bud" that permits any number of x's to be appended to the string. It would be easy, now, to write a definition for the function "plus2".

Zero predicate.   Remember, 0 and F are represented by the same formula. Thus the zero predicate must turn F into T and any other numeric formula into F. (The behavior of *ZeroP* on nonnumeric arguments is undefined. Applying *ZeroP* to a nonnumber is like a type error.) Briefly, the mechanics of this computation work as follows:

- An integer is represented by a formula that is a nest of two lambda expressions.

- *ZeroP* takes its argument, n, and appends two expressions, $\lambda x.F$ and T, to n. These two expressions form arguments for the two lambda expressions in n. The entire unit forms two nested applications.

- We reduce the outermost lambda expression first, using the argument $\lambda x.F$. If n is 0, this argument is "discarded" because the formula for zero does not contain a reference to its parameter. For nonzero arguments, this expression is kept.

- The inner expression (from the original argument, n) forms an application with the argument T. When n is zero, this reduces immediately to T. When n is nonzero, there is one more reduction step and the result is F.

The Order of Reductions

Not every expression has a normal form; some can be reduced forever. But if a normal form exists it can always be reached by some chain of reductions. When each lambda expression in a formula is nested fully within another, only one order of reduction is possible—from the outside in. But it is possible to have a formula with two reducible lambda expressions at the same level, side by side [Exhibit 4.21]. Further, whatever redex you select next, the normal form can still be reached. Put informally, you cannot back yourself into a corner from which you cannot escape. This important result is named the "Church-Rosser Theorem" after the logicians who formally proved it.

Some expressions that do have normal forms contain subexpressions that cannot be reduced to normal form. This seems like a contradiction until you realize that, in the process of evaluation, whole sections of a formula may be "discarded". For

---

Exhibit 4.21.   A formula with three redexes.

Assume that $P3$ (which adds 3 to its argument) and $*$ (which computes the product of two arguments) have already been defined. (They can be built up out of the successor function.) Then the formula

$$(*(P34)(P39))$$

has three reducible expressions: $(P34)$, $(P39)$, and $(*(P34)(P39))$.

---

example, in a conditional structure, either the "then part" or the "else part" will be skipped. The computation enclosing the conditional can still terminate successfully, even if the part that is skipped contains an infinite computation.

By the Church-Rosser theorem, a normal form, if it exists, can be reached by reducing subformulas in any order until there are no reducible subformulas left. However, although you cannot get "blocked" in reducing such an expression, you can waste an infinite amount of effort if you persist in reducing a nonterminating part of the formula. Since any subformula may be discarded by a conditional, and never need to be evaluated, it is wiser to postpone evaluating a subexpression until it is needed. If, eventually, a nonterminating subformula must be evaluated, then the formula has no normal form. If, on the other hand, it is "discarded", the formula in which this infinite computation was embedded can still be computed (reduced to normal form).

A further theorem proves that *if* a normal form can be reached, then it can be reached using the outside-in order of evaluation. That is, at each step the outermost possible redex is chosen. (The formulas in Exhibits 4.20, 4.19, and 4.18 were all reduced in outside-in order.) This order is called the *normal order of evaluation* in lambda calculus and corresponds to *call-by-name reduction order* in a programming language.[17] It may not be a unique order, since sometimes the outermost formula is not reducible, but may contain more than one redex side-by-side. In that case, either may be reduced first.

The Relevancy of Lambda Calculus

Lambda calculus has been proven to be a fully general way to symbolize any computable formula. Its semantic basis contains representations of objects (normal forms) and functions (λ expressions). Because functions *are* objects, and higher-order functions can be constructed, the system is able to represent conditional branching, function composition, and recursion. Computation is represented by the process of reduction, which is defined by the rules for renaming, parameter substitution, and formula rewriting.

Although lambda calculus is a formal logical system for manipulating formulas and symbols, it provides a model of computation that can be and has been used as a starting point for defining programming languages. LISP was originally designed to be an implementation of lambda calculus, but it did not capture the outside-in evaluation semantics.

---

[17]See Chapter 9, Section 9.2.

4.4 EXTENDING THE SEMANTICS OF A LANGUAGE

Let us define an *extension* to be a set of definitions which augment a language with an entirely new facility that can be used in the same way that preexisting facilities are used. Some of the earliest languages were not very extensible at all. The original FOR-TRAN allowed variables to be defined but not types or functions (in a general sense). Function definitions were limited to one line. All modern languages are extensible in many ways. Any time we define a new object, a new function, or a new data type, we are extending the language. Each such definition extends the list of words that are meaningful and adds new expressive power. Pascal, LISP, and the like are extensible in this sense: by building up a vocabulary of defined functions and/or procedures, we ultimately write programs in a language that is much more extensive and powerful than the bare language provided by the compiler.

Historically, we have seen that extensibility depends on uniform, general treat-ment of a language feature. Any time a translator is designed to recognize a specific, fixed set of keywords or defined symbols, that portion of the language is not extensible. The earliest BASIC was not extensible at all; even variable names were all predefined (only two-letter names were permitted). FORTRAN, one of the earliest computer languages, can help us see how the design of a language and a translator can create barriers to extensibility. We will look at types and functions in early FORTRAN and contrast them to the extension facilities in more modern languages.

Early FORTRAN supported a list of predefined mathematical functions. The translator recognized calls on those predefined functions, but users could not define their own. This probably happened because the designers/implementors of FORTRAN provided a static, closed list of function names instead of simply permitting a list that could grow. The mechanics of translating a function call are also simpler if only one- and two-argument functions have to be supported, rather than argument lists of un-limited size.

In contrast, consider early LISP. Functions were considered basic (as lambda expressions are basic in lambda calculus), and the user was expected to define many of them. The language as a whole was designed to accept and translate a series of definitions and enter each into an extensible table of defined functions. The syntax for function calls was completely simple and modeled after lambda calculus, which was known to be completely general. LISP was actually easier to translate than FORTRAN.

Consider type extensions. In FORTRAN, there were two recognized data types, real and integer. These were "hard wired" into the language: variables whose names started with letters "I" through "N" were integers, all other variables were real. On the implementation level, FORTRAN parsers were written to look at each variable name and deduce the type from it. This was certainly a convenient system, since it made declarations unnecessary, but it was not extensible. The system fell apart when FORTRAN was extended to support alphabetic data and double-precision arithmetic.

In contrast, look at Pascal. Pascal has four primitive data types and several ways to build new simple and aggregate types out of the primitive types. The language has a clear notion of what a type is, and when a new type is or is not constructed. Each time the programmer uses a type constructor, a new type is added to the list of defined types. Thereafter, the programmer may use the new type name in exactly the same ways that primitive type names may be used.

Although Pascal types are extensible, there are predefined, nonextensible relationships among the predefined types, just as there are in FORTRAN. Integers may be converted to reals, and vice versa, under specific, predefined circumstances. These conversion relationships are nonextensible; the triggering circumstances cannot be modified, and similar conversion relationships for other types cannot be defined. Object-oriented languages carry type-extensibility one step farther, permitting the programmer to define relationships between types and extend the set of situations in which a conversion will take place. This is accomplished, in C++ for example, by introducing the notion of a "constructor function", which builds a value of the target type out of components of the original type. The programmer may define her or his own constructors. The translator will use those constructors to avoid a type error under specified circumstances, by converting an argument of the original type to one of the target type.

In all the cases described here, extension is accomplished by allowing the programmer to define new examples of a semantic category that already exists in the translator. To enable extension, a new syntax is provided for defining new instances of existing categories. However, the programmer writes the same syntax for using an extension as for using a predefined facility. Old categories are extended; entirely new things are not added. Some languages, those with macro facilities, allow the programmer to extend the language by supplying new notation for existing facilities. However, very few languages support additions or changes to the basic syntactic structure or the semantic basis of the language. Changing the syntactic structure would involve changing the parser, which is normally fixed. Changing the semantic basis would involve adding new kinds of tables or procedures to the translator to implement the new semantics.

What would it mean to extend the syntactic structure of a language? Consider the break instruction in C and the EXIT in Ada. These highly useful statements enable controlled exits from the middle of loops. Pascal does not have a similar statement, and an exit from the middle of a loop can be done only with a GOTO. But the GOTO lacks the safely controlled semantics of break and EXIT. Because it is so useful, EXIT is sometimes added to Pascal as a nonstandard extension. Doing this involves extending the parsing phase of the compiler to recognize a new keyword and modifying the code generation phase to generate a branch from the middle of a loop to the first statement after the loop. Of course, a programmer cannot extend a Pascal compiler like this. It can only be done when the compiler is being written.

The ANSI C dialect and the language C++ are both semantic extensions of C. ANSI C extended the original language by adding type checking for function calls and some coherent operations on structured data. C++ adds, in addition, semantically protected modules (classes), virtual functions, and polymorphic domains. This kind of semantic extension is implemented by changing the compiler and having it do work of a different nature than is done by an old C compiler. These extensions mentioned required modifying the process of translating a function call, adding new information to the symbol table, implementing new restrictions on visibility, and adding type checking and type conversion algorithms.

The code and tables of a compiler are normally "off-limits" to the ordinary language user. In most languages, a programmer cannot access or change the compiler's tables. The languages EL/1, FORTH, and T break this rule; EL/1[18] permitted additions to the compiler's syntactic tables, with accompanying semantic extensions, and FORTH permits access to the entire compiler, including the symbol table and the semantic interpretation mechanisms.

EL/1 (Extensible Language 1) actually permitted the programmer to supply new EBNF syntax rules and their associated interpretations. The translator included a preprocessor and a compiler generator which combined the user-supplied syntax rules with the built-in ones and produced a compiler for the extended language. The semantic interpretations for the new syntactic rules, supplied by the user, were then used in the code generation phase.

A very similar thing can be done in T. T is a semantic extension of Scheme which includes data structuring primitives, object classes, and a macro preprocessor which can be used to extend the syntax of the language. Each preprocessor symbol is defined by a well-formed T expression. With these tools, extensions can be constructed that are not possible in C, Pascal, or Scheme. We could, for example, use the macro facility to define the syntax for a `for loop` expression and define the semantics to be a complex combination of initializations, statement executions, increments, and result-value construction.

4.4.1 Semantic Extension in FORTH

We use FORTH to demonstrate the kind of extension that can be implemented by changing the parser and semantic interpretation mechanisms of a translator. Two kinds of limited semantic extension are possible in FORTH:

- We may add new kinds of information to the symbol table, with accompanying extensions of the interpreter.
- We may modify the parser to translate new control structures.

We shall give an example of each kind of extension below. In both cases, the extension is accomplished by using knowledge of the actual implementation of the compiler and accessing tables that would (in most compilers) be protected from user tampering. FORTH has several unusual features that make it possible to do this kind of extension.

First, like LISP, FORTH is a small, simple language with a totally simple structure. FORTH books explain the internal structure of the language and details of the operation of the compiler and interpreter. Second, the designers of FORTH anticipated the desire to extend the rather rudimentary language and included extension primitives, the words "CREATE" and "DOES>", that denote a compiler extension, and the internal data structures to implement them.

Finally, FORTH is an interpretive language. The compiler produces an efficient intermediate representation of the code, not native machine code. Control changes from the interpreter to the compiler when the interpreter reaches the ":" at the beginning of a definition, and switches back to the interpreter when the compiler reaches the ";" at the end of the definition. Words are also included that permit one to suspend a compilation in the middle, interpret some code, and return to the compilation.

---

[18]Wegbreit [1970].

Thus variable declarations, ordinary function definitions, segments of code to be interpreted, and extensions to the compiler can be freely intermixed. The only requirement is that everything be defined before it is used.

New Types.

Unextended, FORTH has three semantic categories, or data types, for items in the dictionary (symbol table): constant, variable, and function. By using the words CREATE and DOES> inside what otherwise looks like a normal function definition, more types can be added. CREATE enters the name of the new type category into the dictionary. Following it must be FORTH code for any compile-time actions that must be taken to allocate and/or initialize the storage for this new type. This compile-time section is terminated by the DOES>, which marks this partial entry as a new semantic category. Finally, the definition includes FORTH code for the semantic routine that should be executed at run time when items in this category are referenced [Exhibit 4.22].

Exhibit 4.22. Definition in FORTH of the semantics for arrays.

```
0   :   2by3array    ( The ":" marks the beginning of a definition.  )
1       create       ( Compile time actions for type declarator 2by3array.  )
2          2 , 3 ,   ( Store dimensions in the dictionary with the object.  )
3          12 allot  ( Allocate 12 bytes for 6 short integers.  )
4       does>        ( Run time actions to do a subscripted fetch.  )
5       rangecheck   ( Function call to check that both subscripts are )
6       if           ( within the legal range.  )
7       linearsub    ( Function call to compute the effective memory )
8       then         ( address, given base address of array and subscripts.)
9   ;                ( End of data type definition.  )
10
11  2by3array box    ( Declare and allocate an array variable named box.  )
12  10  1 2 box !    ( Store the number 10 in box[1,2].  )
```

Program Notes.

- Comments are enclosed in parentheses.

- The definition of the new type declarator goes from line 0 to line 9.

- "," stores the prior number in the dictionary.

- Lines 5 and 7 are calls on the functions rangecheck and linearsub, which the programmer must define and compile before this can be compiled. Linearsub must leave its result, the desired memory address, on the stack.

- Line 11 declares a 2by3array variable named box. When this line is compiled, the code on lines 2 and 3 is run to allocate and initialize storage for the new array variable.

- Line 12 puts the value 10 on the stack, then the subscripts 1 and 2. When the interpreter processes the reference to box, the semantic routine for 2by3array (lines 5–8) is executed. This checks that the subscripts are within range, then computes a memory address and leaves it on the stack.

- Finally, that address is used by "!" to store the 10 that was put on the stack earlier. "!" is the assignment operation. It expects a value and an address to be on the stack and stores the value in that address.

Having added a type, the FORTH interpreter can be extended to check the type of a function parameter and dispatch (or execute) one of several function methods, depending on the type. New data types are additional examples of a category that was built into the language. However, type checking was not built into FORTH in any way. When we implement type checking, we add a semantic mechanism to the language that did not previously exist. This is true semantic extension.

Adding a new control structure.

CREATE and DOES> provide semantic extension without corresponding syntactic extension. They permit us to extend the data structuring capabilities of the language but not to add things like new loops that would require modifying the syntax. To the extent that the FORTH compiler's code is open and documented, though, the clever programmer can even extend the syntax in a limited way. We have code that adds a BREAK instruction to exit from the middle of a FIG FORTH loop. This code uses a compiler variable that contains the address of the end of the loop during the process of compiling the loop. The code for BREAK cannot be added to FORTH 83. Many compiler variables that were documented in FIG FORTH are kept secret in the newer FORTH 83. These machine- and implementation-dependent things were taken out of the language documentation in order to increase the portability of programs written in FORTH, and the portability of the FORTH translator itself. Providing no documentation about the internal operation of the compiler prevents the syntax from being extended.

EXERCISES

1. Briefly define EBNF and syntax diagrams. How are they used, and why are they necessary?
2. Describe the compilation process from source code to object code.
3. Consider the following EBNF syntax. Rewrite this grammar as syntax diagrams.

```
sneech ::=    '*' |
              ( '(' ⟨sneech⟩ ')' '*' ) |
              [ ⟨bander⟩ ] ⟨sneech⟩

bander ::=    { '+$+' | '#' } | ( '%' ⟨bander⟩ )
```

4. Which of the following "sentences" are not legal according to the syntax for sneeches, given in question 3? Why?

a.	(*)	f.	######**
b.	(+$+*)	g.	(+$+#
c.	*	h.	+$+#*
d.	*****	i.	*+$+#
e.	%%%**	j.	%#*+$+**

5. Rewrite the following syntax diagrams as an EBNF grammar.

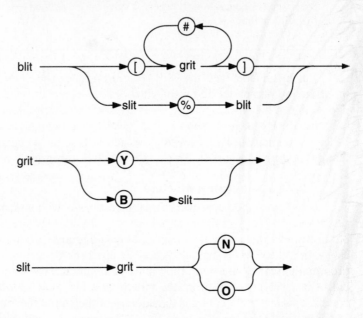

6. What is the difference between a terminal and nonterminal symbol in EBNF?

7. What is a production? How are alternatives denoted in EBNF? Repetitions?

8. Using the production rules in Exhibit 4.4, generate the program called "easy" which has two variables: a, an integer, and b, a real. The program initializes a to 5. Then b gets the result of multiplying a by 2. Finally, the value of b is written to the screen followed by a new line.

9. What are the EBNF productions for the conditional statement in Pascal? Show the corresponding syntax diagrams from a standard Pascal reference.

10. Show the syntax diagram for the For statement in Pascal. List several details of the meaning of the For that are not defined by the syntax diagram.

11. What are semantics?

12. What is the difference between a program environment and a shared environment?

13. What is a stream?

14. Why is lambda calculus relevant in a study of programming language?

15. Show the result of substituting u for x in the following applications. Rename bound variables where necessary.

   a. $((\lambda x.\lambda y.x)u)$
   b. $((\lambda x.\lambda y.z)u)$
   c. $((\lambda x.\lambda u.ux)u)$
   d. $((\lambda x.\lambda x.ux)u)$

16. Each item below is a lambda application. We have used a lot of parentheses to help you parse the expressions. Reduce each formula, until no redex remains. One of the items requires renaming of a bound variable.

    a. $((\lambda x.\lambda y.x(xy))(pq)q)$

    b. $((\lambda x.\lambda y.y)(pq)q)$

    c. $((\lambda z.(\lambda y.yz))(\lambda x.xy))$

    d. $((\lambda x.\lambda y.y(xy))(\lambda p.pp)q)$

17. Verify the following equality. Start with the left-hand side and substitute the formula for *twice*. Then reduce the formula until it is in normal form. This may look like a circular reduction, but the formula reaches normal form after eight reduction steps.

    Let *twice* $= \lambda f.\lambda x.f(fx)$.

    Show that *twice twicegz* $= g(g(g(gz)))$.

Hints: Write out the formula for *twice* only when you are using it as a function; keep arguments in symbolic form. Each time you write out *twice*, use new names for the bound variables. Be careful of the parentheses. Remember that function application associates to the left.

18. Show that 3 is the successor of 2, using the lambda calculus representations defined for integers.

19. Define the function "plus2" using a lambda formula. Demonstrate that your formula works by applying it to the formula for 1.

20. Construct a lambda formula to express the following conditional expression. (Assume that x is a Boolean value, T or F.) Verify the correctness of your expression by applying it to T and F and reducing to get 0 or 2.

    If x is true then return 0 else return 2.

21. How do EL/1 and FORTH allow the semantics of the languages to be extended?

PART

DESCRIBING COMPUTATION

5

Primitive Types

_____ Overview _____

This chapter explains the concept of types within programming languages and the hardware that supports these types. Computer memory is an array of bits usually grouped into addressable 8-bit segments called *bytes*. *Words* are groups of bytes, usually 2, 4, and sometimes 8 bytes long. All data types in programming languages must be mapped onto the bytes and words of the machine. Logical computer instructions operate on bytes and words, but other instructions operate on objects that are represented by codes which are superimposed on bit strings. Common codes include ASCII, EBCDIC, binary integer, packed decimal, and floating point.

A data type is an abstraction: a description of a set of properties independent of any specific object that has those properties. A previously defined type is referred to by a type name. A type description identifies the parts of a nonprimitive type. A specific type is a homogeneous set of objects, while a generic type is a set that includes objects of more than one specific type. Each type is a set of objects with an associated set of functions. A type defines the representation for program objects. Several attributes are defined by the type of an object, including encoding, size, and structure.

Every language supports a set of primitive data types. Usually these include integer, real, Boolean, and character or string. A language standard determines the minimum set of primitive types that the language compiler must implement. Hardware characteristics influence which types a language designer chooses to make primitive. If the hardware does not support a required type, that type may have to be emulated, that is, implemented in the software.

Type declarations have a long history, going back to the earliest languages which supported primitive types built into the instruction set of the host machine. By the late 1960s, types were recognized as abstractions. Type declarations defined value constructors, selectors, and implicit type predicates. In the 1970s, with the emergence of Ada, types were treated as objects in a limited way. There were cleaner type compatibility rules, support for type portability, and explicit constraint on the values of a type. Recent research includes the issues of type hierarchies with inherited properties and the implementation of nonhomogeneous types in a semantically sound way.

5.1 PRIMITIVE HARDWARE TYPES

A translator must map a programmer's objects and operations onto the storage and instructions provided by the computer hardware. To understand the primitive types supported by languages, one should also understand the hardware behind those types.

5.1.1 Bytes, Words, and Long Words

Computer memory is a very long array of bits, normally organized into groups.[1] Each group has an address, used to store and fetch data from it. Modern machines usually have 8-bit bytes and are *byte-addressable*. Bytes are grouped into longer 2- and 4-byte units called *words* and *long words*. Some machines have a few hardware instructions that support *double word*, or 8-byte, operations.

Bytes and words form the basis for all representation and all computation. They are the primitive data type onto which all other data types must be mapped.

Computer instruction sets include some instructions that operate on raw, uninterpreted bytes or words. These are called *logical* instructions. They include right and left shifts, and bitwise complement, and, or, and exor operations.

Most computer instructions, though, are intended to operate on objects other than bit strings, such as numbers or characters. All objects must be *represented* by bit strings, but they have semantics above and beyond the bits that represent them. These objects are represented by codes that are superimposed on the bit strings. Common encodings include ASCII, EBCDIC, binary integer, packed decimal, and floating point.

5.1.2 Character Codes

Long before IBM built computers, it built *unit record equipment*, which processed data recorded on punched cards. Keypunches were used to produce this data, and line printers could copy cards to fanfold paper. Tabulating machines were used to process the data. These had "plug boards", on which a skilled person could build programs

---

[1] The Burroughs memory of the B1700/B1800 series of computers was an undivided string of bits that was actually bit-addressable.

by using plug-in cables to connect holes that represented card columns to holes that represented functions such as "+" and "−".[2]

Punched cards were in common use before computers were invented and quite naturally became the common input medium for computers. The Hollerith character code, used for punched cards, was adapted for use in computers, and called *Binary Coded Decimal*, or BCD. Hollerith code was a decimal code. It used one column with twelve punch positions to represent each digit. (These positions were interpreted as +, −, 0...9.) Alphabetic letters were represented as pairs of punches, one in the "zone" area (+, −, 0), and one in the "digit" area (1..9). This gives 27 combinations, which is one too many for our alphabet, and the 0:1 punch combination was not used for any letter. The tradition was that this combination was omitted from the alphabet because the two closely spaced punches made it physically weak. However, this combination was used to represent "/". Thus the alphabet had a nonalpha character in its middle.

The entire Hollerith character set had no more than 64 codes. Letters and digits accounted for 36 of these; the rest were other punctuation and control characters and were represented by double or triple punches. The BCD code used sixty-four 6-bit codes to represent this character set.

The BCD character code was reflected in various ways in the computer hardware of the 1950s and early 1960s. It has always been practical to make word size a multiple of the character code size. Hardware was built with word lengths of 24, 36, 48, and 60 bits (making 4, 6, 8, and 10 characters per word). Floating-point encoding was invented for the IBM 704; its 36-bit words were long enough to provide adequate range and precision.

Software, also, showed the effects of this character code. FORTRAN was designed around this severely limited character set (uppercase only, very few available punctuation symbols). FORTRAN identifiers were limited to six characters because that is what would fit into one machine word on the IBM 704 machine. COBOL implemented numeric data input formats that were exactly like Hollerith code. If you wanted to input the number −371, you punched only three columns and put the "−" sign *over* the rightmost, giving the *number code* "37J". The number +372 was encoded as "37B". This wholly archaic code is still in use in COBOL today and is increasingly difficult to explain and justify to students.

Dissatisfaction with 6-bit character codes was rampant; sixty-four characters are just not enough. People, reasonably, wanted to use both upper- and lowercase letters, and language designers felt unreasonably restricted by the small set of punctuation and mathematical symbols that BCD provided. Two separate efforts in the early 1960s produced two new codes, EBCDIC (Extended BCD Interchange Code) and ASCII (American Standard Code for Information Interchange).

EBCDIC was produced and championed by IBM. It was an 8-bit code, but many of the 256 possible bit combinations were not assigned any interpretation. Upper- and lowercase characters were included, with ample punctuation and control characters. This code was an extension of BCD; the old BCD characters were mapped into EBCDIC in a systematic way. Certainly, that made compatibility with old equipment less of a problem.

---

[2]These were archaic in the early 1960s, but a few early computer science students had the privilege of learning to use them.

Unfortunately, the EBCDIC code was not a "sensible" code because the collating sequence was not normal alphabetical order.[3] Numbers were greater than letters, and like BCD, alphabetic characters were intermingled with nonalphabetic characters.

ASCII code grew out of the old teletype code. It uses seven bits, allowing 128 characters. Upper- and lowercase letters, numerals, many mathematical symbols, a variety of useful control characters, and an "escape" are supported. The "escape" could be used to form 2-character codes for added items.[4] ASCII is a "sensible" code; it follows the well-established English rules for alphabetization. It has now virtually replaced EBCDIC, even on IBM equipment.

An extended 8-bit version of ASCII code is now becoming common. It uses the additional 128 characters for the accented and umlauted European characters, some graphic characters, and several Greek letters and symbols used in mathematics. Hardware intended for the international market supports extended ASCII.

5.1.3 Numbers

We take integers and floating-point numbers for granted, but they are not the only ways, or even the only common and useful ways, to represent data.

In the late 1950s and early 1960s, machines were designed to be either *scientific computers* or *business computers*. The memory of a scientific computer was structured as a sequence of words (commonly 36 bits per word) and its instruction set performed binary arithmetic. Instructions were fixed length and occupied one word of memory.

Packed Decimal

The memory of a business computer was a series of BCD bytes with an extra bit used to mark the beginning of each variable-length "word". Objects and instructions were variable length. Numbers were represented as a series of decimal (BCD) digits. Arithmetic was done in base ten, not base two.

The distinction between scientific and business computers profoundly affected the design of programming languages. COBOL, a "business language", was oriented toward variable-length objects and supported base ten arithmetic. In contrast, FORTRAN was a "scientific language". Its data objects were one word long, or arrays of one-word objects, and computation was done either in binary or in floating point. Characters were not even a supported data type.

In 1964, IBM introduced a family of computers with innovative architecture, intended to serve both the business and scientific communities.[5] The memory of the IBM 360 was byte-addressable. The hardware had general-purpose registers to manipulate byte, half-word (2-byte), and word (4-byte) sized objects, plus four 8-byte registers for floating-point computation. The instruction set supported computation on binary integers, floating point, *and* integers represented in packed decimal with a trailing sign [Exhibit 5.1].

---

[3]The *collating sequence* of a code is the order determined by the "$<$" relationship. To print out a character code in collation order, start with the code 00000000, print it as a character, then add 1 and repeat, until you reach the largest code in the character set.

[4]It is often used for fancy I/O device control codes, such as "reverse video on".

[5]Gorsline [1986], p. 317.

Exhibit 5.1.   Packed-decimal encoding.

- A number is a string of digits. The sign may be omitted if the number is positive, or represented as the first or last field of the string.
- Each decimal digit is represented by 4 bits, and pairs of digits are packed into each byte. The string may be padded on the left to make the length even.
- The code "0000" represents the digit 0, and "1001" represents 9. The six remaining possible bit patterns, "1010" . . . "1111", do not represent legal digits.

Many contemporary machines support packed-decimal computation. Although the details of packed-decimal representations vary somewhat from machine to machine, the necessary few instructions are included in the Intel chips (IBM PC), the Motorola chips (Apollo workstations, Macintosh, Atari ST), and the Data General MV machines.

Packed-decimal encoding is usually used to implement *decimal fixed-point arithmetic*. A decimal fixed-point number has two integer fields, one representing the magnitude, the other the scale (the position of the decimal point). The scale factors must be taken into account for every arithmetic operation. For instance, numbers must be adjusted to have the same scale factors before they can be added or subtracted. Languages such as Ada and COBOL, which support fixed-point arithmetic, do this adjustment for the programmer.[6]

Base 2 arithmetic is convenient and fast for computers, but it cannot represent most base ten fractions exactly. Furthermore, almost all input and output is done using base ten character strings. These strings must be converted to/from binary during input/output. The ASCII to floating point conversion routines are complex and slow.

Arithmetic is slower with packed decimal than with binary integers because packed-decimal arithmetic is inherently more complex. Input and output conversions are much faster; a packed-decimal number consists of the last 4 bits of each ASCII or EBCDIC digit, packed two digits per byte. Arithmetic is done in *fixed point*; a specified number of digits of precision is maintained, and numbers are rounded or truncated after every computation step to the required precision. Control over rounding is easy, and no accuracy is lost in changing the base of fractions.

In a data processing environment, packed decimal is often an ideal representation for numbers. Most business applications do more input and output than computation. Some, such as banking and insurance computations, require total control of precision and rounding during computation in order to meet legal standards. For these applications, binary encoding for integers and floating-point encoding for reals is simply not appropriate.

Binary Integers

Binary numbers are "built into" modern computers. However, there are several ways that binary numbers can be represented. They can be different lengths (2- and 4-

---

[6]Unfortunately, the Ada standard does not require that fixed-point declarations be implemented by decimal fixed-point arithmetic! It is permissible in Ada to approximate decimal fixed-point computation using numbers represented in binary, not base ten, encoding!

byte lengths being the most common), and be signed or unsigned. If the numbers are signed, the negative values might be represented in several ways.

Unsigned integers are more appropriate than signed numbers for an application that simply does not deal with negative numbers, for example, a variable representing a machine address or a population count. Signed and unsigned numbers of the same length can represent exactly the same number of integers; only the range of representable numbers is different [Exhibit 5.2]. On a modern two's complement machine, unsigned arithmetic is implemented by the same machine instructions as signed arithmetic.

Exhibit 5.2.   Representable values for signed and unsigned integers.

These are the smallest and largest integer values representable on a two's complement machine.

Type	Length	Minimum	Maximum
Signed	4 bytes	-2,147,483,648	2,147,483,647
	2 bytes	-32,768	32,767
	1 byte	-128	127
Unsigned	4 bytes	0	4,294,967,295
	2 bytes	0	65,535
	1 byte	0	255

Some languages, for example C, support both signed and unsigned integers as primitive types. Others, for example Pascal and LISP, support only signed integers. Having "unsigned integer" as a primitive type is not usually necessary. Any integer that can be represented as an "unsigned" can also be represented as a "signed" number that is one bit longer. There are only a few situations in which this single bit makes a difference:

- An application where main storage must be conserved and a 1-byte or 2-byte integer could be used, but only if no bit is wasted on the sign.

- An application where very large machine addresses or very large numbers must be represented as integers, and every bit of a long integer is necessary to represent the full range of possible values.

- The intended application area for the language involves extensive use of the natural numbers (as opposed to the integers). By using type "unsigned" we can constrain a value to be nonnegative, thereby increasing the explicitness of the representation and the robustness of the program.

"Unsigned" will probably be included as a primitive type in any language whose intended applications fit one of these descriptions. C was intended for systems programming, in which access to all of a machine's capabilities is important, and so supports "unsigned" as a primitive type.[7]

---

[7]We must also note that the primitive type "byte" or "bitstring" is lacking in C, and "unsigned" is used instead. While this is semantically unattractive, it works.

Signed Binary Integers.

The arithmetic instructions of a computer define the encoding used for numbers. The ADD 1 instruction determines the order of the bit patterns that represent the integers. Most computers "count" in binary, and thus support binary integer encoding. Most compilers use this encoding to represent integers. Although this is not the only way to represent the integers, binary is a straightforward representation that is easy for humans to learn and understand, and it is reasonably cheap and fast to implement in hardware.[8]

Large machines support both word and long word integers; very small ones may only support byte or word sized integers. On such machines, a compiler writer must use the short word instructions to emulate arithmetic on longer numbers that are required by the language standard. For example, the instruction set on the Commodore 64 supported only byte arithmetic, but Pascal translators for the Commodore implemented 2-byte integers. Adding a pair of 2-byte integers required several instructions; each half was added separately and then the carry was propagated.

Negative Numbers.

One early binary integer representation was *sign and magnitude*. The leftmost bit was interpreted as the sign, and the rest of the bits as the magnitude of the number. The representations for +5 and −5 differed only in one bit. This representation is simple and appealing to humans, but not terrific for a computer. An implementation of arithmetic on sign-and-magnitude numbers required a complex circuit to propagate carries during addition, and another one to do borrowing during subtraction.

CPU circuitry has always been costly, and eventually designers realized that it could be made less complex and cheaper by using complement notation for negative numbers. Instead of implementing "+" and "−", a complement machine could use "+" and "negate". Subtraction is equivalent to negation followed by addition. Negation is trivially easy in one's complement representation—just flip the bits. Thus "00000001" represented the integer 1 and "11111110" represented −1. A carry off the left end of the word was added back in on the right. The biggest drawback of this system is that zero has two representations, "0000000" (or +0) and "11111111" (or −0).

A further insight occurred in the early 1960s: complement arithmetic could be further simplified by using two's complement instead of one's complement. To find the two's complement of a number, complement the bits and add one. The two's complement of "00000001" (representing 1) is "11111111" (representing −1). Two's complement representation has two good properties that are missing in one's complement: there is a unique representation for zero, "00000000", and carries off the left end of a sum can simply be ignored. Two's complement encoding for integers has now become almost universal.

Floating Point

Many hardware representations of floating-point numbers have been used in computers. Before the advent of ASCII code, when characters were 6 bits long, machine

---

[8]Other kinds of codes have better error correction properties or make carrying easier.

words were often 36 or 48 bits long. (It has always been convenient to design a machine's word length to be a multiple of the byte length.) Thirty-six bits is enough to store a floating-point number with a good range of exponents and about eight decimal digits of precision. Forty-eight or more bits allows excellent precision. However, word size now is almost always 32 bits, which is a little too small.

In order to gain the maximum accuracy and reasonable uniformity among machines, the IEEE has developed a standard for floating-point representation and computation. In this discussion, we focus primarily on this standard. The IEEE standard covers all aspects of floating point—the use of bits, error control, and processor register requirements. It sets a high standard for quality. Several modern chips, including the IBM 8087 coprocessor, have been modeled after it.

To understand floats, you need to know both the format and the semantics of the representation. A floating-point number, N, has two parts, an exponent, e, and a mantissa, m. Both parts are signed numbers, in some base. If the base of the exponent is b, then $N = m * b^e$.

The IEEE standard supports floats of three lengths: 4, 8, and 10 bytes. Let us number the bits of a float starting with bit 0 on the right end. The standard prescribes the float formats shown in Exhibit 5.3. The third format defines the form of the CPU register to be used during computation. Exhibit 5.4 shows how a few numbers are represented according to this standard.

Exhibit 5.3.   IEEE floating-point formats.

Format Name	Length	Sign	Exponent	Mantissa
			Bit fields in representation	
Short real	4 bytes	31	30–23	22–0, with implicit leading 1
Long real	8 bytes	63	62–52	51–0, with implicit leading 1
Temporary real	10 bytes	79	78–64	63–0, explicit leading 1

The sign bit, always at the left end, is the sign of the entire number. A "1" is always used for negative, "0" for a positive number.

The exponent is a signed number, often represented in bias notation. A constant, called the bias, is added to the actual exponent so that all exponent values are represented by unsigned positive numbers. In the case of bias 128, this is like two's complement with the sign bit reversed.

The advantage of a bias representation is that, if an ordinary logical comparison is made, positive numbers are greater than negative numbers. Absolutely no special provision needs to be made for the sign of the number. With 8 bits in the exponent, "00000000" represents the smallest possible negative exponent, and "11111111" is the largest positive exponent. "10000000" generally represents an exponent of either zero or one. When interpreted as a binary integer, "10000000" is 128. If this represents an exponent of zero, we say that the notation is "bias 128", because $128 - 0 = 128$. When

Exhibit 5.4.   Floating point on the SparcStation.

The SparcStation is a new RISC workstation built by Sun Microsystems. It has a floating-point coprocessor modeled after the IEEE standard. Using the Sun C compiler to explore its floating-point representation, we find that the C "float" type is implemented by a field with the IEEE 4-byte encoding. A few numbers are shown here with their representations printed in hex notation and in binary with the implied 1-bit shown at the left of the mantissa.

Decimal	Hex	Sign	Binary Representation Exponent	Mantissa
0.00	00000000	0	00000000	0.0000000 00000000 00000000
0.25	3E800000	0	01111101	1.0000000 00000000 00000000
0.50	3F000000	0	01111110	1.0000000 00000000 00000000
1.00	3F800000	0	01111111	1.0000000 00000000 00000000
-1.00	BF800000	1	01111111	1.0000000 00000000 00000000
10.00	41200000	0	10000010	1.0100000 00000000 00000000
5.00	40A00000	0	10000001	1.0100000 00000000 00000000
2.50	40200000	0	10000000	1.0100000 00000000 00000000
1.25	3FA00000	0	01111111	1.0100000 00000000 00000000

"10000000" represents an exponent of one, we say the notation is "bias 127", because $128 - 1 = 127$.

In the IEEE standard, the exponent is represented in bias 127 notation, and the exponent "10000000" represents $+1$. This can be seen easily in Exhibit 5.4. The representation for 2.50 has an exponent of "10000000". The binary point in "1.010000" must be moved one place to the right to arrive at "10.1", the binary representation of 2.50. Thus "10000000" represents $+1$.

Floating-point hardware performs float operations in a very long register, much longer than the 24 bits that can be stored in a float. To maintain as many bits of precision as possible, the mantissa is normalized after every operation. This means that the leading "0" bits are shifted to the left until the leftmost bit is a "1". Then when you store the number, all bits after the twenty-fourth are truncated (discarded). A normalized mantissa always starts with a "1" bit, therefore this bit has no information value and can be regenerated by the hardware when needed. So only bits 2–24 of the mantissa are stored, in bits 22–0 of the float number.

The mantissa is a binary fraction with an implied binary point. In the IEEE standard, the point is between the implied "1" bit and the rest of the mantissa. Some representations place the binary point to the left of the implied "1" bit. These interpretations give the same precision but different ranges of representable numbers.

5.2   TYPES IN PROGRAMMING LANGUAGES

5.2.1   Type Is an Abstraction

An *abstraction* is the description of a property independent from any particular object which has that property. Natural languages contain words that form hierarchies of increasing degrees of abstraction, such as "TRS-80", "microcomputer", "computer", and "electronic device" [Exhibit 5.5]. "TRS-80" is itself an abstraction, like a type, describing a set of real objects, all alike. Most programming language development since the early 1980s has been aimed at increasing the ability to express and use abstractions within a program. This work has included the development of abstract data types, generic functions, and object-oriented programming. We consider these topics briefly here and more extensively later.

Exhibit 5.5. A hierarchy of abstractions.

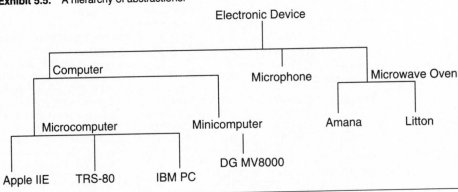

A *data type* is an abstraction: it is the common property of a set of similar data objects. This property is used to define a representation for these objects in a program. Objects are said to "have" or to "be of" that type to which they belong. Types can be primitive, defined by the system implementor, or they can be programmer defined. We refer to a previously defined type by using a *type name*. A *type declaration* defines a type name and associates a *type description* with it, which identifies the parts of a nonprimitive type [Exhibit 5.6]. The terms *type* and *data type* are often used loosely; they can refer to the type name, the type description, or the set of objects belonging to the type.

Exhibit 5.6. Type, type name, and type description.

- Real-world objects: a set of rectangular boxes.
- Type: We will represent a box by three real numbers: its length, width, and depth.
- Type name declared in Pascal: TYPE box_type =
- Possible type descriptions in Pascal:

```
ARRAY [1..3] OF real
RECORD length, width, depth:  real END
```

If all objects in a type have the same size, structure, and semantic intent, we call the type *concrete* or *specific*. A specific type is a homogeneous set of objects. All the primitive types in Pascal are specific types, as are Pascal arrays, sets, and ordinary records made out of these basic types. A *variant record* in Pascal is not a specific type, since it contains elements with different structures and meanings.

A *generic domain* is a set that includes objects of more than one concrete type [Exhibit 5.7]. A specific type that is included in a generic domain is called an *instance* or *species* of the generic domain, as diagrammed in Exhibit 5.8. Chapters 14 and 16 explore the subjects of type abstraction and generic domains.

Exhibit 5.7.   Specific types and generic domains.

Specific types:

- Integer arrays of length 5
- Character arrays of length 10
- Real numbers
- Integer numbers

Generic domains:

- Intarray: The set of integer arrays, of all lengths.
- Number: All representations on which you can do arithmetic, including floating point, integer, packed decimal, etc.

Exhibit 5.8.   Specific types are instances of generic domains.

- The generic domain Number has several specific subtypes, including Real, Integer, and Complex.
- Objects (variables) have been declared that belong to these types. Objects named V, W, and X belong to type Real; objects J and K belong to type Integer, and C belongs to type Complex.
- All six objects also belong to the generic domain Number.

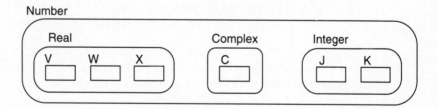

5.2.2   *A Type Provides a Physical Description*

The properties of a type are used to map its elements onto the computer's memory. Let us focus on the different attributes that are part of the type of an object. These include encoding, size, and structure.

Encoding.

The instruction set of each machine includes instructions that do useful things on certain encodings (bit-level formats) of data. For example, the Data General MV8000 has instructions that perform addition if applied to numbers encoded with 4 bits per decimal digit. Because of this "built-in" encoding, numbers can be conveniently represented in packed-decimal encoding in Data General COBOL. Where an encoding must be implemented that is not directly supported by the hardware, the implementation tends to be inefficient.

Size.

The size of an object can be described in terms of hardware quantities such as words or bytes, or in terms of something meaningful to the programmer, such as the range of values or the number of significant digits an object may take on.

Structure.

An object is either simple or it is compound. A *simple object* has one part with no subparts. No operators exist within a language that permit the programmer to decompose simple objects. In a language that has "integer" as a simple type, integer is generally undecomposable.

In standard Pascal, integers are simple objects, as are reals, Booleans, and characters. In various Pascal extensions, though, an integer can be decomposed into a series of bytes. In these dialects "integer" is not a simple type. Primitive types may or may not be simple. In both cases, "integer" is a primitive type; that is, it is a predefined part of the language.

A compound object is constructed of an ordered series of fields of specific types. A list of these fields describes the structure of the object. If the fields of the compound object all have the same type, it is a homogeneous compound. These are commonly called "array", "vector", "matrix", or "string". The dimensions of an array and its base type (the type of its elements) define its structure.

If the fields of a compound object have different types, it is a heterogeneous compound. These are commonly called "records" or "structures". An ordered list of the types of each field of a record defines its structure.

The distinctions among structure, encoding, and size are seen most clearly in COBOL, where these three properties are specified separately by the programmer.

Structure in COBOL.   The internal structure of each data object is defined by listing its fields and subfields, in order. The subfields of a field are listed immediately following the field and given higher level numbers to indicate that they are subordinate to it.

Encoding in COBOL.   Character data has only one encoding: the character code built into the machine hardware. Depending on the compiler, several encodings may be provided for numbers, with DISPLAY being the default. The COBOL programmer may specify the encoding in a USAGE clause. In Data General COBOL, the programmer can choose from the following set:

- DISPLAY   ASCII or EBCDIC characters
- COMPUTATIONAL   binary fixed point

- COMP-2   packed binary-coded-decimal fixed point

- COMP-3   floating point

Double-precision encoding is also provided in some COBOL implementations. Each encoding has inherent advantages, which must be understood by the programmer. Input and output require operands of DISPLAY usage. Arithmetic can be done on all usages except DISPLAY. The most efficient numeric I/O conversion is between DISPLAY and COMP-2. The most efficient arithmetic is done in COMPUTATIONAL.

Conversion from one encoding to another is performed automatically when required in COBOL. If a numeric variable does not have the default usage, DISPLAY, conversion is performed during the input and output processes, as in most languages. If a numeric variable represented in DISPLAY usage is used in an arithmetic statement, it will be converted to packed decimal. (This conversion is fast and efficient.) The arithmetic will be done in packed-decimal encoding, and the result will be converted back to display usage if it is stored in a DISPLAY variable.

Size in COBOL.   Size is defined by supplying a PICTURE clause for every field that has no subfields [Exhibit 5.9]. The PICTURE illustrates the largest number of significant characters or decimal digits that will ever be needed to represent the field. Note that the programmer describes the size of the object being represented, not the size, in bytes, of the representation. Different amounts of storage could be allocated for equal size specifications with different encoding specifications.

Exhibit 5.9.   Size and encoding specifications in COBOL.

Three simple variables are defined, named PRICE, DISCOUNT, and ITEM.

```
01 PRICE      PICTURE 999V99.
01 DISCOUNT   PICTURE V999  USAGE COMPUTATIONAL.
01 ITEM       PICTURE XXXX.
```

PRICE has a numeric-character encoding, indicated by the 9s in the PICTURE clause and the absence of a USAGE clause. The size of this variable is defined by the number of 9s given, and decimal position is marked by the "V". In this case, the number has two decimal places and is less than or equal to 999.99.

DISCOUNT has binary fixed-point encoding (because of the USAGE clause). Its size is three decimal digits, with a leading decimal point.

ITEM has alphanumeric encoding, indicated by the Xs in its PICTURE. Its size is four characters. Any alphanumeric value of four or fewer characters can be stored in this variable.

At the other extreme from COBOL, the language BASIC permits the programmer to specify only whether the object will encode numeric or alphanumeric objects, and to declare the structure of arrays (number of dimensions and size of each). The encoding is chosen by the translator and hidden from the user. Thus BASIC is simpler to use. It frees the programmer from concern about the appropriateness of the encoding. At the same time, it provides no easy or efficient control over precision and rounding. BASIC is thus a better tool for the beginner, but a clumsy tool for the professional.

5.2.3 What Primitive Types Should a Language Support?

The usual set of primitive data types in a language includes integer, real, Boolean, and character or string. However, Ada has many more and BASIC has fewer.

A language standard determines the minimum set of primitive types that must be implemented by a compiler. Choosing this set is the job of the language designer. A language implementor may choose to support additional types, however. For example, Turbo Pascal supports a type string that is not required by the standard. The string type is a language extension.

The decision to make a type "primitive" in a computer language is motivated by hardware characteristics and the intended uses of the language. Compromises must often be made. A language designer must decide to include or exclude a type from the primitive category by considering the cost of implementing and using it [Exhibit 5.10] as opposed to the cost of not implementing it [Exhibit 5.11].

Exhibit 5.10.   Costs of implementing a primitive type.

- Every added feature complicates both the language syntax and semantics. Both require added documentation. If every useful feature were supported, the language would become immense and unwieldy.

- Standardization could become more difficult, as there is one more item about which committee members could disagree. This could be an especially severe problem if a type is complex, its primitive operations are extensive, or it is unclear what the ideal representation should be.

- The compiler and/or library and/or run-time system become more complex, harder to debug, and consume more memory. Literals, input and output routines, and basic functions must be defined for every new primitive type.

- If typical hardware does not provide instructions to handle the type, it may be costly and inefficient to implement it. Perhaps programmers should not be encouraged to use inefficient types.

Exhibit 5.11.   Costs of omitting a primitive type.

- Inefficiency: failing to include an operation that is supported by the hardware leads to a huge increase in execution time.

- Language structure may be inadequate to support the type as a user extension, as Pascal cannot support variable-length strings or bit fields with bitwise operators.

- Some built-in functions such as READ, WRITE, assignment, and comparison are generic in nature. They work on all primitive types but not necessarily on all user-defined types. If these functions cannot be extended, a user type can never be as convenient or easy to use as a primitive type.

- Primitive types have primitive syntax for writing literals. Literal syntax is often not extensible to user-defined types.

Types that are not primitive sometimes cannot be implemented efficiently, or even implemented at all, by the user. For example, the ANSI C standard does not support packed-decimal numbers. A user *could* write his or her own packed-decimal routines in C. To achieve adequate precision the user would probably map them onto integers, not floats. Masking, base 10 addition and multiplication, carrying, and the like could be implemented. However, the lack of efficiency in the finished product would be distressing, especially when you consider that many machines provide efficient hardware instructions to do this operation.

If users are expected to need a certain type frequently, the language is improved by making that type primitive. Packed decimal is not a primitive type in C because the intended usage of C was for systems programming, not business applications. In this case, the cost of *not* implementing the type is low, and the cost of *implementing* it is increased clutter in the language.

As another example, consider the string type in Pascal. It was almost certainly a mistake to omit a string manipulation package from the standard language. Alphabetic data is very common, and many programs use string data. The Pascal standard recognizes that strings exist but does not provide a reasonable set of string manipulation primitives. The standard defines a "string" to be any object that is declared as a "packed array[1..n] of char", where n is an integer > 1. String output is provided by Write and Writeln. String comparison and assignment are supported, but only for strings of equal length. Length adjustment, concatenation, and substrings are not supported, and Read cannot handle strings at all. A programmer using Standard Pascal must read alphabetic fields one character at a time and store each character into a character array.

Virtually all implementations of Pascal extend the language to include a full string type with reasonable operations. Unfortunately, these extensions have minor differences and are incompatible with each other. Thus there are two kinds of costs associated with omitting strings from standard Pascal:

1. User implementations of string functions are required. These execute less efficiently than system implementations could.
2. Because programmers use strings all the time, many compilers are extended to support a string type and some string functions. Using these extensions makes programs less portable because the details of the extensions vary from compiler to compiler.

Including strings in the language makes a language more complex. Both the syntax and semantic definitions become longer and require more extensive documentation. The minimal compiler implementation is bigger. In the case of Pascal and strings, none of these reasons justify the omission.

When language designers do decide to include a primitive type, they must extend the language syntax for declarations, but they have some choices about how to include the operations on that type. The meanings of operators such as "<" are usually extended to operate on elements of the new type. New operators may also be added. Any specific function for the new type may be omitted, added to the language core, or included in a library. The latter approach becomes more and more attractive as the number of different primitive types and functions increases. A modular design makes the language core simpler and smaller, and the library features do not add complexity or consume space unless they are needed.

For example, exponentiation is a primitive operation that is important for much scientific computation. Pascal, C, and FORTRAN all support floating-point encoding but have very unequal support for exponentiation. In Pascal, exponentiation in base 10 is not supported by the standard at all; it must be programmed using the natural logarithm and exponentiation functions ("ln" and "exp"). In C, an exponentiation function, "pow", is included in the mathematics library along with the trigonometric functions. In contrast, FORTRAN's intended application was scientific computation, and the FORTRAN language includes an exponentiation *operator*, "**", as part of the language core.

5.2.4 Emulation

The types required by a language definition may or may not be supported by the hardware of machines for which that language is implemented. For example, Pascal requires the type "real", but floating-point hardware is not included on many personal computers. In such situations, data structures and operations for that type must be implemented in software. Another example: fixed-point arithmetic is part of Ada. This is no problem on hardware that supports packed-decimal encoding, but on a strictly binary machine, an Ada translator must use a software emulation or approximation of fixed-point arithmetic.

The representation for an emulated primitive type is a compromise. On the one hand, it should be as efficient as possible for the architecture of the machine. On the other hand, it should conform as closely as possible to the typical hardware implementation so that programs are portable. The hardware version and the emulation should give the same answers!

When floating point is emulated, the exponent is sometimes represented as a 1-byte integer, and the mantissa is represented by 4 or more bytes with an implied binary point at the left end. This produces an easily manipulated object with good precision. A minimum of shifting and masking is needed when this representation is used. However, it sometimes does not produce the same answers as a 4-byte hardware implementation.

Other software emulations try to conform more closely to the hardware. Accurate emulation of floating-point hardware is more difficult and slower but has the advantage that a program will give the same answers with or without a coprocessor. A good software emulation should try to imitate the IEEE hardware standard as closely as possible without sacrificing acceptable efficiency [Exhibit 5.12].

Exhibit 5.12. An emulation of floating point.

This is a brief description of the software emulation of floating point used by the Mark Williams C compiler for the Atari ST (Motorola 68000 chip). Note that it is very similar to, but not quite like, the IEEE standard shown in Exhibits 5.3 and 5.4.

Bit	31:	Sign
Bits	30–23:	Characteristic, base 2, bias 128
Bits	22–0:	Normalized base 2 mantissa, implied high-order "1", binary point immediately to the left of the implied "1".

Decimal	Hex	Binary Representation		
		Sign	Exponent	Mantissa
0.00	00000000	0	00000000	.00000000 00000000 00000000
0.25	3F800000	0	01111111	.10000000 00000000 00000000
0.50	40000000	0	10000000	.10000000 00000000 00000000
1.00	40800000	0	10000001	.10000000 00000000 00000000
-1.00	C0800000	1	10000001	.10000000 00000000 00000000
10.00	42200000	0	10000100	.10100000 00000000 00000000
5.00	41A00000	0	10000011	.10100000 00000000 00000000
2.50	41200000	0	10000010	.10100000 00000000 00000000
1.25	40A00000	0	10000001	.10100000 00000000 00000000

5.3 A BRIEF HISTORY OF TYPE DECLARATIONS

The ways for combining individual data items into structured aggregates form an important part of the semantic basis of any language.

5.3.1 Origins of Type Ideas

Types Were Based on the Hardware.

The primitive types supported by the earliest languages were the ones built into the instruction set of the host machine. Some aggregates of these types were also supported; the kinds of aggregates differed from language to language, depending on both the underlying hardware and the intended application area. In these old languages, there was an intimate connection between the hardware and the language.

For example, FORTRAN, designed for numeric computation, was first implemented on the IBM 704. This was the first machine to support floating-point arithmetic. So FORTRAN supported one-word representations of integers and floating-point numbers. The 704 hardware had index registers that were used for accessing elements of an array—so FORTRAN supported arrays.

COBOL was used to process business transactions and was implemented on byte-oriented "business" machines. It supported aggregate variables in the form of records and tables, represented as variable-length strings of characters. One could read or write entire COBOL records. This corresponded directly to the hardware operation of reading or writing one tape record. One could extract a field of a record. This corresponded to a hardware-level "load register from memory" instruction. The capabilities of the language were the capabilities of the underlying hardware.

"Type" was not a separate idea in COBOL. A structured variable was not an example of a structured type—it was an independent object, not related to other objects. The structured variable as a whole was named, as were all of its fields, subfields, and sub-subfields. To refer to a subfield, the programmer did not need to start with the name of the whole object and give the complete pathname to that subfield; it could be referred to directly if its name was unambiguous.

FORTRAN supported arrays, and COBOL supported both arrays (called "tables") and records. It would be wrong, though, to say that they supported array or record *types*, because the structure of these aggregates was not abstracted from the individual examples of that structure. One could *use* a record in COBOL, and even pass it to a subroutine, but one could not talk about the type of that record. Each record object had a structure, but that structure had no name and no existence apart from the object [Exhibit 5.13].

Exhibit 5.13.   Declaration and use of a record in COBOL.

We declare a three-level record to store data about a father. If other variables were needed to store information about other family members, lines two through six would have to be repeated. COBOL provides no way to create a set of uniformly structured variables. Field names could be the same or different for a second family member. The prevailing style is to make them different by using a prefix, as in F-FIRST below.

```
1    FATHER.
     2    NAME.
          3    LAST        PIC X(20).
          3    F-FIRST     PIC X(20).
          3    F-MID-INIT  PIC X.
     2    F-AGE           PIC 99.
```

Assume that FATHER is the only variable with a field named F-FIRST, and that MOTHER also has a field named LAST. Then we could store information in FATHER thus:

MOVE 'Charles' TO F-FIRST. MOVE 'Brown' TO LAST IN FATHER.

Note that the second line gives just enough information to unambiguously identify the field desired; it does not specify a full pathname.

LISP **Introduced Type Predicates.**

LISP was the earliest high-level language to support dynamic storage allocation, and it pioneered garbage collection as a storage management technique. In the original implementation of LISP, its primitive types, atom and list, were drawn directly from the machine hardware of the IBM 704. An "atom" was a number or an identifier. A "list" was a pointer to either an atom or a cell. A "cell" was a pair of lists, implemented by a single machine word. The 36-bit machine instruction word had four fields: operation code, address, index, and decrement. The address and decrement fields could both contain a machine address, and the hardware instruction set included instructions to fetch and store these fields.

Here again we see a close relationship between the language and the underlying hardware. This two-address machine word was used to build the two-pointer LISP cell. The three fundamental LISP functions, CAR, CDR, and CONS, were based directly on the hardware structure. CAR extracted the address field of the cell, and CDR extracted the decrement field. (Note that the "A" in CAR and the "D" in CDR came from "address" and "decrement".) CONS constructed a cell dynamically and returned a pointer to it. This cell was initialized to point at the two arguments of CONS.

Note that all LISP allocations were a fixed size—one word. Only one word was ever allocated at a time. However, the two pointers in a cell could be used to link cells together into tree structures of indefinite size and shape.

The concept of "type" was more fully developed in LISP than in FORTRAN or COBOL. Types were recognized as qualities that could exist separately from objects, and LISP supported *type predicates*, functions that could test the type of an argument at run time. Predicates were provided for the types "atom" and "list". These were essential for processing tree structures whose size and shape could vary dynamically.

SNOBOL: **Definable "Patterns".**

SNOBOL was another language of the early 1960s. It was designed for text processing and was the first high-level language that had dynamically allocated *strings* as a primitive type. This was an important step forward, since strings (unlike arrays, records, and list cells) are inherently variable-sized objects.

New storage management techniques had to be developed to handle variable-sized objects. Variables were implemented as pointers to numbers or strings, which were stored in dynamically allocated space. Dynamic binding, not assignment, was used to associate a value with a variable. Storage objects were created to hold the results of computations and bound to an identifier. They died when that identifier was reused for the result of another computation. A storage compaction technique was needed to reclaim dead storage objects periodically. The simplest such technique is called *storage compaction*. It involves identifying all live storage objects and moving them to one end of memory. The rest of the memory then becomes available for reuse.

A second new data type was introduced by SNOBOL: the *pattern*. Patterns were the first primitive data type that did not correspond at all to the computer hardware. A pattern is a string of characters interspersed with "wild cards" and function calls. The language included a highly powerful pattern matching operation that would compare a string to a pattern and identify a substring that matched the pattern. During the matching process, the wild cards would be matched against first one substring and then another, until the entire pattern matched or the string was exhausted.[9]

COBOL permitted the programmer to define objects with complex structured data types but not to refer to those types. LISP provided type predicates but restricted the user to a few primitive types. PL/1 went further than either: its "LIKE" attribute permitted the programmer to refer to a complex user-defined type.

PL/1 was developed in the mid-1960s for the IBM 360 series of machines. It was intended to be the "universal" language that would satisfy the needs of both business and scientific communities. For this reason, features of other popular languages were merged into one large, conglomerate design. Arithmetic expressions resembled FORTRAN, and pointers permitted the programmer to construct dynamically changing tree structures. Declarations for records and arrays were very much like COBOL declarations.

Types could not be declared separately but were created as a side effect of declaring a structured variable. Once a type was created, though, more objects of the same type could be declared by saying they were LIKE the first object [Exhibit 5.14].

5.3.2   Type Becomes a Definable Abstraction

By the late 1960s, types were recognized as abstractions—things that could exist apart from any instances or objects. The fundamental idea, developed by C. Strachey and

---

[9]Compare this to the pattern matching built into Prolog, Chapter 10, Section 10.4.

T. Standish, is that a *type* is a set of constructors (to create instances), selectors (to extract parts of a structured type), and a predicate (to test type identity). Languages began to provide ways to define, name, and use types to create homogeneous sets of objects. ALGOL-68 and Simula were developed during these years.

Exhibit 5.14.   Using the LIKE attribute in PL/1.

The design of PL/1 was strongly influenced by COBOL. This influence is most obvious in the declaration and handling of structures. Here we declare a record like the one in Exhibit 5.13. We go beyond the capabilities of COBOL, though, by declaring a second variable, MOTHER, of the same structured type.

```
DCL 1   FATHER,
        2   NAME,
            3   LAST     CHAR (20),
            3   FIRST    CHAR (20),
            3   MID-INIT CHAR (1),
        2   F-AGE        PIC '99';
DCL 1   MOTHER LIKE FATHER;
```

To create unambiguous references, field names of both MOTHER and FATHER must be qualified by using the variable name:

```
MOTHER.LAST = FATHER.LAST;
```

Simula pioneered the idea that a type definition could be grouped together with the functions that operate on that type, and objects belonging to the type, to form a "class". Thus Simula was the first language to support type modules and was a forerunner of the modern object-oriented languages.[10]

ALGOL-68 contained type declarations and very carefully designed type compatibility rules. The type declarations defined constructors (specifications by which structured variables could be allocated), selectors (subscripts for arrays and part names for records), and implicit type predicates. Type identity was the basis for extensive and carefully designed type checking and compatibility rules. Some kinds of type conversions were recognized to be (usually) semantically valid, and so were supported. Other type relationships were seen as invalid. The definition of the language was immensely complex, partly because of the type extension and compatibility rules, and partly because the design goal was super-generality and power.

Reactions to Complexity: C *and* Pascal

Two languages, C and Pascal, were developed at this time as reactions against the overwhelming size and complexity of PL/1 and ALGOL-68. These were designed to achieve the maximum amount of power with the minimum amount of complexity.

C moved backwards with respect to type abstractions. The designers valued simplicity and flexibility of the language more than its ability to support semantic validity. They adopted type declarations as a way to define classes of structured objects

---

[10]See Chapter 17 for a discussion of object-oriented languages.

but omitted almost all use of types to control semantics. C supported record types (structs and unions) with part selectors and arrays with subscripting. Record types were full abstractions; they could be named, and the names used to create instances, declare parameters, and select subfields. Arrays, however, were not fully abstracted, independent types; array types could not be named and did not have an identity that was distinct from the type of the array elements.

The purpose of type declarations in C was to define the constructors and selectors for a new type. The declaration supplied information to the compiler that enabled it to allocate and access compound objects efficiently. The field names in a record were translated into offsets from the beginning of the object. The size of the base type of an array became a multiplier, to be applied to subscripts, producing an offset. At run time, when the program selected a field of the compound, the offset was added to the address of the beginning of the compound, giving an effective address.

At this period of history, types were not generally used as vehicles for expressing semantic intent. Except for computing address offsets, there were very few contexts in early C in which the type of an object made a difference in the code the translator generated.[11] Type checking was minimal or nonexistent. Thus C type declarations did not define type predicates. Type identity was not, in general, important. The programmer could not test it directly, as was possible in LISP, nor was it checked by the compiler before performing function calls, as it is in Pascal.[12]

Niklaus Wirth, who participated in the ALGOL-68 committee for some time, designed Pascal to prove that a language *could* be simple, powerful, and semantically sound at the same time.[13] Pascal retained both the type declarations and type checking rules of ALGOL-68 and achieved simplicity by omitting ALGOL-68's extensive type conversion rules. The resulting language is more restrictive than C, but it is far easier to understand and less error prone.

Ada: *The Last* ALGOL-*Like Language?*

In the late 1960s, the U.S. Department of Defense (DoD) realized that the lack of a common computer language among its installations was becoming a major problem. By 1968, small-scale research efforts were being funded to develop a core language that could be extended in various directions to meet the needs of different DoD groups. Design goals included generality of the core language, extensibility, and reasonable efficiency.

In the early 1970s, DoD decided to strictly limit the number of languages in use and to begin design of one common language. A set of requirements for this new language were developed by analyzing the needs of various DoD groups using computers. Finalized in 1976, these requirements specified that the new language must support modern software engineering methods, provide superior error checking, and support real-time applications. After careful consideration, it was decided that no existing language met these criteria.

Proposals were sought in 1977 for an ALGOL-like language design that would support reliable, maintainable, and efficient programs. Four proposals were selected,

---

[11] The exception was automatic conversions between numeric types in mixed expressions.

[12] Type checking and the semantic uses of types are discussed at length in Chapter 15.

[13] It is said that he never dreamed that Pascal would achieve such widespread use as a teaching language.

6

Modeling Objects

Overview

This chapter creates a framework for describing the semantics and implementation of objects so that the semantics actually used in any language can be understood and the advantages and drawbacks of the various implementations can be evaluated.

We assume the reader is familiar with the use of objects such as variables, constants, pointers, strings, arrays, and records. When we survey the popular programming languages, we see a great deal of commonality in the semantics of these things in all languages. There are also important differences, sometimes subtle, that cause languages to "feel" different, or require utterly different strategies for use. A program object embodies a real-world object within a program. The program object is stored in a storage object, a collection of contiguous memory cells. Variables are storage objects that store pure values; pointer variables store references.

Initialization and assignment are two processes that place a value in a storage object. Initialization stores a program object in the storage object when the storage object is created. Assignment may be destructive or coherent. Extracting the contents from a storage object is known as dereferencing. Assignment and dereferencing of pointer variables usually yield references to ordinary variables rather than pure values. Managing computer memory involves creating, destroying, and keeping storage objects available. Three strategies are static storage, stack storage, and heap storage.

6.1 KINDS OF OBJECTS

A program is a means of modeling processes and objects that are external to the computer. *External objects* might be numbers, insurance policies, alien invaders for a video game, or industrial robots. Each one may be modeled in diverse ways. We set up the model through declarations, allocation commands, the use of names, and the manipulation of pointers. Through these, we create objects in our programs, give them form, and describe their intended meaning. These objects are then manipulated by the functions and operators of a language.

We start by making a distinction between the memory location in which data is stored and the data itself. The ways of getting data into and out of locations are explored.

A *program object* is the embodiment of an object in the program. It may represent an external object, such as a number or a record, in which case it is called a *pure value*. It may also represent part of the computer system itself, such as a memory location, a file, or a printer. During execution, the program manipulates its program objects as a means of simulating meaningful processes on the external objects or controlling its own internal operations. It produces usable information from observed and derived facts about the program objects.

A program commonly deals with many external objects, each being represented by a pure value program object [Exhibit 6.1]. While all the external objects exist at once, their representing program objects can be passed through the computer sequentially and so do not have to be simultaneously present. For example, an accounting program deals with many accounts. Representations of these accounts are put in some sequence on an input medium and become program objects one at a time.

Exhibit 6.1.   Representing objects.

External object: a length of 2" by 4" lumber.

Program object: a 32-bit floating-point value.
Storage object: a memory location with four consecutive bytes reserved for this number.

External object: a charge account.

Program object: a collection of values representing a customer's name, address, account number, billing date, and current balance.
Storage object: a series of consecutive memory locations totaling 100 bytes.

In order to manipulate program objects, the program must generally store all or part of a program object in memory. It uses a storage object for this purpose. A *storage object* is a collection of contiguous memory cells (bits, bytes, etc.) in which a program object, called its *value* or *contents*, can be stored.[1]

A *reference* is the memory address of a storage object and is the "handle" by which the object is accessed. In older terminology, a pure value is called an *r*-value or right-hand-value, because it can occur to the right of an assignment operator. A

---

[1]A storage object sometimes encompasses more cells than are needed to store the value. These cells, commonly added to achieve word alignment, are called padding.

reference is called an *l*-value or left-hand-value. A reference is created when a storage object is allocated. This reference is itself a program object and may be stored in another storage object for later use [Exhibit 6.2]. A program must possess a reference to a program object in order to use that object.

Exhibit 6.2.   Values, variables, and pointers.

The relationship between storage objects and program objects is illustrated. Boxes represent storage objects, letters represent pure values of type "character", small circles (o) from which arrows emerge represent references, and dotted lines represent dereferencing.

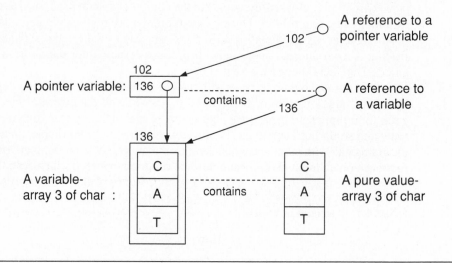

The *allocation* process sets aside an area of unused computer memory to make a new storage object. The process is essentially the same whether it is being carried out by an interpreter, which does the allocation at run time when the command is interpreted, or by a compiler, which deals with addresses of the storage objects that will be allocated at some future time when the program is executed.

Allocation procedures are usually part of the implementation of a language, not part of the language definition, so the actual allocation process often differs from one translator to the next, as well as from one language to the next. Typically, though, the allocation process will include the following actions:

1. The translator must determine N, the number of bytes of memory that are needed. In some languages the programmer communicates this information by specifying the data type of the new object. Size, in bytes, is calculated by the translator and stored as part of the definition of a type. In lower-level languages the programmer specifies the allocation size explicitly.

2. A segment of free storage is located with length $L \geq N$. A reference to the first location in this segment is saved.

3. The address of the beginning of the free storage area is incremented by N, thus removing N bytes from free storage.

4. If an initial value was defined, it is stored in the new storage object.
5. The address, or reference, saved in step 2 is returned as the result of the allocation process. It is the means by which the program is able to find the new storage object.

A *variable* is a storage object in which a pure value may be stored. Pure values and the variables in which they are stored have the same size and structure and are considered to be the same data type in many languages. We distinguish between them here because they have very different semantics. Operations you can perform with variables are to allocate and deallocate them and to fetch values from and store values into them. In contrast, pure values can be combined and manipulated with operators and functions, but not allocated and deallocated.

A *pointer variable* is a storage object, or part of a storage object, in which a reference may be stored. (Often this term will be shortened to "pointer".) Pointers are used to create storage structures such as game trees and linked lists and are an important means of modeling external objects.

6.2 PLACING A VALUE IN A STORAGE OBJECT

6.2.1 Static Initialization

A storage object receives a value by one of two processes: initialization or assignment. Until a value is stored in a storage object, it is said to contain *garbage*, or to have an *undefined value*. (When we wish to indicate an undefined value we will write "?".)

Using an undefined value is a commonly made semantic error which generally cannot be detected by a language translator. For this reason some translators initialize all variables to zero, which is the most commonly useful initial value, or to some distinctive bit pattern, so that the semantic error can be more easily detected. It is poor programming practice to depend on such automatic initialization, however. Different translators for the same language may implement different initialization policies, and the program that depends on a particular policy is not portable.

Initialization stores a program object in the storage object when the storage object is created. Many languages permit the programmer to include an initializing clause in an object declaration. Typical declaration forms are shown in Exhibits 6.3 and 6.4. In each exhibit, declarations are given for an integer variable, a character string, and an array of real numbers, and initial values are declared for each.

Initializing compound objects, such as arrays and records, is restricted or not allowed in some languages. Two problems are involved here: how to denote a structured value, and how to implement initialization of dynamically allocated structured objects. The FORTRAN and C examples (Exhibits 6.3 and 6.4) illustrate two approaches to defining the structure of the initializer.

In FORTRAN, the programmer writes an explicit loop or nest of loops which specify the order in which the fields of an array will be initialized and then provides a series of constants that will evaluate to the desired initial values. A repetition count can be specified when several fields are to be initialized to the same value. Part or all of an array may be initialized this way. This is a powerful and flexible method, but it does complicate the syntax and semantics of the language.

Exhibit 6.3.   Initial value declarations in FORTRAN.

```
CHARACTER*3 EOFLAG
DIMENSION A (8)
DATA EOFLAG, ISUM /'NO ', 0/, (A(I), I=1,8)/ 8.2, 2.6, 3.1, 17.0, 4 * 0.0 /
```

Notes:

- In FORTRAN, simple integers and reals may be declared implicitly. Explicit declarations must be given for arrays and strings.
- Initial values are given in separate DATA declarations which must follow the statements that declare the storage objects.
- A single DATA statement can initialize a list of objects. It must contain exactly as many initial values as fields to be initialized. Initial values may be repeated by using a repeat count with a "*".
- An array may be initialized by giving a loop-controlling expression.

Exhibit 6.4.   Initial value declarations in C.

```
static  char end_of_file_flag [ ] = "no ";
        int isum = 0;
static  float a[8] = {8.2, 2.6, 3.1, 17.0};
```

Notes:

- In C an initial value may be given as part of a variable declaration.
- Static arrays can be initialized by listing the correct number of values for the array enclosed in brackets. (The property "static" is explained in Section 6.3.)
- The programmer may omit the array length specifier from the declaration, as in the top line, and the length of the storage object will be deduced from the length of the initial value list.
- If too few initializers are given to fill an array, remaining elements are initialized to zero.

Contrast this to a C initializer. Its structure is denoted very simply by enclosing the initial values in brackets, which can be nested to denote a type whose fields are themselves structured types. The same simple syntax serves to initialize both records and arrays. Initializers can be constants or constant expressions; that is, expressions that can be evaluated at compile time. In some ways, this is not as flexible a syntax as FORTRAN provides. If any field of a C object is initialized, then all fields will be initialized. If the same nonzero value is to be placed in several fields, it must be written several times. The one shortcut available is that, if the initializer has too few fields, the remaining fields will default to an initial value of zero.

It is likely that the designers of C felt that FORTRAN initializers are too flexible—that they provide unnecessary flexibility, at the cost of unnecessary complication. Applying something akin to the principle of Too Much Flexibility, they chose to include the simpler, but still very useful, form in C.

All data storage in FORTRAN is created and initialized at load time. A translator can evaluate the constant expressions in an initializer and generate store instructions to place the resulting values into storage when the program code is loaded. Modern languages, though, support dynamic allocation of local variables in stack frames. (These are called "automatic" variables in C.) The initialization process for automatic variables is more complex than for static variables.

Suppose a function F contains a declaration and initializations for a local array, V. This array cannot be initialized at load time because it does not yet exist. The translator must evaluate the initializing expressions, store the values somewhere, and generate a series of store instructions to be executed every time F is called. These copy precomputed initial values into the newly allocated area. This process was considered complex enough that the original definition of C simply did not permit initialization of automatic arrays. ANSI C, however, supports this useful facility.

6.2.2   Dynamically Changing the Contents of a Storage Object

Destructive Assignment

In many languages, one storage object can be used to store different program objects at different times. *Assignment* is an operation that stores a program object into an existing storage object and thus permits the programmer to change the value of a storage object dynamically. This operation is sometimes called *destructive assignment* because the previous contents of the storage object are lost. The storage object now represents a different external object, and we say that its *meaning* has changed.

Functional languages are an important current research topic. The goal of this research is to build a language with a clean, simple semantic model. Destructive assignment is a problem because it causes a change in the meaning of the symbol that names the storage object. It complicates a formal semantic model considerably to have to deal with symbols that mean different things at different times.

In a functional language, parameter binding is used in place of destructive assignment to associate names with objects. At the point that a Pascal programmer would store a computed value in a variable, the functional programmer passes that value as an argument to a function. The actions following the assignment in the Pascal program, and depending on it, would form the body of the function. A series of Pascal statements with assignment gets turned "outside in" and becomes a nest of function calls with parameter bindings.[2] This approach produces an attractive, semantically clean language because the parameter name has the same meaning from procedure entry to procedure exit.

Coherent Assignment.

An array or a record is a compound object: a whole made up of parts which are objects themselves. Some but not all programming languages permit *coherent assignment* of compound objects. In such languages an entire compound variable is considered to be a single storage object, and the programmer can refer to the compound object as a whole and assign compound values to it [Exhibits 6.5 and 6.7].

---

[2]A deeply nested expression can look like a "rat's nest" of parentheses; deep nesting is avoided by making many short function definitions.

Exhibit 6.5.   Initializing and copying a compound object in Pascal.

Pascal declarations are given below for a record type named "person" and for two person-variables, a and b. In Pascal, compound objects cannot be initialized coherently, so three assignments are used to store a record-value into b. On the other hand, records *can* be assigned coherently, as shown in the last line, which copies the information from b to a.

```
TYPE person = RECORD age, weight:  integer; sex: char  END;
VAR a, b :  person;
BEGIN
    b.age := 10;
    b.weight := 70;
    b.sex := 'M';
    a := b;
    ...
END;
```

In COBOL any kind of object could be copied coherently. It is even possible to use one coherent READ statement to load an entire data table from a file into memory. In most older languages, though, assignment can only be performed on simple (single-word) objects. An array or a record is considered to be a collection of simple objects, not a coherent large object. The abstract process of placing a compound program object into its proper storage object must be accomplished by a series of assignment commands that store its individual simple components.

An example of the lack of coherent assignment can be seen in the original Kernighan and Ritchie definition of C. Coherent assignment was not supported; to copy a record required one assignment statement for each field in the record. Thus three assignments would be required to copy the information from b to a in Exhibit 6.6. However, coherent initialization of record variables *was* supported, and b could be initialized coherently.

Exhibit 6.6.   Initializing and copying a compound object in K&R C.

A record type named "person" is defined, and two person-variables, a and b, are declared. The variable b is initialized by the declaration and copied into a by the assignment statements.

The property "static" causes the variable to be allocated in the program environment rather than on the stack, so that it can be initialized at load time. K&R C did not support initialization of dynamically allocated structured objects.

```
typedef struct {int age, weight; char sex;} person;
static person a, b = {10, 70, 'M'};
{   a.age = b.age;
    a.weight = b.weight;
    a.sex = b.sex;
    ... }
```

Exhibit 6.7.   Initializing and copying a compound object in ANSI C.

This example is written in ANSI C, which is newer than both K&R C and Pascal. The difference between this and the clumsier versions in Exhibits 6.5 and 6.6 reflects the growing understanding that coherent representations and operations are important.

The type and object declarations are the same in both versions of C, as are initializations. But compound objects can be assigned coherently in ANSI C, so only one assignment is required to copy the information from b to a. Further, dynamically allocated (automatic) structs may be initialized in ANSI C.

```
typedef struct {int age, weight; char sex;} person;
person a, b = {10, 70, 'M'};
{ a = b; ... }
```

Even in languages that support coherent compound assignment, the programmer is generally permitted to assign a value to one part of the compound without changing the others. In such situations, care must always be taken to ensure that a compound storage object is not left containing parts of two different program objects!

Assignment Statements versus Assignment as a Function.

Assignment is invoked either by writing an explicit ASSIGN operator or by calling a READ routine. In either case, two objects are involved, a reference and a value. The reference is usually written on the left of the ASSIGN operator or as the parameter to a READ routine, and the value is written on the right of the ASSIGN or is supplied from an input medium.

Assignment is one of a very small number of operations that require a reference as an argument. (Others are binding, dereference, subscript, and selection of a field of a record.) The purpose of an assignment is to modify the information in the computer's memory, not to compute a new value. It is the only operation that modifies the value of existing storage objects. For this reason, ASSIGN and READ occur in many languages as statement types or procedures rather than as functions. Exhibit 6.8 lists the symbols and semantics for the ASSIGN statements in several common programming languages.

In other languages, ASSIGN is a function that returns a result and may, therefore, be included in the middle of an expression. Exhibit 6.9 shows ASSIGN *functions* in common programming languages. LISP returns the reference as the result of an assignment. C returns the value, so that it may be assigned to another storage object in the same expression or may be used further in computing the value of an enclosing expression. Exhibit 6.10 demonstrates how one assignment can be nested within another.

When ASSIGN returns a value, as in C, a single expression may be written which assigns that value to several storage objects. We call this *multiple assignment*. While this facility is not essential, it is often useful, especially when several variables need to be zeroed out at once. The same end is achieved in other languages, such as COBOL, by introducing an additional syntactic rule to allow an ASSIGN statement to list references to several storage objects, all of which will receive the single value provided.

Exhibit 6.8.   Languages where assignment is a statement.

A "yes" in the third column indicates that compound objects (such as arrays and records) may be assigned coherently, as a single action. A "yes" in the fourth column indicates that one ASSIGN statement may be used to store a value in several storage objects.

Language	Assignment Symbol	Compound Assignment?	Multiple Assignment?
COBOL	MOVE	yes	yes
	= (in a COMPUTE statement)	no	yes
	ADD, SUBTRACT, MULTIPLY, DIVIDE	no	yes
FORTRAN	=	no	no
ALGOL	:=	no	no
PL/1	=	yes	yes
FORTH	!	no	no
Pascal	:=	yes	no
Ada	:=	yes	no

Exhibit 6.9.   Languages where assignment is a function.

A "yes" in the third column indicates that compound objects (such as arrays and records) may be assigned coherently, as a single action.

Language	Assignment Symbol	Compound Assignment?	Result Returned
LISP	`replaca`, `replacd`	some versions	reference
APL	← (also used for binding)	yes	value
C (1973)	=	no	value
C (ANSI)	=	yes	value

Exhibit 6.10.   Assignment as a function in C.

An array length is defined as a constant at the top of the program to facilitate modifications. Then the array "ar" is declared to have 100 elements, with subscripts from 0 to 99. Two integers are declared and set to useful numbers: `num_elements` holds the number of elements in the array, and `high_sub` holds the subscript of the last element.

```
#define MAXLENGTH  100
    float ar[ MAXLENGTH ];
    int high_sub, num_elements;
    high_sub = (num_elements = MAXLENGTH) - 1;
```

The last line contains two assignments. The constant `MAXLENGTH` is stored into the variable `num_elements`, and it is also returned as the result of the assignment function. This value is then decremented by one, and the result is stored in `high_sub`.

6.2.3 Dereferencing

Dereferencing is the act of extracting the contents from a storage object. It is performed by the FETCH operation, which takes a reference to a storage object and returns its value. When a pointer variable is dereferenced, the result is another reference. This could be a reference to a variable, which itself could be dereferenced to get a pure value, or it could be a reference to another pointer, and so forth.

Whereas ASSIGN is always written explicitly in a language, its inverse, FETCH, is often invoked implicitly, simply by using the name of a storage object. Many languages (e.g., FORTRAN, Pascal, C, COBOL, BASIC, LISP) automatically dereference a storage object in any context where a program object is required. Thus a variable name written in a program sometimes "means" a reference and sometimes a pure value, depending on context. This introduces complexity into a language. You cannot just see a symbol, as in lambda calculus, and know what it means. You must first examine where it is in the program and how it is used. To define the dereferencing rules of a language, contexts must be enumerated and described. The commonly important contexts are:

1. The left-hand side of an assignment operator.
2. The right-hand side of an assignment operator.
3. Part of a subscript expression.
4. A pointer expression.
5. A parameter in a function or procedure call.

Note that these contexts are not mutually exclusive but can occur in a confusing variety of combinations, as shown in Exhibit 6.11. Many other combinations of dereferencing contexts are, of course, possible.

Whether or not a reference is dereferenced in each context varies among languages. In context (1) dereferencing is never done, as a reference is required for an ASSIGN operation. But when a subscript expression (3) occurs in context (1), dereferencing will happen within the subscript part of the expression (the subscripted variable itself will not be dereferenced). In contexts (2) and (3) most languages will automatically dereference, as long as the situation does not also involve context (4).

In context (4) languages generally do not dereference automatically. They either provide an explicit FETCH operator or combine dereferencing with other functions. Examples of FETCH operators are the Pascal "↑" and C "*". Examples of combined operators are "->" in C, which dereferences a pointer and then returns a reference to a selected part of the resulting record, and "car" and "cdr" in LISP, which select a part of a record and then dereference it.

In context (5), there is no uniformity at all among languages. The particular choices and mechanisms used in various languages are discussed fully in Chapter 8, Section 8.4 and Chapter 9, Section 9.2.

There are also languages in which storage objects are *never* automatically dereferenced, the most common being FORTH. In such languages the dereference command must be written explicitly using a dereference operator ("@" in FORTH) [Exhibit 6.12]. The great benefit of requiring explicit dereference is simplicity. A variable name always means the same thing: a reference. Considering the kind of complexity

Exhibit 6.11.   Dereferencing by context in Pascal.

We analyze the dereferences triggered by evaluating this expression:

`xarray[ point_1↑.number ] := eval_function( point_2 ) ;`

Assume the objects referenced have the following types:

`xarray:`	An array of unspecified type.
`point_1, point_2:`	Pointer to a record with a field called "`number`".
`eval_function:`	A function taking one pointer parameter and returning something of the correct type to be stored in `xarray`.

A variety of dereference contexts occur. Contexts (1), (3), and (4) occur together on the left, as do contexts (2) and (5) on the right.

Reference	Is it dereferenced here?
`xarray`	No, it is on the left of a `:=` operator.
`point_1`	Yes, explicitly, by the ↑ operator. Although this is part of a subscript expression, explicit dereference must be used because pointer variable names are not dereferenced in a pointer expression.
`point_2`	You cannot tell from this amount of context. It will not be dereferenced if the function *definition* specifies that it is a VAR parameter. If VAR is not specified, it will be automatically dereferenced.

Exhibit 6.12.   Explicit dereferencing in FIG FORTH.

All FORTH expressions are written in postfix form, so you should read and interpret the operators from left to right. The FETCH operator is "`@`". It is written following a reference and extracts the contents from the corresponding storage object.

On lines 1 and 2, variables named XX and Y are declared and initialized to 13 and 0, respectively. Line 3 dereferences the variable XX and multiplies its value by 2. The result is stored in Y, which is not dereferenced because a reference is needed for assignment.

```
1    13 VARIABLE XX
2    0 VARIABLE Y
3    XX @ 2 * Y ! ( Same as Y = XX * 2 in FORTRAN. )
```

The expression XX 2 * would multiply the address, rather than the contents, of the storage object named XX by 2.

(demonstrated above) that is inherent in deriving the meaning of a reference from context, it is easy to understand the appeal of FORTH's simple method. The drawback of requiring explicit dereference is that an additional symbol must be written before most uses of a variable name, adding visual clutter to the program and becoming another likely source of error because dereference symbols are easily forgotten.

6.2.4   Pointer Assignment

Pointer assignment is ordinary assignment where the required reference is a reference to a pointer variable and the value is itself a reference, usually to an ordinary variable. Languages that support pointer variables also provide a run-time allocation function that returns a reference to the newly allocated storage. This reference is then assigned to a pointer variable, which is often part of a compound storage object. Pointer assignment allows a programmer to create and link together simple storage objects into complex, dynamically changing structures of unlimited size.

Multiple pointers may be attached to an object by pointer assignment. The program object of a pointer is a reference to another storage object. When the pointer assignment P2 := P1 is executed, the program object P1, which is a reference to some object, *Cell*1, is copied into the storage object of P2, thus creating an additional pointer to *Cell*1 and enabling P2 as well as P1 to refer to *Cell*1. Thus two objects now store references to one storage object, and we say they "share" storage dynamically. This is illustrated in Exhibits 6.13 and 6.14.

Exhibit 6.13.   Pointer assignments in Pascal.

We assume the initial state of storage shown in Exhibit 6.14.

```
TYPE list = ↑cell;
     cell = RECORD  value:char;  link:list  END;
VAR P1, P2, P3: list;
```

Code	Comments
P2 := P1; P3 := P1 ↑.link;	Dereference P1 and store its value in P2. Dereference P1, select its link field, which is a pointer variable, and dereference it. Store the resulting reference in P3.

P1, P2, and P3 all share storage now. We can refer to the field containing the % as P2↑.link↑.value or as P3↑.value. Note that a pointer must be explicitly dereferenced, using ↑, before accessing a field of the object to which it points.

While such sharing is obviously useful, it creates a complex situation in which the contents of the storage structure attached to a name may change without executing an assignment to that name. This makes pointer programs hard to debug and makes mathematical proofs of correctness very hard to construct. Many programmers find it impossible to construct correct pointer programs without making diagrams of their storage objects and pointer variables.

6.2.5   The Semantics of Pointer Assignment

There are two likely ways in which a pointer assignment could be interpreted: with and without automatic dereferencing of the right-hand side. Pascal does dereference,

Exhibit 6.14. Pointer structures sharing storage.

Storage, diagrammed before and after the pointer assignments in Exhibit 6.13.

Before: **After:**

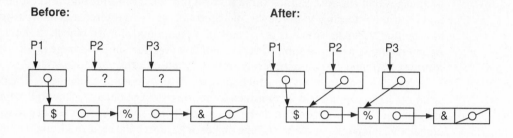

as is shown in Exhibit 6.13. In such a language the statement Q := P is legal if P and Q
are both pointers. This makes Q point at whatever P is pointing at. The assignment P
:= K is *illegal* if P is a pointer and K is an integer. Exhibit 6.15 shows several pointer
assignments in C where the right side is dereferenced.

Exhibit 6.15. Pointer assignments with dereference in C.

The right side of the assignment is dereferenced if it evaluates to a structure or a simple
object.

```
typedef struct { int age; float weight; } body;
body s;                       /* A variable of type 'body'.  */
body *ps, *qs;                /* Two pointers to bodies.  */
int k;                        /* An integer variable.  */
int *p, *q;                   /* Two pointers to integers.  */
p = &k;    /* Store the address of k in p, that is, make p point at k.
              Note: the & operator prevents automatic dereferencing.  */
ps = &s;   /* Make ps point at s. */
q = p;     /* Dereference p to get the address stored in p, and store
              that address in q, making q point at the same thing as p.  */
qs = ps;   /* Make qs point at the same thing as ps.  */
```

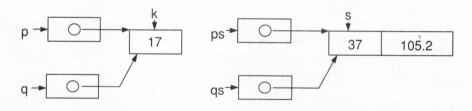

In a hypothetical language, ":=" *could* be defined such that the assignment "p := k" would be legal and would make p point at k. In this case, pointer assignment is interpreted without dereferencing the right side. In such a language we could create a chain of pointers as follows:

```
k := 5.4;    -- k is type float.
p := k;      -- p must be type pointer to float.
q := p;      -- q must be type pointer to pointer to float.
```

These assignments, taken together, would construct a pointer structure like this:

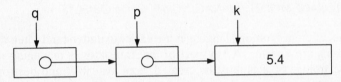

Exhibit 6.16 shows pointer assignments in C which set pointers to an array and a function. In these contexts, in C, the right side will not be dereferenced.

Exhibit 6.16.   Pointer assignment without dereference in C.

We declare an integer variable, k; integer pointers, p1 and p2; an array of five integers, a; a function that returns an integer, f; and a pointer to a function that returns an integer, p3.

The right side of a C assignment is not dereferenced if it refers to an array or a function.

```
int k, *p1, *p2, a[5], f(), *p3();
p1 = &k;        /* Make p1 point at k.  */
p2 = a;         /* Make p2 point at the array.  Note absence of "&".*/
p2 = &a[0];     /* Make p2 point at the address of the zeroth element of the
                   array.  This has the same effect as the line above.  */

p3 = f;         /* Store a reference to the function f in pointer p3.
                   Note that f is not dereferenced.*/
```

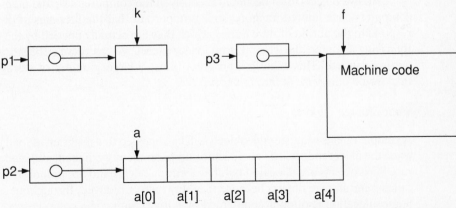

Note that "p2 = &a;" is syntactically incorrect because the name of an array *means* the address of its zeroth element. One must either omit the "&" or supply a subscript.

While either interpretation of pointer assignment could make sense, we would expect to see either one or the other used consistently in a language. One of the unusual and confusing facets of C is that the semantics of pointer assignment depends on the type of the expression on the right. If it denotes a simple object (such as an integer or a pointer) or an object defined as a struct, automatic dereferencing is used [Exhibit 6.15]. If the right-hand object is an array or a function, the second meaning, without dereferencing, is implemented [Exhibit 6.16].

6.3 THE STORAGE MODEL: MANAGING STORAGE OBJECTS

The differences among languages are easier to understand when the underlying mechanisms are known. A key part of any translator is managing the computer memory; storage objects must be created, kept available, and destroyed when appropriate. Three storage management strategies are in common use with all three present in some translators, but only one in others. These are static storage and two kinds of dynamic storage: stack storage and heap storage.

6.3.1   The Birth and Death of Storage Objects

A storage object is *born* when it is allocated, and it *dies* when it is no longer available for use by the program. The *lifetime*, or extent, of a storage object is the span of time from its birth to its death. An object that lives until the program is terminated is *immortal*. Most objects, however, die during program execution. It is a semantic error to attempt to reference a storage object after it has died. The run-time system will typically reuse the formerly occupied storage for other purposes, so references to a dead object will yield unpredictable results.

Deallocation is the recycling process by which dead storage objects are destroyed, and the storage locations they occupied are made available for reuse by the allocation process. Deallocation happens sometime, often not immediately, after death.

All live objects must be simultaneously in the computer's virtual memory. Real computers have limited memory, so it is important that the lifetimes of objects correspond to the period of time during which they are actually needed by the program. By having an object die when it is no longer useful, we can recycle the storage it formerly occupied. This enables a program to use a larger number of storage objects than would otherwise fit into memory.

Static Storage Objects

A compiler plans what storage objects will be allocated to a program at load time, and when the object code will be copied into computer memory, linked, and made ready to run. Such objects are allocated before execution begins and are immortal. These are called *static* storage objects because they stay there, unmoved, throughout execution. Static allocation is often accompanied by initialization. The compiler chooses run-time locations for the static objects and can easily put initial values for these locations into the object code.

The number of static storage objects in a program is fixed throughout execution and is equal to the number of static names the programmer has used. Global variables are static in any language. Some languages (for example, COBOL) have only static objects, while others (for example, Pascal) have no static storage except for globals. Still others (ALGOL, C) permit the programmer to declare that a nonglobal object is to be static. In ALGOL, this is done by specifying the attribute "OWN" as part of a variable declaration. In C, the keyword "static" is used for this attribute.

A language with only static storage is limiting. It cannot support recursion, because storage must be allocated and exist simultaneously for the parameters of a dynamically variable number of calls on any recursive function.

A language that limits static storage to global variables is also limiting. Many complex applications can be best modeled by a set of semi-independent functions. Each one of these performs some simple well-defined task such as filling a buffer with data or printing out data eight columns per line. Each routine needs to maintain its own data structures and buffer pointers. Ideally, these are private structures, protected from all other routines. These pointers cannot be ordinary local variables, since the current position on the line must be remembered from one call to the next, and dynamically allocated variables are deallocated between calls. On the other hand, these pointers should not be global, because global storage is subject to accidental tampering by unrelated routines. The best solution is to declare these as static local storage, which simultaneously provides both continuity and protection.

Finally, the unnecessary use of static objects, either global or local, is unwise because they are immortal. Using them limits the amount of storage that can be recycled, thereby increasing the overall storage requirements of a program.

Dynamic Storage Objects

Storage objects that are born during execution are called *dynamic*. The number of dynamic storage objects often depends on the input data, so the storage for them cannot be planned by the compiler in advance but must be allocated at run time. The process of choosing where in memory to allocate storage objects is called *memory management*. A memory manager *must* be sure that two storage objects that are alive at the same time never occupy the same place in memory. It *should* also try to use memory efficiently so that the program will run with as small an amount of physical memory as possible.

Memory management is a very difficult task to do well, and no single scheme is best in all circumstances. The job is considerably simplified if the memory manager knows something in advance about the lifetimes of its storage objects. For this reason, languages typically provide several different kinds of dynamic storage objects which have different lifetime patterns.

The simplest pattern is a totally unrestricted lifetime. Such an object can be born and die at any time under explicit control of the programmer. Nothing can be predicted about the lifetimes of these objects, which are generally stored in an area of memory called the *heap*. Whenever a new one is born, the storage manager tries to find a sufficiently large unused area of heap memory to contain it. Whenever the storage manager learns of the death of a heap object, it takes note of the fact that the memory is no longer in use.

There are many problems in recycling memory. First of all, the blocks in use may be scattered about the heap, leaving many small unused "holes" instead of one large area. If no hole is large enough for a new storage object, then the new object cannot be created, even though the total size of all of the holes is more than adequate. This situation is called *memory fragmentation*.

Second, a memory manager must keep track of the holes so that they can be located when needed. A third problem is that two or more adjacent small holes should be combined into one larger one. Different heap memory managers solve some or all of these problems in different ways. We will talk about some of them later in this chapter.

Because of the difficulty in managing a heap, it is desirable to use simpler, more efficient but restricted memory managers whenever possible. One particularly common pattern of lifetimes is called *nested lifetimes*. In this pattern, any two objects with different lifetimes that exist at the same time have well-nested lifetimes; that is, the lifetime of one is completely contained within the lifetime of the other. This pattern arises from block structure and procedure calls.

Storage for local block variables and procedure parameters only needs to exist while that block or procedure is active. We say that a block is *active* when control resides within it or within some procedure called from it. A storage object belonging to a block can be born when the block begins and die when the block ends, so its lifetime coincides with the time that the block is active. Blocks can be nested, meaning that a block B that starts within a block A finishes before A does. It follows that the lifetimes of any storage objects created by B are contained within the lifetimes of objects created by A.

Dynamic Stack Storage

Storage for objects with nested lifetimes can be managed very simply using a *stack*, frequently called the *run-time stack*. This is an area of memory, like the heap, on which storage objects are allocated and deallocated. Since, in the world of nested lifetime objects, younger objects always die before older ones, objects can always be allocated and deallocated from the top of the stack. For such objects, allocation and deallocation are very simple processes. The storage manager maintains a stack allocation pointer which indicates the first unused location on the stack. When a program block is entered, this pointer is incremented by the number of bytes required for the new storage object(s) during the allocation process. Deallocation is accomplished at block exit time by simply decrementing the stack allocation pointer by the same number of bytes. This returns the newly freed storage to the storage pool, where it will be reused.

In languages that support both heap and stack storage objects, the stack objects should be used wherever possible because their lifetime is tied to the code that uses them, and the birth and death processes are very efficient and automatic. (This is the reason that stack-allocated objects are called "auto" in C.)

Storage managers typically use stack storage for a variety of purposes. When control enters a new program block, a structure called a *stack frame*, or *activation record*, is created on the top of the stack.) The area past the end of the current stack frame is used for temporary buffers and for storing intermediate results while calculating long arithmetic expressions [Exhibit 6.17, right side].

Exhibit 6.17.   The structure of the run-time stack.

The order of the parts within a stack frame is arbitrary, as is the relationship of global storage and program code to the stack. The diagrams indicate a functional arrangement of the necessary kinds of information.

A single stack frame: **The program and stack at run time:**

| Program Code |
| Global and static storage |
Parameters		Stack frame for oldest block
Return Address		Stack frames for other blocks
Dynamic Link	< **Top of Stack**	Stack frame for newest block
Static Link		< **Top of Stack**
Return Value		Temporary locations
Local Variables		

A stack frame[3] includes several items: parameters, local variables, the return address, and the return value (if the block is a function body). It also contains two pointers, called the static link and dynamic link [Exhibit 6.17, left side].

Let us define the *lexical parent* of a block to be that block which encloses it on the program listing. The lexical parent of the outermost block or blocks is the system. A *lexical ancestor* is a parent or the parent of a parent, and so on. The *static link* points to the stack frame of the current block's lexical parent. At run time, these links form a chain that leads back through the stack frames for all the blocks that lexically enclose the current block. Since the location of a lexical ancestor's frame is not predictable at compile time, the chain of static links must be followed to locate a storage object that was allocated by an ancestor. This is, of course, not as efficient as finding a local object, and it is one good reason to use parameters or local variables wherever possible.

---

[3]The rest of this section explains the structure of the stack for a lexically scoped, block-structured language.

The *dynamic parent* of a block is the block which called it during the course of execution and to which it must return at block exit time. The *dynamic link* points to the stack frame of the current block's dynamic parent. This link is used to pop the stack at block exit time.

The static and dynamic links are created when the stack frame is allocated at run time. During this process, several things are entered into the locations just past the end of the current frame. This process uses (and increments) the *local-allocation pointer* which points to the first free location on the stack. Before beginning the call process, this pointer is saved. The saved value will be used later to pop the stack. The sequence of events is as follows:

1. The calling program puts the argument values on the stack using the local-allocation pointer. Typically, the last argument in the function call is loaded on the stack first, followed by the second-last, and so on. The first argument ends up at the top of the stack.

2. The return address is written at the top of the stack, above the first argument.

3. The current top-of-stack pointer is copied to the top of the stack. This will become the new dynamic link field. The address of this location is stored into the top-of-stack pointer.

4. The static link for the new frame is written on the stack. This is the same as either the static link or the dynamic link of the calling block. Code is generated at compile time to copy the appropriate link.

5. The local allocation pointer is incremented by enough locations to store the return value and the local variables. If the locals have initializers, those values are also copied.

6. Control is transferred to the subroutine.

At block exit time, the stack frame must be deallocated. In our model, the return value is in the frame (rather than in a register), so the frame must be deallocated by the calling program. To do this, the value in the dynamic link field of the subroutine's frame is copied back into the top-of-stack pointer, and the local-allocation pointer is restored to its value prior to loading the arguments onto the stack.

Stack storage enables the implementation of recursive functions by permitting new storage objects to be allocated for parameters and local variables each time the function is invoked. An unlimited number of storage objects which correspond to each parameter or local name in the recursive function can exist at the same time: one set for every time a recursive block has been entered but not exited [Exhibits 6.18 and 6.19]. Each time a recursive procedure exits, the corresponding stack frame is deallocated, and when the original recursive call returns to the calling program, the last of these frames dies. The number of storage objects simultaneously in existence for a recursive program is limited only by the program logic and the amount of storage available for stack allocation, not by the number of declared identifiers in the program.

Dynamic Heap Storage

There are situations in which heap storage must be used because the birth or death patterns associated with stack storage are too restrictive. These include cases in which the size or number of storage objects needed is not known at block entry time and situations in which an object must outlive the block in which it was created.

Exhibit 6.18.   A recursive function in Pascal.

The following (foolish) recursive function multiplies jj inputs together. Exhibit 6.19 traces an execution of this function.

```
FUNCTION product (jj:  integer):integer;
VAR kk:  integer;
BEGIN
    IF jj <= 0 THEN product := 1
    ELSE BEGIN
        readln(kk);
        product := kk * product(jj-1);
    END
END;
```

Exhibit 6.19.   Stack frames for recursive calls.

If the function "product" in Exhibit 6.18 were called with the parameter 2, two recursions would happen. Assume the inputs 25 and 7 were supplied. Just before returning from the second recursion the stack would contain three stack frames as diagrammed. The "?" in a stack location indicates an undefined value.

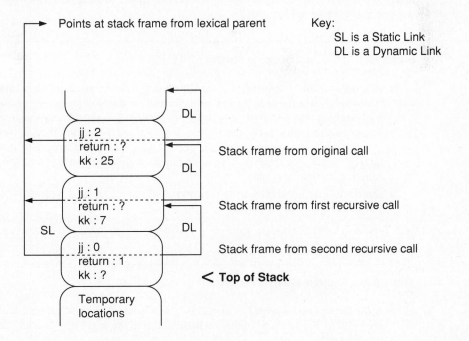

Heap Allocation.

Heap allocation is invoked by an explicit allocation command, which we will call ALLOC. Such commands can occur anywhere in a program, unlike local variable declarations which are restricted to the beginning of blocks. Thus a heap-allocated object can be born at any time. ALLOC reserves storage in the heap and returns a reference to the new storage object. The allocation process for heap storage is somewhat more complicated than that for stack storage, since there may be two places to look in the heap for available storage. Initially there is only a large, empty area with an associated allocation pointer which is incremented (like the stack pointer) when storage is allocated from that area. After some objects have died, there may also be a *freelist* which contains references to these formerly used locations. Clearly, items on the freelist might be scattered all over the heap and be of quite varied sizes. The memory manager must contain algorithms to keep track of the sizes and merge adjacent free areas, and these algorithms must be fast to avoid degrading the performance of the system.

An ALLOC command takes some indication of the required size of the new object and finds and reserves that much memory. Either it returns a reference to the memory location, or it stores that reference in a pointer variable which thereafter gives access to the new object. The ways these actions are incorporated into current languages are truly varied [Exhibits 6.20 through 6.25]. The new storage object is used, later, by dereferencing this pointer, and it remains alive as long as the pointer or some copy of the pointer points at it.

Exhibit 6.20. Dynamic allocation in FORTH.

- **Allocation:** HERE ⟨expression⟩ ALLOT   Storage can be allocated dynamically in the "dictionary", which stores the symbol table and all global objects. The programmer is given access to the top-of-dictionary pointer through the system variable named HERE. The code above puts the current value of HERE on the stack. Then it evaluates the expression, which must produce an integer, N. Finally, ALLOT adds N bytes to the dictionary pointer. The address of the newly allocated area is left on the stack; the user must store it in a pointer variable.
- **Deallocation:** Users must write their own storage management routines if they wish to free and reuse dynamic storage.

Exhibit 6.21. Dynamic allocation in LISP.

- **Allocation:** (cons ⟨expr1⟩ ⟨expr2⟩)   This allocates a new list cell and returns a reference to it. The left field of the cell is initialized to the result of evaluating ⟨expr1⟩ and its right field to ⟨expr2⟩.
- **Deallocation:** Most LISP systems rely on garbage collection.

Exhibit 6.22.   Dynamic allocation in C.

- **Allocation:** In the commands that follow, T and basetype are types, N is an integer. The malloc function allocates one object of type T or size N bytes. calloc allocates an array of N objects of type basetype and initializes the entire array to zero. Both malloc and calloc return a reference to the new storage object. The programmer must cast that reference to the desired pointer type and assign it to some pointer variable.

```
malloc(sizeof(T))
malloc(N)
calloc(N, sizeof(basetype))
```

- **Deallocation:** free(ptr); ptr must be a pointer to a heap object that was previously allocated using malloc or calloc. That object is linked onto a freelist and becomes available for reuse.

Exhibit 6.23.   Dynamic allocation in Pascal.

- **Allocation:** New(⟨PtrName⟩);   The ⟨PtrName⟩ must be declared as a pointer to some type, say T. A new cell is allocated of type T, and the resulting reference is stored in the pointer variable.
- **Deallocation:** Dispose(⟨PtrName⟩);   The object pointed at by PtrName is put onto the freelist.

Exhibit 6.24.   Dynamic allocation in Ada.

- **Allocation:** NEW ⟨type⟩ ' (⟨expression⟩) This allocates an object of the type requested. If the optional expression is supplied, it is evaluated and the result is used to initialize the new storage object. NEW is a function that returns a reference to the new object. The programmer must assign this reference to a variable of an ACCESS type (a pointer).
- **Deallocation:** Explicit deallocation is not generally used in Ada. In most Ada implementations, the dynamically allocated cells in a linked structure are automatically deallocated when the stack frame containing the pointer to the beginning of the structure is deallocated. Some Ada implementations contain full garbage collectors, like LISP.

  When it is necessary to recycle cells explicitly, a programmer may use a generic package named Unchecked_Deallocation.[4] This package must be *instantiated* (expanded, like a macro, at compile time) for each type of cell that is to be deallocated. Each instantiation produces a procedure, for which the programmer supplies a name, that puts that kind of cell on a freelist. (Different cell types go on different freelists.) Use of this facility is discouraged because it may lead to dangling pointers.

---

[4]Generic packages are explained in Chapter 17.

Exhibit 6.25.   Dynamic allocation in Turing.

- **Allocation:** new ⟨collection⟩, ⟨ptr⟩ To dynamically allocate cells of a particular type, the programmer must explicitly declare that the type forms a "collection". The new command allocates one cell from the desired collection and stores the reference in ⟨ptr⟩.

- **Deallocation:** free ⟨collection⟩, ⟨ptr⟩ The object pointed at by ptr is returned to the collection it came from, where it will be available for reuse. The pointer object ptr is set to nil.

Dead Heap Objects.

We call a dead heap object *garbage*. Management of dead heap objects is very different from stack management. A heap object dies either when the last reference to the object is destroyed (let us call this a *natural death*) or when it is explicitly killed using a KILL command.

The run-time system of a language translator must manage heap storage allocation just as it manages stack frame allocation. However, when an object dies a natural death, both the programmer and the run-time system may be unaware of that death. A hole containing garbage is left in the heap at an unknown location.

A KILL command takes a reference to a storage object, kills the storage object, and puts the reference onto the freelist, where it can be recycled. In languages that implement KILL, programmers who use extensive amounts of dynamic storage are strongly urged to keep track of their objects and KILL them when they are no longer useful. (In general, this will be well before the object dies a natural death.) It is only through an explicit KILL command that the system can reclaim the storage.

Recycling a dead heap cell is more complex than recycling stack cells. The system cannot simply decrement the heap allocation pointer because, in general, dead objects are in the middle of the heap, not at the end. A data structure called a *freelist* is generally used to link together the recycled cells and provide a pool of cells available for future reuse. Conceptually, a freelist is just a list of reclaimed and reusable storage objects. However, that is not a simple thing to implement efficiently. The objects might all be interchangeable, or they might be of differing sizes. In any case, they are probably scattered all over heap memory. The language designer or system implementor must decide how to organize the freelist to maximize its benefits and minimize bookkeeping.

Ignore dead cells.   The easiest implementation of KILL is to ignore it! Although this seems to be a misimplementation of a language, it has been done. The Pascal reference manual for the Data General MV8000 explicitly states that the Dispose command is implemented as a no-op. This compiler runs under the AOS-VS operating system, which is a time-shared, paged, virtual memory system.

The philosophy of the compiler writer was that most programs don't gobble up huge amounts of storage, and those that do can be paged. Old, dead storage objects will eventually be paged out. If all objects on the page have died, that page will never again be brought into memory. Thus the compiler depends on the storage management routines of the operating system to "deep-six" the garbage. This can work very well if objects with similar birth times have similar useful lifetimes. If not, each of many pages might end up holding a few scattered objects, vastly increasing the memory requirements of the process and degrading the performance of the entire system.

Keep one freelist.   One possibility is to maintain a single list which links together all free areas. To do this, each area on the list must have at least enough bytes to store the size of the area and a link. (On most hardware that means 8 bytes.) Areas smaller than this are not reclaimable. Many or most C and Pascal compilers work this way.

A compiler could treat this 8-byte minimum object size in three ways. It could refuse to *allocate* anything smaller than 8 bytes; a request for a smaller area would be increased to this minimum. This is not as wasteful as it might seem. Those extra bytes often have to be allocated anyway because many machines require every object to start on a word or long-word boundary (a byte address that is divisible by 2 or 4).

Alternately, the compiler could refuse to *reclaim* anything smaller than the minimum. If a tiny object were freed, its bytes would simply be left as a hole in the heap. The philosophy here is that tiny objects are probably not worth bothering about. It takes a very large number of dead tiny objects to fill up a modern memory.

A fragmentation problem can occur with these methods for handling variable-sized dead objects. With many rounds of allocation and deallocation, the average size of the objects can decrease, and the freelist may end up containing a huge number of tiny, worthless areas. If adjacent areas are not "glued together", one can end up with most of the memory free but no single area large enough to allocate a large object.

Joining adjacent areas is quick and easy, but one must first identify them. Ordinarily this would require keeping the freelist sorted in order of address and searching it each time an object is freed. This is certainly time-consuming, and the system designer must decide whether the time or the space is more valuable.

One final implementation of variable-sized deallocation addresses this problem. In this version, each allocation request results in an 8-byte header *plus* the number of bytes requested, rounded up to the nearest word boundary. At first this seems very wasteful, but using the extra space permits a more satisfactory implementation of the deallocation process.

The 8-byte header contains two pointers that are used to create a doubly linked circular list of dynamically allocated areas. One bit somewhere in the header is set to indicate whether the area is currently in use or free. The areas are arranged on this list in order of memory address. Areas that are adjacent in memory are adjacent in the list. Disposing of a dead object is very efficient with this implementation: one only needs to set this bit to indicate "free". Then if either of the neighboring areas is also free, the two can be combined into one larger area.

When a request is made for more storage, the list can be scanned for a free cell that is large enough to satisfy the new request. Scanning the list from the beginning every time would be very slow, since many areas that are in use would have to be bypassed before finding the first free area. But a scanning pointer can be kept pointing just past the most recently allocated block, and the search for a free area can thus start at the end of the in-use area. By the time the scanner comes back around to the beginning of the list, many of the old cells will have been freed. Thus we have a typical time/space trade-off. By allocating extra space we can reduce memory-management time.

Keep several freelists.   A final strategy for managing free storage is to maintain one freelist for every size or type of storage object that can be freed. Thus all cells on the list are interchangeable, and their order doesn't matter. This simplifies realloca- tion, avoids the need for identifying adjacent areas, and, in general, is simpler and easier to implement. This reallocation strategy is used by Ada and Turing [Exhibits 6.24 and 6.25].

One of the problems with heap-allocated objects is in knowing when to kill them. It is all too easy to forget to kill an object at the end of its useful lifetime or to ac- cidentally kill it too soon. This situation is complicated by the way in which pointer structures may share storage. A storage object could be shared by two data structures, one of which is no longer useful and apparently should be killed, while the other is still in use and must not be killed. If we KILL this structure we create a dangling pointer which will eventually cause trouble. Identifying such situations is difficult and error prone, but omitting KILL instructions can increase a program's storage requirements beyond what is readily available.

For this reason, some languages, such as LISP, automate the process of recycling dead heap objects. In cases where a KILL command does not exist or is not used, heap objects still die, but the memory manager is not aware of the deaths when they happen. To actually recycle these dead heap cells requires a nontrivial mechanism called a *garbage collector*, which is invoked to recycle the dead storage objects when the heap becomes full or nearly full.

A garbage collector looks through storage, locating and marking all the live ob- jects. It can tell that an object is alive if it is static or stack-allocated or if there is a pointer to it from some other live object anywhere in storage. The garbage collec- tor then puts references to all of the unmarked, dead areas on the freelist, where the allocator will look for reusable cells.

While this scheme offers a lot of advantages, it is still incumbent on the program- mer to destroy references to objects that are no longer needed. Furthermore, garbage collection is slow and costly. On the positive side, the garbage collector needs to be run only when the supply of free storage is low, which is an infrequent problem with large, modern memories. Thus garbage collection has become a practical solution to the storage management problem.

6.3.2 Dangling References

The case of a name or a pointer that refers to a dead object is problematical. This can happen with heap storage where the programming language provides an explicit KILL command. The programmer could allocate a heap-object, copy the resulting reference several times, then KILL the object and one of its references. The other references will still exist and point at garbage. These pointers are called *dangling references* or *dangling pointers*.

This situation could also arise if the program is able to store references to stack- allocated objects. Assume that a reference to a stack-allocated variable declared in an inner block could be stored in a pointer from an outer block. During the lifetime of the inner block, this can make good sense. When storage for the inner block is deallocated, though, the reference stored in the outer block becomes garbage. If it were then used, it would be an undefined reference.

Initially, a dangling reference points at the value of the deallocated variable. Later, when the storage is reused for another block, the address will contain useful information that is not relevant to the pointer. Thus the pointer provides a way of accessing and modifying some random piece of storage.

Serious errors can be caused by the accidental use of a dangling reference. Because the storage belonging to any inner block might be affected, the symptoms of this kind of error are varied and confusing. The apparent error happens at a point in the program that is distant from the block containing the dangling reference. If the inner blocks are modified, the symptoms may change; the part that was malfunctioning may start to work, and some other part may suddenly malfunction. This kind of error is extremely difficult to trace to its cause and debug.

Because of the potential severe problems involved, pointers into the stack are completely prohibited in Pascal. Pascal was designed to be simple and as foolproof as possible. The designer's opinion is that all programmers are occasionally "fools", and the language should provide as much protection as possible without prohibiting useful things.

Pascal completely prevents dangling pointers that point into the stack by prohibiting *all pointers to stack-allocated objects*. The use of Pascal pointers is thus restricted to "heap" storage. Linked lists and trees, which require the use of pointers, are allocated in the heap. Simple variables and arrays can be allocated on the stack. Address arithmetic is not defined. Although this seems like a severe restriction, its primary bad effect is that subscripts must be used to process arrays, rather than the more efficient indexing methods which use pointers and address arithmetic.

In contrast, the use of pointers is not at all restricted in C. The "&" operator can be used freely and lets the programmer point at any object, including stack objects that have been deallocated. When control leaves an inner block, and its stack frame is deallocated, any pointer that points into that block will contain garbage. (Examples of such code and corresponding diagrams are given in Exhibits 9.25 and 9.26.)

A language, such as C, which permits unrestricted use of addresses must either forgo the use of an execution stack or cope with the problem of dangling references. Allocation of parameters and local variables on the execution stack is a simple and efficient method of providing dynamically expandable storage, which is necessary to support recursion. Alternatives to using a stack exist but have high run-time overhead.

The other possibility is to permit the programmer to create dangling references and make it the programmer's responsibility to avoid using them meaninglessly. A higher level of programming skill is then required because misuse of pointers is always possible. A high premium is placed on developing clean, structured methods for handling pointers.

One design principle behind the original C was that a systems programmer does not need a foolproof language but does need free access to all the objects in his or her programs. Permitting free use of pointers was also important in the original C because it lacked other important features. Since structured objects could not be passed coherently to and from subroutines, any subroutine that worked on a structure had to communicate with its calling program using a pointer to the structure.

In the new ANSI C, this weakness is changed but not eliminated. It permits coherent assignment of structures, but not arrays. Similarly, structures may be passed to and from functions without using pointers, but an array parameter is always passed by pointer. Thus if C had the same restriction on pointers that Pascal has, the language would be much less powerful, perhaps not even usable.

How, then, can Pascal avoid the need to have pointers to stack objects? It has two facilities that are missing in C:

- Compound stack-allocated objects are coherent. They can be operated on, assigned, compared, and passed as parameters coherently.

- References to objects can be passed as parameters by using the VAR parameter declarator. Unfortunately, returning a compound value from a function is not permitted in the standard language and must be accomplished by storing the answer in a VAR parameter.

Most standard algorithms and data structures can be coded easily within these restrictions, using the fact that compound objects are coherent. Some experts assert that Pascal is a "better" language for these applications because the programmer does not need to exercise as much care.

On the other hand, there are, occasionally, situations in which the pointer restrictions in Pascal prevent the programmer from coding an algorithm at all, and others in which the code would have been much more efficient if the programmer had used pointers to stack objects. One might say that C is a "better" language for these applications.

EXERCISES

1. Define and explain the relationship among: external object, program object, storage object, and pointer object.
2. What is the difference between a variable and a pointer variable?
3. By what two means can a value be placed in a storage object? What is the difference between the two processes?
4. What is the difference between destructive assignment and coherent assignment?
5. What is multiple assignment? How is it used?
6. Why do languages that implement assignment as a function allow the programmer more flexibility than those that implement assignment as a statement?
7. Define dereferencing. Which abstract function implements it?
8. Choose a programming language with which you are familiar. Give a sample of code in which dereferencing is explicit. Give another in which it is implicit.
9. What language contexts must be enumerated in order to define the implicit dereferencing rules in a language?
10. Give some examples of FETCH operators which are used to dereference pointer expressions.
11. How does a pointer assignment differ from an ordinary assignment?

12. Given p1 pointing at this list of integers, write legal pointer assignments for p2 and p3.

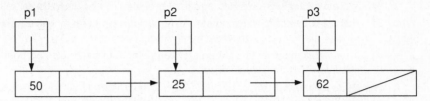

13. In the C language, what are the meanings of "&" and "*" in pointer notation?

14. In C, what is the meaning of the name of an array? Do you need an "&" when assigning a pointer to an array? Why or why not?

15. What is the lifetime of a storage object?

16. What is the difference between a static storage object and a dynamic one?

17. Why is a language that only supports static storage items limiting?

18. What is memory management? Why is it important?

19. What is a run-time stack? A stack-frame? A heap?

20. What are the purposes of the static and dynamic links in a stack frame?

21. Name two languages in which local variables can be declared and are allocated each time a subroutine is entered. Give examples of local variable declarations.

22. Name a language in which local variables cannot be defined.

23. What is static local storage? In what ways is it better than global storage and ordinary local storage? Give an example, in some language, of a declaration that creates static local storage.

24. Suppose a language allows initial values to be specified for local variables, for example, the following declarations which define X and initialize it to 50:

Language	Declaration
Ada	X: integer := 50;
C	int X=50;

When and how often does initialization happen in the following two cases?

    a. X is an ordinary local variable.
    b. X is a static local variable.

25. Explain the differences in lifetime, accessibility, and creation time between:

    a. An ordinary local variable.
    b. A static local variable and a global variable.
    c. A global variable.

26. Name a language that does not support dynamic storage at all. (All storage is static.) Explain two ways in which this limits the power of the language.

27. What is the purpose of an ALLOC command? What is garbage? A freelist? What is the function of a KILL command?

28. Give examples in LISP and C of expressions that allocate nonstack (heap) storage dynamically.

29. Explain the reallocation strategy used by Turing. What are its advantages?

30. What is a dangling reference, and what problems can be caused by it?

31. Name a language in which pointers exist but can only point at dynamically allocated heap objects, not at objects allocated in the stack.

32. Name a language in which a pointer can point at any variable and pointer arithmetic is possible. Give an example of code.

33. Write a paragraph discussing the following questions: In what sense does FORTH or assembly language have pointers? What can be done with them? Are there any restrictions? Name two common errors that can occur with this kind of pointers.

34. Choose three languages from the list: APL, Ada, Pascal, C, FORTH, and assembler. What restrictions are there on the use of pointers in each? What effect do these restrictions have on flexibility and ease of use of the language? What effect do they have on the "safety" of code?

7

Names and Binding

_____ Overview _____

     This chapter discusses the definition, implementation, and semantics
of names. The meaning of a symbol or name in a programming language is its
binding. In most languages, all sorts of entities can have names. Binding creates
an association between a name and its storage object. Binding can be static; the
name is bound to the object when the object is allocated and remains bound
throughout the program. Or, binding can be dynamic. In this case, a name can
be bound to one object, unbound, and rebound to another within the run of a
program. Constant declarations bind a symbolic name to a literal value.

     The scope of a name is that part of the program where a name is known
by the translator. Naming conflicts occur when some name is accidentally used
more than once within a linear program. Modularity and block structure allow
the programmer to limit the scope of a name to a block and all its nested blocks.
It is the job of the interpreter or compiler to determine the proper meaning of
ambiguous names according to the semantics of the language.

7.1 THE PROBLEM WITH NAMES

This section concerns the ways that we define symbols, or *names*, in a programming
language, give those names meaning (or meanings), and interpret references to names.
In lambda calculus this issue is very simple; every name acquires a unique meaning in
one of two ways:

1. Some names are defined, by declaration, to stand for formulas.

2. Parameter names acquire meaning during a reduction step. When a lambda expression is
   applied to an argument, that argument becomes the meaning of the parameter name.

163

Lambda calculus is referentially transparent: wherever a name appears in an expression, the defining formula can be substituted without changing the meaning of the expression. The reverse is also true; the meaning of an expression does not change if a defined name is substituted for a subexpression which matches its defining formula.

Thus lambda calculus makes a simple one-to-one correspondence between names and meanings. Most programming languages, however, are not so simple. This section tries to explain and straighten out all the myriad ways in which real languages complicate the naming problem.

7.1.1   The Role of Names

We use names to talk about objects in a computer. In simplest terms, a name is a string of characters that a programmer can write in a program. Different languages have different rules for the construction of names, but intuitively, a name is just like a word in English—a string of letters. A name must be given a meaning before it can be used. The *meaning of a name* is its binding, and we say the name is *bound* to that meaning.

While *objects* can be created dynamically in most languages, *names* cannot. Names are written in the program, and the text of the program does not change when the program is executed. Bindings, though, change when objects are created or destroyed. They attach the changing collection of objects to the fixed collection of names.

Naming would need little explanation if languages followed a "one object-one name" rule. However, the situation is not so simple. Languages permit a bewildering mismatch between the number of objects that exist and the number of names in the program. On the one hand, an object can have no name, one name, or multiple names bound to it. On the other hand, a name can be bound to no object (a dangling pointer), one object (the usual case), or several objects (a parameter name in a recursive function). This complexity comes about because of block structure, parameters, recursion, pointers, alias commands, KILL commands, and explicit binding commands. In this section, we explore the way names are used in writing programs and the binding mechanisms provided by various languages.

Symbolic names are not necessary for a computer to execute a program: compilers commonly remove names altogether and replace them by references. Nor are names necessary for a person to write a program: the earliest method for programming computers, writing absolute machine code, did not use names. Nonsymbolic programming requires considerable skill and extraordinary attention to detail, and "symbolic assemblers", which permit the programmer to define names for locations, were a great leap forward because names help the programmer write correct code. It is much easier for a human to remember a hundred names than a hundred machine addresses.

In addition, names have an important semantic aspect that is appreciated by experienced programmers. A program that uses well-chosen names that are related to the meaning of the objects being named is much easier to debug than a program with randomly chosen, excessively general, or overused names like "J" and "temp". A program that uses names inappropriately can be terrible to debug, since the human working on the program can be misled by a name and fail to connect the name with an observed error. It is even harder for another programmer, unfamiliar with the program, to maintain that code.

The function definition in Exhibit 7.1 was written with names purposely chosen to disguise and confuse its purpose. The English semantics of every name used are wrong for the usage of the corresponding object. A compiler would have no trouble making sense of this clear, concise code, but a human being will be hindered by ideas of what names are *supposed* to mean and will have trouble understanding the code. You may enjoy trying to decode it before reading further.

Exhibit 7.1.   Bad names.

You may enjoy the challenge of figuring out what this function does without using diagrams. At least one highly experienced Pascal programmer failed on his first try.

```
TYPE
    my_type = ↑x_type;
    x_type = RECORD next:  char; prior:  my_type END;
FUNCTION store_it (temp: my_type, jxq:  char): my_type;
VAR jqx, first:  my_type;
BEGIN
    first := temp;
    jqx := temp↑.prior;
    WHILE (jqx <> NIL) DO BEGIN
        IF jqx↑.next = jxq
        THEN jqx := NIL
        ELSE BEGIN first := jqx; jqx := jqx↑.prior END
    END;
    store_it := first;
END;
```

Several naming sins occur in Exhibit 7.1:

- Two names were used that have subtle differences: jxq, jqx.
- Nonsuggestive names were used: temp, my_type, x_type, jxq.
- Suggestive names were inappropriately used: "store_it" names a search routine that does no storing. "Next" names a value field, rather than the traditional pointer. "Prior" names a pointer field pointing at the next item in the list.
- A name was used that seemed appropriate on first use but did not reflect the actual usage of the object: "first" started as a pointer to the first thing in the list, but it is actually a scanning pointer.

A list of good name substitutions for the program in Exhibit 7.1 is:

my_type = list_type	prior = next	jxq = search_key
x-type = cell_type	next = value	jqx = scanner
store_it = search	temp = letter_list	first = follower

Rewritten with the names changed, the purpose of this code should be immediately apparent. Try reading the code in Exhibit 7.2. Anyone familiar with Pascal and with list processing should understand this code readily.

Exhibit 7.2.   Good names.

```
TYPE
    list_type = ↑cell_type;
    cell_type = RECORD value:  char; next:  list_type  END;
FUNCTION search (letter_list: list_type, search_key: char): list_type;
VAR scanner, follower:  list_type;
BEGIN
    follower := letter_list;
    scanner := letter_list↑.next;
    WHILE (scanner <> NIL) DO BEGIN
        IF scanner↑.value = search_key
        THEN scanner := NIL
        ELSE BEGIN
        follower := scanner; scanner := scanner↑.next
        END
    END;
    search := follower;
END;
```

7.1.2   Definition Mechanisms: Declarations and Defaults

All sorts of entities can have names in most languages: objects and files (nouns), functions and procedures (verbs), types (adjectives), and more. Depending on the rules of the language, the programmer might or might not be permitted to use the same name for entities in different classes. As in English, there must be some way to give meaning to a name and some way to find the meaning of a name when it is used. Declarations, defaults, and the language definition itself are the means used in programming languages to give meaning to names.

The *symbol table* is a data structure maintained by every translator that is analogous to a dictionary. It stores names and their definitions during translation.[1]

A name must be defined before it can be used. In some languages this happens the first time it is used; in others all names must be explicitly declared. A *declaration* is a statement that causes the translator to add a new name to its list of defined names in the symbol table.

Many functions, types, and constants are named by the language designer, and their definitions are built into all implementations of the language. We call these *primitive symbols* [Exhibits 7.3 and 7.4]. These names are not like other reserved words. They do not occur in the syntax that defines the language, and the programmer may

---

[1]This structure has also been called the *environment* or *dictionary*.

define more names in the same categories. They are a necessary part of a language definition because they provide a basic catalog of symbols in terms of which all other symbols must be defined.

Exhibit 7.3.   Predefined names in Pascal.

This is a list of *all* the names that are predefined in UCSD Pascal.

types	integer, real, Boolean, char, text
constants	NIL, TRUE, FALSE, MAXINT
files	input, output
functions	odd, eof, eoln, abs, sqr, sqrt, sin, cos, arctan, ln, exp, trunc, round, ord, chr, succ, pred
procedures	read, readln, write, writeln, get, put, rewrite, reset, page, new, dispose, pack, unpack

---

Exhibit 7.4.   Predefined names in C.

These are the names that are predefined in C.

types	int, long, short, unsigned, float, double, char
constants	NULL (TRUE, FALSE, and EOF are also defined in many versions of ⟨stdio.h⟩, the header file for the standard I/O package.)
functions	Every C implementation has a library, which contains I/O functions, numeric functions, and the like. The libraries are fairly well standardized from one implementation to another and are far too extensive to list here.

In many interpreted languages the programmer is not required to declare types, because allocation decisions do not have to be made in advance of execution, and at execution time, the type of a datum can often be determined by examining the datum itself. Names are generally added to the symbol table the first time they are mentioned. Thus names are typeless. These languages are sometimes called "typeless" because types are not declared and not stored in the symbol table with the names.

Objects, on the other hand, are never "typeless". Every storage object has a fixed size, and size is one aspect of type. Every program object has a defined encoding, another aspect of type. In a "typeless" language, the type of an object must still be recorded. Since the type is not stored with the name, it must be encoded somehow as part of the object itself.

In a compiled language, the type of each name must be supplied either by a declaration or by a default so that the compiler can know how many bytes to allocate for the associated storage object. The type is stored in the symbol table with the name, and remains unchanged throughout the rest of translation. Pascal requires that a type

be declared for each name. FORTRAN permits the programmer to write explicit declarations, but if an identifier does not appear in a declaration, a default type will be
used which depends on the first letter of the name. The original C permitted function
return types and parameter types, but not variable types, to be declared as "integer"
by default.

7.1.3   Binding

In compiled languages, a name exists *only* in the symbol table at translation time and
objects exist only at run time. Names are gone before objects are created; they are not
part of objects. In interpreted languages, names and objects coexist. In both cases, a
name acquires one or more meanings during the course of translation, by a process
called binding.

   Binding creates an association between a name (in the symbol table) and a storage object (an area of memory). We can picture a binding as a pointer from the name
to the storage object. A binding differs from an ordinary pointer, though, because it
reaches from the system's storage area into the programmer's area. Moreover, in compiled languages, the binding spans time as well as space. At compile time it holds the
location where an object will someday be allocated. Finally, bindings are unlike pointers because the translator automatically dereferences bindings but does not dereference pointers. We represent bindings in our diagrams as arrows (like pointers) but
drawn in boldface, because they are not ordinary pointers.

   Binding is invoked by the translator whenever a declaration is processed but can
also be invoked explicitly by the programmer in many languages. A binding is *static* if
it never changes during the lifetime of the program. Otherwise it is said to be *dynamic*.
At any time a name might be *bound* to a particular object to which it *refers*, or it might
be *unbound*, in which case it refers to nothing and is said to be *undefined*, or it might
be *multiply bound* to different objects in different scopes.

   Names of variables, types, pure values, and functions are identified and recorded
in the symbol table during translation of a program. Another column of the symbol
table records the bindings. Like allocation, binding can be static, block structured, or
dynamic.

Typed Languages / Static Binding

Most of the familiar languages (COBOL, FORTRAN, ALGOL, C, Pascal, Ada) belong
to a class called "typed languages". In these languages each name defined in a program
unit has a fixed data type associated with it, and often declared with it.

   In the oldest and simplest of these languages, such as symbolic assemblers and
COBOL, name binding is *static*. A name is bound to an object when the object is
allocated and remains bound to the same storage object until the end of the program.
In such languages, when a meaning is given to a name, that name retains the meaning
throughout the program.

   Static binding occurs in typed languages that are non-block structured. In a static
language, there is no concept of a program block enclosed within another program
block, producing a local program scope in which a name could be redefined.[2] A static

---

[2]However, additional names can be bound to a COBOL object, by using REDEFINES, as explained in
Section 7.1.4.

binding associates a name with a storage object of fixed type and size at a fixed memory address.

Static binding can be implemented simply by using three columns in the symbol table to store the name, type, and binding [Exhibit 7.5]. We can describe this kind of symbol table as "flat"—it has the form of a simple one-dimensional list of entries, where each entry has three fields.

Exhibit 7.5.   A symbol table with static bindings.

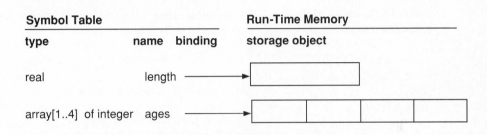

Each declaration (explicit or default) specifies a name and a type. It causes the compiler to select and set aside an area of storage appropriate for an object of that type. Although this storage will not exist until run time, its address can be computed at compile time and stored in the symbol table as the binding for the name. Note, in Exhibit 7.5, that the run-time memory contains only the storage object; the symbol table no longer needs to be present. It was used to generate machine code and discarded at the end of translation.[3]

A Typed Language with Dynamic Binding

FORTH is an interactive, interpretive language embedded in a program development system. A complete system contains an editor, an assembler, an interpreter, and a "compiler". This compiler does not generate machine code, rather, it lexes and parses function definitions and produces an intermediate program form that can be interpreted efficiently.

FORTH is a typed language. Its symbol table, called the "dictionary", is only a little more complex than the simple, flat symbol table used for a static language. The dictionary is organized into several "vocabularies", each containing words for a different subsystem. Each vocabulary is implemented by a simple, flat symbol table. Unlike COBOL and assembler, though, FORTH is an interactive language system. A user wishing to create a new application subsystem is permitted to create a new vocabulary or to add to an existing vocabulary. The user may alternate between defining objects and functions, and executing those functions. The dictionary may thus grow throughout a session.

---

[3]Some translators are embedded in systems that provide a symbolic debugger. These systems must keep the symbol table and load it along with the object code for the program.

The dictionary contains an entry for each defined item [Exhibit 7.6]. Function names, variable names, and constant names are all called "words". Entries for all the primitive words are loaded into the dictionary when you enter the FORTH system. A dictionary entry is created for a user-defined word when a declaration is processed, and it will remain in the dictionary until the user gives the command to FORGET the symbol. The FORTH dictionary is stack-structured; new items are added at the top of the stack and can be defined in terms of anything below them on the stack.

Exhibit 7.6.   Names, types, and bindings in FIG FORTH.

This dictionary segment contains two words, an integer and an array of four integers. The right-hand column has 4 bytes of memory per line in the diagram.

name:	6len gth	(Length of name followed by name.)
link:	-► ?	(Pointer to previous word in dictionary.)
type:	-► int	(Pointer to run-time code for integer variables.)
body:		(4 bytes, properly called the "parameter field".)
name:	4age s	
link:	-► length	
type:	-► int	(Pointer to run-time code for integer variables.)
body:		(16 bytes of storage, enough for four variables.)

Each entry has four fields:

- The *name field* holds the name of the word, stored as a string whose first byte contains the length of the name.
- The *link field* is used to organize the dictionary into a data structure that can be searched efficiently. Searching must be done during translation, when the definition of a function refers to a symbol, or at run time when the interpreter evaluates a symbolic expression interactively. The implementation of the link field and its position relative to the name field varies among different versions and implementations of FORTH. Exhibit 7.6 shows the relationships defined for FIG FORTH.
- The *code field* is the functional equivalent of a type field. It identifies, uniquely, the kind of object this word represents (function, variable, constant, or programmer-defined type).
- The *parameter field*, or body, contains the specific meaning of the word. For constants, it is a pure value. For variables it is a storage object. For functions, it contains code that can be interpreted.

FORTH maintains a rudimentary sort of type information in the "code field" of each dictionary entry. This field is a pointer to a run-time routine that determines the semantics of the name. It is actually a pointer to some code which will be run whenever this word is used at run time. This code defines the interpretation method for objects of this type. Thus constants, variables, and user-defined types can be interpreted differently. Initially only the types "function", "variable", and "constant" are built in, but others can be added. When a new type declarator is defined, two pieces of code are given: one to allocate and initialize enough storage for an object of the new type, and a second to interpret run-time references to the name of an object of this type. A pointer to this second piece of code becomes the unique identifier for the new type, and also becomes the contents of the code field for all objects declared with the new type.

FORTH differs from the simple static languages in one important way: it permits the user to redefine a word that is already in the dictionary. The translator will provide a warning message, but accept the redefinition. Henceforth the new definition will be used to compile any new functions, but the old one will be used to interpret any previously compiled functions. This opens up the possibility of redefining primitive symbols. The new definition can call the original definition and, in addition, do more elaborate processing. The simple relationship between a name and its meaning no longer holds at all.

The FORGET command is an unusual feature that has no counterpart in most language translators. It does not just remove one item from the dictionary, it pops the entire dictionary stack back to the entry before its argument, forgetting everything that has been defined since! This is a rudimentary form of symbol table management which does not have either the same purpose or the same power as the stack-structured symbol tables used to implement block structure. A FORTH programmer alternates between compiling parts of his or her code and testing them. FORGET lets the programmer erase the results of part of a compilation, correct an error in that part, and recompile just one part. Thus FORGET is an important program-development tool.

Typed Languages / Block Structured Binding.

The connection between a name and its meaning is further complicated by block structure. FORTH permits a new definition of a name to be given, and it will permanently replace the old version (unless it is explicitly "forgotten"). A block structured language permits this same kind of redefinition, but such a language will restore the original definition after exit from the block containing the redefinition. Block structure and the semantic mechanisms that implement it are taken up in Section 7.4.

Explicit Dynamic Binding.

Fully dynamic binding is available only in interpreted languages or ones such as LISP with simple, uniform type structures. In such a language, types can be associated with objects, not names, and are stored with the object in memory, rather than in the symbol table. The symbol table has only two columns, the name and its current binding. The type must be stored with or encoded into the object in memory, or discarded altogether as in assembly language. This is illustrated in Exhibit 7.7.

Exhibit 7.7. A symbol table with dynamic binding.

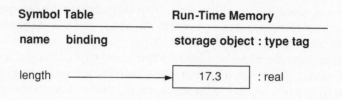

With fully dynamic binding, a name can be unbound from one object and rebound to any other at any time, even in the middle of a block, by explicit programmer command. In such a language, the type of the object bound to a name may change dramatically, and these languages are sometimes called "typeless" because no definite type is associated permanently with a name. SNOBOL and APL are examples of this language class.

These "typeless" languages nevertheless commonly do implement objects of different types. For example, in APL there are two basic types, number and character. These types are implemented by attaching a type tag to the object itself, rather than to the name in the symbol table [Exhibit 7.8]. The symbol table contains only the name and the binding, and the programmer is permitted to bind a name to any object. Thus at different times a name may be bound to storage areas of different sizes, each with an associated type tag.

Exhibit 7.8. Names, types, and binding in APL.

APL is a "typeless" language and so has no permanent association of types with names. Rather, a type tag is associated with each storage object, and the combination may be bound to any name.

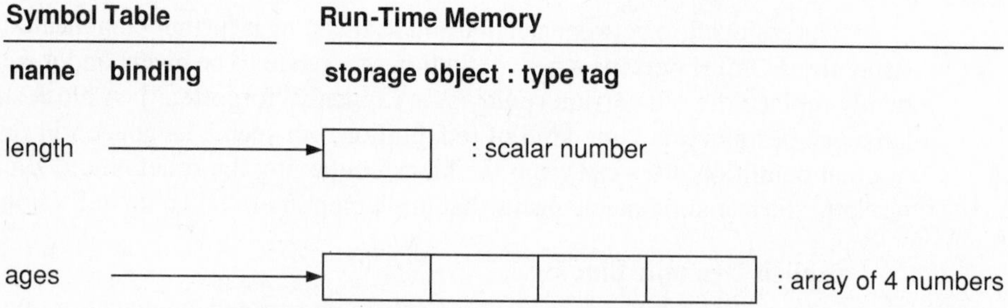

Symbol Table

name   binding

Run-Time Memory

storage object : type tag

length ─────────────────▶ ☐   : scalar number

ages ─────────────────▶ ☐☐☐☐   : array of 4 numbers

In such languages, binding often serves the same purpose as does assignment in Pascal and is often mistaken for assignment. The essential difference is that assignment does not change the storage object to which a name is bound, but changes the program object which is the contents of that storage object. Binding results in a different storage object being bound to a name.

The APL input command is: ← □. Executing □ causes a pure value of some type to be accepted as input from the user's terminal. The input may be a single number or character (called a scalar), or it may be an array (or vector) of any length of either base type. The type of the value is determined, storage is allocated and initialized to this value, and a reference to this storage is returned. The operator ← binds this new object to the name on its left. Exhibit 7.9 uses the □ operator to illustrate the dynamic nature of binding in APL.

Exhibit 7.9.   Dynamic binding in APL.

On two successive executions of the input statement

$$Q \leftarrow \square$$

one could legally supply the following inputs: `'aeiouy'` (which is a character array) and `37.1` (which is a number). Thus we would get first the following binding:

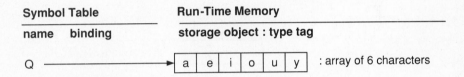

and second the following binding:

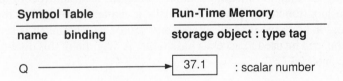

7.1.4 Names and Objects: Not a One-to-One Correspondence

We have seen that although the number of names in a program cannot change dynamically, many applications require that the storage in use expand dynamically. We, therefore, must be able to refer to storage locations that do not have unique names. This need is met by using addresses, or pointers, rather than names to refer to storage, and by binding the same name, recursively, to objects in different stack frames.

Conversely, there are times when it is convenient to bind multiple names to a single storage object or a part of an object. This is often done in order to associate a second data type with that object, or to package logically independent objects together into a group to facilitate their handling. (A full discussion of this topic is in Chapter 14.) The names given to this kind of declaration in some common languages are as follows:

FORTRAN	EQUIVALENCE declaration
COBOL	REDEFINES clause in a declaration
Pascal	Variant record with no tag field
C	Union data type

When multiple-name binding is used, storage is not allocated for the second name, but it is bound to the same address as the first and serves as a second way to refer to the same storage object [Exhibit 7.10]. If used carelessly, this can cause bizarre misinterpretations of data.

Exhibit 7.10.   Sharing through EQUIVALENCE in FORTRAN.

```
DIMENSION P1(3)
EQUIVALENCE (P1, P2), (P1(2), P3)
```

The DIMENSION statement causes an array of length 3 to be allocated and bound to P1. The EQUIVALENCE statement binds a second name to the base address of the array P1, and a third name to a segment of that array, as illustrated below. P1, P2, and P3 now "share" storage.

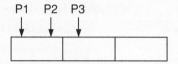

On the other hand, misinterpreting the data on purpose can be an easy way to compute a pseudo-random function. Exhibit 7.11 shows a variant record used as the input to a hashing function. The data is really a character string, but the hashing function is told to construe it as an integer and square it. The result is semantically meaningless but can be used to access a hash table. A diagram of this dual-type object is shown in Exhibit 7.12.

Exhibit 7.11.   A variant record used to compute a hash index.

We define a type that provides storage for 4 bytes, which can be interpreted either as a single integer or an array of four characters. This type is useful in writing a hash function that takes a character array as its parameter and uses integer operations to compute a hash address. Diagrams of the variant-record object are shown in Exhibit 7.12.

```
TYPE twokinds = 1..2;
    hashkey = RECORD CASE twokinds OF
        1: (char_ar: ARRAY [1..4] of char);
        2: (int_way: integer)
    END;
FUNCTION hash (k: hashkey): integer;
BEGIN
    hash := (k.int_way * k.int_way) MOD table_size
END;
```

Exhibit 7.12.   Diagrams of a Pascal variant record.

The storage object for **k** in Exhibit 7.11 would have the following structure:

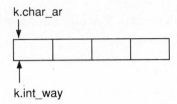

This object has dual semantics. If the actual parameter were the string 'ABCD', the two interpretations of the program object would be as follows:

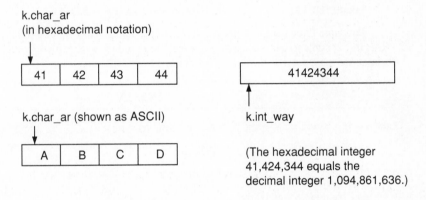

7.2 BINDING A NAME TO A CONSTANT

A constant declaration permits the programmer to attach a symbolic name to a literal value. Although giving a name to a constant does not change the meaning of a program, a judicious choice of names can clarify the programmer's intended meaning to other programmers. Defining the name once and then using it many times in place of a frequently used value also makes it easier to modify a program: only the definition needs to be changed to change all occurrences of that value.

Many but not all languages permit the programmer to name constants. Some place severe restrictions on the kinds of constants that can be named and/or on the ways initial values can be specified. For example, Pascal requires that the value of a constant be a literal value of a primitive type. Constant expressions may not be used as initial values [Exhibit 7.13] even though they could easily be evaluated by the compiler, as they are in FORTRAN 77 [Exhibit 7.14].

In Ada, constant declarations do not have to precede the rest of the program. A constant declaration may come after variable declarations and depend on the initial values given to those variables [Exhibit 7.15].

Exhibit 7.13.   Constant declarations in Pascal.

```
CONST pi = 3.1416;
    max_length = 500;
    max_index = 499;  { Equals max_length - 1 }
```

A real constant and two integer constants are declared. As is often the case, the last one depends on the second, but the dependency cannot be made explicit in Pascal and is indicated only by a comment.

Exhibit 7.14.   Constant declarations in FORTRAN 77.

```
PARAMETER (PI = 3.1416, MAXLEN = 500, MAXIX = MAXLEN-1)
```

The same three constants are created as in the Pascal example of Exhibit 7.13. In FORTRAN it *is* possible to use a constant expression to specify the value of a constant. PARAMETER declarations must precede the executable code.

Exhibit 7.15.   Mixed variable and constant initializations in Ada.

```
pi:  CONSTANT float := 3.1416;
m:   integer;
n:   integer := 5;
max_length:  CONSTANT integer := n * 100;
max_index:   CONSTANT integer := max_length - 1;
```

The real constant pi and two integer variables are declared. The second variable is initialized to 5. The integer constants max_length and max_index are declared and bound, respectively, to 500 and 499. These are legal defining expressions because n is previously initialized. The following constant declaration would not be legal because the value of m is not defined:

```
max_width:  CONSTANT integer := m - 1;  -- Not legal.
```

FORTH, like Ada, permits the declaration of a constant at any point during a program. A constant definition consists of an expression, the word CONSTANT, and the name of the constant. The expression will be evaluated first, and its value will be bound to the name. FORTH, unlike Ada, is interactive. This declaration is translated at run time, not at a prior compile time. Thus there is no need to restrict the initializing expression, which may depend on the current (run-time) value of any name [Exhibit 7.16]. The scope of the constant name is all of the program that follows the declaration.[4]

---

[4]Scope is explained in Section 7.4.

Exhibit 7.16. Variable and constant declarations in FIG FORTH.

```
100 VARIABLE offset
500 CONSTANT max_length
max_length offset + CONSTANT max_index
```

A variable named `offset` is defined and initialized to 100. A constant named `max_length` is defined and initialized to 500. A second constant named `max_index` is initialized to the sum of `offset` plus `max_length`.

The original K&R C contained no special defining word for constants, but a semantics that meets the same needs as the constant declaration in Pascal can be achieved by using the compile-time preprocessor that is part of C. Each #define statement is a macro definition and is expanded by the preprocessor, replacing the defined names by the defining strings before the beginning of actual compilation. [It is conventional, in C, to use capital letters for macro (constant) names and lowercase for other identifiers.]

There is an important difference between using a macro name and using a true constant. In a constant declaration, if the constant value is defined by an expression, that expression will be evaluated once, at compile time. In a macro definition, the expression will be evaluated at run time every time the constant name is used. Of course this is inefficient, but it also leaves open the possibility that the wrong answer might be computed because of unintended interactions between the macro expansion and its context.

In Exhibit 7.17, the parentheses around the expression on the third line prevent unintended interaction between the "–" operator in the expanded macro and other operators in the surrounding program. Assume the parentheses were omitted, and consider this call on the constant `MAX_INDEX`:

```
totsize = MAX_INDEX * 10
```

This macro call would be expanded before parsing, yielding:

```
totsize = 500 - 1 * 10
```

Thus the value of `totsize` would be 490, not the intended 4990.

Exhibit 7.17. "Constant" declarations in C.

```
#define PI 3.1416
#define MAX_LENGTH 500
#define MAX_INDEX (MAX_LENGTH - 1)
const int max_index = MAX_LENGTH - 1;        /* ANSI C only */
```

For two reasons, then, a macro-preprocessor does not wholly take the place of a constant declarator in a language. First, it can lead to unnecessary run-time calculations unless the compiler performs optimization on constant expressions. Second, macros can be tricky and misleading to use. True constants are efficient and simple. Thus a `const` declaration, with semantics similar to that in Ada, was added to the language by the ANSI C standard. The last line in Exhibit 7.17 shows the declaration of a constant integer. The initializing expression will be evaluated once, when storage for `max_index` is allocated, and the result will be stored in the allocated object. Thereafter, the value cannot be changed.

7.2.1   Implementations of Constants

In spite of the differences in syntax, the semantics of constants are nearly identical in FORTH, FORTRAN, and Pascal.[5] In all three languages, a name is entered into the symbol table, a value is provided or calculated and bound to it at compile time, and that binding does not change thereafter.

These semantics can be implemented in two ways. One alternative is to evaluate the defining expression for the constant before compilation, and substitute the result for the constant's name in the source code. There can be no possibility of accidentally assigning a new value to the constant, because constant names are eliminated from the program before compile time. In this case, it might not even be necessary to allocate any run-time storage for the constant. Instead of compiling the code to fetch from a memory address (like a variable), the compiler might make the constant into a part of the compiled code by generating a "load immediate" instruction.

The second implementation for constants permits their names to exist in symbolic form during translation. This is necessary if the constant name is to have a block structured scope. The translator allocates a run-time storage location for the constant, evaluates the defining expression, and stores the result in the allocated space. This is the same way a variable would be initialized. In this case, some mechanism must be embedded in the translator to prevent the programmer from changing the constant by an assignment or read statement. We can say that this implementation provides an *initialized read only variable* (IROV).

Constants are implemented as IROVs in FORTH. The storage set aside for constants and variables is the same, and the initialization process is the same. Different semantic behavior is achieved at run time by associating different semantic routines with constants and variables. The translator puts a constant's *value* on the stack when its name is referenced. But when a variable name is referenced, the *storage address* is placed on the stack and must be explicitly dereferenced to obtain the value of the variable.

7.2.2   How Constant Is a Constant?

The IROV implementation of constants leads to a generalization that is found in Ada and ANSI. We see that the constant names in Pascal can have local scope. (That is, a constant name declared in an inner block or subroutine is only "known" in that block.) It would be logical to evaluate the initializing expression at block entry time, rather than at compile time.

---

[5]Except that the scope of definition of the constant name cannot be restricted to an inner block in FORTH or FORTRAN.

If we defer evaluation and binding for a constant until block entry time, constants can be created and initialized when local variables are allocated. They are essentially initialized read-only variables. An initializing expression can contain references to parameters and variables in outer blocks as well as to literal constants. With this interpretation, the defining expression is reevaluated each time the block is reentered, leading to the situation that a constant might not be constant! (Such a local constant would remain constant for the lifetime of its block, but the name might be bound to a different constant value the next time the block was entered.)

The primary advantage of such a block entry constant is that a constant can be calculated based on input parameters, and yet the language translator guarantees the integrity of the value: it can not be accidentally changed. The cost is more time spent during block entry.

7.3 SURVEY OF ALLOCATION AND BINDING

Early High-Level Languages.

The designers of the earliest high-level languages expected the language users to want to represent certain types of external objects. They made it easy for the programmer to represent those types. COBOL records are a natural representation of a business transaction, being very much like the paper representation of those transactions. FORTRAN makes the representation of numbers and vectors natural. At this historical stage of language development, there was a close relationship among (1) external objects being represented, (2) internal names for those objects, and (3) the storage objects that implemented them. There is no question of what constitutes an object in these languages: it is the combination of all of the above.

Allocation is static, and binding is static except for parameter binding. Each set of similar external objects (policies, dimensions, etc.) is represented by a typed identifier. If the external object has parts and subparts, each part in the representation can be named and referenced. When an identifier is defined by the programmer, a storage object is allocated and bound to that identifier for the life of the program.

Additional names can be bound to a storage object through REDEFINES or EQUIVALENCE statements. Additional names can also be bound to objects temporarily by parameter binding during a call on a subprogram.

Interactive Languages.

An interesting and different set of choices was made in BASIC. Name binding is totally static: subprograms do not have parameters, so unlike FORTRAN, there is no need to deviate from totally static binding. On the other hand, allocation of storage for string variables is dynamic. This is done by statically binding the string identifier to a pointer object and dynamically binding the pointer to a string object in string storage.

Block Structured Languages.

Concern over the difficulty of debugging large programs was beginning to develop in the late 1950s when ALGOL was designed. ALGOL was a remarkably advanced language for those years: it incorporated a clean design, adequate control structures, and recursion.

Block structure, local variables, and parameter binding were devised to ease the problems of name conflicts. With these new semantic mechanisms, the same identifier could be used to correspond to different external objects in different program blocks. This eased the writing of large programs by permitting the programmer to disregard or forget that an identifier had already been used once, so long as the previous use was in an irrelevant context. Block structure is also needed to support recursion.

Dynamic Languages.

With LISP, we see a radically different approach to modeling external objects and processes. LISP objects are implemented by linked structures, called *lists*, of storage objects called *cells*. A list is a pointer to a cell or to a simple object called an *atom*. A cell is a pair of lists. Identifiers do not have data types, but can be bound to any object at any time. Storage is allocated dynamically for parameters and also by calling the allocation function CONS. (CONS takes two parameters. It constructs a cell and initializes its two fields to those parameters.)

We see that the relationship between external objects and storage objects exhibited by the block structured languages breaks down completely in LISP. External objects are represented by lists, which can point at lists that represent smaller external objects. Big objects are made out of references to smaller objects, which are true objects, not subfields. This is in contrast to the COBOL concept that big objects may have many small parts, but these parts are not, literally, at the same level.

Variable names exist in LISP, corresponding roughly to FORTRAN object names. However, the number is not limited to the number of names introduced by the programmer; names can be generated dynamically by a program. Variables may be bound to LISP objects, but the binding is dynamic, not static, so that one variable name may refer to different program objects with different storage amounts and locations at different times. Since storage objects may be dynamically created and pointer assignment is provided, the size of a single program object is bounded only by available storage.

APL, another early interactive language, has dynamic allocation and binding for parameter names and local variables in functions. The basic objects in APL are arrays, either numeric or alphabetic. A tremendous variety of array and matrix operations are predefined. These can produce results of any size and shape, for which storage is allocated dynamically. The resulting references are bound dynamically to untyped identifiers. Global names can be used without declaration. Local variable names, parameter names, and a local name for the function's return value need to be declared in the function header to distinguish them from global names.

Smalltalk is a relatively new language that extends the LISP concept of object by having all objects belong to classes, either system-defined or programmer-defined. With this extension, objects must now contain a class (or type) indicator as well as private storage. Again, big objects are made out of smaller ones. It is significant that, as in APL, this type information is attached to the storage object rather than to an identifier. It is this property that has earned the label *object-oriented language* for Smalltalk.

Combining Static and Dynamic Objects.

In Pascal, ALGOL-like block structured allocation and binding exist side-by-side with LISP-like dynamic creation and pointer assignment, although the two facilities are not closely merged. Pascal programs tend to use either one allocation scheme or the other, with little mixing, because you cannot point at stack-allocated objects.

In C, this restriction on what a pointer may point at is lifted. The address of any storage object and any part of that object is available within the program and can be stored in a pointer. Pointers may, therefore, point at any object.

Identifier binding is block structured in both C and Pascal. An identifier is bound to a new storage object at block entry and remains bound to the same object until it is deallocated. Even though objects can be dynamically allocated from heap storage, these are bound to pointers rather than identifiers.

Data types are associated with identifiers, as in FORTRAN, not with objects, as in Smalltalk and APL. Pointers have a declared base type and should only be bound to objects of the appropriate type. C will give warning errors but still compile if this rule is breached. Pascal will fail to compile.

7.4 THE SCOPE OF A NAME

7.4.1 Naming Conflicts

When symbolic programming languages were new, each identifier stood for one storage object, and there was no need to distinguish between identifiers and internal names. Very soon though, people began to compile programs that included subroutines written by other people. They began to encounter *naming conflicts* when they would accidentally use some name that was used internally by the subroutine.

The first approach to avoiding such name conflicts was to assign a unique prefix to all of the names used in the subroutine. For example, a SIN subroutine that needed a local variable COUNT might use the name SINCOUNT. The programmer needed only to avoid using names with that prefix in other subroutines. To simplify the programmer's task, some early symbolic languages contained a PREFIX statement that would automatically prefix the name, so the programmer could write COUNT and the translator would convert it to SINCOUNT.

As programs became longer, naming conflicts became a problem even within the same program. A programmer working on one part of the program could not easily remember all of the names used in other parts of the program, and accidental duplication of names could lead to bugs that were very difficult to locate.

The concepts of *modularity* and *scope* were developed to alleviate this problem. A program is written as many manageable-sized modules, each with a particular well-defined purpose. Modules interact with each other only in well-defined ways. Names defined within a module, unless explicitly "exported", are not "visible" outside of the module. This introduced the new concept of the *scope* of a name, which is the portion of code in which the name is meaningful. Scoped names could be reused for new objects in different scopes.

The scope of a name is that part of the program in which the name is known and will be recognized by the translator. Scope can be *global*, in which case the name is known throughout the program, or it can be *local*, meaning that it is only known within that program block in which it was defined. In programs with nested scopes, a name, N, may also be *relatively global* by being declared in a block that is neither innermost nor outermost. In programs that are compiled in many modules, names can also have *external scope*, which means that the name is known to all modules.

Along with scoping came the need to distinguish between two concepts that until then had been synonymous—identifiers and complete names. *Identifiers* are the symbols that the programmer writes, and *complete names* are the things that receive bindings. The scope is added to the identifier the programmer writes in order to obtain the *complete name*. Thus if COUNT is defined in two modules SIN and SORT, then the complete names generated by the translator might be written SIN.COUNT and SORT.COUNT. Only one declaration for an identifier may occur per scope, and thus the translator can form a unique name by sequentially numbering the scopes it encounters and concatenating a scope number with the identifier that the programmer used. An attempt to redefine an identifier in the same scope is a translation-time semantic error.

In most modern languages, however, the programmer does not give names to all scopes. Nevertheless, the same rules apply. The identifier COUNT, defined in two different scopes s1 and s2, denotes two different names. When programs are translated, the complete name is formed automatically by the translator. There is no need for the programmer to write the complete names, so complete names are not a part of the syntax for programming languages. However, we still need a way to write a complete name in this chapter, so we will write the name as a pair of a scope number and an identifier, for example, (s1.COUNT) and (s2.COUNT).

The programmer refers to (s1.COUNT) when writing the identifier COUNT within scope s1 and *has no way to refer to this variable elsewhere*. This limitation is intentional and is what gives scope its power. By providing no way to write the complete name (s1.y) outside of the scope s1, we are making accidental references to (s1.y) impossible. The information stored in a named variable is only "visible" or accessible within the scope of the name. It is "hidden" from the rest of the program.

In most languages, each subroutine definition comprises a scope, and thus parameters can be given "dummy names". It is immaterial whether the identifiers used for dummy names are the same as or different from names in the calling program, for the translator will generate different complete names for them.

Language design came full-circle with the invention of object-oriented languages, where programmers, again, have reason to write complete names. Each object class has a name and defines a scope. Within the definition of a class, the programmer uses simple names to refer to the class members (objects and functions). Some class members are private, and are accessible only within the class definition. However, a class may also have public members, which can be used by other parts of the program.[6] When this is done, a double colon symbol, called the *scope-resolution operator* is written between the class name and the member name to form a complete name.

7.4.2 Block Structure

The idea of *block structure*, introduced in ALGOL-60, permitted the programmer to define nested modules called *blocks*. In a block structured language, the programmer can introduce additional blocks at quite arbitrary places, wherever they are convenient. Identifiers declared within a block are translated to complete names whose scope is

---

[6]Object-oriented scope and referencing rules are explained in Chapter 16, Section 16.4 and in Chapter 18, Section 18.2.

that block *and all nested blocks*. A well-written program uses many short blocks, and names are declared in the smallest possible block. Each block corresponds to a scope. Thus several sets of declarations might be relevant to a particular use of a name in the program.

This situation can arise in C because a new block be opened anywhere, using "{", and names may be defined at the beginning of any block.

In Pascal, blocks cannot be opened and closed at arbitrary places. But each function or procedure body is a block, and it may be nested inside other function or procedure definitions.[7] Thus we arrive at nested scopes by a different path. The simple program in Exhibit 7.18 has three scopes which are outlined by boxes. One scope is created by the main program, and two by functions within it. Let us call the scopes A, B, and C. Scope A is the lexical parent of scopes B and C.

Exhibit 7.18.   Nested scopes in Pascal.

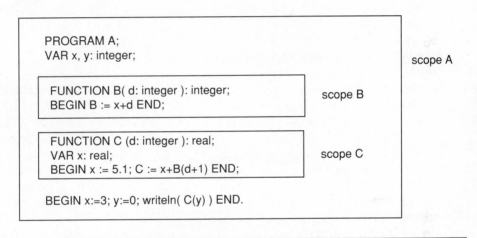

```
PROGRAM A;
VAR x, y: integer;                                                    scope A

    FUNCTION B( d: integer ): integer;                   scope B
    BEGIN B := x+d END;

    FUNCTION C (d: integer ): real;
    VAR x: real;                                         scope C
    BEGIN x := 5.1; C := x+B(d+1) END;

BEGIN x:=3; y:=0; writeln( C(y) ) END.
```

Nested blocks reintroduce ambiguity into the naming rules that scopes were invented to avoid. We said previously that although an identifier might refer to different names in different scopes, the identifier together with the scope in which it was contained was enough to disambiguate it. Now, however, we see that scopes can be nested, so an instance of an identifier can appear simultaneously in the several scopes of its enclosing blocks. Once again we are faced with an ambiguity. We must determine which scope identifier to use in forming the complete name.

To resolve this ambiguity, we introduce yet another concept—that of a *defining occurrence* of an identifier. Each identifier is given meaning by a declaration.[8] At that point, the identifier, with its type, is entered into the symbol table. All other occurrences of that identifier are *nondefining occurrences* and are called *uses*. Uses are found in executable statements and initial value clauses.

---

[7]All function definitions in C are at the top level. They may not be nested within each other.

[8]In some languages a name is defined by default when the translator sees the identifier for the first time.

An identifier can be redefined by a new declaration in a nested block, and this introduces a new complete name. The scope of each complete name is the smallest scope that contains its declaration. In order to translate a use of an identifier, the compiler must decide which complete name corresponds to it. The rule used is called *lexical scoping*.[9] The complete name to which a use, U, refers is the one produced by the nearest declaration for U. The nearest declaration is the one in the smallest enclosing block.

Exhibit 7.18 has a short program with a nest of three scopes, defined by the main program (scope A), and the two subroutines (scopes B and C). The object identifiers in use are x, y, and d. Each parameter or local variable declaration defines a complete name, thus the complete names formed from these identifiers are: (A.x), (A.y), (B.d), (C.x), and (C.d). Subroutine names are visible in the scope of the enclosing block (so that they may be called from that block). Thus the complete names of the subroutines are A.B and A.C. This program is rewritten using complete names in Exhibit 7.19. Exhibit 7.20 shows the contents of the stack during execution of function B.

Exhibit 7.19.   Complete names in Pascal.

```
PROGRAM A;
VAR (A.x), (A.y): integer;

    FUNCTION B( (B.d): integer ): integer;
    BEGIN B := (A.x)+(B.d) END;


    FUNCTION C(C.d: integer ): real;
    VAR C.x: real;
    BEGIN (C.x):=5.1; A.C:= (C.x)+A.B((C.d)+1) END;


BEGIN (A.x):=3; (A.y):= 0; writeln(A.C(A.y)) END.
```

Since x is not redefined in scope B, the x referred to in that scope is the one in the lexically enclosing scope, which is scope A.

A straightforward implementation of lexical scoping works as follows. When a block or subprogram is entered, storage for its parameters and local variables is allocated in a stack frame on the run-time stack. The stack frame also includes the return address for the subprogram and a pointer to the stack frames of the lexical and

---

[9]The word "lexical" is used because the scope of a name is a static property determined by how the program is laid out on the listing.

Exhibit 7.20.   A stack diagram for nested scopes.

This diagram shows the contents of the stack during execution of the program in Exhibit 7.18, at the point that the main program has called function c and c has called function b, but b has not yet returned.

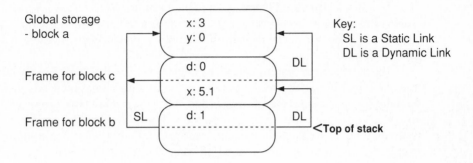

dynamic parents of the block. The pointer to the lexical parent is called the *static link*, and the pointer to the dynamic parent is called the *dynamic link*.

The static links are the means of implementing complete names, and they provide an easy way to describe lexical scoping. To find the correct complete name for a use, U, the compiler must start at the stack frame for the block that contains U. If there is no declaration for U in that stack frame, start following the chain of static links backward through the stack. The first declaration for U that you find is the relevant one. Following the static link can bypass a variable number of stack frames that were allocated for blocks called by the lexical parent of the current block.

Once the compiler determines which scope defines U, the chain of stack frames can be short-circuited so that run-time references will be more efficient. If the definition is found at a global level, the address to which it is bound is static and may simply be compiled into the code. If the definition of U is neither local nor global, but occurs in some scope between local and global, extra storage can be allocated in the local stack frame for a pointer to the defining reference. At block entry time the actual address of the proper binding can be determined by tracing through the frames by the above method, then copied into this pointer area. A use of a relatively global variable then becomes like a use of a VAR parameter, causing an automatic dereferencing of the pointer. (VAR parameters are explained in Chapter 9, Section 9.2.)

A final, confusing aspect of nested scopes must be mastered: the phenomenon of masking. Redeclaration of an identifier locally will *mask* any definitions of the same identifier that are relatively global to it. By this we mean that the object created by the declaration in the enclosing block cannot be accessed within the enclosed block because every use of that identifier in the enclosed block will be associated with the object created in the smaller scope. In the Pascal example [Exhibits 7.18 and 7.19], the object (A.y) is accessible within function C because it was declared globally. But the object (A.x) cannot be accessed within C because the local declaration for x will "swallow up" all references to x.

A Block Structured Symbol Table.

Let us say that a complete name is *born* when the compiler begins translating the block in which it is defined. It *dies* at the end of that block. The symbol table must include only names that are alive, since dead names must not be used to interpret any references.

In a block structured language, a name becomes *visible* when it is born and *invisible* again when it dies. However, a living name also becomes temporarily invisible when it is masked by a declaration in an inner block, and it becomes visible again when the masking variable dies.

Block structured binding cannot be implemented with a "flat" symbol table (that is, a one-dimensional list) because bindings for invisible names must be retained, and bindings for dead names must be discarded. Thus the symbol table grows and shrinks, and we can describe it as "stack-structured". For each name declared in a block, a type and binding are pushed onto the stack for that name when the compiler begins translating the block and are popped off when the translator reaches the lexical end of the block. There are two ways to organize the stack—either the bindings for the block can be inserted as a group, or each variable name can have an associated stack of bindings. Exhibit 7.21 shows a program in which several variables are declared in more than one block. Note that a function name is in the scope of its enclosing block, not the block created by the function definition. Exhibit 7.22 shows this stack-structured symbol table with a stack of bindings for each multiply defined name.

Exhibit 7.21.   A Pascal program demonstrating block structure.

This program contains a function within a function. During translation of the innermost function block, block III, three sets of bindings are recorded in the symbol table. This is diagrammed in Exhibit 7.22. However, only the bindings for the innermost block are active, or *visible*, at this time.

```
program demo_bind;                                       I
const a=10;
var b, c:  real;

    function d (a:real):  real;                          II

        function c (b:integer):  real;                   III
        begin c:=b/2 end;

    begin d := a+c(b) end;

begin writeln(a+trunc(d(c))) end.
```

7.4.3   Recursive Bindings

The number of names in a particular program is determined by the programmer and does not change after the program is translated. However, any language with recur-

Exhibit 7.22.   A symbol table with block structured bindings.

We depict a block structured symbol table using columns for the object's type, block identifier, name, and binding. The symbol table entry for each name is a stack of types and bindings. These are pushed onto and popped off of the symbol stacks at the beginning and end of translation of the relevant program block.

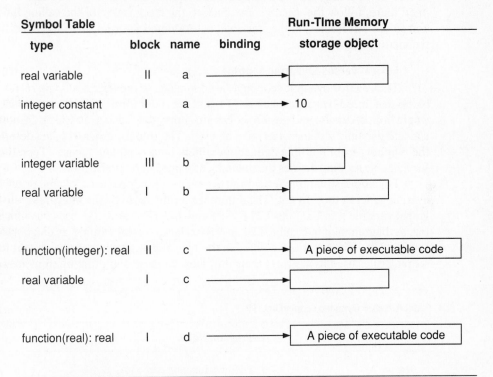

Symbol Table				**Run-Time Memory**
type	block	name	binding	storage object
real variable	II	a	⟶	▢
integer constant	I	a	⟶	10
integer variable	III	b	⟶	▢
real variable	I	b	⟶	▢
function(integer): real	II	c	⟶	A piece of executable code
real variable	I	c	⟶	▢
function(real): real	I	d	⟶	A piece of executable code

sion permits creation of an unlimited number of stack-allocated objects at run time. On each invocation of a recursive function, new storage is allocated, in a new stack frame, for parameters and local variables. This new storage is bound to the parameter and local names and remains bound to them until control exits from the subprogram. We say that each stack frame corresponds to one *dynamic scope*.

Thus each name declared in a recursive function must be bound simultaneously to several objects in different dynamic scopes. If a subprogram has called itself five times and not yet returned once, there are six sets of storage objects simultaneously bound to the local names (one for the original call and one for each of the five recursive calls).

Recursively bound names are ambiguous, and this ambiguity is not like the static ambiguity introduced by block structure. In a block structured program, a name may be simultaneously within the scope of several definitions [Exhibit 7.18]. But we are able to identify and resolve the resulting ambiguity at *compile time* by identifying the lexical scope of each name and forming a unique complete name from the block identifier and object identifier.

This method for disambiguation will not work for the dynamic, run-time ambiguity caused by recursion, because the recursive invocations all come from the same lexical block. A single symbol declaration, such as the declaration for jj or kk in Exhibit 6.18, produces more than one allocation and binding. The disambiguation rule that applies here is the rule for *dynamic scoping*: the *most recent* active binding is used. To find that binding, start searching in the current stack frame. If the name is not defined there, follow the *dynamic link* back to the stack frame of the calling function, and so on. All frames on the stack will be examined in order, until the definition of the identifier is found.

Lexical versus Dynamic Scoping.

The rule for dynamic scoping is used in place of the lexical scoping rule in non-block-structured languages such as APL and the older forms of LISP. In any language where both recursion and nested scopes are supported (such as Pascal or C), both lexical and dynamic scoping rules must be used. The rule for lexical scoping determines the mapping from multiply defined identifiers onto complete names. Then the rule for dynamic scoping defines the meaning of names in recursive scopes.

For simple situations, lexical and dynamic scoping produce the same result. However, in general, they do not. The difference is illustrated by the interpretation of the global variable x in Exhibits 7.23 (LISP) and 7.25 (Pascal). LISP uses dynamic scoping, as diagrammed in Exhibit 7.24, and Pascal uses lexical scoping, as diagrammed in Exhibit 7.26. The functions defined in the two languages are identical except for the scoping rules used to interpret them, but they compute and print different answers.

Exhibit 7.23. Dynamic scoping in LISP.

	Program Notes
`(defun A`	Define a function named A,
`    (x y)`	with two parameters, x and y.
`    (printc (C y)))`	The function prints the result of calling a function
	named C on the parameter y.
`(defun B`	Define a function named B,
`    (d)`	with one parameter, d.
`    (+ d x))`	The function returns the result of adding d and x. Since
	x is not defined locally, it is a global reference .
`(defun C`	Define a function named C,
`    (d)`	with one parameter, d.
`    (let (x '5.1))`	Set local variable x to value 5.1.
`    (+ x (B (+ d 1))))`	Return the result of adding x to the result
	of executing function B
	on the parameter d incremented by 1.
`(A 3 0)`	Call function A with parameters 3 and 0. It will
	print the number 11.2.

Exhibit 7.24.   Diagram of bindings in dynamic scoping.

Stack frames (with dynamic links) are shown for the stage of execution at which all the functions in Exhibit 7.23 have been called and none has returned. The name x is used but not defined in function B, so its meaning is determined by following the dynamic links backward until the definition of x in function C is encountered.

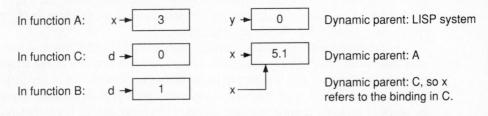

Exhibit 7.25.   Lexically scoped functions in Pascal.

```
PROGRAM a;
VAR x, y: integer;
FUNCTION b(d: integer):integer;
BEGIN b:= x+d END;
FUNCTION c(d: integer):real;
VAR x: real;
BEGIN x:= 5.1; c:= x + b(d+1) END;
BEGIN x:= 3; y:= 0; writeln(c(y)) END.
```

We define a main program, named a, and two functions, b and c. The program is the lexical parent of both functions. When this is executed, a calls c which calls b. The number 9.1 will be printed.

Exhibit 7.26.   Lexical scoping in Pascal.

At one point during execution, the main program has called function c which has called function b, so stack frames for all three coexist. Program a is the dynamic parent of c, which is the dynamic parent of b.

Pascal is a lexically scoped language, so one follows the static link from the current stack frame to find the meaning of nonlocal names. The x referred to in function b is not the object in c's frame, but the one in a's frame, because a is the lexical parent.

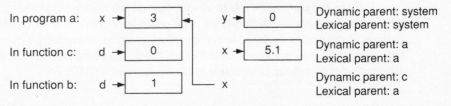

7.4.4   *Visibility versus Lifetime.*

The scope of a name is not necessarily the same as the lifetime of the object to which it is bound. This mismatch of scope and lifetime can happen in several ways. The most familiar is by using a reference (VAR) parameter in a subroutine call. During the procedure call the dummy parameter name is bound to an actual parameter. Storage for a calling block has a longer lifetime than the called block, since the called block will exit first. Thus, within the procedure, the parameter name refers to an object with permanence greater than the scope of the name.

In languages with dynamic allocation, such as Pascal and C, list and tree structures can be built out of heap-allocated objects. As each new cell of the structure is allocated, a reference to it is stored in its predecessor. A reference to the first cell of the structure must be stored in a named, stack-allocated, pointer variable. Frequently the scope of these pointers is less than global, while heap storage is permanent. Thus the head-pointer points at an object that could live longer than itself and could be passed outward by copying its reference into a pointer with a longer lifetime.

Nonhierarchical Sharing.

A serious shortcoming of lexical scoping is its strict hierarchical nature: names defined within a block cannot be exported and made known outside the block. In a language that is limited to hierarchical scoping, there are useful protection and sharing mechanisms that cannot be defined or emulated. Examples of such data facilities are "named common" storage in FORTRAN and "packages" in Ada. Such facilities can be superimposed on lexical scoping only by expanding a language's semantic basis to include more than one kind of scoping.

An Ada package has two classes of names, some which are known outside the scope of the package, some known only within the package.[10]

In FORTRAN, access to a storage object may be shared by several subroutines. To do this you place the object's name in a COMMON statement and include identical COMMON declarations in all subroutines that need access to the object. The user can create and name several independent COMMON areas. These named COMMON areas can be used to set up a nonhierarchical sharing structure [Exhibit 7.27]. This sharing structure cannot be built in a strictly block structured language, since block structure and lexical scoping either permit no sharing of data at all, or indiscriminate sharing among all subroutines at the same level.

A COMMON area does not "belong" to any single subroutine, but is allocated in the program environment area where it can be accessed by any subroutine containing the right declaration. The declaration for a COMMON statement supplies names (with associated types) which will be bound to successive locations in the common area.

It is the programmer's job to ensure that all subroutines that share a common area contain compatible declarations. The compiler will not check that. If the order or types of the names declared in two subroutines differ, everything will compile and link, but compute nonsense. On the other hand, the particular names declared in different subroutines are completely arbitrary and can be different.

---

[10]See Chapter 16 where this topic is fully developed.

Exhibit 7.27.   Named common in FORTRAN.

Just the COMMON declarations are given here for three subroutines that share storage in a nonhierarchical fashion.

```
SUBROUTINE POINT
COMMON /POINTBLANK/ X, Y(100)
COMMON /CHECKPOINT/ JJ, KK, LL

SUBROUTINE BLANK
COMMON /POINTBLANK/ X, Y(100)
COMMON /BLANKCHECK/ F(5), G

SUBROUTINE CHECK
COMMON /BLANKCHECK/ F(5), G
COMMON /CHECKPOINT/ J, K, L
```

An example of the use of COMMON to achieve nonhierarchical sharing is shown in Exhibit 7.27. There are three common areas, and matching common declarations are included in the pair of subroutines that share each area. Subroutines POINT and BLANK share the storage area named POINTBLANK which contains the variables X and Y. Likewise, subroutines POINT and CHECK share area CHECKPOINT and BLANK and CHECK share BLANKCHECK. The common areas and bindings created by these definitions are diagrammed in Exhibit 7.28. Note that CHECK and POINT call the variables in area CHECKPOINT by different names, but the data types of the components do match.

Static Local Storage.

ALGOL OWN variables and C variables with the "static" storage class are examples of another kind of mismatch between lifetime and scope. These variables are statically allocated and are immortal like global variables, but the scope of the names of these objects is block structured. Each time a block is entered in which a static variable is declared, the variable name becomes known again and refers to the static object, which becomes accessible. The run-time system ensures that the name always refers to the same storage address. At block exit time the name becomes undefined, and outside the block, no name refers to the object. The object is then invisible and remains inaccessible and unchangeable until its block is reentered.[11]

This is an important facility. It permits the value of a variable to be retained between executions of a subprogram and yet protected from external tampering. The need for this is apparent if you consider an output buffering procedure which must remember how full it left the buffer in order to know where to store the next value. The buffer pointer must be retained between calls on the output function, yet it should be "hidden" from all other parts of the program to ensure unhindered operation. The ability to "hide" information is now recognized as a cornerstone of good programming practice.

In a language such as Pascal, which does not support static local objects, the buffer pointer would have to be declared globally (all globals are static). This works,

---

[11] An extended example of the use of static storage in C is given in Chapter 16.

but it increases the scope of the pointer to the entire program and creates the possibility that the value of the pointer can be accidentally changed by some remote and irrelevant section of code.

Exhibit 7.28.   A diagram of common storage in FORTRAN.

This is a storage diagram of the common areas created in Exhibit 7.27. An arrow represents a binding.

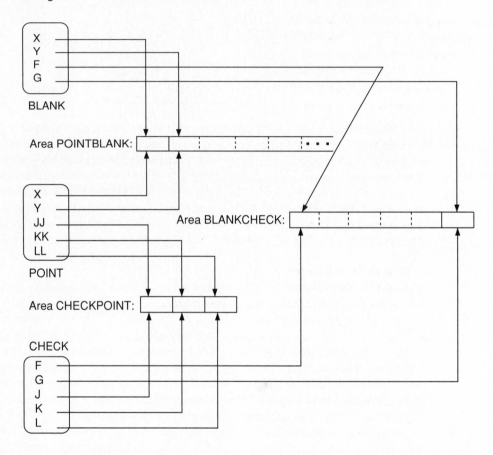

7.5 IMPLICATIONS FOR THE COMPILER / INTERPRETER

A language translator must determine the proper meaning of an ambiguous name according to the semantics defined for that language. We need to make a distinction here between the way interpreters and compilers handle the task.

One of the essential differences between interpreters and compilers stems from the fact that more information is often available at run time than at compile time. An interpreter can query the user about the required amount of data on each run and allocate arrays exactly as long as they are needed. A compiler must allocate storage before actual data values are known, and therefore, perhaps, before actual storage requirements are known. The programmer using a compiler must, therefore, establish array lengths adequate for the maximum size data set the program will ever process. If a program is to process data sets whose size is highly variable, its array lengths will be excessive on most runs, and considerable storage will be allocated that is never used or needed.

Typed languages can be translated by a compiler. Type declarations permit a compiler to anticipate how much storage will be needed in the future to hold program objects. Commands can be compiled to increment and decrement the stack allocation pointer by the appropriate amounts when control enters and leaves program blocks at run time. Typeless languages cannot be compiled in the same sense; the source code can be parsed and symbol tables can be set up, but storage management must be done dynamically because the size of the storage objects that will be needed is not predictable.

In an interpreter, translation and execution proceed at the same time. Dynamic allocation with *dynamic binding* is the natural and easy method to implement. The symbol table exists during execution, and binding of allocation address to symbol is done when the allocation happens. Each symbolic reference is interpreted just before it is executed, in the context of the results of prior computations, and thus the most recent binding of a symbol is used. The path of execution of any program may depend on inputs and conditionals and, therefore, be impossible to predict. Consequently, dynamic binding may bind a name differently from run to run, causing inconsistent interpretations of global references and errors that are hard to track down or identify.

In a compiler, on the other hand, all symbolic names are discarded at the end of compilation, before execution begins (except when a symbolic debugger is in use). All binding of symbolic name to storage location is done within the compiler, even for local variables that become allocated in the middle of execution. For locals, the compiler determines the address, relative to the current stack frame, that they will occupy in the future when they become allocated. Thus, for an ambiguous name, a compiler must maintain a stack of bindings that is parallel to the stack of allocation areas that will exist in the future when the program is executed. A binding is pushed onto the stack at the time the compiler begins to translate a subprogram and is popped off it when the end of the subprogram is compiled. The binding used to interpret a symbolic reference in the program is the one on the top of the stack. This translation scheme implements lexical scoping: the binding used to interpret a name is the one in the smallest enclosing block in which the symbol is defined. Lexical scoping is the *only* method that can be implemented by a compiler. A compiler can determine how definitions are nested, but it cannot guess the order in which they will be executed.

Lexical scoping is considered to be superior for two reasons. First, the binding that will be used is always predictable, and, therefore, programs with lexical scoping are easier to debug. Second, there are languages, for example LISP, for which it is common to write both interpreters and compilers. The interpreter is used while a program is being developed and debugged, then the compiler is used to produce code that executes faster. Since dynamic and lexical scoping produce different semantics, it has often been the case that a program, fully debugged under an interpreter using dynamic scoping, will not work when it is compiled and will have to be debugged again. The scoping discipline affects the meaning of a program and, therefore, *should* be part of a formal definition of any programming language.

Interpreting Block Structure.

Block structure is implemented using stack allocation and block structured binding. The following is a description of the operation of block structure in an interpreted language:

1. Storage objects are allocated on the run-time stack whenever a block is entered. One object is allocated for each locally declared name or parameter. Local variables are usually not initialized. Parameter storage is initialized to the actual parameter values or references to variable parameters.

2. The new storage object is bound to the local name, giving the name an *additional binding*. If the block is a recursive procedure, the name could have bindings created in the enclosing blocks, in which case more than one storage object is bound to the same name, and the meaning of the name is the most recent (dynamic) binding. If control leaves the block and then reenters it, the name will be bound to a different storage object.

3. Local bindings remain static until control leaves the block at *block exit* time. A given name refers to the same storage object from block entry until block exit. At block exit, all local storage objects are deallocated and local identifiers revert to their prior bindings (possibly "undefined"). The freed storage is made available for reuse by "popping" the run-time stack.

The number of storage objects on the stack changes only when blocks are entered or exited, and then only changes by the number of names (locals + parameters) declared in that block.

Compiling Block Structure.

The implementation of block structure in a compiled language is not quite the same as the implementation in an interpreted language. The difference is that the compiler deals with storage that *will be* allocated rather than storage that *is* allocated. The address at which a stack frame will start is completely unpredictable at compile time. However, the number, size, and order of the items in each future stack frame is known to the compiler.

A common frame-management scheme is to have a central "core" in each stack frame that contains everything except parameters and local variables. A calling program puts parameters on the stack and increments the stack pointer (which is kept in a machine register which we will call the *SP*). Then the calling program fills in the static link, dynamic link, and return address in the core area of the stack frame. It puts a pointer to the dynamic link field of the new frame into a machine register. (Let us call this register the *FP*, for frame pointer.) The contents of the new *dynamic link* is the current value of FP. Finally, the program branches to the subroutine.

The subroutine can now find its stack frame because the address is in the FP. It can use the SP to find the top of the stack. The first action of the subroutine is to increment the SP to allocate space for local variables. The subprogram code is compiled to refer to its parameters and local variables *using addresses that are relative to the FP*. The last parameter might be FP − 2, and the first might be FP − 12. The local variables will be in locations such as FP + 4 and FP + 20. Stack locations past the SP are available for use as a scratch pad and will be used for temporary storage during calculations.

At block exit, several things happen:

- The return value, if any, of the subprogram is loaded into a machine register. (It is often called the return register.)
- The dynamic link field is copied back into the FP.
- The SP is decremented by the size of the stack frame.
- A branch is taken to the return address.

This erases all trace of the subprogram.

EXERCISES

1. What is a name? What is the meaning of a name? Do languages follow a one object-one name rule? Explain.
2. Do compilers need names to execute a program? Explain. What is the semantic aspect of a name? Why is this important for human interpretation of a program?
3. What is the role of the symbol table? How are new names added to it?
4. In APL, why are names typeless?
5. What are primitive symbols? Why are they necessary?
6. How do names relate to objects in a compiled language? In an interpreted one?
7. What is binding? How is it invoked?
8. What do we call storage that is allocated once at load time and remains until program exit, but whose usage is restricted to one function?
9. Define and contrast static binding, dynamic binding, and block structured binding.
10. In modern functional languages, assignment is not supported, and in APL, it is rarely used. Dynamic binding takes the place of assignment. Explain how this is implemented.
11. In block structured languages, when is a name visible? Invisible?
12. This question and the next seven involve the following skeletal program written in C. How many name scopes are defined in this program skeleton? Draw a box around each block and label these blocks with the letters A, B, C, etc.

```
int x, y, z;
fun1()
{   int j, k, l;
    {   int m, n, x;
        . . .
    }
}

fun3()
{   int y, z, k;
    . . .
}
main()
{ . . . }
```

13. Name a block that is nested within another block.
14. In which scopes are the global variables x, y, and z all accessible?
15. What variables are accessible to the main function?
16. Are k in fun1 and k in fun3 the same variable? Why or why not?
17. Are the global variables y and z accessible in fun3? Why or why not?
18. In which blocks does j refer to a global variable? In which blocks is j a local variable?
19. In which block or blocks can we use both m and k?
20. Name a language in which storage can be shared by two functions, neither of which is enclosed within the other, but kept private from all other functions and from the main program. Explain how to accomplish this goal in your language.
21. How are FORTRAN's "named common storage" and Ada's "packages" examples of non-hierarchical data facilities?
22. What is the function of a constant declaration? Why is it useful to the programmer?
23. What is the difference between defining a true constant whose meaning is a constant expression and using a macro to define a symbolic name for that expression?
24. How are constants implemented in these languages: Pascal, Ada, FORTRAN, FORTH?
25. What is a naming conflict?
26. How did the concept of scope and modularity resolve the problem of naming conflicts? What is the difference between an identifier and a complete name?
27. What is a block structure? What are nested blocks? What is the scope of the complete name of identifiers declared within a block?
28. Consider a language in which all variables must be declared with fully specific types. Is this language more likely to be interpreted or compiled? Why?
29. Why is the scope of a name not equal to its lifetime? Explain.
30. Explain how the compiler and interpreter each determine the semantics of an ambiguous name.

8

Expressions and Evaluation

Overview

This chapter introduces the concept of the programming environment and the role of expressions in a program. Programs are executed in an environment which is provided by the operating system or the translator. An editor, linker, file system, and compiler form the environment in which the programmer can enter and run programs. Interactive language systems, such as APL, FORTH, Prolog, and Smalltalk among others, are embedded in subsystems which replace the operating system in forming the program-development environment. The top-level control structure for these subsystems is the Read-Evaluate-Write cycle.

The order of computation within a program is controlled in one of three basic ways: nesting, sequencing, or signaling other processes through the shared environment or streams which are managed by the operating system.

Within a program, an expression is a nest of function calls or operators that returns a value. Binary operators written between their arguments are used in infix syntax. Unary and binary operators written before a single argument or a pair of arguments are used in prefix syntax. In postfix syntax, operators (unary or binary) follow their arguments. Parse trees can be developed from expressions that include infix, prefix, and postfix operators. Rules for precedence, associativity, and parenthesization determine which operands belong to which operators.

The rules that define order of evaluation for elements of a function call are as follows:

- Inside-out: Evaluate every argument before beginning to evaluate the function.
- Outside-in: Start evaluating the function body. When (and if) a parameter is used in the body, evaluate the corresponding argument. There are two variants, as follows:

1. **Call-by-name:** An argument expression is evaluated each time the corresponding parameter is used. This is inefficient and may result in different values for the argument at different times.

2. **Call-by-need:** An argument expression is evaluated the first time its parameter is used, and the result is stored for future use.

Inside-out evaluation has been used for most block structured languages; outside-in has recently been efficiently implemented, in the form of call-by-need, for functional languages. Some languages, however, use a mixture of strategies. Call-by-value-and-return is used in order to facilitate concurrent, multitasked operations.

8.1 THE PROGRAMMING ENVIRONMENT

Each program module is executed in some environment. In these days that environment is rarely the bare machine; almost all machines run under an operating system (OS). The OS forms an interface between the hardware, the user, and the user's program, and it creates the environment in which the user's program runs.

Compiled Language Systems

When working with a compiler, a programmer either works in the environment provided by the OS or uses a *development shell*, often provided with the translator, to tailor the OS environment to current needs. An editor, linker, file system, and the compiler itself are included in this environment. Together they enable the programmer to enter, compile, and link/load programs. The programmer can give OS commands to execute his or her own program or others, and when execution is done, control returns to the OS or to the shell.

If the OS supports multitasking (making it an M-OS) there may be other programs, or tasks, in this context, and the M-OS will mediate between them. It supervises messages, controls signals, and manages shared memory. A task might run indefinitely, putting itself to sleep when it needs information from another task and waking up in response to an interrupt generated when that other task supplies the information.

Interactive Language Systems

The category of interactive languages includes APL, FORTH, the functional languages, Prolog, Smalltalk, and many others. These languages are embedded in subsystems that take the place of the OS in forming the user's program development environment. Many of these contain independent file systems and editors, and a separate interactive control cycle.

Access to the enclosing OS is almost always restricted. For example, just one language is generally supported, with no possibility of interaction with subprograms written in a different language. Also, even if the OS supports multitasking, the language subsystem may not give access to it. It also may not support use of an outside text editor and may restrict file system access, allowing fewer kinds of operations than the OS.

These language subsystems implement a top-level control structure known as the *Read-Evaluate-Write (REW) cycle*. When the programmer enters this environment she or he sees a prompt on the terminal and the interpreter is in control, waiting for programmer input. The programmer enters expressions which the interpreter reads and evaluates. It then writes the value of the expression, if any, and a prompt on the user's terminal. The user initiates all actual execution.

Three kinds of items are entered to form a complete program: (1) definitions of objects (name-value pairs), (2) definitions of functions, with parameter names, and (3) expressions or function calls with actual arguments. Items of type (1) are handled by the interpreter. Names are entered, with their value bindings, into the program environment.

For items of type (2), the interpreter will call a *half-compiler*, which reads the expression, lexes it, parses it, and converts it to an internal form which represents the semantics of the expression in a form that is convenient for later evaluation. This form might be a computation tree or a linear list of actions in postfix order. (A full compiler would also generate native machine code.)

For items of type (3), the interpreter evaluates the expression and leaves the result on the stack. During execution, this expression may call functions that are defined in its program environment. After returning from the top-level call, the value left on the stack is generally printed out by the REW cycle for inspection by the programmer.

8.2 SEQUENCE CONTROL AND COMMUNICATION

A program specifies a set of actions that must be done with a set of representations of objects. In some cases the order of these actions is not important, but generally order matters, particularly when interaction with the outside environment (user or file system) is involved. The words the programmer writes in the program to invoke this ordered series of actions must be arranged in a way that specifies this order, or the programmer might specify that the order is not important. In any case, the connection between the way the programmer writes things and the order of resulting outputs must generally be predictable, easy to control, and stable.

Three basic ways have been developed for specifying the order in which computation will happen:

- Nesting of expressions, lexically or symbolically.
- Sequencing of statements and procedure calls.
- Signaling to other tasks.

8.2.1 Nesting

Individual symbols are the lowest-level construct in any programming language. These are formed into expressions (see Section 8.3) which are contained in larger expressions and, in the end, organized into some larger unit. In some languages these units are statements, written in sequence. In others they are function definitions, written sequentially or in nested form.

Lexical Nesting by Parenthesization

Each function call is a function name with expressions as arguments, which might themselves be function calls. When a call does contain another function call, we say that it is a *nested expression*.

A nested expression can be evaluated using only a stack for intermediate results, and without use of assignment or nonstack variables.[1] Here we consider in detail how the stack works. Before a function call can be evaluated, its argument expressions must be evaluated. Evaluation of arguments thus proceeds inward through the nest of function calls, until there are no more enclosed expressions. As each argument expression is evaluated, its value is left at the top of the stack. When all arguments for a function call have been evaluated, the function can be called. The values on the stack will be bound to parameter names within the function. The function will run, compute an answer, and leave it on the stack for later use by an enclosing expression.

Parameter binding enables communication of information in and out through the hierarchical nest of function calls. During execution, the position on the stack where an expression's results will be stored corresponds directly to the position in which the programmer wrote the subexpression in the program, and to the position in the program of the expression that will use the results.

Symbolic Nesting by Declaration

A function call with function calls in its parameter list, which, in turn, have embedded function calls can become quite incomprehensible. This is so even if indentation and spacing are used to clarify the structure of the whole unit.

Declarations are used (among other reasons) to reduce the apparent nesting depth of expressions. A local variable declaration permits the programmer to define a name for the result of a subexpression. A subroutine declaration permits one to isolate and name some part of the program code. These defined names can then be used to build routines with a lower apparent degree of nesting, which are easier for a human to cope with than a deeply nested program. Modularizing a program by defining local names and short functions helps a programmer create a correct program more easily.

Programs in functional languages tend to be highly modular because of this. Since parameter binding, not assignment, is used to give names to computed values, a new function must be defined whenever the programmer wishes to name an intermediate result. Further, when a nested expression has many nesting levels, humans tend to become confused about the meaning of the code. Subroutines are used to minimize the depth of nesting in a single program unit.

8.2.2   Sequences of Statements

A *statement* is an expression that leaves no return value on the stack and thus cannot be used as the argument to a function. Statements are executed for their *side effects*, not for their return values. Side effects include changing the value in a storage object and changing the status of anything in the program environment, the shared environment,

---

[1]All the familiar older languages use a stack. Some of the modern functional languages use a more complex data structure that avoids evaluating arguments that are not actually used in the function code.

or the streams. To be useful, a statement must use one of these channels to affect the world, since it does not change the program stack. Either it must alter program memory or produce input/output activity.

A *procedural language* is one in which a program is a sequence of statements. Procedural languages commonly contain statement forms to do the following tasks:

- **Assignment statement:** Changes the value of a variable.
- **Binding statement:** Enters a named value into the symbol table.
- **Procedure call:** A call on a user-defined function that returns no result.
- **Input statement:** Changes the values of some variables.
- **Output statement:** Changes the state of the external world.
- **Control statement:** A compound of other statements which implements a loop or conditional structure.

Procedural and functional languages both contain expressions. Within an expression, one function communicates its result directly to the enclosing function without using the program environment. This is done by taking arguments from the program stack and leaving results on it.

In *functional languages*, the expression is the outermost control structure, and the stack is the only form of communication between the parts of a program. Modern functional languages do not support data objects in the program environment. In contrast, in *procedural languages* (ALGOL, FORTRAN, Pascal, APL, etc.) all expressions eventually become part of some statement, and a program body is a series of statements, written top to bottom in the order they are to be executed. Communication between one statement and another can go through variables in the program environment; each statement finds its inputs in a set of variables and leaves its results in variables for possible later use [Exhibit 4.9].

8.2.3   Interprocess Sequence Control

When all computers had small memories and single, slow processors, it was adequate to design languages for writing independent programs. Such a program would follow one control path during execution, which was independent of all other programs. Its memory was its own, and it could interact with the world only through input and output. But as multiprocessor systems and networks have become common, we have had to expand our area of consideration from a single, isolated program (or *process* or *task*) to a group of asynchronous processes that are actively interacting and communicating.

A single process, no matter how large, can communicate through global variables and parameters. If that process were to be compiled in several modules, each module could have external symbols (variables and functions) that would be defined in other modules. In this case, the linking loader would connect each external reference from one module with the definition of that object or function in another module, creating a single, connected unit that could communicate through variables and subroutine calls.

Communication for two separate interacting processes is quite different. No compiler or linking loader links up external references in one process to symbols defined in the other. In a modern system, one process may not know the location of another process with which it is interacting. All communication must take place through the operating system or systems which host the two processes, or through the file system. In terms of our formal model, communication must be through the shared environment or through streams, and both of these areas of storage are managed by the OS. The specific kind of communication possible depends on the operating system host.

One common mechanism is message passing. A message is a string of bytes that is written into an OS buffer and either broadcast to all processes or addressed to one particular process whose process-ID is known to the sender. To send a message, a program calls the operating system's message sending routine. To receive a message, a process makes a corresponding call to the operating system, signaling that it is ready to process a message either from anyone or from a particular sender. The message is then copied into a buffer belonging to the receiver.

Another common communication mechanism is the semaphore. This is a storage location in protected OS memory, accessible to a program only through system calls. Semaphores come in many varieties, but they basically function as pigeonholes that contain one of two signals meaning either "wait until I'm ready" or "go ahead". These are commonly used to control and synchronize access to files and buffers that are shared among interacting processes.

8.3 EXPRESSION SYNTAX

An expression is a nest of function calls (or operators, in some languages) that returns a value. The syntax for writing an expression varies among languages. Exhibit 8.1 shows examples of function calls drawn from several languages which illustrate the various kinds of syntax in common use. In all cases, the action represented is adding one to an integer, A, and returning the result.

Exhibit 8.1. Syntax for expressions.

Lambda calculus
    An application   (S A)   – Compute the successor of A.
LISP
    An expression   (+ A 1) – Add the value of A and 1.
    An expression   (1+ A)   – Add 1 to the value of A.
Pascal
    A function call   succ(A) – Compute the successor of A.
    Use of an operator   A + 1   – Add the value of A and 1.
APL
    An expression   A + 1   – Add the value of A and 1.
    (APL has no other syntax for function calls.)

8.3.1 Functional Expression Syntax

In the most basic syntax, one writes an expression by writing a function name, with its actual arguments, enclosed in parentheses. In lambda calculus and in LISP the function name is *inside* the left paren [Exhibit 8.1]; in most languages it is *outside* the left paren. We will call the first variant *lambda calculus function-call syntax* and the latter variant *normal function-call syntax*.

In modern languages, an actual argument is an expression. It is evaluated, in the context of the calling program, either before control is transferred to the function or during evaluation of the function. The value of each argument expression is used to initialize the corresponding formal parameter.

There are two ways that the correspondence between arguments and parameters can be specified: positionally or by keyword. With positional notation, which is supported in virtually every language, the first argument value initializes the first parameter name, the second argument corresponds to the second name, and so on. To call a function positionally one must know the number and order of the parameters, and know the type and semantics of each, but not its declared name.

A few languages support a second parameter correspondence mechanism, sometimes called *correspondence-by-keyword*, or *named parameter association*. To use named association, the argument expression in the function call is preceded by the dummy parameter name as defined in the procedure definition. This mechanism has the advantage that the arguments in a call may be written in any order, and it is useful for implementing functions with optional arguments (Section 9.1.1). It is syntactically more complex, though, than positional correspondence, and more complex to implement. Further, the parameter names, which are otherwise arbitrary and local to the function, must be made known to all users.

Some confusion of terminology has developed among different programming languages. In LISP "+" is called a "function" and is written with lambda calculus function-call syntax. In Pascal it is called an "operator" and written with *infix operator syntax*; that is, each operator is written between its operands. In APL "+" is called a "function" but written in infix operator syntax.

Operators are just a syntactic variant of functions; the underlying semantics are the same. Both denote an action which, when applied to some objects (the arguments), will produce another object (the function result). Some languages include only the function-call syntax; some include only the operator syntax; some include both. There are two minor differences between operators and functions. First, functions may have any number of arguments, while operators are almost universally limited to one or two. Second, in languages that include both functions and operators, it is generally not possible to define new operators; all newly defined verbs are functions.

8.3.2   *Operator Expressions*

An operator with two arguments is called *binary* or *dyadic*. It is generally called using infix operator syntax; that is, the operator is written between its arguments. A single-argument operator, known as *unary* or *monadic*, is generally called using *prefix syntax*; that is, the operator is written before its argument. Some languages also have monadic postfix operators, which are written after the operand. C has a diverse collection and even has one two-part operator with three operands!

Any expression specifies a *computation tree*, which is the *meaning* of the source expression. The task of a compiler (specifically, the parsing phase of a compiler) is to take the source syntax of an expression and produce the computation tree, or *parse tree*, that it denotes.

For normal function-call syntax, producing a parse tree is an easy task. Each function call corresponds to a node in the tree, and each argument corresponds to a child of that node. If some argument position contains a nested function call, then that child is itself a node with children [Exhibit 8.2].

Developing a parse tree from an expression that includes a combination of infix, prefix, and postfix operators is much more complex. Two sets of rules (the rules for precedence and the rules for associativity), plus explicit parenthesization, determine which operand belongs to which operator.

Exhibit 8.2.   Nested function calls and parenthesized infix expressions.

An expression written in LISP, using functional notation, and in Pascal, using fully parenthesized infix notation. Both denote the same computation tree.

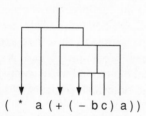

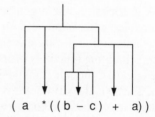

(* a (+ (– b c) a))   (a * ((b – c) + a))

LISP: a nested expression.   Pascal: fully parenthesized infix notation.

Parenthesization

Languages that have infix operators permit the programmer to use explicit parentheses to surround an operator and its one or two operands. Like an expression written using nested function calls, a fully parenthesized infix expression explicitly and unambiguously specifies which operands belong to each operator. Exhibit 8.2 shows the parse trees derived from a LISP expression that is a nest of function calls, and the analogous Pascal expression, written with operators. The trees are identical except for the order of the operator and the first operand.

Postfix and Prefix:
Unambiguous Unparenthesized Expression Syntax

The parentheses in LISP, or in a fully parenthesized infix expression, group each function or operator with its operands. This permits one to draw a parse tree with no further information and no knowledge of the meaning of the operator. In a language where each operator has a fixed number of operands, these parentheses are nice but not necessary. They guide the eye and the parser, and permit us to check whether each operator has been written with the correct number of operands. There are other ways, however, to indicate which operands belong to which operator.

We can actually eliminate the parentheses if we are willing to restrict each operator to exactly one meaning and require that its number of operands be fixed. (This eliminates the possibility of an ambiguous operator, such as "−" in FORTRAN, which exists in both unary and binary forms.)

With this restriction, there are two forms for expressions, called *prefix order* and *postfix order*, that unambiguously specify the computation tree without the use of parentheses or precedence. In a prefix expression, each operator is written before its operands, like a LISP expression without the parentheses [Exhibit 8.3].

Exhibit 8.3.   Unambiguous ways to write an arithmetic expression.

This is how the expression (a * ((b − c) + a)) would be written in prefix and postfix notations.

    Prefix: * a + − b c a   This is like LISP, but without parentheses. The scope of each operator is the two operands or subexpressions following it.

    Postfix: a b c − a + *   This is used in FORTH. The scope of each operator is the two operands or subexpressions preceding it.

In *postfix order*,[2] an operator is written after its operands. The FORTH language and Postscript[3] use postfix notation exclusively. This order corresponds to the actual order of machine instructions needed to compute the value of an expression using a stack machine. The evaluation process is illustrated in Exhibit 8.4, and works like this:

- Evaluate the expression left-to-right.
- As each symbol is encountered, put its current value on the stack.
- For each operator, take two values off the stack and execute the operation. Put the result back on the stack.

Exhibit 8.4.   Evaluation of a postfix expression using a stack.

We evaluate the expression a b c − a + *   from Exhibit 8.3. Assume the stack is initially empty and the names a, b, and c are bound to constant values: a = 5, b = 4, c = 7.

Evaluation Step	Stack Contents (top is at right)
a	5
b	5, 4
c	5, 4, 7
−	5, −3
a	5, −3, 5
+	5, 2
*	10

One might ask why LISP uses both prefix order and parentheses if prefix order is unambiguous without the parentheses. The parentheses in LISP permit its functions

---

[2] Also known as reverse Polish notation.
[3] A language for controlling graphic output devices. Adobe Systems [1985].

and operators to take a varying number of operands [Exhibit 8.5, line 6]. Several
primitive LISP functions can have variable-length argument lists, including one at the
core of the language. The LISP conditional expression, COND, is a variable-argument
function.

Exhibit 8.5.   Bracketing used to permit variable-argument expressions.

Seven forms are given of an expression which sums four items. In the first four forms the + operator must be written three times, because it is "built into" these languages that the + operator
takes two operands.

Forms 5 and 6 show an analogous expression written in LISP. Form 5 has two operands
for each +, but version 6 takes advantage of the fact that + can accept a variable number of
arguments.

Form 7 is a statement, not a function: it modifies the value of C rather than returning a
value. Note that it uses the reserved words ADD and TO, rather than parentheses, to bracket the
variable-length list.

1. Fully parenthesized infix:	(((a + b) + 3) + c)	Pascal or C
2. Infix without parentheses:	a + b + 3 + c	Pascal or C
3. Postfix notation:	a b + 3 + c +	FORTH
4. Prefix notation:	+ + + a b 3 c	
5. Use of + in binary form:	(+ (+ (+ a b) 3) c)	LISP
6. Multiple arguments for +:	(+ a b 3 c)	LISP
7. A statement that modifies C:	ADD A B 3 TO C.	COBOL

Note the similarity between form 4, prefix notation, and form 5, written in LISP.
If functions in LISP were restricted to a fixed number of parameters, the parentheses
would not be necessary. But LISP has variable-argument functions, including +. In
form 6, the expression is rewritten using the variable-argument form of +, and parentheses are used to delimit the scope of the +. It can be cogently argued that this is the
clearest way to write this expression.

Form 6, in LISP, strongly resembles form 7, in COBOL, which adds a variable
number of items to the last item. Reserved words are used in COBOL instead of parentheses to bracket the variable-length parameter list, but the principle is the same; it
is possible to parse a language that has variable-length parameter lists as long as the
lists are bracketed somehow.

Precedence

The early computer languages FORTRAN and ALGOL-60 were designed for use by scientists and engineers who were accustomed to traditional mathematical notation for
expressions.[4] Engineers wanted a "natural" way to write formulas in their programs;
that is, they wanted the formulas in their computer programs to look as much as possible like formulas on paper. Engineers and mathematicians have never considered full
parenthesization, prefix order, or postfix order to be "natural" ways to express a for-

---

[4]This is evident from their names. FORTRAN was derived from FORmula TRANslator, and AL-
GOL from ALGOrithmic Language.

mula. The familiar way of writing expressions using operator precedence was used in FORTRAN and ALGOL-60 because it had been in use in mathematics for many years. Since then precedence expressions have been implemented in all their descendents.

Without parentheses or additional parsing rules, infix notation is ambiguous. The symbols written on the page do not indicate which operands belong with each operator. Consider the expression in Exhibit 8.6, where *op*1 and *op*2 are two unspecified binary operators. Two parses of this expression are possible and correspond to the two trees shown. The rule of operator precedence was adopted from mathematics to disambiguate the nonparenthesized parts of infix expressions. The precedence rule determines which parse is correct, and thus whether the scope of *op*2 includes the result of *op*1 or vice versa.

Exhibit 8.6.   Infix notation is ambiguous without precedence.

Source expression: A *op*1 B *op*2 C
  Possible parse trees:

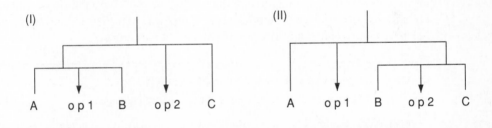

In a precedence language, each operator is assigned a precedence level. These levels can be arbitrary integers; only their order matters. The standard precedence rule can now be stated:

- If $prec_{op1} > prec_{op2}$ then the meaning is parse tree I.
- Else if $prec_{op1} < prec_{op2}$ then the meaning is parse tree II.
- Else $prec_{op1} = prec_{op2}$. Use the rule of associativity to determine which parse is correct.

Associativity

Associativity is used as a tie-breaking rule in languages with precedence. It is also used in APL as the only added parsing rule to disambiguate infix expressions. Associativity governs the choice of parse trees when there are consecutive binary operators with equal precedence. Associated with each precedence class is an associativity direction, either left-to-right or right-to-left. All operators with the same precedence must have the same associativity. This direction is used as follows:

- If the associativity of *op*1 and *op*2 is left-to-right then the meaning of the expression is parse tree I.
- Else (the associativity of *op*1 and *op*2 is right-to-left) the meaning of the expression is parse tree II.

The associativity of each operator is determined by the language designer and is usually chosen to seem natural to mathematicians. For example, in C, the associativity of – (subtraction) is left-to-right, but the associativity of = (assignment) is right-to-left. The programmer can write: X= Y= Z-1-X to compute the value ((Z-1)-X) and store the answer in both Y and X.

In APL there were so many operators that the language designer evidently felt that establishing precedence classes for them would cause more confusion than help. Therefore, although APL functions are written with infix notation, only an associativity rule, right-to-left, is used for disambiguation.

8.3.3   Combinations of Parsing Rules

Existing languages use varying combinations of rules to define the meaning of an expression. Very different effects can be achieved by combining these few simple rules, as illustrated by Exhibits 8.7, 8.8, and 8.9. Exhibit 8.7 gives brief summaries of the parsing rules in some of the languages previously mentioned. Exhibit 8.8 shows how the arithmetic expression $((b*c)/((a+1)*(b-2)))$ would be written in each language using as few parentheses as possible. Exhibit 8.9 shows the computation tree into which all of these expressions will be translated. Note the similarities and contrasts in these languages, especially the contrast in placement of parentheses.

Exhibit 8.7.   Varying rules for parsing expressions.

Summaries of the parsing rules are given below for several languages.

- FORTH: postfix notation, no precedence, no associativity, no parentheses. Operators are executed left-to-right. Parameter lists are not delimited at all.
- APL: infix notation for all functions, no precedence, right-to-left associativity. Parentheses may be used to override associativity.
- Pascal: infix notation for operators, with precedence and left-to-right associativity. Parentheses may be used to override precedence or associativity.
- C: infix, prefix, and postfix operators, with precedence. Left-to-right or right-to-left associativity, depending on the operator. Parentheses may be used to override precedence or associativity.

Exhibit 8.8.   Varying syntax for the use of operators.

Each expression below illustrates the rules summarized in Exhibit 8.7 and will translate into the computation tree in Exhibit 8.9. A, B, and C are integer variables.

- FORTH: B @ C @ * A @ 1 + B @ 2 - * /

  Note: A variable name in FORTH is interpreted to mean the address of the variable. The symbol @ must be used explicitly to fetch the value from that address.
- APL: $(B \times C) \div (A + 1) \times B - 2$
- Pascal: B * C / ((A + 1) * (B - 2))

  Relevant precedence values, with highest precedence listed first: (*, /) > (+, -).

Exhibit 8.9.   A computation tree.

This tree represents the computation $((b * c)/((a + 1) * (b - 2)))$. Each leaf represents the value of an integer variable, and each interior node represents an operation to be applied to the values returned by its children. The expressions in Exhibit 8.8 will all translate into this computation tree.

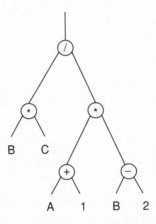

The language syntax, parentheses, precedence, and associativity all help the translator to parse a program and produce a parse tree. After the parse tree is produced, it is interpreted, or code is generated that will later be executed to evaluate the parse tree. It is perhaps surprising, but true, that the same parse tree can have very different meanings in different languages. There are still semantic issues to be resolved *after parsing* that determine the meaning of the expression.

8.4 FUNCTION EVALUATION

A function call (like a lambda calculus application) consists of a literal function or a function name, with formulas representing actual arguments, and an indication that the function is to be applied to those arguments. In many languages, the actual arguments may contain function calls, producing a hierarchy, or nest, of calls. The order and method of evaluation of such a nest depends on the programming language and sometimes also on the compiler writer.

8.4.1   Order of Evaluation

Two very different evaluation rules are in use which govern the order of evaluation of the elements of a function call:

1. *Inside-out evaluation:* Evaluate every actual argument before beginning to evaluate the function itself. In a given language, arguments might be evaluated left-to-right, right-to-left, or in an order determined by the compiler writer.

2. *Outside-in evaluation:* Start evaluating the function call first. The first time the value of an argument is needed, evaluate that argument and remember the answer in case that argument is used again.

Rule (1) has been used for LISP, Pascal, ALGOL-60, C, and most other languages designed since block structure was developed for ALGOL-60. Implementations of these languages are based on the use of a stack to store arguments and local variables.

Recently, efficient implementation methods for rule (2) have been developed, leading to a new class of languages called "functional languages" (Miranda, Haskell, etc.). Let us examine the relationship between evaluation order, stacks, and block structure.

The *substitution rule* of lambda calculus says that if an expression, E, contains a nonprimitive symbol, S, the meaning of the E is the same as if each occurrence of the symbol S were replaced by its definition. This rule applies in the following two situations:

- S is a symbol whose meaning is defined by the user in a declaration.
- S is a parameter of E, and S is given a meaning by applying E to a list of arguments. (The meaning of S is the expression that forms the argument corresponding to S.)

This seems to be an obvious definition and clearly something that should be part of the implementation of any programming language. But implementing it directly causes some trouble for two reasons. Let Exp be the meaning of S. Exp may contain *unbound* symbols, that is, symbols whose meaning is not defined within Exp. We say there is a *name conflict* if one of these unbound symbols also occurs in E. If we simply substitute Exp for S in E, these unbound symbols will be *captured* and given spurious meanings by bindings declared in E. Thus symbols involved in name conflicts must be renamed. The substitution rule is stated formally in Exhibit 8.10.

Exhibit 8.10. The substitution rule.

The "substitution rule" of lambda calculus defines the semantics of arguments. It is stated here using the familiar terms "function", "argument", and "parameter" instead of the usual lambda calculus terminology.

- Let P be a parameter for function F.
- Let Exp, an expression, be the corresponding actual argument.
- Declarations in F must not capture unbound variables in Exp. If some variable, V, defined in F has the same name as an unbound symbol in P, rename it with a unique name, say $V2$, and replace all Vs in F by $V2$.
- Now the meaning of $F(Exp)$ is found by replacing every occurrence of P in F by Exp.

The need for renaming complicates the substitution rule. A second problem is presented by recursion. A recursive definition would lead to an infinite number of substitutions if you actually tried to physically substitute the definition of S into the expression E.

At this point we can take a shortcut. To the extent that every copy of S is identical, a single copy is able to emulate multiple copies. Thus we only need to copy the *variable* parts of S. We are thereby led directly to making a distinction between "pure code", which never varies, and "data," which does. Multiple copies of "pure code" may be implemented efficiently by making one copy and accessing it with a "jump to subroutine" instruction. On the other hand, a correct implementation of the substitution rule implies that multiple copies of data and argument values must exist simultaneously.

The oldest computer languages, FORTRAN and COBOL, use only static storage, with one storage location for each variable or parameter. For this reason neither language can support recursion. When ALGOL-60 was first designed no one knew how to implement it efficiently, because an efficient implementation for multiple copies of local variables had not been invented.

Within a few years, however, a significant insight was gained. No matter how many copies of the variables for a function S exist, the real computer has only one processor and, therefore, can be actively using only one copy at a time. All that is necessary to implement the substitution rule efficiently is to make *one* copy (the one needed at the moment) of S's variables conveniently available and bind them to the local names defined in S. When a copy of S is fully evaluated we no longer need its corresponding variables. They can be forgotten, and the names in S can be bound to some other copy. All is well so long as the *correct* copy of the variables always gets bound to the names.

When function evaluation rule (1) is used, the groups of variables are allocated, used, and deallocated in a last-in-first-out manner. The only set of variables needed at the moment are those for the current function. They can be created at the beginning of function execution and forgotten at the end. The stack of our abstract machine is able to perform all the required allocation, binding, and deallocation operations efficiently. But to use a stack like this we must *always evaluate the arguments to a function before evaluating the function*. At first sight this restriction seems to prohibit nothing of importance, and the evaluation order it requires is intuitively appealing. Actually, it is an important and fundamental restriction, as we shall see.

The *evaluation rule of lambda calculus* specifies that the order of evaluation of parts of an expression is undefined, but that parameters must be evaluated if and when they are used (if not earlier). It can be shown that anything that can be computed using this unconstrained evaluation order can also be computed using outside-in order, but some computable things cannot be computed using inside-out order.

The outside-in evaluation rule is: evaluate as much of an expression as possible before using the substitution rule, then replace a symbolic parameter by its definition. This strategy has one very nice property: a parameter that is never used does not ever have to be evaluated. This can happen when the only references to that parameter are in a part of the program that is skipped over by a conditional.

Outside-in evaluation also has one awkward property: the simple stack implementation for parameters won't work. A different parameter evaluation method named *call-by-need* has been developed which produces an efficient implementation of outside-in evaluation. It avoids both the unnecessary evaluation of unused parameters that is inherent in call-by-value, and the repeated evaluation of the same parameter inherent in call-by-name. It is often referred to as *lazy evaluation*, because all unnecessary parameter evaluation is avoided.

In call-by-need evaluation, every function is evaluated until the point that it refers to one of its parameters, *P*. That parameter is then evaluated, and its value is saved. Evaluation then proceeds until the next parameter reference. All future references to *P* in the same function will be interpreted to have this saved value.

A programmer can exploit the lazy nature of this evaluation order by using, as arguments, expressions that are erroneous or nonterminating under some conditions. The programmer must then use these parameters in guarded ways, checking for the dangerous conditions and being sure not to evaluate the argument if they occur. Lazy evaluation can also be used to build a useful kind of data structure called an "infinite" list. These lists have a head section that is like an ordinary list, and a tail that is a function that can be evaluated to produce the next item on the list. Evaluating it *N* times extends the list by *N* elements.

An if..then..else conditional is actually a function of three arguments, but a very special kind of function. The intent and meaning of a conditional is that either the second argument or the third, but never both, is evaluated. Thus, by its very nature, a conditional *must* be evaluated outside-in. All languages use a variant of lazy evaluation for conditional statements and expressions. Thus a programmer can emulate lazy evaluation in any language by using conditionals liberally. Exhibit 12.14 shows the use of if in Pascal to emulate the lazy evaluation built into Miranda.

8.4.2 Lazy or Strict Evaluation

The most important issue concerning order of evaluation is whether an expression will be evaluated outside-in or inside-out. The modern functional languages are the only ones that apply either rule consistently; they use outside-in evaluation order. Other languages use a mixture of strategies, inside-out for most things, but outside-in for conditionals and sometimes also for Boolean expressions.

Ordinary inside-out evaluation is called *strict evaluation*. An evaluator is strict if it evaluates all the arguments to a function before beginning to evaluate a function. Its opposite is *lazy evaluation*. Evaluation is lazy if subexpressions are evaluated only when necessary; if the outcome of an expression does not depend on evaluation of a subexpression, the subexpression is skipped. In modern functional languages, all function calls are interpreted using call-by-need, a kind of lazy evaluation. Each argument expression is evaluated the first time the function body refers to the corresponding parameter. The resulting value is bound to the parameter name and is available for future use. If an argument is not used, it will not be evaluated.

In general, to evaluate an arithmetic expression one must first evaluate all its subexpressions. (For example, to calculate a + b one must first know the values of a and b.) But Boolean expressions are different. Exhibits 8.11 and 8.12 show that it is sometimes possible to know the outcome of a logical AND or OR operation after evaluating only one of its subexpressions. Thus evaluation of the second subexpression can be skipped and execution time can be saved. Some languages, for example, MAD and C, use lazy evaluation for Boolean expressions (also called *short circuit evaluation*) because it is more efficient.

Exhibit 8.11. Lazy evaluation of AND.

Value of L	Value of R	Value of L AND R
T	T	T
T	F	F
F	T	F
F	F	F

We see that if L is FALSE, the value of the expression is always FALSE, and R does not need to be evaluated.

Exhibit 8.12. Lazy evaluation of OR.

Value of L	Value of R	Value of L OR R
T	T	T
T	F	T
F	T	T
F	F	F

We see that if L is TRUE, the value of the expression is always TRUE, and R does not need to be evaluated.

Boolean expressions in many other languages, for example, Pascal, are evaluated inside-out. Thus parts of a program that could, under some circumstances, cause run-time errors must be enclosed inside a control statement (an IF or a WHILE) which checks the error condition and determines whether or not to execute the code.

For example, in Exhibit 8.13, an extra control statement must be used to check for a subscript-out-of-bounds error before executing the subscripted expression. There are two possible reasons for leaving any search loop: either the key item was found, or the array to be searched was exhausted. We would like to test both conditions in the following WHILE statement:

```
WHILE (scan < 101) and (a[scan] <> key) ...
```

But this would cause the program to "bomb" when scan exceeded 100, and a[101] was tested. This happens because Pascal uses inside-out evaluation order, and *both comparisons are made before performing the WHILE test.*

To code this function in Pascal, the two tests must be written separately. An extra Boolean variable is then introduced to effect exit from the loop when the second condition becomes true. We see that the Pascal version requires an extra control statement and makes exit from a simple loop awkward.

Exhibit 8.13. Extra code needed with inside-out evaluation.

```
TYPE array_type = array[0..100] of char;
FUNCTION search (a:array_type, key:char):integer;
VAR done_flag:  boolean;
    scan:  -1 .. 101;              (* An integer in the range -1 to 101.  *)
BEGIN
    done := FALSE;                 (* Flag to control loop exit. *)
    scan := 0;
    WHILE ( scan < 101) and not done DO
        IF a[scan] = key
        THEN done := TRUE          (* Leave loop next time. *)
        ELSE scan := scan + 1;
    IF scan = 101 THEN search := -1 ELSE search := scan;
END
```

Compare this to the parallel form in Exhibit 8.14 written in C. C uses lazy evaluation for Boolean expressions, with arguments evaluated in a left-to-right order. Further evaluation is aborted as soon as the outcome of the expression is determined.

Exhibit 8.14. Simpler control structures with outside-in evaluation.

```
int search (char a[], char key);
{   int scan;
    scan = 0;
    while ( scan < 101 && a[scan] != key ) ++scan;
    if (scan == 101) return -1; else return scan;
}
```

The expression that controls the while statement can, therefore, encompass both the subscript-out-of-range test and the search test. The error condition is tested first. If the subscript is too large, the rest of the expression (including the part that would malfunction) is not evaluated. This greatly simplifies construction of the loop.

8.4.3 Order of Evaluation of Arguments

One final design decision is whether to specify that arguments are evaluated left-to-right or right-to-left, or leave the order unspecified. This makes no difference when inside-out evaluation is used and the subexpressions have no side effects. But when expressions can produce output or modify memory, the order of evaluation can determine the outcome of the program.

In the modern functional languages, this order is unspecified. These languages do not implement destructive assignment, and, therefore, there is no problem with side effects *except* where output is concerned. For these situations, the languages provide a way, called *strict evaluation*, to specify an ordered evaluation of all subexpressions.

In languages such as Pascal where functions and operators cannot have side effects, there is also no problem. All side effects (assignment, input, output) are restricted to statements, whose order is clearly specified. It is impossible to tell whether a Pascal compiler evaluates expressions left-to-right or right-to-left.

Finally, there are languages such as C and APL where expressions can have side effects. Assignment, input, and output are all expressions in these languages. In addition, C has an increment operator. The language definition in these cases must clearly specify what the evaluation order is. APL does specify right-to-left.

In C, though, the decision was left to the language implementor, and both right-to-left and left-to-right evaluation are permitted and considered to conform to the standard. It is, therefore, incumbent upon a C programmer to avoid using any variable in an expression whose value is changed by a preceding or following subexpression with a side effect [Exhibit 8.15]. The result of such an expression is called *indeterminate*; that is, it may vary from compiler to compiler, even on the same hardware.

Exhibit 8.15. Expressions whose values are indeterminate in C.

```
int x, z, a[10];
int throwaway (int b, int c) { return c };
x = 3;    z = x * ++x;          /* z could be 9 or 12. */
x = 3;    z = throwaway(++x, x); /* z could be 3 or 4.  */
x = 3;    a[x] = x++;            /* 3 is stored in either a[3] or a[4].  */
```

EXERCISES

1. What is the programming environment? How is it provided?

2. What is the Read-Evaluate-Write cycle? How is it implemented?

3. What are the three basic methods that specify order of computation?

4. Explain how an expression can be nested.

5. How is a stack used in evaluating a nested expression?

6. What is an expression? How does the role of expressions differ in procedural and functional languages?

7. What is "message passing," and how is it accomplished between two separate interacting processes?

8. Parameters allow program modules to communicate with each other. Name at least three mechanisms or data structures that must be a part of the semantic basis of a language to implement parameter passing for recursive subroutines.

9. Is there a difference between operators and functions? Explain.

10. Define infix, prefix, and postfix operator syntax.

11. What is the role of parentheses in an expression?

12. How do prefix and postfix order for expressions eliminate the need for parentheses?

13. Using a stack, evaluate the following postfix expression. Assume the stack is initially empty and that x=2, y=3, and z=4. Show the contents of the stack after each push or pop.

    x y + z - x z * -

14. Draw a computation tree for the following infix expression:

    ((x/y) * (((3*z) + (2 + y)) +7))

15. Rewrite the expression of question 14 with the minimum number of parentheses, using the precedence rules in C or Pascal.

16. Draw a computation tree for the following prefix expression:

    * / x y + 3 * * z 2 + y 7

17. Explain the two evaluation rules which govern order of evaluation of elements of a function call.

18. What is the difference between call-by-need and call-by-name?

19. What is automatic dereferencing? Give a specific example.

20. In FORTRAN, call-by-reference is the only mechanism for passing parameters. Why is this now considered poor design?

21. When should call-by-reference be used instead of call-by-value? Give two distinct situations.

22. In APL, parameter names are declared but their types are not specified. What is the purpose of the parameter declarations? How can communication work without parameter type specifications?

9

Functions and Parameters

Overview

A function call consists of a name and actual arguments. These correspond to the declared function name and its formal parameters. Functions may be defined with a fixed or variable number of arguments, depending upon the language. Missing or extra parameters are handled by the translator of the particular language.

Arguments are passed to a function by the function call. They are usually matched up with parameter names positionally; the nth argument in the function call becomes the value of the nth parameter name in the function definition. Correspondence-by-keyword is also used. In this method, the dummy parameter name is written next to the argument expression in the function call. This parameter passing mechanism is very useful for functions that expect variable-length argument lists.

After the argument is passed, it is interpreted by the receiving function. In ALGOL-60, parameter interpretation mechanisms were limited to call-by-name and call-by-value. Call-by-reference was used in early FORTRAN. Call-by-need and call-by-pointer have since been devised as methods for passing and interpreting parameters.

A higher-order function is one that takes a function as an argument and/or returns a function as a result. Pure functional languages fully support higher-order functions. Flexible code and mapping are two common applications of functional arguments.

Currying is a way of looking at a function of two or more arguments, so that it is considered to be a higher-order function of one argument that returns a function.

Closure is an operation that binds the free variables of an expression. It creates and returns a function. The most common application of closure is partial parameterization.

9.1 FUNCTION SYNTAX

9.1.1 Fixed versus Variable Argument Functions

Many languages require that a function be defined with a fixed number of parameters of specified types. The required parameters and types for predefined functions are specified in the syntax of the language. The elements required for a control statement are similarly defined by the language syntax.

The parser requires every statement and function call to be well-formed: it counts the arguments, checks their types, and binds them to the defined dummy parameter names. If either the number or the type of arguments is wrong, the program is not well-formed and the translator gives an error comment. If some element is misplaced or missing, the translator cannot, in general, know the intended meaning of the program. For example, if an END statement is missing, it is impossible in many languages for a translator to guess, accurately, where it was supposed to be.

Because the parser rejects programs that are not well-formed, being well-formed can be seen as a syntactic requirement. But the syntax merely reflects semantic requirements: the code that defines the semantics of these statements and functions is not prepared to handle a variable number or type of argument.

A function *uses* a certain number of parameters; that is, it refers to their names. There are several ways in which there might be a mismatch between the number of arguments passed and the number of parameters that are actually used, as follows:

Unused arguments: Parameters might be named and passed but not referred to anywhere in the function. In a procedural language, an unused argument might as well be omitted. In functional languages, however, there are situations in which this is useful. (Consider the lambda calculus functions T and F, which each discard one parameter.)

Optional parameters: A parameter might be named and used, but no corresponding argument passed. This can be meaningful if default values are defined for missing arguments, and the argument-parameter correspondence is unambiguously specified.

Indefinite-length argument lists: Parameters might be passed but not named. These can be useful if some way is supplied by the language for referring to them.

Optional Parameters.

Several modern languages support optional parameters. If the number of actual arguments passed is smaller than the number of parameters called for, some parameters cannot be given a meaning in the normal way. If this is permitted, the meaning of such an omission must be defined by default or explicitly within the function. Every parameter must have a meaning *if and when* it is actually used in a computation. One solution, used in Ada, is that parameters may be defined to have default values. If an actual argument *is* supplied, its value is used for that parameter, otherwise the default value is used [Exhibit 9.1].

Exhibit 9.1.   An Ada function with a default value for one parameter.

Imagine that this function is a small routine inside a chef's program for figuring out ing[...] quantities when the quantity of a recipe must be changed. The usual case is to double a re[...] so the program has an optional parameter with a default value of 2.0.

```
function CONVERT ( quantity:real,
                   proportion: real := 2.0
              )  return real is
        begin  return quantity*proportion  end CONVERT;
```

Legal and meaningful calls on CONVERT:

```
CONVERT(3.75)            -- Double the amount, result is 7.5.
CONVERT(3.75, .5)        -- Halve the amount, result is 1.675.
```

9.1.2   Parameter Correspondence

When calling a function with optional parameters, arguments may (or may not) be omitted. This complicates the problem of matching up argument values and parameter names, and makes the simple positional correspondence syntax inadequate. The problem can be handled in three ways:

- Permit the user to use adjacent commas to "hold the place" for an omitted argument.
- Require all arguments that *are* supplied to precede the ones that are omitted.
- Use correspondence-by-keyword for all arguments after the first one that is omitted, or for all optional arguments.

All three ways have been used. For example, command line interpreters commonly use the first and third conventions, and Ada supports the second and third. The Ada CONVERT function from Exhibit 9.1 had one optional parameter. Because it was the last parameter, we could use positional argument correspondence to call the CONVERT function.

If a function has several optional parameters, however, which could be included or omitted independently, positional correspondence cannot be used. Exhibit 9.2 shows how correspondence-by-keyword can be used to specify the correct parameter values. The rule in Ada is that all positional arguments in a call must precede all keyword arguments.

Pros and Cons.

Whether or not a language should support optional parameters reduces to the usual question of values. Adding syntax and semantic mechanisms to support correspondence-by-keyword does complicate a language and its compiler. Sometimes the effect of optional parameters can be achieved in some other way, without adding special syntax or semantics. For example, the functional languages support higher-level functions (functions that can return functions as their result). In these languages, a *closure* is the function that results from binding some (or perhaps all) of the arguments

A function and a set of closures made from that function are like a default values for some parameters.

ndence-by-keyword in Ada.

function Wash_Cycle is built into the controller of an automated wash-
parameters that describe the character of a load of laundry and executes
cle. Only the first parameter, the load size, is required; default values are
(We show a possible function header and omit the function body.) As-
, soil_type, and error_type are previously defined enumerated types.

```
FUNCTION Wash_Cycle
(   Weight:  IN integer;
    Fabric:  IN clothtype := cottonknit;
    Soil_level:  IN soiltype := average;
    Dark:  IN Boolean := False;
    Delicate:  IN Boolean := False;
) RETURN error_type IS ...
```

Following are several calls on Wash_Cycle that would process different kinds of loads.
Note the mixed use of positional and keyword correspondence.

```
Result:= Wash_Cycle(10);              -- A large load of T-shirts.
Result:= Wash_Cycle(4, denim, Dark => True);
                                      -- A small load of jeans.
Result:= Wash_Cycle(8, Soil_level => filthy, );
                                      -- Lots of dirty socks.
Result:= Wash_Cycle(Weight => 2, Delicate => True, Fabric => wool);
                                      -- Two winter sweaters.
```

Using optional parameters has a mixed effect on semantic validity. When a programmer omits an optional parameter, the code is less explicit and more concise. This
may or may not be a wise trade-off; explicit code is usually easier to debug and easier
to modify. Being forced to write out all the arguments every time prevents a programmer from accidentally omitting one that was needed. On the other hand, if a
function has a dozen parameters that are usually called with the same values, writing
them all out every time hides the variable parts of the program and makes it harder
to comprehend.

9.1.3 Indefinite-Length Parameter Lists

Some languages permit a function call to pass more arguments than the number of
parameter names defined in the function. Such indefinite-length parameter lists are
useful in functions that apply some uniform process to a variable number of objects,
such as read and write in Pascal.

A Pascal programmer cannot write such a function in Pascal, because all Pascal
function calls must be well-formed. The syntax of Pascal treats read and write as spe-

cial cases. In contrast, C and FORTH do not require function calls to be well-formed. A FORTH function definition does not specify either parameter names or the number of parameters. Parameters are left explicitly on the parameter stack before calling a function, and the function manipulates the stack directly, removing parameters if and when they are needed. Thus a function can be written, such as SumN in Exhibit 9.3, that reads its first parameter(s) and uses it (them) to determine how many optional parameters to read.

Exhibit 9.3.   A FORTH function with a variable number of arguments.

```
:  SumN   ( Sums N numbers.  N must be on top of parameter stack,  )
          ( with numbers to be summed below it.  )
   0      ( Put an initial sum (zero) on top of the stack.  )
   swap   ( Exchange positions of N and initial sum.  N now on top.)
   0 DO   ( Do loop removes 0 and N from stack,  and will iterate )
          ( from 0 through N-1.  )
   +      ( + adds top two items on stack and leaves result there.  )
   LOOP   ( Terminates loop that began with DO. )
   ;      ( End of definition.  Answer is on top of stack.  )
```

Exhibit 9.4 shows legal and meaningful calls on SumN. In every case, the number of arguments provided equals the number consumed by the function, and removed from the stack.

Exhibit 9.4.   Meaningful calls on a variable-argument function in FORTH.

Note: Execution is strictly left-to-right.

```
21 4 55 62   4 SumN      ( Sum the four numbers 21, 4, 55, and 62.  )
32 5         2 SumN      ( Sum the two numbers 32 and 5.  )
32 5         2 SumN 5 *  ( First sum the two numbers 32 and 5, then )
                         ( multiply the result by 5.  )
```

Compare the meaningful calls in Exhibit 9.4 with the first meaningless one in Exhibit 9.5. If this call were made beginning with an empty stack, the result would be a run-time stack underflow. If the stack was nonempty before this call, a value left there for some other purpose would be consumed, and the inevitable stack underflow would be postponed indefinitely.

Too many arguments are supplied in the second meaningless call. This leaves garbage (the extra argument) on the stack. This garbage may or may not interfere with future program operation and can lead to a run-time error. In any case, leaving garbage lying around is undesirable.

Note that FORTH is a postfix language and has no syntactic markers for the beginning and end of a parameter list. Moreover, there is no way to tell how many

---

Exhibit 9.5.   Meaningless calls on a variable-argument function in FORTH.

```
32 5         3 SumN  ( Consumes one more parameter than was supplied, )
                     ( causing immediate or eventual stack underflow.  )
21 4 55 62   3 SumN  ( Fails to consume a parameter, leaving garbage )
                     ( on the stack.  )
```

---

parameters will be used by a function without executing it on specific data. It is impossible, therefore, for a FORTH translator to help the programmer achieve semantic validity by checking that she or he has called functions in meaningful ways.

FORTH's stack operations are extremely low-level. Higher-level languages do not normally let the programmer manipulate the translator's internal data structures because the semantics of this kind of operation are unclear and unpredictable at compile time. If the number of parameters actually supplied is fewer than the number needed, the program will crash. If too many parameters are supplied, junk will build up on the stack.

Although C functions do specify how many parameters they expect, it is possible to call a C function with a different number of parameters. In general, it would not be very useful to pass extra parameters to a function, but that is how the printf function works [Exhibit 9.6]. It uses the number of arguments specified by the information in its first argument (which is the format specification) to determine how many more arguments to process.

Exhibit 9.6.   A call on a variable-argument function in C.

The call on printf below has three arguments—a format string and two numeric items. The format, in quotes, contains two % fields; each one directs that an integer is to be converted to ASCII and written to the output stream.

```
printf ("The sum is %d and the average is %d\n", sum, sum/count);
```

This call will execute correctly because the number (and types) of conversions specified in the format matches the rest of the argument list. The format string is not actually checked at all at compile time. Rather, it is passed on to the run-time system to be interpreted when printf is called. A mismatch in number or type between the format fields and the actual arguments will cause a run-time error or simply produce garbage.

C will translate programs containing calls with missing or extra parameters, and such programs will behave much like similar programs in FORTH. All is well if the program actually uses the number of parameters that are supplied. If *too few* are supplied, the program will either access garbage, causing unpredictable behavior, or it will stop with a stack underflow.

Supplying *too many* parameters will not cause C to malfunction. In current C implementations, parameters are removed from the stack by the calling program, not by the subroutine. This produces a longer calling sequence but avoids creating a serious problem by passing too many parameters. Excess parameters will sit on the stack unused until the subroutine exits, but then they will be removed. Junk will not pile up on the stack.

Pros and Cons.

The examples cited previously help us answer the question, "To what extent is it good and/or bad to permit argument lists of indefinite length?"

Putting syntactic markers around parameter lists in a program makes them easier for humans to work with, and thus is good. Once these markers are required by a language, it is easy for a translator to check that the right number of parameters is used in every call. Doing so prevents the programmer from writing nonsense that will cause programs to malfunction or crash. Thus a parameter checking mechanism in the translator can be a powerful aid to writing correct programs.

On the other hand, there is a real cost involved. Once in a while it is very useful to write a function, such as `printf`, that accepts a variable number of parameters. This can be done by the programmer in C but not in a language such as Pascal that requires well-formed function calls. The Pascal I/O procedures do accept a variable number of parameters, but they are predefined and no functions like them can be defined by the programmer.

Whether or not a restriction is severe depends partly on whether the useful things it prohibits can be achieved some other way. For example, a function in a list-oriented language might accomplish the same end more simply by taking a single argument that is a variable-length list.

Thus the question of whether to require function calls to be well-formed can be reduced to making a set of value judgements about the relative importance of (1) semantic validity and (2) unrestricted flexibility. The answer also depends on what other mechanisms are included in the language.

Most language designers placed a higher value on communicating and preserving semantic intent than the designers of FORTH and C, who valued flexibility more highly. Neither of these languages enforces the very helpful restriction that a function must be called with a semantically meaningful number of parameters. Both are considered to be systems programming languages, and both provide nearly full access to the machine hardware. Both permit programs to be written that can crash easily and in spectacular ways.

9.2   WHAT DOES AN ARGUMENT MEAN?

Chapter 8, Section 8.4.1, discusses the order in which arguments are evaluated. Here we examine how an argument is passed to a function and interpreted within the function.

ALGOL-60, the first formally defined higher-level language, was defined with inside-out expression evaluation and both call-by-value and call-by-name parameter passing mechanisms. Since then, other call mechanisms have been devised: call-by-need, call-by-reference, call-by-value-and-return, and call-by-pointer. The syntax and the semantics of these call mechanisms differ in important ways, which we explore in this section.

9.2.1 Call-by-Value

Call-by-value is the simplest and cleanest parameter passing mechanism, both in terms
of its semantics and its implementation. In call-by-value, an expression written as an
actual parameter is evaluated before beginning the execution of a subprogram. The
resulting value is written into the stack area reserved for the subprogram and bound to
the corresponding formal parameter name within the subprogram. Exhibit 9.7 shows a
Pascal procedure named `test1` which has call-by-value parameters. Exhibit 9.8 shows
the relevant storage allocated for both the calling program and for `test1` at the beginning of execution of the call:

```
test1( J1, A1[J1], P1↑.next );
```

Exhibit 9.7.   A procedure using call-by-value in Pascal.

```
PROCEDURE test1 (J2, A2:  integer; P2:list);
BEGIN
    writeln (J2, A2, P2↑.value);
    J2 := J2 + 1;
    P2 := P2↑.next;
    writeln (J2, A2, P2↑.value)
END;
```

Exhibit 9.8.   Result of parameter binding by value in Pascal.

Double arrows represent bindings; plain arrows represent pointers. The "∨" symbol marks the
current stack frame.

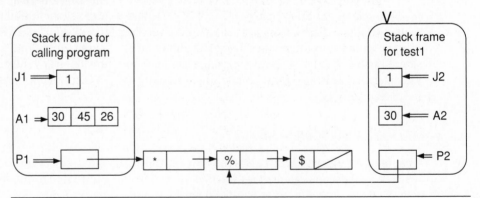

Exhibit 9.9 shows the result of executing `test1`, just after the procedure return
and after deallocation of the stack frame for `test1`. Two lines of output are produced
by this call:

```
1   30   %
2   30   $
```

Exhibit 9.9. Result of execution with value parameters.

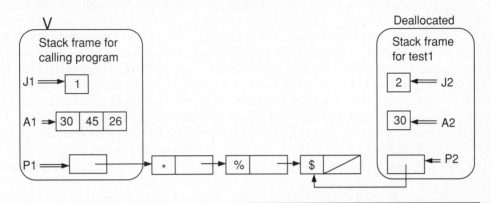

Assigning a value to the dummy parameter affects only the stack storage for the subroutine; it does not change anything in the storage area belonging to the calling program. Note, in Exhibit 9.9, that nothing in the stack frame of the calling program has been modified. The call-by-value mechanism is, thus, a powerful tool for limiting unintended side effects and making a program modular. Call-by-value guarantees that no subroutine can "mess up" the values of its nonpointer arguments in the calling context. For this reason, it is the most useful of the mechanisms for passing parameters and should be used wherever it can do the job.

Passing a pointer, by value, to a subroutine will not permit the pointer itself to be changed, but it permits modification of storage owned by the calling program and *accessible through the pointer*. In Exhibit 9.7 it would have been possible to modify contents of the list by assigning a new value to P2↑.value or P2↑.next. This is demonstrated in Section 9.2.6. A pointer argument, therefore, partially breaches the protection inherent in call-by-value.

9.2.2   Call-by-Name

In the vocabulary of programming languages, lambda calculus uses a *call-by-name* parameter interpretation rule. This is defined formally in Exhibit 8.10. Briefly put, each occurrence of a call-by-name formal parameter in an expression is to be replaced by the *entire actual argument expression* written in the function application or call.

Two function passing mechanisms were implemented in ALGOL-60 because it was recognized that call-by-value parameters do not permit information to be passed back from a function to the calling program.[1] While a single value may be returned as the value of a function, this is often not adequate. Many common applications, such as the swap routine, require passing back more than one datum.

The common swap subroutine takes two arguments, both variables, and uses a temporary storage object to exchange their values. Since the values of two variables

---

[1]This is true unless the language supports pointer types. ALGOL-60 did not have pointers.

are changed, this cannot be done with a function return value. What is actually necessary is to pass the two storage objects (not just the values in those objects) into the subroutine. The values in these objects can then be interchanged. We can pass a storage object by passing its name, its address, or a pointer pointing to it.

ALGOL-60 was developed at the same time as LISP, when lambda calculus was strongly influencing programming language design. This was before reference parameter binding was well understood and accepted, and before the concept of a storage object was well understood. It was not surprising, then, that the ALGOL-60 designers included call-by-name as a means of implementing swap and similar procedures.

In a call-by-name system, entire formulas are passed as arguments, to be evaluated within the called function, but using the symbols defined in the calling program. Thus one could pass a *variable name* to a subroutine, and inside the subroutine it would evaluate to the variable's address and provide access to that variable's storage object.

Symbols in an argument expression are evaluated *in the context of the calling program*. This means that if a symbol, S, occurs in an argument expression and is redefined as a local symbol in the subprogram, the global meaning (not the local meaning) is used in evaluating the argument. To implement this rule, name conflicts must be eliminated. This requires lambda-calculus-like renaming [Exhibit 8.10], which is somewhat hard to implement.[2]

Call-by-name semantics has two more nasty properties. Suppose that the definition of a function, F, contains three references to the parameter P, and that we call F with an expression, E, as the actual parameter corresponding to P. If we use call-by-value or call-by-reference (defined on page 228), then E will be evaluated once, before evaluating the function, and its value will be bound to P. When F is evaluated, that single value will be used three times. But if we use call-by-name, then the original expression, E, will be evaluated every time the code of F refers to P. In this example, E will be evaluated three times. Of course, this is not very efficient, particularly if E is a large expression.

Worse yet, if the process of evaluating E has a side effect (such as producing output or changing the value of a global variable), the side effect will happen more than once, and the results of the first time might affect the value of the expression the other times or might produce extra output. Thus call-by-name on a parameter with a side effect is semantically messy as well as inefficient and hard to implement.

Pascal does not support parameter binding by name. In order to produce an example of binding by name that can be compared to the binding examples in Exhibits 9.7 and 9.13 we must use an imaginary extension of Pascal that includes the keyword NAME, placed before a dummy parameter, to indicate that the parameter is to be passed by name. Exhibit 9.10 shows a procedure, test2, written in this imaginary language. Exhibit 9.11 shows the bindings created for test2 and the relevant storage allocated for the calling program, just after parameter binding and before procedure execution.

The result, just after the procedure return, of executing test2 is shown in Exhibit 9.12. The bindings for the subroutine have been undone. Note that, unlike test1, test2 modifies the linked list—it unlinks one cell. The value of J1 is also changed. The following two lines of output are produced by this call. The second line

---

[2]The difficulty of translating call-by-name contributed to the unpopularity of ALGOL-60 in this country.

differs from the call-by-value results because the argument expression A1[J1] was evaluated a second time after the value of J1 had been changed.

```
1   30   %
2   45   $
```

Exhibit 9.10.   Parameter binding by name.

In our imaginary Pascal-like language, only the procedure header would differ from the version in Exhibit 9.7. The header for the call-by-name version of test would be:

```
PROCEDURE test2 (NAME J2, A2:  integer; NAME P2:list);
```

Execution of the procedure call

```
test2( J1, A1[J1], P1↑.next );
```

is traced in Exhibits 9.11 and 9.12.

Exhibit 9.11.   Result of parameter binding by name.

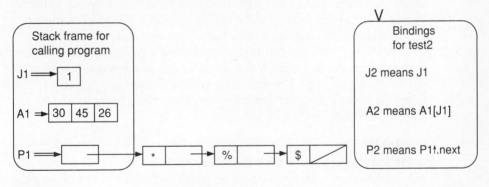

Exhibit 9.12.   Result of execution with by-name binding.

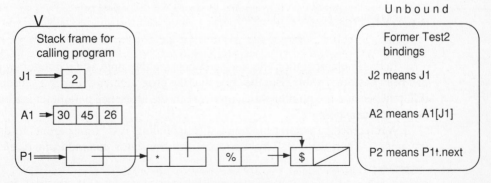

Call-by-name proved to be a mistake and a headache. It was awkward to implement, inefficient to execute, and more general than necessary to implement routines such as "swap". Since the mid-1960s a better way (call-by-reference) has been used to implement the desired semantics. Ordinary call-by-name has not been incorporated in a language since ALGOL-60, as a primary function call mechanism. Macro languages, such as the C preprocessor, use something akin to call-by-name to interpret parameters when a macro definition is expanded. Argument strings are substituted bodily for occurrences of the parameters. This can result in multiple copies of the argument string. If the argument string is an expression, it will be compiled several times and executed several times.

9.2.3 Call-by-Reference

The call-by-reference parameter passing mechanism is also called *call-by-address* and, in Pascal, *VAR parameter passing*. A reference parameter is used to pass a storage object to a subprogram. An actual argument must be a variable name or an expression whose value is an address.

To implement a reference parameter, the compiler allocates enough storage for a pointer in the subprogram's stack area and binds the dummy parameter name to this stack location. A pointer to the actual parameter is stored in this space. During procedure execution, the dummy parameter name is indirectly bound to the argument's storage object (which belongs to the calling program). The value in this storage object may be changed by assigning a value to the dummy name.

When the attribute VAR is used to declare a dummy parameter name in Pascal, the parameter is generally translated as call-by-reference.[3] Exhibit 9.13 shows the function header for a by-reference version of the test procedure. Exhibit 9.14 shows the relevant storage allocated for both the calling program and for test3, after parameter binding but before procedure execution.

Exhibit 9.13. A procedure using call-by-reference in Pascal.

Only the procedure header differs from the version in Exhibit 9.7. The keyword VAR indicates call-by-reference.

```
PROCEDURE test3 (VAR J2, A2:  integer; VAR P2:list);
```

Execution of the following call on test3 is traced in Exhibits 9.14 and 9.15:

```
test3( J1, A1[J1], P1↑.next );
```

In this implementation the stack contents are the same as if a pointer argument had been passed by-value. But the code that the programmer writes in a subroutine is different because the pointer which implements the reference parameter is a binding, not an ordinary pointer.

A reference parameter binding is a true binding; it is "transparent" to the programmer. When using call-by-reference, the translator *automatically dereferences*

---

[3]Call-by-value-and-return is the other possible implementation for a VAR parameter. See Section 9.2.5.

Exhibit 9.14. VAR parameter binding in Pascal.

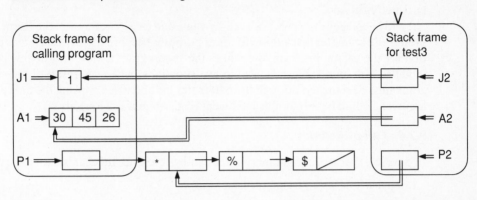

every occurrence of a by-reference parameter. A naive user does not even realize that the binding pointer exists. In the stack diagram in Exhibit 9.14, this extra automatic dereference is indicated by the double binding arrows from the slots allocated for the parameters to the actual arguments. Thus we can say that the reference parameter is *indirectly bound* to the argument. As with any binding, the programmer cannot change the binding by executing an assignment.

The results of call-by-reference differ from both call-by-value and call-by-name. Exhibit 9.15 shows the stack just after the procedure return, and after deallocation of the stack frame for test3. Note that two things have been modified in the storage diagram: the value of J1 and a cell in the linked list. These changes are like the ones produced by test2, using call-by-name. But the output produced differs from the test2 output, and is like the test1 output:

$$
\begin{array}{ccc}
1 & 30 & \% \\
2 & 30 & \$
\end{array}
$$

Exhibit 9.15. Result of execution with a VAR parameter.

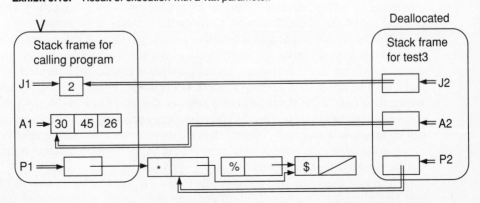

All parameters are passed by reference in FORTRAN, as are all array parameters in C. Call-by-reference is optional in Pascal and is used to implement output parameters in Ada.

In languages that have both call-by-value and call-by-reference, the former is the preferred parameter mechanism for most purposes because it provides greater protection for the calling program and makes the subprogram a more thoroughly isolated module. Call-by-reference is used in two situations: when the result of the subprogram must be returned through the parameter list and when copying the entire actual argument would be intolerably inefficient (e.g., when it is a long array).

9.2.4   Call-by-Return

In practice, Pascal programmers use the call-by-reference mechanism for two reasons:

1. So that a value may be returned.
2. To avoid consuming the execution time and stack space necessary to pass a very large argument by value.

Using a VAR parameter for the first reason is semantically sound and in keeping with the intent of the language designer. Using a VAR parameter for the second reason is not semantically sound, even though it may be necessary to achieve acceptable performance from a program. Call-by-value semantics is the only sound semantics for a parameter that does not carry information out of the subroutine.

This illustrates a defect in the design of Pascal; the only efficient mechanism for passing large arguments (call-by-reference) is tied to the semantics appropriate for return values. In Ada, this design defect was partially corrected by permitting the programmer to specify the desired *semantics* and letting the translator choose an appropriate *mechanism*. Thus an Ada parameter has a declared *mode*. The mode is declared to be "in" if the parameter carries information into the subroutine or "out" if it carries information back to the calling program. A two-way parameter is declared to be "in out".

The mode in is like a value parameter except that, within the subroutine, it has the semantics of a constant and a new value cannot be assigned to it. This is more restrictive than call-by-value, since most languages permit a value parameter to be used as a local variable and receive assignments. For this reason, we will refer to this mode as *call-by-constant*. This can be implemented by using call-by-value and prohibiting the use of the parameter name on the left side of an assignment.

The Ada mode out is also referred to as *call-by-return*. A call-by-return parameter is write-only; it carries information *out* of the subprogram but not *into* the subprogram. Within the subprogram, an out parameter can be implemented by a local variable. The program is allowed to store information in this variable but not fetch information from it. When the function returns, the final value of the out parameter is stored in the location specified by corresponding argument. For output parameters, call-by-return is semantically cleaner than call-by-reference because access to the location in the calling program is write-only and can happen only at function return time. Call-by-return is therefore preferred.

The Ada mode in out corresponds to the VAR parameter mechanism in Pascal. Unfortunately, the Ada standard does not fully specify the semantics that must accompany an in out parameter. A compiler is permitted to implement either call-by-reference or call-by-value-and-return. A program that depends on the difference between these two calling mechanisms is only partially defined. As seen in the next section, this is a truly unfortunate shortcoming in a language that was designed to support multitasking!

9.2.5   Call-by-Value-and-Return

We can combine call-by-value and call-by-return to achieve two-way communication between called and caller, with no accessing restrictions inside the subroutine. At first look, *call-by-value-and-return* seems more complex than call-by-reference, and it seems to offer no advantages. While this is true in an isolated program on a simple machine, it does not hold in more complex environments. Two factors, hardware complexity and concurrency, make call-by-value-and-return the preferred mechanism.

Consider a machine with a partitioned memory, or a program that is being executed on a networked system. In such hardware environments, nearby memory is fast (and therefore cheap) to access, and more distant memory costs more. A function that executes using only local storage will be more efficient than one that accesses data in another memory segment. When call-by-value is used, the data is copied from the caller's memory into the local memory. Although this copying operation takes time, much more time may be saved by avoiding out-of-segment references to the parameter. Call-by-value is simply more efficient once the argument has been copied. This is true on any partitioned architecture, even an IBM PC, although the savings may be minor. However, for a program on a network that is processing data stored at a remote location, the savings would be substantial, and the difference in response time would be important.

The difference between call-by-reference and call-by-value-and-return is very important in an application where two or more processes concurrently access the same data object. Suppose that processes P1 and P2 both have received argument ARG as a reference parameter. Using call-by-value-and-return, the answer is always one of three things:

- If the first process to begin, P1, ends before the second one, P2, starts, the final value in ARG is just the result of ordinary, sequential execution.
- If P1 starts, then P2 starts, then P1 returns, then P2 returns, the result of P1's execution is wiped out. The value in ARG is the answer from P2, as if P1 had never been called.
- If P1 starts, then P2 starts, then P2 returns, then P1 returns, the result of P2's execution is wiped out. The value in ARG is the answer from P1, as if P2 had never been called.

In any case, the final result is some value that was correctly and meaningfully computed. It may seem very undesirable to have the possibility that the result of calling a procedure could be totally wiped out. However, that situation is better than the alternative; call-by-reference can cause real trouble in a concurrent application. If both P1 and P2 read and modify ARG several times, and if their actions are interspersed, the final value of ARG can be completely unpredictable.[4] Worst of all, the

---

[4]Most textbooks on operating systems cover this problem in a chapter on concurrency.

value left in ARG could be different from any legal value that could be computed by either process alone, or both processes executed in either sequence.

The modern call-by-value-and-return semantics should be used for Ada because Ada was specifically designed to be used:

- On any machine architecture.
- On networks of machines.
- With concurrent, multitasked applications.

9.2.6   Call-by-Pointer

Call-by-pointer is a subcase of call-by-value. The contents of the pointer variable in the calling program is an address. During parameter passing this address is copied into the corresponding pointer variable in the stack frame for the subroutine. Now two pointers, one in each stack frame, point at the same object. Because the argument is the address of a storage object belonging to the calling program, it can be used to return a value from the subroutine. Unlike a by-reference parameter, though, a pointer parameter must be explicitly dereferenced within the subprogram.

Three versions of a swap subroutine are given here in two languages. These illustrate the similarities and differences between call-by-reference and call-by-pointer. In all three, the programmer indicates that a variable address, not a value, is passed into the subroutine so that the swapped values can be passed outward. Exhibit 9.16 shows a procedure named swap1 which uses call-by-reference. Exhibit 9.17 shows the storage allocated for execution of swap1.

Exhibit 9.16.   A swap routine using reference parameters in Pascal.

The VAR keyword is used before the parameter name to indicate a reference parameter. Assuming that j and k are integers, an appropriate call would be: swap1 (j, k);

```
PROCEDURE swap1 (VAR a, b:  integer);
VAR t:integer;
BEGIN
    t:=a;   a:=b;   b:=t
END;
```

The subprogram stack frames for call-by-pointer [Exhibit 9.21] and call-by-reference contain the same information, but that information has a different meaning because of the extra automatic dereference that accompanies call-by-reference. When call-by-pointer is used to implement the same process, the programmer must write an explicit dereference symbol each time the pointer parameter is used, as shown in Exhibits 9.18 and 9.20.

Contrast Exhibit 9.17 to Exhibit 9.21. Note the double binding arrows in the former, and the single pointer arrows in the latter. These semantic differences account for and correspond to the absence of explicit dereference symbols in Exhibit 9.16 and their presence ("↑" in Pascal and "*" in C) in Exhibits 9.18 and 9.20.

Exhibit 9.17. The implementation of reference parameters in Pascal.

Stack diagrams for `swap1` are shown here, just before the code in `swap1` is executed and after return from the subroutine. The arrowhead at the top of the stack frame indicates the current stack frame.

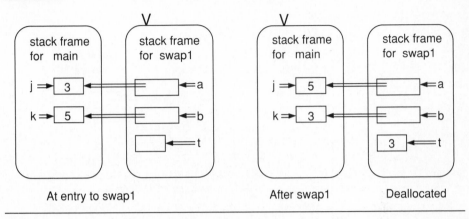

At entry to swap1   After swap1   Deallocated

Exhibit 9.18. A swap routine using pointer parameters in Pascal.

The pointer parameters are passed by value and explicitly dereferenced within the subroutine.

```
TYPE int_ptr = ↑ integer;
VAR jp, kp: int_ptr;
PROCEDURE swap2 (a, b:  int_ptr);
VAR t:integer;
BEGIN
    t:=a↑ ; a↑:=b↑ ; b↑:=t
END;
```

Assume that the following code has been executed. The last line is an appropriate call on `swap2`. Execution of this call is traced in Exhibit 9.19.

```
NEW(jp);  jp↑ := 3;
NEW(kp);  kp↑ := 5;
swap2 (jp, kp);
```

Moreover, although a by-reference binding cannot be changed, the address stored in the pointer parameter can be changed by an assignment statement, as shown on the last line of Exhibit 9.22.

Use of call-by-pointer is severely restricted in Pascal. Since Pascal pointers can never point at objects on the stack, one can only use call-by-pointer to process dynamically allocated storage objects. This accounts for the difference between Exhibit 9.19 and Exhibit 9.23. C does not restrict use of pointers; the programmer can use the "&" operator to get the address of (a pointer to) any variable. Thus call-by-pointer can be used in C to pass an argument allocated in either the stack or the heap.

Exhibit 9.19.   Storage for swap2.

This diagram shows the storage allocated for swap2 and the calling program, just after exit from the call on swap2. Note that the values of pointers jp and kp were copied into swap2's stack frame, and provide access to objects that were dynamically allocated by the calling program.

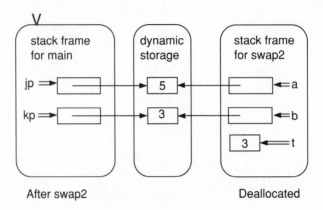

After swap2   Deallocated

Two versions of the swap routine can be written in Pascal, with the use of the second restricted to heap-allocated objects. In contrast, only one version is possible in C because C does not support call-by-reference. In its place, call-by-value is used to pass the value of a pointer (an address). We call this parameter passing method *call-by-pointer* [Exhibit 9.20]. In this version of the swap routine, the type of the dummy parameters is "int *" (pointer-to-integer). The parameters must be explicitly dereferenced (using the * symbol), just as ↑ is used in the Pascal swap2 routine.

Exhibit 9.20.   Pointer parameters in C.

```
void swap3 (int *a, int *b)
{ int t;
    t = *a;   *a = *b;   *b = t;
}
```

Two distinct kinds of calls on this one function are possible. In the first, shown in Exhibit 9.21, we use the "&" operator to pass the addresses of the two integers whose values are to be swapped. This is not possible in Pascal, as Pascal does not have an "&" (address of) operator.

Note that only the values in the variables j and k are swapped; the pointers a and b point at the same variables throughout. A reader who is confused by this should note, in Exhibit 9.22, that an assignment statement that changes a pointer is quite different from an assignment that changes a value.

Exhibit 9.21.   Call-by-pointer using & in C.

```
main(){
    int j=3, k=5;              /* Declare and initialize two integers. */
    swap3 (&j, &k);
}
```

The stack diagram on the left shows execution of this call just after creation of the stack frame for swap3. The diagram on the right shows storage after exit from swap3.

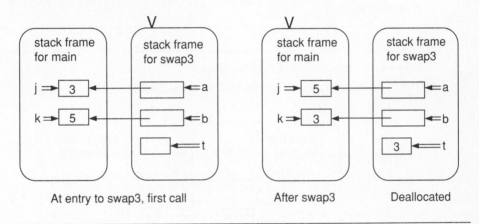

| At entry to swap3, first call | After swap3 | Deallocated |

Exhibit 9.22.   Assignments using pointers in C.

```
int j=3, k=5;       /* j and k are integer variables.    */
int *p= &j;         /* Make the pointer p point at j.     */
*p = k;             /* Variable j now contains a 5.       */
p = &k;             /* Make p point at k instead of j.    */
```

The second call, shown in Exhibit 9.23, corresponds to the call on swap2 in Pascal. In the main program, we initialize pointers to the two integer variables and pass those pointers (by value, of course) to swap3. The result is the same as the first call: the stack frame for swap3 contains two pointers, initialized at block entry to the addresses of j and k. The only difference between these two kinds of call-by-pointer is the presence or absence of the pointer variables in main. If these pointers are useful for other reasons, the second call would be stylistically better. Otherwise the first call should be used.

There are two important practical differences between reference parameters and pointer parameters. The first has already been noted: pointers must be explicitly dereferenced. Experience has shown that a common error is using one too few or one too many dereference symbols. The call-by-reference mechanism is inherently less error prone.

Exhibit 9.23.   Call-by-pointer using pointer variables in C.

```
main(){
    int j=3, k=5;              /* Declare and initialize two integers. */
    int *jp = &j, *kp = &k;   /* Make pointers point at the integers. */
    swap3 (jp, kp);
}
```

The stack diagram in Exhibit 9.24 shows execution of this call just after creation of the stack frame for swap3.

Exhibit 9.24.   Stack diagram for call-by-pointer.

This diagram shows execution of the code from Exhibit 9.23.

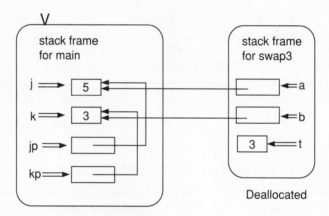

After exit from second call on swap3

Second, once you are permitted to point freely at items allocated on the stack, it is possible to create dangling pointers. This is why the "address of" operator was omitted from Pascal. Wirth's intent was that Pascal should prevent the programmer from making many semantic errors by providing only semantically "safe" operators.

There are two simple ways to create a dangling pointer in a language such as C that permits an "address of" operation to be applied to any object. First, it can be done by passing an argument which is *the address of a pointer to an object*. Assume pk is a pointer to an object. Then &pk is the address of a pointer. By passing &pk to a subprogram we permit the subprogram to change the value of pk. Inside the subprogram, pk can be set to point to a local variable. Second, a dangling reference may be created by returning the address of a local variable from a function. Upon returning from the function in either case, the local variable will be deallocated and the calling program will point to a storage object that no longer exists. This is illustrated in Exhibits 9.25 and 9.26.

Exhibit 9.25.   Creation of two dangling pointers in C.

```
int * dangle (int ** ppp) /* The parameter is the address of a pointer.  */
{    int p=5;
     int m=21;
     *ppp = &p;              /* Dereference ppp to get the pointer whose address
                                 was passed.  Make it point at local p.  */
     return &m; }            /*  A second dangling pointer.  */
main()
{    int k = 17;
     int *pm, *pk = &k;  /* pk is a pointer pointing at k.  */
     pm = dangle(&pk);   /* Upon return, pk and pm point at */
}                        /* deallocated spaces.  */
```

Exhibit 9.26 shows storage before and after returning from the call on `dangle`.

Exhibit 9.26.   Creating a dangling pointer.

The stack before execution of `dangle`, showing parameter bindings and local allocation.

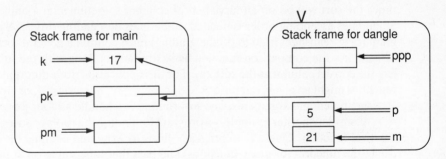

The stack, after return from `dangle`, showing results of execution.

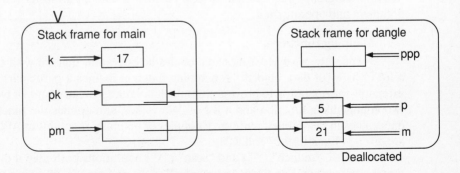

9.3 HIGHER-ORDER FUNCTIONS

A *higher-order function* is one that takes a function as an argument or returns a function as its result. Lambda calculus has higher-order functions—it makes no distinction between a functional object and a nonfunctional object. The pure functional languages, which are modeled after lambda calculus, give full support to higher-order functions, and this is the basis of much of their power. Other languages give partial support or no support, because of the difficulties involved. In this section we look at some of the applications of higher-order functions and consider some of the difficulties involved in their implementation.

9.3.1 Functional Arguments

It is not too difficult and it is very useful to support functions as arguments to other functions. Let us consider two of the more common applications of functional arguments, flexible code and mapping functions.

Flexible Code.

Sometimes a complex general process can have several variants. For example, consider a spreadsheet that consists of one line of data per student and one column for each assignment or exam, in which the student's grade is recorded. In the process of assigning grades, an instructor will sort that data many times in many ways. Sometimes the sort will be on an alphabetical column, sometimes on a numeric column. Sometimes ascending order is needed, sometimes descending order. A grading program (or spreadsheet used to do the grading) must contain a general sort procedure, which takes the comparison function as its argument, along with the function to select the correct column as the sort key. For this application, four different comparison functions might be given, numeric "<", alphabetic "<", numeric ">", or alphabetic ">". By using functional arguments, one sort routine can handle all four jobs.

Consider another example—a program for finding the roots of an arbitrary mathematical function. One way to program this is to write and compile the code to calculate the function (or many functions) and pass that function as an argument to the general root-finding procedure. This permits the root-finder to be kept in a library and used for many applications without modification. The general graphing facilities of packages such as Lotus must also be able to take an arbitrary function as its argument and operate on it.

Mapping Functions.

Frequently, we have a monadic or dyadic operation that we wish to apply to a list or array of data objects. A mapping function defines a particular pattern for extending the operation to process multiple data values instead of one or two. It takes two arguments, a function and a list of data values, and applies the function to the data values in the defined pattern. Examples of mapping functions in APL and LISP are given in Exhibits 9.27 and 9.28.

The APL "reduce" ("/") and "scan" ("\") operations both take a dyadic functional argument and an array argument. Reduce computes a "running operation". The result is the same as if the functional argument were written between each pair of

Exhibit 9.27.   Mapping functions in APL.

Code	Operation	Results
A ← 1 1 0 1		Bind A to an array of four Boolean values.
+/ A	plus reduce	3 (Count true values.)
+\A	plus scan	1 2 2 3
∨/ A	logical-or reduce	1 (At least one true exists.)
∧/A	logical-and reduce	0 (Some value is false.)
∧\A	logical-and scan	1 1 0 0 (Find first false.)

Exhibit 9.28.   Some applications of `mapcar` in LISP.

Assume x is the list (4 9 16 25), y is (1 2 3 4), z is NIL, and w is ((3 4 5) (2 1) (7 9 3 6)), which is a list of lists. The quote mark before the function name causes the actual, executable function (not the result of evaluating it) to be sent to `mapcar`.

Expression	Comments	List Returned
`(mapcar '+1 x)`	Increment each element.	(5 10 17 26)
`(mapcar '+ x y)`	Add corresponding elements.	(5 11 19 29)
`(mapcar '+1 z)`	The empty list is no problem.	NIL

`(mapcar '(lambda (a b)`
`    (- (* 3 a) b) ))`
`     x y)`
	Apply the function ((3*a)-b)
	   to corresponding elements
	   of lists x and y.
		(11 25 45 71)

`(mapcdr 'caar w)`	The first item of each sublist.	

values from the data array, and the entire expression were then evaluated. Thus if the function argument is "+", reduce totals the array. The scan operation works similarly, except that its answer is the same length as the input array and contains all the partial "sums". These operations are fundamental to giving APL its power and are also essential operations in modern parallel algorithms.

There are several mapping functions in LISP, that iterate a functional argument over a list argument or arguments. In all cases, the number of list arguments must match the number of parameters in the functional argument; a monadic function needs one list, a dyadic function needs two. Let us use the function `mapcar` as an example; `mapcar` goes down the argument lists, selecting the next value from each list argument at each step and applying the functional argument to those values. The result becomes the next item in the result list. A null argument produces a null result, and a list of any other length maps onto another, transformed list of equal length. Iteration stops when the end of the shortest list-argument is reached. If the functional argument returns a list, the final output is a list of lists [Exhibit 9.28].

The function mapcdr is similar to mapcar, except that the parameter of the functional argument must be of type list, and at each step, the function is applied to the entire list and then the head of the list is discarded. (The remaining list argument is one value shorter after each iteration.) The result of each step is appended to the output list.

Implementation.

A functional argument can be passed to another function easily and efficiently by passing a pointer to the function, not the function itself. The only implementation problem concerns type checking—the type of the functional argument, that is, the types of all its arguments and the type of its result, must be known before code can be compiled to call that function. This accounts for one major difference between the functional languages and Pascal or ANSI C. All support functional parameters, but the functional languages are interpreted and do not require the declaration of the full type of a functional argument since its type can be deduced, when necessary, from the function's definition.

A short Pascal function with a functional argument is shown in Exhibit 9.29. It is a very limited version of APL's reduce operator. The capabilities of this code are much more restricted than the "reduce" operation in APL because Pascal is a strongly typed, compiled language, and APL is not.[5] Note that the functional parameter, f, is declared with a full header, including dummy parameter names x and y which are meaningless and never used.

Exhibit 9.29.   A Pascal version of "reduce".

This function will apply any dyadic integer function to reduce an array of ten integers.

```
Type row_type = array[0..9] of integer;
Function Reduce( Function f(x:integer, y:integer):integer;
                   ar: row_type)integer;
Var sum, k:  integer;
Begin
    sum := ar[0];
    For k=1 to 9 do
        sum := f(sum, ar[k]);
    Reduce := sum;
End;
```

9.3.2 Currying

In functional languages,[6] every function of two or more arguments is considered to be a higher-order function of one argument that returns another function. This way of

---

[5]A similar version of "reduce" with some type flexibility is given in C in Exhibit 15.4.

[6]We will use Miranda syntax, because it is simple and elegant, to illustrate the properties common to all functional languages.

looking at functions is called *currying*.[7] The returned function represents a function of one fewer argument which is the same as the original function in which the first argument has been fixed to the given value. This pattern is repeated until all but one of the arguments have been used, and the final function returns a data-object.

An example should help make this clear. Consider the Miranda function `pythag` `a b = sqrt (a * a + b * b)`, which uses the Pythagorean theorem to compute the length of the hypotenuse of a right triangle whose base and height have lengths a and b respectively. `Pythag` is considered by Miranda to be a function that takes one numeric argument and returns a function. That function takes a numeric argument and returns a number. Thus the result returned by `pythag 3` is a function that finds the hypotenuse of any right triangle whose base has length 3. The following Miranda expressions all return the length of the hypotenuse ($= 5$) of a right triangle with base 3 and height 4:

- `pythag 3 4`
- `(pythag 3) 4`
- `f 4` if we have previously defined `f = pythag 3`

In the last expression above, we have given a temporary name `f` to the function returned by `pythag 3`. `f` is itself a legitimate function and can be used like any other function. For example, the expression

    (f 4) + (f 7)

computes the sum of the lengths of the hypotenuses of two right triangles, one with base 3 and height 4 and the other with base 3 and height 7. See if you can figure out what is computed by this Miranda expression:

    f (f 4) where f = pythag 3

The notation for expressing a curried function type is:

    ⟨function name⟩ ::⟨argument type⟩ → ⟨result type⟩

The type of a higher-order function is written by repeated uses of the → notation. The "→" sign is right associative, as shown below, permitting us to write the type of an ordinary numeric function without using parentheses. These two type expressions are equivalent and denote the type of `myfunc`:

    myfunc :: num → num → num
    myfunc :: num → (num → num)

We can use this notation to write the type of a function that takes a function as a parameter. For example, Exhibit 9.30 shows the type of a Miranda version of the `reduce` function. (The function itself is shown and discussed in Chapter 12, Exhibit 12.15.) This version of `reduce` takes a binary arithmetic operator, a list of numbers (possibly null), and an identity value, and returns a number. The identity value must

---

[7]Named after Haskell Curry, an early logician who used this device extensively in his work on semantics.

be appropriate for the given operator; it is used to initialize the summing process and is returned as the value of reduce when the list argument is a null list.

Exhibit 9.30.   The type of reduce in Miranda.

```
reduce ::                        The function reduce takes three arguments,
       (num → num → num )        a binary operator,
       → [num]                   a list of numbers,
       → num                     and an identity element.
       → num                     It returns a number.
```

Notes:

- Type num means number and is a primitive type in Miranda.
- A function type is denoted by use of parentheses.
- We denote the type of a list with base type T as " [T] ".

9.3.3   Returning Functions from Functions

C supports functional arguments, in the form of pointers to functions, and C++ carries this further to permit the predefined operators to be named and used as arguments also. Both languages permit the programmer to return a pointer to a function as the result of a function. However, a C or C++ function cannot do one thing that distinguishes functional languages from all other languages: create a function within a function and return it as the result of the function. At first sight, this facility might seem esoteric and not very useful; it is, however, a powerful and concise way to achieve several practical ends, including composition functions, closures, and infinite lists. We discuss closures here and infinite lists in Chapter 12.

Closures

Closure is an operation that can be applied to an expression. We close an expression by binding each of its free variables to the value of another expression. A closure creates a function, which is returned as the result of the closure process. The most useful and easily understood application of closure is known as *partial parameterization*. In this process we take a function of n arguments, bind one to a locally defined value, and produce a function of $n - 1$ arguments.

For example, we can partially parameterize "+" by closing its first argument; the result is a one-argument function that adds a constant to its argument. If the closed argument is bound to 1, the result is commonly known as "+1", or increment. Exhibit 9.31 shows the types and definitions, in Miranda, for two functions produced by closing the first argument of plus. The result is always a function of one argument, whose type is the same as the type of plus, with the first clause omitted.

An Application of Closures.

As an example of the possible use of closures, consider the currency conversion problem. An international bank has a general currency-conversion function, Convert, that takes a conversion rate and an amount of currency and returns an amount in a different currency. The bank has a second program that is run each morning. It reads the current conversion rates for all currencies the bank handles, then creates two closures of the `convert` program for each rate. For example, after reading the fact that one mark = .6 dollars, two closures would be created:

- MarksToDollars = Convert 1.67
- DollarsToMarks = Convert .6

The resulting closures would be accessed through a menu offering dozens of specialized conversion routines. These could be called up during the business day, as needed.

Exhibit 9.31.   Partially closing a function to make new functions.

We define a simple function of two arguments in Miranda and produce two new functions from it by closing its first argument. Assume the symbol x is bound in the enclosing context.

```
plus :: num → (num → num )
plus a b = a + b
add1 :: num → num
add1 = plus 1
plusx :: num → num
plusx = plus (x * 10)
```

Implementation of Closures.

Closure is a useful device for taking general, library code modules and tailoring them to the needs of a particular environment. Although it produces a new function, it does not require translating new code; the function code for the closure is just like the code of an existing function. Thus we can implement closure using a record containing bindings for symbols, together with a pointer to a function.

When we close a function with a constant value, as in the function `add1` [Exhibit 9.31], there is no question about what the meaning is or how to construct the closure. In this case the closure would contain a pointer to the function `plus` and the information that the symbol a in `plus` is bound to 1.

However, a problem arises when we close `plus` with an expression such as x * 10: what should be recorded in the closure? Should that expression be evaluated and the result stored in the closure, or should the expression itself become part of the closure? The answer is, we can still be lazy. We can safely defer evaluation of the expression until the value is needed. There is no need to evaluate the expression when we make a closure, because the result of evaluating the expression will always be the same. Each symbol used in the expression has one meaning from the time it becomes defined until the end of its lifetime; assignment doesn't exist and can't change that meaning. So we defer evaluation, and compute x * 10 when it is used, if it is used.

The symbol x may have some other meaning in the surrounding program, and the closure, which is a function, might be passed around and executed in that other context. Whatever happens, though, when `plusx` is used, x must mean whatever it did when plus was closed. To make this work, the closure must contain the current binding for x, and the data-part of the closure must have a lifetime longer than the lifetime of the block that created the closure.

Except for the lifetime problem, the data-part of a closure is identical to the stack frame that would be created for a function activation; it contains the local context in terms of which local symbols must be interpreted. The difference between a closure and a stack frame is that stack frames have nested lifetimes and closures do not. A stack frame is deallocated before deallocating the stack frame for the block that created it, but a closure must outlive that block. For this reason, closure is a process that can only be done in functional languages or in other languages that have a special closure facility.

The student must get a clear understanding of the difference between a closure and the functions that can be written in traditional languages. The Pascal programmer can write (and then compile) a function that calls another function with a constant parameter. For example, MySum, defined in Exhibit 9.32, calls the function Reduce, from Exhibit 9.29 with its first argument bound to a locally defined function, MyOp. A function such as MySum is not like a closure for two reasons:

- This code must be compiled before it becomes a function! The binding of f in Reduce to MyOp is created by the compiler, not at run time.
- The lifetime and visibility of MySum are limited. It can be used only within the block in which MyOp and Mysum are defined, and it will die when that block dies.

Exhibit 9.32.   We can't make closures in Pascal.

The function MySum calls the function Reduce from Exhibit 9.29 with the first argument bound to a specific operation.

```
Function MyOp(x:  integer, y:integer):integer;
Begin   MyOp := abs(x) + abs(y)   End;

Function MySum(ar:  row_type):integer;
Begin   MySum := Reduce( MyOp, ar)   End;
```

Most things that can be done with closures, and with higher-order functions in general, can also be done in Pascal. To emulate a closure, the programmer would write a program with the necessary bindings in it at a global level, then compile the code. When executed, the result will work just like a closure. However, the ability to create closures during execution gives a more concise and efficient way to accomplish the job.

EXERCISES

1. What is the difference between an argument and a parameter?
2. What is a well-formed function call? Explain the following statement: K&R C is a language in which function calls do not need to be well-formed. Is this an advantage or disadvantage for C programmers?

3. In Ada, a function may be called with fewer arguments than the number of parameters in the function definition. Explain how. Why is this useful?

4. In FORTH, function definitions do not include parameter declarations. This permits the programmer to write a function that uses different numbers of arguments on each call. Explain one benefit and one drawback of this design.

5. How does call-by-value afford protection to the calling program?

6. Why is a call-by-value method of parameter passing ineffective for a swap routine that intends to swap values in the calling program?

7. Why does Pascal refuse to bind a VAR parameter to a constant?

8. Why does Pascal need VAR parameters, but C functions can communicate as well using only value parameters?

9. The attributes "in", "out", and "in out" that are specified in Ada parameter declarations have a basic good property that Pascal cannot achieve with its declarations of VAR or value parameter passing. What is it? (Note: The fact that Ada permits optional parameters is not relevant here.)

10. Explain why a language that supports multitasking will be likely to support call-by-value-and-return rather than call-by-reference.

11. A short program is given below in Pascal with one procedure definition. Show the storage allocated for the main program and the stack frame (activation record) created for the call on the subroutine. Note that one parameter is a reference (VAR) parameter, and one is a value parameter.

```
Program ParameterDemo;
Var I: integer;
    A: array[1..3] of integer;
Procedure Strange (Var X: integer; Y: integer);
    Var temp:  integer;
    Begin temp:=X; X:=X+Y; Y:=temp  End;
Begin (* main program *)
    For I := 1 to 3  Do A[I] := 10-I;
    I := 2;
    Writeln ( 'Initial values ', I, A[1], A[2], A[3]);
    Strange( A[I], I );
    Writeln ( 'Final values ', I, A[1], A[2], A[3]);
End.
```

12. Use the stack frame diagram from question 11 to trace execution of this program. Write values in the storage locations, and show how the values change during execution of the program. Show the output produced.

13. Change both of the parameters of the procedure named Strange, in question 11, to VAR parameters. Answer questions 11 and 12 again showing the storage setup, data changes, and output.

14. What is lazy evaluation? Why is it used?

15. What is call-by-pointer? Why is it a subcase of call-by-value and different from call-by-reference?

16. Explain the differences between call-by-reference (as in a Pascal VAR parameter) and call-by-pointer, with respect to the following:

    a. What is written in the procedure call.
    b. What is written in the procedure header.
    c. How the parameter is used within the procedure body.

17. What is a dangling pointer?

18. Write a short piece of Pascal or C code that creates a dangling pointer.

19. Fill in answers to the twelve questions in the following chart. To name times, use the phrases "load time", "block entry time", "block exit time", "program termination", "any time", or "other" (please explain other). To label accessible locations, use the phrases "anywhere except where masked", "in the declaring block" or "other".

Type of variable	Time of creation?	Time of death?	Where is it accessible?
global variable	1.	2.	3.
static local variable	4.	5.	6.
ordinary local variable	7.	8.	9.
dynamic heap object	10.	11.	12.

20. What is printed by the following Pascal program? Make diagrams of storage for both the main program and subroutine, showing the initial contents and changes in contents. Distinguish between VAR and value parameters in your diagram. This is trickier than tricky. You are being tested on comprehension of name scoping and VAR and value parameters.

```
PROGRAM trick (INPUT, OUTPUT);
VAR J, K, L: INTEGER;
    FUNCTION F(J: INTEGER;  VAR L: INTEGER):CHAR;
    VAR K: INTEGER;
    BEGIN
        K := L + J;
        L := K;
        J := K;
        IF K > 10 THEN F := 'Y' ELSE F := 'N'
    END;
BEGIN   (* main program *)
    J := 3;  K := 15;  L := 4;
    WRITELN( F(L, J) );
    WRITELN (J, K, L)
END.
```

21. What is a higher-order function? Explain two uses for higher-order functions.

22. Name two languages that do not support higher-order functions in any way. Explain how you found the information to give the answer.

23. Explain what a closure is.

24. C gives some support for higher-order functions: pointers to functions may be passed as parameters and returned from functions. Explain what kind of support is missing in C—that is, what can a programmer do with higher-order functions in a functional language that C does not support?

25. Express the type of the function `search` from Chapter 8, Exhibit 8.14 in Pascal type notation, as if it were to be passed as an argument to another function.

26. Express the type of the function `search` from Chapter 8, Exhibit 8.14 in curried notation.

10

Control Structures

This chapter treats the subject of control structures. A control structure is a language feature which defines the order of evaluation of expressions or larger units. Control structures exist in a variety of forms, the lowest level being the primitive control instructions which are defined by the hardware. These include instruction sequencing, conditional and unconditional jumps, and subroutine calls. Control structures in high-level programming languages developed out of and are implemented in terms of these instructions.

Above the expression level, there are four kinds of control structures. These are subroutine call with parameters, statement sequence, conditional execution, and repetition. In order to be useful, programs must be able to perform a section of code for one particular set of inputs and a different set of actions for another. Functional languages have only control expressions: that is, expressions that contain one or more conditions, and for each condition, an expression to evaluate when the condition is true. Procedural languages, on the other hand, have both control expressions and control statements.

Conditional forms are basic and absolutely essential in a programming language because they are inherently outside-in control structures. The conditional lets us test whether it is safe to proceed with a computation before doing so. Various conditional forms are discussed, ranging from very primitive to very general. The generalized conditional is shown to be the most flexible, and the CASE statement the most efficient.

The simplest decision structure is the conditional IF ⟨condition⟩ GOTO ⟨label⟩. Unfortunately, its usage often leads to spaghetti code because the GOTO may lead anywhere in the program. This problem is largely resolved by using structured conditionals such as If..Then..Elseif..Else. The CASE statement is an efficient structured conditional control statement with multiple branches. There are three ways to implement the CASE statement to achieve greater efficiency than a structured conditional. Many languages support the CASE; several of these (including the forms in Pascal, C, and early COBOL) have defects which make the CASE statement cumbersome to use.

Iterative control structures are used to process homogeneous data structures such as arrays, lists, and files. The most primitive loop is the infinite loop, which is a one-in/zero-out structure. The two simplest finite loops, formed with a conditional GOTO, are the repeat loop (with its test at the end of the loop) and the while loop (with a test at the top). These correspond to the structured REPEAT and WHILE statements found in most languages. Ada, Turing, and FORTH have combined these forms into a more general loop in which the loop termination test may appear anywhere in the loop.

If the length of a data structure is known, automatic processing can be performed by a counted loop. The FOR loop has two parts:

- A control element, containing an initial value for the loop variable, a goal, and an increment.

- A scope, containing a sequence of statements to be iterated.

Most languages restrict the expressions that may be used in the control element, and most prohibit changing the loop variable within the scope. The iteration element is a generalization of the counted loop with no restrictions on the expressions within the control element or use of the loop variable. It is not, strictly, a counted loop, and it cannot be implemented as efficiently.

Some languages support implicit iteration. Their basic data structure is a set, array, or list of some sort, and they support a variety of iterative functions to process an entire compound object and return a simple or compound result. Implicitly iterative expressions add great power to a language and permit many complex operations to be expressed briefly and clearly.

10.1 BASIC CONTROL STRUCTURES

A *control structure* is a language feature defined in the semantics of the language (not in syntax only) that defines the order of evaluation of expressions or larger program units.

The *primitive control instructions* defined by the hardware in all computers are listed on page 250. The control structures in higher languages developed out of these and are implemented in terms of them. Execution starts when the computer is turned on or receives a RESET signal. A boot sequence is built into the computer hardware which causes actual execution to start somewhere, in a location defined by the hardware. In modern computers, the boot sequence initializes whatever is necessary, loads the operating system (the OS), then transfers control to it. The OS then accepts a series of commands and carries them out by loading and transferring control to other system programs or to application programs. The transfer of control to a program is represented graphically by the arrow leading into the top of its control diagram.

10.1.1   Normal Instruction Sequencing

Normally, instructions are executed in the order that they are loaded into memory. This is carried out by the instruction cycle of the machine. A typical version of the cycle is as follows:

1. **Instruction fetch:** Load the CPU's instruction register from the memory address stored in the instruction counter register (IC).
2. **Instruction counter increment:** Add 1 to the address stored in the IC, in preparation for fetching the next instruction.
3. **Decode the instruction:** Connect all the appropriate registers and logic circuits. If the instruction references memory, load the memory address register with the address.
4. **Execute:** Do the current instruction. If it references memory, do the fetch or store. If it is an arithmetic instruction, perform the operation.

   Machine instructions are executed in the order in which they are loaded into memory unless that order is changed by a jump instruction. A sequence of instructions that does not include jumps will be diagrammed as a simple box, as in Exhibit 10.1.

Exhibit 10.1.   Diagram of a sequence of statements.

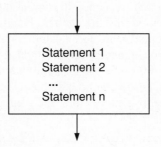

   Sequences are a basic control structure in procedural languages. The code section of a program in a procedural language is a sequence of statements; execution starts at the first and progresses to the next until the end is reached. Programmers are trained to analyze their problems as ordered sequences of steps to be performed on a set of objects. The pure functional languages do not support statement sequences. Rather, sequences are eliminated by use of nested function calls and lazy evaluation. Chapter 12 discusses this approach to programming.

10.1.2   Assemblers

A symbolic assembly language is built on the semantic basis provided by the raw machine, machine language, a symbol table, and ways to define variables, labels, and functions. A macro assembler provides source code macros in addition. This semantic basis is completely flexible: using it you can express any action that your machine can do. But it is not a very powerful semantic basis because it lacks any way to convey the programmer's semantic intent to the translator, and the translator has no mechanisms for ensuring that this intent is carried out.

Macros ease the task of writing code but do not extend the semantic basis, since all macros are expanded, that is, replaced by their definitions, *before* translating the program.

Assemblers impose no restrictions, good or bad, on the programmer; they permit the programmer to write good code or totally meaningless code. Higher-level languages impose many kinds of helpful restrictions, including some that can be checked at compile time and others that must be checked at load-link time or at run time. These restrictions help the translator identify meaningless code.

Two of the primitive semantic features supported by assemblers cause a lot of difficulty in debugging and in proving that a program is correct. These are (1) the GOTO, and (2) destructive assignment. The GOTO introduces complex data-dependent flow patterns which cannot be predicted at compile time, and assignment to variables introduces dependency on time and the order of evaluation into the meaning of an expression. Both make proofs of correctness hard to construct.

In the rest of this chapter, we examine aspects of control structures that are supported by higher-level programming languages. Two kinds of control structures above the expression level are basic: subroutine call with parameters and conditional execution (discussed in Section 10.2). Procedural languages have two more basic kinds of control: execution of a sequence of statements and repetition (discussed in Section 10.3). Many languages, especially older ones, provide a fifth kind of control structure: a GOTO (discussed in Chapter 11, Section 11.1), which is more or less restricted depending on the language. Finally, some languages contain primitives for communication between concurrent, asynchronous processes, such as the task names and `accept` statement in Ada.[1]

10.1.3   Sequence, Subroutine Call, IF, and WHILE Suffice

In 1968 Dijkstra[2] wrote an important and provocative paper that advocated that the GOTO statement should be dropped from programming languages because it was the cause of far too many program errors. This position was based on earlier work by Jacopini[3] which showed that any flow diagram can be written, without arbitrary GOTOs, in terms of conditionals, while loops, and sequences [Exhibit 10.2].

Dijkstra did not claim that programs limited to these control structures would be maximally efficient, merely that they could be written, and written more rapidly and with less likelihood of errors. His evidence was drawn from real industrial experience and from personal observation.

Each of these control structures is comprised of a group of boxes with connecting arrows. Each group is a *one-in/one-out* structure; that is, on a flowchart, one line comes into the control structure and one line goes out of it. This is an important property: programs limited to these formation patterns are easier to debug because the effects of any transfer of control are confined to a small and defined part of the algorithm.

---

[1]Concurrency primitives are beyond the scope of this book.

[2]Dijkstra's ideas were published first in Europe: Dijkstra [1965]. His ideas became known in the United States after he published a second short paper: Dijkstra [1968].

[3]Cf. Böhm and Jacopini [1966].

Exhibit 10.2. A sufficient set of basic control structures.

These are the traditional flow diagrams for Dijkstra's three control structures.

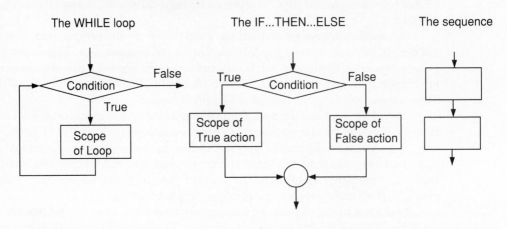

Restricting control to one-in/one-out structures also makes mathematical proofs about the correctness of the program much easier to construct. Such a program can be decomposed into a series of short one-in/one-out sections, and correctness conditions can be written that relate the program state at the top of a section to the state at the bottom. Next, the correctness of each section can be proved independently. Finally, these short proofs can be combined into a whole, yielding a proof of correctness of the entire program whose structure matches the program structure.

The term *structured programming* has no single definition but is generally used to mean a top-down style of program development. The first step is to state the high-level purpose, requirements, and general process of a program. Each process step is then refined by elaborating the definition and adding more detail. In the end, procedures and functions are written to correspond to each portion of the problem definition, and these must be written using only the one-in/one-out control structures provided by the programming language.

Pascal is the "structured" language most widely used now for instruction. It contains recursive functions and procedures, the three control structures just discussed (conditionals, WHILE loops, sequences), two additional loop control structures (FOR and REPEAT loops) [Exhibits 10.27 and 10.23], and a badly designed multibranching conditional structure (CASE) [Exhibit 10.18]. These extra control structures are not necessary in a complete language, but they are certainly nice to have. Pascal also contains a GOTO instruction, but students are often not told that it exists and are seldom taught how or why to use it.

10.1.4 Subroutine Call

This instruction, also called *jump to subroutine*, saves the current value of the IC, then stores the entry address of the subroutine in the IC. *Subroutine return* restores the saved address and brings control back to the instruction after the call. A simple sub-routine call box is shown on the left in Exhibit 10.3. This is diagrammed as a two-part box, divided horizontally, with the subroutine name written above the line and the parameters written below [Exhibit 10.3]. Where a subroutine call is nested within another call or within a statement, these boxes can be used to show the nesting structure. For example, the box on the right in Exhibit 10.3 represents the following nested function calls:

```
c := Foo(a, Goo(3), b) + Goo(17);
```

Exhibit 10.3.   Diagram of a subroutine call with parameters.

The left diagram represents a procedure call (a function call statement); the right diagram shows three function calls nested within an expression.

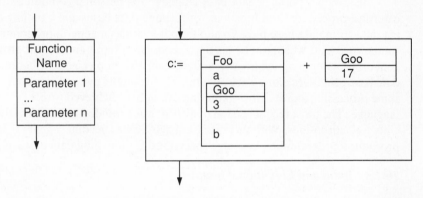

All modern programming languages provide the ability to define and call sub-routines with parameters. Without subroutines, it is nearly impossible to write and debug a large program. The programmer must break a large problem into concep-tually manageable pieces. Subroutines are the programmer's tool for implementing each part in such a way that the interfaces are clearly defined and the interactions among parts are limited. This methodology, of decomposing a problem into clearly defined parts with limited and clearly defined interactions, then building a program by implementing each, is called "top-down programming". It is now recognized to be the basis of good program design.

To understand why there is no real substitute for subroutines with parameters, let us look at a pair of languages that did not, initially, support them: BASIC and dBASE.

BASIC was originally defined[4] lacking a crucial feature. It had a GOSUB xxx state-ment which did a subroutine jump to statement number xxx, and a RETURN statement which returned control to the calling program, but parameters and results had to be passed through global variables. The programmer could emulate the normal param-

---

[4]Dartmouth [1965].

eter passing mechanism by storing each parameter value in a global variable, calling the subroutine, and using the same global variable name inside the subroutine. There were no "dummy parameter" names. The subroutine would likewise store its results in global variables. Thus what is easy in most languages became cumbersome in BASIC, and the programmer had to be careful not to use the same name twice for two different purposes. Worse, the subroutine's actions and those of the main program were not well isolated from each other.

BASIC was recently revised and updated by the author of the original BASIC language, John Kemeny. The new version is called True BASIC[5], perhaps to distinguish it both from the original language and from the dozens of nonstandardized extended BASIC implementations that were developed. This new version upgrades the original language extensively, but perhaps the most important improvement is the inclusion of subroutines with parameters.

dBASE is a popular data base language for personal computers that includes extensive procedures and functions for forming data bases and handling and extracting data from data base files. In addition, it includes a general programming facility similar to BASIC which can be used to create fancy input and output programs. This general programming facility was added to dBASE in pieces, as it became clear that data base primitives alone were not enough. Flexibility in handling input, output, and some processing and statistics gathering can only be achieved with a general-purpose language. The most recent version of dBASE was extended to include a parameter facility for subroutines. With this extension dBASE has become a general, interpretive, procedural programming language specialized for handling data bases.

10.1.5   Jump and Conditional Jump

Jump and conditional jump instructions change the next instruction to be executed by storing a new address into the IC. They differ from a jump to subroutine instruction in that they do not save or restore the address from which the jump originates. The GOTO is an unconstrained transfer of control to some other part of the program. It is diagrammed as an arrow, as in Exhibit 10.4.

Exhibit 10.4.   Diagram of the computer's primitive GOTO instruction.

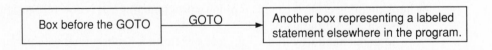

A test or condition will be diagrammed as a trapezoid [Exhibit 10.5]. Control enters at the top of this box. Control leaves to the right through the diagonal side (along the horizontal arrow) if the condition is true. It leaves through the bottom (the

---

[5]Kemeny [1985].

downward arrow) for a false condition. The arrows are not normally written on the diagram and are shown here and in subsequent diagrams only to emphasize the flow of control.

Exhibit 10.5.   Diagram of the primitive conditional.

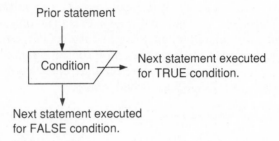

10.1.6   *Control Diagrams*

In order to visualize and compare the wide range of control statements in different languages, we need a language-independent representation for each basic kind of control. Flowcharts provide a graphic representation of control flow but cannot represent the difference between GOTO and structured transfers of control. We define a new kind of diagram, called a *control diagram*, that can represent the limited branches inherent in modern control structures.[6] Simple diagrams are defined for each of the primitive control structures. These diagrams will be elaborated and extended to develop higher-level control structures.

Modern control structures are one-in/one-out units, that is, control can enter the unit at exactly one place and leave the unit at exactly one place. Within a control structure, control may jump around, skip sections, and form repetitive loops.

Our control diagrams represent this control flow implicitly and/or explicitly. Each control diagram has a frame with one entry arrow and one exit arrow. Smaller boxes may be nested within the outer frame. Control flows downward, implicitly, unless an arrow or a branch (indicated by a box section with a diagonal side) directs it elsewhere.

The control diagram for a sequence of statements was shown in Exhibit 10.1. The single entry is indicated by an arrow along the top edge of the sequence box. When control enters this box it progresses downward through any enclosed statements until it reaches the bottom line, then exits on the single exit arrow.

The control diagram for a subroutine call was shown in Exhibit 10.3. When control enters a subroutine call box, the arguments are evaluated and bound to the parameter names; then, control goes to the subroutine code and eventually returns to the bottom of the subroutine call box. Then it leaves by the exit arrow.

Control diagrams for conditionals, loops, and limited control transfers will be presented with these control structures in the remaining sections of this chapter.

---

[6]These diagrams are modeled after, but are not the same as, Nassi and Schneiderman's system.

10.2 CONDITIONAL CONTROL STRUCTURES

All programming languages must contain some control structure that permits conditional execution of a section of code or selection among two or more alternative sections of code. This is obviously fundamental to programming: a program that performs the same actions for all inputs is of limited use.

The kinds of control structures included in a language are, in part, determined by whether the language is functional (nested), or a mixture of functional and procedural (sequential). Functional languages contain only expressions—they have no statements, and, therefore, all control structures in these languages are control expressions. Procedural languages all have control statements, and some also include control expressions. Let us explore the difference between control expressions and control statements by looking at conditionals.

10.2.1 Conditional Expressions versus Conditional Statements

The *conditional expression* is the control structure most intimately associated with the functional languages. It is an expression that contains one or more conditions and, for each condition, an expression to evaluate when the condition is true. A final expression is included to evaluate when all the conditions are false. The conditional expression returns, as its result, the value of whichever expression was evaluated. The simplest conditional expression has the general form:

if ⟨condition⟩ then ⟨expression 1⟩ else ⟨expression 2⟩

For example, the value of the following expression is B or C, whichever is smaller:

if B < C then B else C;

Because a conditional expression returns a result, it may be embedded in a larger expression. Exhibit 10.6 shows the syntax and usage of the conditional expression in C.

Exhibit 10.6.   Syntax and uses of a conditional expression in C.

Syntax: ⟨condition⟩ ? ⟨expression⟩ : ⟨expression⟩
Two examples of usage:

```
a = b<c ? b : c;            /* Store the smaller value in a.  */
printf("%d\n", b<c ? b : c);   /* Print whichever is smaller, b or c.  */
```

Contrast this to the *conditional statement*, which returns no result. A simple conditional statement has the basic form:

if ⟨condition⟩ then ⟨statement 1⟩ else ⟨statement 2⟩;

No result is returned, and the conditional statement is used by including entire statements in its clauses and by placing the entire unit in a sequence of statements. To be useful, the included statements must either do I/O or store their results in a set of variables, as illustrated by Exhibit 10.7.

Exhibit 10.7.   Syntax and uses of a conditional statement in C.

Syntax: if (⟨condition⟩) ⟨statement⟩ else ⟨statement⟩;
Usage: these statements are equivalent to the conditional expressions in Exhibit 10.6.

```
if (b<c) a=b; else a=c;                /* Store the smaller value in a. */
if (b<c) printf("%d\n", b); else printf("%d\n", c);
```

It is not necessary for a language to provide both a conditional expression and a conditional statement, although some do. Anything that can be written using a conditional expression can also be written (more redundantly) using a conditional statement, statement sequencing, assignment, and a temporary variable, V. To do this, the conditional expression is first extracted from its context and its THEN and ELSE clauses modified to store their results in V:

if ⟨condition⟩ then V = ⟨expression 1⟩ else V = ⟨expression 2⟩

Then the outer expression, in which the conditional expression was embedded, is written with V substituted for the conditional expression. Exhibit 10.7 shows the result of applying this process to the expressions in Exhibit 10.6.

The opposite transformation is much more complex. Rewriting an entire conditional statement as an expression may not be possible to do mechanically if it contains several statements in the THEN and ELSE clauses. In the simple case, the transformation is done by "factoring out" the common portion of the THEN and ELSE clauses. If what remains of the clauses can be written as two expressions, ⟨Texp⟩ and ⟨Fexp⟩, and both return the same type result, we can finish the transformation. The common part extracted from the THEN and ELSE clauses is written once (instead of twice), with a "hole" left where ⟨Texp⟩ and ⟨Fexp⟩ had been. Then the new conditional expression is formed by writing

if ⟨original condition⟩ then ⟨Texp⟩ else ⟨Fexp⟩

and is embedded in this hole.

The Effect of Conditional Expressions on Programming Style.

A Pascal program cannot be written in nested, LISP-like style because Pascal does not support conditional expressions. The IF in Pascal is a statement—it does not return a result and therefore may not be used in an argument to a function. The IF statement must communicate through the the program environment and not through parameters on the stack. In contrast, the LISP conditional, COND, is an *expression* that returns a result which can be used in an enclosing expression. LISP conditionals can, therefore, communicate with the rest of the program using parameters. It is this difference, not the presence or absence of many parentheses in the syntax, that is the root of the difference between the LISP and Pascal programming styles.

Most languages are not purely sequential or purely nested. LISP is primarily a nested language, but it also contains a rplaca (destructive assignment) function and the progn control structure. These enable the programmer to use variables and to list a series of expressions to be executed sequentially. Further, all the major sequential languages permit nested function calls, stack allocation, and parameter binding, and some, for example C, contain a conditional expression.

In spite of this extensive overlap in the actual semantic features supported by languages in the two classes, LISP programs tend to be written as nests of function calls, and C programs tend to be written as sequences of statements.

In the late 1970s several people decided that all those parentheses in LISP were "bad". They wrote *front-end processors* which accepted programs written in a much more ALGOL-like or C-like syntax and translated them to ordinary LISP. These preprocessors supported arithmetic expressions with infix operators and conditionals that started with IF. But the programs written for these front-ends still used the modular, nested programming style, common with LISP, with little or no use of variables.

On the other hand, consider C. Theoretically a C programmer *could* write using a LISP-like style, but most do not. One can only speculate on the reasons for this. A few possibilities come to mind:

1. The loop control structures in C are useful. C programmers often use arrays and files. Looping statements are a natural way to process these data structures. But loops in C are statements, not functions. If a programmer uses them, he or she cannot write in a purely nested style. In contrast, LISP programmers often use list- and tree-structured data. Recursion, with nesting, is a natural way to process these structures.

2. A programmer using C *expects* to write in a sequential rather than nested style, and a programmer writing in a LISP variant *expects* to write in a nested style. The expected style dominates the program even though either style could be used in either language.

3. Sequential processing may be more natural for humans than highly nested function calls. Breaking the code into statements and storing intermediate results in variables helps the programmer keep things straight in his or her mind.

It is likely that some combination of these reasons works to keep C programmers writing programs that are more heavily procedural than the typical LISP program.

10.2.2 Conditional Branches: Simple Spaghetti

The simplest, most primitive decision structure is the simple Conditional GOTO, or IF-GO, diagrammed in Exhibit 10.8. This statement exactly implements the conditional branch instruction built into the hardware of most computers, and it was the only conditional control structure in the original BASIC.

Exhibit 10.8.   Syntax and diagram of the simple IF-GO.

Possible source syntax: IF ⟨condition⟩ GOTO ⟨label⟩;   (Keywords vary.)

Diagram:

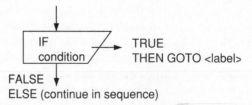

The IF-GO is often used to create "spaghetti code", or code that contains many IF-GO instructions with overlapping scopes that form intertwined threads of code. Spaghetti code is easy to write but hard to debug. It has poor lexical coherence and poor locality of effects. Visually, the spaghetti is the GOTO arrow in the diagram, which may end anywhere in the program.

The IF-GO causes poor lexical coherence because it permits the THEN and ELSE clauses to be placed at widely separated places in the program. Further, if statement labels are distant and not in numeric or alphabetic order, they can be hard to locate in a large program. These problems can, of course, have greater or smaller impact, depending on the style of the programmer. The lexical coherence problem is reduced considerably by using the IF-GO to emulate a structured IF...THEN...ELSE [Exhibit 10.9]. The important semantic problems created by use of IF-GO are discussed in Chapter 11, Section 11.1.

Exhibit 10.9.   The IF in BASIC.

Two control skeletons are shown here. On the left side, the THEN clause is placed at the end of the program, far distant from the related IF and ELSE clauses. On the right, the THEN clause is placed directly after its related ELSE clause. The number of GOTO instructions and labels required for both cases is the same, but the right version has shorter spaghetti strands and, therefore, better lexical coherence.

	Poor lexical coherence		Better lexical coherence
	IF ⟨condition⟩ GO 300		IF ⟨condition⟩ GO 100
	⟨else clause⟩		⟨else clause⟩
	. . .		. . .
200	⟨rest of program⟩		GO 200
	. . .	100	⟨then clause⟩
	END		. . .
300	⟨then clause⟩	200	⟨rest of program⟩
	. . .		. . .
	GO 200		END

10.2.3   Structured Conditionals

Conditional Diagrams.

Conditionals will always be diagrammed by boxes (or box sections) with one diagonal side. Normally, control flows through that diagonal side when the condition is true, but this default can be overridden by drawing a horizontal arrow labeled "FALSE" or "F" that crosses the diagonal side. The other condition (normally "FALSE") causes control to continue flowing downward. Sometimes the diagrams are explicitly labeled for emphasis, even when the default defines the desired direction of control flow.

Structured conditionals are one-in/one-out units, and the corresponding control diagrams have a single entry at the top and a single exit somewhere along the bottom.

The conditional is built out of a series of condition clauses, which are rectangles divided in the middle by a diagonal line. The condition is written to the left of the diagonal line, the actions to be performed when the condition is true are written on the right.

The jump around the ELSE clause or clauses is diagrammed by using a *control frame* along the right and bottom edges of the box. Just as control structures replace GOTOs, these frames replace long twisting control transfer arrows. Control enters a frame by way of a horizontal arrow after completing a TRUE clause, then flows down to the bottom and out by the exit arrow. If control reaches the final ELSE clause, it then goes downward into the frame and, again, out at the bottom [Exhibit 10.10].

Exhibit 10.10.   Diagrams of the structured conditional.

In both diagrams, the GOTO of the simple IF-GO has been replaced by a block of statements, to be executed when the condition is true. After executing this block, control passes to the right into the frame of the control diagram. If the condition is false, control passes downward into the frame.

In the diagram on the right, a box section is added for the ELSE clause. If the condition is FALSE, control flows into this section, and from there downward into the frame.

This is a one-in/one-out structure. The second exit of the simple conditional branch has been "captured" by the frame of this structure. However control reaches the frame, it leaves the frame by the single downward exit.

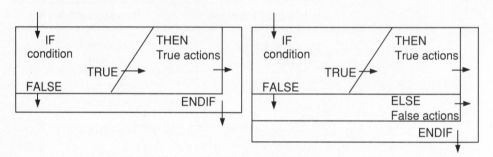

The Basic Forms.

Any of the forms of the structured conditional can be implemented either as a conditional expression (as in LISP) or as a conditional statement (as in Pascal). They differ from the simple conditional branch statement by being one-in/one-out structures. Contrast the diagram of the conditional branch in Exhibit 10.8 to the diagram of the structured IF-THEN conditional on the left in Exhibit 10.10. The difference is that a surrounding frame has become a part of the control structure, delimiting the scope of the TRUE clause. The conditional provides two ways to enter this frame, but there is only one way to leave it: downward.

A more general form of this same control structure also includes a scope of actions for the FALSE case, giving the full IF. . . THEN. . . ELSE control structure on the right in Exhibit 10.10. Use of this control diagram is illustrated in Exhibit 10.11.

Exhibit 10.11.   A structured conditional statement in Pascal.

A Pascal conditional statement is shown on the left and diagrammed on the right.

```
if index <= max then begin
    writeln( name[index] );
    index := index + 1 end
else
    writeln('Index out of range');
```

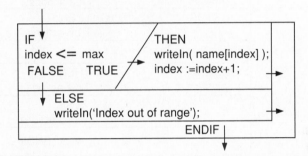

All modern procedural languages provide a conditional control structure with at least two clauses, although the keywords and punctuation vary from language to language. The greatest difference is the way the scopes of the THEN and ELSE are delimited. There are two possibilities:

1. The scopes of the THEN and ELSE are each restricted to a single statement. If more than one action is required, a compound statement may be used. This is a series of statements delimited by BEGIN...END or equivalent bracketing symbols. This kind of syntax is used in Pascal and C.

2. An explicit ENDIF is provided. The series of statements between the THEN and the ENDIF (or the optional ELSE) is the TRUE-scope. The series of statements between the ELSE and the ENDIF is the FALSE-scope. This syntax is used in FORTRAN, Ada, and Turing.

The advantage of choice 1 is that it has fewer keywords and the language syntax is simpler. A disadvantage is that the syntax is ambiguous if one IF is nested inside another, and only one has an ELSE clause. An extra rule in the grammar forces this lone ELSE to be parsed with the nearer IF.

The advantages of choice 2 are that the program does not become filled with BEGIN...END pairs which can interfere with indenting and can be a source of clutter. Also, the ambiguity problem for nested conditionals is solved by the ENDIF. If ENDIF is placed before the lone ELSE, that ELSE parses with the outer IF; otherwise, it goes with the inner IF.

Finally, this IF...THEN...ELSE control structure can be extended again to permit a series of conditions to be tested [Exhibit 10.12]. This produces the most general and flexible possible conditional control structure. Exhibit 10.13 shows a use of the general conditional in LISP. In other languages, conditional clauses after the first are often denoted by the keyword ELSIF or ELSEIF, as shown in Exhibit 10.14.

Exhibit 10.12. Diagram of the generalized structured conditional.

This is a one-in/one-out structure. Any number of conditions may be listed in series, each associated with a scope of actions to be executed if that condition is TRUE. The conditions are tested in the order written, and the actions for the first true condition are executed. If no condition is true, the FALSE scope at the bottom is executed. After executing a scope, control passes into the frame.

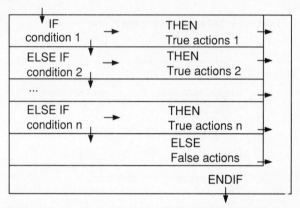

Exhibit 10.13. Use of the general conditional expression cond in LISP.

This call on the print function takes one piece of information, an age, and prints a word describing that age. Its control diagram is the same as the diagram in Exhibit 10.14.

```
(print (cond ((< age 5) ( "young child"))
             ((< age 13)( "child"))
             ((< age 18)( "adolescent"))
             ( T        ( "adult"))))
```

Some languages support the IF...THEN...ELSE but not the ELSEIF clause. To write a generalized conditional in these languages, one writes a series of conditionals, nesting each successive IF inside the prior ELSE clause. The Pascal code fragment in Exhibit 10.15 does the same thing as the LISP and Ada versions in Exhibits 10.13 and 10.14. Note the similarity to Ada code. The same Pascal statement is shown indented in two ways. The version on the left shows the actual nesting depth of the IFs. The version on the right reflects the semantics of the situation, a choice among several parallel cases.

A Short History of Conditionals.

At about the same time as the simple IF...THEN...ELSE was introduced in ALGOL-60, the generalized conditional came into use in MAD[7] and in LISP.[8] The

---

[7]Michigan Algorithm Decoder, Arden, Galler, and Graham [1963]. This language was based on the preliminary ALGOL report (1958) and implemented at the University of Michigan in about 1959.

[8]LISt Processing language, McCarthy et al. [1962]. This language was implemented at M.I.T. in the late 1950s.

Exhibit 10.14.   Use of the general conditional statement in Ada.

I/O in Ada is too complex to be explained here. Please simply assume that the user has defined a procedure named "pr" that takes one string argument, and prints it, followed by a carriage return. This code fragment then does the same thing as the LISP version in Exhibit 10.13. Its diagram is on the right.

```
IF age < 5 THEN
    pr("young child");
ELSIF age < 13 THEN
    pr("child");
ELSIF age < 18 THEN
    pr("adolescent");
ELSE
    pr("adult");
END IF;
```

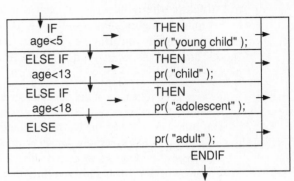

Exhibit 10.15.   Using Pascal to emulate ELSEIF.

Indentation shows nesting depth. Each IF is within the prior ELSE.	Left-justified ELSE IF shows semantic structure—a series of equal choices.
```IF age < 5 THEN writeln('young child') ELSE IF age < 13 THEN writeln('child') ELSE IF age < 18 THEN writeln('adolescent') ELSE writeln('adult');```	```IF age < 5 THEN writeln('young child') ELSE IF age < 13 THEN writeln('child') ELSE IF age < 18 THEN writeln('adolescent') ELSE writeln('adult');```

---

generalized form was later included in PL/1[9] but then was omitted from many new languages (e.g., C and Pascal) which instead included the simpler IF...THEN...ELSE from ALGOL-60.

The original FORTRAN did not include any structured conditionals at all. All forms of IF used GOTOs to transfer control. The ANSI committee in charge of revising the FORTRAN standard resisted all urging to include a structured conditional in FORTRAN II and even in FORTRAN IV. Many nonstandard extensions of FORTRAN IV included IF...THEN...ELSE...ENDIF, though, and finally, with FORTRAN 77, the

---

[9]Programming Language 1, implemented by IBM in 1967 and intended to be the language that would fill everyone's needs. B. Galler, one of the designers of MAD, was on the committee that designed PL/1.

full structured IF with ELSEIF was included because of popular demand. This illustrates both the trouble with design-by-committee, and the slowness with which good new ideas are accepted by people accustomed to doing things in other ways.

The syntax of a language is certainly simplified (and translation is therefore made easier) by omitting the ELSEIF. The ELSEIF adds no "power" to the language, since the same flow of control can be created using the simple IF... THEN... ELSE control structure where the scope of each ELSE is another IF statement.

Opinions about what is most important in language design vary from community to community and change often. In this case, there is no agreement whether a "good" language should include an ELSEIF clause. The ELSEIF statement has some nice properties:

- It is a good reflection of the semantics of a series of parallel choices, a commonly occurring control pattern.
- It combines well with the ENDIF to delimit a series of conditional clauses without need for BEGIN... END bracketing, which clutters the code.
- A series of IFs has each IF nested within the ELSE clause of the preceding IF. This causes many programmers to indent each IF more than the prior one, as shown in the left column of Exhibit 10.15. In contrast, the ELSEIF statement encourages programmers to indent scopes uniformly, in a manner consistent with their status as equally important alternatives.

Thus factors relating to human engineering are the primary reasons for including the more complex ELSEIF syntax in a language design. It is not theoretically necessary or even helpful.

10.2.4   The CASE Statement

While the generalized conditional is maximally flexible, it is not always maximally efficient or convenient to write. Consider the situation in which one of a set of N actions must be taken depending on the value of a single expression [Exhibit 10.13]. It is redundant to write that expression $N - 1$ times as part of N conditions, and it is inefficient to evaluate the expression $N - 1$ times, especially if it is a long expression. Some efficiency can be gained by evaluating the test expression once and storing the answer in a variable, but that still requires fetching that value $N - 1$ times. In assembly language, a programmer would write only one fetch.

This need was met in nonstructured procedural languages by the *computed GOTO statement*. APL, COBOL, and FORTRAN all contain versions of a computed GOTO. In this control structure, an expression is evaluated and its result is used to select one statement label from a list of labels. Control then goes to that label.

Essentials of the CASE Statement.

What is needed here is a structured conditional control statement with multiple branches that implements this common control pattern in an efficient way. The single expression can be evaluated once at the top of the control structure and its value loaded into a machine register where it can then be used to index a transfer vector or be compared efficiently to a series of constants to determine which set of actions to execute. This general CASE structure is illustrated in Exhibit 10.16.

Exhibit 10.16.   The CASE statement.

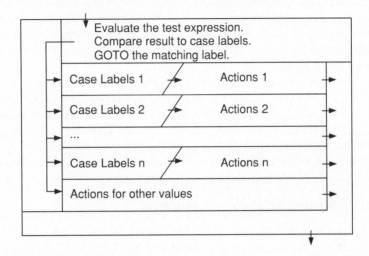

This is the control structure implemented by the CASE in Ada. It is a complex control structure whose semantics are defined by the following list of rules:

1. Each set of case labels is a series of constants or constant expressions of the same discrete type as the result of the test expression.
2. The actions executed are the ones following the case label that is equal to the value of the test expression. The same constant may not be included in two sets of labels.
3. If no label equals the test value, the "other values" clause is executed.
4. After executing a set of actions, control passes to the right, into the "frame", and from there to the single exit.

Possible variations of the general CASE structure involve the rules for the type of value returned by the test expression and the rules for labeling cases. The value must, in any case, be a discrete value. Real numbers such as 3.91 would not make meaningful case labels because of the approximate nature of real arithmetic.

Some languages require that every possible value of the test expression occur exactly once as a case label. If a type with a large number of possible values, such as integer, is permitted, some way must be provided to avoid listing all possible values. This might be done by using subranges of the type as case labels or by using an OTHERS clause to cover nonexceptional cases.

There are three good implementations of the CASE structure. In all three, the test expression is evaluated once at the top and loaded into a machine register. An easy implementation is possible if the machine instruction set includes a computed goto instruction, and the range of values of the control expression is small and matches the range that the hardware is built to handle.

The second implementation, a transfer vector, is exceptionally fast but possibly requires a lot of space. It uses the register containing the test expression value to index an array of code addresses. The compiler generates this array by first sorting the case labels into ascending order, then storing the address of the object code for a case action in the array position corresponding to the value of its case label. To execute case N, the translator generates a simple indirect GOTO through the Nth position of the label array. With this implementation, every possible value in the type of the test expression must occur as a case label, and the transfer array will be as long as the number of possible case labels.

A third implementation of the case is possible if one of the above conditions does not hold. If a possible case label may be omitted or a very large type (like integer) is permitted for the case labels, the CASE must be translated into a series of conditional GOTOs. A series of case labels can be compared very efficiently to the register containing the test value, and a GOTO taken to the first label matching the value in the register. This is not as fast as use of a transfer vector, but it is a big improvement over the code that would be generated (by a nonoptimizing compiler) for a series of IF statements.

Defective Versions of the CASE Statement

COBOL's CASE.

The CASE statement was introduced into COBOL a long time ago when the programming community did not understand that GOTOs cause unending trouble. Unlike the modern CASE, the COBOL CASE is a multiway conditional GOTO, and a program containing a CASE becomes one massive nest of GOTOs. Procedure calls and GOTOs interact in a curious way in COBOL; the same block of code can be entered either way. If a block is entered by a procedure call, control returns to the caller at block end. But if it is entered by a GOTO, control continues on to the next lexical program element. Using the CASE in such an environment makes a program even harder to debug than it would be in FORTRAN or in BASIC. Control can shoot off in any direction if the programmer is not careful.

A good CASE statement is particularly useful in modern data processing applications where on-line data entry is expedited by menu-driven programs. The general CASE is ideal for menu handling. COBOL 85[10] introduced a new statement type, called EVALUATE, which implements the general case structure [Exhibit 10.17]. It is an especially nice version of the general control structure because it allows range expressions to be used as case labels.

The introduction of the EVALUATE statement in COBOL fixes an old defect and illustrates the way languages can grow and adapt to an increasingly sophisticated public. It also illustrates one negative aspect of language growth and restandardization: the proliferation of keywords. Rather than redefine the keyword CASE to have a modern semantics, a new keyword was introduced. The standardization committee had no choice about introducing a new keyword: if they redefined the old one, *all existing programs* that used CASE would become obsolete overnight. In the business world this is certainly unacceptable. Many companies have programs in use that were written ten years ago and are simply modified every time the company's needs change. Reworking all those programs to eliminate the CASE GOTOs is not reasonable. The old CASE statement must now be categorized as an archaic feature that should never be used. Perhaps in twenty years it can be dropped from the language.

---

[10] A good presentation of the changes in the language can be found in Stern and Stern [1988].

Exhibit 10.17.   The COBOL EVALUATE statement.

General Syntax	Code Sample

EVALUATE ⟨expression⟩
    WHEN ⟨condition-1⟩ ⟨action-1⟩
    WHEN ⟨condition-2⟩ ⟨action-2⟩
    . . .
    WHEN ⟨condition-n⟩ ⟨action-n⟩
    WHEN OTHER ⟨action-other⟩
END EVALUATE
	EVALUATE EXAM-SCORE
	    WHEN 90 THRU 100 PERFORM A-ROUTINE
	    WHEN 80 THRU 89 PERFORM B-ROUTINE
	    . . .
	    WHEN 0 THRU 59 PERFORM F-ROUTINE
	    WHEN OTHER PERFORM ERROR-ROUTINE
	END EVALUATE

Pascal's CASE.

Perhaps because the CASE statement is inherently complex, some languages contain variants of it that can be considered to be faulty. That is, they fail to include some important part of the general structure.

Experience has shown that a CASE conditional structure needs to include an OTHERS clause which is to be executed if none of the case labels matches the test value. For example, a very common application for a CASE statement is to handle character data. In such situations, it is often desirable to provide special handling for a few special characters, and one or two routines to be executed for most of the other possible characters. The potential efficiency of a CASE statement makes it attractive in implementing this situation. With an OTHERS clause, this structure requires writing out case labels only for cases that require special handling. But without an OTHERS clause, case labels would have to be written and tested for all 128 possible ASCII characters. This is messy and cumbersome, and most programmers will end up using a series of half a dozen IFs instead of writing a CASE statement with 128 case labels.

Standard Pascal fails to provide an OTHERS clause for its CASE statement. It has the logical structure shown in Exhibit 10.18. Because it lacks this clause, the Pascal CASE statement is rarely appropriate for real situations. Many Pascal implementations are extended to contain an OTHERS clause. Unfortunately, there is no single standard way to add such an extension, and the extensions often have slight syntactic differences, making a program containing a CASE nonportable.

If the value of the test expression is *not* included among the case labels, it is an "error" according to the ISO Pascal standard. (That is, it is a violation of strict Pascal semantics.) In this situation the person who builds a translator has several choices:

- Detect the error at compile time and give an error comment.
- Detect the error at run time and halt execution.
- Make clear in the documentation that the error will not be detected.

Handling a case error in the third way makes it legal (by the standard) to implement one sensible default: if no case label matches, do nothing. Occasionally this is even what the programmer wants to do. But failing to detect a language error is just

Exhibit 10.18. The Pascal CASE with no default clause.

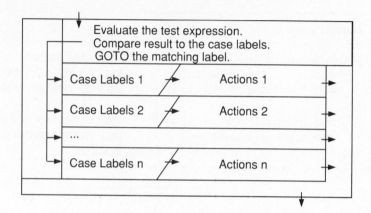

not a good way to get around the defects in the language. Ideally, this defect will be corrected in the next Pascal standard.

C's switch **Statement.**

The switch statement in C does have an OTHERS clause, marked by the keyword default. However, C omits a different part of the general CASE control structure: the exit into the frame after completion of the CASE actions. The general CASE is like a series of simple conditionals, each with an accompanying scope. The C switch is not. It is like a computed GOTO, where all target statements are within the scope of the switch statement. Restricting the targets to the scope of the switch *is* a great improvement over the semantics of a computed GOTO, since it enforces locality of effects and lexical coherence. Nonetheless, the C switch is less than a true CASE structure.

The switch differs from the general CASE structure because once C "goes" to a case label and completes its corresponding actions, it keeps on "going", doing, in turn, all the actions for the succeeding cases! [See Exhibit 10.19, first column.] This is rarely, if ever, what the programmer wants. The switch lacks the frame on the right which is part of the CASE structure.

The C switch would be unusable except for the existence of the break statement, which can be used to attach a frame to any C control structure. Executing a break statement sends control into the frame and thus immediately terminates the switch statement in which it is embedded. Thus the break is like a structured GOTO *out of* the control structure.

C forces the programmer to explicitly write the break which should be an integral part of the CASE control structure. This does provide some flexibility. The programmer may choose to leave the control structure (break) or continue with the actions for the other cases. But this is a case of too much, error prone flexibility. It is a very rare situation in which one would want to continue with all the rest of the case actions.

Exhibit 10.19.   The C `switch` statement without and with `break`.

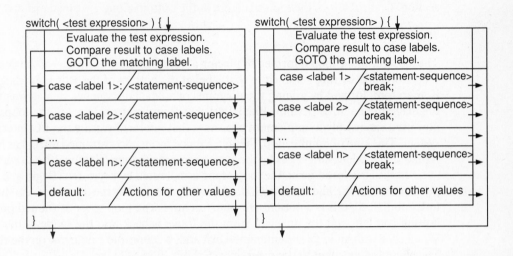

One can only guess at the reasoning of the C designers when they defined the `switch` this way. Since the `break` exists, all the internal mechanisms must be included in the translator to implement the general CASE structure. The reasoning that the combination of `switch` and `break` is more flexible than the general CASE is specious, since an added control command "`don't-break`" could just as well be combined with the CASE to produce the same flexibility as `switch` plus `break`, and be less error prone in the common case. Perhaps this strangeness is simply an accident of history, and a reflection of the fact that C is a twenty-year-old language. In any case, by the principle of *Too Much Flexibility*, we can say that it is a design error.

10.3 ITERATION

Iterative control structures are used to process homogeneous aggregate data structures such as arrays, lists, and files. In procedural languages, iteration is accomplished through explicit loop statements which do not return values although they may modify variables or arrays in memory. In functional languages, iteration is done through functions in which repetition is implicit, such as the LISP `map` functions. These often return lists that were lengthened by one element on each iteration.

Diagramming Loops.

Iterative control structures are one-in/one-out units, and the corresponding control diagrams still must have a single entry at the top and a single exit somewhere along the bottom. The nonsequential transfers of control in a structured loop are diagrammed by using a *control frame* around parts of the box. Control enters the frame by "falling through" from the bottom of the scope, then continues in a clockwise direction, to the left across the bottom, and upward on the left. Control reenters the scope along a horizontal arrow, near the upper left, that leads into some enclosed box section. Control leaves the loop structure at the bottom along a vertical exit arrow.

10.3.1   The Infinite Loop

The most primitive loop is formed by placing a statement label at the top of the desired loop scope and writing a branch to that label at the bottom of the scope. Its diagram is, therefore, formed by joining the diagrams of a labeled sequence of statements to the diagram of a GOTO [Exhibit 10.20, left]. Far from being useless, infinite loops are now used extensively to implement processes that interact by using the I/O interrupt system. This kind of infinite loop, though, formed by an unconstrained GOTO, has been replaced in modern languages by the structured infinite loop [Exhibit 10.20, right].

In the structured form, the loop scope is delimited by keywords (Begin and Repeat are used here), and the branch statement is generated by the translator. As shown in Exhibit 10.20, this is a one-in/*zero*-out structure! The loop scope is framed on the bottom and left, and the only exit from the frame is back into the scope at the top. When used with an exit statement, the exit adds a frame and exit arrow on the right. The result is equivalent to the diagram in Exhibit 10.25.

Exhibit 10.20.   The simplest loop: an infinite loop.

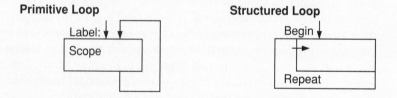

10.3.2   Conditional Loops

Two different simple conditional loops can be formed with a single conditional GOTO. The first form is the same as the primitive infinite loop except that the GOTO at the bottom of the scope is a conditional GOTO [Exhibit 10.21, left]. This is frequently called a REPEAT LOOP.

In the second form, usually called a WHILE LOOP, the conditional branch is placed at the top of the scope [Exhibit 10.21, right]. This form is more frequently useful. Loops are used to process files, lists, and arrays, and it is usually necessary to prepare for the possibility of empty files and zero-length data structures.

Corresponding to the two kinds of conditional GOTO loops are the two structured loops shown in Exhibit 10.22. Their translations into machine code will be the same, but the structured form automatically generates a semantically correct branch instruction. In the structured loop, the programmer marks the beginning and end of

Exhibit 10.21.   The simplest finite loops, formed with a GOTO.

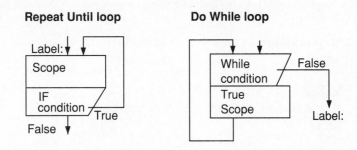

Exhibit 10.22.   Structured conditional loops.

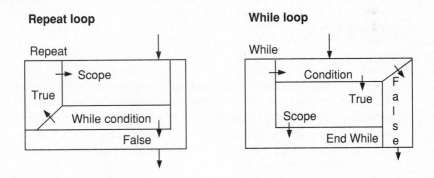

the loop scope with the exit test and a keyword or special character. The compiler then generates the GOTO that forms the loop.

A WHILE loop has the exit test at the top of the scope, a REPEAT loop at the bottom. The WHILE loop was one of the control structures recommended by Dijkstra to be used in eliminating GOTOs. Structured loops are easier and faster to translate than the GOTO versions,[11] and they are less error prone in the hands of any programmer.

The REPEAT is not a very useful loop form because the scope is always executed at least once. In almost all situations some case can arise in which the scope should be skipped. Often these cases correspond to faulty input data. The WHILE makes it easier to check for these errors. For example, the REPEAT loop in Exhibit 10.23 will malfunction if the input, n, is less than 1.

With either of these loop forms, the loop test may have a positive or a negative sense; that is, it may loop on TRUE and exit on FALSE, or loop on FALSE and exit on TRUE. The former type is called a *While test* and the latter type is called an *Until test*. This is a detail that must be checked when learning a new language. Exhibit 10.23

---

[11]See Chapter 11, Section 11.1.

Exhibit 10.23.   REPEAT and WHILE loops in Pascal.

These loops both print out the first n elements of the array a. The repeat loop will malfunction unless $n >= 1$.

Repeat loop:	**While loop:**
`Readln(n);`	`Readln(n);`
`i:= 1;`	`i:= 1;`
`Repeat`	`While i<=n Do Begin`
`    writeln(i, a[i])`	`    writeln(i, a[i])`
`Until i=n;`	`End;`

---

shows samples of the REPEAT and WHILE loops in Pascal. Note that the REPEAT loop ends with an *Until* test.

The WHILE loop is an appropriate basis for an iterative expression as well as for an iterative statement. It is built into LISP's family of map functions and into iterative constructs in modern functional languages such as Miranda. This topic is taken up more fully in Section 10.4.

10.3.3 The General Loop

Restricting loops to a single exit at either the top or the bottom of the scope is artificial. It leads to awkward programming practices such as the "priming read"—a read instruction given to bring in the first line of data before entering the main processing loop (see Exhibit 11.5). The main loop then must end with a duplicate of that read instruction. There is no reason why a loop should not have its exit test at any arbitrary place within its scope, as in the FORTH program in Exhibit 10.24.

Exhibit 10.24.   The general loop in FORTH 83.

Assume getn has been defined to be a function that reads an integer from the keyboard and leaves it on the stack.

```
VARIABLE sum
:  read&add              ( Print a prompt and read a value.  )
                         ( If it is positive, sum it and repeat, else quit.  )
    0 sum !              ( Initialize sum to zero.  )
    BEGIN
        ." Please enter a number and type a CR."
        getn 0 >         ( True if input is a positive number.  )
        WHILE            ( Exit loop if prior expression is not True.  )
        sum @ + sum !    ( Fetch sum, add input, store back in sum.  )
    REPEAT
    sum @ .              ( Fetch value of sum and print it.  )
;                        ( End of function definition.  )
```

Let us define the *general loop* [Exhibit 10.25] to be a structured loop that merges the two common loop forms (REPEAT and WHILE) into a single more flexible looping form. The loop termination test in the general loop is not constrained to occur at the beginning or end of the loop. The beginning and end of the scope will be bracketed by the keywords LOOP and END LOOP, and statements of the scope may come both before and after the termination test. The termination test could be either a While test or an Until test, or the language might provide both forms, giving the programmer an option.

Exhibit 10.25.   The general loop.

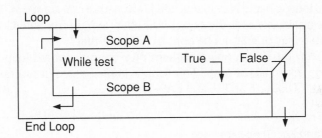

This very nice loop form is supported in FORTH, Turing, and Ada [Exhibit 10.26]. It is likely to become more widely used since REPEAT and WHILE loops are simply special cases of this general structure, and language translation is simplified by reducing the number of special cases. Providing the extra flexibility costs little or nothing.

Exhibit 10.26.   The general loop in Ada.

This function does the same thing as the FORTH function in Exhibit 10.24. Assume that write_prompt is a programmer-defined procedure that writes a message to the screen, and get_number is a function that reads an integer from the keyboard and returns it.

```
FUNCTION read_add RETURN integer IS
    n:  integer;
    sum:  integer := 0          -- Initialize sum to zero.
    LOOP
        write_prompt("Please enter a number and type a CR.");
        n:= get_number ;
        EXIT WHEN n<=0 ;
        sum := sum + n;
    END LOOP;
    return sum;
END read_add
```

10.3.4 Counted Loops

Finally, we can add some mechanism to any of the loop forms (REPEAT, WHILE, or LOOP) to automate sequential processing of a data structure whose length is known. We call the result a *counted loop* because the number of iterations is fixed at the beginning of the loop, and the loop exits when the iteration count reaches that number. Counted loops differ from general loops because the number of repetitions of a general loop may depend on the result of computations within the loop.

There are nearly as many variations in the details of the counted loop as there are languages that support it. In general, though, a variable, called the *loop variable*, must somehow be defined. It is initialized at the top of the loop, incremented at the bottom of the loop, and tested by a loop test. Within the scope of the loop, the value of the loop variable is available and is often used as a subscript. When the value of the loop variable exceeds the preset limit, the loop is terminated. An additional "cleanup" step may or may not be done at loop exit time.

Exhibit 10.27 gives a diagram of a typical counted loop with the loop test at the top, like a WHILE loop. This form is implemented in several languages, including Pascal, COBOL, FORTH, and BASIC.[12]

Exhibit 10.27.   The counted loop.

Syntax in various languages.

FORTH:
```
    10 0 DO ⟨scope⟩ LOOP
```
Pascal:
```
    For J:=1 to 10 Do Begin
        ⟨statement sequence⟩
    End;
```
BASIC:
```
    FOR J=1 TO 10
        ⟨sequence of lines⟩
    NEXT J
```
COBOL:
```
    PERFORM ⟨paragraph-name⟩
        VARYING J FROM 1 BY 1
        UNTIL J > 10.
```

For

Initialize counter.

Does counter meet or exceed goal?

Scope of loop.   False

Increment counter.

End For

True

The nature and implementation of the loop variable has evolved through the years. FORTRAN and COBOL had only static storage, and loop variables were ordinary global variables. PL/1, an old language, permits the loop variable to be declared in any scope surrounding the loop. As the years passed, the special nature of the loop variable was better recognized, and various special restrictions were applied to it.

---

[12]The for loop in C is not a counted loop by our definition; it is dealt with in the next section.

Pascal, for example, requires that the loop variable be declared locally in the block that contains the counted loop. Some languages restrict the use of the loop variable. Pascal and all versions of FORTRAN say that the programmer must not assign a value to the loop variable within the loop. This is done for efficiency. During execution of the loop, the loop variable can be temporarily implemented by a machine register, instead of or in addition to an ordinary memory location. This makes it very fast to test, increment, and use the loop variable. The typical loop refers to its loop variable many times. Thus many machine cycles are saved by not fetching and storing this value every time it is referenced or updated.

FORTH *predeclares* a local identifier, I, to name the loop variable. (If two loops are nested, I is the index for the inner one and J for the outer one.) The loop variable is kept on top of the return stack, rather than in an ordinary storage object, and it is deallocated automatically at loop exit.

Two newer languages, Ada and Turing, go further in this direction. They open a local declaration scope at the beginning of the counted loop and automatically declare the loop variable name as a local variable in that scope. The loop variable is used within the loop and deallocated when the loop terminates. This arrangement has one real advantage: a loop variable, by its nature, has only local meaning, and that meaning is obvious from the context. (This is reflected in the fact that programmers still like to use single-letter names for loop variables.) Declaring the loop variable as a local variable within the loop increases the modularity of the program and minimizes chances of accidental error.

A question now arises about the meaning of the loop variable after exit from the loop. If the loop variable was local to the loop, the answer is clear and easy to implement: since the loop variable was deallocated at loop exit time, its value is undefined. That means that it is completely implementation-dependent, and the programmer should never attempt to use the loop variable after a loop exit. This makes it easy for a compiler writer to implement the language—she or he can use a register for the loop variable, to gain execution efficiency, and does not need to store the final value back into a memory location.

In most languages the loop variable is not local to the loop. However, there is still a question about its meaning after loop exit. Does it contain its original value? Its value on the final time through the loop? A value that is one greater than the goal? In FORTRAN II, the loop variable was kept in a machine index register and its value was officially undefined after loop exit. The ISO Pascal standard also states that the value is *undefined* after loop exit.

This design decision has been called a "victory of religious fervor over common sense".[13] It is easy to define in a formal semantic definition and easy to implement efficiently. However, the programmer often needs to know the value of the index after an abortive loop exit. If that information is not available, the programmer is forced to introduce yet another variable and assign the index value to it inside the loop. This is surely neither efficient nor desirable.

FORTRAN 77 illustrates a more practical design. The language standard defines what the index value will be after an exit. The index value may still be stored in a machine register during the loop, but if so, an *epilogue*, or clean-up step, must be

---

[13]B. Kernighan, informal comment.

executed before leaving the loop normally or by a GOTO. The epilogue will copy the current value of the loop variable back into its ordinary memory location. The loop variable may, thus, have either of two values after exit. If the loop exited normally after completing N iterations, the loop variable equals the initial value plus N times the step size. (This is at least one greater than the goal value.) If a GOTO is used to leave the loop, the loop variable will contain the value current at the time of exit.

The counted loop requires several arguments: the size and sign of the increment, the initial and terminal values for the loop variable, the beginning and end of the scope to be iterated, and the exact termination condition. Different languages provide more or less flexibility in specifying these things and have different rules about the times at which each element is evaluated. Some ways in which counted loop statements differ from language to language are trivial syntactic details; others are more major semantic differences that determine the power and flexibility of the control structure.

FORTRAN II is an example of a language that has differed in a major semantic way from most. It placed the execution of the scope before the loop test so that every loop was executed at least once. That is now recognized to be a mistake, and all modern languages place the test at the top, before the loop scope.

In all languages, control must enter a counted loop through the initialization code (you cannot GOTO into a counted loop). But there are differences in the rules about what happens at loop entry and loop exit, and the ways that control is allowed to leave a loop. Further, treatment of the loop variable, increment, and goal expressions can be different.

All languages increment or decrement the loop variable after executing the scope and before retesting the exit condition. Most of the time, programmers write loops that increment or decrement the value of a variable by 1, so Pascal and Ada restrict the increment to be either $+1$ or -1. This shortens the language syntax a little but is an unnecessary and annoying restriction.

Some languages exit when the loop variable meets the goal, some when the goal is exceeded, and some permit the programmer to write his or her own test using relational operators. Among the latter group, some exit when the test expression evaluates to TRUE and others when it evaluates to FALSE.

If the language allows the programmer to write an expression (rather than a constant) as the goal, it must also specify when that expression will be evaluated. The original FORTRAN, designed for efficiency, permitted the goal to be a constant or simple variable name. The value was fetched once and loaded into a register. Changing the value of the goal variable within the loop did not affect loop termination. Modern FORTRAN permits the goal to be specified by an expression, but the meaning remains the same: it is evaluated only once, before entering the loop. At that time, the *tripcount*, or number of loop repetitions, is fixed. Changes to values of variables within the loop cannot affect the tripcount.

This restriction does not apply to the PL/1 FOR loop. Its goal is specified by an arbitrary expression that is reevaluated every time around the loop. If the values of some of its variables change, the loop termination condition changes. This is also true in COBOL.

Three things must be fixed before loop entry in order to determine a tripcount: the initial value of the loop variable, the goal value, and the increment value. If any one of these can be changed within the loop, the number of iterations is unpredictable. In Pascal, all three are fixed. The increment value is always $+1$ or -1. The language standard states that the loop variable may not be modified within the loop. The goal expression is evaluated only once, at the top of the loop. These three together determine the tripcount [Exhibit 10.28].

Exhibit 10.28.   Pascal computes a tripcount.

Assume i and k have been declared to be local integer variables in the program that contains this code fragment. It is not clear from looking at this loop whether it will produce three lines of output or an infinite number. To know the answer you must know that Pascal *does* compute a tripcount before entering the loop.

```
k := 3;
FOR i := 1 TO k DO BEGIN      { A tripcount of three is computed here.  }
    writeln(i, k);
    k := k + 1                { Changing k does not change the tripcount.  }
END;
writeln(i);                   { Answer is unpredictable; i is undefined.  }
```

A small change in the definition of the semantics of a counted loop can radically affect its behavior. If either the goal value or the increment value can be changed inside the loop, the tripcount cannot be determined ahead of time. FORTH has two counted loop forms, DO...LOOP and DO...+LOOP. In both of these, the beginning and ending index values are computed before the loop. The DO...LOOP has a constant increment value of $+1$, and so has a fixed tripcount. But the DO...+LOOP uses whatever value is left on the top of the stack as the increment value, producing completely unpredictable behavior.

Clearly, in order to understand the semantics of the counted loop in any particular language, all of these matters must be clarified. The counted loop is thus a very interesting statement type. While its general intent is obvious, knowing its actual meaning requires knowledge of many small details. Programmers changing to a language with different details make lots of errors writing counted loops.

10.3.5   The Iteration Element

The most general form of the FOR loop is called the *iteration element*.[14] It was developed in 1963 and was incorporated into the MAD language at that time. Dennis Ritchie, who used MAD at Harvard, later incorporated it into his own language, C. The iteration element generalizes the semantics of each part of the FOR statement and is equally implementable as a loop statement and as a loop expression. It has two sections: a control element and a scope, diagrammed in Exhibit 10.29. The control element contains:

---

[14]Galler and Fischer [1965].

a. A list of arbitrary expressions to be evaluated before entering the loop (initializations). Control passes to expression (b) after executing these expressions.

b. An arbitrary expression whose result must be interpretable as a truth value. This is evaluated before executing the loop scope. Iteration continues until this value is FALSE. At that point control passes out of the iteration element.

c. A list of expressions to be executed after the scope of the loop (increments). Control passes to expression (b) after executing these expressions.

Exhibit 10.29.   The iteration element.

Syntax: Iterate (⟨a⟩;⟨b⟩;⟨c⟩) ⟨scope⟩;

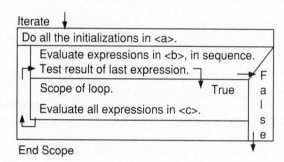

The scope begins at the end of the control element. In an iteration statement, the scope contains a single statement or a compound statement, consisting of a sequence of statements delimited by begin-scope and end-scope symbols. Executing the scope results in a side effect such as input, output, or assignment. In an iteration expression, a program object is computed each time the scope is executed. These program objects are collected into an aggregate (a list or an array) that becomes the result of the entire iteration expression.

Iteration in C.

The C for statement implements the iteration element. The syntax for for is:

for(⟨expression⟩; ⟨expression⟩; ⟨expression⟩) ⟨statement⟩

Exhibit 10.30 shows examples of the use of the for. For these loops, assume identifiers have been declared as follows:

- A cell has two fields, named value and next.
- current and list are pointers to cells.
- k and N are integer variables.
- ar is an array of integers with subscripts 0...max.
- scanf stores the data in the address given as an argument and returns an error/success code which will equal EOF when end-of-file is found.

The biggest difference between the iteration element and ordinary FOR loops is the totally unrestricted nature of the pieces of the control element. This leads to all sorts of unusual constructs, like the last loop in Exhibit 10.30 in which *all* of the work of the loop is done by the control element, and the scope is empty.

Exhibit 10.30.   Uses of the iteration element in C.

```
/*  Read a file of subscripts and print corresponding array elements.  */
    for( ; scanf("%d",&k)!=EOF; )
        if (k>=0 && k<=max) printf("%d\n", ar[k]);
/*  Read N, then read and sum N numbers.  */
    for (sum=count=0, scanf("%d",&N); count<N;  count++)
        { scanf("%d", &k); sum+=k;}
/*  Sum the numbers in a linked list.  */
    for (current=list, sum=0;
        current!=NULL;
        sum+=current->value, current=current->next);
```

The notation current->value on the last line means to dereference the pointer current and select the value field of the resulting cell. It is equivalent, in C, to (*current).value.

When using a normal FOR statement, there is generally one way to set up the initialization, goal, increment, and scope to achieve the desired result. When using the iteration element, there can be several ways to do the same thing [Exhibit 10.31]. This flexibility confuses programmers who are accustomed to restricted forms of the FOR. Many want to be told what the *right* way is, but, of course, there is no single right way. At best we can give rough guidance:

- Put all the initializations relevant to the loop in part (a). Don't initialize loop variables or accumulators earlier, for instance, in the declarations. (This follows from the principle of Local Effects.) Don't put an action here that is repeated in some other loop part.
- Part (b) should contain the loop test. If some action, such as reading data, needs to be done before the test on every iteration (including the first), put it there also. If you have no loop test here, use an explicit infinite loop.
- Part (c) normally contains the statement that changes the loop variable, in preparation for the test. If more than one linear data structure is being processed, increment the "current element" pointers for all of them here.
- The loop body should contain any actions that are left, such as output, function calls, and control statements.

Because the initialization, test, and increment parts of the iteration element are arbitrary expressions, evaluated every time around the loop, super-efficient implementations are not feasible. The FORTRAN implementation (where the loop variable is kept in an index register) makes both incrementation and use as a subscript very fast. This cannot be done if the increment clause is an arbitrary list of expressions to evaluate.

Exhibit 10.31.   Many ways to write the same iteration.

These for loops do the same thing as the last loop in Exhibit 10.30. (Note: When two C expressions are connected by a ",", they become the syntactic equivalent of a single expression.)

```
sum=0;
for (current=list; current!=NULL; current=current->next)
    sum+=current->value;       /* One action in each slot. */

for (current=list, sum=0;  current!=NULL; current=current->next)
    sum+=current->value;       /* The usual way to write it in C. */

current=list, sum=0;
for ( ; current!=NULL; )
    sum+=current->value, current=current->next;

current=list, sum=0;           /* Very bad style. */
for ( ; ; ) if (current==NULL) break;
    else sum+=current->value, current=current->next;
```

The following two loops do the same process and work correctly on nonempty lists. Both will cause a run-time error if current is the NULL list.

```
for (current=list, sum=0;
    (current=current->next)!=NULL;
    sum+=current->value);   /* Ugly but efficient. */

current=list, sum=0;           /* A total misuse of the for loop. */
for ( ; current=current->next; sum+=current->value )
    if (current==NULL) break;
```

On the other hand, this iteration element has total flexibility and no other forms of iteration are necessary. It could serve as the only iterative form in the language. C does have a while statement, but it is equivalent to a degenerate for loop [Exhibit 10.32].

Exhibit 10.32.   Equivalent loop forms in C.

```
while ( ⟨condition⟩ ) ⟨scope⟩ ;
for ( ; ⟨condition⟩ ; ) ⟨scope⟩;
```

10.4 IMPLICIT ITERATION

Some languages support particularly powerful operations on aggregates of data in which iteration is implicit. In the modern functional languages this is the only kind of iteration supported, and it plays an important role. To be useful, an iterative construct in a functional language must return a value, since using destructive assignment to modify the contents of an array is prohibited and there is no other way to communicate the results of the iteration.

10.4.1   Iteration on Coherent Objects

Implicit iteration is one of the most striking features of APL. Most operators in APL are defined for numbers but are applied iteratively to their arguments if the arguments are arrays or matrices. Operators defined for arrays are iterated if the arguments are matrices. How iteration is performed on an APL object depends on its number of dimensions and on the operation being iterated.

Compare the first few examples in Exhibit 10.33 to the LISP code in Exhibit 9.28, and compare the last line to the C code in Exhibit 10.34. (The APL operator "=" performs comparison, not assignment.)

When coupled with dynamic storage allocation, automatic implicit iteration is tremendously powerful. Code that would fill many lines in a language with explicit loops can often be written in one line of APL. Compare the last expression in Exhibit 10.33 to its (partial) C equivalent in Exhibit 10.34. The difference in length illustrates the power of implicit looping when used to process all the elements in a data aggregate.

Exhibit 10.33.   Use of implicit looping in APL.

```
▽   ANSWER ← A FUNC B            ⍝ Define a two-argument function named FUNC.
[1] ANSWER ← (3 × A)- B          ⍝ Return 3 times A minus B.
▽

    X ← 4 9 16 25                ⍝ Bind X and Y to integer vectors.
    Y ← 1 2 3 4
    Z ← (3 4) ρ 1 2 3 4 1 4 9 16 1 8 27 64    ⍝ A 3 by 4 matrix.
```

Expression	Value Computed
X + 1	(5 10 17 26)
X + Y	(5 11 19 29)
X FUNC Y	(11 25 45 71)
(X + 1) = X + Y	(1 0 0 0)
Z = 1	((1 0 0 0)(1 0 0 0)(1 0 0 0))
+/ Z=W	If W is a scalar, the result is a vector containing the number of occurrences of W in each row of Z. If W is the same shape as Z, the result is a vector whose length is the number of rows in Z, containing the number of positions in each row where corresponding elements of W and Z match.

Exhibit 10.34.   Explicit looping in ANSI C takes more writing.

```
int j, k, count[3];
int w          /* Assume w is initialized before entering loops.  */
int z[3][4] = {{1, 2, 3, 4}, {1, 4, 9, 16}, {1, 8, 27, 64}};
```

Given these declarations, the double loop and `printf` statement below do more or less the same thing as the final line of APL code in Exhibit 10.33.

```
for(j=0;  j<3;  j++)
{
    for (k=count[j]=0; k<4; k++)
        if ( z[j][k] == w   ) count[j]++;
}
printf("%d %d %d\n", count[0], count[1], count[2] );
```

A more important benefit of implicit looping is its flexibility. Any size or shape of arrays can be accommodated, so long as every operator is called with arguments whose shapes make sense when combined. APL defines iteration patterns for scalar/scalar, scalar/vector, scalar/matrix, vector/vector, vector/matrix, and so on through higher and higher dimensional objects. The APL code that counts the occurrences of W in Z (+/ Z=W) will work on any shape matrix, and it also will provide a meaningful answer if W is a simple integer. Different C code would have to be written for those cases.

The primary data aggregate type supported by functional languages is the list, and the implicit iterative functions in these languages process lists. In APL the data aggregate type is the array, and operators are iterated over arrays. A data base language such as dBASE also makes extensive use of implied iteration to process all data elements of its basic aggregate type, which is "file".

dBMAN, a dBASE look-alike for the Atari computer, supports many operations that test or manipulate each record in a file, in turn, possibly producing a new file as the result. Examples of such operations are `display` and `sum` [Exhibit 10.35].

Exhibit 10.35.   Implicit looping in dBMAN.

Assume the current record type has fields named `lastname`, `sex`, `hours`, `grosspay`, and `withheld`, and that the current file contains records of this type for each employee. Statistics can be gathered on subsets of the file selected by simple statements which access each record in the file and test or process it. Examples of dBMAN commands follow:

1. `display all for lastname = 'Jones' and sex = 'M'`
2. `copy to lowpay.dat all for grosspay < 10000`
3. `sum grosspay, withheld to grosstot, wheldtot all for hours > 0`

Line 1 finds and displays all male employees named Jones. Line 2 creates a new file that contains copies of some of the records in the current file. Line 3 sums the current gross pay and withholding fields for all employees who have logged some working hours.

The term "fourth-generation language", sometimes applied to data base languages, recognizes the great ease with which large volumes of data can be manipulated using implicitly iterative statements.

10.4.2   Backtracking

A few languages exist that not only support implicit iteration, but combine it with a trial-and-error backtracking algorithm to enable the programmer to write pattern matching expressions. Prolog will search a data base of relations and extract items, one at a time, that match a pattern specified by the programmer. SNOBOL and its successor, ICON, search text strings for the first section that matches a specified pattern (these patterns can be very complex).

In all three languages the semantics of the search command requires that all possibilities must be examined before returning a FAIL result. In some cases this can be done only by making a trial match, then continuing the matching process. If the process later fails, then the system must back up to the point it made the trial match, discard that possibility, and search for a different trial match. This process is called "backtracking". The implementation of backtracking uses a stack to store pointers to the positions at which each trial match was made. It is a well-understood recursive process but nontrivial to write and potentially very slow to execute.

We can illustrate this process by a Prolog example. Prolog maintains a data base of facts, and relations. It searches this data base in response to queries, looking for a set of facts that match the user's requirements. Each query is one or a series of patterns to be matched, in order. As each pattern is matched, any variables in the pattern become bound to the corresponding values in the fact, and a marker is left pointing to that fact. If some later pattern cannot be matched, Prolog will come back to this marker and try to find another match. All searches start at the top of the data base and move sequentially through it. If the end of the data base is reached and a matching fact is not found, Prolog returns the answer "no".

Exhibit 10.36 contains a brief data base about a group of teenagers, their current crushes, and their favored activities. The numbers listed are not part of the data base but are for the purpose of tracing the pattern matching operation. The reader should keep in mind that this data base and the query we will trace are both very simple. Prolog can express far more complex relationships with multiple, nested dependencies.

Exhibit 10.36.   A data base of Prolog relationships.

1. likes(Sara,John)	7. likes(John,Jana)	13. does(John,skating)
2. likes(Jana,Mike)	8. likes(Sean,Mary)	14. does(Sean,swimming)
3. likes(Mary,Dave)	9. does(Mike,skating)	15. does(Mary,skating)
4. likes(Beth,Sean)	10. does(Jana,swimming)	16. does(Beth,swimming)
5. likes(Mike,Jana)	11. does(Sara,skating)	
6. likes(Dave,Mary)	12. does(Dave,skating)	

The owner of this data base is looking for a compatible couple to share an afternoon of sport with himself and his date. Exhibit 10.37 gives his query, which contains four goals to be satisfied together. When and if a match is found, Prolog will tell him the girl, the guy, and the activity he wants. The chart below the query traces the steps Prolog would follow in trying to match all the patterns.

Exhibit 10.37. Answering a Prolog query.

    Query: ?- likes(X,Y), likes(Y,X), does(X,Z), does(Y, Z)

Marker for Goal 1	Bind X to	Bind Y to	Marker for Goal 2	Marker for Goal 3	Bind Z to	Marker for Goal 4	Next Step
1	Sara	John					Try goal 1.
							Try goal 2.
			7? no				Retry goal 1.
2	Jana	Mike					Try goal 2.
			5? yes				Try goal 3.
				10	swimming		Try goal 4.
						9? no	Retry goal 3.
				no			Retry goal 2.
			no				Retry goal 1.
3	Mary	Dave					Try goal 2.
			6? yes				Try goal 3.
				15	skating		Try goal 4.
						12? yes	Solution found.

    Answer: X=Mary, Y=Dave, Z=skating

    String processing and artificial intelligence application programs commonly need to perform exhaustive searches. Thus the implicit iteration plus backtracking provided in ICON and Prolog make them very appropriate and very powerful languages for these application areas.

EXERCISES

1. What is a primitive control instruction?
2. What is the difference between a jump and a conditional jump?
3. What is the purpose of using subroutines in a program?
4. Why is "sequence" considered to be a basic control structure in procedural languages but not in functional ones?
5. What is a one-in-one-out unit? Give a specific example.
6. Of what does a sufficient set of basic control structures consist, according to Dijkstra? Why are these structures easier to debug than programs that use the unconstrained GOTO?
7. What is the difference between a conditional statement and a conditional expression? Give an example of each.
8. How are structured conditionals different from simple conditional branch statements?

9. In what two ways are THEN and ELSE clauses delimited in modern procedural languages?

10. What are the advantages of each method discussed in question 9?

11. What is a CASE statement?

12. Why can a CASE statement be implemented more efficiently than a series of conditionals?

13. Why is an infinite loop considered a one-in-zero-out control structure?

14. What are the two simple conditional loops that can be formed? How are they implemented as structured loops?

15. What is a general loop? How is it different from the other structured loops? What are its advantages?

16. What is a counted loop? When is it used?

17. What is the loop variable? How has it evolved through the years?

18. What happens to the loop variable upon exit from the loop?

19. What is a tripcount? How do changes to the loop variable affect the tripcount?

20. What is an iteration element? How does it differ from a counted loop? (Both have been called FOR loops.)

21. To understand exactly how a for loop operates you must know several details about what happens in what order and under what conditions. Make a list of questions which you must answer to interpret the meaning of a for.

22. The for loop in Pascal is superficially similar to the for loop in C but has very different semantics. List three ways in which the Pascal loop is restricted when compared to the C loop.

23. Diagram all five of the following FORTH loops, and write the keywords in appropriate places on each diagram.

    a. begin...again
    b. begin...while...repeat
    c. begin...until
    d. do...loop
    e. do...+loop

24. What is implicit iteration? What is its purpose?

25. Name two programming languages that support iteration without the use of explicit control structures such as FOR, WHILE, GOTO, or recursion. What kind of iteration is supported?

26. Why is implicit iteration often combined with backtracking? How is it used?

11

Global Control

_____ Overview _____

This chapter deals with several kinds of nonlocal control structures that have come into common use. They range in sophistication from the ubiquitous GOTO to continuations, a form of control transfer based on higher-order functions. Between these extremes are some very useful and practical constructs: BREAK, labeled loops, and exception handlers.

The GOTO instruction is supported in many languages but completely absent in others. There are three faults inherent in the GOTO: bad effects on translation, bad effects on proofs of correctness, and bad human engineering properties. In spite of the fact that GOTO is out of favor, most procedural languages provide a GOTO instruction because sometimes it is the most efficient and practical way to implement a control pattern.

In the late 1960s, there was considerable controversy about using GOTO within a program. Dijkstra advocated that programs should be limited to a set of three basic control structures: sequence, conditional, and while loop. Each is a one-in/one-out structure, making it possible to debug a program by debugging a series of shorter sections of code.

Nonlocal transfers of control can be important when a programmer needs to abort execution of a loop or recover from an error. In some languages, this can only be done by using a GOTO. In more modern procedural languages, the break instruction and exception handlers have been introduced to meet this need. In functional languages, nonlocal transfers of control can be accomplished by using continuations.

11.1 THE GOTO PROBLEM

GOTO is ancient, simple, and efficient; it mirrors the primitive jump instruction built into all machine hardware. To understand why we need modern forms of control transfer, the student must first understand what is wrong with the GOTO.

When the GOTO was first introduced into higher-level languages, it was thought to be both basic and necessary. It was considered basic because it directly reflected the branch instructions of all computers. It was considered necessary because it was used to compensate for the nonexistence of an important semantic mechanism that was not well understood until the late 1960s. Early languages such as assembly language, APL, FORTRAN, FORTRAN II, COBOL, and BASIC did not embody the abstraction "scope". Labeled statements and/or the GOTO were used in place of begin-scope and end-scope markers. APL, FORTRAN II, and BASIC provided no other way to delimit the required scopes. COBOL was different. It had a more complex system with a murky kind of semantics that caused or permitted a tremendous variety of subtle errors.

Since then, there has been considerable argument about the wisdom of using GOTO in a program, or even including GOTO in a programming language. More foolish assertions have been made about this issue than about almost any other programming language feature. Use of any kind of GOTO instruction does cause some problems. We need to examine how this can lead to trouble, why some programmers want to use such a flawed control structure, and whether the need could be eliminated by better language design.

11.1.1 Faults Inherent in GOTO

We can divide the faults of the GOTO control structure roughly into three categories: bad effects on translation, bad effects on proofs of correctness, and bad human engineering properties.

Bad Effects on the Translation Process.

GOTOs are harder to translate than structured control statements. Backward and forward branches require different techniques. A backward branch is used to form loops. To translate it, the location of each label in the object code of a program must be remembered until the end of the code has been reached, since any instruction at any distance could branch back to it. Thus the global symbol table becomes cluttered if many labels are used.

Forward branches are used to implement IF control structures. One conditional branch is needed at the location of the test, and an unconditional branch is needed to skip around the ELSE clause, if it exists. A label is needed just after the last line in the scope of a conditional. These statements are true whether applied to the code a programmer would write in BASIC or the code produced by a translator for a Pascal IF. But a forward branch cannot be translated when it is first encountered, since the location of the target label in the object code is not known at that time.

In the case of a forward GOTO, the location of the forward branch itself must be remembered, and later, when a label is found, the list of incomplete forward branches must be searched and any branch that refers to that label must be patched up and deleted from the list. Again, in a program with a lot of labels, this is slow and inefficient. Translation of the forward branches in an IF is easier and much more efficient. The locations of the forward branches can be kept on a stack. Each ELSE and ENDIF can patch up the branch on the top of the stack. (An ELSE also places an item *on* the stack, to be patched by the ENDIF.) No searching is necessary, and since exactly one end-scope exists for each begin-scope, the stack can be popped when the top item is used.

Correctness Is Hard to Prove with GOTOs.

The bad mathematical properties of GOTO are all related to modularity. Correctness proofs start by breaking the program into one-in/one-out sections and proving that whenever some correctness property is true at the beginning of a section, it is also true at the end. Such proofs become much easier when the size of each section is small. But a program cannot be divided between a GOTO and its target label. Thus the more that GOTOs are used, and the more tangled they become, the harder it is to prove that the program does its intended job.

Some "pragmatists" are not deterred by this reasoning. They believe that mathematical proofs of correctness are seldom, if ever, useful, and that proofs are not used in "real" situations. Unfortunately, the same properties that make a program a bad candidate for a mathematical proof make it hard for a human to understand and debug. Proof and debugging have similar goals and face similar problems.

Some of the GOTOs might be data-dependent conditional branches. With these, the flow of control cannot be predicted by looking at the program, and the number of possible control paths that must be checked is doubled by each IF. With many such branches we get a combinatorial explosion of possible control paths, and complete debugging of a long program becomes highly unlikely.

The best policy for a programmer who must use GOTO because the chosen language lacks an essential control structure is to use GOTO only to emulate properly nested, one-in/one-out control structures. All forward and backward branches are kept short. This takes self-discipline and does not make translation any easier, but it avoids the debugging problems.

Bad Human Factors Inherent in the Best Use of GOTOs.

When scopes are defined by labels and GOTO there is often poor visual correspondence between the true structure of the program and its apparent structure, represented by the order of lines on the page. FORTRAN II and BASIC had only an IF...GO, not a full IF...THEN...ELSE structure. The latter can be emulated using GOTO, but this has the effect of putting the ELSE clause under the IF (where control goes when the condition is false) and putting the THEN clause at some remote program location, often the end. The end of such a program tends to be a series of stray clauses from a bunch of unrelated IFs. Things that belong together are not placed together in the source code, and the code has poor lexical coherence [Exhibit 10.9, the IF in BASIC].

Writing such code is error prone because the programmer will often write an IF and simply forget to write the code for the remote section. Debugging such code is also more difficult because it requires lots of paging back and forth. Patching or modifying code after it is written usually introduces even more remote sections. Eventually the flow of control can become simply too confusing to follow.

Why Spaghetti Is Unpalatable.

The most difficult situation for either proof or debugging is one in which the scopes of different IFs or loops overlap partially, in a non-well-nested manner, and unconditional GOTOs thread in and out through these merged scopes. In this situation there may be a very large number of ways that control could reach a particular statement. This kind of program is called *spaghetti code* because of its tangled nature. Spaghetti code is easy to write but tricky to debug. The outstanding characteristic of spaghetti code is that virtually everything has global effects.

If one simply sits down and writes out lines of code as they occur to the conscious mind, adding afterthoughts, corrections, and improvements as needed, the result will probably be spaghetti code, even if a "structured language" is used. The lack of clarity is caused by too many IF statements asking redundant questions about obscurely named global variables. Disorganized thinking produces disorganized code, and disorganized code is hard to understand and hard to debug.

The bugs in most programs can be eliminated by cleaning up the code. The truth of this has been demonstrated over and over by beginning students, coming to a professor with programs whose bugs they cannot locate, let alone fix. The professor can look at such a program, fail to see the error right away, and suggest that a few messy parts be cleaned up and rewritten, keeping all routines short and all variables local. Having no other recourse, the student follows these orders. The student comes back an hour later with a working program. The bug never was found, but it disappeared when good "hygiene" was applied to the program. The irony is that the programmer accomplished in an hour of clean-up what had not been achieved in a whole evening of debugging through patches and modifications.

The performance of many spaghetti programs can be improved by cleaning them up. For small jobs and quick answers, the stream-of-consciousness programming method is usable and may even be fastest in the long run. For large or production jobs, it is disastrous. The resulting program is usually "loose": it is longer, more complex, and less efficient than a well-thought-out, well-structured program.

A spaghetti program has a short useful lifetime and poor portability. In a spaghetti program with ill-defined scopes and global variables, it is difficult to define or understand how the parts of the program interact. It is, therefore, difficult to modify or extend the program in even minor ways without introducing errors into parts that formerly worked.

It is for these reasons that the business and defense communities have given their full backing to structured system design and structured programming techniques. Any program is expensive to develop, and one with a short lifetime is too expensive. Most managers do not understand programming, and they are at the mercy of their staff unless they can establish some sort of criteria for the "right way" to do things. To this end, they often require or forbid the use of certain language features, require a certain style of programming, and require extensive documentation of every step of the program development process.

Rigid rules about methodology and style often do stand in the way of modernization. New and better languages and methods are not accepted until a new generation of managers takes over. But firm application of these rules protects a manager against unscrupulous programmers like one professional who bragged to a class that he had "tenure" at his company because his program code was both crucial to operations and undecipherable by anyone else. Perhaps to defend against programmers like this, one local company has a program that turns spaghetti code written in COBOL into modern structured COBOL code.

11.1.2   To GOTO or Not to GOTO

Against the GOTO.

On the one hand it is amply clear that excessive use of GOTO and highly unrestricted GOTO instructions make programs error prone, hard to read, hard to debug, and perhaps impossible to prove "correct" by mathematical methods. The simple existence of a label in a program slows down translation. For these reasons, the computing community has largely adopted Dijkstra's position that the use of GOTO is bad, and that structured programming, *without* GOTO, is better.

Many of the newer computer languages contain no GOTO at all [Exhibit 11.1]. The omission of GOTO is particularly interesting in the cases where a new language is basically a revision of an old one, as Icon is a revision of SNOBOL. Both are general languages, designed by R. Griswold, with particular adaptations and many functions included to make string processing easy.

Exhibit 11.1.   Some languages with no GOTO and no labels.

Icon: Has ordinary WHILE and UNTIL loops and an IF...THEN...ELSE control structure.

Prolog: Uses the REW cycle and nested functions like LISP.

FORTH: Has structured loops and conditionals only. An assembler is an integral part of a FORTH system, but even the FORTH assembly language does not provide an arbitrary GOTO; it has only limited-distance forward and backward jumps.

Turing: Has a structured conditional and structured loops, with break.

SNOBOL, designed in the early 1960s, is built around an unusual one-in/three-out control structure. Each line of a SNOBOL-4 program invokes a series of function calls, name bindings, and pattern matches. Depending on the success or failure of this series of actions, processing can continue at any of three lines [Exhibit 11.2]. Even a short program can become a rat's nest of intertwining GOTOs.

Exhibit 11.2.   The unique control structure in SNOBOL-4.

SNOBOL-4 was built on a unique one-in/three-out control pattern. Control flowed in at the left side of a line. Function calls, pattern matches, and explicit bindings were executed in left-to-right order. At the right end of the line, the process produced either a "success" or "failure" result, which determined the next line to be executed:

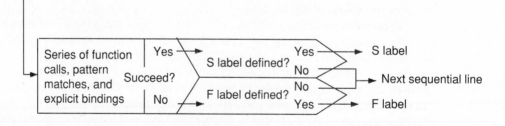

Icon is the modern successor to SNOBOL-4. The string-processing orientation remains, but the curious GOTO structure is gone. It is replaced by structured control statements, including WHILE, UNTIL, and IF... THEN... ELSE. Icon programs look more like C than like SNOBOL.

In Favor of the GOTO.

In spite of the fact that GOTO is currently out of favor, most procedural languages do provide a GOTO instruction. This is because using a GOTO is sometimes the only efficient or practical way to implement an essential control pattern. Articles appear regularly in the popular computing magazines hotly debating the merits of the GOTO instruction and exhibiting programs that cannot be written efficiently (in languages such as Pascal) without it.

It is important to understand that if the control structures of a language reflect the commonly occurring process control patterns, then the programmer will be happy to use them instead of GOTO. Some languages are clearly deficient in control structures. For example, FORTRAN lacks a WHILE loop and a CASE statement, and BASIC lacks a WHILE loop, an IF... THEN... ELSE conditional, and procedure parameters. Textbooks for beginning programmers in these languages have been rewritten to preach the use of structured programming, even though adequate one-in/one-out control structures are not provided by the language.

Authors of textbooks for both languages advocate achieving "structure" by restricting the use of labels and GOTO to emulate the standard IF and WHILE control structures in Exhibit 10.2. Unfortunately, this produces FORTRAN code that is awkward, cluttered, and unmotivated by any real need. Dijkstra's control structures are not the only possible "good" ones and are not the most appropriate to superimpose upon a GOTO language.

Pascal contains all of Dijkstra's control structures, but these form a very limited tool bag for the expert programmer. One might suggest that limiting the programmer to WHILE, FOR, REPEAT, IF... THEN... ELSE, and CASE is like limiting a skilled carpenter to the use of a screwdriver, hammer, wrench, saw, and a broken chisel. Perhaps the programmer can do the job required, but not in a very pretty way. These five control structures satisfy programming needs much of the time, but there are many common situations in which they fall short. Pascal programmers who use GOTO do so primarily when they wish to implement the following four control structures efficiently:

- An OTHERWISE clause in the case statement.

- A loop statement whose exit test can be placed anywhere in the scope [Exhibit 11.4].

- A break statement [Exhibit 11.9] to be used in loops, or a two-exit loop, returning a "success" or "abort" result.

- A way to terminate a nest of loops all at once after an error [Exhibit 11.10, Ada loop labels].

As long as programmers work with languages such as FORTRAN and Pascal, GOTO will be used to emulate important missing control structures, and we will continue to hear arguments from naive programmers about the value and indispensability of GOTO. In a properly designed language, GOTO has few, if any, uses.

Ada has the control primitives, missing in Pascal, to handle the needs described. Consequently, there is little demand for the GOTO in Ada. It is not possible to give a list of all the control structures that might sometime be useful, but we can provide enough structures to satisfy 99.9% of the needs, and make 99.9% of the uses of GOTO unnecessary. It remains a design issue whether a language should provide GOTO to allow the programmer to write efficient code for that remaining .1% of situations.

11.1.3 Statement Labels

A discussion of GOTO must cover the target of the GOTO—a statement label. Programming languages have used a variety of methods to define labels, including label declarations, simple use, and merging labels with source code line numbers.

Line Numbers Used as Labels.

Some interactive languages, notably BASIC and APL, took a shortcut approach to statement labels: the same line numbers that define the sequence of statements were used as the targets for GOTO. Like all shortcuts, this caused real semantic trouble.

First, it deprives the programmer of any way to distinguish lines that form the top of a program scope from lines that are simply in the middle of some sequence of commands.[1] A programmer normally knows which lines of code should and should not become the target of a GOTO. Even a programmer who chooses to create spaghetti code with tangled scopes knows where each thread should and should not begin. A language that provides no way to communicate this information is not offering the programmer a good vehicle for modeling a problem.

Second, as discussed in Chapter 2, Section 2.3.3, line number/labels are a compromise because the semantics needed for line numbers are different from those needed for labels. If the semantics defined for them are appropriate for use by the on-line editor, then the semantics are inappropriate for defining flow-of-control, and vice versa.

Defined Labels.

Most languages avoid these problems by having a programmer simply write a label at the beginning of any line. In Pascal, the label must also be declared at the top of the program. (This permits Pascal to be compiled easily in one pass through the source code. Languages without declared labels either require two passes or some complicated patching-up of the generated code at the end of the first pass.) Exhibit 11.3 summarizes the rules for defining and using labels in several common languages.

Conclusions.

The uses and misuses of GOTO and statement labels have been considered, along with a variety of ways to minimize the use of GOTO. These include the obvious ways— inclusion of structured loops and conditionals in the language, and ways that have only recently been appreciated, including providing more flexible loop control structures and a structured BREAK statement which replaces the unstructured GOTO.

---

[1]Discussed more fully in Chapter 2, Section 2.3.3.

Exhibit 11.3. The form and definition of labels.

Language	Form	Rules for making and using labels
Ada	alphanumeric	Place << label_name >> before any statement. Use in the GOTO statement.
APL	alphanumeric	Place label followed by ":" before any statement. Use in "→" statement.
COBOL	alphanumeric	Place beginning of label in columns 8–11 (ordinary statements cannot start before column 12). Use in the GOTO or PERFORM statements.
FORTRAN	numeric	Place in columns 1–5 at the beginning of any executable statement. Use in the GOTO statement.
LISP	alphanumeric	Labels and "go" expressions are legal only within a "prog" or a "do" body. The label is defined by an expression that forms part of the body of the prog. The expression "(go label_name)" within a prog body causes transfer of control to the expression after label_name.
Pascal	numeric	Declare label at top of program and place it, followed by ":", before any statement. Use in GOTO statement.
PL/1	alphanumeric	Place label followed by ":" before any statement. Use in GOTO statement.
SNOBOL-4	alphanumeric	Place label and ":" at the left side of any statement. Use labels by placing their names in the "succeed" or "fail" field of any statement.

11.2 BREAKING OUT

Many loops have two possible reasons for termination, not one. The basic search loop is a good example: control will leave the loop after all data items have been searched and the key item is not found anywhere. This is called a *normal exit*, or FINISH. On the other hand, if the item is in the data base, a search loop should terminate as soon as it is found, before examining all the remaining items. This is called an *abortive exit*, or ABORT. In a search loop, a normal FINISH is associated with failure and an ABORT with success.

As another example, an input loop will ABORT if a premature end-of-file is encountered and will FINISH if the number of input items meets expectations. In this case, the FINISH is associated with success and the ABORT with failure.

A loop syntax that provides two ways to leave the loop is important. It is applicable to the large number of situations in which a repeated process can either FINISH or ABORT. To write such a loop using GOTO is easy. The normal termination condition can be placed in the loop control element; the ABORT condition is placed in an IF-GO within the loop [Exhibit 11.4].

Exhibit 11.4.   An input loop with an exit in the middle.

A simple interactive read loop is shown here in FORTRAN, demonstrating a common situation in which the loop exit is placed at a position other than the top or bottom:

```
100 PRINT ('Please type your name.')
    READ *, (NAME)
    IF (NAME .EQ. 'Quit') 200
    PRINT ('Hello ', Name, 'Nice to see you.')
    GOTO 100
200 PRINT ('Goodbye.')
```

Compare this code to the Pascal version in Exhibit 11.5.

To accomplish the same thing without using IF-GO is more complex. In the case of an input loop, this is generally handled by using a priming read [Exhibit 11.5]. The prompt and input statements are written twice, once just before the loop, guaranteeing that the loop variable will be initialized, and once at the end of the loop, to prepare for the next test. This is correct and executes efficiently, but it is clumsy to write.

Exhibit 11.5.   The Pascal input loop with a redundant priming read.

```
Writeln ('Please type your name.');
Readln (Name);
While Name <> 'Quit' do begin
    Writeln ('Hello ', Name, 'Nice to see you.');
    Writeln ('Please type your name.');
    Readln (Name);
end;
Writeln ('Goodbye.');
```

Compare this code to the FORTRAN version in Exhibit 11.4.

An inexperienced programmer thinks that he can solve this problem by using an UNTIL loop instead of a WHILE loop. Unfortunately, this just leads to a different kind of repetition: the loop exit condition has to be tested within the loop (as well as at the end) in order to avoid processing nondata when the end-of-file condition occurs [Exhibit 11.6]. This is even less elegant than the priming read, since it introduces an extra level of nested logic and it causes unnecessary duplication of work on every iteration.

Sometimes two exit conditions can be combined into a single loop control expression using AND. In other cases this is not possible, either because some action must

Exhibit 11.6.   The Pascal input loop with an extra test.

```
Repeat
    Writeln ('Please type your name.');
    Readln (Name);
    If Name <>'Quit' Then Writeln ('Hello ', Name, 'Nice to see you.');
Until Name = 'Quit';
Writeln ('Goodbye.');
```

be done between testing the conditions, or because the second condition would cause a run-time error whenever the first is true [Exhibit 11.7].

The WHILE loop in Exhibit 11.7 translates into the following steps:

1. (k<=max) is evaluated (call the result t1).
2. (a[k]>0) is evaluated (call the result t2).
3. (t1 and t2) is evaluated (call the result t3.)
4. If t3 is false the loop exits, otherwise sum = sum + a[k] and k := k + 1 are executed.
5. Control returns to step 1.

Exhibit 11.7.   Some Pascal code that will stop with a run-time error.

Assume k is an integer, and a is an array with subscripts from 1 to max. This code sums the items in a up to but not including the first negative or zero element.

```
k := 1;   sum := 0;
While ( k<=max ) and ( a[k]>0 ) Do Begin
    sum := sum + a[k];
    k := k + 1
End;
```

This code segment will "bomb" with a "subscript out of range" error at the end of summing any array whose elements are all positive. What happens is this: when (1) is false, (2) is evaluated anyway, and since k is too large, this causes an error. (In fact, that is why test (1) was included.)

To program such a loop correctly in Pascal one must put condition (1) in the loop control element and condition (2) in a separate statement inside the loop. A superfluous Boolean variable is declared, and an IF statement within the loop sets it to TRUE if the ABORT condition happens. Then the test in the loop control element is modified to test this flag also. This will cause an exit from the loop at the beginning of the iteration after the ABORT condition was discovered. After loop exit, some other mechanism must be found to determine what condition caused the exit and take appropriate action. This awkward program idiom is illustrated in Chapter 8, Exhibit 8.13, where a flag named done is introduced to permit an abortive loop exit.

In more complex situations a Pascal programmer might use several Boolean flags, set in several places, and combined into a complex expression for the exit condition. This is logical spaghetti just as surely as if we used many GOTOs to create this control pattern. Our goal is to eliminate the need for spaghetti in our programs.[2] To do this we need a structured way to exit from the middle of a loop. Such an exit mechanism is provided by the BREAK statement (or its equivalent) in many languages. The BREAK is simply a structured GOTO to the end of the control unit. It may be placed anywhere within a loop, and it transfers control immediately to the statement following the loop. Its control diagram [Exhibit 11.8] is an immediate exit into the frame of the statement. (A frame is added if the control structure does not already have one.)

Exhibit 11.8.   Structured conditional loops with BREAK.

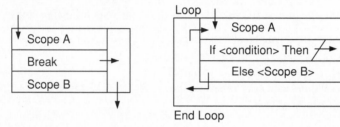

BREAK exits to the right.   A loop with a conditional BREAK.

C[3] and the newer procedural languages, Ada and Turing, all include some form of the BREAK statement for aborting a loop in a structured manner. In Ada and Turing it is called EXIT. This is shown on a control diagram as a frame along the right side of the box which is connected to the bottom frame, from which control leaves the entire diagram. Control enters this frame along a horizontal arrow wherever a break occurs in the program.

Exhibit 11.9 gives one final version of our print routine, written in C using break, which causes immediate exit from a loop. By putting a break instruction inside an if and embedding the whole thing in an infinite loop, we can achieve the same thing as in the original FORTRAN example, simply and efficiently.

11.2.1   Generalizing the BREAK

In addition to statement labels, for use with the GOTO instruction, Ada also has loop labels, which are used to create double-exit loops and to allow immediate, one-step exit from a nest of loops. The simple BREAK statement takes control immediately out of the enclosing control structure, and into the control scope that surrounds it. The Ada EXIT is a generalization of this idea; it can cause an immediate exit from an entire nest of loops (or any part of a nest) by naming the loop label of the outermost loop. It can be used for any kind of loop (FOR, WHILE, or infinite)[4] [Exhibit 11.10]. We will

---

[2]See Section 11.1.

[3]C also has a continue statement, which can be used inside any loop. It transfers control immediately to the top of the loop and begins the next iteration.

[4]Ada is the only major language that lets you name a loop scope so that you can exit from it.

Exhibit 11.9.   The input loop implemented using `break` in C.

```
char *name;                    /* This is a string variable.  */
for(;;)                        /* An explicit endless loop.   */
{
    printf ("Please type your name.   ");
    scanf ("%s", name);
    if (name[1] == '\0') break;  /* Exit if no name was entered.  */
    printf ("Hello %s, Nice to see you.\n", name);
}
printf ("Goodbye.");
```

call this control structure the FAR_EXIT. The canonical example of an application for the FAR_EXIT is a search loop over a two-dimensional data structure such as a matrix or a list of lists. A double loop is used to process the structure, and when the key item is found, control must leave both loops.

Exhibit 11.10.   Loop labels in Ada.

In the following code, a dictionary is represented as a linked list of words, and each word is represented as a linked list of characters. The double loop searches a dictionary for the first word containing the character '#'. Upon loop exit, word_pointer and char_pointer either point to the required word and the '#', or to null, if no such word was found. These variables must be defined outside the outer_loop.

```
outer_loop:  WHILE dictionary_pointer /= null
                word_pointer := dictionary_pointer.word;
                char_pointer := word_pointer;
                WHILE char_pointer /= null
                    IF char_pointer.letter = '#'
                        THEN EXIT outer_loop;
                        ELSE char_pointer := char_pointer.next
                    END IF;
                END LOOP;
             END LOOP outer_loop;
             -- Control comes here from the EXIT above.
```

Implementing this exit actually requires more than a simple GOTO. When an Ada FOR loop is entered, stack space is allocated for the loop variable. This obviously must be deallocated upon exit from the loop. A FAR_EXIT can be placed at any nesting depth. When executed, it will terminate all loops in the nest, up to and including the labeled loop, and any other loops that were placed within that outer loop. The obvious implementation of this action is to scan backwards through the stack, deallocating everything up to and including the storage for the labeled loop. This kind of sudden exit can be quite useful for error handling but must be accompanied by some way to pass information outward, to the calling program, about the reason for the sudden exit. Variables that are global to the outer loop are used for this purpose in Ada.

11.3 CONTINUATIONS

All the nonlocal control structures discussed so far have been defined in terms of sequences of statements. Functional languages do not have such sequences but must supply some way to accomplish the same ends in a functionally acceptable manner. Programmers who use functional languages still must write search loops and make sudden error-exits. The continuation is a functional object that meets this need.

Briefly, a *continuation* is a function which "acts like" the remainder of the program which is still to be executed. For example, suppose a programmer writes a program to compute $\sqrt{2}$ and then print out the answer. We can think of this program as having two parts:

1. The job of the square root function is to compute a real number which, when multiplied with itself, equals 2.

2. The print routine waits to receive a number from the square root function, at which time it prints the number it receives on the user's screen.

Step 2—the part of the program that will make use of the answer provided by part 1— is called the continuation of the program. You can think of the term "continuation" just as a fancy name for "the rest of the program still to be executed".

The concept of a continuation exists in all programming languages and is of concern to the language implementor, but only languages that support higher-order functions are able to give the programmer explicit access to the continuation. This is because the continuation acts like a function. It waits to receive a value and then performs an action or computation which depends on that value. Manipulating a continuation is like manipulating a function. If functions are already first-class objects, then continuations can be treated like any other function. If not, then special language primitives would be required. It is not surprising that most languages elect to omit such facilities.

Even in a language that supports higher-order functions, a primitive is needed to package up the current continuation in a form that the program can use. Packaging the continuation is like establishing a *checkpoint*—everything must be saved that is needed in order to safely restart execution at a later time. This typically includes the program counter, the stack, the environment, and so forth. Saving the current continuation can be quite an expensive operation indeed!

We will use Scheme syntax to illustrate the formation, semantics, and use of continuations. In Scheme, this primitive is called *call-with-current-continuation*, which is often shortened to *call/cc*. It is a higher-order function which takes another function, f, as its single argument. It creates a one-argument function, cc, from the current continuation and then calls f with argument cc. Function f is an arbitrary program, usually written by the programmer, which may or may not make use of the function cc. If cc is ever called, the current environment is discarded and replaced with the one saved when cc was created, and the argument to cc is passed back as the value returned by call/cc.

In Exhibit 11.11, we show how to use `call/cc` to store the current continuation in a global variable, gcc. The argument given to `call/cc` is the nameless function defined by "`(lambda (cc) (set! gcc cc) '())`". Call/cc applies this lambda expression to the current continuation, which results in the local symbol cc (in the body of the lambda expression) being bound to the current continuation. This lambda expression doesn't do much—it just assigns its argument to a global variable named gcc, which exports the continuation into the surrounding environment. Finally, the lambda expression returns a null list to `call/cc`, which passes the value on to its caller, the `let` expression, which binds the symbol x to the return value, in this case, the null list. The display statements cause the comment "`returned value`" and the value of x to be printed on the terminal.

Exhibit 11.11. Packaging a continuation in Scheme.

```
(define (makecc)
    (let ((x (call-with-current-continuation
          (lambda (cc) (set! gcc cc) '()) )))
    (display "returned value: ")
    (display x) ))
```

After returning from `call/cc`, the name gcc can be used, any time, to call the saved continuation. If the user types in the command "`(gcc 3)`", she or he will see the response "`returned value:  3`". The reason this happens is that gcc returns control to the previous control point where `call/cc` was about to return with the null list, but this time `call/cc` returns 3 instead. Thus x gets bound to 3. Execution now continues as before, printing the comment and the current value of x.

This example just demonstrates how a continuation may be formed and called; it does not do anything very useful. However, the `call/cc` is a powerful control structure which can be used to emulate other control structures, including WHILE loops and BREAK. This ability to break out of a piece of code is the most common use for `call/cc`. If one thinks of execution over time, the continuation is created when you execute the `call/cc`, *just before* f is called, and the continuation consists of the code that will be executed *after* f returns. The execution of f itself is not included in the continuation; thus calling the continuation from within f has the effect of causing control to jump ahead to the point it would be if f were allowed to finish normally.

In the Scheme code in Exhibit 11.12, the function named search implements the search procedure by making a continuation which is used to break out of the search process when the search key is found in the data list. Search creates a continuation, binds it to the symbol cc, then calls scan with cc as an argument. Scan performs a recursive search and uses its continuation-argument (which it calls foundf) to break out when the key is found. Scan returns the rest of the list starting with the key.

The continuation requires an argument, so when it is called by scan, the answer found by scan is passed to the continuation, which in turn passes it on to the calling

environment. A transcript of a test of search is shown in Exhibit 11.13. You can see
that calling the continuation really does abort the recursive search.

Exhibit 11.12.   Call/cc used in Scheme to break out of a loop.

```
; Search a list, break when found.  Returns tail of list, starting
; with the atom equal to the key.
(define (search key ls)
    (call-with-current-continuation      ; label break point
      (lambda (cc) (scan key ls cc))))   ; calling cc causes break
; Perform actual search.  Called like search, but "foundf" is a
; functional argument that is applied to the part of the list
; starting with the first occurrence of the search key.
(define (scan key ls foundf)
  (if (null? ls)                         ; if end of list
   '()                                   ; return failure token
   (begin                                ; else
     (display "examining element ")      ; document progress
     (display (car ls))
     (newline)
     (if (eq? key (car ls))              ; test list head
       (foundf ls)                       ; break out if found
       (scan key (cdr ls) foundf)))))    ; else recursively scan tail
```

A transcript of a test run is shown in Exhibit 11.13.

Exhibit 11.13.   Testing the break routine.

This is a transcript of a test run of the code from Exhibit 11.12, translated by MIT Scheme. The
characters "1]=>" are Scheme's prompt.

```
; Define some test data
1 ]=> (define boys '(tom dick harry bob ted))

1 ]=> (search 'dick boys)
examining element tom
examining element dick
;Value:  (dick harry bob ted)

1 ]=> (search 'john boys)
examining element tom
examining element dick
examining element harry
examining element bob
examining element ted
;Value:  ()
```

In the search example, the continuation was used to do a forward jump, skipping over work that would otherwise have been done. However, there is nothing in the definition of a continuation that restricts its use to jumping forward in time. It can also be used to return to a previously visited point of the computation. Suppose, in the above example, that $cc(w)$ were called, not while executing f but while executing cc itself. This seems circular, and indeed it is! This causes cc to start over again, but this second execution is given argument w, whereas the first execution might well have been with some other argument. (If not, the program will be in an infinite loop!)

The next two examples show how call/cc can be used to emulate WHILE. Although Scheme has an iterative control structure, it is not a pure functional construct. Call/cc can be used instead, in order to make Scheme truly behave like a pure functional language.

Exhibit 11.14 shows a simple counting loop, implemented using a continuation. At the top of the routine, a continuation is formed and bound to the name "cc". The continuation marks the spot to return to later. (This is analogous to what a compiler must do to translate the beginning of a WHILE loop.) The result of call/cc is a list containing this continuation and a number. The code analogous to the body of the loop starts with let; the first thing it does is to give names to the items in the list that was returned by call/cc; the continuation is named gcc, and the number is named n. Now, this number is tested. If it exceeds the limit, a "!" is displayed and execution ends because there is nothing more to do. If n is less than the limit, it is displayed and the continuation is called (with n incremented) to continue the looping process. Test results are shown at the bottom of the exhibit; the command (count 5) does, indeed, count to 5.

Exhibit 11.14. Using call/cc to make a loop.

```
; (count n) prints the numbers 1...n !  on a line.
(define (count limit)
    (let ((x (call-with-current-continuation
                 (lambda (cc) (cons cc 1)))))
         (let ((gcc (car x))
               (n (cdr x)))
              (cond
                ((> n limit) (display "!"))
                ((begin
                  (display n)
                  (display " ")
                  (gcc (cons gcc (1+ n))))))))))
1 ]=> (count 5)
1 2 3 4 5 !
;No value
```

Exhibit 11.15 shows another function: one that computes factorial. Compare this to the Pascal version of factorial in Exhibit 11.16.

Exhibit 11.15. A Pascal-like implementation of factorial, using a continuation.

```
(define (fact n)
    (let ((x (call-with-current-continuation
                   (lambda (cc) (list cc 1 1)))))
         (let ((gcc (car x))
               (k    (cadr x))
               (p    (caddr x)))
              (cond
                ((> k n) p)
                ((gcc (list gcc (1+ k) (* k p)))))))))
1 ]=> (fact 5)
;Value:  120
```

Exhibit 11.16. The factorial function in Pascal.

```
function fact (n:  integer) :  integer;
var
   temp:  integer;
   i:  integer;
begin
  temp := 1;
  for i := 1 to n do temp := temp * i;
  fact := temp
end;
```

When used in this manner, the continuation becomes like a WHILE statement: it returns repeatedly to a fixed starting point, each time bringing with it a value that can be tested and can potentially stop the repetitions. Each time the continuation is called, the new context *replaces* the old context, just as the new value of the WHILE loop variable replaces the old value. Here is a wolf in sheep's clothing: destructive assignment disguised as a higher-order function in a form that is "politically correct" for a functional language.

This kind of "backing-up" behavior is appropriate in several real-life situations. The Prolog interpreter backs up whenever the tentative instantiation it has been trying fails. A transaction processing system backs up if the transaction it is in the middle of processing is forced to abort. An operating system backs up the I/O system when a disk read error occurs and tries the read again.

11.4 EXCEPTION PROCESSING

11.4.1 What Is an Exception?

An *exception* is a situation that makes it impossible for a program to proceed with normal processing. It is an unpredictable situation with which the program must cope.

Exceptions happen frequently enough so that a robust system cannot ignore them, but seldom enough so that they are unusual. There are three major ways in which exceptions arise:

1. A hardware error occurs and triggers a hardware interrupt signal. Examples of hardware errors are highly varied and well known to all programmers. These include: an attempt to divide by zero, numeric overflow during an arithmetic operation, an attempt to access protected memory or a nonexistent address, a disk-read error, I/O device not ready, and others.

2. A system software module identifies an error situation. Examples include: a nonnumeric character entered in a numeric input field, an attempt to use a subscript outside of defined array bounds, an attempt to store an out-of-range value in a subrange-type variable, an attempt to open a file that does not exist, an attempt to write a file on a device that has no available space, an end-of-input file, and so on.

3. A user function identifies a logically impossible or inconsistent situation. Examples, of course, are specific to the application. Some might be: a request for processing on a data item that is not in the data base, illegal data value in input stream, and the like.

A program that ignores exceptions invites disaster. For example, arithmetic overflow can be ignored in COBOL, and will be, unless the programmer explicitly tests for it. The result is that the COBOL program continues its normal computations using a meaningless bit pattern that looks like data and is likely to print out a meaningless answer. Ignoring an end-of-file condition in a C program will generally result in an infinite loop processing the last data item repeatedly. The worst possible thing to do about an exception is pretend that nothing is wrong and keep processing.

A second possible response to an exception is to terminate the program immediately and return control to the system. This action is what the Pascal standard *requires* as a response to a subrange error, subscript error, or arithmetic overflow. While this may be an acceptable way to manage faulty student programs, abrupt termination is not acceptable for a production system. At the very least, relevant information about the state of the system and the cause of the error should be made available.

In the old days, a sudden termination of this sort would usually be followed by an octal or hexadecimal dump. The programmer could then manually decode and trace the action of the program and perhaps find the cause of the sudden termination. A more modern response, typical in Pascal systems, is the "call traceback", which dumps the chain of dynamic links from the run-time stack. Unfortunately, a dump is a primitive tool for tracing errors, and a "call traceback" offers too little information. Further, even if the programmer can decode these communications, the end user, who must handle the error, generally cannot.

Robust systems must be able to recover from errors. Ignoring exceptions and sudden death are both unacceptable alternatives. Exceptions must be identified, if possible, and their effects controlled and limited as much as possible. Often, if the exception is handled at the right level, corrective action can be taken and the program can finish normally. For example, if a user of an interactive program types an illegal input, it should be identified, and the user should have an opportunity to retype the data. Sometimes the length of the code to handle exceptions exceeds the length of the code to process normal data.

11.4.2   The Steps in Exception Handling

There are four steps in processing an exception condition:

- Detect the exception.
- Pass control to the unit that is able to take action.
- Handle the exception by taking constructive action.
- Continue with normal execution after correcting the problem.

The last two steps are straightforward and can be done with ordinary program code, so long as the language provides support for the first two steps. Unfortunately, support for steps 1 and 2 is spotty and limited in most current languages.

Detecting Hardware and Software Exceptions.

Computer hardware detects many kinds of errors automatically and generates hardware interrupts to signal that an exception has happened. An interrupt is processed by the operating system which generally sets a status flag in response. These status flags can be read by application programs at run time, but many languages do not provide language primitives to do so. Thus the warning provided by the hardware and the operating system is simply ignored.

Even in languages as early as COBOL, the importance of error containment was recognized. Arithmetic commands could contain an optional ON SIZE ERROR clause which provided a way to send control to an error routine. After processing the error, control could return to the next step and the program could continue. PL/1 was another early language with some support for exception handling. It has defined names for system-generated hardware and software exceptions. The user can define handlers for these exceptions using an ON CONDITION clause. In case of an error, control would come to a user-defined routine, giving the programmer an opportunity to print appropriate error comments. For most errors, however, the programmer cannot prevent program termination after printing comments.

One of the glaring omissions in standard Pascal is any way to test hardware status codes. Arithmetic overflow, division by zero, and the like cannot be either detected or handled within the user program. Because error detection and recovery is an essential part of a production program, most commercial Pascal implementations extend the language by introducing predicates which test the system status flags.

Some languages use error codes, returned by system subroutines, to provide the programmer with information about exceptions. This is a common way to handle I/O errors. For example, in the standard C library, input, output, file-open, and dynamic memory-allocate commands all return error codes for exceptional conditions. The user's program may ignore these codes, which is risky, or take action.

Finally, some languages provide a general exception-handling control structure, along with a list of predefined exception names. The programmer may test for these names in the program, and the control structure delivers control to user-defined exception-handling code. In Section 11.4.3 we examine this exception facility in Ada.

Passing Control.

The user often knows what can and should be done to recover from or correct an exception error. However, a good program is written as a series of modules; the exception may be discovered in a low-level module that is called from many places. That module often cannot take constructive corrective action because it does not have access to important data objects. Intelligent processing can be done only in a context where the meaning of the data objects is known and the severity of the exception can be evaluated. For example, in an interactive program, an "invalid input" exception may be detected in a deeply nested subroutine, but only the main interactive module can interact with the user.

Knowledge of the exception must be passed back from the routine that discovered the exception to the point at which it can be handled gracefully. There are two ways that control can be transferred in a language with no special exception control mechanism: by using GOTO or a continuation, or by propagating an error code back up a chain of nested subroutine returns.

GOTO is not a good solution. Although it passes control, it cannot pass information about the exception with that control. Any such information has to be passed through global variables. Further, most languages have restrictions about the target of a GOTO; for example, control cannot pass into the middle of a loop or a conditional, and it can only go to a label that is visible in the scope of the GOTO. The result is that exception handlers end up being defined at the top level, so that they are accessible. After taking action, it is then difficult to resume normal operation.

In a functional language, continuations can be used to handle exceptions in much the same way as a GOTO can be used.

Passing an error code back up a chain of calls can be done in any language, and the return value can encode information about the exact nature of the exception. We call this process *error propagation*. Control can be passed backwards to the right level for handling the problem. One difficulty of this approach is that the error handling code must be intermixed with the code for normal processing, making the logic for both cases harder to write and comprehend. A more serious difficulty is that the error propagation code must be present in every subroutine in the chain between the detecting module and the handling module. These intermediate routines have no interest in the error; they did not cause it and don't know how to handle it, yet they have to pass it on. This greatly clutters the code and obscures its logic. The code itself is very error prone.

For example, a well-written C program that uses the standard I/O library will check the code returned by every I/O statement and take corrective action if the result differs from the expected result. In Exhibits 11.17 and 11.18, two versions of an I/O routine are given—a robust version and a clear version. The error-trapping code makes the robust version much longer and more obscure; the actual I/O operations are buried in a mass of exception code. This demonstrates the importance of an exception control structure in a modern language.

11.4.3 *Exception Handling in* Ada

The facility for exception handling in Ada provides a real contrast to the do-it-yourself versions we have discussed. Ada provides excellent support for detection of both hardware and software generated exceptions. It provides reasonable, clean solutions to the problems of passing control, handling exceptions, and restarting normal processing.

Exhibit 11.17.   I/O with error checking in C.

```
void silly()
{   int age, code;
    char * name;
    FILE * infile, outfile;
    if ( !(infile = fopen("myinput", "r"))
        { fprintf(stderr, "Cannot open input file.\n"); exit(1);}
    if ( !(outfile = fopen("myout", "w"))
        { fprintf(stderr, "Cannot open output file.\n"); exit(1);}
    if ( fscanf(infile, "%s%d", name, &age) < 2)
        fprintf(stderr, "Bad data record ignored\n");
    if ( fprintf(outfile, "Hi %s; I hear you are %d years old!\n", name, age)
        = = EOF
      { fprintf(stderr, "Cannot write to file myout!\n");  exit(1);}
}
```

The system call exit(1) causes the program to abort gracefully, flushing all buffers and closing all open files.

Exhibit 11.18.   I/O without error checking in C.

```
void silly()
{   int age, code;
    char * name;
    FILE * infile, outfile;
    infile = fopen("myinput", "r");
    outfile = fopen("myout", "w");
    fscanf(infile, "%s%d", name, &age);
    fprintf(outfile, "Hi %s, I hear you are %d years old!\n", name, age);
}
```

The exception facility includes four kinds of statements:

- A declaration form for user-defined exception names.
- A command to signal that an exception has happened.
- A syntactic word, "EXCEPTION," to separate the regular program code from the exception handlers.
- A syntax for defining a procedure to handle one kind of exception.

Exhibit 11.19 shows samples of each kind of exception statement. In the following discussion, we examine the usage of each part of the exception system.

Exhibit 11.19.   Handling an integer overflow exception in Ada.

The simple program `Circles` accepts interactive input and calls procedure `One_Circle` to process it. `One_Circle` calls an output routine, `Print_Circle`, which is omitted here for brevity. If an arithmetic overflow occurs during execution of `One_Circle`, normal processing of that data is aborted: `Print_Circle` is not called, and the normal prompt is not printed. Instead, the user is prompted to reenter the data, and processing proceeds with the new data.

```
WITH Text_IO; USE Text_IO;  PACKAGE Int_IO is NEW Integer_IO(integer);
-- -- -- -- -- -- -- -- -- -- -- -- -- -- -- -- -- -- -- -- -- -- -- --

PROCEDURE Circles IS
    Diameter: Integer;
BEGIN
    Put ("Please enter an integer diameter.");
    LOOP
        BEGIN
            Int_IO.
            Get(Diameter);
            EXIT WHEN Diameter<=0;
            One_Circle(Diameter);
            Put ("Please enter another diameter (0 to quit):    ");
        EXCEPTION
            WHEN Diameter_Too_Big_Error =>
                Put("Invalid input--diameter too large.  Please reenter: ");
        END
    END LOOP;
    Put ("Processing finished.");
    Put New_line;
END Circles;
-- -- -- -- -- -- -- -- -- -- -- -- -- -- -- -- -- -- -- -- -- -- -- --

PROCEDURE One_Circle (Diam:  Integer) IS
    Radius, Circumference, Area : Integer;
BEGIN
    Circumference := Diam * 22 / 7;
    Radius := Diam / 2;
    Area := Radius * Radius * 22 / 7;
    Print_Circle(Diameter, Radius, Circumference, Area);
EXCEPTION
    WHEN Numeric_Error =>
        RAISE Diameter_Too_Big_Error;
END One_Circle;
```

User-defined Exceptions.

Descriptions of the Ada language and the standard library packages list the names and semantics of the exceptions that the Ada system might generate. In addition, programmers can define their own exceptions, which will be handled the same way as those defined by the system. A simple declaration defines a name as an exception:

⟨exception name⟩ :   EXCEPTION;

To signal a user-defined exception, we use the RAISE statement:

RAISE   ⟨exception name⟩;

Exception Handlers.

An *exception handler* is a body of code labeled by the name of an exception. A program can have handlers for user-defined exceptions and/or for system-defined exceptions. A programmer writing code that must be reliable needs to define handlers for any of those exceptions that might be raised by that job. Any block of code (BEGIN...END) can have local exception handlers, which are declared at the bottom of the block. The syntax for defining an exception handler is:

```
BEGIN
    ⟨code for processing normal case⟩
EXCEPTION
    WHEN ⟨exception name⟩ =>
            ⟨action for that exception⟩
    WHEN ...
    WHEN OTHERS =>
END
```

The exception portion of the block can contain as many WHEN clauses as needed, and their order does not matter. (These clauses must be mutually exclusive, though; one exception name cannot be used to trigger two clauses.) A program that wishes to be sure to catch all exceptions, even unexpected ones, can include a handler labeled WHEN OTHERS =>. In the Circles example, both the main program and the subprogram have one exception handler.

Passing Control and Resuming Normal Processing.

The code of a handler is translated in the context of its enclosing block; that is, variable bindings and visibility are the same as for the rest of the code in the block. The block BEGIN...END also defines the scope of the abort action associated with each exception: all code is skipped from the point at which the exception is raised until the end of the block, and the exception handler is executed in its place. If an exception is raised during execution of a subroutine call, all statements in the block after the call will be skipped.

Raising an exception starts an abort action. If there is no local handler for the exception, the current block is aborted and its frame is removed from the run-time stack. The exception is then raised in the routine that called the aborted routine. If that routine has a handler, it is executed. Otherwise, it is aborted and the exception is passed backward another level. This aborting continues, removing one stack frame each time, until a stack frame is found that contains a handler for the exception. The handler is executed and stops the popping. If a program has no handler for an exception, all frames will be popped, the main procedure will be aborted, and control will return to the system.

Raising and Propagating Exceptions.

In procedure `One_Circle`, the computation of `Area` is likely to overflow with relatively small inputs.[5] The code to check for this overflow is not placed immediately after the exception-prone statement; rather, it is separated and put into the `EXCEPTION` section of the block. Thus the flow of control for normal processing is clear and uninterrupted. If arithmetic overflow does happen, the system will raise the `Numeric_Error` exception flag and abort the block from the point of * 22. Control will pass directly to the statement `RAISE Diameter_Too_Big_Error`, then leave the enclosing block, which, in this case, is the body of the `One_Circle` procedure.

The command `RAISE Diameter_Too_Big_Error` renames the exception condition, an action which seems pointless in a short example. However, this can be an important way to communicate information. In a large program, there might be many situations in which a `Numeric_Error` could be generated, and many different potential responses. Renaming the exception provides more information to the receiver about the cause of the problem and the context in which it arose and makes it possible to take more specific corrective action.

The act of raising the new exception sends control back to procedure `Circles` with the information that the diameter was too large. This procedure takes corrective action by asking the user to reenter the data. At this point, the exception handling is complete. The exception has been "caught", and it is not passed up to the next level. The problem has no further repercussions; normal processing is resumed.

EXERCISES

1. What is spaghetti code? What causes it?
2. What are the three faults inherent in the GOTO control structure?
3. Why was GOTO initially used in the development of programming languages?
4. Name two programming languages in which any line of the program may be the target of a GOTO, whether or not that line has a declared statement label.
5. Name two programming languages that do not support GOTO at all.
6. What are the current arguments against using GOTOs? For using GOTOs?
7. What is a statement label? Why is it necessary?
8. What are the two ways to leave a loop? Give a specific example of each.
9. Explain the difference between BREAK and GOTO. Why is BREAK a superior control structure?
10. Explain why Ada has loop labels in addition to an EXIT statement.
11. Explain why labels in FORTRAN are more semantically sound than labels in BASIC.
12. Briefly, what is a continuation?
13. Why are continuations interesting?
14. Describe two applications of continuations.
15. How do exceptions arise? What is the result of ignoring them?
16. Compare exception handling in Pascal and in C.

---

[5]On our system, integers are 2 bytes, and overflow occurs for diameter = 205.

17. Explain why exceptions are connected to nonlocal transfers of control.

18. Compare I/O error handling in C and in Ada. Comment on lexical coherence and human engineering.

19. Compare an exception name declaration in Ada to a label declaration in Pascal. Comment on purpose and likely implementation.

20. Why is an exception control structure superior to a GOTO for containing and recovering from errors?

PART

III

APPLICATION MODELING

12

Functional Languages

___ Overview ___

This chapter presents the goals and attractions of functional programming. Functional languages have developed as semantically clean ways to denote objects, functions, and function application.

The concept of denotation, as opposed to computation, is introduced. Functional constructs denote objects, in contrast to procedural constructs which specify methods for constructing objects.

Development of functional languages started with lambda calculus, which was extended to denote types, literals, and operations for primitive data domains. Lazy evaluation and the absence of destructive assignment were also carried over from lambda calculus into the modern functional languages.

Functional languages have a minimum of explicit control structures. Explicit loops are replaced by tail recursion and implicit iterative constructs. Sequences of statements can be replaced by lazy evaluation, nested context blocks, or nested procedure calls because there is no destructive assignment.

Miranda is presented as an example of a functional language because of its generality, power, and simple, attractive syntax. List comprehensions and infinite lists are explained, and applications are given.

12.1 DENOTATION VERSUS COMPUTATION

During the 1960s, several researchers began work on proving things about programs. Efforts were made to prove that:

- A program was correct.
- Two programs with different code computed the same answers when given the same inputs.

313

- One program was faster than another.
- A given program would always terminate.

While these are abstract goals, they are all, really, the same as the practical goal of "getting the program debugged".

Several difficult problems emerged from this work. One was the problem of *specification*: before one can prove that a program is correct, one must specify the meaning of "correct", formally and unambiguously. Formal systems for specifying the meaning of a program were developed, and they looked suspiciously like programming languages.

Researchers began to analyze why it is often harder to prove things about programs written in traditional languages than it is to prove theorems about mathematics. Two aspects of traditional languages emerged as sources of trouble because they are very difficult to model in a mathematical system: mutability and sequencing.

Mutability.

Mathematics is a pure denotational system; a symbol, once defined in a given context, means one thing. The truth or falsity of a mathematical statement is a permanent property of the statement; it does not change over time. But programming languages have variables, whose contents can be changed at any time by a remote part of the program. Thus a mathematical proof about a program that uses assignment is necessarily nonmodular and must consider all parts of the program at once.

Programming language functions are not like mathematical functions because of the mutability of variables. In mathematics, a function is a mapping from one set of values (the domain) onto another (the range). To use a function you supply an argument from the domain, and the function returns an element from the range. If the function is used twice with the same argument, the element returned will be the same. We can thus say that a mathematical function f denotes a set of ordered pairs $(x, f(x))$.

It is easy to write a program that does not correspond to any mathematical function. Exhibit 12.1 shows a definition of a C function that, if called twice with the same argument, returns different answers. This function increments a static local variable each time it is called, and returns the sum of the argument and the value of that variable. Although this code uses a static variable, which is not supported by many languages, the same function could be written in almost any language by using a global variable instead.

Exhibit 12.1.   A nonfunctional function in C.

```
int my_func(int x)
{   static int z = 0;       /* Load-time initialization.  */
    return x+(z++);         /* Value of z increases after each call.  */
}
```

Sequencing.

When a mathematician develops a theorem, she or he defines symbols, then writes down facts that relate those symbols. The order of those facts is unimportant, so long as all the symbols used are defined, and it certainly does not matter where each fact is written on the paper! A proof is a static thing—its parts just *are*, they do not *act*.

In contrast, a program is a description of a dynamic process. It prescribes a sequence of actions to be taken, not a collection of facts. Sometimes the order of a pair of program statements does not matter, but other times it does. Some statements are in the scope of a loop and are evaluated many times, each time producing a different result. To fully describe a program during execution (which we call a *process*), we need not only the program code, but a copy of the stack, the values of global and static variables, the current values of the computer's program counter and other hardware registers, and a copy of the input.

12.1.1 Denotation

Functional languages are an attempt to move away from all this complexity and toward a more mathematical way of specifying computation. In a functional language, each expression of the language *denotes* an object. Objects are pure values and may be primitive data elements such as integers, functions, or higher-order functions. Thus each expression can be thought of as a description of a static, mathematical entity rather than of a dynamic computation.

Some examples will help make this clear. The expression 3 denotes the integer 3, as do the expressions $2 + 1$ and $5 - 2$. The meanings of these expressions are fixed for all time and do not change depending on what has happened elsewhere in the program. In functional languages, these same properties are extended to functions. (Remember that a function is a set of ordered pairs.) The factorial function, `fact(n)`, takes an integer argument n and returns a number $n!$, which is the product of the first n natural numbers. This mathematical function might be described in a functional way by a pair of *recurrence equations*, for example,

$$\text{fact } 0 \;=\; 1$$
$$\text{fact } n \;=\; n * \text{fact } (n-1) \text{ if } n \geq 1$$

The first equation describes the value of `fact` for argument 0. The second equation describes how the value of `fact` n is related to the value of `fact(n - 1)`. It takes some effort to show that there is a unique function (on the natural numbers) that satisfies these equations and hence that the equations do in fact specify a function, but it is clear from the form of the equations that whatever the meaning is, it does not depend on the history of execution up to this point. We say that this pair of equations denote the mathematical function $n!$.

Denotational semantics is a way of describing the meaning of a programming language construct by giving the mathematical object that it denotes. In the above examples, the meaning of $2 + 1$ is the integer 3, and the meaning of the two equations specifying `fact` is the factorial function. Contrast this style of description with the Pascal program for computing factorial shown in Exhibit 11.16.

What this Pascal expression denotes is the process of successively multiplying `temp` by the integers $1, 2, 3, \ldots, n$. In this case, the result of that process happens to be functional, and the program does indeed compute the factorial function, but it is not obvious without careful inspection of the code that the program in fact computes a function.

Functions are denoted by λ-expressions. For example, consider the function G denoted by the expression

$$\text{Let } G \text{ be } \lambda f.\lambda x.(\text{ if } x = 0 \text{ then } 1 \text{ else } x * f(x - 1)).$$

G denotes a function of two arguments, f, a function, and x, an integer. Suppose p is the function $p(n) = 3n$. Then $Gp5$ denotes the value of the expression

$$\text{if } 5 = 0 \text{ then } 1 \text{ else } 5 * p(5 - 1)$$

which is equal to $5 * p(4) = 5 * 12 = 60$.

Fixed Points.

The function G above has a curious property: namely, if h is the mathematical function factorial(n), then $G(h)$ is also the factorial function. We say that the factorial function is a *fixed point* of G because $h = G(h)$. Moreover, it is the least fixed point in the sense that any function h' satisfying the equation $h' = G(h')$ agrees with factorial at all of the points where factorial is defined (the nonnegative integers). We can use this fact and the "least fixed point operator", Y, to write an expression that denotes the factorial function, namely YG, or equivalently,

$$Y\lambda f.\lambda x.(\text{ if } x = 0 \text{ then } 1 \text{ else } x * f(x - 1))$$

Intuitively, $Y\lambda f$ just means, "in the following expression, f refers recursively to the function being defined".

A curiosity of lambda calculus is that Y itself can be denoted by a (rather complicated) lambda expression. Hence Y does not have to be added to the language as a special primitive for defining recursive functions. In practice, it almost always is added for efficiency reasons. Rather than replace Y by the equivalent lambda expression, it is much more efficient in the implementation to allow pointers to functions; then $Y\lambda f \ldots$ simply binds f to the function being defined by the $\lambda x \ldots$ expression. Lambda calculus is a sufficient semantic basis for expressing all computations *because* it is able to express the Y operator as a formula.

The fact that pure lambda calculus lacks types is not an oversight; it is necessary in order to define Y. The reason is that Y works with *any* function as its first argument, not just with functions of a specific type.[1] Imposing a type structure on lambda calculus, as many functional languages do, weakens the lambda calculus and makes it necessary to introduce additional constructs to allow for recursive definitions. Convenience of use also dictates the addition of other constructs. Still, it is elegant that so simple a system as the untyped lambda calculus could be the basis of a powerful programming language!

12.2 THE FUNCTIONAL APPROACH

Abstractly a functional language is simply a system of notation for denoting primitive values and functions. Lambda calculus, which was already proven to be a fully general formal system in which any computable function could be defined, was used as

---

[1]The type of a function is defined by the types of its argument and return value.

a notation for early functional languages. However, lambda calculus has two serious shortcomings as a language for programmers: it lacks any concept of types and it is hopelessly clumsy to use.

Nevertheless, lambda calculus has been taken as the starting point for the development of most real functional languages. The earliest practical language in this family was LISP, which now has two important descendants, Common LISP and Scheme.

Another class of languages has been developed recently, which we will call *pure functional languages*. These languages follow lambda calculus and functional principles much more closely. This family includes ML, Miranda, and Haskell. An extended version of lambda calculus was developed which includes types and operators and literals for the underlying data domains. This system forms the semantic basis upon which the pure functional languages are built. Functional programs are parsed and translated into computation trees which represent lambda applications. At execution time, the lambda evaluator crawls over these trees, binding arguments, evaluating expressions as needed, and replacing expression trees by constant values wherever possible.

Pure functional languages come extremely close to implementing the semantics that Church defined for lambda calculus. They share many traits with the older functional languages, specifically, functions are first-class objects, conditional expressions are used, rather than conditional statements, and repetition is done implicitly or with recursion, not by explicit loops. The key differences between the newer and the older functional languages are:

- The prohibition on destructive assignment.
- The complete absence of statement sequences.
- The use of lazy parameter evaluation.

We will consider each of these issues and show how denotational constructs can take the place of procedural language elements.

12.2.1 Eliminating Assignment

Destructive assignment causes semantic problems because it creates a time- and sequence-dependent change in the meaning of a name. Prohibiting destructive assignment does not imply that a programmer cannot give a name to a value, merely that a name, once bound to a value, must remain bound to the same value throughout the scope of the name. Thus the meaning of a name is constant, and not dependent on the order of execution. This greatly simplifies the task of understanding the program and proving that it is correct.

In procedural languages, assignment is used for several purposes:

1. To store the result of computing a subexpression.
2. In conjunction with conditional statements.
3. With a loop variable, to mark the progress of a loop.
4. To build complex data structures.

To show that assignment can be eliminated, we must show how each of these things can be accomplished, with reasonable efficiency and style, in a functional way.

Programmers store the results of subexpressions, goal (1), for many good reasons. When an expression is complex, a local name can be used to "break out" and name a portion of it, so that the structure and meaning of the entire expression can be made clearer. Local names are also used in Pascal for efficiency; rather than write a common subexpression several times, the subexpression is evaluated first, and its result is assigned to a local variable. The local name is then used in further computations. Both uses of local variables can reduce the complexity of expressions and make a Pascal program easier to understand and debug. It is easy to devise a functional method for goal (1). We simply need to let the programmer open a local context block in which to define local names for expressions. Miranda provides three ways to define a symbol:

- As a global symbol, by declaring the name with an "=", just as symbols are defined in lambda calculus.
- As a parameter name. The name is bound to an argument expression during a function call.
- As a local symbol, by using a `where` clause.

A Miranda `where` clause defines one or more local names and gives an expression for the meaning of each. The entire group of definitions forms a local context and can be implemented by a stack frame. `Where` clauses can also be nested, producing block structured name-binding.

Goal (2) is satisfied by using a conditional expression, which returns a value, instead of a conditional statement. The value returned by the conditional expression can be bound to a name by parameter binding or by a `where` clause.

Extensive support for list data structures, including list constructors, whole-list operations with implied iteration, and expressions that denote complex lists all combine to minimize the need for loops, goal (3). Sequences of data values are represented as lists, and operations that process such sequences are written by mapping simple operations over lists. This device eliminates the need for most explicit loops and many statement sequences. The remaining repetitive processes are programmed using recursion. These topics are discussed at length in Sections 12.2.2 and 12.3.

Goal (4) is the only real difficulty. Prohibiting destructive assignment means that a data structure cannot be modified after it is created. For small data structures this is no problem, as a new copy of the structure can be created that incorporates any desired change. This, in fact, is how call-by-value works: objects are copied during the function call, and the new copies are bound to the parameter names within the function. Most list processing and a lot of processing on records and arrays can be done efficiently this way. The exception is when a large data structure, such as a 1000 element array, is used as a parameter and slightly modified within the subroutine. Copying it all in order to modify one element might produce unacceptable inefficiency.

Efficient implementation of arrays in a functional language is a current research topic. Work centers on the question of whether the *original* and *modified* versions of the array are both used. If not, then the language system can perhaps avoid the copy operation. It can *do* a destructive assignment to an array element "on the sly" and pretend that it didn't. This trick will succeed if the program never again asks to see the original version of the array. Because of the efficiency problem with large arrays, existing pure functional languages are all list-oriented.

When (and if) ways are found to circumvent these problems, careful design efforts will be needed to integrate arrays into functional languages. APL is an array-processing language that has many things in common with functional languages and lets the programmer use a functional programming style to do complex combinations of whole-array operations. To support this style, APL has a large and complex set of array operations [Exhibit 12.2]. The set of primitive composition and decomposition operations needed to make arrays usable without constant use of assignment is large compared to the set provided for list handling in Miranda [Exhibit 12.11]. Today's list-oriented functional languages are small and simple; tomorrow's languages, with arrays added, will be larger and more complex.

Exhibit 12.2.   Primitive operations for arrays in APL.

APL (*Array Processing Language*) was designed to make working with arrays easy. It contains more kinds of array primitives than other languages, including operations such as generalized cross-section, concatenation, lamination, and whole-array arithmetic. It gives excellent support for all sorts of array manipulation.

In these examples, the variables named ar and br are 3 by 3 arrays.

Array Primitive	Example in APL
Exhibit a literal array	17 18 19
Fetch dimensions of array	ρ ar
Create and initialize an array	ar $\leftarrow$ 3 3 ρ 0
Subscript (random access)	ar[1;3]
Cross-section	ar[1 2; 2]
Change one array item	ar[1,1] $\leftarrow$ 17
Prepare for sequential access	ix $\leftarrow$ 1
Access current item	ar[ix; iy]
Whole-matrix operations	ar + 1
Concatenation on dimension n	ar ,[1] br
Lamination (makes more dimensions)	ar ,[.5] br

12.2.2 Recursion Can Replace WHILE

In Chapter 10, we discussed the fact that all programs can be written in terms of three control structures: statement sequence, IF...THEN...ELSE, and the WHILE loop. That is, these three control structures are *sufficient* for all programming needs. However, they are not *necessary*; both WHILE and sequence can be eliminated. An alternative set of *necessary control structures* is:

- IF...THEN...ELSE
- recursive procedure call

Repetition of sections of code is certainly fundamental to programming; problems that do not involve repetition are usually solved by hand, not by computer. But repetition does not have to be achieved with an explicit loop. It is possible to implement repetition without a GOTO or any kind of looping statement, by using tail recursion.

A *tail recursion* is a recursive call to a function, in such a position within the function that will always be the last thing executed before the function return. Frequently, this will be at the lexical end of that function, but it could also be nested within a control structure [Exhibit 12.3]. Tail recursion produces the same result as a simple infinite loop or simple backwards GOTO. Combined with a conditional, tail recursion can emulate a WHILE or FOR loop. The parallel between tail recursive functions and loops is so straightforward that either form can be mechanically translated to the other form, either by a programmer or by a compiler.

Exhibit 12.3.   Recursive implementation of repetition.

The following procedure prints the values of an integer array. We would call print _out(LL, N); to print out the first N items of array LL. The outer procedure is a shell that initializes a parameter for the inner, recursive procedure, print_out_recursive. The recursive procedure will be called N times and will create and initialize one copy of the parameter count each time. No copy of count is ever incremented. After the last item is printed, all N calls on print_out_recursive return, and all N copies of the parameters are deallocated.

```
Procedure print_out ( list: list_type; list_size: integer);
Procedure print_out_recursive (count:integer);
Begin
    writeln( list [count] );
    if ( count < list_size ) then print_out_recursive (count+1);
End;
Begin
    print_out_recursive (1);
End;
```

To use recursion to emulate a loop, one writes the body of the recursive function as an IF statement that tests the loop-termination condition. The answer returned by the function, if any, can be returned by the THEN clause, and the body of the loop is written as the scope of the ELSE clause. (A procedure that returns no value can put the loop body in the THEN clause and eliminate the ELSE clause.) The loop variable in the loop version is replaced by a parameter in the recursive version. On each recursive call, the parameter is increased or decreased by the value of the loop's increment expression.

The iterative and recursive mechanisms that implement repetition are quite different. In an iterative implementation, the contents of a single machine address, associated with the "loop variable," is changed during each repetition, and execution continues until the value of that variable reaches some goal. Exhibit 12.4 shows an iterative procedure to print the contents of part of an array. One storage object is allocated for the parameter count, and the value in that location is changed once for each item printed out.

In a tail-recursive implementation of repetition, each recursion causes allocation of additional storage on the stack for the current value(s) of the parameter(s) and for the function return address. New stack frames are piled on top of old ones. The recursive descent ends when the value of some parameter reaches a goal; thus

Exhibit 12.4.   Iterative implementation of repetition.

The following procedure uses iteration to print the values of an integer array. We would call print_out(LL, N); to print out the first N items of array LL. The outer procedure is a shell that initializes a parameter for the inner, iterative procedure, print_out_iterative. The iterative procedure will be called once. It creates one copy of the parameter count, which is incremented N times.

```
Procedure print_out (list: list_type; list_size: integer);
Procedure print_out_iterative (count:integer);
Begin
    While (count <= list_size) Do Begin
        writeln( list [count] );
        count := count + 1
    End
End;
Begin
        print_out_iterative (1);
End;
```

this parameter must be different in each successive stack frame. When the value in the newest stack frame reaches the goal, repetition stops, and all the accumulated stack locations are freed, one frame at a time. Each parameter value is only used during the cycle that placed it on the stack. Values in locations below the top of the stack are never used again, and all are popped off together when the termination condition eventually happens.

A recursive version and an iterative version of a print_out procedure are given in Exhibits 12.3 and 12.4. Both routines are written in Pascal, and the implementations described are those produced by a typical Pascal compiler. These routines print out the elements of an array starting at the subscript count. The array, called list, has list_size elements. (To work correctly, list_size must be $>= 1$.) Let N be the number of items to be printed; $N =$ list_size $-$ count $+1$. The appropriate calls for the two inner procedures, to print out all list items, are identical:

```
print_out_recursive(1);
print_out_iterative(1);
```

The stack allocations for both are shown in Exhibit 12.5.

Repetition through recursion does use more storage space and more overhead time than repetition through iteration. Stack overflow could limit the number of repetitions. But coupled with some kind of conditional control structure and some form of sequential execution, recursion forms an adequate semantic basis for a programming language; explicit loops are not needed. Further, even when the programmer writes repetition using recursion, a translator can recognize tail recursion and generate iterative, not recursive, code. Translators for many languages descended from LISP do exactly that.

Exhibit 12.5. Stack diagrams for a tail recursion and a loop.

Assume that the global variable `list` is this array of four real numbers:

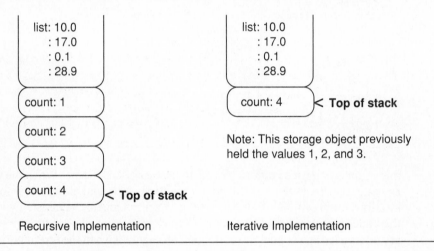

The stacks for `print_out_recursive(1)` and `print_out_iterative(1)` are shown just as the last item on the list is being processed, but before the function return.

Recursive Implementation   Iterative Implementation

Whether or not to include iterative control structures in a language thus depends on some value judgements. The questions are:

- Is the iterative syntactic form better, more natural, or more appropriate than the recursive form for communicating some problems?
- Is iterative syntax better enough to warrant including nonnecessary statements in the language syntax?
- Will programmers be likely to write better code with the extra iterative forms?

If the answers are yes, iterative control structures should be included in a language. If not, they are excess baggage. The older LISP-like functional languages included explicit map functions which implement iteration over lists. Newer functional languages include extensive collections of list operators that do implied iteration.

12.2.3 Sequences

Traditional languages define the flow of control in terms of sequences of statements (control statements, procedure calls, and assignments). These languages also support nested expressions and function calls; some even include conditional expressions. The programmer often has a choice about whether to use heavily nested code, or to break that code into a sequence of statements. Writing a sequence of statements is often the simplest, clearest, and most direct way to express an idea. We have found by experience that pulling out the parts of a highly nested expression and writing them as separate steps often clarifies the meaning of a program. It also permits the programmer to do a better job of attaching comments to obscure parts of the code.

Lambda calculus has shown us that statement sequences are really unnecessary in a theoretical sense. Everything can be done by nesting functions and function calls. However, lists of statements do provide the programmer with a second tool, in addition to function definitions, for breaking up code into comprehensible units. Modern functional languages meet the need for separating out parts of the code without supporting statement sequences at all. In this section, we examine how this is accomplished.

Nesting Replaces Assignment Sequences.

A sequence of assignment statements *that does not assign two different values to the same variable* and, therefore, does not destroy information, can be emulated by a nest of functions with parameter bindings and local symbol definitions taking the place of the assignments. This is true in traditional languages as well as in functional languages. Exhibit 12.6 shows a simple series of assignment and output statements, written in Pascal. In such a sequence, each line forms the context in which the next line is interpreted.

Exhibit 12.6.   A sequence of statements in Pascal.

```
c := a + b;
s := sin(c*c);
write (a, b, c, s);
```

To form nested contexts in a functional language, one can use a nest of function calls and/or block declarations. Exhibit 12.7 shows how the Pascal assignment sequence might be rewritten in LISP using symbols defined in nested blocks. The first assignment in the Pascal sequence forms the outermost context block in LISP, creating the context for the rest of the nest. The final write in Pascal is innermost in the LISP version, so that its symbols are interpreted in the context of all the surrounding bindings.

Lazy Evaluation Replaces Sequences.

In a Pascal program, the programmer must write statements physically in the same order that they will be evaluated. If statement B depends on the result of statement A, then A must come first. In contrast, when lazy evaluation is used, the sequence in which expressions are evaluated can be completely different from their order on the written page, because no expression is evaluated until its result is needed. When we look at this situation one way, we see that we have no direct control over the order of evaluation. When looked at from the other side, though, we see that we do not have to worry about that order!

Exhibit 12.7. A LISP function nest emulating a sequence.

```
(print (let ((c (+ a b)))
           (let ((s (sin (* c c))))
              (list a b c s))))
```

Miranda provides the keyword **where** to permit the programmer to define and initialize local symbols. Local names and their defining expressions are written at the end of a Miranda definition, following **where**. These expressions are evaluated using lazy evaluation, an important difference from both Pascal and LISP. This frees the programmer from concern about the order in which the definitions are written within the **where** clause. Exhibit 12.8 defines a function called Answers that is analogous to the Pascal function in Exhibit 12.6. In Answers, the symbols s and c are both defined, but s, which depends on c, is defined first. This causes no problem. When s is used, its definition will be evaluated; in the middle of that process, where s refers to c, the expression for c will be evaluated. The order of the definitions on the page is immaterial.

Exhibit 12.8. Defining local symbols in Miranda.

This code is more or less like the Pascal and LISP examples in Exhibits 12.6 and 12.7. The function Answers returns a tuple of values, which will be printed if the function is called from the top level.

```
Answers a b = (a b c s)
             where
             s = sin(c * c)
             c = a+b
```

Note, also, that the explicit nesting present in LISP is gone. Miranda does not require each symbol to be defined before it is used. The set of **where** clauses, taken together, form a context for each other and for the function code. This is different from LISP semantics, which require that each clause be explicitly nested within the context formed by the definitions of all its symbols.

Guarded Expressions.

In traditional languages, all statements must be written in one sequence or another. Frequently, though, the sequence of a short group of statements does not matter, so long as all are executed before the next part of the program. Some newer procedural languages, such as Concurrent Pascal,[2] provide a *parallel execution* control structure, consisting of scope markers enclosing a series of statements. The semantics of parallel execution are that the statements in the scope may be executed in any sequence, or all at the same time, on different processors. No statement in such a scope

---

[2]Brinch Hansen [1975].

computes a value that is referenced anywhere else in the group, and no two statements compute the same value.

This concept is carried over into the functional languages in the form of guarded expressions and where clauses. A *guarded expression* is a generalized conditional control structure in which the condition clauses are evaluated in parallel. It is very much similar to the generalized conditional in LISP. However, there is a critically important difference: the clauses of a LISP cond are evaluated sequentially, and the first true condition triggers evaluation of its corresponding clause. In contrast, a guarded expression is evaluated in *parallel* . This does not affect the outcome if only one guard is true. However, if two (or more) guards are true, either corresponding clause might be evaluated; a nondeterministic choice is made by the translator. Thus the value of a LISP conditional with more than one true clause is defined and deterministic because all clauses following the first true clause are ignored. In contrast, the value of a Miranda expression with two or more true guards is undefined. (Using such an expression is therefore risky.)

Output Sequences.

The use of conditional expressions eliminates the need for conditional statements. Using recursion we can eliminate explicit loops. Using symbol definitions, nested contexts, and lazy evaluation we can eliminate sequences of assignments. Having done these things, the only remaining kinds of statements in traditional languages are those related to input and output.

The premise of lazy evaluation is that no expression is ever evaluated unless its result is needed. For most computations this works nicely, but it is not well suited to producing output. By definition, it is the side effect of the output process that is wanted, not the value returned. One device is to permit the programmer to specify that *strict evaluation* should be used. With strict evaluation all arguments are evaluated, even if they would be skipped using the rule for lazy evaluation. This permits the programmer to cause the evaluation of an expression whose result is not used by the rest of the program, and whose only effect is output.

Another way to produce an output sequence is to use the sequencing built into data objects in place of a sequence of statements. The compound data types, lists (sequences of values, all of the same type) and tuples (nonhomogeneous sequences of values), are both ordered sequences of values. Both can be constructed dynamically. Since structured objects are first-class objects in functional languages, any kind of output supported by the language (interactive output or file output) can also be used for lists and tuples.

12.3 Miranda: *A FUNCTIONAL LANGUAGE*

Miranda is a simple and elegant functional language that illustrates both the principles and the attractiveness of the functional approach.[3] This section deals with the basic elements of Miranda; several advanced features are discussed in Chapter 18.

A program in Miranda is a collection of definitions, called a *script*, that define and name objects. Like lambda calculus, each definition has (on the left) the symbol being

---

[3]Turner [1986].

defined and (on the right) several clauses that comprise its definition. An object can be a simple data type, a list, a tuple, or a function. A very simple script which defines and calls the `square` function is shown in Exhibit 12.9.

Exhibit 12.9. A simple Miranda script.

Miranda	Lambda Calculus
`sq n = n * n` `z = sq x / sq y`	`sq = λ n. * n n` `z = / (sq x) (sq y)`

A function call is written by writing the function name followed by one or more arguments, which can be simple items, lists, or tuples. No parentheses or delimiters of any kind are used to enclose the arguments. Note the similarity between the definition and calls on the function `sq`, shown on the left in Exhibit 12.9, and the corresponding definitions, expressed in lambda calculus, on the right. Note that Miranda uses infix notation for ordinary arithmetic operators and uses end-of-line rather than a character such as ";" to end the expression.

The primitive types in Miranda are characters (type `char`, written in single quotes), truth values (type `bool`, values `True` and `False`), and numbers, which include both integers and reals (type num). The basic data structures in Miranda are the list and the tuple. A list is an ordered sequence of homogeneously typed values and is written by enclosing the list values in square brackets. A string is a list of characters, and a literal string can be written as a list of characters, or as characters between double quote marks. A tuple is a nonhomogeneous sequence of values, and it is written by enclosing the values in parentheses.

12.3.1 Data Structures

Tuples

Miranda supports two compound data structures, tuples[4] and lists. A *tuple* is simply a list of objects whose types do not have to be alike. It could be implemented by a record data type or by a list of pointers to the members of the tuple. In Miranda we denote a literal tuple by enclosing a series of values in parentheses. The argument list of a function is also a tuple, although it is written with no punctuation at all.

Tuples are used in Miranda to define enumerated data types and to form complex data structures, just as records are used in traditional languages. The methods for defining and accessing tuple types involve a powerful pattern-matching mechanism. They are dealt with in Chapter 18.

---

[4]"Tuple" rhymes with "scruple", and it comes from the mathematical term "n-tuple", which comes from the family of words "quadruple", "quintuple", etc.

Lists

Miranda lists can be denoted in several ways. The simplest list is a sequence items enclosed in square brackets [Exhibit 12.10]. However, this notation is cum some for long lists and impossible for infinite lists, so Miranda also provides shorthan ways to denote lists. We can denote a list of consecutive values by giving the first and last value. Thus [1..5] means the same thing as [1,2,3,4,5]. This notation can be extended to denote any arithmetic progression of values. The first two values are written, followed by ".." and the last value. This is enough information to define the list; the difference between the first value and second value is taken as the step size for the progression. An *infinite list*, such as "all the numbers greater than 10", is denoted by giving just the first value or the first two values. A list may also be denoted by a powerful kind of expression known as a list comprehension, which is discussed below.

Exhibit 12.10.   Denoting lists in Miranda.

```
[]                                       The null list.
[1..n]                                   The integers from one to n.
odd_numbers = [1,3..100]                 Odd numbers from one to one hundred.
evens = [ 10,12 .. 100]                  The even numbers between 10 and 100.
eleven_up = [11 .. ]                     All numbers greater than 10.
evens_up = [12,14 ..]                    All even numbers greater than 10.
week_days = ["Mon","Tue","Wed","Thur","Fri"]
                                         A list of 5 strings is bound to week_days.
```

12.3.2   Operations and Expressions

The usual arithmetic operators (+, -, *. /, div, mod) are defined with the usual precedence and are written in infix notation. Miranda has some basic operators for building and decomposing lists, as well as several powerful operations that work on list arguments. Exhibit 12.11 shows the use of the five basic list operators, which are:

L1 ++ L2	Concatenate list L2 onto the end of L1.
item : List	Add the item to the head of the List.
List ! n	Select the *n*th item from the List.
L1 -- L2	Remove values in L2 from list of values in L1.
# List	Return the number of items on the List.

12.3.3   Function Definitions

A function definition is called an "equation" because it does look like a mathematical equation. The simplest functions can be written on one line, like the function sq in Exhibit 12.9. The function name is written, followed by a dummy parameter list, followed by "=" and an expression which is written in terms of the dummy parameters. If the definition requires more than one line of code, succeeding lines must be indented.

list operations in Miranda.

	Result
n","Tue","Wed","Thur","Fri"]	5
++ ["Sat","Sun"]	a list of 7 days.
	[0,1,2,3]
week_days ! 2	"Wed" (0-based subscript.)
week_day -- "Fri"	["Mon","Tue","Wed","Thur"]

In Miranda, guarded expressions are used for conditional control. A guarded expression consists of a series of lines, each with an expression on the left, followed by a comma and a Boolean guard on the right. The interpretation is this: The guard expressions are evaluated in parallel. If the result of any guard is true, the corresponding expression is evaluated and returned. If more than one guard is true, any one of the corresponding values might be returned. An "otherwise" clause is permitted at the end.

A recursive definition of the greatest common divisor algorithm, implemented using a guarded expression, is shown in Exhibit 12.12. This shows the proper use of guards—exactly one guard is true, and the set of guards explicitly cover all possibilities.

Exhibit 12.12. A guarded expression.

```
gcd a b = gcd (a-b) b,    a>b
        = gcd a (b-a),    a<b
        = a,              a=b
```

In a functional language, binding must take the place of assignment. Of course, a function call offers an opportunity for evaluating expressions and binding the results to parameter names. However, a nest of many function calls can be completely unreadable and difficult for the programmer to construct. Miranda provides parameter binding plus a second way to bind a value to a name: the where clause. Within a function definition, "where" is used to define a local name for the value of an expression. The Miranda programmer uses where in the same way that a Pascal programmer uses assignment, to give a name to a subexpression that will be used more than once. Where clauses may be nested to arbitrary depth, producing block structured name binding. Indentation of inner blocks is compulsory, because layout information is used by the parser.

Compare the Miranda code in Exhibit 12.13 to the more-or-less equivalent Pascal code in Exhibit 12.14. Both functions compute the two roots of a quadratic equation, but the Pascal code is twice as long and far more complex. This is due to several factors:

- Guarded expressions are syntactically briefer than nested if...then...else statements.
- Miranda frees the programmer from concern about evaluation order. The local symbols are defined in a group at the bottom. They will be evaluated if needed and in whatever order they might be needed. The order in which the `where` clauses are written is immaterial.
- The Pascal code uses nested conditionals to implement lazy evaluation of the local variables. In Miranda, lazy evaluation just happens—the programmer does not have to force it by carefully ordering and nesting the code. If a subexpression is not needed, its `where` clause is not evaluated.
- The goal of implementing denotational philosophy forced Miranda's designers to provide an assignment-free method for returning a list. The result is that Miranda lets the programmer denote variable-length lists with ease; the programmer simply writes a list of expressions within brackets. In Pascal, however, the list must be constructed and initialized piece by painful piece.

Exhibit 12.13.   `Where` takes the place of assignment.

```
quadroot a b c = error "complex roots",        delta < 0
              = [term1],                        delta = 0
              = [term1+term2, term1-term2],     delta > 0
                where
                delta = b*b - 4*a*c
                radix = sqrt delta
                term1 = -b/(2*a)
                term2 = radix/(2*a)
```

Higher-order Functions

Like all functional languages, Miranda supports higher-order functions. Thus Miranda programs often use partial parameterization through closures and functional parameters. A Miranda version of the "reduce" function is given in Exhibit 12.15; compare its simplicity to the Pascal version in Exhibit 9.29.

12.3.4   List Comprehensions

Loops that use explicit loop variables are inherently nonfunctional; both FOR and WHILE loops depend on statement sequences and assignment. In contrast, a *comprehension* is a pure functional construct which provides a way to specify iteration without using assignment or sequences of statements.

A *list comprehension* is an expression that denotes a finite or infinite list with an arbitrarily complex structure.[5] A comprehension has two parts: on the left is an expression, and on the right are a series of clauses called a *qualifier list*, consisting of generators and filters separated by semicolons. The qualifier list specifies an ordered series of values to bind to the free variable(s) in the expression. The syntax for list

---

[5]This terminology is from Haskell; the term used in Miranda is "Zermelo Frankel expression", or ZF expression. This form was named after two early logicians who developed set theory.

Exhibit 12.14. Assignment used to name subexpressions in Pascal.

```
type root_list= ↑root_type;
type root_type = record  root: real;  next:  root_list  end;
function quadroot(a, b, c:  real):    root_list;
var delta, radix, term2:  real;
    roots, temp:  root_list;
begin
    roots := NIL;
    delta := b*b - 4*a*c;
    if delta < 0
    then writeln('Error:  complex roots')
    else begin
        new(roots);
        roots↑.root:= -b/(2*a);
        if delta = 0
        then roots↑.next := NIL
        else begin
            radix := sqrt(delta);
            term2 := radix/(2*a);
            new (temp);
            roots↑.next:= temp;
            temp↑.root := roots↑.root - term2;
            roots↑.root := roots↑.root + term2;
            temp↑.next := NIL
        end
    end;
    quadroot := roots
end;
```

comprehensions is shown in Exhibit 12.16 and an example is shown in Exhibit 12.17. The clauses that form the qualifier list consist of one or more list-expressions called "generators" followed by zero or more Boolean expressions called "filters".[6]

In many ways a comprehension is like a FOR loop control structure. The expression is like the body of the loop, its free variable(s) is (are) like the loop control variable(s), and the generators and filters specify a series of values for the free variable, much as a loop control element specifies a series of values for the loop variable. A comprehension differs from a loop because a comprehension returns a list as its result, whereas a loop does not return a value. A comprehension with one generator is like a single loop; with two generators (for two free variables) a comprehension is like a pair of nested loops.

_____

[6]The use of generators and filters goes back to an early low-level language named IPL/5, Newell [1961]. Notation similar to that shown here was used by Schwarz in his set-processing language, SetL.

Exhibit 12.15.   The reduce function in Miranda.

The reduce function may be defined in Miranda to take three parameters: a function, a list, and a number. The third argument is the identity value for the given function; its value is used to initialize the summing process and is returned as the value of reduce when the list argument is a null list.

```
reduce f [] n = n
reduce f (a:x) n = f a (reduce x n)
```

The type of reduce, as discussed in Chapter 9, Section 9.3, is:

```
reduce ::  (num → num → num )
           → [num]
           → num
           → num
```

Exhibit 12.16.   The syntax for a list comprehension.

```
ZF expr ::=     '[' ⟨body⟩ '|' ⟨qual-list '] '
qual-list ::    generator { generator | filter }
generator ::    ⟨variable⟩ ← ⟨list-expression⟩
filter ::=      ⟨Boolean expression⟩
body ::=        ⟨list expression⟩
```

Exhibit 12.17.   A list comprehension.

Expression: [n+2 | n ← [1..10]]
Read this as: the list of all values for n+2 such that n takes on the list of values 1 through 10.

For simplicity, let us first examine simple comprehensions with just one generator. A generator is used to produce and name an ordered set of values. It specifies a symbol and a list expression. The list expression generates a series of values which are bound, in sequence, to the symbol. Then the symbol with its value is passed through all of the filters; if any filter evaluates to FALSE, the value is discarded and the next value is generated. If the value passes all the tests, it is substituted for its variable in the expression on the left side of the comprehension and used to compute the next value in the output list.

Let us look at a series of list comprehensions to see how generators and filters work. Line 1 in Exhibit 12.18 is a very simple example. A single generator is used to produce a list of even numbers from 2 to 10. This list is "fed into" the expression on the left, producing a list of multiples of 4 from 4 to 20. In line 2, the result is an infinite list of square numbers.

Exhibit 12.18.   Some list comprehensions.

	Expression	Result
1	[n*2 | n ← [2,4.. 10]]	[4, 8, 12, 16, 20]
2	[n*n | n ← [1, 2 ..]]	All perfect squares; 1, 4, 9, etc.).
3	[x+y | x ← [1..3]; y ← [3, 7]]	[4, 5, 6, 8, 9, 10]
4	[x*y | x ← [1..3]; y ← [1..3]; x>=y]	[1, 2, 4, 3, 6, 9]

The combination of generators and filters can specify a list whose structure is considerably more complex than the control element of a FOR loop, because a generator can start with any existing list, and any number of filters can be applied to the elements on that list. To use a comprehension, the programmer specifies a list of values that contain all the ones of interest and perhaps some other, unwanted values. Then filters are appended to specify subsets of values to remove from the result. Several filters may be needed if the values to be excluded form a complex pattern.

A comprehension with two free variables needs two generators. In this case, the generators are executed in a nested fashion; the second generator runs through all of its values for each value generated by the first. The number of value-pairs generated is the product of the lengths of the two generator lists. In line 3, two lists are generated and the final result is the pairwise sum of those lists. Even though two generators are nested here, the final result is a linear list, not a multidimensional structure. A filter may test just one member of the value-pair, or it may combine them in a test [Exhibit 12.18, line 4]. Thus the length of the output from a comprehension can be anything from zero up to the product of the lengths of all the generated lists.

When list comprehensions are used in a program, the result is often a concise, clear statement of the algorithm. For example, consider the quicksort program in Exhibit 12.19. The function sort takes a list as its argument and returns a sorted list. Line 1 defines the action of sort on a null-list argument—it simply returns the null list. This is the base case for the recursive definition of sort. Lines 2 through 4 define sort on all other lists. The fact that the argument must be a list is denoted by the parentheses between the function name and the "=" sign which terminates the header. (Remember, parentheses are not used to enclose parameter lists.) Within these parentheses, the ":" notation is used to give local names to the head and tail of the argument. Thus the name "pivot" will be bound to the first element, or head, of the list, and "rest" will be bound to the rest (or tail) of the list.

The sort function works by separating its argument (a list) into three sections: the first element, named pivot, one new list containing all elements from the rest of the list that are less than or equal to the pivot (line 2), and a second new list containing all elements that are greater than the pivot (line 4). The result returned by sort is these three parts, concatenated (lines 2 through 4) in the correct order, after the sublists have been recursively sorted.

Exhibit 12.19.   Quicksort in Miranda.

```
1.  sort [] = []                                          y
2.  sort (pivot:rest) = sort [ y | y ← rest; b ≤ pivot ]
3                       ++ [pivot] ++              z
4.                      sort [ z | z ← rest; b > pivot ]
```

The program differs from a quicksort program written in a procedural language because it does *not* define the procedure for finding "all the elements of the list that are less than the first element, pivot". Instead, a list comprehension is used to *denote* those elements and supply them as an argument to a recursive call on the sort function. Implementation of the actual process of finding those elements is left to the system.

This definition of quicksort is certainly brief and is relatively easy to understand. Further, a proof of its correctness is straightforward because the program is simply a statement of what it means to be "sorted". However, note the inefficiency involved in processing each element of the input list twice, once to find small elements, and again to find large ones!

12.3.5 Infinite Lists

Some of the lists denoted in Exhibits 12.10 and 12.18 are infinite lists; that is, they go on forever. In this section we examine how an infinite list can be represented in a real computer, and why we might want to use one.

Think of an infinite list as having two parts, a finite head, consisting of values that have already been computed, and an infinite tail, consisting of code for generating the rest of the list. We will be lazy about constructing this list—new values will only be computed when they are needed. The program may access this list like any other, for example, by using subscripts. When the program needs a value at the head of the list, the desired value is found and returned.

The infinite tail of the list will not be represented as data (obviously). Instead, it will be a functional object. When the program needs a value on the tail of the list, the function on the tail is used to extend the head of the list as follows. When it is called, it computes the next list item and constructs a new functional object for computing the rest of the list. The value and the function become the new tail of the list, replacing the old functional object. (The list has now grown by one data item.) This process is repeated until the required list item is generated.

These functional objects can be implemented by closures, consisting of a context that remembers the current position in the list, and a function that, given the current position, can calculate the next list item. The new functional object that is created is just a new closure, whose context is the new position on the list.

Memo Functions

A generally useful device that can be used in any language is called *memoizing*. We do it to increase efficiency when a function is called repeatedly on the same inputs. For example, consider the process of ASCII-to-floating-point number conversion, which must be done each time a floating-point number is read from the input stream. The last step in the conversion is to divide the intermediate result by a power of 10 that corresponds to the number of decimal places in the input. We can write a function pow10(d) that returns 10 to the power d. If many numbers are to be read, though, we would expect to need the same result many times, and computing powers is a slow job. The obvious answer is to make a table of powers of 10 ahead of time, then just use a subscript to extract the right power. We can conceive of this in a lazy way. How many powers of 10 do we need? That isn't really known ahead of time. Should we just calculate a bunch and hope that our table is long enough? What happens if it isn't? Infinite lists provide a straightforward solution to this problem. We can use an infinite list to memoize our Pow10 function. When a particular power of 10 is needed for the first time, the infinite list will be extended that far (and no farther). If a power is called for that is already on the list, it will be returned directly. Exhibit 12.20 shows a version of this function memoized by using an infinite list.

Exhibit 12.20.   A memoized function.

```
pow10 0      = 1
pow10 (n+1)  = 10 * powlist ! n
powlist = [ pow10(x)  |  x <- [0..]  ]
```

Input and Output

Input and output are obvious necessities for any programming language, including a functional language. However, both are inherently time-dependent. The usual concept of input, that a storage object takes on a series of values brought in by executing READ requests, is not consistent with the functional approach. However, infinite lists provide a functionally acceptable way to model I/O.[7] The input stream is modeled as an infinite list of values. Each time you poke the input stream, a new value is appended to the list of inputs and can then be accessed by a program.

We can also model the output stream as an infinite list. It is important, though, that real output starts to happen before the entire list is evaluated. This can be guaranteed, even in a lazy system, by having the output function return a "success" or "fail" response and then testing that response. The act of testing forces the output function to be evaluated, which has the side effect of making the output happen.

EXERCISES

1. Explain what it means to denote a function as opposed to writing code for a function.
2. Define "mutability" and explain why it is undesirable.
3. Explain the sense in which a Pascal or C programmer must "over-sequence" code.
4. How does lazy evaluation eliminate much of the concern about sequencing?

---

[7]Continuations can also be used to implement I/O.

5. How does recursion differ from iteration?

6. Name three mechanisms or data structures that must be part of the semantic basis of a language that supports recursion.

7. FORTRAN supports local variables and parameters in functions. What semantic mechanism is missing that makes FORTRAN unable to support recursion?

8. What is tail recursion?

9. How can recursion be used to eliminate the need for the WHILE construct?

10. What is the minimal set of necessary control structures? Name a language that contains these alone.

11. What is the difference between lazy and strict evaluation?

12. What is a guarded expression? How can it be misused?

13. What is the difference between a tuple and a list in Miranda?

14. What is an infinite list? How can it be used to model I/O?

15. What is a list comprehension? Qualifier? Filter?

16. How does a list comprehension differ from a traditional loop?

17. What is memoizing? Why is it used?

18. Write a Miranda script for Euclid's greatest common divisor algorithm. Compare your code to the gcd programs in Prolog [Exhibit 13.13] and C [Exhibit 13.14].

13

Logic Programming

____ Overview _____

This chapter presents the goals and applications of logic programming and the historical and theoretical context in which it was developed.

In a logic language, the programmer defines predicates and writes logical formulas involving these predicates, constants, and variables. In this way, a data base of facts and relations is constructed.

Central to logic programming are the logical operation of implication and the process of inference. The programmer states rules which the language interpreter may use to infer new facts from those in the data base. This inference is done by a powerful reasoning technique called resolution.

Prolog is introduced as an example of a logic language. It was the first and is still widely known and used today. The relationship between deduction in an axiomatized system and computation is explored by comparing short Prolog programs to analogous programs in a procedural language.

In a procedural language, we define constants and variables and accept input data. We describe computation by defining functions and/or procedures which call preexisting functions and operators to compute new values from existing data. Assignment or binding is used to store the new data for future use. Because a program consists of a series of control units which will be executed sequentially, the order of computation is largely determined by the programmer. Within each control unit are other control units and function calls which largely (but not completely) define the sequence in which the actions and computations will be done.

In a logic language, we also define constants and variables. However, computation is done by finding data objects that satisfy a set of constraints. The programmer states facts, or relationships, about data objects, as well as inference rules by which conclusions may be drawn about those objects. A query may then be written—a statement whose truth or falsity the programmer does not know. The language interpreter attempts to prove that statement from the facts and rules previously provided.

The programmer does not define either the nature of the computational process or the exact order in which computations will happen. Those aspects are defined by the theorem-proving mechanisms built into the logic language interpreter. For this reason, logic languages are often described as "declarative" rather than "imperative".

The traditional languages based on arithmetic, assignment, and sequential computation force programmers to over-specify the sequencing of their nonsequential algorithms and nonordered data. For some applications—for example, language recognition, artificial intelligence, data base query languages, and expert systems—it is easier and more comfortable to model the application declaratively. Interest in logic programming languages is, therefore, especially strong in these areas.

13.1 PREDICATE CALCULUS

The predicate calculus is a formal logical system for symbolizing facts about data structures and reasoning about them. It is also the basis on which logic programming languages are built. Before one can understand logic programming languages, one must be familiar with the symbols and concepts of logic. We review them here briefly.

13.1.1 Formulas

The components of the *first-order predicate calculus* are symbols for constants, variables, logical operations, functions, predicates, and quantifiers. Symbols may be combined to make formulas.

Constants

A constant denotes one specific object, which belongs to some specific domain, or set, of real or mathematical objects. This domain is also called a *universe of discourse*. Normally, several domains are involved in a single logical system, and different symbols are defined for each. In this discussion, we generally take the domain to be the set of numeric integers, and we will denote the integers by ordinary base-10 numerals. Names of other constants will be written using lowercase letters (including the underscore).

Variables

A variable ranges over a particular domain and represents some unspecified object from that domain. During a deduction, a variable may be *instantiated*, that is, bound to one constant object from its domain. In general, several variables will be simultaneously instantiated, each to a different value, and we use the term "instantiate" in this more general sense. We will use uppercase letters to name variables.

Functions

Symbols are used to name functions and may have parameters. A function name written with the appropriate collection of arguments denotes the result of executing that function on those arguments and is called a *term*. The arguments to functions may be constants, variables, or other terms. We will use lowercase letters (with the underscore) to name functions.

Predicates

A *predicate* is a symbol that denotes some property that an object, or several objects, might have. Thus if gummy and biggerthan are predicates and j and k are objects, then gummy(k) is an assertion that k has the property gummy, and biggerthan(j,k) asserts that j is biggerthan k. We will use lowercase letters to name predicates.

The arguments to a predicate are terms. A predicate applied to constants, or to variable-free terms, is called a *sentence* or a *proposition*. It has a truth value (true or false), depending on whether or not the predicate is true of the objects denoted by its arguments. A predicate may also be applied to variables, or to terms containing variables, but it does not form a sentence until all those variables are instantiated. If the instantiated predicate is true, then we say the predicate *is satisfied by* the instantiation.

A predicate may have one, two, or more arguments [Exhibit 13.1]. We use the word *arity* to denote the number of arguments and describe a predicate with arity N as an *N-ary* predicate. Thus the predicate divide in Exhibit 13.1 has arity 4 and is a 4-ary predicate.

Exhibit 13.1.   Predicates and arity.

Predicate	Arity	Intent
odd(X)	1	X is an odd number.
father(F,S)	2	F is the father of S.
divide(N,D,Q,R)	4	N divided by D gives quotient Q and remainder R.

Instantiated Predicate	Truth Value
odd(2)	False.
father(David, Solomon)	True.
divide(23, 3, 7, 2)	True.
divide(23, 3, 7, N)	Neither true nor false until we instantiate N.

Quantifiers

Variables let us denote arbitrary objects in a domain; quantifiers let us denote sets of objects. There are two kinds of quantifiers: existential and universal. The *existential* quantifier is written ∃X and read as "there exists an X such that", and the *universal* quantifier is written ∀Y and read as "for all Y". Quantifiers are written at the beginning of a formula and bind all occurrences of the quantified variable within the formula.

The formula to which the quantifier is applied is called the *scope*. Thus, in Exhibit 13.2, both occurrences of the variable X on the third line are bound by the quantifier ∀X. The scope of the quantifier is X = 2 * Y + 1 → odd(X).

Exhibit 13.2.   Quantified predicates.

	Quantified Predicate	Truth Value
1.	∀X odd(X)	false.
2.	∃X odd(X)	true, satisfied by X=3.
3.	∀X (X=2*Y+1 → odd(X))	true.
4.	∀X ∃Y divide(X, 3, Y, 0)	false for X=2.
5.	∃X ∃Y divide(X, 3, Y, 0)	true, satisfied by X=12, Y=4.
6.	∃X ∀Y divide(X, 3, Y, 0)	false, but harder to prove.

A quantified formula containing no free variables is a sentence and has a truth value. An existentially quantified formula is true if the scope of the quantifier(s) can be satisfied, that is, if there is at least one way to instantiate the variables (each from its proper domain) so that the resulting proposition is true. It is therefore easy to show that the quantified predicates on lines 2 and 5 in Exhibit 13.2 are true—we simply find suitable values for the variables.

Proving the truth of a universally quantified predicate is more difficult, especially if the universe of discourse is large or infinite. One must demonstrate that the scope is true for all objects in the universe. On the other hand, the negation of a universally quantified predicate is an existentially quantified predicate, as shown in Exhibit 13.3. Thus it is easy to show that a universally quantified statement is *false*; one just needs to find a single instantiation of the variables that makes the scope false, as shown on line 4 of Exhibit 13.2.

Exhibit 13.3.   Quantified formulas.

	Quantified Predicate	Negation
1.	∀ X odd(X)	∃ X not odd(X)
2.	∃ X odd(X)	∀ X not odd(X)
3.	∀ X X=2*Y+1 → odd(X)	∃ X not(X=2*Y+1 → odd(X))
		∃ X not(not(X=2*Y+1) or odd(X))
		∃ X (X=2*Y+1) and not odd(X))
4.	∀ X ∃ Y divide(X, 3, Y, 0)	∃ X ∀ Y not divide(X, 3, Y, 0)
5.	∃ X ∃ Y divide(X, 3, Y, 0)	∀ X ∀ Y not divide(X, 3, Y, 0)
6.	∃ X ∀ Y divide(X, 3, Y, 0)	∀ X ∃ Y not divide(X, 3, Y, 0)

Logical Operations

Formulas can be combined to build bigger formulas using logical operations. Only a small number of logical operations, "and", "or", and "not", are needed. The semantics of these operations are defined by the truth tables in Exhibit 13.4. Other logical operations such as "implies" are often used and can be defined in terms of the three basic operations.

Exhibit 13.4.   Semantics of not, or, and, and implies.

p	q	not p	p or q	p and q	q or not p / p implies q
true	true	false	true	true	true
true	false		true	false	false
false	true	true	true	false	true
false	false		false	false	true

13.2 PROOF SYSTEMS

When we use the predicate calculus to represent some problem area, we start by defining symbols to represent objects, functions, and predicates from our external domains [Exhibit 13.5]. Then we write a set of sentences in terms of these symbols that represent facts about our system. These formulas, called *axioms*, usually capture only a portion of the logician's semantic intent: that portion relevant to the current problem. Other aspects of semantic intent may be stated in the form of comments.

Exhibit 13.5.   Logical symbols and sentences.

```
Constants:    17, gnu, apple_tree
Variables:    X, YY
Functions:    successor(X), product(Y,Z)
Predicates:   even(X), even(successor(17)), cousin(Y,Z), remainder(X, Y, Z)
```

A *proof system* is a set of valid deduction rules that can be applied to axioms to deduce theorems. A *deduction* is an application of one of the valid inference rules of the proof system. In a simple deductive step, we derive a conclusion from the axioms and previously deduced theorems according to that rule. A *proof* is a series of sentences, ending with the sentence to be proved, such that each sentence is either an axiom or a valid deduction from some subset of the previous sentences in the proof. If there are N sentences in a proof, we will call it an *N-step proof*. A *refutation* is a proof of the negation of a sentence, which is the same as a proof that the sentence is inconsistent with the given axioms.

Two proofs of the same proposition can differ drastically in length and complexity. A logician constructs a proof or a refutation using insight, pattern recognition, and a bit of luck. With more insight (and luck) a proof is clear and brief; with less it can be tedious and murky. Even the clumsiest proof, however, takes some skill to construct.

A sentence that can be deduced from the axioms is called a *valid sentence*. Any valid sentence can also be called a *theorem*.[1] The set of all theorems derivable from a set of axioms is called a *theory*. We say that a theory is *consistent* if it does not contain contradictory theorems.

Classical Logic

Logicians have invented several different valid proof systems with very different deduction rules. One such system, often called *classical logic*, has been in use for centuries. It is based on the ancient deduction rule called "modus ponens" (the way of the bridge), which is the primary rule used to reason about conditional sentences. A *conditional sentence* is of the form:

$$C1 \rightarrow C2$$

where the arrow symbolizes the logical operation "implies", and $C1$ and $C2$ are sentences. $C1 \rightarrow C2$ is read "$C1$ implies $C2$"; $C1$ is called the *premise* and $C2$ is called the *conclusion*. Modus ponens says,

> If the truth of the premise can be established, then one can infer that the conclusion is also true.

In symbols, this lets one derive the theorem $C2$ if both the conditional sentence $C1 \rightarrow C2$ and the sentence $C1$ have been previously proved (or are axioms).

Other proof rules are needed in order to deal with quantified sentences and with formulas containing free variables. For example, the rule of generalization says that if a formula $C(X)$ containing a free variable X can be proved (meaning that C is true no matter how X is instantiated), then one can infer the sentence $\forall X C(X)$.

Clausal Logic and Resolution

Clausal logic is an alternative to classical logic. It is based on a powerful deduction rule called *resolution* which is described in Section 13.4.1. *Resolution* often allows much shorter proofs because one resolution inference can take the place of many simple modus ponens inferences.

Prolog itself is a proof system which uses clausal logic and resolution. Clausal logic generally writes "implies" using the left arrow, so that the conditional sentence $C1 \rightarrow C2$ becomes

$$C2 \leftarrow C1$$

and is read "$C2$ if $C1$".

---

[1] In other contexts this word is used only for particularly interesting or useful valid sentences.

13.3 MODELS

Recall that a theory is a set of formulas derivable from a set of axioms. Given a theory, we can try to find a *model* for it. A model is not something that can be written or discussed within a formal system. Rather, it is one possible interpretation of the semantic intent of a theory and is presented in a metalanguage. To make a model, we find interpretations for each constant, function, and predicate symbol in the axioms, so that the axioms are all true statements about those interpretations. Specifically, we must define each universe of discourse and show the correspondence between members of a universe, or domain, and the constants in the axioms. The predicate symbols in the axioms must also be assigned to properties of objects in these domains, and the function symbols must be assigned to functions that operate on objects from the specified domains. An inconsistent theory has no models because it is impossible to find interpretations that simultaneously satisfy contradictory theorems.

Because a set of axioms only partially "defines" the functions and predicates of a theory, one theory may have several models. For example, consider the very simple theory in Exhibit 13.6, which we will call the "Theory of Ugliness". To find a model for this theory we must find a domain of discourse which contains interpretations for the constant symbols "1" and "2", for the function symbol "+", and for the predicate symbol "ugly". This is easily done.

- Let our domain of discourse be the integers. Let "1" represent the integer one and let "2" represent the integer two.
- Let "+" represent the function of addition on the integers.
- Now there are two possible interpretations for "ugly": the integer predicate "odd" or the integer predicate "even".

Exhibit 13.6.   A simple theory: The Theory of Ugliness.

Axioms for the Theory of Ugliness:

```
1.  ∀ X ugly(X)          → not ugly(X+1)
2.  ∀ X not ugly(X+1)    → ugly(X)
3.  2 = 1 + 1
```

Theorems from the Theory of Ugliness:

```
1.  ∀ X ugly(X)          → ugly(X+2)
2.  ∀ X ugly(X+2)        → ugly(X)
```

We can now make two models for the Theory of Ugliness. In one model, all odd numbers are ugly, even numbers are not. In the other model, all even numbers are ugly, odd numbers are not. Both models are completely consistent with the axioms, yet the axioms do not let us identify even one ugly number with certainty. Nevertheless, we can reason about ugly numbers and prove, for example, that if X is ugly, then so is X+2. (This is the theorem mentioned in Exhibit 13.6.) The fact that a set of axioms can have more than one model is a very important matter in logic programming applications; we do not have to axiomatize all aspects of a model in order to reason about it.

13.4 AUTOMATIC THEOREM PROVING

Symbolic logic was first formulated by Frege[2], at the end of the nineteenth century. This work was extended during the next fifty years by several pioneers. Certain properties of logical theories have been central to this work. The first is completeness: a theory is *complete* if every sentence that is true in all models of the theory can be proved from its axioms by using its deductive rules. We say that such a sentence is a *logical consequence* of the axioms.

A second property, first studied by Hilbert, is *decidability*. A theory is decidable if one can decide (that is, prove) whether any given sentence is or is not valid in that theory. This is equivalent to saying that, for any sentence, either it or its negation can be proved. A theory can be complete but not decidable if there are sentences that are true in some models but not in others. Such sentences are not logical consequences of the axioms. For example, in the Theory of Ugliness, the sentence ugly(3) is true in one model, where the predicate ugly corresponds to the integer property odd, but not in the alternate model where ugly represents even. Thus ugly(3) is not a logical consequence of the theory, and neither ugly(3) nor not ugly(3) can be proved from the axioms.

By 1940, the logical foundations of mathematics had been thoroughly established and explored. The central theorems are as follows:

1. The predicate calculus is complete. That is, the proof techniques of the predicate calculus can be used to develop a formal proof for every logically true proposition. (Goedel, Herbrand, 1930.)

2. If a proposition can be proved at all, then it can be proved "in a direct way", without requiring insight. That is, a mechanical proof method exists. (Gentzen, 1936.)

3. There is not, and cannot be, an algorithm that correctly identifies propositions that are *not* true and *cannot* be proved. Even though a proof procedure exists for true propositions, a proof may take an indefinitely long time to produce by this procedure. There is no time at which we can conclude that a proof will *not* be discovered in the future. As a consequence, Hilbert's decision problem is unsolvable for the predicate calculus. (Church, Turing, 1936.)

Since the invention of electronic computers, there has been interest in automating the proof process. At first this was only of academic interest. More recently, however, the community has come to understand that deduction and computation are analogous processes—indeed, computations can be written as deductions, and vice versa. Since 1940, logicians have been working on the problem of automatic theorem proving programs:

- We know that we can devise an algorithm (or write a program) that will take a set of axioms and enumerate and prove all possible propositions that can be derived from those axioms.

- Of more interest, we would like an automatic system which, given a single interesting proposition, will prove it.

- We would like this system to be efficient enough to be useful.

---

[2]Frege [1879].

- We would like a language in which to express propositions, and a language processor that will find proofs for these propositions, if they exist.

As a consequence of the completeness result, we know that it is theoretically possible to build a program that can prove any theorem that is a logical consequence of a set of axioms. However, if we simply generate and prove propositions systematically, most of them will be simple variations of similar propositions and any interesting theorems would be buried in an avalanche of trivia. Moreover, the process would take forever. This is analogous to the old question of the monkeys and the typewriters: if you put 1000 monkeys in front of 1000 typewriters, and they all randomly type, day and night, will they ever produce any great literature? The answer is yes: eventually the random process will produce a poem, or more, but the valuable information will be lost in a sea of garbage. Finding the "great" stuff would be impractical.

Once we restrict our attention to proving a single proposition, the main problem is efficiency. If we start with the axioms and make every inference possible, a few might be relevant to our chosen proposition, but most are not, and we have no automatable way to tell which. Further, any deduction we make can lead to several other deductions, creating multiple, branching lines of reasoning. Visualize all possible deductions from a set of axioms as a tree structure. The width and bushiness of the tree are determined by the number of alternative deductions possible at each stage. A sentence at level one of the tree represents an axiom. A sentence at level two is a theorem with a two-step proof, and the sentences at level N are theorems with N step proofs.

If we could build an automatic theorem-prover to start with a set of axioms, make every possible inference, and follow every possible line of reasoning, our proof method would be complete. However, that would create an impossibly bushy and impossibly deep tree-structure of lines of deduction. We say that there is a *combinatorial explosion* of possible lines of reasoning, because of the huge number of different combinations of inferences that we might make.

We could try to generate proofs by constructing this tree in a breadth-first manner; that is, make all two-step deductions before starting on the three-step proofs. If we do so, we build a very bushy tree. By the time we have made all ten-step deductions, we could have so many possibilities that remembering and extending them all becomes unmanageable. And ten-step proofs are material for student exercises! Hundred-step proofs would be practically impossible. On the other hand, we could try to generate proofs in a depth-first manner; that is, we could follow one line of reasoning to its logical conclusion before exploring other lines. However, using this approach, we could get trapped in an infinite, circular line of reasoning, and our proof process would never terminate.

Some propositions which can be easily proved by a human with insight are very difficult to prove by constructing the entire reasoning tree. For example, Exhibit 13.7 states a very uninteresting proposition: "The number 65534 is a good number". This is proved from axioms that the number zero is good and conditional rules about good numbers that use the arithmetic operations of addition, multiplication, and exponentiation to the base two. The complete line-of-reasoning tree for this foolish proposition would be immensely bushy, since four or five rules can be applied at each step and, usually, only one of them leads to this twenty-one-step proof or to a similar short proof. Moreover, one branch of the tree is at least 32,767 lines long. Finally, rules 3 and 4 can be applied alternately to create an infinite chain of deductions that makes no progress. Whether we search this tree breadth first or depth first, any systematic exploration of it will become mired in masses of uninteresting inferences. Admittedly, propositions like this are pathological cases and are of no real interest to anyone. However, they illustrate that, in order to be truly useful, a general proof algorithm must be able to avoid trouble when given such a proposition to prove.

Exhibit 13.7.   A proof that 65,534 is a good number.

- Let the predicate good(X) mean that the number X is good.
- Let the predicate powtwo(Y,Z) mean that 2 to the power Y is Z.
- Prolog syntax is used below to write the propositions. The comma in axiom 6 should be interpreted as the logical operator "and".

Axioms.

1.	good(0).	
2.	powtwo(0,1).	
3.	good(A-2)	← good(A).
4.	good(A+2)	← good(A).
5.	good(A*2)	← good(A).
6.	good(A)	← powtwo(B,A), good(B).
7.	powtwo(P+1,A*2)	← powtwo(P,A).

The shortest proof of the proposition that 65,534 is a good number:

8.	good(2)	by rule 4, A=0, with line 1.
9.	good(4)	by rule 5, A=2, with line 8.
10.	powtwo(1,2)	by rule 7, P=0, A=1, with rule 2.
11.	powtwo(2,4)	by rule 7, P=1, A=2, with line 10.
12.	powtwo(3,8)	by rule 7, P=2, A=4.
13.	powtwo(4,16)	by rule 7, P=3, A=8.
14.	good(16)	by rule 6, A=16, B=4.
15.	powtwo(5,32)	by rule 7, P=4, A=16.
16.	powtwo(6,64)	by rule 7, P=5, A=32.
17.	powtwo(7,128)	by rule 7, P=6, A=64.
18.	powtwo(8,256)	by rule 7, P=7, A=128.
19.	powtwo(9,512)	by rule 7, P=8, A=256.
20.	powtwo(10,1024)	by rule 7, P=9, A=512.
21.	powtwo(11,2048)	by rule 7, P=9, A=1024.
22.	powtwo(12,4096)	by rule 7, P=9, A=2048.
23.	powtwo(13,8192)	by rule 7, P=9, A=4096.
24.	powtwo(14,16384)	by rule 7, P=9, A=8192.
25.	powtwo(15,32768)	by rule 7, P=9, A=16384.
26.	powtwo(16,65536)	by rule 7, P=9, A=32768.
27.	good(65536)	by rule 6, A=65536, B=16, with lines 14, 26.
28.	good(65534)	by rule 3, A=65536, with line 27.

13.4.1   Resolution Theorem Provers

Early in the history of automatic theorem proving, it was clearly understood that a brute-force, enumerate-them-all approach could never be practical. A usable automatic theorem-prover would have to use techniques that were different from the step-by-step deductions that humans were accustomed to making. Two breakthroughs happened. First, it was shown that a highly restricted form of the predicate calculus, called *clausal logic*, was still complete. In clausal logic, all sentences are a series of predicates, possibly negated, connected by "or" operators.

Second, a new proof technique named *resolution* was invented. The goal of *resolution* was to collapse many simple modus-ponens-like deduction steps into one large inference, thereby eliminating whole sections of the unmanageable deduction tree. Resolution operated on clausal sentences and relied on a pattern-matching algorithm called *unification* to identify sections of a proposition that could be simplified.

The process of resolution on two clauses is analogous to algebraic simplification; it is a way to derive a new, simpler fact from a pair of related facts. First, unification is used to identify portions of the two clauses that are related and can be "simplified" by a *cut operation*. Specifically, given the two assertions:

$$A \rightarrow (B \text{ or } C)$$

and

$$(C \text{ or } D) \rightarrow E$$

then resolution lets us infer that

$$(A \text{ or } D) \rightarrow (B \text{ or } E)$$

Before making this inference, though, we must establish the correspondence between the C parts of the two formulas. Since these subformulas might be quite complicated and involve many predicates with variables and constants, unification (the process of establishing the correspondence or showing that no correspondence exists) is not a trivial matter.

A *resolution deduction* is a sequence of resolution inferences. A *resolution proof* is a resolution deduction whose conclusion is "false"; it establishes that the premises, taken together, form a contradiction. A resolution proof can be used to prove that the *negation* of any single premise can be deduced from the other premises by ordinary logical deduction.

The original resolution methods were better than the brute-force method of enumerating and testing all possible lines of reasoning but were still not practical or useful in real applications. For example, the proposition in Exhibit 13.7 would cause an early resolution-theorem-prover to become mired in irrelevant deductions. Since then, it has been shown that we can restrict the kinds of propositions even further, in ways that make the resolution more efficient. Happily, these restrictions affect only the way a proposition is stated; they do not affect the completeness of the system.

Some interesting theorems are easily derived using ordinary resolution. However, the computation for most theorems is very extensive and is still not of any practical use. A more advanced method, named *hyperresolution*, was developed that operates on Horn clauses, which are even more highly restricted sentences. It is this form of resolution on which logic programming languages are built.

Implementing Resolution Efficiently

Horn Clauses.

A *Horn clause* is a clause with at most one unnegated predicate symbol. As shown in Exhibit 13.8, this is equivalent to saying that a sentence may contain a single "implies" operator, whose premise is several predicates connected by "and" and whose conclusion contains only one predicate symbol.

Exhibit 13.8. Ways to write a Horn clause.

We show that a Horn clause can be rewritten as an implication whose premise is a series of predicates connected by "and" operators and whose conclusion is a single predicate. Let each capital letter in the following derivation stand for a predicate symbol with its required arguments.

A Horn clause is a clause with at most one nonnegated predicate, such as:

$$\text{not } P \text{ or not } Q \text{ or not } R \text{ or } S \text{ or not } T$$

Because "or" is associative and commutative, we can move all the negated predicates to the right:

$$S \text{ or not } P \text{ or not } Q \text{ or not } R \text{ or not } T$$

Using DeMorgan's law, this expression can be transformed to the form:

$$S \text{ or not } (P \text{ and } Q \text{ and } R \text{ and } T)$$

The operator "implies" is defined in terms of "not" and "or", and can be written with either a right-pointing arrow or a left-pointing arrow. Thus the two expressions

$$B \leftarrow A \qquad A \rightarrow B$$

are defined to mean

$$B \text{ or not } A$$

We use the left-pointing "implies" arrow here to conform to the order of terms in Prolog syntax. Now we can rewrite the Horn clause as follows:

$$S \leftarrow (P \text{ and } Q \text{ and } R \text{ and } T)$$

Unification.

Most of the time spent in finding a resolution proof is actually spent in identifying related phrases in two sentences that can be simplified, or cut. A hyperresolution inference depends on the result of a unification procedure. Hyperresolution says that, from the premises

$$A1 \text{ and } A2 \text{ and } \ldots \text{ and } An$$

and

$$(B1 \text{ and } B2 \text{ and } \ldots \text{ and } Bn) \rightarrow D$$

we can infer D, where all variables in D have been instantiated with expressions that unify the set $\{\{A1,B1\}, \{A2,B2\},\ldots,\{An,Bn\}\}$.

The unification algorithm finds a set of substitutions for the variables in the two formulas so that, after making the substitutions, the two clauses are equal. This is a kind of pattern-matching process. Exhibit 13.9 shows examples of simple unification problems and their results.

Exhibit 13.9.   Unifying clauses.

	Formula 1	Formula 2	Most General Unification
1.	pp(a,b)	pp(X,Y)	X=a, Y=b
2.	pp(Q(c,d),Z)	pp(Y,e)	Y=Q(c,d), Z=e
3.	pp(X,Y) and qq(Y,a)	pp(a,b) and qq(Z,W)	W=a, X=a, Y=b, Z=b
4.	qq(pp, gg(X,Y), X, Y)	qq(Y, Z, hh(U, kk), U)	U=pp, X=hh(pp,kk)
			Y=pp, Z= gg(hh(pp,kk), pp)

We use the unification algorithm to determine whether or not a conditional Horn clause, C, can be used in a resolution, given the current set of unconditional clauses in the data base. To perform a hyperresolution step, we need to find a set of unconditional clauses that *cover* all the predicate symbols in C, and a single set of instantiations for all the variables in these clauses that unifies each unconditional clause with the corresponding predicate. Let us describe the process of unifying an unconditional clause whose predicate symbol is P, and a single predicate symbol, Q, in the conditional clause C as follows:

- A cluster is a set of terms that have been mapped into one equivalence class and must be unified.
- To begin the unification process, map P and Q into a cluster.

   1. Choose any cluster. Look at all the terms in the cluster. (In unifying M items, there will be M terms.)
   2. If one term is a constant and if another term is a predicate or a constant that does not match, no unification is possible and the process fails. If all terms are matching constants, this branch is successfully unified. Otherwise proceed.
   3. If two or more terms are predicates and they are different, no unification is possible and the process fails. Otherwise, proceed, and let N be the arity of the cluster.
   4. We know we are merging a combination of one constant or one predicate with one or more variables. Merge all terms in the cluster into a single unified super-term. Temporarily, the super-term will inherit all the arguments from the predicate terms in the cluster, so that it will have M first arguments, M second arguments, ..., and M Nth arguments.
   5. We must replace each collection of M Nth arguments that was created in step 4 by a unified term. For j from 1 to N, look at all the Nth arguments that belong to this super-term. (If we are unifying M terms, there will be M arguments to consider.) Make a new cluster by mapping together all the terms that are the jth arguments of the super-term. During this process, we may find that one of the terms to be mapped was mapped to a different cluster by a previous operation. In that case, the two clusters are mapped into one.

6. Replace the cluster we have been processing by the super-term created in step 4 with its arguments replaced by the argument clusters from step 5.
7. Repeat steps 1 through 6 until there are no remaining clusters in the formula.

- The process will end when it has descended through all levels of argument nesting.

13.5 Prolog

13.5.1 *The* Prolog *Environment*

Prolog is an interactive language for expressing predicates, relations, and axioms. The programmer may state facts or make queries about those facts. In response to a query, Prolog will attempt to find one instantiation of the query's variables that makes the formula true.

In addition to the language for writing logical assertions and queries, a Prolog system includes a metalanguage for managing the data base of facts and rules. Large data bases can be entered either from a file or from the keyboard by calling the input function `consult(filename)`. Once in the system, parts of the data base can be listed (by using `listing(predicate_name)`) or edited (by using `retract(Z)`), and the data base can be extended (by using `asserta(X)` or `assertz(X)`).

After entering a data base, the programmer may interactively enter queries, test hypotheses, and assert more facts. In response to a query, Prolog executes its proof-procedure and searches for a set of instantiations that satisfies a query's variables. If this search succeeds, Prolog responds by writing out the instantiations that were found. The programmer can indicate that she or he is satisfied (by typing a carriage return), and Prolog responds by saying "yes" and giving a new prompt. Alternatively, the programmer may ask Prolog to search for additional instantiations (by typing a ";" and a carriage return). This search process continues until the programmer decides he or she has seen enough or the entire data base has been searched and no further set of instantiations can be found, at which time Prolog responds by writing "no" and a new prompt.

13.5.2 *Data Objects and Terms*

The basic components of a Prolog program are objects (constants, variables, structures, lists), predicates, operators, functions, and rules.

- Constants: Integers are predefined and represented in base 10. User-defined constants, or *atoms*, have names that start with lowercase letters. Remember that a Prolog program, like a theory, may have many models (or none) and a Prolog atom may correspond to different objects in different models.
- Variables: All variable names start with uppercase letters. All occurrences of the same variable in a rule will be bound to the same object. The symbol "_" can be used in place of a variable name in cases where the program does not need to refer to this same object twice. If the "_" symbol occurs several times in a rule, it may be bound to several different objects.
- Structures: Compound data types (record types) may be defined by specifying a *functor* (the type name) and a list of *components* (fields), in parentheses:

$$\langle\text{type name}\rangle(\ \langle\text{component}\rangle, \dots, \langle\text{component}\rangle\ )$$

- Lists may be denoted by using square brackets. The empty brackets "[]" denote the empty (null) list. The notation [a,b,c] denotes a list of three terms whose head is a and whose last item is c. The notation [A|X] denotes a list of length one or greater with head A and tail, or remainder, X, which may be a list, a single atom, or null. This notation is often used in function definitions to give local names (A and X) to the parts of a list.

  This bracket notation is a "sugaring" of a less attractive basic syntax; "[Head|Tail]" is a syntactic variant of ".(Head,Tail)" and "[x,y,z]" is a variant of ".(x, .(y, .(z, [])))". We will call both forms *list specifications*. A list specification can denote a fully defined list, such as [a, b, c], a fully variable list, such as [Head|Tail], or a list with a defined head and a variable tail, such as [a,b|Z]. The term *open list* refers to a list with a variable tail. During the proof process, an open list may be unified (matched) with any list that has the same constant as its head. The selector functions head(x) and tail(x) are defined to return the head and tail of a list argument.

- Predicates =, \=, <, =<, >, and => are defined. Users may introduce their own predicate symbols, which are written in lowercase. Again, remember that the semantics of these symbols remains largely in the programmer's mind. Within Prolog they have no meaning except that captured by the axioms, or rules, the programmer supplies.

- The integer operators +, -, *, /, and mod are defined and may be written either in standard functional notation: "+(3,X)", or in infix form: "3+X". When infix form is used, the operators have the usual precedence. These operators may be used in an "is" formula, thus: "X is (A+B) mod C". When Prolog processes such a formula it performs the computation using the current bindings of A, B, and C, and binds the result to X. An error is generated if any variable on the right of the "is" is not bound to a number.

A *term* is a predicate symbol or operator or function symbol, together with a parenthesized list of the right number of arguments.

13.5.3 Horn Clauses in Prolog

Deductive Rules

Rules are the axioms that form the basis for deductions in Prolog. A *rule* represents a statement of the form

> **If** a set of premises are all true,
> **then** we may infer that a given conclusion is also true.

The conclusion is written on the left, followed by a ":−" sign, and the premises are written on the right, separated by commas. The variables in a rule are implicitly, universally quantified. A rule is also called a *conditional clause*. Examples of rules are given in Exhibit 13.10.

A *fact* is an assertion that some object or objects satisfy a given predicate. Formally, a fact is a rule which has a conclusion but no conditions, and it is, therefore, sometimes called an *unconditional clause*. Examples of facts are given in Exhibit 13.10. The programmer adds a new fact to the data base by *asserting* it. If X is a fact, then the predicate asserta(X) appends the fact X to the beginning of the data base, and the predicate assertz(X) appends it to the end.

Prolog rules and facts are Horn clauses. The conditions of a rule are a conjunction of terms, even though we write commas between the terms rather than "and"

Exhibit 13.10.   Prolog rules and facts.

Conditional clauses
(rules)
	`pretty(X) :- artwork(X).`
	`pretty(X) :- color(X,red), flower(X).`
	`watchout(X) :- sharp(X,_).`

Unconditional clauses
(facts)
	`color(rose, red).`
	`sharp(rose, stem).`
	`sharp(holly, leaf).`
	`flower(rose).`
	`flower(violet).`
	`artwork(painting(Monet, haystack_at_Giverny)).`

operators. Each single rule represents the "and" of a series of conditions. The conclusion is a single positive term, and the ":−" represents a ← sign. An underscore is a wild card. Thus a Prolog rule is a Horn clause written in the form shown on the last line of Exhibit 13.8. Prolog facts are unconditional Horn clauses.

Typically, one predicate may have several rules defined for it [Exhibit 13.13]. A list of rules for one predicate represents the "or" of those conditions—only one rule will be used to interpret a given call on that predicate, and the one used will be the first one that can be satisfied. Thus we can use a sequence of rules to express a generalized conditional semantic structure.

Rules may be recursive and thus may be used to implement repetition in an algorithm. A recursive predicate must, of course, have at least two rules (the base case and the recursive step).

Queries

A query in Prolog is a request to Prolog to prove a theorem. Because the question posed is the goal of the proof process, a query is also called a *goal*. Syntactically, a query is a list of terms, separated by commas [Exhibit 13.11]. Semantically, the commas represent "and" operators. If the query has no variables, Prolog will attempt to prove it from the rules and facts previously given. Thus, in Exhibit 13.11, the query "?- pretty(rose)" can be proved from the second rule taken together with the first and fourth facts in Exhibit 13.10.

If the query does contain variables, the Prolog theorem-prover attempts to find a set of instantiations that satisfy the query. All variables in the query are, implicitly, quantified by "∃"; that is, a query asks whether any set of objects exists that can satisfy the clause. Thus to respond to the query "?- pretty(Y)", Prolog tries to find some object, Y, that has the property "pretty". It will begin by using rule 1, the first rule given for the predicate "pretty", and will combine this with fact 5, instantiating Y to a painting, and producing the output "Y = painting(Monet, haystack_at_Giverny)". If the programmer types ";" to ask for another instantiation, Prolog will continue to search its data base and find the second instantiation, "Y = rose". If the search is continued again, no further instantiations succeed, and the answer "no" is printed.

Exhibit 13.11.   Prolog queries.

```
?- pretty(rose).
yes
?- pretty(Y).
Y=painting(Monet, haystack_at_Giverny).
Y=rose
no
?- pretty(W),sharp(W,Z).
W=rose      Z=stem
no
```

A query may contain a series of predicate terms which will always be processed in order, left to right, and processing will be aborted if any one predicate cannot be satisfied [Exhibit 13.12]. This built-in conditional sequencing is used where "`if`" statements and sequences of assignments would be used in a procedural language.

Exhibit 13.12.   Interpreting Prolog rules.

Rules 2 and 3 from the gcd algorithm (Exhibit 13.13) are dissected here. In both rules, A and B are input parameters and D is an output parameter.

```
gcd(A, B, D) :- (A<B), gcd(B, A, D).
```

This right side is the analog of a Pascal IF...THEN statement. Prolog interprets it as follows: test whether (A<B) is true. If so, call predicate gcd with arguments (B, A, D). If that succeeds, D will be bound to the answer.

```
gcd(A, B, D) := (A>B), (B>0), R is A mod B, gcd(B, R, D).
```

This performs the equivalent of two Pascal if statements, an assignment, and a function call. Prolog interprets it thus: test whether (A>B) is true. If so, test (B>0). If both conditions hold, calculate A mod B and bind to R. Finally, call predicate gcd with arguments (B, R, D). If all succeed, D will be bound to the answer.

13.5.4   *The* Prolog *Deduction Process*

A query establishes a goal for the deductive process, in the form of a conjunction of terms. To satisfy this goal, Prolog first takes each individual term in the goal, in order, as a subgoal, and recursively attempts to satisfy that subgoal.

The subgoal is a predicate with arguments. Prolog begins by finding, in the data base, the rules for that predicate which have the right arity for the subgoal, and then starts with the first rule. It attempts to unify the head (conclusion) of the rule with the subgoal; if there is a conflict because constant terms do not match, Prolog will go on to the next rule for that predicate. If the head can be unified with the subgoal, it means that this rule is, potentially, applicable.

Prolog then tries to satisfy each of the condition terms on the right side of that rule. To do this, it searches for a set of facts that "cover" the terms of the goal. If this process succeeds, the rule is applied to the goal, the goal's variables are instantiated to the objects discovered by the unification algorithm, and the set of instantiations is returned to the calling context. At the top level, the instantiations are printed out.

We can summarize the operation of the Prolog proof process as follows:

1. Work on the leftmost subgoal first.
2. Select the first applicable rule.
3. Search the facts in the order they appear in the data base.

Careful attention to the order in which goals are written, rules are given, and facts are asserted can improve the performance of the proof system substantially. It makes good sense, when defining a multirule predicate, to make the first rule the one that will be used most frequently, if that is possible. For example, in the gcd algorithm [Exhibit 13.13], the rule that ends the recursion must be written before rule 2, to prevent rule 2 from being invoked with a zero divisor, which would generate an error. However, rules 2 and 3 could be written in either order, and rule 3 is placed last because it will be executed at most once, to swap the arguments on the first recursion, in the case that the first argument is smaller than the second.

The programmer must also be careful of the order of the conditions within a rule. Since these conditions are taken, in order, as subgoals, and variables become instantiated as the subgoals succeed, a condition that is intended to instantiate a variable must precede all conditions that expect that variable to be instantiated. This is like saying, in a procedural language, that variables must be initialized before they are used. Further, because the conditions are tested in order, a series of conditions is very much like a nested conditional. Sometimes a condition is simple to test; sometimes satisfying it can involve a great deal of computation. Where two conditions must both be true before proceeding with a rule, it is prudent to write the simple one first, so that, if it is false, it will abort the rule before making the costly test. A simple condition can thus "guard" a complex or difficult condition.

Backtracking

The recursive descent from goal to subgoal ends successfully when a subgoal is reached that corresponds to a known fact in the data base. The instantiations used to satisfy the subgoal are passed back up and are used to instantiate the variables in the goal.

The recursive descent ends in failure if the fail predicate is encountered while processing a rule, or if the entire data base has been searched and no relevant information was found. Failure of a goal does not mean that the goal is false, only that it cannot be proven from the facts given. When a subgoal fails, control *backtracks*, that is, it passes back up to the level of the goal above, and Prolog attempts to find a different set of instantiations that satisfy the original goal. In terms of the tree of possible proofs, this amounts to backing up one path until an unexplored branching point is found, then going down the new branch of the tree. Exhibit 10.36, at the end of Chapter 10, illustrates this recursive backtracking.

13.5.5 Functions and Computation

A programmer trying to solve a problem or model a system starts with a set of inputs, in some given form, and wishes to derive from them a set of outputs. In a language like C, this is done by defining functions to carry out a series of calculations and manipulations on the data that produce a result in the desired form. We call this procedural programming.

We might view the same problem in a different way. Instead of specifying the method to reach the desired output, we could describe the output desired, in a declarative, axiomatic language. Prolog is a language for axiomatizing a desired result. The process of computation, in a C program, is replaced by the process of proof in Prolog, where a proof consists of *finding* a data object that satisfies the formula for the result. Thus ordinary computation, as well as data base searches, can be expressed in Prolog.

Computation

In place of a C function that returns an answer, a Prolog programmer writes a predicate with one additional parameter, which will be used for returning the answer. It is customary to write the output parameter or parameters last. Instead of instructions to perform a computation, the Prolog programmer writes axioms to verify that the answer is correct. During the proof process, the output parameter names become bound to values that have been verified, and these values are then returned to the calling environment. If the predicate involves an actual arithmetic computation, one of its rules will contain an is clause, which directs Prolog to actually evaluate an expression and bind its result to a variable so that it can be returned.

An example of ordinary computation expressed as a Prolog predicate is the implementation of Euclid's algorithm for calculating the greatest common divisor of A and B [Exhibit 13.13]. This recursive definition has three rules. The first rule stops the recursion when the gcd has been found. The second rule does the work. It is a recursive axiom that says that the gcd of two numbers, A and B, is also the gcd of B and (A mod B), and the gcd of every remainder calculated. The third rule is invoked only when the second argument is larger than the first, and it simply reorders the arguments so that the larger one is first.

Exhibit 13.13. Euclid's algorithm in Prolog.

These three rules axiomatize Euclid's greatest common divisor algorithm. The numbers on the left are for reference only; they are not part of the Prolog code.

```
1.  | gcd(A, 0, A).
2.  | gcd(A, B, D) :- (A>B), (B>0), R is A mod B, gcd(B, R, D).
3.  | gcd(A, B, D) :- (A<B), gcd(B, A, D).
```

Let us compare the Prolog gcd program with the same algorithm expressed in C [Exhibit 13.14]. We see that the C program requires more syntactic details—such things as type declarations for the parameters and an explicit return statement. As in Miranda, Prolog variables are untyped, but objects are typed and their types are deduced by the system. Return values are implemented as output parameters in Prolog, and the value is returned by Prolog's action (during unification) of instantiating the output parameter.

Exhibit 13.14.   Euclid's algorithm in C.

```
int gcd(int A, int B)
{   int D;
    if (B >A) D=B, B=A, A=D;   /* swap */
    do D=(A % B), A=B, B=D;
    while (D >0);
    return A;
}
```

The three Prolog rules for gcd are exactly echoed in the remaining three lines of the C program. Rule one corresponds to the while—both stop the recursion/iteration when the answer has been calculated. Rule two corresponds to the do—both perform one mod operation and shift the arguments to the left for the next recursion/iteration. Finally, rule three corresponds to the if—both just swap the inputs. Thus we see that an axiomatic expression of an algorithm can look and work very much like a procedural formulation.

Sorting

Algorithms, such as sorts, that manipulate data can also be expressed axiomatically. An axiomatization of quicksort is shown in Exhibit 13.15. The quicksort function is expressed as a recursive function with three rules. Rules 4 and 5 are the base cases for the recursion, and they stop it when the list to be sorted has zero elements or one element. Rule 6 does most of the work. It separates the argument (a list) into three parts (smaller values, pivot, and larger values), sorts the parts, then appends them together in sorted order. Quicksort calls a subroutine, named split, that actually does the separation.

The task of split is to separate the list into a sublist of small values and a sublist of large values by comparing each list element to the Pivot. The input arguments are Pivot, the first value on the sublist that is being sorted, and Unsorted, the rest of that sublist. The value of Pivot will be compared to each element of Unsorted, and the elements of Unsorted will be divided into two lists, those smaller than Pivot and those that are larger. The last two arguments, Small and Large, are output parameters that split will use to return the sorted Small and Large sublists.

Split is implemented recursively, by three rules. Rule 1 is the base case for the recursion; if the argument is the null list, it will return immediately with null lists as its output parameters. Each time split is called with a list of at least one item, either the second rule or the third will be used. In both cases, the symbol Head is bound to the first item remaining on the unsorted list, and Tail is bound to whatever remains. On the next call, the first item of Tail will be peeled off. This will continue until the remaining tail is null, at which time the first rule for split will terminate the recursion.

Exhibit 13.15.   Quicksort in `Prolog`.

```
1.  |  split(_,[],[],[]).
2.  |  split(Pivot, [Head|Tail], [Head|Sm], Lg) :-
    |      Head<Pivot, split(Pivot, Tail, Sm, Lg).
3.  |  split(Pivot, [Head|Tail], Sm, [Head|Lg]) :-
    |      Pivot<Head, split(Pivot, Tail, Sm, Lg).
4.  |  quicksort([],[]).
5.  |  quicksort([Head|[]], Head).
6.  |  quicksort([Pivot|Unsorted], AllSorted) :-
    |      split( Pivot, Unsorted, Small, Large),
    |      quicksort(Small, SmSorted),
    |      quicksort(Large, LgSorted),
    |      append(SmSorted, [Pivot|LgSorted], AllSorted).
```

The second rule for `split` is applied whenever the first item on the `Unsorted` list is smaller than the `Pivot`. This first item is peeled off and remembered, then `split` calls itself recursively to process the remaining unsorted list. When this recursive call returns, all items smaller than the `Pivot` will be on the list `Sm`, and all larger ones will be on the list `Lg`. Since the `Head` element was smaller than `Pivot`, it belongs on the `Sm` list, and so it is appended to the front of that list. The extended `Sm` list and the `Lg` list are then returned to the calling routine.

The third rule for `split` is applied whenever the first item on the `Unsorted` list is larger than the `Pivot`. Its operation is just like the second rule, except that, because the `Head` element is bigger than the `Pivot`, it is concatenated to the `Lg` list.

Let us look at how the Prolog proof system is being used here to implement a sort procedure, and compare it to a quicksort program written in a procedural language. In C, the code for `quicksort` uses recursion, explicit iteration, explicit conditionals, comparisons, pointers, and assignments [Exhibits 13.16 and 13.17]. In contrast, the Prolog code uses only recursion and comparison. How is the rest of the work done? First, note that in both languages, the main `quicksort` routine is recursive. However, the `split` routine is tail-recursive in Prolog but iterative in C, for efficiency. The act of calling a routine recursively looks just the same in the two languages, and it has the same semantic effect.

The data structures used are different; the Prolog version sorts a list, while the C version sorts an array. The action of moving through the elements of the list is accomplished in Prolog by recursively binding a local name, `Tail`, to the list with its head removed. This recursive binding takes the place of the increment ("++") and decrement ("--") operations in C, both of which have assignment as a side effect.

Binding and concatenation are used in Prolog in place of the assignment operations in C. As Prolog's `split` pulls each item off the unsorted list, it binds the item to a local variable name, `Head`. Since the function is called recursively, once for each element on the unsorted list, enough bindings are created to hold all the list elements. As each call to `split` returns, the bound item is appended to the list returned by the lower level. In contrast, the C version uses iteration instead of recursion to perform the split operation. New storage is not created; rather, assignment is used to swap pairs of values in the original storage area.

Exhibit 13.16.   Quicksort in C.

Notes on this code are given in Exhibit 13.17.

```
int * split( int *first, int *last )
{   int *small;                     /* small is a left-to-right scanner. */
    int *large;                     /* large is a right-to-left scanner. */
    int swap, pivot = *first;
    int *scan;

    for( small=first, large=last+1; ; )
    {
        while (* ++small < pivot);  /* Scan until large item is found. */
        while (* --large > pivot);  /* Scan until small item is found. */
        if (small >= large) break;  /* Quit if scanners have crossed. */
        swap =*large; *large=*small; *small=swap;
    }
    *first = *large;  *large = pivot;
    return large;                   /* This marks the split point.  */
}
void quicksort(int * first, int * last)
{   int * split_point;

    if (last<=first) return;        /* Only one item -- no action needed.  */
    split_point = split (first, last);
    quicksort (first, split_point-1);
    quicksort (split_point+1, last);
}
```

Exhibit 13.17.   Notes on the C quicksort.

1. The parameters first and last must be pointers to the beginning and end of an array of integers. On exit from quicksort, the values in this array are in sorted order. Pointers, rather than subscripts, are used to index the array.

2. A sentinel value equal to maxint must follow the last data element to stop the left-to-right scanning pointer in the case that the pivot value is the largest value in the array.

3. The inner while loops identify the leftmost and rightmost elements that are stored in the wrong part of the array. These two elements are then swapped.

4. After exit from the for loop, all items to the left of small are small (less than or equal to pivot value) and all items to the right of large are large. The large scanner points to a small element, and small either points to the same thing or points to the large element on large's right.

5. Before returning, the pivot element is swapped into the middle, between the small and large elements. This is its final resting place. The small and large areas remain to be sorted by future recursive calls on quicksort.

The sequential execution of C statements is echoed exactly in the sequential application of the subgoals in each Prolog rule. Thus the main routine, quicksort, looks almost the same in the two languages.

Finally, in the C code, explicit if statements are used to end recursion in quicksort and to end the split operation, and while statements are used to determine whether an element belongs in the small or the large part of the array. In Prolog all this is accomplished by the elaborate pattern matching algorithm (unification) that is built into the proof system. Prolog uses unification to select which rule to apply when split is called, which determines whether the next step will add an element to the small list or the large list, or end the recursion.

13.5.6 Cuts and the "not" Predicate

Two major theoretical results have had a strong bearing on Prolog: clausal logic is *complete* but *not decidable*. So although every true clausal theorem can be proved, no effective procedure can ever exist that will always produce a proof and terminate in a finite amount of time. This means that if the Prolog proof system relied on resolution alone, a programmer might not know whether a given query would ever be answered. Prolog does have a way, called a cut, to control the proof process so that a programmer can avoid being trapped in lengthy deductions that seem likely to be fruitless. However, when the cut operation is used for this purpose in Prolog, it destroys the completeness of the proof system and leaves open the possibility that a provable goal might fail.

Cuts

A cut is written as "!" and may appear as one of the conditions in a rule.[3] Informally, a *cut* prunes off one branch of the proof-search tree by telling the proof system to abandon a chain of reasoning under certain conditions. In some ways it is analogous to a break instruction.

Perhaps the best way to think of a cut is to imagine that it is a barrier, placed by the programmer in a rule, to stop fruitless backtracking. Consider a rule with several terms:

$$P: -Q, R, S, !, T, U, V.$$

In trying to satisfy this rule, the proof system starts by searching for a unification of conditions Q, R, and S. Backtracking might occur several times during this search, and control might go back as far as condition Q. If Prolog fails to satisfy this part of the rule, it will go on to try the next rule for P. However, if the conditions Q, R, and S on the left are eventually satisfied, control passes through the cut to the conditions T, U, and V on the right. At this point, all variable bindings for conditions Q, R, and S are frozen, or committed, and the information that would permit Prolog to backtrack back through these conditions is discarded.

The proof system now begins to try to find a unification for conditions T, U, and V that is consistent with the frozen bindings. Again, a great deal of backtracking can

---

[3]Do not confuse this meaning of the term "cut" with the meaning of "cut" in a resolution step of clausal logic.

happen among these clauses, and, perhaps, some unification of the whole rule may be found. In this case, the rule succeeds, and a unification is returned. If (during backtracking) control ever returns to the cut, it means that the attempt to unify conditions T, U, and V with the frozen bindings has failed. At this point, the two pruning actions of the cut take place:

1. Instead of returning to reinstantiate the left part of the rule, the entire rule fails immediately.

2. The goal that caused this rule to be processed also fails and no more attempts are made to satisfy the predicate, even if there are more, untried rules for it.

Safe Cuts.

A safe cut is one that cannot possibly cause a provable goal to fail. These are used for the sake of efficiency, in situations where the conditions that guard the various rules for a predicate are mutually exclusive. This is illustrated by the code in Exhibit 13.18, which determines whether a student should be put on academic probation. (Students are listed in Exhibit 13.19.) The grade point average needed to avoid probation becomes higher each year. Thus one rule is included in the `probation` predicate for each grade point level involved.

Exhibit 13.18.   "Cutting" off a search.

These predicates axiomatize what it means to be on academic probation at a hypothetical university. Loosely, the requirement is that the closer a student is to graduation, the closer the student's grade point average must be to the minimum gpa for graduation, which is 2.00. (We use the integer form, 200, rather than the decimal form, 2.00, in this code.) Each student is represented in the data base by a fact of the form shown in Exhibit 13.19.

```
1. |   year(S, Y) :- student(S,Y,_).
2. |   gpa( S, G) :- student(S,_,G).
3. |   probation(S, X):-year(S,fr), !, gpa(S,X), X<150.
4. |   probation(S, X):-year(S,so1),!, gpa(S,X), X<160.
5. |   probation(S, X):-year(S,so2),!, gpa(S,X), X<170.
6. |   probation(S, X):-year(S,ju1),!, gpa(S,X), X<180.
7. |   probation(S, X):-year(S,ju2),!, gpa(S,X), X<190.
8. |   probation(S, X):-year(S,se), gpa(S,X), X<200.
```

Exhibit 13.19.   Data for the probation predicate.

```
student(ali, so1, 195).    student(dale, ju2, 189).    student(jan, fr, 372).
student(jess, fr, 142).    student(ken, fr, 199).      student(les, so2, 315).
student(mark, so1, 152).   student(nan, so2, 170).     student(pat, ju1, 175).
student(rae, se, 195).     student(sal, ju2, 298).     student(tal, se, 400).
```

If we ask "`probation(tal)`", the query will fail, because tal is a fine student. In the process of answering this query, Prolog will have looked at all the rules for the predicate probation and will have failed to satisfy the "year(S,Y)" term on all but the last rule. In this case, the cuts in the prior rules have no effect. Similarly, the cuts have no effect during processing of the query "year(S,se), probation(S,G)", and Prolog will return with the instantiation "S=rae, G=195" indicating that rae is, indeed, in trouble.

Similarly, there is no inefficiency problem if we ask "probation(jess,G)". Prolog tries rule 3 first, finds that it describes jess well, and succeeds with the instantiation G=142. No backtracking ever happens.

However, if we ask "probation(jan,G).", Prolog finds that rule 3 for probation should be processed because jan is a freshman. It then finds jan's gpa, compares it to the minimum for freshmen, and fails. This failure initiates backtracking, and control backs up to the cut without finding any other instantiations for X. If the cut were not there, backtracking would continue; rule 3 would then fail, and rules 4 through 8 would all be tried and fail on the year condition. All this work is nonproductive because a student who is a freshman cannot simultaneously fall into any of the other categories. The presence of the cut in rule 3 acts like an else clause and eliminates the fruitless testing of all the other rules. In a chain of exclusive conditions, therefore, each rule except the last should be written with a cut.

Cuts Implement the Operator not.

Perhaps the reader has noted the conspicuous absence of "not" in any of the examples given. One of the restrictions placed on both rules and queries is that the conditions must all be *nonnegative*. This is required in order to permit the use of resolution as a proof system.

Of course, several of the built-in predicates have a negative form also—for example, we have both "=" and "\=". The Prolog language does include a built-in not operator which can be applied to a condition term. However, not is problematical and the results obtained by using it can be misleading. Consider what happens during processing of not, whose definition is shown in Exhibit 13.20:

- If X is false, rule 1 fails before passing through the cut.
- In that case, rule 2 is used. This rule always succeeds, no matter what its argument is, and it instantiates nothing.
- If X is true, control passes through the cut in rule 1 and comes to the fail. This term always fails, initiating backtracking.
- When the backtracking reaches the cut, rule 1 fails, and since rule 2 is not used because of the cut, the predicate fails.
- The result is that not(X) succeeds if X fails and fails if X succeeds.

Exhibit 13.20. The "not" in Prolog.

Definition of not:

```
1. |  not(X) :- X, !, fail.
2. |  not(_).
```

The condition not(X) succeeds if X fails, and fails if X succeeds.

The disturbing fact about not is that the results of evaluating the predicates P and not(not(P)) are not necessarily the same, and the results of evaluating the predicates P and not(P) are sometimes the same! This is illustrated by the simple example in Exhibit 13.21. This difficulty is caused by the fact that not is implemented using a cut, and when we backtrack to a cut, the goal fails. Thus we see that the last query in Exhibit 13.21 fails, even though it seems that it should not.

Exhibit 13.21.   The trouble with "not".

Suppose we have the simple predicate test:

```
test(S, T) :- S = T.
```

The problems with not are illustrated by this transcript of a test run:

```
?- test(3, 5).
no
?- test(5, 5).
yes
?- not( test(5, 5) ).
no
?- test(x,3), R is x+2.
x=3
R=5
?- not( not( test(x,3))), R is x + 2.
! error in arithmetic expression: not a number
```

The responses to the first four queries are exactly what one expects. However, the final one is a surprise, since the query is the double-not of the preceding query, but the response is different!

One last difficulty with not arises from the fact that clausal logic is not decidable. In practical terms, this means that sometimes we can prove a theorem, T, sometimes we can prove its negation, not T, and sometimes we cannot prove either! In the last case, the theorem is true in some models of the theory but not in others, and we certainly cannot conclude that T is false just because we cannot prove that T is true. However, when Prolog cannot prove that T is true, the predicate not(T) succeeds. This is so, even if the reason for the failure of T is that the data base contains too little relevant data or that the programmer made a program-sequencing error! Obviously, we must be extremely careful when using not.

Unsafe Cuts.

Sometimes a programmer might decide to use a cut when implementing some heuristic part of a computation. In this case, the programmer knows that there is some possibility that the desired solution may lie on that part of the proof-tree that is being cut off. Use of the cut for such purposes is considered to be "impure", since it destroys the completeness of the proof system. However, in many artificial intelligence and optimization problems, it may not be possible, because of time constraints, to fully explore the proof-tree. Pruning the tree might eliminate the best solution, and it might even eliminate the only solution, but if the heuristics are skillfully chosen, these unhappy outcomes can be largely avoided. On the positive side, skillfully used heuristic cuts can dramatically speed up processing and reduce the memory requirements of a computation to be within practical limits.

13.5.7   *Evaluation of* Prolog

Prolog will not be appropriate in applications where efficiency is a major consideration. Its performance is limited by its interactive, interpretive nature, and by the lack of destructive assignment operations. All computation is done through parameter binding, and parameter binding is done by the complex and relatively slow unification algorithm. Further, the programmer has only limited control over execution order. Ordinary applications that can be programmed directly in a procedural language such as C will be more efficient than the same applications in Prolog.

However, Prolog is a very attractive language for applications in which the programmer does not know how to organize the data or the computational process. It can be used to express some kinds of information much more directly than the common procedural languages, and it makes it possible to integrate procedural program elements with nonprocedural ones.

Finally, because order of evaluation is left largely unspecified, Prolog is useful for applications in which parallel evaluation is required. It will be an appropriate language for implementation on computers with highly parallel architecture, such as the Connection Machine.

EXERCISES

1. What is the difference between computation and deduction? In what sense are they analogous processes?
2. What is a universe of discourse?
3. What does it mean to instantiate a variable? How are variables instantiated in the process of deduction?
4. What is a term? A predicate? A sentence? Make clear what the differences are among these concepts.
5. Give an example of a 3-ary predicate.
6. Given the predicates in Exhibit 13.1, are the following instantiated predicates true or false?
    a. odd(13)
    b. odd(7+3)
    c. divide(45,5,9,0)
    d. divide(56,5,11,3)
    e. father(Isaac, Abraham)
7. What is the difference between the meaning of $\exists X$ and $\forall X$?
8. Which of the following quantified predicates is true? What is the negation of each?

    a. $\forall Y$ even(Y)
    b. $\exists X$ even(X)
    c. $\forall X$ X=X+0
    d. $\exists X \forall Y$ X=Y+1
    e. $\forall X \exists Y$ X=Y*1

9. Define and explain the relationship between axioms and theories.

10. How is it possible for a theory to have more than one model?

11. What is a proof? A refutation?

12. Write an example of a Horn clause in the form of a disjunction of terms. Write a logical sentence that is not a Horn clause.

13. If a theory has only unconditional axioms (no conditional axioms), the theory has very few theorems and all the proofs are quite boring. Explain.

14. Write examples of conditional and unconditional Horn clauses. Write a Prolog sentence that corresponds to each.

15. What are the elements of the Prolog programming environment?

16. A Prolog rule specifies a set of constraints that must be simultaneously true to draw a conclusion. Explain how each part of a rule fits this description.

17. Given the data base in Exhibit 13.10, how would Prolog respond to the following queries?

    a. pretty(violet).
    b. watchout(holly).
    c. watchout(X),pretty(X).
    d. watchout(X),color(X,green).

18. Prolog cannot always prove a true assertion and it cannot always disprove a false assertion. Explain.

19. In Prolog, a fact is a single nonnegated term, such as pretty(mary). The same term, or a similar one such as pretty(pat) or pretty(X), can be a query. However, a term that is a fact and one that is a query have different meanings. Explain.

20. Given these facts and rules,

Facts	Rules
flower(crocus, spring, white).	color(F,C) :- flower(F,S,C).
flower(violet, spring, blue).	color(T,green) :- tree(T).
flower(iris, summer, blue).	pretty(F) :- color(F,red).
flower(rose, summer, red).	pretty(F) :- color(F,blue).
flower(marigold, summer, orange).	grows(X) :- tree(X).
tree(holly)	grows(X) :- flower(X,Y,Z).

find all sets of instantiations that unify each of the following pairs of clauses:

    a. flower(F,spring,Y), pretty(F).
    b. flower(F,summer,Y), pretty(F).
    c. grows(X), pretty(X).
    d. flower(Z,Y,orange), pretty(Z).

21. Discuss the difference in efficiency between the C quicksort [Exhibit 13.16] and the Prolog version [Exhibit 13.15].

22. Compare and contrast the operation and efficiency of the Miranda gcd algorithm [Exhibit 12.12] and the Prolog version [Exhibit 13.13].

23. Compare the clarity of code in the C quicksort [Exhibit 13.16] and the Prolog version [Exhibit 13.15]. Which do you think is easier to understand? Why?

24. What are the syntactic similarities and differences between the Miranda quicksort script [Exhibit 12.19] and the Prolog quicksort [Exhibit 13.15]?

25. Compare and contrast the operation and efficiency of the Miranda quicksort script [Exhibit 12.19] and the Prolog quicksort [Exhibit 13.15].

14

The Representation of Types

_____ Overview _____

We began the discussion of types in Chapter 5 by considering the primitive types supported by languages and their connection with the hardware types supported by typical computers. In this chapter we consider the implementation of both primitive and user-defined types. Finally, we continue, in Chapter 15, with a discussion of the semantics of types.

To augment the primitive types, most languages permit types to be defined by the programmer. A type definition enables the programmer to define the physical properties of a new type and to name it. A type object represents this type information inside the translator. It is composed of three parts: a name, a type, and a body of information. Various types of types include: primitive, array, record, and enumerated. Each kind of type has its own declaration syntax and corresponds to a distinct type of type object within the translator.

We consider simple types (enumerated types, constrained types, pointer types), compound types (arrays, strings, sets, records), and union types (free and discriminated).

Operations which can be performed on compound objects include value construction, the combination of a set of components into a single compound object, selection, which enables the programmer to reference a part of the compound object, and dereferencing, which maps a reference into a program object or value. Modern programming languages implement some or all of these to various degrees.

14.1 PROGRAMMER-DEFINED TYPES

A data type is a set of objects with an associated set of functions that permit us to manipulate the objects. To use a type we must be able to represent those objects and

365

functions in our source code and in the computer. A type definition gives us ways to do both. It supplies all information about the physical properties of the new type, and gives names to the type itself, and, if it is a structured type, to its parts. From this information, a translator can build constructors, selectors, and predicates that let us create and manipulate objects of the new type.

In this section, we examine the ways in which types can be represented in the source code and within a translator.[1] A new type representation may be defined by:

- Listing all its members.
- Placing restrictions on an existing type.
- Combining elements from existing types into an aggregate.

We will look at typical forms for these kinds of type declarations and see how a translator uses the information they provide.

14.1.1   Representing Types within a Translator

Whether a type is primitive or defined by the programmer, the properties of the type are stored by the translator when the type is defined. For the time being, let us imagine that all this information is stored in one place, and let us use the term *type-object* to refer to the collection of information that the translator stores about a type. In reality, depending on the language being implemented, the type information could be stored coherently in a type-object, or it could be scattered throughout various translator tables. Moreover, the amount and nature of the information stored varies from language to language, even for similar data types.

There are various types of types: primitive types, array types, record types, enumerated types, and others. For each type of type, a different collection of information must be supplied by the programmer and stored by the translator. Thus a type-object can be seen as a three-part entity, having a name (usually[2]), a type, and a body of information, which we will refer to as the *body*. The *type of a type* tells us how to interpret the body of the type, and the body of the type tells us how to interpret objects of that type. Every kind of type declaration supported by a language corresponds to a distinct type of type within the translator.

A data object also consists of a name, a type, and a body of information. The name is kept in the symbol table, and the type, represented by a pointer to a type-object, may be attached either to the name or to the body, depending on the language. Let us diagram objects as shown in Exhibit 14.1. The object is represented by a "*T*" shaped figure, with the object's name (if there is one) written on top, the type on the left, and the body on the right. The type of an object is always a pointer to some type-object. The body of a variable is a storage object and will be diagrammed as a box. The body of a constant or a type is a series of data values.

The body of a type must contain enough information to support whatever semantics are defined for the type. The nature and amount of this information varies

---

[1]Chapter 15 covers the semantics of types and the ways in which distinct meanings, or semantics, can be given to types with the same representation. In this section we are concerned primarily with the representation of types, not the semantics of similarly represented types.

[2]In some languages, it is possible to create a type with no name.

Exhibit 14.1. Object diagrams.

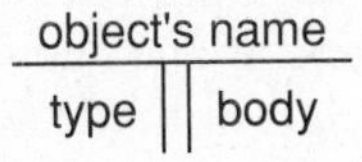

object's name

type || body

among the different types of types, and from language to language. Examples are: the base type of a pointer or array type, the dimension of an array, and the order, types, and names of the fields of a record type. In addition, a type body might contain extra or redundant information, designed to make use of the type more efficient. One such redundant fact might be the total size, in bytes, of an object of this type. While this might be calculated from other information, it is used frequently and should be kept "handy".

We will define (somewhat arbitrarily) general and useful type-objects for each type of type as we consider it. Although examples of type declarations are drawn from several languages, we should emphasize that the type-objects diagrammed do not necessarily reflect existing translator mechanisms for those languages. However, they would be appropriate as part of the semantic basis of a new object-oriented language with similar features.

Type-objects for the primitive types are defined by the compiler itself. We will diagram a primitive type body by listing only the size, in bytes, and denote the rest of the type's definition as a "code definition". An integer variable named "year" is diagrammed, with its type, in Exhibit 14.2.

Exhibit 14.2. An integer object and its type.

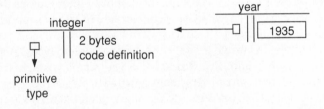

14.1.2 Finite Types

When a type is semantically unrelated to existing types and has a small number of members, it is practical to define it by simply listing, or *enumerating*, identifiers for the members of the type. These are called the *type constants*.

If a language supports enumerated types, it must also provide some functions that are automatically defined for every enumerated type. Comparison for equality must be supported. Other useful and common functions include comparison for inequality, successor, and predecessor. Input and output routines are sometimes supplied.

The programmer supplies only identifiers for the type constants; the translator must create an encoding for them. The obvious encoding is to use the integers, in order, starting with zero, to represent the type constants. This encoding makes it easy to implement comparison and successor functions; the corresponding integer functions are simply carried over to the new type. The standards for both Pascal and ANSI C explicitly state that the enumerated type will be represented by integers.[3]

As is common when languages are compared, type declarations that are syntactically very similar can create types with widely varying semantics. C is a language at one extreme. The enumerated type declaration is no more and no less than a convenient way to define identifiers for integer constants. An enumerated type, in C, is implemented by type int and has semantics identical to int. This is consistent with the use of types in C primarily to allocate and access data objects, rather than as a vehicle for semantics. Enumerated type constants are represented as integers and are considered to be integers. Characters and truth values, the two primitive enumerated types, are integers in C.

The treatment of enumerated types in Pascal is like C, with one very important exception: the enumerated type is semantically distinct from the type integer, which is used to represent it. Type integer is incompatible with enumerated types in Pascal. This means that you cannot, for example, multiply two values of an enumerated type in Pascal, as you could in C! Nor can you mix values of two different enumerated types in an expression.

There are some functions that are predefined for any enumerated type in Pascal. These are: Succ (successor), Pred (predecessor), Ord (conversion to type integer), assignment, and all the comparison operators. An enumeration constant or variable may also be used as a subscript. These functions are enough to make enumerated types useful, but not enough to make their use convenient. Unfortunately, Pascal lacks convenient means to read in and print out enumerated constants. Thus every program that uses an enumerated type must contain code to perform input and output conversions. Often this takes the form of two rather tedious CASE statements.

We can only speculate why enumerated I/O is not supported in Pascal. One possibility is that the idea was so new when Pascal was designed that Wirth did not realize that omitting I/O would limit the uses of enumerated types. A more likely explanation is the quest for simplicity. Pascal I/O is very simple and less flexible than the formatted I/O functions provided by many languages. Pascal provides less control over detail than FORTRAN, C, or APL. Adding enumerated I/O would have complicated a simple and elegant design, and may have been considered too unimportant to justify this cost.

To provide I/O for enumerated types, as is done in Ada, a language definition must include format descriptors for type constants. A translator needs the constant identifiers available at run time, so that inputs can be encoded and outputs decoded, automatically. Thus a type-object for an enumerated type would need to contain a list of pointers to the names (represented as character strings) [Exhibit 14.3].

Sending type constants to the output stream is easy enough, but some uniform way would be needed to recognize them in the input stream. All of these things are easy enough to define and implement, and support for input and output would make enumerated types considerably more useful.

---

[3]C permits programmers to use the default codes or assign their own integer codes.

Exhibit 14.3.   A type-object for an enumerated type.

```
TYPE warm = (red, maroon, magenta, pink, coral);
```

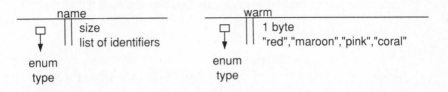

An implementation of enumerated type I/O would increase the complexity of the compiler's I/O system and increase the amount of system code that would be included with a program at run time. In a program that used enumerated types, there would be a corresponding decrease in programmer-generated code, because programs would not need to manually encode and decode the enumerated constants. Overall, the costs seem modest and the benefits real.

14.1.3   Constrained Types

Some languages permit a programmer to define a new type by applying constraints to an existing type. This is a powerful tool for expressing semantic intent. If a language supports constrained types, the run-time system for that language must check each value of the type to ensure that it obeys the constraint. The type-object must therefore include the base type and the limiting values.

Pascal and Ada provide subrange type declarations which define a new type whose members are a consecutive subset of an existing simple type. The programmer specifies the initial and final values that will belong to the new type. (The base type of these values is implicit.) Exhibit 14.4 shows a type-object for a Pascal subrange type.

Exhibit 14.4.   A constrained type in Pascal.

```
TYPE age = 0..150;
```

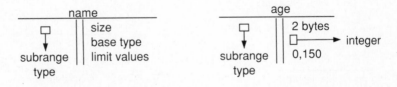

Values of the constrained type and the underlying base type are compatible and may be combined in operations. Functions for either type may be applied to the other. However, a computed value is checked (at run time) before assigning it to a constrained variable; any violation of the constraints causes a run-time error.

C does not support subrange types. This is consistent with the general philosophy that C types are used to define storage configurations, not semantics. A constraint has no effect on the size or the encoding of the representation; it is relevant only to the semantics of values of that type. (A value may be acceptable or not in the constrained type, while all representable values are legal for the base type.)

14.1.4 Pointer Types

All pointers represent machine addresses, so the semantics of a pointer type do not depend on the semantics of its base type. (The *base type of a pointer* is the type of the object to which the pointer points.) Moreover, the size of a pointer is quite independent of the base type, so no storage layout information is needed in the body of a pointer type except the size of pointers on the target machine. Any pointer value will physically fit into any pointer variable.

This innate relationship among pointer types is exploited in FORTH. It supports pointers in the sense that the address of any object can be obtained and stored in an integer variable. Pointer arithmetic (implemented in terms of integer arithmetic) is possible, and integer variables may be declared and used for pointer values. However, no distinction is made between pointers with different base types.[4]

Most languages, however, require the programmer to declare the base type of every pointer. Therefore we will diagram a pointer type as shown in Exhibit 14.5. Information about the base type of a pointer is not needed for allocation or for access. It is required only by languages whose compilers use that type information to determine the semantics of the program. Even among languages that require declaration of a pointer's base type, that type information may be used in the following different ways:

1. To compile the correct meaning of ambiguous operators, such as "+".
2. To determine the number of bytes to fetch when a pointer is dereferenced and used in an expression.
3. To determine the type of the result of a dereference, so that it may check for type errors.
4. To dynamically allocate space for an object of the base type.

Exhibit 14.5.   A C pointer and its type-object.

We declare and initialize an integer pointer, pk, to point at an integer, k, which is initialized to the value 5.

```
int k=5, *pk=&k;
```

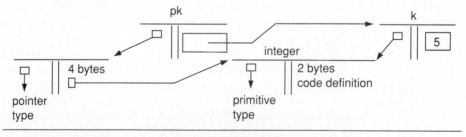

---

[4]Indeed, no distinction is made between pointers and integers!

Similar declarations can have very different meanings in different languages. For example, in C, the base type is used only for purposes 1 and 2. In the following list, assume p is a pointer whose base type is BT:

1. Arithmetic on pointers is defined in terms of the base type. The expression p+1 will cause p to be incremented by the length of an object of type BT.

2. The meaning of dereference and fetch depends on the base type. The expression *p +1 will cause a fetch operation from the memory location stored in p and increment that value by 1. The number of bytes fetched will depend on BT, which must be a simple, primitive type.

3. In general, C does not perform type checking.

4. The type of the pointer is not used for allocating base-type objects. To allocate a base-type object dynamically, one refers directly to the name of the base type, not to the pointer.

In contrast, Pascal uses the same information for the last three purposes. In the following list, assume p is a pointer whose base type is BT, and b is an object of type BT:

1. There are no operations on pointers whose meaning depends on the base type. Dereferencing is the only pointer operation that is supported, and its meaning is the same for all pointers.

2. Any type of pointer may be dereferenced and used in an assignment. The statement "b := p↑;" copies n bytes, where n is the size of BT.

3. Pascal is a fully type-checked language. In the expression "b + p↑ * 2", the base type of p is checked to ensure that it is appropriate for the surrounding expression.

4. The argument to a call on NEW (which performs dynamic allocation in Pascal) must be a pointer, p. An object is allocated of p's base type, and the resulting reference is stored in p.

14.2 COMPOUND TYPES

14.2.1 Arrays

Modern languages permit simple types to be combined to form compound, or structured, types. These combinations can be positional (arrays, strings) or not (sets), and homogeneous (arrays, strings, sets) or heterogeneous (records). They can have fixed size (arrays, records) or variable size (strings, sets). Let us look at typical type declarations, type-objects, and accessing methods for these compound types.

An array is a fixed-length sequence of elements of a single type, called the *base type*. The length of the sequence is called its *dimension*. Elements of an array are accessed by position, and the position values of the first and last elements are called the *array bounds*. In theory, array positions and bounds could be values of any simple, discrete type, called the *index type*. Possible index types include the integers and any type that is implemented by mapping onto the integers. In practice, various languages are more or less restrictive about the index types that can be used. For simplicity, in this discussion, let us presume that integers are used for the index type.

To access an individual element of an array, we append a *subscript* to the array name. This is an expression (usually enclosed in parentheses or square brackets) whose value falls within the bounds of the array. The subscript, base address, and base type of the array are used to compute the *effective address*, or address of the desired component. This computation is simplest and most efficient if the language requires *zero-based subscripting*. In this system, if an array has dimension D, its bounds are $0 \ldots D - 1$. The effective address formulas for zero-based and arbitrary-based subscripting are shown in Exhibit 14.6.

Exhibit 14.6.   Formulas for the effective address computation.

Let ba be the base address of the array A, and let $size$ be the number of addressable units (bytes) required to store a value of the base type of A. Then the effective address corresponding to $A[s1]$ is:

- Zero-based subscript: $ba + size * s1$
- Other-based subscript: $ba + size * (s1 - lower\ bound\ of\ A)$

For a multidimensional array, with zero-based subscripting and declared dimensions $d1, d2, \ldots, dn$, the effective address corresponding to $A[s1, s2, \ldots sn]$ is:

$$ba + size * ((((s1 * d2 + s2) * d3 + s3) \ldots) * dn + sn)$$

In the old days, when all computer memory was a series of "words" (not bytes) and all numbers were one word long, arrays of numbers were implemented very simply and efficiently. The array's base address was loaded into the computer's memory address register and the subscript was loaded into an index register. Then the computer's indexed-fetch or indexed-store instruction dynamically computed the desired effective address.

Multidimensional Arrays

Some older languages, such as MAD, FORTRAN, and APL, specifically supported arrays of two or more dimensions. (Following APL terminology, let us use the word *rank* to mean the number of dimensions of an array.) The rank was limited, in FORTRAN, to the number of index registers available on the host computer, since each subscript was kept in a register for efficiency's sake. However, computing an effective address for an array of rank n cannot be done simply by adding together all the subscripts; it requires $n - 1$ multiplications and additions, plus one index operation [Exhibit 14.6]. An example of a three-dimensional subscript computation for Pascal arrays is shown in Exhibit 14.7.

Support for multidimensional arrays is important in languages that are intended for use by scientists and engineers who work regularly with matrices. In these older languages, special syntax and semantics were provided to support higher-rank arrays [Exhibit 14.8].

Type declarations were invented in the late 1960s, and this changed the way that higher-rank arrays were implemented. Languages designed since then have array type declarations that define arrays in terms of an *arbitrary* base type. Thus a two-dimensional array became, simply, an array of arrays. Special syntax and special semantic rules were no longer needed to handle higher-rank arrays; they could be handled by iterating the type definitions and type accessing syntax for rank one arrays, as shown in Exhibit 14.9, item B.

Exhibit 14.7.   Effective address computation for Pascal arrays.

Here we give declarations for two arrays of rank 3. Assume that storage for `Matrix` starts at location 1000 and storage for `Box` starts at location 2000. In this implementation, the size of a real is 4 bytes and the size of an integer is two bytes.

```
VAR Matrix: array[0..1] of array [0..2] of array [0..4] of real;
    Box: array[1..2] of array [5..7] of array [-2..2] of integer;
```

`Matrix` has zero-based subscripts, so we use the simpler form of the formula to compute the effective address corresponding to `Matrix[1][2][3]`.

```
1000 + 4 * (((1*3 +2)*5 + 3)) = 1000 + 4 * 33 =  1132
```

`Box` does not have zero-based subscripts, so the lower bound for each dimension must be subtracted from the corresponding subscript. Here we compute the effective address for `Box[2][7][-1]`:

```
2000 + 2 *(( (2-1)*3 + (7-5) )*5 + (-1--2) ) =
2000 + 2 *( 5*5 + 1 )     =     2000 + 2*26    = 2052
```

Exhibit 14.8.   A three-dimensional array in FORTRAN.

```
REAL AR3
DIMENSION AR3[5, 2, 4]
* Store a number in one element of the array.
AR3[2,2,1] = 17.0
```

Exhibit 14.9.   Basic and sugared notation for arrays in Pascal.

A. Sugared notation:

```
VAR Sugared:  array[1..3, 1..10, 0..3] of char;
c := Sugared[1, 5, 2];
```

B. Equivalent array declared using basic notation:

```
VAR Plain:  array[1..3] of array [1..10] of array [0..3] of char;
c := Plain[1][5][2];
```

This is a real simplification in the language. The syntax is simpler because the brackets written to declare and use subscripts need to delimit only a single expression, not a list of expressions. The semantics is simpler because the complex formula for computing a higher-rank effective address is replaced by iterating the simple formula for computing a one-dimensional effective address. The size of the various base types replaces the declared dimensions in the formula [Exhibit 14.10]. C was designed with streamlined simplicity in mind. It supports only zero-based subscripting and only one-dimensional arrays. A higher-rank array is defined and referenced as an array of arrays.

Exhibit 14.10. Effective address computation for a four-level type.

Assume that storage for the variable named `Plain` from Exhibit 14.9 starts at address 1000. Let us compute the effective address for `Plain[1][5][2]`.

	Type	Dimension	Total Size
1.	char		1 byte
2.	array [0..3] of (1)	4	4 bytes
3.	array [1..10] of (2)	10	40 bytes
4.	array [1..3] of (3)	3	120 bytes

```
Effective address = base address of Plain +
   (1-1)*40 bytes + (5-1)* 4 bytes + (2-0)*1 byte =
   1000 + 0 + 16 + 2   = 1018
```

Pascal, on the other hand, made an interesting concession to custom. Pascal has type declarations and supports arrays with an arbitrary base type, so it does not need to have FORTRAN-like array notation. However, programmers were used to the multisubscript FORTRAN notation shown in Exhibit 14.8. So Wirth compromised. The semantic basis of Pascal is like C: it supports only one-dimensional arrays. But the syntax of Pascal was extended to include FORTRAN-like subscript notation, with all subscripts (optionally) included between a single pair of brackets. This "extra" declaration form is called *syntactic sugar* because it is unnecessary but makes the language sweeter and more attractive for many users. The multidimensional notation that the programmer writes is converted by the parser to the basic notation [Exhibit 14.9]. Of course, the programmer may always choose to write directly in the basic notation. A Pascal code generator contains semantic interpretation routines for the one-dimensional notation only.

Ada **Arrays and Slices.**

In the treatment of arrays, as in many other ways, Ada is like a greatly complicated (and more capable) version of Pascal. Like Pascal, Ada provides syntactic forms for declaring both arrays of arrays and multidimensional arrays. Unlike Pascal, though, the two forms are not equivalent! Ada provides an operation called "slicing"[5] for arrays of arrays that cannot be applied to multidimensional arrays.

---

[5]This term was introduced by ALGOL-68.

A *slice* of an array is the contents of a consecutive series of locations, denoted by the array name with a range of subscripts. If `Ar` is an array with bounds 1...10, then the slice from positions 3 through 5 is denoted thus:

`Ar(3..5)`

A slice can be used in an assignment or a function call. Slicing provides a nice way to do some array operations coherently that would need to be written with a loop in Pascal or C. However, Ada slices are not as flexible or as powerful a tool as the APL subscripting facility, described in Section 14.3.2.

Type-Objects for Arrays

We see that the type-object for an array type in a modern language only needs to have information about one dimension. For that dimension it must store the total size, the index type, the bounds, and a pointer to the base type. For efficient use in various computations, it might also contain the dimension and the size of the base type. Exhibit 14.11 shows diagrams of two array type-objects, representing an array of arrays in a language with non-zero-based subscripts. Exhibit 14.12 shows the simpler type representation possible with zero-based subscripts. One number, the dimension, takes the place of three: dimension, lower bound, and upper bound.

Exhibit 14.11.   Diagrams of array type-objects.

The type declaration is given using Ada syntax.

`type Matrix is array(-5..5, 1..5) of float;`

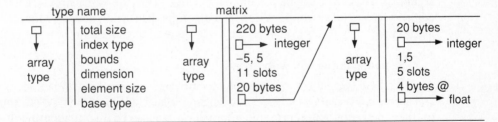

Exhibit 14.12.   Diagram of a zero-based array type-object.

The type declaration is given using C syntax.

`typedef float [5] vector;`

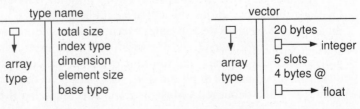

Arrays with Undeclared Bounds.

In certain situations it makes sense to declare an array but not specify the array bounds. This is permitted in some languages if either

1. The omitted information can be deduced from the context, or
2. The omitted information is not needed by the compiler.

Where structured initializers may be given for arrays, and a particular lower bound is either required or is the default, as in C and Ada, the upper bound of an array can be deduced from an initializer if one is given as part of the declaration. In this situation, omitting the bounds from the declaration reduces the redundancy and eliminates the chance that the programmer might miscalculate the dimension needed. However, it also eliminates the chance that the compiler can detect a faulty initializer. (This is another example of the general rule that redundancy is a pain to write into a program, but can serve as a double check on the typist's accuracy.)

An example of the second principle is seen in C. An array parameter may be declared with an unspecified dimension because C does not use the dimension information for parameters. All C arrays are passed by reference, so only a pointer is allocated for the array in the function's stack frame. Further, C does not perform bounds checks of any sort. Thus the dimension of an array parameter is immaterial within the function. Within the C subroutine, only the base type of an array is ever needed.

Contrast this to Pascal which does pass arrays by value, if desired, and does check array bounds. Both of these facilities can be used to make programs more reliable and easier to debug; however, this security comes at a high price. The bounds of a Pascal array parameter must be declared and fixed at compile time. Therefore each function can accept, as arguments, only one fixed size of array. In C, any length array of the appropriate base type can be passed to a function. Thus the Pascal programmer must edit and recompile subroutines if the length of the data array changes, whereas the C programmer only needs to change the declaration of the data array in one routine.

Semantic Protection with Arrays.

We have seen how array type-objects are used to allocate array storage objects and access individual elements. Some languages, such as C, use the type information for these purposes only. This same information can also be used to identify run-time errors, as it is in Pascal and Ada. These languages compare the value of the subscript expression to the declared array bounds, and halt with an error comment if the bounds are violated. Of course, this slows down execution. However, this cost is probably justified. Semidebugged C programs often "run wild" and erase the contents of memory, forcing the user to reboot the workstation. Pascal programs seldom do.

Bounds checking is most useful during program development and debugging. Omitting the checks during this phase would be penny wise and pound foolish. Although the checking code consumes execution time and memory space, a single error caught pays for many tests. However, one might assert that finished production programs should not incur the run-time overhead of bounds checking because fully debugged programs just don't run wild. (Of course, one can debate whether any program is ever fully debugged.) Most programs perform well with these checks included.

Occasionally, a bounds check in an inner loop can cause a significant slowdown and is therefore undesirable.

The Ada language includes a way to turn off unwanted checking, called a suppress PRAGMA. If a compiler honors a suppression request (it is not required to do so), type checking is suppressed throughout the block that contains the pragma declaration. The design of Ada encourages very limited and selected use of suppression pragmas. A separate declaration is needed for each kind of check that is to be suppressed. The programmer is urged to use these only in fully debugged code that is unacceptably slow, and then to place the suppression declaration in the smallest block that contains the slow code section. A PRAGMA declaration to suppress bounds checking has this format:

```
PRAGMA Suppress (Index_Check);
```

14.2.2 Strings

A string is a variable-length array of characters. In many languages (for example, Pascal and Ada) the type string is treated as a special case of an array, with an integer lower bound of 1 and a base type of character. This treatment does not really capture the essence of strings. Strings are different from general arrays because:

1. The length of a string is, in general, unknown at compile time.
2. Strings of many different lengths are commonly used together.
3. A string variable should be able to "contain" any string.
4. A string function should be able to work on any string.
5. Strings have special semantics, such as the rule for alphabetic-order comparison of strings with unlike lengths.

The "strings" supported by Ada and Pascal are not variable-length objects. A string variable has a declared length and can only contain string values that are short enough to fit within this maximum. Strings shorter than that must be manually padded with blanks. Using fixed-length arrays to represent variable-length strings doesn't really work.

A good representation for strings must embody their essential variable-length nature, use storage efficiently, provide for efficient processing, and have reasonable error-recovery properties. There are two representations for string values that meet these criteria: the *counted string* and the *terminated string*.

In a *counted string* the first byte (in subscript position 0) is an unsigned integer which gives the length of the string. String functions must calculate the length of a newly constructed string and store it in the first byte. With this representation, strings can be processed easily using for loops. The error recovery potential is not ideal, but it is adequate. If a program error happens and the count byte is changed to a garbage value, any loop that uses the garbage will still terminate after no more than 255 iterations. No runaway loop in a string function will be infinite and force the user to reboot a machine.

A *terminated string* contains only characters, but following the last data character there is a terminator, probably the null character (ASCII code 0) (strings cannot contain the terminator). Functions must be written to add a terminator to the end of any newly constructed string. Strings are normally processed by looping while the data is nonnull. This representation for strings works well for error recovery. If a program error happens and a null terminator gets "wiped out", it is highly likely that another zero byte is somewhere nearby in memory and will terminate the runaway operation soon.

Both of these representations make efficient use of storage and support efficient string processing. The null terminated string, used in C, seems to have slightly better error recovery properties. Exhibit 14.13 shows appropriate type-objects for strings.

Exhibit 14.13.   A type-object for a null terminated string.

```
char *str1 = "This is a string literal.";
```

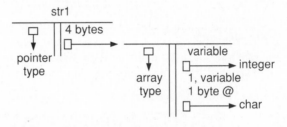

Once the representation of a string value is decided, we can deal with the question of string variables. In a compiled language, storage for variables in run-time stack frames is laid out at compile time. The size of each allocation is fixed then and is not variable. This conflicts with the variable-length nature of strings. One good solution is to use a dynamically allocated string storage area, and let a string variable be a pointer into this area. This is how BASIC and SNOBOL IV are implemented. All the string functions take pointer arguments and return pointer results. Storage for newly created strings is taken automatically from the system-managed string store.

C implements a version of strings that is half way between the fully functioning string store and the fixed-length strings of Pascal. Like BASIC, a string in C is a pointer to an array of characters. Unlike BASIC, the semantic basis of C does not include a string store, and the string functions do not allocate new storage. C functions such as "strcat", or string concatenate, require that one argument be a pointer to a preallocated storage object long enough to store the result. The effect of this mixed approach is that C's extensive and powerful string library is less easy to use than the string facilities in SNOBOL.

There is a good reason why C does not supply automatically managed dynamic storage: simplicity and execution efficiency were both design goals in C. Managing dynamic storage is not simple, and it requires some sort of string compaction or garbage collection facility. These facilities are all slow and costly. Using a compaction algorithm becomes necessary when available storage has all been used and is now occupied largely by dead strings. (A dead string is one that is no longer bound to any live name or pointer.)

Rather than include a complex dynamic storage management system, the designers of C chose to let programmers implement whatever portion of such a system might really be needed. One standard technique used in C string programs is to implement a dynamic string store similar to that which is built into BASIC.

14.2.3   Sets

The "set" types supported by Pascal are variants of Boolean arrays. A set value is like a packed array of Booleans, where each index position, or slot, represents one constant of a subrange type or enumerated type, called the *base type of the set*.

The number of constants in the base type determines the number of Booleans in the set value; the first Boolean in the set value corresponds to the first constant in the base type, and so on. A set with one member is represented by a Boolean array with one element which is TRUE and all the others FALSE. A set with several members is represented by an array with several TRUE elements [Exhibit 14.14].

Exhibit 14.14.   A set type in Pascal.

We declare an enumerated type, color, and a set type, combo, whose base type is color. Some variables of type combo are declared and initialized. The Boolean array representations of these variables are diagrammed below.

```
TYPE   color = (red, pink, orange, yellow, green, blue, violet,
               magenta, brown, black, gray, white);
       combo = set of color;
VAR    tree, daffodil, iris: combo;
       palette, common: combo;
daffodil := [white, yellow, orange, green];
iris := [white, yellow, blue, violet, green];
tree := [white, gray, brown, black, green];
palette := iris + daffodil;          { '+' means set union.  }
common := iris * tree * daffodil;    { '*' means set intersection.  }
```

In the following representations, a "0" represents a FALSE value, and a "1" represents a TRUE value.

- Cardinality of base type (color): 12
- Number of elements in a combo value: 12
- Size of each element: 1 bit
- Representation of daffodil: 001110000001
- Representation of iris: 000111100001
- Representation of palette: 001111100001
- Representation of common: 000010000001

The "in" operation in Pascal is the selector function for a set. The operands of in are a value of the base type, v, and a set value, S. The result of the expression v *in* S is the Boolean value stored in the position of S that corresponds to v. For example, in

Exhibit 14.14, "common" is a set variable of type "combo". We would write "IF green IN common" to find out whether "green" is a "common" color.

The standard mathematical set operations union, intersection, and difference are denoted by the Pascal operators "+", "*", and "−", respectively. These take operands of a specific set type and return a result of the same set type. These operators are implemented by applying Boolean operations to corresponding elements of the two operand arrays. Union is implemented by or, and intersection by and. Set difference ("−") is implemented by the composition of "complement" and "and".

A Boolean value can be represented by a single bit. In an efficient representation of a Boolean array, we *pack* the bits into a series of bytes, so that every bit is used. By packing the Boolean array, we are able to use the efficient bitwise logical operations to implement set operations. These operations let you "turn on" and "turn off" bits singly, or several at a time. Turning a bit on corresponds to adding a member to a set. The diagram on the left in Exhibit 14.15 shows an appropriate type-object for a Pascal set type.

Exhibit 14.15.   Type-objects for set types.

The diagram on the left is a type-object for a Pascal set type. On the right is a type-object appropriate for an Ada-like implementation of sets as Boolean arrays. We use the type-object defined, above, for zero-based arrays. The symbols used in these type-objects are defined thus:

- E, an enumerated type, is the base type of this set type.
- N is the number of enumeration constants in E.
- L is the smallest integer greater than or equal to (N/8).

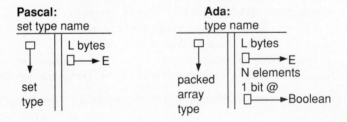

Although sets are included in Pascal, most languages do not have a corresponding set type constructor. This is not surprising, since both the semantics and the representation for sets are somewhat complex. One of the design goals for Pascal was simplicity, and it is interesting to ask why Wirth included this nonsimple type of type in his design. The reason was a combination of three factors: completeness, validity, and simplicity.

Completeness.

A powerful language should contain constructs that support standard mathematical notation. It should also reflect as many as possible of the capabilities of the typical modern computer. Including a set type in Pascal, with the representation described, "completes" the language in two ways.

The bitwise operations on a computer are vital for applications such as number conversion, using hardware switches, and packing and unpacking data values. With sets, Pascal provides "access" to the bitwise hardware instructions; that is, it provides a type constructor and some operators that translate into the bitwise operations.

Sets are a standard mathematical notion that can be used to model quite a variety of applications. By including an efficient implementation of sets and set operations, Pascal supports an important mathematical notation.

Why, then, does C not support sets? The design goals for C were significantly different from those for Pascal. The fact that mathematicians use sets was of little importance in designing a language for systems programming. The need for access to the bitwise operations was compelling, but it was met in a different, and simpler, way. C includes the bitwise operators "&" (and), "|" (or), "^" (exor), and "~" (complement), which can be applied to any type of value.

If a C programmer wanted to implement set semantics, she or he would define a set value as an array of unsigned integers, where each integer represents 16 or 32 index positions in the set. To implement the set operations, the programmer would simply iterate the primitive bitwise operators as many times as necessary to process each byte of the array. This is a simple and straightforward implementation. There is no particular need to make sets a primitive type constructor.

Validity.

Support for semantic validity was one of Wirth's most important design goals. All primitive operations that he included were semantically valid for some primitive type. Strong type checking ensured that validity was maintained by every operation.

Wirth would have considered the semantics for the bitwise operators in C to be unacceptable. An unsigned integer type should be used to store unsigned integers, not bit strings. The bitwise logical operators have no semantic validity when applied to integers. Basically, they can only be meaningfully applied to packed arrays of Booleans, and that is what Pascal supports.

But semantic validity and completeness were also of primary importance in the design of Ada, and Ada does not have a set type constructor. It does provide an easy way to implement the set semantics, though. In Ada, the type one-dimensional array of Booleans is given special semantics. The logical operators and, or, xor, and not may be applied to one-dimensional Boolean arrays. The relational operators =, <=, and the like may be applied to any one-dimensional array. Thus sets can be easily implemented as Boolean arrays. The diagram on the right in Exhibit 14.15 shows an appropriate type-object for this set implementation. Exhibit 14.16 shows a set of Ada type declarations to implement types analogous to the Pascal color example from Exhibit 14.14. Exhibit 14.17 shows how corresponding set selection operations would be written in Pascal and Ada.

Simplicity.

Wirth intended Pascal to be a powerful but simple and minimal language. Highly complex semantic mechanisms did not fit this purpose. He also wished to have a clean, general design with few special cases and few restricted, special-purpose capabilities.[6]

---

[6]Note that the special semantics for strings in Pascal is an example of what Wirth wished to avoid. String types break many of the type rules that govern the rest of the language.

Exhibit 14.16.   Implementation of sets in Ada.

We declare an enumerated type, `color`, and a set type, `combo`, whose base type is `color`. Some variables of type `combo` are declared and initialized. The Boolean-array representations of these variables are diagrammed below.

```
type  color is (red, pink, orange, yellow, green, blue, violet,
             magenta, brown, black, gray, white);
type  combo is array(red..white) of boolean;

T: constant boolean := TRUE;
F: constant boolean := FALSE;

tree:  constant combo := (F,F,F,F,T,F,F,F,T,T,T,T);
daffodil:  constant combo := (F,F,T,T,T,F,F,F,F,F,F,T);
iris:  constant combo := (F,F,F,T,T,T,T,F,F,F,F,T);
palette, common:  combo;

palette := iris or daffodil;
common := iris and tree and daffodil;
```

Exhibit 14.17.   Selecting a member of a set.

In Pascal we select a member of a set using "`in`":

```
if green in common then ...
```

In Ada we use a subscript to select a set member:

```
if common(green) then ...
```

A language with suitably powerful array operations would not need a special type of type to implement the semantics of Pascal sets, as shown by the array-of-Booleans implementation in Ada. APL also supports coherent array operations which make the Boolean-array implementation of sets easy and straightforward.

But the powerful, general array operations in APL do not meet the criteria of simplicity and minimality. The solution in Ada (including primitive bitwise operators that are defined only for one-dimensional Boolean arrays, and coherent array operations that apply only to one-dimensional scalar arrays) is too nongeneral and special-purpose to meet Pascal's design goals. While Pascal sets are not a simple type of type, they are less complex than APL array operations, more elegant than the Ada solution, and more valid than the C approach.

14.2.4   Records

A record is a compound object consisting of an ordered series of components of heterogeneous types. These objects are usually implemented by contiguous blocks of memory, in which the fields of a record object are stored in the order specified by the programmer.[7] A modern language permits the programmer to manipulate a record object coherently or to access its components and process them individually.

Type-Objects for Records

The type-object for a record will contain all the information needed to allocate and access the record. For allocation, only the total size of a record storage object is needed. Intuitively, a record object is no more and no less than the sum of its parts. However, in real implementations, the storage object for a record may contain more bytes than are needed to store the components, and the extra bytes will generally contain garbage. This happens because many computers require all numbers to be *aligned on word or long-word boundaries*. With word alignment, all objects start at even byte addresses; with long-word alignment, all addresses are evenly divisible by 4. Padding is inserted into a record type if the size of some field in a record declaration would cause the following field to break alignment rules. The amount of padding included (if any) depends on the hardware. Thus all we can say about the size of a record is that it is at least as great as the sum of the sizes of its parts.

To access a record component, a compiler needs to know its *offset*, that is, the number of bytes between the beginning of the record object and the beginning of the desired field. Each offset is the sum of the sizes of all preceding fields, plus any preceding padding bytes. When the compiler processes the list of component types in a record declaration, it calculates these offsets and binds each one to the corresponding record part name. We will represent all this information (offsets, part names, component types) as part of the type-object for a record [Exhibit 14.18].

Exhibit 14.18.   A type-object for a record.

```
struct personcell{char* name; char sex; float salary; personcell* next};
```

We would diagram the type `personcell` as follows:

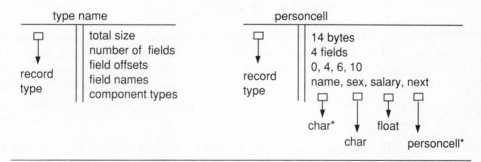

Part Selectors

The part names for a record type are selector functions. Like functions, each one takes an argument (a reference to a record), performs an action (increments that ref-

---

[7]This order is by no means necessary unless a language permits the programmer to circumvent the usual accessing methods and access the record's representation directly.

erence by an offset amount), and returns a reference to another object (one component). The nature of part names can be seen most clearly in FORTH. FORTH has no special provision for records, but it permits the programmer to allocate storage manually, manipulate references to objects, and do address arithmetic. When a FORTH programmer wants to use records, he or she defines an allocation function and a set of selector functions [Exhibit 14.19]. These selectors are used very much like Pascal part names; compare the FORTH expression from the last line of the exhibit to the equivalent expressions in Pascal and C:

```
FORTH:   89700 employee @ .salary D!
Pascal:  employee↑.salary := 89700
C:       employee->salary = 89700
```

Exhibit 14.19.   Defining a record type in FORTH.

We define functions to allocate and access a record type named `personcell`. Objects of this type will be allocated dynamically and attached to linked lists.

```
:  new_personcell
     here 10 allot;     ( Allocate 10 bytes; leave address on stack.   )
( Selector functions for the record type personcell. All expect a      )
( single argument which is a pointer to a record. All leave on         )
( the stack a reference to one component.                              )
:  .name ;              ( Zero offset for first field.                 )
:  .sex    2 + ;        ( Assume string pointers take 2 bytes.         )
:  .salary 4 +;         ( One byte for sex, one for padding.           )
:  .next   8 +;         ( Leave four bytes for double-length integer.  )
```

Assume that the variable `employee` is a pointer to a `personcell` record. If we wish to store a number in the `salary` field of this employee's record, we write the following expression. (The operator `D!` performs a double-length assignment.)

```
89700 employee @ .salary D!
```

So we see that part names can be defined as functions in a language that gives access to low-level information. Why, then, do most languages provide special declarations? There are several reasons: convenience, economy, portability, and semantic safety.

Convenience.

The part name function definitions in FORTH are simple and brief, but even so, they are somewhat of a nuisance to write out. The record type declaration is clearly a more convenient way to convey this information. A type declaration conveys all the relevant information concisely.

Economy.

Implementing selectors as ordinary functions is overkill. Associating a selector name with an offset takes very little storage, and putting these pairs in the type-object gives an extremely brief way to represent the information. Moreover, we do not need the full generality of functions for this purpose. Selectors are constant functions that are applied and expanded by the compiler. Compiled code contains address arithmetic, not function calls.

Most languages permit the same part name to be used in multiple record definitions. Storing the part name/offset mappings in the type-object is an easy way to implement the required kind of ambiguity; it allows the same part name to be bound to different offsets in different types. It is interesting to note that very old C compilers did not work like this. They probably stored the part names in the symbol table with the function names and other identifiers. The result was that each part name could only be used to mean one offset. A part name could be used in more than one struct declaration, but each use had to correspond to the same offset amount! This has been modernized by the ANSI C standard.

Portability.

To define the FORTH selectors we had to know exactly how many bytes would be required to implement each primitive type. But this varies from machine to machine. Whatever constants we use for the offsets, they will be wrong for some FORTH implementations.

C provides the same access to low-level information as does FORTH, so one could define record selectors the same way in C. However, this would be foolish, because then the user would have to worry about inserting padding bytes and accommodating varying sizes for the primitive types. If the user writes a struct declaration, the compiler takes care of all this.

Semantic Safety.

The part selectors defined in FORTH are accompanied by absolutely no checking. If an offset was one too large, the boundary between successive parts would be violated. A program that tried to access that component would get the last byte(s) of it and the first byte of the next component! These bytes do not form a valid object of any sort. Moreover, a FORTH function is not restricted to use with the correct type of argument; any selector could be used on an entirely inappropriate type of record, producing a garbage answer.

Pathnames

Let us define the term *pathname* to mean the sequence of identifiers, starting with the name of an object and continuing with a series of selectors (part names or subscripts). A pathname designates a particular field, fn, of a particular object, Ob.

When a compiler translates a pathname, it uses the series of selectors to compute the address of the specified component, or the *effective address*. Initially, the effective address is set to the *base address*, that is, the address of the first location in Ob. The current type-object is set to the type-object of Ob, and the current selector is set to the first selector in the pathname.

The compiler looks for the current selector in the current type-object. This field has an associated type $t1$, and an offset amount, $n1$. For records, $n1$ is listed explicitly in the type-object. For arrays, $n1$ is found by multiplying the component size (from the type-object) by the array index minus the array's lower bound. The compiler then adds $n1$ to the effective address, sets the current type-object to $t1$, and goes on to the next selector in the pathname. This process is iterated until all selectors are used, and a final offset amount is calculated. A pathname that contains no variable subscripts can be processed entirely at compile time. Otherwise, the constant portions of the computation are done at compile time, and the rest must be deferred until run time.

Partial Pathnames.

When part names are simply entered into the symbol table, as they are in COBOL, PL/1, and old versions of C, the programmer must be careful about using the same part name in two different record types. We eliminate this problem by storing the record part names in the type-objects. This makes them into local names, that is, names whose meaning within the type is quite independent of any other meanings in other contexts. Localizing names makes it easier to write correct code. However, one "feature" present in older languages was lost by this change.

In PL/1, the programmer could refer to a sub-subfield without specifying a full pathname; the programmer wrote only the name of the object itself and the name of the sub-subfield. This kind of short-cut naming can shorten and simplify code, especially where a record type contains a structured component, and so on, for several levels.

Pascal has one statement type that partially compensates for this loss of convenience. A "with" statement allows the programmer to establish a local context, within which the initial portion of a pathname can be omitted. The form of a with statement is as follows:

$$\text{with } \langle\text{partial pathname}\rangle \text{ do } \langle\text{scope}\rangle$$

When the compiler begins to translate a with statement, it evaluates the effective address, $Ea_p p$, for the partial pathname. (If there are variable fields in the pathname, code is generated to complete this process at run time.) During compilation of the with scope, $Ea_p p$ is the starting point for computing effective addresses of components, and the current type-object is set to the type of the last field in the partial pathname. Within the scope, all references to field names defined for this type are legal and will be interpreted as offsets added to $Ea_p p$.

At run time, any variable fields in $Ea_p p$ are evaluated once, when control enters the with block. Within the block, only the "tail" section of each pathname must be specified and evaluated, saving both execution time and space [Exhibit 14.20].

The principle here is valid and important: when doing several operations with one part of a large compound object, it is more efficient (in several ways) to mark the beginning of that component and make local references relative to that mark. Looking at other programming languages, we see more general ways to solve the same problem.

A C programmer does not need a special statement type to accomplish this; she or he simply sets a pointer to the desired component (at entry to the block) and makes references within the block relative to that pointer [Exhibit 14.21]. The with statement is included in Pascal because C's simple solution is not available. (Recall that, in Pascal, pointers to stack-allocated variables are prohibited.) Moreover, the

Pascal solution is semantically cleaner because, in C, the pointer is not constrained to be constant within the local scope.

Exhibit 14.20.   Partial pathnames using with in Pascal.

With is used here to simplify the source code and reduce execution time for access to one part of a complex data structure, a stack of student records. When the with block is entered, the effective address of the top student on the stack is calculated. All references to the field names defined for StudentType will be interpreted relative to this address.

```
Type NameType =    packed array[1..20] of char;
     StudentType = record LastName, FirstName:  NameType;
                        Sex:  char;
                        Id:  integer
                   end;
     ClassType =    record { A class is a stack of students.  }
                        Top:  integer;
                        Member:  array[1..50] of StudentType;
                   end;
Var  N: Integer;
     CS101:  ClassType;
     Stu:  StudentType;
...
With CS101.Member[ CS101.Top ] Do Begin
     Writeln( Id, FirstName, LastName );
     If Sex='F' Then FemaleTotal := FemaleTotal + 1
                     Else MaleTotal := MaleTotal + 1
End;
```

LISP incorporates what might be called the "right" way to solve the problem. Using "let", the programmer can create a new block with a local symbol and bind that symbol to any object. (The programmer would bind the new symbol to a pointer to the Ea_pp.) C-style references relative to this pointer could then be used within the local scope.

Records Are Much Like Arrays

There are many similarities between records and arrays; both are compound types with a series of parts, accessed by selector functions. Their type-objects contain similar information, except that an array type-object is simpler because all fields of an array are the same size and type. Where an array type-object contains one piece of information about a component, a record type-object contains a list.

However, the familiar syntax for subscript (with parentheses or brackets) is markedly different from the syntax for record part selection (with a dot). This is partly an accident of history; neither subscript notation nor dot notation is engraved in stone. A language designer could choose to use either syntax, as shown in Exhibit 14.22.

Exhibit 14.21.   Using a pointer in C to emulate "`with`".

```
typedef struct  {
                char last_name[20], first_name[20];
                char sex;
                int id;
        } student_type;
typedef struct  {
                int top;
                student_type member[50];
        } class_type; /* A class is a stack of students.  */
...
{   int female_total, male_total;
    class_type cs101;
    student_type *stu;
...
    stu = &cs101.member[ cs101.top ];
        printf("%d %s %s\n", stu->id, stu->first_name, stu->last_name );
        if(stu->sex=='F') ++female_total; else ++male_total;
...
}
```

Exhibit 14.22.   Alternative syntax for part selection.

Let `Student` be a `StudentType`, as declared in Exhibit 14.20, and let `Class` be an array of `StudentType`. There could be many clear and unambiguous ways to denote part selection. A few possibilities are listed here.

	Array Selection	Record Selection
Traditional syntax	Class[5]	Student.FirstName
Possible syntax	Class.5	Student[FirstName]
Uniform syntax	Class@5	Student@FirstName
Functional syntax	Subscript(Class,5)	Select (Student, 'FirstName')

There is a more important difference between arrays and records than the syntax used for part selection. That is the fact that the traditional array selectors are numeric and record selectors are not. Let us consider the twin questions:

1. Why don't we use symbolic names to select array components?
2. Why don't we use integers to select record components?

The essence of an array is that its components are semantically uniform. They represent objects from the same domain, and we expect to apply the same operations to each, in turn. The number of array elements and position of a particular element in the array is of secondary importance, at most. Because these elements have uniform meaning to the programmer, a uniform way to name them is needed. Giving them numbers is a good solution. Giving individual names to a series of similar objects would be silly.

In contrast, the components of a record are not semantically uniform. They represent different aspects of the same object, not separate objects. Even when components are the same type, they represent different concepts and can easily be given different names. Defining symbolic names for record components is, therefore, natural and functional.

However, constant numeric selectors could be used for records. Allowing numeric (as well as symbolic) selection could have some advantages, especially for writing library or utility routines. Variable numeric selectors cannot be used in a strongly typed compiled language because the type of the result of every expression must be determined at compile time. Suppose R is a record variable with five components. Then a compiler can determine the type of $R[3]$ by looking at the third entry in the list of component types in the type-object for R. But a compiler cannot know the type of $R[i]$, where i is a variable; it could be any one of the component types of the record. Thus a variable can't be used to select a record part in a statically type-checked language.

Some languages are interpreted, not compiled. These languages eliminate the restriction that the type of the result of an expression must be known ahead of time. If such a language also permitted the programmer to use the information in a record's type-object, some very useful and powerful routines could be written. For example, we could write a general debugging package with a routine that could print out and label the components of any record. Such a routine would use the type-object to find out how many components were in the record, then execute a loop that used the field name and field type information in the type-object to print out the record's value.

This kind of code is *polymorphic*, that is, the type of a function argument is tested at run time in order to know how to execute the function.[8]

14.2.5   Union Types

Two kinds of types are called *unions* because the semantics of a given storage object can vary. There are actually two kinds of unions, with very different semantic properties, known as *free* unions and *discriminated* unions.

A *free union* is a semantically unsound type. An object of a free union type has two or more possible semantic interpretations, and there is no field, either in the object itself or in its associated type-object, that defines which set of semantics is currently valid. A free union type declaration is not a way to build a compound type out of simpler types. Rather, it is a way to create objects with ambiguous semantics. A free union type-object is shown in Exhibit 14.23. Its form is like the type-object for a record. Its semantics differ from a record in that only enough space for the longest field is allocated, and all fields have an offset of 0 bytes (the offsets, therefore, do not need to be part of the type-object.) Many languages, including Pascal and C, support

---

[8]We will cover polymorphic code in Chapter 17.

free union types. These will be dealt with fully in Chapter 15, Section 15.7, after the discussion of type checking.

Exhibit 14.23.   A type-object for a free union type.

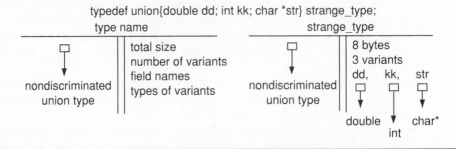

A *discriminated union* is, in theory[9], a semantically sound type, because the alternative semantic interpretations are controlled by a field that contains a *case specifier*. The general form of a discriminated union is: Common part—key—set of variant parts. The Pascal *variant record* declaration is an example of a discriminated union type constructor. It defines a record type with three sections: an initial section with fields that are common to all variants, a tag field that is a code for the variant currently stored in the variable, and a set of variant parts, each having any number of unrelated parts [Exhibit 14.24]. The clear intent of variant types is to conserve storage by permitting mutually exclusive information fields to occupy the same positions in the record. This reduces the total amount of storage needed for variant objects to the amount needed for the longest variant. We can say that the variant fields *share storage*.

If storage is plentiful, there is no need for this type of type. The same semantics can be achieved by using an ordinary record which contains all possible fields and a tag field to say which subset of the fields is currently meaningful. Storage for all fields would then exist all the time, and some subset would contain meaningless garbage.

There are some curious, perhaps faulty, aspects of Pascal's variant records. The tag field controls which set of field names is defined at any given time and should always correspond to the information actually stored in the record. To assign a value to a variant record, the variant tag must be stored first. This causes the corresponding field names to "become defined". However, nothing forces a programmer to finish the job. A value of one variant type, with its tag, could be stored in the variable. Then the tag could be changed. At this point, the tag label does not match the contents of the variable, and if the variable is used, the bits will be given an invalid interpretation! The rules of Pascal allow this to happen, and thus the variant record is a gaping hole in Pascal's type system.

Ada also supports discriminated variant records that are similar to Pascal's, but with an important difference that corrects the loophole in Pascal's semantic rules. Assignment is restricted so that a variant storage object can never contain a case specifier for one variant and a value of another.

---

[9]We say "in theory" because the implementation in Pascal is faulty and semantically unsafe.

Exhibit 14.24.   A type-object for a discriminated union type.

A discriminated union type has two parts. The first part is essentially an ordinary record ending with the discriminant field; the second part is a free union. This is an appropriate type-object for the type declared in Exhibit 14.25.

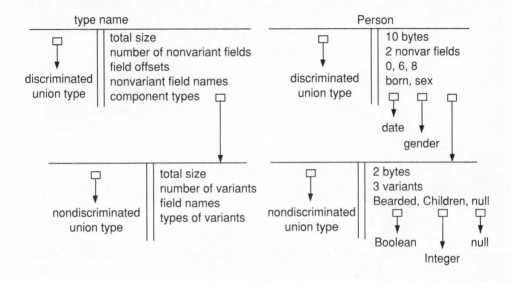

In Exhibit 14.25, we declare a discriminated union type with one common field (Born), a discriminant named "Sex" whose default value is "Unknown", and three sets of variant fields, labeled by the elements of type Gender. We may construct a value of type Person by supplying a list of relevant data items, thus:

```
(Male, (1970,Jan,3), FALSE)
```

Exhibit 14.25.   The discriminated variant record in Ada.

```
type Gender is (Male, Female, Unknown);
type Person(Sex:Gender:=Unknown) is
    record
        Born:  Date;
        case Sex is
            when Male => Bearded: Boolean;
            when Female => Children: Integer;
            when Unknown => null;
        end case;
    end record;
Sam:  Person;   -- A variable of type Person.
```

We may assign such a value to a Person variable. But we may not assign values to the tag field or the variant field independently, These rules forcibly maintain the consistency between the tag field and the information stored. Let Sam be a variable of type Person. Then the whole-record assignment on the first line of Exhibit 14.26 is permitted, but the partial-record assignment on the second line is not. The third assignment is not permitted because the field name Children is not defined for objects with the tag Male. These constraints in Ada close the loopholes present in Pascal.

Exhibit 14.26.   Legal and illegal uses of a discriminated variant record.

```
Sam := (Male, (1970,Jan,3), FALSE);     -- This is ok.
Sam.Sex := Female;                       -- Prohibited.
Sam.Children := 2;                       -- Undefined, Sam is Male.
```

14.3   OPERATIONS ON COMPOUND OBJECTS

14.3.1   Creating Program Objects: Value Constructors

A program object of a primitive type is created initially by executing a function or by writing a literal in a program. For example, the result of performing an addition operation is a program object. Arithmetic expressions and most functions create program objects as their results. (Sometimes these program objects are references.) These values are kept on a run-time stack.

Programming language conventions have developed to allow the writing of literal values of all the primitive types. Most languages have distinguishable syntactic forms for types real, integer, and character, and sometimes for Boolean. Additional primitive types, such as short integer, packed decimal, and byte, are sometimes supported. Sometimes the same program object may be denoted by more than one literal expression. For example, C lets the programmer write an octal, hexadecimal, or decimal literal to denote an integer value.

A language that permits a programmer to define new types should provide some way to write literals for these types. Pascal does not do this; the programmer cannot, therefore, define a constant of a user-defined type. C permits such a literal value to be written as an initializer, in a declaration, but not in any other context. This is a wholly unnecessary restriction.

A language could include a constructor function which we will call "MAKE" to solve this problem. The first argument of MAKE is a type. Following this is a variable number of literals or expressions appropriate in number and composition for program objects of the specified type [Exhibit 14.27]. MAKE takes the separate pure values in this list, bundles them into an object of the given type, and returns this value as its result. It is important to note that this result should be a coherent object, temporarily residing on the run-time stack. It can, therefore, be dealt with or manipulated as a whole even if it is a record or an array.

Another possible approach with the same semantics but slightly different syntax was used in Ada. Each defined type name becomes a constructor function automatically. To construct a program object of the new type, the new type name is written preceding the appropriate series of components, listed in parentheses [Exhibit 14.28].

Exhibit 14.27.   Making a record object from its components.

Assume that the type `complex-pair` has been defined as a record containing real and imaginary components, and that imaginary numbers are made out of reals. Then a `complex-pair` would be constructed by executing the following:

```
MAKE( complex-pair, 0.0, MAKE( imag, 5.6) );
```

Exhibit 14.28.   Making a record object from its components in Ada.

```
type imag is new float;        -- Floats will be used to represent type imag.
type complex_pair is          -- A complex pair is a float and an imag.
    record rp: float;
           ip: imag
    end record;
complex_pair(0.0, imag(5.6))  -- Make a float into an imag, then
                              -- use it with another float to make
                              -- a complex pair.
```

14.3.2   The Interaction of Dereferencing, Constructors, and Selectors

Dereferencing maps a reference into a program object, or value. This reference/value relationship is complicated by the introduction of compound data-objects (arrays and records), selection functions, and constructors. A *selection function* takes, as parameters, a compound object and a part specification. It returns a reference to the specified part of the compound [Exhibit 14.29]. A *constructor* combines a set of components into a single compound object.

Exhibit 14.29.   Pascal selection functions.

In Pascal, the part names associated with record types are selection functions. We define these functions when we make a type declaration. The following declaration creates two new selection functions, named `top` (line a) and `store` (line b).

Subscript is a selection function that is predefined for all arrays, but depends on the declared array bounds. Line b defines the legal range of subscripts for the `store` component of a `stack`, and fully determines the meaning of subscript on this kind of object.

```
TYPE stack = RECORD
                 top: integer;                          {a}
                 store: array [1..100] of StackItem  {b}
             END;
```

The selection functions in many familiar languages (e.g., FORTRAN and Pascal) take references to compound objects as parameters and return references to simple objects as results. The simple reference is then dereferenced if the context requires. Simple selection functions are combined to build the essential accessing functions for abstract data types such as stack in Exhibit 14.30.

Exhibit 14.30.   Using selection functions in Pascal.

We combine the selection functions subscript, top, and store to build a "pop" function for a stack.

  a. The parameter to the pop function is the address of the beginning of a stack storage object. (The keyword VAR indicates that a Pascal parameter is a reference.)

  b. All three selection functions are composed, to arrive at the address of the element at the "top" of the stack. This address is dereferenced because it appears on the right side of an assignment. This yields a program object which is later returned by the function.

  c. A different stack component, the top-of-stack index, is then selected twice. The right-hand occurrence is dereferenced and decremented. The resulting value is stored in the address given on the left (the same location), modifying the value of the compound object.

```
FUNCTION pop(VAR S:stack):StackItem;        {a}
BEGIN
    pop := S.store[ S.top ];                {b}
    S.top := S.top - 1                      {c}
END;
```

A constructor creates a compound program object from a set of pure values on the run-time stack. It can leave the resulting compound object on the stack or allocate a variable of the correct shape and initialize it to the given set of pure values. We call the former a *value constructor* and the latter a *reference constructor*.

Several languages give partial support to value constructors; for example, C permits them in initializing expressions and Ada supports a similar notation for compound literal expressions. APL, however, is one of the few languages that supports explicit, run-time value construction with no restrictions. Use of APL's value constructor, comma, is shown in Exhibit 14.31. The reshape function, ρ, is a combined type cast and constructor; its use is illustrated in Exhibit 14.35.

Reference construction implies dynamic allocation and the use of pointers. It is not supported at all in many common languages, but it has a basic and central importance in LISP. The LISP "cons" function is a reference constructor which allocates a new cell and initializes it to the two arguments on the stack.

The possible relationships among references, program objects, compound objects, and their components are captured in Exhibit 14.32. Each arrow represents a type of function, pointing from the type of its argument to the type of its result. Thus the arrow for "value selector" starts at "compound program object" and ends at "simple program object", and the arrow for "reference constructor" starts at "simple program object" and goes to "compound reference". No arrow in the graph leads from a collection of simple references to a compound reference. This is because programs deal with real storage. Whereas compound storage objects must occupy contiguous blocks of memory, a set of individual storage locations normally are not allocated contiguously and, therefore, cannot be combined directly into a coherent compound object.

Exhibit 14.31.   Value constructors in APL.

- Using a literal or a variable name causes the corresponding value to be placed on the stack.
- Assume N is bound to a numeric value; it will be automatically dereferenced and placed on the stack between the other two numbers.
- We use the concatenate operator, comma, to construct a one-dimensional numeric array, or vector, from the three simple values on the stack.

      2, N, 5.1

Exhibit 14.32.   Selection and dereferencing.

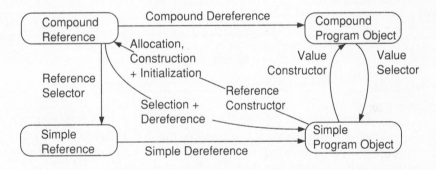

Selection and Compound Objects in Pascal.

Most languages do not support all of these kinds of selection and dereferencing functions. Pascal incorporates a limited subset of these possible function types as diagrammed in Exhibit 14.33. Moreover, Pascal only supports some of these function types in a highly restricted fashion. (The letters in the diagram key it to the following explanation of these restrictions.)

a: Reference selectors. Like most common languages, Pascal provides selection functions that return references when used on the left side of an assignment statement. This permits a single part of a compound storage object to be changed without manipulating the entire compound. Subscripting an array (or selection of one field of a record) returns a reference to the selected part.

b: Simple dereference. Dereferencing is automatic when a reference appears to the right of an ":=", or in an expression, or as an actual argument corresponding to a value parameter.

c: Selection with dereference. The result of a subscript or selection operation is a simple reference. Like any reference, this is automatically dereferenced unless it is on the left side of an assignment operator or is used as an argument to a function with a VAR parameter. Thus a reference to part of an object cannot be obtained and stored or manipulated by the programmer.

d: Compound dereference. Any Pascal variable, even a compound variable, may be passed as a value parameter. This causes the variable to be dereferenced. Otherwise, Pascal's support for compound dereference is severely restricted. Record variables will be dereferenced when they are compared for equality, or when the value of one record variable is copied into another. Array variables can be copied but not compared.

Exhibit 14.33. Pascal selection and dereferencing.

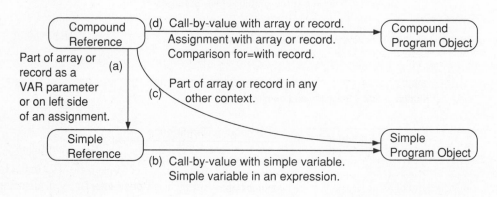

Pascal does not support the other three kinds of functions at all. It provides dynamic storage allocation and pointers, but not reference constructors. A series of separate operations is required to allocate a new compound storage object and initialize its fields. Nothing like the LISP cons is supported.

Value constructors are not supported at all in Pascal, not even those which construct compound literal values as in Ada and C. A compound value can only be constructed by storing its components, one at a time, into a compound storage object. Compound values may not even be returned from functions in the standard language.

With no value constructors, value selectors are not needed. All compound values are created, piece by piece, by storing components in a compound variable. Reference selection may then be used to decompose the value, if needed.

Selection and Compound Objects in APL.

The power of APL comes from its generalized ability to manipulate compound program objects. Here we will look at the selectors and constructors in APL and note how they differ from those in most languages.

Many APL operations, including the selection functions, can result in compound pure values being left on the stack for further processing by other operators. All the selection operators can be used as value selectors, to select some portion of a compound value that was just computed. A complex expression might perform several computation steps, each time creating, on the stack, an answer of a new size or new number of dimensions. This is in stark contrast to Pascal, where every compound value must be created by a series of assignments, and the size and shape of every result must be known at compile time.

APL **Selectors.** In FORTRAN, C, and Pascal, selection functions operate only on variables. The question of selecting a part of a compound program object never occurs because these languages do not support either literals of compound types or functions that return objects of compound types. In contrast, APL supports compound program objects and selection functions on both variables and program objects, and APL incorporates a much more extensive and less restricted subset of the possible function types from Exhibit 14.32.

APL compounds are limited to arrays (records do not exist in APL), but the programmer can do many more things with arrays than in Pascal [Exhibit 14.34]. APL gives full support to compound dereferencing (arrow d), value selectors (arrow e), and value constructors (arrow f).

Exhibit 14.34.   APL selection and dereferencing.

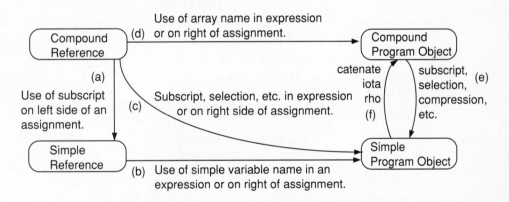

Simple dereferencing (arrow b) works similarly in Pascal and APL; anything on the right side of an assignment arrow, and any variable name in any other kind of expression, is automatically dereferenced. Both languages prohibit storing and calculating with a reference to part of an object. Compound dereferencing (arrow d), though, is much less restricted in APL than in Pascal. Compound variables, like simple variables, can be used in most expressions. Using a compound variable name as an operand causes compound dereferencing and leaves a compound object on the stack.

APL is like Pascal where reference selection (arrow a) is concerned. Selection results in a reference in APL only when subscripts are used to the left of an assignment arrow; selection is followed by dereferencing (arrow c) for all other uses of subscripts. Unlike Pascal, though, APL lets the programmer write a subscript expression that denotes any subset of the rows and columns of a matrix. All of these locations will be selected and receive assignments or be dereferenced [Exhibit 14.36].

Exhibit 14.35.   Constructing matrices in APL.

These lines create two literal matrices and bind them to the identifiers M1 and M2. Diagrams of these matrices are shown below.

```
M1 ← 3 5 ρ 11 12 13 14 15 21 22 23 24 25 31 32 33 34 35
M2 ← 4 4 ρ 0
```

M1:	11	12	13	14	15
	21	22	23	24	25
	31	32	33	34	35

M2:	0	0	0	0
	0	0	0	0
	0	0	0	0
	0	0	0	0

Exhibit 14.36.   Selecting a submatrix in APL.

Reference selection and two operators that perform value selection are illustrated below. These operations use the matrix values M1 and M2 created in Exhibit 14.35. The first line selects two characters, "no", from the string "random" and binds the resulting value to M3. The second line selects six values from M1 (rows 1 and 3, columns 2, 4, and 5) and assigns them to six selected locations in M2 (rows 1 and 4, columns 1, 2, and 3). The result is diagrammed.

```
M3 ← 0 0 1 0 1 0 / "random"
M2[1 4; 1 2 3] ← M1[ 1 3; 2 4 5]
```

Result of value selection:

12	14	15
32	34	35

Result of reference selection
and assignment of a compound
value to parts of M2:

12	14	15	0
0	0	0	0
0	0	0	0
32	34	35	0

Unlike Pascal, subscript is not the only selection function that operates on arrays; there are several selection operators that take an array or matrix operand and an operand that specifies which part of the array is to be selected, and compute a new array of a different shape. These are listed in Exhibit 14.37.

APL Constructors.   A value constructor takes two or more values, on the stack, and combines them into a compound value, which it leaves on the stack. APL relies everywhere on value constructors. All APL operators, when given compound arguments, can construct compound values as their results. An array literal is denoted simply by writing a series of simple literal numbers (without any delimiters or punctuation), and an array may be input by typing a similar series of numbers. In addition, there are two operators whose sole purpose is to construct array values [Exhibit 14.38], and one operator that can be used to "cast" a one-dimensional array into any multidimensional shape.

Exhibit 14.37.   APL selection functions.

We give the most basic meaning of APL's selector functions. The "/" has additional meanings when used in other contexts.

Symbol	Name	Semantics
N ↑ V	take	Select N values from V and include them in the answer. If N is positive, take the first N values; if N is negative, take the last N.
N ↓ V	drop	Eliminate N values from V and include the rest of V in the answer. If N is positive, drop the first N values; if N is negative, drop the last N.
V1 / V2	select	The two array operands must have the same length, and the value in each position of V1 should be a positive integer, N. Then N copies of the value in the corresponding position of V2 will be selected and included in the result.
[...]	subscript	Works for matrices of any number of dimensions. An array element is selected if all of its indices (row, column, etc.) are included in the subscript list.

Exhibit 14.38.   Using value constructors in APL.

We give the most basic meaning of APL's three constructors. All three symbols have additional meanings when used in other contexts.

Symbol	Name	Semantics
ι N	iota	Create an array value consisting of the numbers 1 through N.
A1 , A2	catenate	If A1 and A2 are arrays, form a new array value by concatenating the elements of A1 and A2.
D ρ A	reshape	D is an array of dimensions, and A is an array of values. Form a new matrix, whose shape is specified by D, containing the values in A. If there are too few values in A, use them cyclically until the new matrix is filled up.

Because APL supports compound selectors, compound dereferencing, and value constructors in very general ways, compound objects can be processed as easily as simple objects. APL combines these unusual and powerful data-handling facilities with implicit iteration[10] The result is that many algorithms can be written succinctly or as "one liners" in APL that would require several lines of code and explicit loops in most other languages.

14.4 OPERATIONS ON TYPES

Often a systems programmer wants to design and write library functions or general implementations of common, useful algorithms. He or she is faced with a type-declaration dilemma:

- The actual size and structure of an argument must generally be known to process that structure correctly.
- But a generally applicable program should be usable for many variations of a data structure. For example, a package of stack functions should work on stacks implemented by arrays of any length or base type.

Binding time becomes a problem in a compiled language. Data types for all objects must be *bound* (fully specified and fixed) before code can be compiled; allocation and selection functions depend on this information. In Ada the binding time problem is solved by putting the library code in a *generic package*, which is a code schema with one or more type-parameters. To use such a package you first *instantiate* the package with particular type-arguments. This binds the types and creates fully specified code which can then be compiled normally.

But there is still a problem. Code often depends on some particular property of a type, such as the size of objects of that type or the number of elements in an array. The code in the body of a generic package needs to have access to this kind of information about the type-arguments used in the instantiation process. Even when we write library functions for an interpreted language, we need *type predicates* that can test the types of arguments and conditionally execute the appropriate code.

Type-objects provide a clean solution to these problems. They are objects and can be passed as arguments, just like data objects. A pointer to a type-object serves as a unique identifier for the type, providing an easy implementation for a type-predicate. A type-object has a body that stores specific information about the properties of objects of that type. To find the *attributes* of a type, we need the ability to access the information stored in its type-object. Thus we need selectors *for the type-objects*.

The actual selectors that are meaningful for a type-object depend, obviously, on the type of the type. The type pointer in a type-object provides a way to find out what selectors are appropriate. Finally, the language definition must list the selector functions that may be used for each type of type.

C provides us with one example of a type operation. The `sizeof` operator in C may be applied to any type or any object. It accesses the type-object and returns the value of the "size" field. The `sizeof` operator is necessary in C to provide program portability. It is most commonly used in conjunction with the dynamic allocation

---

[10]See Chapter 10.4.

functions, `malloc` and `calloc`, which require the programmer to tell the allocator how many bytes to allocate [Exhibit 14.39]. Since the size of any structure can vary from machine to machine, an operator was provided that would return the size of a type in the current implementation.

Exhibit 14.39.   The lone type operation in C.

Assume that `T1` is a defined type name. Line (a) declares two pointers of type `T1*`, or pointer-to-`T1`. Line (b) allocates one storage object large enough to hold a value of type `T1`. The result of `malloc` must be explicitly cast to type `T1*` before it is stored in the pointer variable, `pt1`. Line (c) allocates an array of `n` such objects and stores the reference in `pt2`.

```
T1 *pt1, *pt2;                          /* a */
pt1 = (T1*)(malloc(sizeof T1));         /* b */
pt2 = (T1*)(calloc(n, sizeof T1));      /* c */
```

Ada supports generic packages and, therefore, must provide a variety of type-selectors. These are referred to as *attributes*, and they give a package access to many kinds of important information. Some, but by no means all, of these attributes are listed in Exhibit 14.40. The first one is the analog of C's `sizeof`. The last selectors listed apply to any array type and return the bounds of the Nth dimension. These type-selectors let the library programmer write code that can process any type array.

Exhibit 14.40.   Some of the type operations supported by Ada.

Attribute	Meaning
For any type:	
'storage_size	Total number of storage units needed
'size	Number of bits needed for type or allocated for object
For integer types, subranges, and enumerated types:	
'first	Minimum value in the type
'last	Maximum value in the type
For floating-point types:	
'digits	Number of decimals in mantissa of representation
'emax	Largest exponent value
'epsilon	Difference between two successive representable values
'large	Largest positive value
For array types:	
'first(N)	Lower bound for Nth index position
'last(N)	Upper bound for Nth index position

Many of these attribute selectors define the limits inherent in an implementation of the basic types. Note the similarity between the third selector, `'last`, and Pascal's implementation-dependent constant `maxint`. The type-objects for the basic types in Ada are more complex than those we diagrammed, since they must also contain the limit information. The ability to get this kind of information about an implementation can be an important ingredient in writing reliable, portable code.

EXERCISES

1. What is the difference between a primitive and a programmer-defined type?
2. What is a type object? What are its components?
3. The process of type-checking in Pascal is very simple and fast, even if the types being compared are complex and nested. Explain. How is this related to type objects?
4. What is a type constant? Why is it used?
5. What information is necessary to represent a pointer type? Explain two ways that this information might be used by the compiler.
6. What is a compound type?
7. What information is necessary to represent an array type?
8. What is an index type? What is its role in an array?
9. How is an effective address computed for a one-dimensional array?
10. How was the implementation of multidimensional arrays simplified in the late 1960s?
11. What is a slice of an array?
12. Compare the highly flexible arrays in APL and the much more restricted ones in Pascal. Comment on: selection functions, coherent operations, use as parameters, and returning arrays as function results.
13. What is bounds checking? What is the advantage of having it in a language? The disadvantage?
14. What is a string? A counted string? A terminated string?
15. What is the difference in representation between a C string and a Pascal string?
16. Why was the set type included in Pascal?
17. What are the similarities between an array and a record?
18. What are the differences between an array and a record? Explain why a representation of a record type is more complex than a representation of an array type.
19. Explain why the fields of a record cannot be accessed by subscript (like elements of an array) in a strongly typed compiled language.
20. How can a record component be accessed?
21. What is a pathname?
22. What is the difference between a free union and a discriminated union?
23. How has Ada closed the loophole found in Pascal's variant record?
24. How are literal objects of primitive types created in a program?
25. How are literal objects of user-defined types created in Pascal? C?
26. What is a selection function? What does it return?
27. How does a value constructor create a compound object?
28. Why is binding time a problem in compiled languages?
29. How can we find the attributes of a type?
30. Give an example of a type operation in C and Ada.

15

The Semantics of Types

In this chapter we explore the semantics of types. In addition to describing physical properties of objects, types can be used to define the domain of a function and thereby control its application. There are several different approaches to domains and domain or type checking.

We consider the use of types and the development of type checking from the earliest languages, in which checking was largely absent, to modern strongly typed languages. Types are properties of data objects and they describe data size, structure, and encoding. Types may also be associated with identifiers to restrict the domain of objects to which an identifier may be bound. Type restrictions can be enforced at compile time or at run time.

In early languages, types were used primarily for storage allocation, storage access, and to control application of predefined functions. Two types were considered compatible if they described the same storage format. This definition of compatibility became inadequate when newer languages began using types to carry semantic information. The translators for the newer strongly typed languages use domain or type checking to ensure the semantic validity of function calls. A major research problem has been to find semantically meaningful extensions of the type compatibility rules.

A distinction is made between external domains, those within a programmer's application area, and internal domains, the semantic groupings of objects or types identified by the language translator. While older languages had a fixed number of distinct domains, type constructors in modern languages permit programmer-defined domains.

Type casts cause a change in the semantics of an object—the domain label is changed, but the bits are not. A conversion is a change in the physical properties of an object—size, encoding, or reference level. A coercion is a conversion or cast that is automatically invoked by the translator.

While type checking aids the programmer, it creates an inflexible environment. A programmer who needs to convert from integer to floating point or to compute a hash index, for example, would be hampered by strong type checking. Modern languages often provide escape hatches so that the experienced programmer can evade the type matching rules.

15.1 SEMANTIC DESCRIPTION

Types can be used to embody both the physical properties and the semantic properties of objects. In Chapter 5, we explored the use of types to describe physical properties. In this chapter we look at the other use of types: to define the domain of a function and thereby to control function applicability. A *domain* is the set of objects over which a function is defined. Objects in this set must share common physical properties (size, structure) and semantic properties (encoding, intent).

Functions defined for a domain depend on the common properties of its elements. If the size or structure of a function parameter differed from what the function expected, the results of the computation would probably be wrong. Similarly you would get nonsense if the meaning of an actual parameter was different from the meaning of objects for which the function was designed. Data type definitions were developed as a way to specify the size and structure of variables, so that translators could allocate appropriate amounts of storage. Type checking is a way the translator can use the same information to help the programmer eliminate errors and inconsistencies in code.

Checking was minimal in early languages, but it has become more sophisticated through the years. In this section we look briefly at several different approaches to domains and domain checking. We consider the typing rules in a series of languages, from very old to fairly new.

15.1.1 Domains in Early Languages

Assemblers, the earliest computer languages, had implicit domains rather than explicit domains: addresses, integers, indices, and the like [Exhibit 15.1]. The programmer used elements of these domains, but their properties and relationships were part of the programming lore, not part of the language. All assembly language objects were represented by storage locations (or blocks of locations), each location big enough to store an integer. The type of the object (integer, address, or index) was not part of the program—it existed only in the programmer's mind. Computers typically had some instructions intended to do useful things on each domain. However, the language translator had no way of knowing whether a variable represented a true integer, an address, or an index. Thus the translator could not ensure meaningful use of instructions. Some higher-level languages, such as FORTH, also use a single domain to represent integers, addresses, and indices, and provide no way to ensure their appropriate use.

Exhibit 15.1.   Operations defined for assembly language domains.

Domain Name	Operations Defined
machine address	Goto, fetch a value, store a value.
integer	Arithmetic and comparison operations.
index	Load index register, add to base address of an array.

Early Typed Languages.

Languages designed in the 1950s, such as FORTRAN and ALGOL, embodied fixed sets of *primitive*, or predefined, domains. The language and the translator made distinctions among these domains. The domain of each variable was defined (by default in FORTRAN, by declaration in ALGOL) and became permanently associated with the variable identifier.

The original FORTRAN was a very primitive language. It did not have variable declarations; the type of a variable was derived by default from the first letter of its name. Names were restricted to six letters; this is so short that meaningful names were hard to devise. The domains "integer" and "real" were supported as unrelated numeric types that could not be used in combination.

The ALGOL domain structure was much richer than FORTRAN. Integers and reals became related domains [Exhibit 15.2]. Automatic type conversions were introduced so that values of either numeric type could be mixed in arithmetic statements. The external domain "real" was commonly represented internally by single machine words in floating-point encoding.[1] Integers were also commonly represented as single machine words in binary sign and magnitude encoding. With this representation, the internal domain "integer" is not a strict subset of the internal domain "floating point". Some numbers can be represented exactly both ways, some cannot. Very large integers have too many digits of accuracy and can only be approximated in floating-point representation. Nonintegral floating-point numbers can only be approximated in integer representation.

ALGOL introduced `Boolean` as a distinct domain. Boolean values were produced by comparison operators and used by conditional statements. All variables were declared, and the declaration was used for both allocation and type checking. ALGOL had too many primitive types to make FORTRAN-style defaults useful.

15.1.2   Domains in "Typeless" Languages

Some languages, which are called *dynamically typed languages*[2], support dynamic allocation of storage objects whenever they are needed to contain an input value or the

---

[1]These were 36 bits long on the IBM 704.
[2]The less precise term *typeless languages* has also been used.

result of a computation.[3] Identifiers are *typeless* in the sense that types are not permanently attached to them. Rather, a type tag is attached to each storage object when it is created. The storage object is then bound dynamically to an identifier. Thus the type that is indirectly associated with an identifier may change dynamically. Examples of such languages are LISP, APL, and SNOBOL.

Exhibit 15.2.   Domain relationships in ALGOL.

Unrelated.

The domains "Boolean" and "integer" were independent. No relationship existed between integer values and Boolean values.

Intersection.

The external domain "integer" is a subset of the external domain "real"; all integers are reals, and some reals are integers. However, in a typical 4-byte implementation, the domains integer and real intersect, but neither is a subset of the other.

Numbers Not Exactly Representable as Integers

5,000,000,000	Larger than maximum 4-byte integer.
3.25	Has a fractional part.

Numbers Exactly Representable as Integer and Float

2,147,481,880	No bits in low-order byte of this integer.
3	No bits in high-order byte of this integer.

Number Not Exactly Representable as a Float

2,101,111,111	Integer has "1" bits in both high- and low-order bytes.

Number Exactly Representable as Neither

1/3	Has fractional part that is infinite when expressed in binary.

In these languages, the programmer does not *declare* types for variables and function parameters. However, all those variables *have* types, which are necessary to describe the data size, structure, and encoding. These languages all incorporate the various data encodings supported by typical computer instruction sets (character, integer, floating point, bitstring). Further, the domain of an object is usually tested, at run time, before a primitive operation is applied to it. Exhibit 15.3 gives examples of domain-checking in APL, a dynamically typed language. A run-time error comment is generated if the domain is not appropriate.

Types are not used to control function applicability in these languages. Any *programmer-defined* function can be applied to any object. The language does not support the concept that a function might be meaningful for some arguments but not for others. However, even though the domains of arguments to programmer-defined functions are not checked, many (but not all) semantic errors are detected when the program eventually calls a primitive operation with an inappropriate parameter.

---

[3]These languages are usually interpreted, not compiled.

Exhibit 15.3.   Domains are checked by APL primitive operators.

The domain of an argument is checked by primitive operators. Use of an operand belonging to the wrong domain results in an error comment.

Programmer Writes	APL's Output	Note Below
A ← 2.11 34.2 17 18.1		(a)
□ ← A [3]	17	(b)
□ ← A ['N']	Domain Error	(c)

a. An array of four numbers is created and bound to the variable A.

b. "□ ←" means to output the value of the expression on the right side of the arrow. The value of the third element of the array A is selected and printed.

c. A subscript in APL must belong to the domain "integer". A character may not be used as a subscript.

In Exhibit 15.4 we define a simple APL function named DEMO that accepts a parameter, S, passed by value. At function exit, the value of R will be returned as the value of the function. Meaningful and meaningless calls on DEMO (and their results) are shown in Exhibit 15.5. The domain mismatch in the second call is not detected when control enters DEMO. However, it is detected during the subscript computation, because subscript is a primitive function.

Exhibit 15.4.   A simple APL function.

Note that the domain of the programmer-defined function is not declared and therefore cannot be checked.

```
∇ R ← DEMO S
[1] A ← 2.11  34.2  4.8  18.1
[2] R ← A[S]
∇
```

Line 1 We define a length-4 array.

Line 2 The parameter, S, is used to subscript A. If the subscript is in the range 1..4, the corresponding item in the array will be selected and bound to R, the local name for the result.

Dynamically typed languages often supply domain predicates for the primitive domains, so that programmers may write their own domain checks. The most general kind of domain predicate is a Boolean function of two parameters; let us call it IN. One parameter is an object, Ob, the other is a domain name, D. The predicate IN(Ob, D) returns TRUE if D is the domain of Ob.

Exhibit 15.5.   APL does not check domains of programmer-defined functions.

Programmer Writes	APL's Response	Notes
☐ ←DEMO 3	4.8	(a)
☐ ←DEMO 'N'	Domain Error, line 2 of DEMO	(b)
☐ ←DEMO 5	Index error, line 2 of DEMO	(c)

  a. A correct function call. A [3] is returned.

  b. The domain is checked on a call to a primitive function.

  c. The subscript range is also checked. 5 is too large for array A.

Some languages do not permit a domain name to be used as a parameter. Such a language might supply a separate domain predicate for each domain. In this case the domain name is made part of the predicate name, and each predicate tests whether its single argument belongs to a specific domain. This is well illustrated by the domain predicates in LISP [Exhibit 15.6].

Exhibit 15.6.   Types and domain checking in LISP.

The information given here is for the dialect Common LISP.

> Automatic domain checking: primitive functions check the domains of their arguments.
>
> Primitive domains: number (integer), symbol (the name of an object), atom (any nonlist entity), list (a sequence of lists and/or atoms, delimited by parentheses).
>
> Primitive domain predicates: numberp, symbolp, atom, listp, null (true for empty lists). Example: "(numberp s)" returns T (for true) if s is a number, and F otherwise.

If a dynamically typed language supports domain predicates, a programmer can do manual domain checking within functions. A function will accept, as arguments, objects of any domain. Within the function the programmer writes conditional statements that test the domain and take one of several branches. Conditionals can be set up that will emulate the checking done automatically in Pascal. Thus, whatever operations are ultimately applied to the data, they are sure to be appropriate for the data encoding. Domain testing becomes another form of data-validity checking, similar to checking for an absurd data value or a table index that is out of range.

15.1.3   Domains in the 1970s

Early C: Domains Checked for Primitive Operators Only

Type compatibility is a complex question in C. First, we must distinguish among various versions of C, especially between the old semistandard version of C which is described in the Kernighan and Ritchie book (we refer to this as K&R C) and ANSI C. There are far-reaching differences in the typing and type checking rules between the oldest versions and ANSI C. Here we discuss both K&R C and the ANSI standard.

Second, some, but not all, implementations of K&R C have an accompanying program named LINT, which may be used by the programmer to examine programs and locate Pascal-style type errors. A LINT program defines many things as errors that the accompanying C compiler would let go, and thus LINT defines a language with different semantics than C, but the same syntax. LINT implements type constructors and domain identity checking similar to that in Pascal.

Third, many recent non-ANSI compilers generate nonfatal "warning messages" for Pascal-style type errors, but compile the code anyway. It amounts to a semantic quibble whether the warning messages or the generated code defines the semantics of the language.

Finally, type compatibility for array and record types in K&R C was almost a moot point. There was nothing that you could do coherently with a compound object except store its address into a pointer. Thus the question of type checking for function parameters was reduced to a question of what could be done with pointers.

A rough generalization about early C translators is that types were used primarily for storage allocation and access, as described in Chapter 5. Types were declared so that the compiler could know the number, position, and encoding of the fields of an object. This is essential information for producing object code. The types of arguments to primitive functions and operators were checked. But, as in APL, arguments to programmer-defined functions were not checked at all. A function call could have the wrong number, wrong type, or wrong sequence of arguments, and the violation would not be detected.

Further, the rules for pointers created a gaping hole in the type structure. A pointer, declared to point at one type, could be set to point at an object of a different type. Older C compilers would not comment on this type violation. In newer compilers, this would trigger a warning message, but object code will be generated anyway. In Exhibit 15.7, the pointer r is made to point at an object whose type does not match r's declared type. Then a field is selected from r's object and interpreted as if it were the proper type for r, which is untrue. This technique can be used to "fool" the compiler into compiling code that would cause a type error if it were executed without the pointers. Thus the language definition and the compiler provide no sure control over whether or not a pointer is pointing at an object of the appropriate type.

Programmer-Defined Domains

Time and experience have influenced design philosophy. The historical trend has been to give domains an increasingly important role in programming languages because they are a great aid to producing semantically sound programs. In older languages, all domains were predefined, and their relationships (if any) were predefined and not modifiable. No domain checking was done that distinguished between objects of similarly represented domains. For example, in C (which was developed by Ritchie in about 1972), integers and truth values are the same domain. More important, the types of the arguments to programmer-defined functions were not checked.

Exhibit 15.7.   Pointer assignments in K&R C.

Two types named funny and runny are defined and are used to declare two pointers (named f and r) and an ordinary structured variable (named ff). Note that these types are structurally different. The following statements will compile without causing a fatal error. Recent non-ANSI C compilers are likely to produce a warning message for the last assignment.

```
struct runny {int a; int b;}  *r;
struct funny {int a; float c;} *f, ff= {2, 3.1};
f = & ff;    /* This makes f point at the variable ff.  */
r = f;       /* This sets r to point at the same thing as f,
                which is, of course, the wrong type for r.  */
```

After executing these lines, storage will contain:

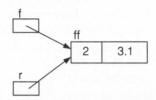

The first expression, below, is normal. The second field of a funny object is selected. It is expected to be, and is, a float. The second expression, though, selects the second field of a runny object, which is expected to be an integer, but is actually a float that will be interpreted as an integer.

```
f->c    Select 2nd part of f's struct; float result is interpreted as float.
r->b    Select 2nd part of r's struct; float result is interpreted as int.
```

In newer languages, such as Pascal (released by Jensen and Wirth in 1974), ways were provided to define new domains, and more elaborate domain-matching rules were implemented. In addition to the usual record, array, and pointer types, Pascal included several new kinds of type definitions: subrange type, enumerated type,[4] set type, and type mapping [Exhibit 15.8]. Domain relationships began to become important. In Pascal, these were pre-defined and unmodifiable. Let us consider the four types of relationships in Pascal.

Intersection.
The domains real and integer intersect in Pascal as they did in ALGOL. Set domains can intersect with other set domains over the same base type.

Unrelated.
Domains created by array or record or pointer type declarations are unrelated to any other domain. Domains defined by enumeration (including the primitive domains char and Boolean) are unrelated semantically to any other domain. However, all enumerated types are represented by integers and can be converted to the domain integer by explicit use of the primitive function ord.

---
[4]Enumerated types were not supported by early versions of C.

Exhibit 15.8. Diagrams of the domain relationships in Pascal.

```
TYPE index = 0..100;
     age= integer;
```

- Boolean, integer, and real are primitive types.
- The domain Boolean is semantically unrelated to integer, e͟͟͟͟͟͟͟͟͟͟͟͟͟ mapping onto a subset of the integers.
- Integer and real intersect; that is, some reals can be converted to integers; most or all integers (depending on the implementation) are also representable as reals.
- The domain index is a subset of the domain integer, and fully compatible.
- The domain age is merged with the domain integer. There is no distinction.

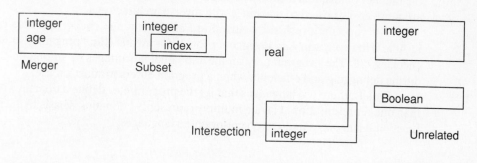

Subset.

Subset.

The Pascal subrange declaration narrows a domain to a compatible smaller domain with the same representation. Variables of a subrange type are restricted to storing values in the subrange. Attempting to store a value outside this range results in a run-time error and program termination. Using a subrange variable incurs run-time overhead due to automatic range-checking every time a value is stored in it! While the protection provided by subranges is valuable, especially during program debugging, the cost is great. Further, because a range error causes a Pascal program to "bomb", subranges cannot be used for ordinary input validation. They are primarily useful for trapping subscript values that have unintentionally become too large or too small.

Merger.

Compatibility rules were very loose in the original K&R C; they are far tighter in Pascal. For example, truth values, integers, and addresses comprise different domains, and a pointer to a real is incompatible with a pointer to an integer. The compiler checks the domains of all function arguments and requires that the formal and actual parameters have the same domain identity (not just the same representation, as in C).

However, even in Pascal, the relationships among types, structures, and domains are not easily stated. In Pascal, we may have merged domains, that is, more than one type name associated with one domain [Exhibit 15.18], and more than one domain associated with one structural description [Exhibit 15.14]. The number of distinct domains is equal neither to the number of names nor to the number of different structures defined.

15.1.4 Domains in the 1980s

Languages newer than Pascal embody a clearer view of the nature and uses of domains. For example, Ada gives the programmer more control over the relationships among new domains (see Section 15.3).

In C, the programmer specifies the physical size of variables by declaring them to be "long int", "short int", or "int" (meaning either one). In contrast, Ada encourages the programmer to declare domains abstractly, by specifying characteristics (range, precision) of the values to be represented, rather than concretely, by specifying the number of machine locations needed. Programs containing abstract specifications are more easily ported to machines with diverse architectures.

The run-time overhead incurred in Pascal for range checking is also incurred in Ada. However, the Ada designers provided a means (the "pragma") to turn this checking off. The programmer can have the dual advantages of automatic checking during debugging and efficiency when a program enters production use.

Finally, there are languages that let the programmer define a domain with more than one representation. Having multiply represented domains is basic to the modern functional languages and the object-oriented languages.[5]

15.2 TYPE CHECKING

Translators use *domain checking* (often called *type checking*) to ensure the semantic validity of function calls. In a domain-checked language, the domain of each formal parameter of a function is declared to be a specific or generic data type. When the programmer tries to apply a function to a set of actual parameters, the translator verifies that the type of each actual parameter is appropriate; the type of the actual parameter must be contained in the domain of the corresponding formal parameter. If this is true we say the actual and formal parameters are *type compatible*, or that their types *match*.

If any parameter fails this test, the function call will not be carried out and an error comment will be generated. This process can be done dynamically, rejecting meaningless function calls at run time, or statically, detecting *type errors* at compile time. The actual rules for determining whether two types match can be confusingly complex and vary greatly from language to language. The rest of this chapter discusses and contrasts the compatibility rules for a few languages.

15.2.1 Strong Typing

The term *strongly typed language* means, roughly, a language that checks the semantic validity of all function calls. There is considerable confusion, though, about the exact meaning of this term. In this section we will go through a series of increasingly sophisticated definitions of strong typing.

---

[5]These are discussed in Chapter 17.

Some early authors called a language "typed" (abbreviated as ST#1) if the programmer used declarations to specify the types of variables. By this definition, APL and BASIC are not ST#1 and C and Pascal are. This definition classes languages such as BASIC (where the data type is implicitly declared by the form of the variable name) with languages such as APL which do not associate types with identifiers at all. A better definition (ST#2) is: a language is typed if there is a type associated with each variable name, and only objects of that type can be stored in the variable. APL is not ST#2 and BASIC, C, and Pascal are.

It became clear that the important distinction was not whether every object had a declared type, but whether those types were used to support semantic validity. A new name and a third, stricter definition evolved: A *strongly typed language* (ST#3) is one in which the compiler enforces these type compatibility rules:

- All objects (variables, values, and formal parameters) are divided into sets called *types*, usually labeled by type names. Types can be built in or programmer defined. Each object belongs to exactly one type.

- A type may have two or more variants. The variant to which an object belongs can be ascertained by a program at run time. Perhaps it is encoded by a tag field associated with the object.

- A variable can only store values of the same type.

- In a legal function call, the type of each actual argument must match the type of the corresponding formal parameter. The exact definition of compatibility is language-dependent. Roughly, though, two types are usually compatible if they are the same type or are overlapping subsets of the same type.

- If an argument belongs to a type with variants, the programmer must explicitly test which variant is present and write code that handles each variant appropriately.

APL is not ST#3. Neither is the original Kernighan and Ritchie version of C, because calls to user-defined functions are not type-checked. Pascal, Ada, and ANSI C are ST#3 except for some "escape hatches". These are Pascal's nondiscriminated variant record and the analogous union data type in C, as well as ANSI C's continued support of K&R C's original function definition syntax and semantics. BASIC is ST#3, in a rather uninteresting way, because it will never let you apply numeric operators to strings or vice versa.

When using the method of top-down programming, a programmer begins by working with a very general description of a problem and then making several passes over that description. On each pass the programmer specifies more details of both the data representation and the method for computation. In the middle of this process an abstract solution for the problem has been described. The algorithms and data are defined in a rough fashion but nothing is specified fully yet. Finally, after several passes, the programmer arrives at a fully specified algorithm which can be coded.

Languages that are ST#3 offer limited support for top-down programming, primarily because they require the full specification of data representations too early in the process. Functions can only be written to accept parameters of fully specified types. In order to define functions over abstract data types, a language must permit postponement of the time at which representation details need to be pinned down.

15.2.2   Strong Typing and Data Abstraction

An *abstract data type*, or *ADT*, is a combination of one or more abstract domains together with a set of functions that operate on them, and related data items that characterize the domain. An ADT is an abstraction. We can define an abstraction in English by specifying its required properties. For example, we can define a "tire" as a resilient covering for the rim of a wheel. This definition is a generic definition because it includes "tires" of many sizes, shapes, and materials. Similarly, we can use English to define an ADT; to define "stack" we define the semantics of "push" and "pop" when applied to a stack object.

Only part of this information can be expressed explicitly within a programming language: the intent and semantic properties of the ADT must remain implicit. For example, the fact that the push and pop operations for the stack ADT implement a last-in-first-out accessing pattern is not expressible in any way except a comment. What we can express in a program are abstract functions (function headers without accompanying bodies) and abstract domains (domain names without accompanying data type definitions). For example, Exhibit 15.9 defines the ADT `array_stack` in an Ada-like language. An `array_stack` is an array-based data structure capable of storing multiple data items, together with the functions Push and Pop that implement a LIFO accessing pattern, the function Top that returns a copy of the most recently pushed item, and predicates Empty and Full.

We can make a specific implementation of an ADT in an ST#3 language by defining a specific data type to represent each abstract domain in the ADT, and a specific function to carry out each abstract function. For example, to make a specific implementation of a stack, we first define a specific data type to represent the stack. Functions "push" and "pop" are then defined that operate on that type to carry out the semantics defined for the ADT operations. We are able to define a stack of 100 characters in Pascal (to be represented by an array [1..100] of char), or a stack of integers (to be represented by a linked list of integers). However, we cannot define the abstract data type itself in these languages.

This is because, by definition, an ST#3 language has disjoint (nonoverlapping) types.[6] There is no general provision for talking about groups of types or defining a function that would apply to more than one type, or to a partially unspecified type. A function definition in an ST#3 language specifies the types of its arguments, so every ST#3 function depends on a previously defined specific type and cannot be written in a general way to operate on a generic domain. Thus a program in Pascal that uses two kinds of stacks requires two sets of type declarations and two separate but nearly identical definitions of each stack function.

Many Pascal students have asked why they could not make one set of definitions for a stack and its operations, then have it automatically applied to stacks of any kind of object. The best that can be done in Pascal is to write a set of stack definitions and store them in a source code library. To use the stack code, the source code must be edited to change the type definitions, then compiled. The language does not support compiled modules with type flexibility, and it does not even provide an automated way to do the editing job.

---

[6]Variant records and unions are inadequate support for generic types.

Exhibit 15.9.   Definition of the ADT "`array_stack`".

We define the abstract data type `array_stack` by declaring a parameterized generic domain and listing the relevant abstract functions. We use syntax modeled after Ada, but extended by several constructs that are not supported by Ada.

```
ADT array_stack Begin
    ParamType Stack(
        T:type;               -- Type of data objects to be stored.
        L:integer);           -- Maximum number of simultaneous objects.
    Function Top(
        S: in Stack)          -- Stack itself is unchanged.
        return T;             -- Returns copy of most recently pushed data.
    Function Pop(
        S: in out Stack)      -- Top item is removed from S.
        return T;             -- Returns most recently pushed data.
    Function Push(
        item:  in T,          -- Store item at top of stack.
        S: in out Stack)
        return Boolean;       -- Return true if push executed successfully.
    Function Full(
        S: in Stack )         -- Stack itself is unchanged.
        return Boolean;       -- Return TRUE if S.store is full.
    Function Empty(
        S: in Stack )         -- Stack itself is unchanged.
        return Boolean;       -- Return TRUE if stack contains no data.
End ADT array_stack;
```

When Ada was developed, a facility was included to automate this tailoring process. A set of definitions called a *generic package* can be defined in Ada, which contains the type declarations and function definitions for an abstract data type such as "stack". These definitions are written in terms of a type parameter. Later, the package must be instantiated with a concrete type during the first phase of compilation. This process generates ordinary program code that is ST#3, and it is then compiled. Generic packages for standard algorithms on commonly useful data structures can be included in libraries. These are called in and instantiated when needed. The need to write and debug new code is minimized. However, the end product is the same as if the programmer had written fully concrete code in the first place. Thus Ada's generic facility adds real convenience but not significant flexibility to the language.

Chapter 17 describes Ada generic packages and examines the support for data abstraction in more modern languages such as Miranda and C++, which permit the user to define generic types and functions over these types. Chapter 17 also presents a fourth definition of "strong typing" which admits automatic type checking for these nonhomogeneous types.

15.3 DOMAIN IDENTITY: DIFFERENT DOMAIN/ SAME DOMAIN?

15.3.1 Internal and External Domains

There is generally not a one-to-one relationship between type names and distinct domains. Most languages use type names to define domain membership, but a translator may implement two type names as the same domain or as distinguishable domains. It is possible in some languages to define two different type names which have identical semantics and, therefore, denote the same domain, and also to define different semantics for structurally identical types, so that they become distinct domains.

We must first distinguish between external domains and internal domains. *External domains* are those that occur in the programmer's application area. *Internal domains* are the semantic groupings of objects or types that are recognized and maintained by a language translator. These are not necessarily the same thing. Two types, A and B, form *distinguishable internal domains* if the translator implements different semantics for them. Operationally that means that some function is defined differently for type A than it is for type B. Two distinguishable domains are *independent* if no function defined for one is applicable to objects from the other, and vice versa. If this property holds in one direction but not in the other, we say the domains are *semi-independent*. If the implementations of two external domains have the same internal semantics, we say they are *internally merged*.

15.3.2 Internally Merged Domains

Some languages maintain no semantic distinction among domains that have the same internal representation. For example, in FORTH and C, integers, truth values, and characters are represented identically. In these languages, an integer *is* a truth value *is* a character, and a truth value or a character *is* an integer. A value belonging to any one of these external domains can be used in a context appropriate for any other one. An integer operation may be applied at will to a truth value or a character. No "conversion" process is needed to go between these domains.

This is one of the very convenient aspects of C: the translator lets the programmer decide whether it is meaningful to use a truth value as if it were an integer, and thus does not prevent the programmer from exploiting an implicit relationship between domains [Exhibit 15.10].

Of course, one could also claim that this kind of code is obscure and ought to be well documented if it is written at all. In fact, C and FORTH programmers use these tricks frequently, and the very commonness of such code reduces the difficulty of understanding it.

A more serious cost associated with internally merged domains is that the translator has no way of knowing which objects belong to which external domain, and so cannot help the programmer avoid unintended and meaningless operations. This is illustrated by the very strange C code in Exhibit 15.11. Let us trace the execution of this odd expression:

- The ASCII codes for 'a' and 'b' are compared. 'a' is not greater than 'b', so the answer is FALSE, which is represented by 0 (4 bytes).
- The character 'c' (one byte) is interpreted as an integer. Its ASCII code, 99, must be lengthened to 4 bytes to match the length of the integer 5.

- We add 5 to 99 giving 104 (4 bytes).
- The truth value, 0, from item (1) is interpreted as an integer and divided by 104, giving 0 (4 bytes).
- This integer 0 is now interpreted as the truth value FALSE, and used in the "if" test, selecting the else clause.
- Finally, we store 1 in the variable t.

Exhibit 15.10.   Merging the domains "truth value" and "integer".

Neither C nor FORTH distinguishes between integers and truth values. There are many situations in which this is convenient. Programmers using C and FORTH commonly use the "tricks" below to shorten their code. (The examples are written in both languages.)

Using a truth value as an integer.   Your process compares two input streams, item by item, and gives a TRUE answer if the items are not equal. You wish to count the number of nonmatching item pairs. This is easy: just "add up" the TRUE values. (TRUE is represented by 1 in C and by −1 in FORTH.)

> C: difference_count = difference_count + (item1 != item2);
> FORTH: item1 item2 = NOT difference_count @ + difference_count !

Using an integer as a truth value.   You wish to terminate a loop when the input variable, an integer, equals zero. Easy! Remember that 0 is the representation for FALSE, and write:

> C: While (input_variable) { ⟨process⟩ } ;
> FORTH: BEGIN input_variable @ WHILE ⟨process⟩ REPEAT

Exhibit 15.11.   Many misinterpretations!

The "/" and the "+" are nonsensical operations. They would be flagged as errors in Pascal, but they are accepted in C because integers, characters, and truth values belong to one internally merged domain.

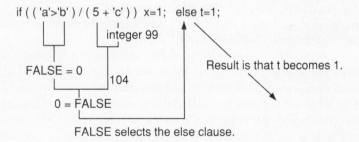

FALSE selects the else clause.

This example illustrates the variety of ways that C values can be interpreted, but it is so artificial that it does not provide a convincing example of the cost of internally merged domains. However, this kind of domain merging does frequently lead to errors, especially for programmers who commonly use more than one language. Exhibit

15.12 illustrates a common and galling error that most former Pascal programmers make when they begin to write code in C.

Exhibit 15.12.   The bane of the former Pascal programmer.

The Pascal comparison operator is "=", but C uses "==" for comparison and "=" for assignment. Intending to repeat a process many times, as long as the variable named "a" remains equal to zero, the absentminded programmer writes:

```
do ⟨process to be repeated⟩ while ( a=0 );
```

Unfortunately, this process will be executed exactly once. The first time the expression a=0 is evaluated, the value zero will be stored in the variable a, and also returned as the value of the assignment expression. The while test interprets the 0 as FALSE and terminates the loop.

Moreover, when the perplexed programmer looks at the value in a, she or he will see the number zero and be unable to understand *why* the loop did not repeat!

As a general rule, the language that has distinct internal domains representing distinct external domains is easier to learn and easier to use. A compiler with full type checking is a powerful ally in the battle to debug a large program. The price paid for this assistance is that the programmer must explicitly indicate domain conversions.

15.3.3   Domain Mapping

An existing domain may be used to implement a new domain by mapping the elements of the new domain onto the elements of the old. This produces two domains with a common implementation but dissimilar semantic intent. For example, one could represent the imaginary numbers by mapping each imaginary onto the corresponding real and leaving implicit the fact that each one represents that real multiplied by i.

When a new domain, D', is implemented by mapping it onto an old domain, D, we say that every element of D' is *represented by* an element from D. In this case, the object from D' can be "converted" into an object from D, or vice versa, by changing only the domain identifier attached to the object. The physical form of the value does not need to be changed. The same domain, D, may be used to implement other domains also, making a many-to-one relationship between implemented domains and an implementing domain [Exhibit 15.13].

Although a D-object is structurally identical to a D'-object, different sets of functions are probably appropriate for D and D'. For example, bit strings are sometimes used to represent both integers and arrays of switches. Division is meaningful for integers but not for switches, and masking operations may be meaningful for arrays of switches but not for integers. Concatenation might be a meaningful operation for bit strings that are neither integers nor switches. Thus the semantic intent of the object's domain, not just its physical representation, determines what operations are meaningful. The intent should be considered before applying a function to the object.

Mapped Domains with Distinct Identities

The primitive types in Pascal demonstrate domain mapping where all domains have separate identities. Several Pascal primitive types are actually represented in the computer as integers [Exhibit 15.13]. Pascal also permits the programmer to define an "enumerated type". To do this, the programmer enumerates names for the elements of a finite type, and the type is implemented by mapping the elements, in the order given, onto the integers.

Exhibit 15.13.   Domains mapped onto integers in Pascal.

Semantic Intent	Typical Implementations
integer numbers	full-word bit strings
alphabetic characters	full-word integers (8-bit if packed)
machine addresses	integers 0 .. virtual memory size
truth values (false, true)	integers (0=false, 1=true)
enumerated type	integers 0 .. cardinality of the type

The computer hardware itself defines the mappings for integers, addresses, and characters. Integers are defined by the operation of the machine language add, negate, and comparison instructions. Addresses are mapped onto the integers by the memory mapping hardware of the machine; one computes the next machine address in a sequence by using the integer "add 1" machine instruction. The mapping from characters to bit strings is defined by the I/O devices, most of which implement a common character code such as ASCII.

Truth values are mapped onto bit strings by a language implementor. "False" is virtually always represented as a string of 0 bits. Anything nonzero is therefore taken to be "true". When a "true" value must be generated by the translator, most languages generate the string 00000001 with a number of leading zeros appropriate to fill a memory location. (Some translators generate a string of all 1 bits.)

Pascal defines primitive functions and procedures for these primitive domains. Although the representations of these domains are structurally compatible with each other, the primitive functions only accept arguments from the defined domain. A Pascal translator checks the declared data type of each argument against the declared domain of a function and enforces what is, ideally, the programmer's semantic intent. If the programmer wants to do some operation that would violate the type rules, he or she must first explicitly convert the argument to a different type.

15.4 PROGRAMMER-DEFINED DOMAINS

15.4.1 Type Description versus Type Name

In the historical progression from ALGOL, through C, Pascal, and Ada, to C++ and ML, types have become the basis for increasingly powerful semantic mechanisms and have been given increasingly clear semantics. Languages have supported programmer-defined types since the 1960s. During this time the relation between the type description, the type name, and the type's semantics have varied greatly. In the older languages, such as K&R C, a type name was no more and no less than a shorthand notation for the type description. All types with the same description were merged into one internal domain. In such a language two structurally identical objects belong to the same domain even if they were declared using different type names.

A more modern approach is to give meaning to the type name over and above the meaning of the type description. In such a language the programmer may use the type name to help express semantics. Thus the same type description may be associated with more than one type name to express semantically different types that happen to have the same representation [Exhibit 15.14]. The compiler can then use these differentiated type names to help the programmer achieve semantic validity. In this situation, type checking can catch errors that checking only for structural properties cannot detect.

Exhibit 15.14. Two types with the same description.

In writing a graphics program one might use two related but distinct types:

- A set of points in the Cartesian plane
- A set of points in the polar coordinate plane

Both of these types are normally represented by a pair of real numbers. In the Pascal type declarations below, both are given the same structure. The two type names will not be synonyms, since functions defined for one cannot be applied to the other.

```
TYPE cart_point = ARRAY [1..2] OF real;
     polar_point = ARRAY [1..2] OF real;
```

15.4.2 Type Constructors

Old languages had a fixed number of distinct domains. In modern languages, type constructors are provided to permit the programmer to define new domains. Each new domain may be, and normally is, bound to a new type name. The new type name can be used to declare objects that belong to the domain and to declare the domain of function parameters.

A *type constructor* is a keyword or syntactic construct whose use creates a new domain. Not all ways of declaring new types are type constructors. Type constructors are chosen by a language designer and vary greatly among languages. For example, "array" and "↑" are type constructors in Pascal but the analogous "[⟨dimension⟩]" and "*" in C do not construct domains. However, struct in C and the analogous record in Pascal are both type constructors.

Constructed Domains and Type Checking

When a programmer uses a type constructor in a type declaration, the declared type name is bound to the newly formed domain. Thereafter, other program statements can declare objects and function parameters in that domain by referring to the type name directly or indirectly [Exhibit 15.15].

Exhibit 15.15.   A type constructor in Pascal.

The keyword `array` is a type constructor in Pascal; each use of `array` builds a new domain. Here we construct a new domain and bind the name `BoxDimensions` to it. We use this type name to define a function, `vol`, that operates on `BoxDimensions`.

Giving a new name to a type does not construct a domain in Pascal. The type name `Tank` names the same domain as `BoxDimensions`.

```
TYPE   BoxDimensions = array [1..3] of Real;
       Tank = BoxDimensions;
VAR    p, q:  BoxDimensions;
       t:  Tank;
FUNCTION vol(d:  BoxDimensions):  real;
       BEGIN vol := d[1] * d[2] * d[3] END;
```

The function `vol` may be legally applied to variables p and q. The types match because p, q, and d were all declared to be `BoxDimensions`. This function may also be applied to t, since it was declared using the same instance of `array` as was `BoxDimensions`.

In an ST#3 language, a domain, D, created by a type constructor is *independent*; that is, it is functionally incompatible with all existing or future domains.[7] No functions may be applied to objects from D unless they are explicitly defined for D, and functions defined for D may not be applied to objects from any other domain. An object is type-compatible with a formal parameter if and only if both were declared to belong to the same domain.

Every occurrence of a type constructor constructs a different domain. If types $D1$ and $D2$ are declarations with identical type definitions containing a type constructor, $D1$ and $D2$ are incompatible. In some languages, a type constructor may be used in a variable or parameter declaration. This constructs a domain that is incompatible with everything because the new domain has no name, and other parts of the program are unable to refer to it. The only variables that can ever belong to this domain are those created by the same declaration.

Thus the variables p and q in Exhibit 15.16 have the same (unnamed) domain. Variables r and s have the same domain, structurally identical to the domain of p and q, but semantically distinct because they were declared with different uses of the type constructor `array`. No other variables or parameters can belong to the same domain as p and q, or as r and s. Specifically, variable v does not belong to the same domain as any of these other variables.

An object and a parameter belonging to different domains are incompatible, even if they have the same structural description. A type constructor, therefore, is never used to declare the parameters of a function: no variable could ever match the type of the parameter, and the function could never be called. In Exhibit 15.16, the function `NoGood` can never be called because the type of its parameter, t, can never match the type of any variable. Specifically, t is not in the same domain as p, r, or v, but belongs to a fourth domain with distinct semantics.

---

[7]In more modern languages, this incompatibility may be modified by rules for domain inheritance.

Exhibit 15.16. Incompatible domains in Pascal.

Four incompatible domains are constructed here, by using the type constructor `array`
four times. Each of the identifiers p, r, v, and t belongs to a different domain. The function
NoGood cannot ever be called because its parameter, t, is not in the same domain as any other
object.

```
TYPE  VitalStats = array [1..3] of real;
VAR   p, q: array [1..3] of real;
      r, s: array [1..3] of real;
      v   : VitalStats;
FUNCTION NoGood(t:  array[1..3] of real):real;
      BEGIN NoGood := t[1] + t[2] + t[3] END;
```

15.4.3 Types Defined by Mapping

Nonindependent Mapped Types

In some languages, a type defined by mapping does not construct a new, independent
domain. Rather, the new type name is an alternative way to refer to an existing domain. The `typedef` declaration in C is an example. It defines the new type name as a
synonym for its definition, which is often a structural description [Exhibit 15.17]. Although `typedef` does not create a new domain, a `typedef` declaration is useful in C
because the syntax for using `typedef` names is clearer and more convenient than the
syntax for using their descriptions.

Exhibit 15.17. Merged domains defined using `typedef` in C.

A point in a plane can be represented as a pair of real numbers. We define a record type using
the C type constructor `struct`. The identifier pt is called a *type tag* and can be used to refer to
the constructed domain.

We use `typedef` here to map three type names onto the domain pt: `polar_point`,
`xy_point`, and `twisted_point`. We now have four names by which we can refer to the same
domain, and they are used, below, to declare a group of type-compatible variables: pp, xp, tp,
and sp.

```
typedef struct pt {float c1, c2;} polar_point,  xy_point;
typedef pt twisted_point;
polar_point pp;
xy_point xp;
twisted_point tp;
struct pt sp;
```

C was one of the earliest languages developed that permitted the programmer
to declare new types. At that time, the relationships among the name of a type, its
representation, and its semantics were only partially understood. This is probably

why C has fewer type constructors than newer languages, and why `typedef` is not a type constructor.[8]

Pascal was developed at about the same time as C. Although Pascal does support several type constructors ("array", "record", "↑", and enumeration), it does not permit the programmer to define a mapped domain with distinct semantics. A new type, D', can be mapped onto an old type, D, as shown in Exhibit 15.18. Objects belonging to D' are compatible with functions defined for D, and objects of type D are compatible with functions defined for D'. The two external domains are merged into one internal domain. Exhibit 15.19 shows examples of function calls on three Pascal types that belong to the same domain.

Exhibit 15.18.   Merged domains in Pascal.

We declare two new type names (`LengthInFeet` and `LengthInMeters`) by mapping them onto the domain `Real`. These two types are synonyms for each other and for `Real`.

```
TYPE  LengthInFeet = Real;
      LengthInMeters = Real;
```

Exhibit 15.19.   Function calls with merged domains in Pascal.

Three variables are declared, one of each type defined in Exhibit 15.18. A new function, `FeetToMeters`, is defined for lengths. It accepts a length, in feet, and converts it to the corresponding length, in meters.

```
VAR r:  Real;
    f:  LengthInFeet;
    m:  LengthInMeters;
FUNCTION FeetToMeters( f:LengthInFeet):LengthInMeters;
    BEGIN  FeetToMeters := f * 12 * 0.00254  END;
```

These variables are fully type-compatible; they belong to the same internal domain. Real functions, such as "*" and "/", and length functions, such as FeetToMeters, can legally be applied to any combination of lengths and reals. The following function calls and assignments are all legal although those in the second row are semantically invalid.

```
r := FeetToMeters(f);       r := f          f := 3.89;
f := FeetToMeters(m);       r := m * 5.0;   m := f / 2.0;
```

In this situation, Pascal does not help the programmer to make the semantic distinction between variables that represent reals and lengths, nor between different kinds of lengths. The type names are full synonyms in all contexts, and the semantics of the two external domains are merged. The fact that the type definitions in Exhibit 15.18 are not type constructors can be attributed to the lack of full understanding of domains and mapping in the early 1970s.

---

[8]The `typedef` declaration was added to C after the language had been in use for some years.

The connection among domains, type names, and representations in Pascal and C is confusing. We may have one domain associated with more than one type name, and more than one domain associated with one structural description, as in Exhibit 15.14. The number of distinct domains is equal neither to the number of type names nor the number of different structures defined.

Mapped Types That Form Distinct Domains

The confusing connection among domains, type names, and representations was "cleaned up" in Ada. The type structure in Ada is richer than either Pascal or C. Ada permits the programmer to declare a type D', mapped onto D, but choose whether D and D' will be synonyms or name distinct domains. Ada provides two different declaration forms for using an old type to represent a new one.

The first form, marked by the keyword "subtype", creates a new name for part (or all) of the old domain [Exhibit 15.20]. The names become synonyms as they would in the corresponding Pascal [Exhibit 15.18] and C [Exhibit 15.17] declarations.

Exhibit 15.20.   Creating a compatible type name by mapping.

The new type name `length` is declared as a synonym for `real` or `float`.

Ada	`subtype length is float;`
Pascal	`TYPE length = real;`
C	`typedef float length;`

The second Ada form, marked by the keyword "new", creates a *derived type* [Exhibit 15.21]. A derived type is a new domain that is at least partially distinct from the old domain.

Exhibit 15.21.   An Ada derived type is a new domain.

The type name `new_type` will represent a domain that is only partially compatible with the domain named `old_type`.

```
type new_type is new old_type;
```

An issue arises with using a new domain that was created by mapping. If the new domain were completely incompatible with existing domains, no functions would be defined on it, and you couldn't define any! We must use existing function definitions to define the set of operations appropriate for the new domain.

The primitive operations of subscript, part selection, and dereferencing are defined for all domains that are constructed using the type constructors "array", "record", or "↑". Given an object, O, of a new domain, we can use these primitives to "extract" parts of O that belong to old domains. Then we can use the functions defined for the old domains to implement the primitive functions for the new domain.

We need a similar way to go from new domain to old for mapped domains. This could be in the form of a general casting operation, "REP", that would take an object of a new mapped domain and "extract" the object that represents it in the old domain. REP would be a compile-time operation, changing only the domain label and not the representation. An inverse cast, "MAKE", would also be needed to relabel values computed in the old domain as elements of the new domain. REP and MAKE are analogous to the Pascal functions ord and chr, but they describe the general relationship between a mapped domain and its representation, rather than the specific relationship between characters and integers.

Ada supports type casts between representing and represented types. A cast is called by putting the target domain name in front of the value to be relabeled. REP and MAKE casts are both written this way [Exhibit 15.22].

Exhibit 15.22.   Type casts in Ada.

The domain tonnage is derived from the domain float. Casts are predefined in Ada for derived types. Two casts are used here in order to permit mixed-domain arithmetic.

```
type tonnage is new float;
t1, t2:  tonnage;     -- Two variables of type tonnage,
ff :  float1;         -- and one of type float.
ff := 3.2;
t1 := tonnage( float(t2) * ff );
```

Derived types could have been defined in Ada as completely independent new domains, but they were not. One-way compatibility was retained. We summarize the compatibility rules here, for a new type T derived from an old type R:

- Literals of type T are written exactly like R literals.
- Functions predefined for type R can be applied to type T.
- Functions defined for type T cannot be applied to type R.
- A value of type R can be explicitly cast to type T, and vice versa.
- Such a cast *must* be done before values of types R and T can be mixed in an expression or an assignment statement.

These rules implement one-way semantic protection. Objects of new_type can use functions for old_type, but not vice versa [Exhibit 15.23]. The advantage of this partial compatibility is that the basic definitions for a new ADT can be a bit shorter, because explicit casts are not required. Literal values, also, don't need to be cast to the new type. The costs of this compatibility are that the Ada programmer must learn a complex set of type compatibility rules, and that the compiler is unable to detect half of the unintentional type errors. Further, after the basic functions for a new domain have been defined, those functions can and should be used *exclusively* in defining further operations. Compatibility with the old type is no longer needed or desirable, but it is still permitted by Ada. This seems to be a real defect in Ada's type system.

Exhibit 15.23. Domain compatibility rules in Ada.

Two new types are defined to be represented by floats. Length is a synonym for float, and distance is semantically distinct. Variables are defined of the three types.

```
subtype length is float;
type distance is new float;
flo:  float;
len:  length;
dis:  distance;
```

The following expressions are all legal (put is an output procedure predefined for floats).

```
flo := 8.1;          len := 8.1;          dis := 8.1;
flo := flo+2.0;      len := len+2.0;      dis := dis+2.0;
put(flo);            put(len);            put(dis);
flo := flo * flo;    len := len * len;    dis := dis * dis;
                     len := flo;
                     len := len + flo;
```

The following statements have type errors.

dis := flo;   An explicit type cast, as in: dis := distance(flo);
                         must be done before the assignment.

dis := dis + flo;   Mixed type arithmetic is not allowed. One operand must
                         be cast before the operation.

15.5 TYPE CASTS, CONVERSIONS, AND COERCIONS

In the previous section we mentioned the topic of type casts briefly [Exhibit 15.23]. Here we explore the nature of casts and also examine other kinds of conversion processes. We examine what happens to the physical type and the semantic properties of the converted object during the conversion. In Section 15.6, the type compatibility and conversion rules in a number of common languages are described in detail.

Conversion processes can be classified into two categories: conversions and casts. Processes in both categories change some property of their parameter. Both might be called for explicitly or invoked automatically. The words "cast", "conversion", and "coercion" are all in common use, but have fuzzy meanings.[9] We use all three terms, and give them distinct meanings. We define the terms briefly here and explain them at length in the following sections. A *type cast* is a change in semantic labeling involving one domain that is mapped onto another. A *conversion* is a change in the size, encoding, or reference level of an argument. A *coercion* is a conversion or a cast that is invoked automatically by the translator.

---

[9]The word "cast" is used in books about C to include all explicitly written casts and conversions.

15.5.1 Type Casts

Section 15.3.3 dealt with the domain relationship called "domain mapping", in which a new domain is implemented by setting up a correspondence between its members and members of some existing domain. Typically, the old and new domains are semantically unrelated. Several domains, D_1', D_2', etc., may all be mapped onto one representing domain, D. Mapped domains can thus form a tree-structured hierarchy [Exhibit 15.24].

Exhibit 15.24.   A hierarchy of mapped domains.

The following set of domains are all represented internally as floats, but they have different operations defined.

- Dimensions (but not distances or ages) can be multiplied to compute areas and volumes.
- Distances (but not ages) can be added to compute a total distance.
- Neither dimensions nor distances can be added to floats.
- Ages can be subtracted from each other to yield a float (age difference) and added to floats to produce another age.

The domains "length" and "age" were defined by mapping directly onto "float". Domains "dimension" and "distance" were defined by mapping onto "length". We have thus created this tree of domains:

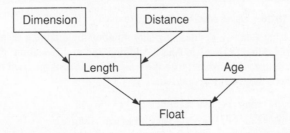

A *type cast* is a "conversion" between mapped domains. It is a curious thing: it leaves the bits of a value unchanged but alters its domain label, thereby changing the semantics of the object. Type casts convert values in a represented domain, D', to or from values in the representing domain, D. For example, binary integers are used to represent characters in Pascal. The function chr, which takes an integer and returns the corresponding character, is a cast; so is its inverse, ord [Exhibit 15.25].

The operation of casting happens entirely at compile time. A cast actually does nothing to its argument except relabel the argument value with a different type-object. The purpose of a cast is to communicate to the compiler that it is meaningful to use an object in what would appear to be the wrong domain context. This prevents the compiler from generating a type-error comment. The compiler does not generate run-time code for a cast operation—the physical representation of the cast argument is already appropriate for the target domain and does not need to be changed.

Exhibit 15.25.   Pascal casts for integer-mapped domains.

Represented Domain D'	Representing Domain D	Casting Functions	
		D' to D	D to D'
enumerated type	integers	ord	Not primitive
character	integers	ord	chr
addresses	integers	Prohibited	Prohibited
truth value	integers	ord	Not primitive

Once the basic functions and data structures of an ADT are defined, an application program works within the defined domains and rarely needs casts. However, the ability to cast a value between the represented domain and the representing domain can be very important in defining the basic ADT functions. For example, with the mapped domains "imaginary" and "real", one needs to use "real" operations in order to define "imaginary" arithmetic. To do this one needs to cast the "imaginary" operands to "real", do "real" arithmetic, then (in some cases) cast the result back to "imaginary" [Exhibit 15.26].

Exhibit 15.26.   Using casts in a mapped domain.

Using Ada, we define imaginary numbers by mapping them onto the reals. (The real domain is called "float" in Ada.) Addition and multiplication of imaginary numbers is then defined in terms of arithmetic on the reals. Explicit casts are used here to clarify the semantics, even where they could be omitted.

```
type imag is new float;
function "+" (q,r:  imag) return imag is
    begin return imag( float(q) + float(r) ) end "+";
function "*" (q,r:  imag) return float is
    begin return -1 * float(q) * float(r)  end "*";
```

Pascal places limitations on casting which make the language clumsy or inappropriate for systems programming. Certain important type casts are not supported at all. In one such case, we can write a simple function that converts integers to truth values [Exhibit 15.27]. But the casts for address to integer and integer to address are prohibited altogether and cannot be implemented *within* the defined semantics of the language. Thus any kind of address arithmetic is prohibited in Pascal, causing some systems programmers to avoid the language.

We say that a cast is a *promotion* if it moves from domain D to domain D', like chr. A *demotion*, such as ord, casts a value from D' to D. A *promotion cast* adds a layer of semantics to the object that it did not formerly have. With *demotion casts*, there is a loss of semantic information. The cast strips off the semantics of domain D', like an extra suit of clothes, exposing the underlying semantics of the domain D.

Exhibit 15.27.   Implementing a cast in Pascal.

If we accept the semantics that 0 represents FALSE and all nonzero integers represent TRUE, the following code converts an integer to a truth value:

```
FUNCTION IntToTv (k: integer): Boolean;
BEGIN if k = 0 then IntToTv := FALSE else IntToTv := TRUE END;
```

If D was itself a represented domain, another demotion cast would strip off another layer of semantics.

Casts Are Essential.

Both demotion and promotion casts are essential during the bootstrapping process that creates the functions for a new domain. Demotions permit operations defined for the old domain to be used on demoted members of the new domain. One must demote a value and operate on the underlying representation since there are, initially, no functions for the new domain. A promotion cast must be applied to the result of the computation to "lift" it back to the level of the new domain [Exhibit 15.28].

Exhibit 15.28.   Using casts in Ada.

Here we declare two mapped domains, length and area, and variables from the new and old domains:

```
type length is new integer;   -- Length and area form new domains.
type area is new integer;     -- Area and length are independent domains.
k:   integer := 15;           -- Declare and initialize integer k.
x:   length;                  -- x is a variable in the domain "length".
a:   area;                    -- a is a variable in the domain "area".
```

A type cast is called for by writing the name of the target type followed by parentheses enclosing an element from the original type. We may create a length-value out of an integer by using a promotion cast:

```
x := length(i)
```

A demotion cast must be used to define basic operations for lengths. Here we define an additional method for the primitive operator "*".

```
function "*"( x, y: length) return area is      -- Note a
begin
    return area(integer(x) * integer(y));       -- Notes b, c
end "*";
```

a. The function returns a value of type area.
b. The demotion cast, is used twice, integer(x) and integer(y), so that the meaning of length multiplication may be defined in terms of multiplication on the underlying domain, integer.
c. The promotion cast, area(z), is used to promote the underlying integer representation to the appropriate mapped domain. Note that length is not the appropriate domain.

After this bootstrapping process is finished, elements of the new domain can and should be manipulated only by functions defined for the new domain. It would be desirable then to "seal off" the mapping relationship and prohibit further demotion and promotion casts.

Casters Beware!

Casts are inherently dangerous operations; changing the meaning of an object should not be done lightly. It is legitimately done only in the process of implementing new domains, and in systems programming environments where the programmer is forced to deal with the underlying representations of objects in order to achieve acceptable efficiency.

Many languages use type coercion to change the type of an argument to the type expected by an operator. This is semantically meaningful if the two domains have related semantics, like integers and reals. But a type cast, by its nature, relabels a value with the identity of a domain that is usually unrelated, and thus changes the meaning of the value. A programmer writing an explicit cast presumably knows what she or he is doing and is taking responsibility for the meaning of the result. A flexible language must support explicit casts. However, a compiler has no understanding of the meaning of anything. It certainly cannot discern those contexts in which it is appropriate to change the meaning of an object.

A complication of promotion casts makes them particularly dangerous to invoke automatically. Many domains can be mapped onto a single representing domain. When a demotion cast is used on any of these mapped domains, it exposes the semantics of its single underlying domain. But a promotion cast might go in any of several directions. If a promotion cast is done by a compiler that cannot understand the code, it may utterly distort the meaning of a value. A combination of automatic demotion and promotion casts is likely to produce total nonsense, as in the PL/1 example in Exhibit 15.29.

Consider what has happened here. The second item relates a mapped domain to its underlying representation and maps truth values onto length-1 bit strings; '1'B represents TRUE and '0'B represents FALSE. These domains do not have the same semantic intent. When a demotion cast is made, the semantic intent of the mapped domain is lost. (In this example, when FALSE or TRUE is represented as a single bit and demoted to type "bit string", it causes the original intent to be "forgotten". It is no longer possible to tell that this bit string originally represented a truth value.

In the third and fourth steps, the single bit is promoted to integer and lengthened to the size of the integer c by padding it with leading zero bits. Lengthening is a semantically safe operation, but promotion is not. In the fifth step, the former truth value is used as an integer, even though this meaning is wholly inappropriate. The nonsense result of "a <= b <= c" is a result of the automatic invocation of semantics-changing casts, a demotion followed by a promotion.

15.5.2 Type Conversions

A *type conversion* changes one or more of the physical properties of the object: its size, its encoding, or its reference level. Examples of *encoding conversion* routines are the FORTRAN functions INT and NINT, which change a number from floating-point

Exhibit 15.29.   Mangled meaning in PL/1.

Let us examine the automatic conversions triggered by the expression: a <= b <= c

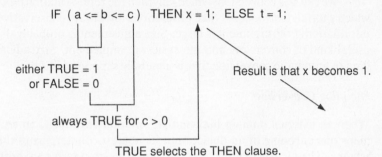

IF (a <= b <= c)   THEN x = 1;   ELSE t = 1;

either TRUE = 1
or FALSE = 0

Result is that x becomes 1.

always TRUE for c > 0

TRUE selects the THEN clause.

1. Compare a to b; the answer is a truth value, represented as a bit.
2. Demote the domain of the truth value to the domain "bit string".
3. Promote the domain of the bit string to the domain integer, to match the integer c and the definition of "<=".
4. Promote the length of the integer to the length of c.
5. Compare the resulting integer to c. As long as c is positive, the result will always be TRUE.
6. Use this TRUE in the "if" test, selecting the "then" clause.
7. Store 1 in the variable x.

---

encoding to binary integer encoding, using truncation and rounding, respectively. Changing a short integer to a long integer, or vice versa, is a *size conversion*. A *reference conversion* substitutes a value where an address or pointer is given (by fetching) or an address where a value is given.

We are often concerned whether a conversion preserves all the information in a value, or whether some information is lost. We use the term *conservative* for conversions in which all of the information originally present is retained in the converted form, and *information-losing* for conversions that do not preserve all information.

Size Conversion

Size conversion changes the number of bytes used to represent a value without changing the value's encoding or its semantics. Some modern machines support integers of three or four lengths, and floats of two lengths. Many languages reflect this hardware structure by supporting types with the same encoding and different sizes. This produces a flexible language that can be used to achieve both time and space efficiency. However, when operands of different sizes are mixed in an operation, their sizes must generally be adjusted to match.

For example, C provides integers of at least three lengths, 1 byte, 2 bytes, and 4 bytes. The 1-byte size, called "char", and the 2-byte size, called "short int" or "short", are needed to achieve acceptable storage efficiency. Moreover, short integers correspond to the hardware capabilities of personal computers, and so can be faster to fetch and faster in arithmetic operations than longs. Four-byte integers, called "`long int`" or simply "`long`", are needed to store many pointers and numbers greater than 32,767.

We call size conversions which lengthen the representation *promotions*, and those which shorten it *demotions*. Size promotions are always conservative; demotions lose information if the argument is large. Size adjustment is probably the safest and most useful kind of conversion, and the easiest to implement. Size adjustment is the only kind of automatic conversion that is generally supported in Ada.

Encoding Conversion

When an external domain has multiple internal encodings, an *encoding conversion* maps one encoding of an object onto its nearest counterpart in the other encoding scheme. The ideal is that unconverted and converted forms are both representations of the same external object. This is more or less true for the conversions integer-to-floating point and floating point-to-integer that are predefined in many languages. If the machine implementation of floating point uses more bytes than implementation of integers in the same machine, the conversion from integer to floating point is conservative; all integers can be represented exactly in a long enough floating-point encoding.

In the other direction, floating point-to-integer conversion is defined to give as good a mapping as possible, although information is necessarily lost if the number has a fractional part or a large exponent. The answer returned from a conversion can be either the integer value nearest to the real value (conversion by rounding) or the first integer value closer to zero than the real value (conversion by truncation). Some languages (for example, FORTRAN and Pascal), provide primitives for both versions, others provide only one. For example, Ada supports only conversion by rounding.

Reference Conversion

Let us define the *reference level*, or *ref-level*, of an argument to be the number of times a dereference operation must be applied to arrive at a pure value. Thus the ref-level of "3" is 0, and the ref-level of a pointer pointing to a variable that contains this "3" is 2 [Exhibit 15.30]. A *reference conversion* takes an argument of one reference level and returns a result with a difference reference level (but the same encoding and size).

A reference demotion takes a storage object and returns a program object. A reference promotion takes a program object and returns a storage object. Demotions are used all the time; promotions are rare.

15.5.3 Type Coercion

Conversion processes can be invoked two ways: explicitly or automatically. A call on a conversion function or a type cast that is written in the source code is an *explicit conversion process*. A *coercion* or *automatic conversion* is one that is invoked by the compiler but does not appear in the source code. Language definitions generally specify a set of possible coercions, which is a subset of the conversions that can be applied explicitly.

Exhibit 15.30.   Reference level in C.

We use C to define and initialize several objects that have integer encoding, long length, and various ref-levels.

```
#define   SAMPLE 50000L    /* "L" makes this a long integer, ref-level 0. */
long int  k     = SAMPLE, /* Ref-level 1:  a variable.  */
          *pk   = &k,     /* Ref-level 2:  a pointer.   */
          **ppk = &pk;    /* Ref-level 3:  a pointer to a pointer.  */
```

A translator will attempt to coerce an argument when the source code does not "make sense" as written, because the domain of some argument fails to match the domain of an operator or function applied to it. If one (or a series) of the permitted coercions will make the argument fit the context, it (they) will be invoked [Exhibit 15.31]. Coercions are used in many languages to change the encoding, the size, and/or the reference level of an argument.

Exhibit 15.31.   Coercions and explicit conversions in Pascal.

Line (a) contains two explicit type casts. The function ord casts its argument from the domain "char" to the underlying domain "integer".

The addition in line (b) will trigger a coercion from integer encoding to real (floating point) encoding. The compiler will invoke the encoding conversion because no machine instruction can add an integer to a real without conversion. Converting the value "makes sense" of the source code.

The right sides of lines (a) and (b) trigger reference coercion, to extract values from the variables c, Number, and DigitValue.

```
    Var c:  char;
        Number:  real
        DigitValue:  integer;
    DigitValue := ord(c)-ord('0');          { a }
    Number := Number*10.0 + DigitValue;  { b }
```

These two lines could appear in an input conversion routine that manually converts numbers in an ASCII input stream to floating-point encoding. (This is not the best way to do the job, though.)

When a coercion must be done because of mixed-type operands, a translator could theoretically choose to convert either argument to the type of the other. However, it is usually true that one direction is conservative and the other is not. A conservative conversion process is always preferred over the inverse information-losing process because it is unlikely to distort the meaning of the argument. This is particularly important when the translator (which does not and cannot understand the meaning of the code) is invoking the conversion. A programmer might find that the nonconservative conversion does exactly what is needed when it discards some information. But the translator has no way of knowing all of a programmer's intent, and it must always "play it safe" by choosing a conservative transformation when possible.

Size Coercion

When a language supports multiple sizes of types with the same encoding, keeping track of the size of objects and manually converting between sizes is burdensome and distracting. It becomes more burdensome as the number of related types grows. Such languages typically use size coercion (promotion) in any context where the argument sizes are mixed. Size demotion is not a conservative operation, so arguments are only coerced to the smaller size when a long value must be stored in a small storage object.

For example, numbers may be declared in COBOL to be from one to many digits long, with a decimal point anywhere, either within these digits or any number of places before or after the string of digits. A "PICTURE" clause which conveys all this information is included in each variable declaration [Exhibit 15.32]. COBOL's type flexibility is actually important in many business applications where the number of decimal places maintained before rounding is vital. But in order to use two numbers of different sizes in an arithmetic expression, one number must generally be converted to the size of the other. COBOL does this automatically; it would be a distracting and awkward process for a programmer to manage.

Exhibit 15.32. COBOL fixed-point size specifications.

PICTURE	Type Denoted
999	A three-digit integer.
9V99	A three-digit number with two decimal places.
999PP	A number with two implied trailing zeros, in the range from 100 to 99,900.
PP999	A number with a leading decimal point followed by two implied zeros, in the range from .00999 down to .00001.

Finally, a modern language must support the use and manipulation of character strings, either as part of the language or as part of a standard library. The string facility must conveniently provide for reading strings of varying lengths, storing them in variables, and for operating on strings of different lengths.

Storage can be handled in two ways. Dynamically typed languages (APL, SNOBOL) and BASIC store strings in a dynamically allocated string storage area and implement string variables by binding the variable name to a string value. This permits string length to vary as needed. Typed languages (C, Pascal, FORTRAN, Ada) preallocate storage for all variables and allocate fixed-size areas to hold strings. Strings stored in these areas are adjusted in length by truncation, marking the right end with a string termination symbol or padding the right end with blanks.

A language (or string library) should handle input, output, padding (lengthening), and truncation (shortening) operations automatically. Unhappily, many languages do not. Pascal, for example, forces programmers to write their own string input routines and manually pad or truncate strings to make them fit into the fixed-length spaces.

Encoding Coercion

Encoding coercions are important when a program deals with semantically related domains with different encodings. FORTRAN originally did not implement automatic conversions in arithmetic expressions. (That is, mixed type expressions were prohibited.) This prohibition was dropped in FORTRAN 77 because of popular demand. Experience showed that it was a terrible nuisance for programmers to concern themselves with explicitly converting a 1 to a 1.0 for a computation or a 4.0 to a 4 in order to use it as a subscript.

APL and BASIC go farther. They don't even require a programmer to make a distinction between integer numbers and real numbers but choose an appropriate encoding dynamically and coerce numbers when necessary.

Integer-to-real and real-to-integer conversions are both applied automatically in many languages (FORTRAN, C) but under different circumstances. The conservative conversion is always used in cases where arithmetic is done on operands of mixed type. This implements the intuitive requirement that information, and therefore meaning, should be preserved during all operations in order that the ultimate result be meaningful and as accurate as possible.

The information-losing conversion is only applied automatically when absolutely necessary, that is, when the programmer orders that a floating-point number be stored in an integer location. If the programmer did this purposely, she or he is likely to be using this assignment command as an easy way to invoke the truncation function. If the programmer did not realize this was a mixed type assignment, the conversion is likely to result in a program error.

One might claim that such an information-losing conversion function should never be automatically invoked and that a programmer should explicitly invoke an information-losing conversion if one is needed. This is, in fact, the rule adopted by Pascal. Ada goes even further—it does not, in general, invoke encoding coercions of any kind.[10]

Reference Coercion

A reference coercion happens when a program object is supplied in a context that requires a storage object, or vice versa, and the translator "makes good" the discrepancy. Automatic dereferencing, invoked by language translators in most languages, is a downward coercion; an address is supplied in a context that requires a value [Exhibit 15.35]. The translator fetches the required value from the given address. In simple contexts, such as the arithmetic statements in Exhibit 15.31, reference coercion is a real convenience and eliminates the explicit dereferences that would otherwise clutter the code. However, in linked list programs, which contain many situations in which automatic and explicit dereferencing must be mixed, reference coercion leads to endless confusion. It requires great care to write the correct combination of explicit and implicit dereferences in complex situations. The last two lines of code in Exhibit 15.35 illustrate the nonintuitive nature of expressions that combine explicit dereference ("*") and reference coercion.

---

[10]Curiously, there is one exception to this in Ada; an integer value will be coerced to a real type if it is multiplied by a real value.

As seen in Chapter 6, languages exist that do not do automatic dereferencing. However, it is so omnipresent that programming students tend to accept it as the only normal convention and forget that a conversion process is happening.

The opposite coercion, from value to reference, is rare, since it amounts to creating a nameless variable and storing a value in it. Under restricted circumstances it is done automatically in FORTRAN. All function parameters in FORTRAN are passed by reference, but a programmer *is* permitted to call a function with a pure value as the argument. In this situation FORTRAN must coerce the value to an address by storing it somewhere and passing the address to the function.

Although this is the extent of reference coercions in the familiar languages, other languages (EL1, Aleph) have been designed which apply a second reference coercion automatically when needed to fit the context. We are all familiar with the automatic dereferencing of variables to get values. These languages will dereference a pointer to get a value, if it fits the context.

15.6 CONVERSIONS AND CASTS IN COMMON LANGUAGES

This section gives a description of the type transformations that are implemented in COBOL and in five languages from the ALGOL family (FORTRAN, C, PL/1, Pascal, Ada). In all except Ada, if a conversion is conservative it will be performed automatically when operands of mixed type are used in an expression. A nonconservative conversion will only be performed when the programmer directs that a value be stored in a variable of the lesser type. Ada has more restrictive conversion rules.

15.6.1 COBOL

Both size and encoding conversions are performed automatically whenever they are necessary to perform a specified operation. In practice this means almost constantly, for the following reasons: first, objects of many sizes are usually declared; second, the encoding ASCII-string is used for most numeric variables, but the encoding packed-decimal or binary-integer must be used for arithmetic. Thus the language processor is constantly involved in adjusting sizes and changing encodings. The conversions it uses are normally conservative. An information-losing size conversion will only be performed when the programmer directs that a value be stored in a variable too small to hold it, in which case the value will be truncated.

Because COBOL does use automatic size demotion, it is possible to lose the high-order digit(s) of a number by attempting to store it in a field that is too short. When this happens in an arithmetic statement, an error indicator is turned on. The programmer may (or may not) choose to test the overflow indicator in the program. In a simple assignment statement (MOVE), though, no indication of error is given. The programmer must be careful to avoid this, as the language does not provide a reasonable level of error checking.

15.6.2 FORTRAN

The standard language supports a variety of types. In addition to the usual CHARACTER, LOGICAL, INTEGER, and REAL, there are two numeric types, DOUBLE (double-precision floating point) and COMPLEX. No conversions or casts are defined for the type LOGICAL.

Two explicit casts are provided as standard functions in FORTRAN 77. These are never applied automatically.

ICHAR(ch)   Demotes a character to the underlying ASCII code.

CHAR(i)   Promotes an integer in the range 0..127 to a character.

Only two primitive types share both semantics and encoding; thus only one pair of size conversion functions is built into the language. The conversion marked "*" is conservative.

* DBLE(r)   Promotes the size from real to double precision.

REAL(d)   Demotes the size from double precision to real.

Encoding conversions are more numerous because three distinct numeric types are available, integer, floating point (real and double), and complex. The conversions marked "*" are usually conservative.

INT(r)   Converts real, double, or complex to integer by truncation.

NINT(r)   Converts a real or double to an integer by rounding.

* REAL(i)   Converts an integer to single-precision floating point.

REAL(c)   Converts complex to real by discarding the imaginary part.

* DBLE(i)   Converts from integer to double-precision floating point.

* CMPLX(x)   Converts from integer or real to complex.

CMPLX(d)   Converts from double precision to complex.

15.6.3 Pascal

The standard language supports a few encodings that can occur in types of different sizes: character strings can be declared to be of any length, and character strings and Boolean arrays can be either packed or unpacked. String lengths are adjusted for comparison and assignment as necessary. Character strings and Boolean arrays are packed and unpacked automatically, when necessary, in a way that is quite transparent to the programmer.

Standard Pascal provides two types, integer and real, that implement domains with related semantics. The conversion functions accessible to the programmer are:

round(r) converts a real to an integer by rounding.
trunc(r) converts a real to an integer by truncation.

No function is provided to explicitly convert an integer to a real. Integer literals are also considered to be real literals, and the values of integer variables are converted automatically when necessary. Reals are never automatically converted to integers, because that is usually an information-losing conversion. This conversion must always be done explicitly.

Implementations of Pascal for microcomputers typically support two more types with integer encoding, a second size (so that both 2-byte and 4-byte integers are provided) and the type "unsigned integer" (frequently used to implement bit masks). Conversions are provided that promote short integers to longer ones. These are conservative operations and are applied automatically in some common implementations. Casts from unsigned to integer may also be performed automatically. When these are combined with the normally safe length changes, they can result in unintended changes of meaning, as is typical with automatically applied casts. It is in these areas that Turbo Pascal deviates most strongly from the standard language. Standard Pascal's semantic protection is lost in order to gain access to the underlying representation and convenience in handling mixtures of the three integer-encoded types.

15.6.4 PL/1

In order to understand Ada's restrictions on automatic type conversion, it helps to understand the effects of the generalized conversion rules in PL/1. Extensive, generalized, automatic conversion is supported, so that a PL/1 translator will convert any type to any type. The language designers perceived meaningful domain relationships between several pairs of primitive types (real—integer; bitstring—anything; numeric character string—number; bit—truth value; shorter object—longer object of same encoding). Conversions were defined for all of these relationships and are invoked automatically by the translator, singly or in series, whenever the programmer codes a mixed-type operation. Because the conversion from any type to any type is defined, expressions that are syntactically illegal in many other languages become legal in PL/1 and produce some surprising or nonsensical results [Exhibit 15.29].

Since any PL/1 object is type compatible (by conversion) with any other object, the language and translator cannot use domain checking to help the programmer achieve semantic validity. This is a great loss, and it far exceeds the value of automatic conversion mechanism. Coercions are convenient but not necessary, since explicit conversions could be used instead.

15.6.5 C

Basic Types in C.

C implements a large variety of types semantically related to integers. Integers may come in three lengths, short int (2 bytes in the ANSI C standard), long int (4 bytes), and char (1 byte). The type name int refers to either long or short, whichever is more efficient for the hardware.[11] The type name "char" means "1-byte integer"; the semantics of chars are not differentiated from the semantics of integers. Integer operations can be applied to chars and vice versa. The external domains "character" and "1-byte integer" are thus merged internally in C.

An integer of any of the three lengths may have a sign or not; unsigned objects are created by including the type modifier unsigned in the declaration. Taken together then, there are six integer domains with eight type names.

The unsigned and signed types form distinguishable but not independent domains. In some cases different code will be generated for values of the two varieties. In particular, the methods for promoting the length of signed and unsigned integers are different (details are given below). On the other hand, the machine instruction for integer "+" will be used by C to translate "x + y" whether these numbers are signed

---

[11] In K&R C, the lengths of short and long integers were not fixed. The only rule was that shorts could not be longer than integers and longs could not be shorter.

or unsigned. This will normally carry out the programmer's intent.[12] A general rule for the safe use of these types is to use signed integers for numeric computation and unsigned for everything else (especially bit masks and addresses). Because unsigned types directly reflect the bit-string nature of computer storage, we considered them to be the basic domain and assert that signed values are mapped onto the unsigned. Thus we consider an int-to-unsigned cast to be a demotion, and unsigned-to-int a promotion.

Floating-point numbers of two lengths are implemented: float (usually 4 bytes) and double (usually 8 bytes).

Truth values exist and are mapped onto the integers. They have no separate type name but are created by comparison operators and used by conditionals, as in any language. FALSE is represented by "0", TRUE by any nonzero integer. A "1" is generated when the system must create a TRUE value. Truth values do not form a distinguishable internal domain, as their semantics are not differentiated from the semantics of the underlying type, int.

Casts in C.

C does not distinguish between conversions and casts, although neither the processes nor their semantics are similar. Both are called "casts" in reference books, which are likely to explain that "a cast performs a type conversion". All conversions and casts may be explicitly invoked using the same syntax; the name of the target type is written in parentheses before the name or expression denoting the value that is to be changed [Exhibit 15.33].

Size Conversions in C.

Size promotions may be done explicitly and are also done automatically when operands of mixed lengths are combined. Also, short integers (int and unsigned) are promoted to integer, and floats are promoted to double[13] when they are passed as parameters to a function. Within the function, parameters may be declared using the promoted or the original, nonpromoted, type. When the latter is done, the argument will be automatically demoted again. Characters are promoted and demoted at the convenience of the translator, whenever they are manipulated.

An unsigned value (integer or character) is promoted by padding it with 0 bits. A signed integer is promoted by sign-extension; that is, by padding the high-order end with copies of the high-order bit of the value. This retains the sign of the object and its absolute value if it is an integer. It is thus the semantically correct way to promote a signed integer. Signed characters may be promoted by either method, depending on the translator. Values are demoted by truncating the high-order end, an inherently risky operation.

Encoding Conversions in C.

Two encoding conversions are implemented to convert floating-point numbers to integers and vice versa. These may be invoked automatically, or explicitly using the

---

[12]A nice aspect of two's complement encoding for negative numbers is that no special provision needs to be made for the sign during an addition operation.

[13]Non-ANSI only.

Exhibit 15.33. Syntax and semantics for casts and conversions in C.

```
int i;
unsigned u;
char c;
float f, g;
```

`(int)u`	Promote an unsigned to an int, no change in bit pattern. The result is undefined if the unsigned value is larger than the maximum int value. However, the operation will almost certainly be carried out by doing nothing! The high-order bit will simply be reinterpreted as a sign.
`(unsigned)i`	Demote an int to an unsigned, no change in bit pattern. The result is undefined for negative integers. However, the bits of a negative number will probably be unchanged, and the sign bit will be reinterpreted as a large positive power of 2.
`(int)c`	A size promotion from one byte to int (2 or 4 bytes).
`(float)i`	Convert from integer encoding to a floating point.
`(int)f`	Convert encoding from float to integer by truncation.
`(int)(f+g)`	Convert the sum from float to integer by truncation.
`i = (int)f+g`	Convert the float f to an integer by truncation, then convert it back to a float in order to add it to g. The result is a float; convert it to an int by truncation and store it in i.

"casting" syntax in Exhibit 15.33. The conservative conversion, from integer to floating point, is applied automatically when mixed type operands are used in an expression. This conversion might be automatically applied in combination with promoting the length of one of the operands.

Coercion in C.

One of the anomalies of C syntax can be best understood in terms of reference coercion. A pointer may be set to point at a variable by assigning the address of the variable to the pointer. One indicates that the address, not the value, of the variable is to be used by writing an "&" before the variable name. This inhibits the reference coercion that normally would have been applied to the variable. Pointers may also point to arrays and functions, but in these cases no reference coercion ever happens, and the "&" must not be written [Exhibit 15.34].

Pointers, explicit dereferencing, reference coercion, and inhibited coercion are all combined in Exhibit 15.35. Arithmetic operators in C operate on numeric values, not on addresses. A commonly useful complex data structure involves a pointer to an array of pointers which in turn index an array of data objects. Here we declare such a structure and show some code that uses the structure. Note that in C, adding two values is a legal operation but adding two addresses is not. Adding an integer to a pointer which represents an array index is also legal.

Exhibit 15.34.   Coercion complications in C.

Here we declare a variety of variables and pointers. The C syntax for setting a pointer to point at an object is shown on the fifth line. The "&" operator means "address of". Note that we do not use "&" on the last two lines.

`int k, *kk, *aa;`	Declare an integer and two pointers to integers.
`int a[5];`	An array of 5 integers.
`int f();`	This declares a function f (to be defined elsewhere) that returns an integer.
`int *ff();`	A pointer to a function such as f.
`kk = &k;`	Pointer kk is set to point at k, an integer variable.
`aa = &a[0];`	Pointer aa points at the first element of a, an integer.
`aa = a;`	This also makes aa point at the beginning of array a, because the name of an array is coerced to mean its first element.
`ff = f;`	Set ff to point at the beginning of function f.

Comments on the right in Exhibit 15.35 document the dereferences; each assignment statement is echoed, with code letters replacing the variables. The code "*E*" marks each explicit dereference, "*I*" marks each inhibited dereference, "*N*" marks contexts in which no dereference takes place, and "*C*" marks each variable where C applies reference coercion. Where multiple dereferences happen, a list of code letters is used; these should be read left-to-right.

Note that most ordinary expressions are marked by "*C*". For example, in the expression (`index1 < index2`), both pointer operands represent storage objects and both are coerced to pointer values which are then compared.

The C language does not provide for handling array values coherently, nor for handling pure values of function types. When the programmer writes an assignment involving an array or a function, the translator makes sense of the request by inhibiting the automatic coercion (dereference) that normally would have taken place on the right side of an assignment statement. This is a double negative situation: automatic inhibition of an automatic coercion results in no action at all. The result is that the address originally given is assigned to the pointer.

The expression on the last line of Exhibit 15.35 is daunting; its meaning can best be ascertained by making careful diagrams. This illustrates the complexity inherent in the C approach to references and coercion!

15.6.6   Ada *Types and Treatment of Coercion*

Basic Types in the Standard Type Definition Package.

As with C, a profusion of type definitions is included in the standard Ada package. These implement four external domains: truth value, character, integer, and real. The numeric domains are both implemented by several primitive types.

Exhibit 15.35.   Explicit dereference and reference coercion in C.

```
int j, k, m;                    /* Integers.  */
int value_array[100];           /* An array of integers.  */
int *scanner, *temp;            /* Pointers to integers.  */
int *index_array[10];           /* An array of pointers to integers.  */
int **index1, **index2;         /* Pointers to pointers to integers.  */
/* Initialize three pointers.  */
scanner=value_array;            /* N = N  */
index1=index_array,             /* N = N  */
index2=&index_array[10];        /* N = I  */
/* Make elements of the index array point at every tenth value.  */
while (index1 < index2)         /* C < C  */
/* Compare the values of the pointers, not the values they point at!  */
{   index1; scanner+=10;        /* N = C + 1 ;  N = C + 10 */
    *index1 = scanner;          /* E  = C  */
}
/* Input two integers between 0 and 9; set pointers to those slots.  */
scanf("%d%d", &j, &k);          /* I, I  */
index1=&index_array[j];         /* Set a pointer to jth index.  */
index2=&index_array[k];         /* N = I */
/* Swap two pointers in index_array.  */
temp=*index1;                   /* N = E,C  */
/* index1=*index2;              /* E = E,C  */
/* index2=temp;                 /* E = C /*
/* Add an int value to 3 times another int.  */
m= **index1 + *((*index2)+j)*3; /* N = E,E,C + E((E,C) + C) * N  */
```

All implementations support type integer, whose length, as in C, may vary from implementation to implementation. Types natural (like unsigned, range 0.. max_representable), positive (like natural but excludes 0), long_integer, and short_integer might also be implemented.

If the programmer simply specifies the range of values that she or he intends to store in a variable, the translator will choose an appropriate size for the variable. Note the similarity to COBOL. The practical reason for using this facility is illustrated by Exhibit 15.36. The range of values that can be stored in the variable line_no is fixed and does not depend on the implementation. In contrast, the ranges of the other three variables depend on the translator. Using the type declaration with a range clause, therefore, produces more portable code and is considered better programming style. An attempt to store an out-of-range number, such as 85, into line_no would cause the run-time error "CONSTRAINT_ERROR" (called an "exception" in Ada).

As with the integer types, reals are implemented by a group of types whose lengths depend on the implementation. These come in two varieties, *floating-point types* (like reals in Pascal and floats in C) and *fixed-point types* (as in COBOL). The primitive type names are float, long_float, and short_float [Exhibit 15.37].

Exhibit 15.36.   Ada integer type specification.

Here are two type declarations that will map two new domains onto some primitive integer type with an appropriate length.

```
type line_count   is range 0..66;
type fathom       is range -5_000 .. 0;
```

If we declare an object of one of these constrained types, we can be sure of the range of values that can ever be stored in it. The variable line_no can hold only values between 0 and 66.

```
line_no: line_count;
```

In contrast, these declarations for objects of the primitive integer types define variables whose range of values can vary from one implementation to another.

```
count:        integer;
population:   long_integer;
index:        short_integer;
```

Exhibit 15.37.   Ada real type specification.

Use of the keyword digits indicates that the new type is to be a floating-point type; delta indicates fixed point. The new type will be mapped onto a primitive real type with an appropriate length and encoding. The precision of a 4-byte floating-point value is about 7 digits; 8-byte floats provide about 16 digits of precision.

Floating-Point Declarations.

```
type mass       is digits 15;                      -- Needs double length.
type pressure   is digits 7  range 0.0 .. 25.0;  -- Single length ok.
```

For fixed-point numbers, the declaration completely determines the minimum size of the representation, as does a COBOL PICTURE clause. The delta clause specifies the required number of decimal places of accuracy, and the range clause shows the number of places needed to the left of the decimal.

Fixed-Point Declarations:

```
type dollars  is delta 0.01  range 0.0 ..  10_000.0;
type voltage  is delta 0.1   range -12.0 ..  24.0;
```

The variable dollars can take on values between 0 and 10,000. These values will be binary approximations to these values 0.01, 0.02, etc. Successive elements in the approximation must not differ by more than .01.

Truth values are supported: the Ada type Boolean is defined as the enumerated type (FALSE, TRUE). No physical or semantic relationship exists between Boolean and any other type and, therefore, no conversions or casts are defined for Booleans.

Characters, specifically the ASCII characters, are the other predefined enumerated type. The mapping between the ASCII character sequence and the integers 0..127 is defined, but no functions are defined to cast characters to integers or vice versa.

Ada **Conversions and Casts.**

Ada is the only language we have considered here whose designers made careful distinctions among the various ways an object of one type may be "changed" into an object of another type.

Ada provides type casts that move between a programmer-defined mapped type and its underlying type. These are for the purpose of defining the semantics of the mapped domain and are never applied automatically. No casts are defined that move between predefined mapped types and their representations.

Explicit conversions are not needed between different size objects of the same encoding. The "safe" conservative size promotions are used freely and automatically, without any involvement on the part of the programmer. Indeed, when using the recommended programming style the programmer may not even be aware which size of a primitive type is used to implement his or her objects. Ada will promote the size of the smaller object automatically when objects of different sizes are mixed in an expression.

Representation conversion functions are defined for all numeric types to convert among the three basic numeric encodings, integer, fixed point, and floating point. A conversion is invoked by writing the name of the target type like a function name, and writing the value to be converted as the argument of the function. Example: integer(123.9).

These representation conversions are available for explicit programmer use, but they are never used for automatic coercion. This greatly simplifies the problem of maintaining protected semantic domains. If conversions and casts are not applied automatically, the programmer's semantic intent cannot accidentally be violated. The cost of this simplicity is inconvenience to the programmer, since mixed-type arithmetic is, therefore, not predefined. The Ada programmer must either use explicit type casts to do mixed-type arithmetic, or explicitly define each operator for each desired combination of mismatched argument types [Exhibit 15.38]. At best, this is a nuisance; at worst, it causes time and space inefficiency to translate and store the code for these simple and repetitive function bodies.

Exhibit 15.38.   Mixed type addition in Ada.

We extend the operator "+" to operate on one integer and one float by supplying an additional computation method for "+".

```
function "+" (x:  integer; y:float) return float is
begin
    return (float(x) + y)
end "+";
```

Nonextensible Domain Relationships

We have seen that many languages have predefined domain relationships and will use these relationships when they invoke automatic conversions. PL/1 is the most permissive of the group, as it will automatically convert anything to anything. Ada is the most discerning of the group, and it will invoke only casts and length conversions automatically.

None of these languages permit programmers to limit or control application of a built-in relationship, and none permit them to define domain relationships of their own that will be automatically invoked. For example, a programmer could define a new representation for numbers and write a type conversion routine to convert integers to the new representation. But none of these translators will use the conversion automatically, the way the integer-to-real conversion is used.

Chapter 17 explores more modern and sophisticated type systems that permit the programmer to define more kinds of domain relationships.

15.7   EVADING THE TYPE MATCHING RULES

Type checking is an immense aid to the programmer. The more strict the type rules are, the fewer stupid mistakes and oversights will go undetected. The cost of this protection, though, is inflexibility. Occasionally a programmer needs to perform an operation that breaks the rules. Applications that can use such flexibility include conversion of integer to floating point and efficient computation of a hash index.

Users do not normally write integer-to-floating-point conversion routines because compilers normally supply them as primitive functions. A systems programmer, though, needs a language that will permit her or him to deal with hardware-dependent number representations. The bits of an integer value must be tested, shifted, and masked during the conversion process. The value starts out as an integer, ends up as a float, and is nothing recognizable in between. A systems programming language needs the flexibility to refer to this object as both an integer and a float. Let us say that the number being converted must have a *dual type*.

Another example of the use of dual-typed objects is hashing. The intent of a hash function is to generate a random-looking but repeatable integer within a specified range. Think of the argument to the hash function as a bit pattern. Hashing should scramble these bits so that the various inputs generate uniformly distributed integers as outputs. An easy way to do this is to apply an operation that is normally meaningless for the data and take the resulting scrambled bits. For example, adding the right and left halves of a character string using integer addition would randomize its bits in a repeatable, efficient, and possibly useful way.

Languages that are ST#3 (all objects are typed, types do not overlap, and all function calls are type checked) do not let a program do such operations in a straightforward way. Many, however, provide declaration forms that function as an "escape hatch" by which the programmer can get around the normal typing restrictions. By using such an escape hatch, a programmer declares that a normally meaningless operation is meaningful in a program. These declarations bind multiple names (with different types) to a single storage object or to part of an object. This gives the programmer a way to circumvent restrictions imposed by the type checking system of the translator.

When doing this kind of operation, it is up to the programmer to make sure that the result is semantically valid. Further, any time a program depends on a particular underlying representation, and exploits that representation in a computation, it becomes nonportable code. Different compilers and different machines use different representations. An obvious example is the order of two bytes in the representation of a short integer. On an IBM PC, they will be arranged low-order, high-order. But on a Macintosh, they will be high-order, low-order. Any code that depends on the order of these bytes is nonportable.

Examples are given here in several languages of declarations that can bind dual types to a single object.

FORTRAN.

The EQUIVALENCE declaration is an entirely unrestricted way to map one object onto another. No restrictions are placed on the relative sizes of these objects, or on the relative positions of their beginning bytes. EQUIVALENCE is used in a very restricted way in Exhibit 15.39 to associate two types with one variable. Lines (a) and (b) of Exhibit 15.39 declare four names: a real, an integer, a one-dimensional integer array, and a two-dimensional integer array. In line (c) we use EQUIVALENCE to map the real variable Z and the integer variable INTZ onto the same storage location.

Exhibit 15.39.   EQUIVALENCE in FORTRAN.

EQUIVALENCE may be used to bind an additional name and type to any variable or any part of a subscripted variable. (The letters on the right relate each declaration to its explanation.)

```
REAL Z                          (a)
INTEGER INTZ, M1(100), M2(4,25) (b)
EQUIVALENCE (INTZ, Z)           (c)
EQUIVALENCE (M1(1), M2(1,1))    (d)
```

The following pairs of lines refer to the same storage locations:

```
X = Z         Copy the dual-type value into a real variable.
K = INTZ - 1  Interpret the dual-type value as an integer and subtract 1.
K = M1(29)    Copy an array item into K.
K = M2(1,8)   Does the same thing as the line above.
```

Note that the subscript in the last line is (1,8) rather than (2,4) because FORTRAN arrays are stored in column-major order, not row-major order like most other languages.

Line (d), similarly, maps the two arrays onto the same space. These two arrays have a different number of dimensions but an equal total number of elements. We now have two names for the same array, allowing us to refer to it using either linear or two-dimensional subscripts.

COBOL.

The REDEFINES declaration is like EQUIVALENCE except that the original object and the redefined type are required to be the same size. The redefinition must immediately follow the original declaration.

Pascal.

In FORTRAN, we declare two variables, then say, as an afterthought, that they are one and the same object. This serves the purpose of attaching two types to an object but certainly does not implement the abstraction "dual type". In Pascal, we can explicitly declare a type with two meanings, then use it to declare variables.

This is done with a nondiscriminated variant record. The common portion of the variant record and the tag field are omitted altogether, producing a record that consists entirely of two or more variant parts. Outside of the context of Pascal, this kind of dual type is called a *free union type*. It is impossible to tell, at run time, what the semantics of a nondiscriminated variant object is supposed to be. A program may use an object as first one type, then another, without using any conversions or casts.

The examples used above for FORTRAN EQUIVALENCE are rewritten in Exhibit 15.40 in Pascal as nondiscriminated variant records. Analogous type declarations are given for an integer-real variable (line b) and an array that can be accessed using either one or two subscripts (line c). The Pascal variant record syntax requires declaration of an enumerated type (line a) with the correct number of variants.

Exhibit 15.40.   Variant records in Pascal.

```
TYPE TwoVariants = 1..2;                          {a}
     IntReal = RECORD CASE TwoVariants OF         {b}
                    1:  (IntName:  integer);
                    2:  (RealName:  real );
               END;
     OneDim  =   ARRAY [1..100] OF integer;
     TwoDim  =   ARRAY [1..4, 1..25] OF integer;
     DualDim =   RECORD CASE TwoVariants OF       {c}
                    1:  ( vector:  OneDim );
                    2:  ( matrix:  TwoDim );
               END;
```

Exhibit 15.41 shows examples of the use of these records to implement dual-type objects. We declare an IntReal variable, R, and a DualDim array, A. When R is used in a context that requires a real number, we refer to "R.RealName". In an integer context we write "R.IntName". Similarly, A.vector[3] and A.matrix[1,3] refer to the same location.

C Has Two Escape Routes.

In C, the union type constructor builds a free union type, like the nondiscriminated variant record in Pascal. The syntax for the union is similar to but simpler than the Pascal syntax for variant records. Exhibit 15.42 shows how the union type constructor can be used in C to accomplish the same goal as the FORTRAN code in Exhibit 15.39 and the Pascal code in Exhibit 15.41. Type declarations are given (line 1) for an integer-real variable and (line 4) for an array that can be accessed using either one or two subscripts.

- In line 1, type `int_real` is defined to be either a long integer or a floating-point number. Enough storage will be allocated to store whichever variant is longer. (They are often the same length.)
- Line 2 creates an object, `r`, of type `int_real`. To access it as a long integer we use the name `r.int_name`. To access it as a float we use the name `r.real_name`.
- Line 3 defines a type named `dual_dim` that can be either a one- or two-dimensional array. In either case, it has 100 integer elements.
- Line 4 declares an object, `a`, of type `dual_dim`. We may access this array with either one or two subscripts, thus: `a.vector[k]` or `a.matrix[m][n]`.

Exhibit 15.41. Use of a Pascal nondiscriminated variant record.

```
VAR R: IntReal;
    A: DualDim;
    X: Real;
    K: Integer;
X = R.RealName        Copy the dual-type value into a real variable.
K = R.IntName - 1     Reinterpret dual-type value as integer; subtract 1.
K = A.vector[29]      Copy the second array item into K.
K = A.matrix[2,4]     Does the same thing as the line above.
```

Exhibit 15.42. Union data type in C.

```
typedef union {  long int_name;
                 float real_name;}  int_real;         /* 1 */
int_real r;                                            /* 2 */
typedef int one_dim [100];
typedef int two_dim [25][4];
typedef union {  one_dim vector;
                 two_dim matrix;}  dual_dim ;         /* 3 */
dual_dim a;                                            /* 4 */
```

Interestingly, the `union` type constructor is not the only way, or the easiest way, to create a dual-type object in C. This same end can be achieved by making two pointers (an integer pointer and a float pointer) point at the same object [Exhibit 15.43]. When the program needs an int, it can access the object through the integer pointer. To get a float, it can use the float pointer.[14] This is demonstrated in Exhibit 15.43. Here we allocate one storage object, named `k`, and make two pointers, `plong` and `pfloat`, point at it. Both pointers are initialized to point at `k`.

Any pointer in C can be cast to any other pointer type. This causes no change except a relabeling of the domain of the pointer. Specifically, a pointer cast does not convert the representation of the object to which the pointer points.[15]

---

[14]This "trick" is the basis of the object-oriented function dispatching in C++.

[15]The explicit cast on the initialization is not necessary at all in many older C implementations, and it is used only to avoid a warning message in newer compilers. The code would compile, run, and produce the same answer without the cast.

Exhibit 15.43.   Using pointers in C to attach two types to an object.

In C, long integers and floats are usually the same length, so we use these two types to create a dual-type object, k. Then we compute a hash function by referring to k first as, a float, and then as an int. We store a float value into k using pflot, and take it out using plong. This does not cause a representation conversion. Applying integer division to the misinterpreted value will not cause a representation conversion either. The result is scrambled bits; it is complete nonsense to divide a float value by an integer. Thus we have "hashed" the original number.

```
#define TABLESIZE 1000
long int j, k;
long int *plong=&k;
float *pflot = (float*)(&k);

*pflot = 3.1;              /* Put a floating-point value into k. */
j = *plong % TABLESIZE;   /* Apply mod to k to calculate a value between
                             zero and the size of the hash table.  */
```

The programmer who uses this coding trick must do so carefully; any code that casts the type of a pointer, or depends on the representations of two types to be the same length, is nonportable.

Ada Closes the Loopholes.

The designers of Ada put a high value on designing a semantically "safe" language, that would be wholly and completely ST#3. Free union types and unrestricted casts are ways to evade the constraints imposed by strong typing, and they are not permitted in Ada.

Ada does support type casts, specifically, those necessary casts between types that are related by mapping. Type conversions are also supported between pairs of numeric types such as integer and real. These conversions must be invoked explicitly, using the same syntax as for type casts. But, unlike C, Ada does not support unrestricted casts from any type to any type. Thus the pointer trick will not work in Ada.

This surely increases both the readability and the portability of Ada programs. Type changes must be explicitly stated, eliminating confusion about intent. By eliminating free union types, access to the actual bit-level implementation of Ada objects is shut off, forcing programmers to write implementation-independent code. The cost is that flexibility to do some useful things is lost. The advantage is more reliable code.

EXERCISES

1. What is a domain?
2. How were implicit domains represented in early computer languages?
3. What is a predefined domain? Which ones were supported by the original FORTRAN? What determined the domain of each variable?
4. How did ALGOL enrich the domain structure of previous languages?
5. Why is "typeless" sometimes used as a synonym for "dynamically typed" language?
6. When is the domain of a variable tested in a dynamically typed language? Why is it tested? Why is it tested at that time?

7. Can function applicability be controlled in dynamically typed languages? Explain.

8. Why can early C be considered a weakly typed language?

9. Why were domains given increasingly important roles as programming languages developed?

10. What is a subrange declaration? Why is it useful?

11. How has Ada enhanced the use of domains beyond Pascal?

12. What is type checking?

13. Briefly define strong typing, and explain how it can be, at the same time, a boon and a burden.

14. How has the definition of "strongly typed language" evolved?

15. What is an ADT? Why can't we define an ADT in C or Pascal?

16. What is an external domain? Internal domain?

17. What are internally merged domains?

18. What are the problems associated with internally merged domains?

19. When a new domain has been mapped onto an old one, is the semantic intent of the two domains identical? Why or why not?

20. Name two domains whose semantics are totally different, even though they are both sometimes represented as integers. Give an example of two values that might be represented by the same integer.

21. Why is Pascal considered a strongly typed language? Explain.

22. What is a "type constructor"? Give an example. How does a type constructor permit the programmer to define new domains?

23. Why are some domains which have the same structural description considered incompatible in Pascal?

24. What is the role of a `typedef` declaration in C?

25. How does Ada improve upon the type structure found in C and Pascal?

26. What is a type cast? Conversion? Coercion? Give an example of each in a language that is familiar to you.

27. For each of the following kinds of type "conversions", say whether the original and converted objects represent the same thing and whether the representation (bit pattern) is changed.

    a. integer to real
    b. the result of an addition used as a truth value
    c. long integer to short integer

28. Give and explain an example of automatic type conversion destroying the semantics of an object. The example may be drawn from any language that uses automatic conversion, but please say what language you are using.

29. What is an encoding conversion? Size conversion? Reference conversion?

30. Name two domains that contain some elements that have the same meaning. As an example, show a pair of values that correspond.

31. Explain the following statement: A conversion involves a run-time computation, but a cast happens entirely at compile time.

32. A data value in one domain is changed to a corresponding value with the same (or similar) meaning in a second domain. Is this a conversion or a cast?

33. Consider the Pascal statements given below. What semantic action is implicit in this fragment?

```
jj:  integer;

ff:  real;
begin
    ff := 3.0
    jj := 1;
    ff := ff + jj;
end
```

34. Would the following code in Ada (analogous to the Pascal code in question 33) be legal? Why or why not?

```
rr:  float := 3.0;
jj:   integer := 1;
begin
    rr := rr + jj;
end
```

35. What is the difference between a promotion and demotion cast?

36. Why are casts considered dangerous operations?

37. Consider these equivalent expressions, where b is an integer:

```
In APL:  8 > b > 3
In C or Pascal:  3 < b < 8
```

The Pascal expression causes a compile-time error. What is it?

38. The APL and C expressions in question 37 will compile and run without errors. Evaluate the expression in either language using the value b = 2. What semantic distortion is committed by the translator that causes the result to be different from the programmer's apparent semantic intent? Why does it not produce a type error in these languages?

39. APL objects retain their type tags on the stack, and data types are checked by all primitive operators (unlike FORTH). Nonetheless, because statement labels are mapped onto integers, APL will sometimes execute code that is semantic nonsense and would be identified as a type error in other languages. Give an example of code that is legal in APL but that computes nonsense. Explain briefly what semantic error is being made. (Note: The fact that identifiers do not have types is not a semantic error.)

40. Explain what the semantic problem can be when a language applies two-way automatic conversion between a user-defined data type and the primitive data type used to represent it.

41. Explain or give an example of one way that C will permit a programmer to make a semantically absurd calculation.

42. Describe or give an example of a situation (other than that described in answer to questions 37 and 38) that would cause a compile-time error in Pascal but that would be legal at compile time in C.

43. Describe or give an example of a situation that would cause a run-time error comment in Pascal but that would not be considered to be an error in C.

44. Give an example of an error that Pascal cannot identify at compile time but will identify at run time. Why can't this error be identified at compile time?

45. What is meant by a conservative conversion?

46. When does a translator attempt to coerce an argument?

47. Why is size coercion essential in the use and efficiency of computer languages?

48. When are encoding coercions used?

49. In what sense is automatic dereferencing a downward coercion?

50. Why is it sometimes necessary to evade type compatibility rules?

51. Give an example of a "loophole" in a strongly typed language.

52. How have Ada designers created a semantically "safe" language?

53. Because FORTH objects lose their types when they are put on the stack, FORTH permits the programmer to violate the semantic intent of these objects, either by accident or on purpose. Explain and give an example of such a violation.

54. Happy Hacker is using a version of FORTH in which integers occupy 4 bytes. He has extended the semantics of the language to include a new type declarator, REALVAR, for real (floating-point encoding) variables, each taking 4 bytes. Happy wants code to compute the same function as in the Pascal code in question 33, and has written this:

```
1 VARIABLE JJ
3 REALVAR FF
FF @ JJ @ + FF !
```

Would this code work? If so, what answer would be left in FF? If not, why not?

16

Modules and Object Classes

_____ Overview

For clarity and easy debugging, a small program should be written as a collection of functions. However, use of subprograms alone is inadequate for a large, complex system. Encapsulated modules were developed as tools for managing team efforts and complex tasks. An encapsulated module is bigger than a function definition, yet smaller than a program. These modules facilitate the creation of code libraries, separate compilation, the grouping of logically related elements for the implementation of abstract data types, the sharing of public data, and the protection of private information.

Separately compiled C files, Ada packages, and object classes in C++ are three strategies for achieving modularity. Before module-related facilities were included within programming languages, files and separate compilation were used to achieve the goals of modularity. In a modularized C program, an object or function in one file can be shared by a program in another file by using an "extern" specification, and kept private through the use of the keyword "static". The operating system's linking loader completed the connections among the program's parts. An automated method, the makefile, was invented to make linking UNIX applications easier and more foolproof.

Packages in Ada provide the framework to group the variables and functions of an abstract data type. A package consists of a header which declares shared data and a body which defines private symbols and the ADT functions. Unlike C, Ada's goals of modularity are achieved from within the language.

In C++, the class serves a similar role as the package in Ada. Classes contain both functions and data. C++ also allows classes to be constructed in a hierarchical fashion so that they are related to each other and can inherit data and functions. Within a class, the definition of a function is called a method. The C++ class is a template that must be instantiated by the use of the class name in a declaration. The result is an object whose fields will be initialized if the class contains an initialization function called a constructor.

Some relationships among classes are difficult to achieve using only public and private parts. There are times when we would like parts shared with some modules but not all. C++ provides a solution for this problem: a class or a function may be declared to be a friend of another class. Access is then shared by the parent class and the friend class.

16.1 THE PURPOSE OF MODULES

It is universally accepted by computer scientists that programs should be designed and implemented in a modular fashion. For small programs, this merely means that a program is written as a collection of function calls. Each function definition must be short, its purpose clearly defined, and its interface clearly declared and documented. Global variables are avoided in order to minimize unwanted interaction between functions and side effects.

When writing large systems programs, though, this basic modular methodology is helpful but inadequate. The complexity of a large system is so great that it must be organized as something other than a list of thousands of function definitions. Another level of program structure is needed so that things that belong together can be grouped and isolated from all possible outside interference. The semantic bases of many modern languages have been extended to support a unit that is larger than a single function but smaller than a program. Such units are called by varied names [Exhibit 16.1] but have similar purposes and properties, which we examine here. Sample modules are given in Ada and in C++.

Encapsulated modules were developed in response to several needs that have been mentioned earlier. These are:

- To facilitate separate compilation and creation of code libraries.
- To enable the logical grouping of type declarations and relevant representation-dependent functions.
- To support implementation-independent abstract data types.
- To implement private information (static local data).
- To implement controlled, nonhierarchical sharing of data.

Exhibit 16.1.   Terms for modules.

C	a separately compiled file
Ada	package
Modula	module
CLU	cluster
C++, Simula, Smalltalk	class

Grouping Logically Related Elements.

A module provides a framework for grouping together a set of related functions and is thus an ideal way to implement an ADT. Within the module, the details of the implementation and functions are defined that access specific fields in the representation. The module must include all representation-dependent functions that are needed to use the ADT domains. These can be written, compiled, and tested in relative isolation. The ADT functions often call each other and might use information that is private within the module. Their interdependence is documented by their inclusion in the same module. The `array_stack`, defined in Exhibit 15.9, is a good example; in Section 16.3 we give an implementation of this ADT in Ada.

Sharing Public Facilities.

To be useful, a module must have some functions or data objects that are public and can be accessed by other parts of the program. These symbols are "made known" to other modules, on demand. If a program, P, wishes to use a module, M, then P must contain a command to *include* M. Then within P, the public symbols in M can be referenced.

Protecting Private Information.

An encapsulated module contains declarations for types, functions, and data objects. These declarations are separated into two groups, of *public* and *private* symbols. Public symbols may be accessed by other modules and form the interface between a module and the rest of the world. In an ADT implementation, the ADT functions would be declared to be public symbols, so that other parts of a program could call them. In addition, the module might contain private functions which are called by the ADT functions but cannot be called from outside the module.

The `array_stack` ADT is particularly simple and does not require any locally defined types. To implement more complex ADTs, however, we must be able to make private type declarations. Having the possibility of internally defined types also enables the representation of the ADT to be changed easily, simply by changing the private type declaration. The effects of that change are limited to the scope of the module definition. Once the module's functions are redefined to work on the new representation, all code that depends on those functions would automatically work. For example, suppose a module were used to define a stack, and the representation chosen initially was an array. Later, it became clear that a linked list representation would fit the data characteristics better. To make this change, the data type of the stack storage and definitions of the stack functions (all within the module) would have to be changed. However, when the outer program called push or pop, the call would function as expected and store or return a value. The caller would never know that the representation of the ADT had been changed.

A module must provide for private data. Many large systems have modules that operate as coroutines, acting asynchronously to carry out a set of related concurrent tasks. For example, an application that uses dynamic storage allocation will often have a separate memory management module which gets storage from the operating system in efficient quantities and manages lists of new and freed cells. I/O buffering and caching are done by coroutines. To support coroutines we need private data objects with a static lifetime that can be shared among all the functions in the module. These must be created and initialized when the module is first entered.

Often, a group of private data declarations can be used in a module in place of a single object of a record type. In Pascal, for example, a stack is usually implemented as a record consisting of an array of data slots and an integer top-of-stack subscript. We declare a record data type with these parts so that a stack can be passed around as one coherent argument. However, when we implement a stack module, the stack-data-object is internal to the module, and within the module it is global to all the module's functions. It is not passed anywhere as a parameter. In such cases, there is no real advantage to gathering the two parts of the stack into one record.

The data parts of the ADT would be declared in the private part of the module. Private symbols can be used only within the module; we say they are *hidden* within it. In an ordinary function, the local variables are similarly hidden. However, local variables cannot do all that is needed. By concealing the data-parts of the ADT, we force the programmer to access them *only* through the ADT functions. The nature, type, extent, and value of all private data are concealed from the program outside the module. This organization forces the programmer to use an implementation-independent coding style, making the entire package easier to debug and modify.

Implementation Strategies.

We will examine three basic strategies for achieving modularity that are in common use:

1. C's separately compiled files.
2. Ada packages.
3. Object classes in C++.

16.2 MODULARITY THROUGH FILES AND LINKING

Before module-related facilities were included within programming languages, files and separate compilation were used to achieve the goals of modularity. This was not an altogether satisfactory solution, since it relied on the operating system environment, specifically the linker, to complete the connections among the parts of the program. The structure of the application as a whole was not expressed anywhere within the program code! Instead, the user determined this structure by telling the system linker which modules to include.

Giving complex commands to a linker is error prone and cumbersome, so an automated method, the *makefile*, was invented for linking UNIX applications. Currently, several systems support some kind of "make" facility. The example we give and explain here is written in ANSI C and UNIX.

A modularized program in C consists of four or more files. We list their purposes here, then examine an example of each written in C. The files are as follows:

- A makefile, which represents the entire program. It lists the components and describes how each depends on the others. The contents of this file are not C code. Rather, they are operating system commands, interpreted by the system's "make" facility. When you "make" a program, any necessary compilation and linking is done, according to the instructions given in the makefile. The result is a machine-code module that is ready to load and run.

- A header file, containing declarations and definitions of symbols that must be shared by two or more code modules in order to attain consistency.
- A main module, containing the main program, where execution begins. Any declarations in the main program are local to it and are not shared by other modules.
- One or more modules containing functions that are called by main. These share the header file with main, but are compiled separately and may contain private declarations of any sort. These modules often are used for coroutines that handle buffering and storage management.

Library Packages

We present a short interactive C application consisting of four files to show how the parts of an application are written and combined. The header file [Exhibit 16.2] must be included in the other files when they are compiled; note the #include statements at the top of Exhibits 16.3 and 16.4. A header file provides a way to coordinate the assumptions made in the code modules. In this example, the code modules both need to know the length and base type of the arrays that will be processed. Using the particular constant definitions in Exhibit 16.2, we would work with arrays of four long integers and print the answers out in a "%ld" (long decimal) format field. However, we could change these three declarations to handle any other length and base type. For example, to work with arrays of ten floating-point numbers, we would edit the header file to say:

```
#define LEN 10
#define D "%f"
typedef float NUMBER;
```

Exhibit 16.2.   Header file: "modules.h".

```
/* Set this constant to the number of data items in your array.  */
#define LEN 4
/* Set these definitions to the desired data type and format specifier.  */
/* NUMBER must be defined to be a standard numeric type.  */
#define D "%ld"
typedef long int NUMBER;
extern NUMBER reduce(NUMBER (*)(), NUMBER)
```

Note the extern declaration for the function reduce. When this line is included in the main module, it tells the compiler two things:

- The reduce function is defined in another module.
- It takes two arguments, a pointer to a function and a number, and returns a number.

This information permits the compiler to compile correct and meaningful calls to a function it has never seen.

Exhibit 16.3.   Main module: "sumup.c".

```
#include <stdio.h>
#include "modules.h"
/* This constant is the number of array operations that are defined.  */
#define OPS 6
NUMBER fi_plus(a, b)      NUMBER a, b; {return a + b;}
NUMBER fi_times (a, b)    NUMBER a, b; {return a * b;}
NUMBER fl_or(a, b)        NUMBER a, b; {return a || b;}
NUMBER fl_and(a, b)       NUMBER a, b; {return a && b;}
NUMBER fb_or(a, b)        NUMBER a, b; {return a | b;}
NUMBER fb_and(a, b)       NUMBER a, b; {return a & b;}
static NUMBER (*op_ar[OPS])() = {fi_plus,fl_or,fb_or,fi_times,fl_and,fb_and};
static char *label[OPS] = {"plus ", "logical or ", "bitwise or ",
                          "times ", "logical and", "bitwise and"};
main()
{ /* Header file must define NUMBER to be a standard numeric type.  */
    NUMBER ar[LEN];                /* Declare an array of numbers.  */
    NUMBER *ar_last = &ar[LEN-1];  /* Mark the last slot of the array.  */
    NUMBER *p;                     /* A scanning pointer for the array.  */
    int k;                         /* An index for the function array.  */
    puts("This program demonstrates some whole-array operations.\n\n");
    do {
        printf ("Please enter %d integers separated by spaces.\n", LEN);
        p=ar;                      /* Start input at head of array.  */

        while( p<=ar_last && scanf(D, p)==1 ) ++p;
        if (p <= ar_last)
            printf("Premature EOF or conversion error; job terminated.\n"),
            exit(1);
        while (getchar()!='\n');   /* Flush rest of input line. */
        putchar ('\n');            /* Prepare for output.   */
        /* Apply each operation in the op array to the number array.  */
        for(k=0; k<OPS; k++)
            printf ("%s "D"\n", label[k], reduce(op_ar[k], ar));
        printf("\nDo you want to enter more data?  (y/n)\n");
        }
    while (getchar() == 'y');
}
```

Keeping Private Information

In a modularized C program, a programmer can create both shared functions and private functions by judicial use of header files and "static" declarations. The modifier "static" is the opposite of "extern". The keyword extern is used to denote an ob-

Exhibit 16.4.   Subroutine module: "reduce.c".

```
#include "modules.h"                                /* a */
NUMBER reduce(NUMBER (*op)(), NUMBER ar)           /* b */
{   int k;
    NUMBER sum;                                     /* c */
    sum = ar[0];
    for(k=1; k<LEN; k++) sum = (*op)(sum, ar[k]);  /* d */
    return sum;
}
```

ject or function that is to be shared by other modules, while static denotes a private item. A global symbol (function or data object) that is not declared to be either one is extern.

The main module, shown in Exhibit 16.3, is intended only as a demonstration of how the parts of a modularized program work together.[1] It sets up an array of integers, then sends the array to reduce to be processed, in turn, by each of six dyadic integer functions. Finally, it prints all the answers and queries the user about more data.

Sharing Information

The subroutine module shown in Exhibit 16.4 contains the function reduce.[2] This performs a "running operation", using whatever dyadic function is passed to it as an argument. For example, if the argument operation is "+", reduce computes the running sum: a[0] + a[1] + a[2] + ... + a[n]. If the argument function is "*", the answer is the "running product".

Note that this module includes the header file (line a). Thus the local variable, sum (line c), will be type long or short or integer or float, whichever is selected in the header file. The important thing is that it will be the same type as the array elements created in main, and an appropriate type for the function argument. Each time the header file is modified, both the subroutine module and the main module, which depend on it, must be recompiled.

The type declaration "NUMBER (*op)()", in the header of reduce, declares "op" to be a pointer to a function that returns a NUMBER. We can refer to this function through the pointer by writing its name with a dereference operator: "(*op)". Thus line d calls the function which was passed to reduce as an argument. The arguments to *that* function are the current partial sum and the current array element.

Defining the Application

The #include commands in the two code modules express the relationship among the three files, but not in a coherent way. By reading all the files, a user could deduce the relationship, but that relationship is not presented in a single place or in a way that

---

[1]This main program is for demonstration purposes—it does not do anything that is particularly useful.

[2]Compare the syntax for functional parameters in C to the Pascal syntax shown in Exhibit 9.29.

is convenient to process. Although the problem is small for a program with only two code modules and a header, it can become considerable with a large many-module application. The UNIX "makefile" makes the relationships and dependencies explicit. A makefile is a file of executable system commands; the example shown here contains UNIX commands to compile and link a program.

The makefile is the root of a tree of files that comprise the application, and it is the basis of an automated version-control system which serves two purposes:

- The most recent version of every file involved will be used to construct the executable module. No object module will be sent to the linker if a corresponding source or header file has been modified after the last compilation for that module.
- If any step in the compiling and linking process is unnecessary, it will be skipped. No compiling or linking operation will ever be redone unless the files on which it depends have been modified.

A makefile explicitly defines how the final application depends on separately compiled object modules, and how each of these depends on source code and header files. In our example [Exhibit 16.5], the first line tells the linker that the finished program will be called "sumup", and that it can be produced by linking two user-created object files, main.o and reduce.o. (The object files that belong to the C library do not need to be listed.) The third and fifth lines define the source files on which the two user-defined object modules depend.

Exhibit 16.5.   The makefile for the sumup program.

```
sumup:  main.o  reduce.o
    cc -o sumup main.o reduce.o
main.o:  main.c  modules.h
    cc -o main.o  main.c
reduce.o:  reduce.c  modules.h
    cc -o reduce.o  reduce.c
```

The second line of the makefile contains a call to link the object files that comprise this application and to produce an executable file named "sumup". The fourth and sixth lines contain calls on the compiler to produce the necessary object files.[3] These lines are invoked only when needed. The make facility checks the date-last-modified on source files, object files, and executable files. If a linked module already exists, and none of its component object files have been modified or need modification, the linker can return immediately without wasting the effort to redo a job that is already done. An object file needs to be recompiled if any of the source files on which it depends have been changed since the creation time of the object file. These dependencies are defined by the last two lines in the makefile, where we see that the object file main.o depends on main.c and modules.h, and, similarly, reduce.o depends on

---

[3]These two lines are not strictly necessary because they only state explicitly what the system would do by default if no compile commands were given.

a code module and a header module. If one of these three files were modified, the relevant object module or modules would be recompiled.

To use a makefile, that is, to compile and link the program, the programmer simply says "`make`", or "`make sumup`". (The longer form is needed if the user's file directory contains makefiles for more than one application.) Any source module that has been edited since the last call on `make` will be recompiled, then the object modules will be linked and the result stored as an executable file named `sumup`. To run the compiled program, the programmer will say "`sumup`".

Makefiles, separate compilation, and declarations for external and static symbols thus combine to provide a language/system that achieves the goals of grouping, sharing, and protection.

16.3   PACKAGES IN Ada

Grouping Related Elements

Packages in Ada provide a framework under which to group together the variables and functions of an ADT, uninterrupted by unrelated variables and code. An Ada package has much better lexical coherence than a comparable set of definitions in Pascal. A package has a header, which declares all the externally visible symbols, and a body, which can include type definitions, static local variables, definitions for the publicly accessible functions, and private local functions. We will show how an Ada package definition can be used to implement the ADT `array_stack` [Exhibit 16.6].[4] This package contains definitions for a stack representation and the representation-dependent stack functions, PUSH, POP, and TOP.

Sharing Public Facilities

Any symbol declared in the header of an Ada package can be shared by other modules. In our example, this includes the functions PUSH, POP, and TOP. To use an Ada package, the programmer writes a `with` command within the main program [Exhibit 16.7]. Having done this, one can refer to a part of that module by its complete name: the module name followed by the function or data name (see the left side of the exhibit). Using complete names avoids a possible problem caused by using the same identifier for parts of different modules.

Because packages are used extensively in Ada programs, this syntax for naming the parts of a package becomes annoying. Ada provides an alternate syntax that can usually be used and is more convenient. Using the `use` command causes all the public names in a package to be included with the local symbols in the calling program, eliminating the need to use the module name in every reference (see the right side of the exhibit).[5]

By selectively including modules where they are needed, we can construct a non-hierarchical sharing structure. Each part of a program can be given access to exactly

---

[4]In Chapter 17 we show how a package can be embedded within a generic framework which allows for varying the base type of this ADT.

[5]Much like the "`with`" command in Pascal.

those other parts it needs. The possibility of many kinds of unintentional interactions between functions and data can be minimized, and the resulting software becomes easier to debug and maintain.

Exhibit 16.6.   Defining a stack package in Ada.

```
-- The package header declares the externally visible symbols of the ADT.
package STACK is
    function PUSH(k:  integer) return boolean;
    function POP return integer;
    function TOP return integer;
end STACK;
-- The package body defines private symbols and the ADT functions.
-- The private variables cannot be referenced outside this package.
package body STACK is
    STKLEN: constant:= 10;
    stk:  array(1..STKLEN)of integer:    -- static local storage.
    tos:  integer range -1..STKLEN;      -- Negative 1 is an error code.
    -- These functions can be called from outside package because they
    -- have been declared as external symbols in the package header.
    function PUSH(k:  integer) is
    begin
        if tos<STKLEN then
            tos:=tos+1;    stk(tos):= k;
            return true;
        else return false;
        end if
    end PUSH;
    function TOP return integer is
    begin
        if tos >0 then return stk(tos);
        else return SYSTEM.MIN_INT;      -- Use value from package named SYSTEM.
        end if;
    end TOP;
    function POP return integer is       -- Remove & return top stack item.
        ans:  integer;
    begin
        ans:= TOP;  tos:=tos-1;
        return ans;
    end POP;
-- This code is run at load time; it initializes the package data.
begin
    tos:=0;
end STACK;
```

Exhibit 16.7.   Using an Ada package.

Basic Syntax:	Sugared Syntax:

```
    with STACK;                                    with STACK;
                                                   use STACK;

    procedure MyJob is                             procedure MyJob is

       ...                                            ...
       STACK.push(MyValue);                           push(MyValue);
```

Private Information

Any symbol declared in the package body but not listed in the header is private and can only be accessed from within the package. In our Ada example, the stack-array and the stack-pointer are declared as pieces of private data, and the length of the stack is a private constant [Exhibit 16.6, lines 10 to 12]. The stack-pointer (tos) and the array (stk) are not grouped into a record-object, as they would be in Pascal, because there is no advantage to that grouping. The two variables are global within the package and invisible outside it, so they will never be passed anywhere as arguments.

Private variables declared in a package are static; that is, the value computed during one activation of a stack function remains until the next stack function is called. Package variables are not deallocated when control leaves the package, and they are not reinitialized when control returns. This permits the programmer to declare protected, local objects that can be used globally. This system is a tremendous improvement over the way similar problems must be handled in Pascal. In a Pascal program, data structures that are to be used throughout the program must be declared globally. They are usually initialized by the main program at the beginning of program execution. Pascal provides no way to protect the data structures from the rest of the program, or to ensure that they are accessed only through the proper functions.

Many variables and most data structures must be initialized when they are allocated. If a data structure is local and private within a package, the package itself must initialize it. The code on the last three lines of this Ada package serves this purpose [Exhibit 16.6]. At load time, before beginning to execute the main program, storage is allocated for all private variables in all included packages. The "main" initializing code in each of these packages is then executed.

Comparison to C

The goals of grouping, sharing, and privacy are achieved much the same way in an Ada package as they are in a C module. The primary differences between the two systems is that Ada packages have been brought entirely within the Ada language, whereas the C system relies on using a command file that is outside the C language.

16.4 OBJECT CLASSES

In object-oriented languages, the class serves much the same roles as the package does in Ada: it organizes things that belong together and allows for private information. In addition, the classes can be constructed so that there are hierarchies of classes, all related to each other.[6] The best-known object-oriented languages are Simula, (the first such language), Smalltalk, and C++. In all of these, a class may contain data fields and functions, which we will call *members of the class*. Like Ada packages, classes may have private and public members.

Terminology varies somewhat among these languages. The term *method* was invented for Smalltalk,[7] and it means one definition, in one class, for a function. This term is useful, and we will use it whenever we need to distinguish between an entire function and a single definition for that function. A function name represents a conceptual process. A class function might be (and usually is) given different (but related) method definitions in various parts of a class hierarchy.[8]

Terminology used for function definitions and calls is also variable. Simula has procedures, C++ has functions, and Smalltalk has messages. In Simula and C++, we speak of calling a procedure or function, while in Smalltalk we "send a message to an object". In this discussion, we will use the terms "function" and "function call".

16.4.1   Classes in C++

For the rest of this discussion, we will focus attention primarily on the semantics and syntax of C++, since it promises to become the most widely used object-oriented language.

A C++ class has the same elements as an Ada package, and it is declared with similar syntax.[9] A sample class, named "`char_stack`", is defined in Exhibit 16.8. It has four private data-members and four public function-members.

Instances and Naming

A C++ class is a template, like a type declaration in Pascal, and must be instantiated to create objects. To instantiate a class, you use the class name in a declaration, as you would use a Pascal type name. The result of instantiation is an *object*, which is represented by a record-type storage-object with one field for each of the class variables. Those fields will be initialized if the class contains an initialization function.

When we instantiate a class, we bind the resulting object to a name. The object's name is used to refer to both data fields and the function members. For example, in Exhibit 16.9, the object `stk1` is an instance of the C++ class `char_stack`, and it has the function-members `stk1.push` and `stk1.pop` and the data members `stk1.size`, `stk1.top,` `stk1.s,` and `stk1.end`.

Within the context of the class, the members may be referenced by using a simple name. A public member can be referenced outside the class using a dotted notation:

⟨class_name⟩.⟨function_name⟩ (⟨argument_list⟩)

For example, the last three lines in Exhibit 16.9 call functions defined in the class `char_stack`.

---

[6]See Chapter 18.

[7]This term is not generally used in describing Simula and C++.

[8]Virtual functions are covered in Chapter 18.

[9]In C++, a "`struct`" data type is also a kind of class. It may contain function declarations, and any `struct` declaration actually defines a class. However, it is a class with no private parts. The difference between a `struct` variable and a class variable is the accessing restrictions on the private data and functions. We will limit further discussion to classes declared as `class`.

Exhibit 16.8.   Defining a class in C++.

```
class char_stack {              // Here are the private parts of the class.
    int size;
    char *tos, *end;
    char* s;
public:                         // All remaining symbols are public.
    char_stack(int sz)          // This is the class's constructor.
    {   s=new char[size=sz];    // Allocate an array of sz chars.
        tos=s;                  // Initialize top to point at first char.
        end=tos+(size-1);       // Mark last slot in stack.
    }
    ~char_stack() { delete s; } // This object destructor is used when
                                // control leaves the object's scope.

    int push(char c)            // Return 0 if stack is full.
    {   return ( tos<=end ?  (*tos++ =c) :  0 ); }

    char pop()                  // Return null char if stack is empty.
    {   return ( tos>s ?  *--tos :  '\0' ); }

    char top();
};                              // End of class char_stack.
char char_stack::top()          // Return top but don't pop.
{   return ( tos>s ?  *tos :  '\0' ); }
```

Exhibit 16.9.   Instantiating a C++ class.

```
main ()
{   char c;
    char_stack stk1(100);       // We can instantiate a class more than once,
    char_stack stk2(10);        // and get multiple copies of the objects.
    ...
    stk3 = new char_stack(20);
    stk1.push('#');             // We must specify which "push" to use.
    stk2.push('%');
    c = stk2.pop();
}
```

The Implicit Argument.

When we call a function that is a class member, we must specify which instance of the function we are calling. To do this, we write an object name followed by the member function name. (In Smalltalk, these are separated by spaces, while Simula and C++ use dotted notation, as in Exhibit 16.9.) The data members of an object do not need to be passed as arguments to the function members: each function may operate on the data fields of its own instance. Thus the record of data-members is an implicit argument to all of its function members.

As a result of having an implicit argument, each class function needs one fewer explicit argument. However, the name of the object that includes both the function instance and the implicit argument must be specified as part of the function name. To a programmer accustomed to traditional languages, such as Pascal, this looks like writing the name of the first argument on the left side of a function name instead of on the right side with the rest of the argument list. For example, in Pascal, the name stk1_stack would be written as part of the argument list to push or pop, but in an object-oriented language it is written as part of the name of the function [Exhibit 16.9].

Having an implicit argument leads to one difficulty. Unlike an explicit argument, the syntax provides no way to give a local name to this record. Yet some functions, particularly recursive ones, must refer explicitly to the implicit argument. This problem is solved by a keyword that can be used to refer to any implicit argument. In Smalltalk, the keyword is self. In C++, the keyword "this" refers to a pointer to the implied argument.

Implementation

Classes contain both functions and data. The functions are declared within the class definition and may be either public or private. Theoretically, a "copy" of each class function is made each time the class is instantiated. The newly instantiated functions are part of the new class-object and are the only functions that have access to its private data fields. In practice, though, there is no need to duplicate the code of the class functions for every class instance. Thus an instance of a class can be implemented by a record variable with one field for each class data-member. This differs from an ordinary record-type variable because the access to the private fields is restricted to member functions.[10] Initialization is done by a member function called a constructor, which must have the same name as the class.

Constructors and Initialization.

Each class may contain a set of constructor functions.[11] A class variable may be created in a declaration or by using the new operator, which creates a storage object dynamically. In both cases, a constructor function is called to initialize the new object. Like Ada (see Exhibit 14.28), C++ permits the programmer to call a constructor function in an expression to create a pure value of the class out of its components.[12] This is often done inside a function to create a return value of the new type, and it is also used in declarations to create appropriate initializers.

Constructors are ordinary functions, with or without parameters. The only restriction is that all the constructors in a class must have different types of argument lists.[13] If a constructor has parameters, an argument list must be supplied in a declaration, a call on new, or in an explicit call on the constructor. Exhibit 16.9 creates three instances of the class char_stack with different arguments and binds them to the names stk1, stk2, and stk3. The class char_stack must have a definition for

---

[10]A Simula class has an associated "main procedure", like that in an Ada package, which is called when a class object is constructed to initialize it.

[11]In current terminology, the name of the constructor function may be "overloaded".

[12]Review Chapter 14, Section 14.3.1.

[13]The power of C++ constructors goes well beyond initialization, and will be further developed in Chapter 18, Section 2.5.

its constructor which takes an integer argument. This function is freely definable and can perform any appropriate initialization.

A C++ class may also have a destructor function, which does the opposite of the constructor function. If a destructor is defined for the class, it is invoked automatically at block exit to dispose of any class instances that were created at block entry or during execution of the block. This permits automatic recovery of storage locations that were created using new, a major improvement over C and Pascal.

Function Declarations and Definitions.

A function is a class member if it is *declared* within the class. Remember that a function declaration is simply a header line—stating the return type, the function name, and the argument types. Compare the C++ code in Exhibit 16.8 to the Ada code in Exhibit 16.6. Ada requires the programmer to write each function declaration twice: once to declare whether it is public or private, and once with the definition. C++ syntax is simpler. It permits the function definition either to follow the declaration immediately, or to be given elsewhere. Practical considerations determine whether the definition should be with or separated from the declaration. Definitions written *with* the declaration are expanded as an in-line code; that is, the translator replaces each function call, in line, by a new copy of the compiled code for the function. All the time and space overhead of stack frames, jump-to-subroutine, and subroutine return is avoided.

If a member function is declared but not defined in a class, its definition must eventually be given; often, this is done just after the end of the class. Defining a method outside the class does not affect the status of the method as a class member. The method still has member's access rights. The difference is practical, not semantic; functions defined this way are compiled separately using the ordinary function call and return mechanism.

Giving a definition outside its class has one effect on syntax. Because some functions have multiple defining methods, we must specify the full name of the method when we define it, so that the compiler can tell with which class the method belongs. To denote the full name of a method we use the *scope resolution operator*, "::". It can be used in dyadic or monadic form:

⟨class_name⟩::⟨function_name⟩(⟨argument_list⟩)
::⟨function_name⟩(⟨argument_list⟩)

Thus the full name of the method for pop in the class char_stack is char_stack::pop, and the constructor function for the class is char_stack::char_stack.

Denoting a Single Method.

The meaning of the scope resolution operator, "char_stack::push", is easily confused with the dotted notation used in a function call, "stk1.push", but they do not mean the same thing. The first notation denotes a particular method which is a member of a particular class. Every reference to a method outside its defining class must be written using "::". Methods in programmer-defined classes are denoted using the dyadic "::", and globally defined methods are denoted by using "::" in its monadic form.

In contrast, the dotted notation is used to refer to a function, not one of its methods. It is important to be able to denote a single function method, as opposed to the entire function, which is a collection of methods. A function call must be dispatched,[14] while a method may simply be called directly. The dotted reference "stk1.push" means "Start with the object stk1. Run the function dispatcher to select the most appropriate method for the function push, then call that method with stk1 as its implied argument." If no method for push is defined in the class of its implied argument, some other method, higher in the class hierarchy, will be dispatched.

The most common reason for using a method name instead of a function name is that one method for a function is being defined in terms of another. The philosophy of object-oriented programming dictates that we should be able to use a single function name for both old and new methods, so long as they implement a common external function. For example, a customized printing function might be defined for a user-defined type by making several calls on one of the predefined print functions. Within the definition of the new print method, we must be able to denote the old method by its method name, in order to avoid a hopeless circular definition.

16.4.2   Represented Domains

Chapter 15, Section 15.4.3, discusses the problems inherent in using one domain to represent another. Briefly, the language must allow some connection between the domains in order to permit the programmer to define functions intrinsic to the new domain. However, once these are defined, all further compatibility between the domains is undesirable. In Pascal, this unwanted compatibility is unavoidable. In Ada, one-way protection is provided, as described in Exhibits 15.22 and 15.23. In C++ we have more control over the situation.

A language with classes provides a different and much more satisfactory approach to this problem. Where in Ada, we would define a new represented domain, in C++ we would define a class with one private data member from the old domain. The class imag in Exhibit 16.10 is an analog of the Ada type imag defined in Exhibit 15.26. The information provided by the programmer and even the syntax are similar in the two languages. The important difference is the semantics.

Exhibit 16.10.   A represented domain in C++.

```
class imag
{   im:  float;
    operator float() { return im; }
public:
    imag(){ im=0.0; }
    imag(float f){ im=f; }
    friend imag operator+(imag a, imag b){imag( float(a)+float(b) ); }
    friend float operator*(imag a, imag b){ -1*(float(a) * float(b)); }
}   // Operators + and * are friends of this class.
```

---

[14]The distinction cannot be fully understood until the material in Chapter 17 is mastered. However, we give a brief explanation here.

No casts or compatibilities are predefined for C++ classes, so the programmer is not stuck with unwanted ones. In return, the two casts that are needed to define arithmetic for imaginary numbers must be defined explicitly. The first is the constructor imag(float), which changes a float value to type imag.[15] Because these two functions are private, the relationship between types float and imag is completely hidden from the outside world, and the semantics of type imag are fully protected. In contrast, the semantics of the Ada type in Exhibit 15.26 make the cast imag(float) public, and make the cast float() automatic. (That is, an imag is acceptable in any context that requires a float.)

The other cast needed in our package is one that changes an imag number to its underlying float representation so that we may operate on it. This is the *operator function* named "float", defined in Exhibit 16.10.[16] In C and C++ syntax, a cast is (syntactically) a prefix operator, not a function, and it is called by placing the name of the cast to the left of the expression which is its operand. Since the name of a cast is a type name enclosed in parentheses, this looks like a function call with the parentheses around the wrong thing. The designer of C++ gave the option of calling any operator, including a cast, using either operator syntax or standard function call syntax. Thus we can call operator float() either of these two ways:

```
float(17); float (x+2)
(float) 17; (float)(x+2)
```

16.4.3   Friends of Classes

The class mechanism lets the programmer impose restrictions on type compatibility, object visibility, and access to parts of objects. These restrictions are immensely powerful and can be a huge help in achieving semantically valid programs. However, when one uses a restricting mechanism, it is often difficult to achieve exactly the right degree of restrictions.

This is true of classes, also. There can be relationships among classes that are important but hard to capture using only public and private parts. This gives us tree-structured sharing among classes. However, sometimes graph-structured sharing is needed. We could say that, sometimes, we want "semiprivate" parts: parts that can be shared with some other program modules but not with all.

We use classes to make programs more modular and more reliable. The important semantic mechanism for achieving these goals is accessing restrictions. The data type of a class is *hidden* within the class, and other functions are forced to work through the accessing functions defined for the class. By using this methodology, we can easily change the representation of a class without affecting the correctness of other parts of the program. However, each function call has a cost in time and space efficiency. Although the cost of a single function call is small, these costs add up. The cost of doing everything through function calls can be great. When the access operation itself is trivial, like the pop function in Exhibit 16.8, the cost of calling the function can exceed the cost of executing it. Thus applying modular methodology throughout a program could introduce unacceptable inefficiency.

---

[15]Conversion functions are treated more fully in Chapter 18, Section 18.1.
[16]The word "operator" in lines 3, 7, and 8 is a keyword.

Two solutions are provided in C++ for this problem: friends and in-line code. A method may be declared to produce *in-line code*, like a macro, rather than a separately compiled code module. If the method is actually defined between the begin-class and end-class brackets, it will be expanded in-line. If it is declared inside the class but defined elsewhere, it will be compiled as a separate code module. The semantics and syntax are otherwise the same, as is the ability to access the private members of the class. With short functions, such as push and pop, in-line code is preferred, because it is more time- and space-efficient than separate compilation. For long functions, in-line code would still be faster, but it could make the compiled program much longer if there are two or more calls on the function. Thus in-line compilation is a bad idea for moderate-length and long functions, and separate compilation is more commonly used.

The *friend* mechanism can also be used to avoid the inefficiency involved in constant calls to trivial functions. A class will share its private members with friend functions, but not with other functions. Friendship is given, not taken. A class declares who its friends are; a function cannot declare which classes are its friends. The friendship relationship can be declared function-by-function, or an entire class can be declared to be a friend, which means that all its functions are friends.

For example, assume that we have defined two classes, "forest" and "tree". A forest is to be a collection of trees, in this case an array. In general though, whether it is a set, an array, or a list, it would be hidden within the class forest [Exhibit 16.11]. Both constructors for class tree are called by function forest::grow_tree; this would be permitted even if forest were not a friend, because these constructors are public in class tree. However, grow_tree also sets the value field of the new tree node it creates. To do this, it uses the member name value, which is private to class tree. This is permitted because class forest is a friend of class tree.

Exhibit 16.11.   Friend classes.

```
class tree
{   tree * l_son;
    tree * r_son;
    char value;
public:
    tree(){ l_son= r_son= NULL; value= '\0'; }
    tree(tree *a, tree *b){ l_son =a; r_son =b; value= '\0'; }
    friend class forest;
}
class forest
{   int n;
    tree woods[100];
public:
    forest(){ n=0; }
    forest(tree * t)
    {   if( n==100 ) cout <<"Forest is full.";
        else woods[n++] = t;
    }
```

```
      void grow_tree(int n, char c)
      {   tree * t = new tree;
          t->value = c;
          forest[n] = tree(t, forest[n]);
      }
  }
```

Comparisons

The class mechanism in C++ differs from the Ada package mechanism in many ways. Among the most important are the use of classes to form type hierarchies and govern function inheritance and automatic type conversion, as explained in Chapter 17. These facilities grow directly from the fact that the C++ class is an extension of the facility for defining record types.

The Ada package has one property, though, that is lacking in the class. A package can contain objects, functions, and more than one type declaration. Thus if we were writing a package, both types `tree` and `forest` would be written in the same package. Having done this, the right of forests to access tree parts would be established. A back door mechanism, such as the `friend` mechanism, is not needed to establish a relationship of "trust" between the two types.

EXERCISES

1. Why should programs be modularized?
2. What are the dangers in using global variables?
3. What is the purpose of encapsulating a module?
4. How can a module share data and yet protect private information?
5. How do private type declarations make an ADT representation invisible to the programmer?
6. How does C use files and separate compilation to achieve the goals of modularity?
7. What is the role of the makefile facility? A header file? The main module?
8. What is the role of `extern` and `static` in C declarations?
9. How did Ada and C++ extend the goals of grouping, sharing, and protection to their languages?
10. How does Ada distinguish between public and private symbols?
11. What is a method in Smalltalk?
12. A C++ class is a template. How is it instantiated? Initialized?
13. Explain two ways in which constructor function might be treated differently than other functions in a C++ class (Refer to Chapter 18, Section 2.5).
14. What is an implicit argument? How is it used in C++?
15. What is the role of a destructor function?
16. What are the differences in the declaration of a function in C++ and Ada syntax?
17. What is the role of the scope resolution operator?
18. How does C++ give the programmer more control than Ada over semantics and compatibility when using one domain to represent another?

19. What is the role of a friend class?

20. What is in-line code? When is its usage preferred? Not preferred?

21. Contrast classes in C++ and packages in Ada.

17

Generics

Overview

Generic domains are domains which include more than one specific type of object. They are used to express abstractions, to make code reusable, and to support top-down programming. There are four kinds of generic domains: parameterized, subdomains, polymorphic, and ad-hoc.

Several issues must be considered when implementing generic domains. They have been considered in the support for generics that has been built into various languages. The solutions vary in flexibility, preservation of semantic validity, binding time, and efficiency. Approaches to this problem include: overloaded operators, flexible arrays, polymorphic types, parameterized domains with instantiation, class hierarchies with inheritance, and declarable domain relationships.

A corresponding tool for expressing procedural abstractions is the virtual function. A virtual function is a function name, header, and description but no code. An ADT can be represented in a programming language by a generic domain together with virtual function declarations.

A generic function is a single abstract operation defined over a generic domain. Most languages have a few primitive generic functions for all primitive types, which are automatically extended to user-defined types. However, user-defined generic functions create semantic problems. The code that implements any process must be appropriate for the type of its arguments; what works for one type does not for another. The translator, therefore, must be able to handle multiple definitions for a generic function, and it must decide which method to use for each function call. This process is known as dispatching.

An ad hoc generic domain has subdomains that are related by semantics rather than by structure. Definitions of a function over two specific domains with an ad hoc relationship may look different if they depend on representation. However, they perform the same semantic action on objects of the different specific domains.

Many older languages support some predefined generics for forms of nonhomogeneous domains. These include union data types, overloaded names, fixed sets of generic definitions with coercion, extending predefined operators, flexible arrays, parameterized generic domains, domains with type parameters, preprocessors, and generic packages. These are far more limited than support for generic types found in object-oriented languages because final binding of the type parameters happens at precompile time.

17.1 GENERICS

17.1.1 What Is a Generic?

Chapter 15 discussed domains, type checking, and type conversions in several familiar strongly typed languages. In these languages, types are used to define domains such that each new type constructed, with a few exceptions, defines a distinct domain incompatible with other domains, and each domain contains only one type of object. In this chapter we examine the ways to declare and use generic domains, that is, domains that include more than one type of object. We see how generic domains can be used to express abstractions, to make code reusable, and to support top-down programming.

We say the domain of a function is *specific* if every argument to the function is defined to be a single specific type. The properties of a specific domain are fully defined by the specific type definition used to define the function, and the function makes use of these properties in order to perform meaningful computations. The opposite of "specific" is "generic". A function domain is *generic* if some argument can be of two or more different specific types. There are four ways in which a domain, D, may be *generic*:

- D may be defined by a type expression with components of an unspecified type and/or an array with unspecified array bounds. We call such a type expression a *parameterized type*. Several languages provide some support for this kind of generics. The domain it defines is a *parameterized generic domain*.[1]
- D may have a subdomain, D'. This occurs when D is defined as a type for which subtypes have been declared. For example, the Pascal subrange type "1..10" is a subtype of the type `integer`.
- D may be defined by a polymorphic type. A *polymorphic* type is a single type with internal variability, like a discriminated union.
- D is an *ad hoc* generic domain if it includes objects of more than one specific type, such that all of the specific types are representations of the same external domain. The semantic relationships among these species are important, but the species are related in an ad hoc manner, not by structure or representation. For example, the generic domain "number" includes at least two specific domains "integer" and "real" in most languages, and the generic domain "tree_node" can be defined to include specific types "leaf_node" and "interior_node". Ad hoc generics are a topic of current research interest.

Consider the domains listed in Exhibit 17.1. The domains "number" and "matrix of numbers" are generic because they include both integers and reals. "Matrix" and

---

[1]Implementations of generics over parameterized domains are discussed in Section 17.3.

"string" are generic because their dimensions are not specified, so these types include matrices of all shapes and strings of all lengths. "Set" is generic because the base type of the set is not specified and, therefore, sets of reals, characters, cells, and any other type are all included. "Stack" is generic for the same reason, and also because the size and structure of stacks can vary.

Exhibit 17.1.   Generic domains and functions on them.

Domain	Generic Functions on the Domain
number	+, -, *, /
matrix of numbers	inverse, transpose, +
character string	concatenation, substring
set of ?	union, intersection
stack of ?	push, pop, top

17.1.2 Implementations of Generics

There are several ways that generic and polymorphic functions may be supported within a programming language, but all approaches must provide answers for the same syntactic and semantic problems. The issues to be considered include:

- What kind of generic and/or polymorphic domains may we define? Parameterized domains? Structurally related domains? Domains with a small number of variants? Unlimited ad hoc generics?
- How and under what conditions may we define a generic or polymorphic function? May we define functions over generic domains?
- How do we translate calls on functions with more than one specific method? What information is considered by the translator when it chooses a method? Can this choice be deferred until run time or is it always made at compile time?
- If we permit run-time type variability, is it possible to compile code with reasonable efficiency?
- How do generic domains and generic functions interact with type coercion?
- What does it mean to call a function which has a generic formal parameter? (See Exhibit 17.3.) What type matching rules should apply? How can we implement such calls?

Support for generics has been achieved to different degrees for domains with subdomains, parameterized domains, and ad hoc generic domains. The solutions provided by various languages vary in their flexibility, their ability to preserve semantic validity, their time of binding, and the inefficiency inherent in the implementation. We will examine several approaches to this problem in some detail.

Overloaded Operators.

A few generic arithmetic operators are built into the language. A programmer can define new methods for these operators but cannot define any new operators or functions that are generic in the same way. Ada's operators are an example and are discussed in Section 17.2.

Flexible Arrays.

A programmer can use array parameters whose bounds are not defined at compile time. Either the array length must be passed as a separate parameter, or the code for the function must work correctly for all possible values of the array length. Several older languages support flexible arrays, including FORTRAN, C, and Pascal. These are covered in Section 17.2.

Parameterized Domains with Instantiation.

The generic module is kept in the form of parameterized source code. A preprocessor is used to instantiate the parameterized code with actual type arguments and generate fully specific, ordinary code which is bound to a unique name and then compiled. The programmer uses the unique name, not the generic name, in the code. This kind of generic module is supported by Ada and can be implemented in C using macros. It is discussed in Section 17.3.

Class Hierarchies with Inheritance.

Objects belong to classes, as do function methods. The symbol table is available at run time, and the class of the actual arguments to a function can be examined. One name is given to an abstract function, and many methods can be defined for that name, so long as each method is defined in a different class. A function method has one implied argument, and the translator uses the class of that argument to determine which method to dispatch for each function call. This kind of support for generics is present in Simula, Smalltalk, and C++. Because generic dispatching must sometimes be postponed until run time, these languages are at least partly interpreted. This is discussed in Chapter 18, Section 18.2.

Polymorphic Types.

The type of each symbol can be determined at run time. Functions are polymorphic, and each part of a function definition is controlled by a predicate. These predicates may be used to test the type or the value of the actual argument for each call. The translator will use a powerful pattern-matching facility to determine which predicate is true and select the corresponding action. Miranda and Haskell support this kind of generics. They are discussed in Chapter 18, Section 18.3.

Declarable Domain Relationships.

Generic function calls are interpreted, not compiled. The type information for generic objects is kept available at run time. One name is given to an abstract function and is used to refer to all of its methods. A generalized graph of relationships between domains can be created or declared, and is used to dispatch functions. In a generic function call, the arguments might be of any specific type which is a subdomain of the generic domain, according to the graph. A function call with generic parameters translates into code that will look at the argument types at run time and execute the function method that is most appropriate for those types, using coercion if necessary.

Examples of this approach to dispatching are drawn from C++ and Miranda and are discussed in Chapter 18, Section 18.4.

The extent to which a language supports generics is an important issue. The greater the extent, the more flexible and adaptable a program can be at run time. The smaller the extent, the more difficult it is to create reusable code and code libraries. Generic domains are supported to a minimal extent in most languages, but the kind of support provided, the restrictions, and whether support extends to programmer-defined domains and functions vary dramatically from one language to another. Traditional typed languages such as Pascal usually have some predefined generic domains with predefined relationships, but they lack any way for programmers to define their own generic domains or domain relationships. For example, a general matrix multiplication function cannot be defined in Pascal or FORTRAN because there is no way in these languages to define the generic domain "matrix of integers or reals".

Programmer-defined subdomains and domains with integer parameters are relatively easy to implement and are supported in many languages. Domains with type parameters are more difficult to implement in a strongly typed, compiled language because ordinary type checking requires that the specific type of each function argument be known (or deduced) at compile time. Ad hoc generic domains are the most difficult to implement because there is no structural relationship among the variants that can be exploited.

17.1.3   Generics, Virtual Functions, and ADTs

A generic domain is an abstraction that represents the shared structural and/or semantic properties of its subdomains. Thus a language that permits programmers to declare their own generic domains provides a powerful tool with which to express data abstractions. A corresponding tool for expressing procedural abstractions is the *abstract function*, or *virtual function*. This is a function name, a function header (or "prototype"), and a description of the intent of the function, with no accompanying code. The header defines the number and types of the function parameters and return value. The accompanying description defines the intended semantics of each, and any relevant assumptions or restrictions.

An abstract data type can be represented in a programming language by a generic domain together with a collection of virtual function declarations. A virtual function would be included for each essential representation-dependent process to be performed on members of the domain. This set of virtual functions explicitly describes the common behavior of all objects of the generic domain and is, thus, a description of the semantics of the generic domain. The virtual functions would be "guaranteed" to exist for every subdomain and would form the basis for defining all functions on the generic domain. In a few languages, a programmer is able to explicitly declare and name a generic domain, D, then use a single method to define a generic function, GF, over D. The function header for GF would refer to D, and the code for GF could call the virtual functions defined for D and rely only upon properties that are common to all specific domains contained in D.

A *realization* of a generic domain is some specific, fully defined type that implements the semantics of that domain. All realizations of a generic domain must have methods defined for all of the domain's virtual functions. A program could contain several realizations of the same generic domain. For example, in Pascal, `integer` and `real` are both realizations of the domain "number". The translator and linker must guarantee that, by run time, realizations of all promised functions for all subdomains must exist.

17.1.4   Generic Functions

A *generic function* is a single abstract operation that is defined over a generic domain. In most languages, FETCH, STORE, and comparison for equality are primitive generic functions that are defined for all primitive types. Most languages developed since the early 1970s extend these primitive generics automatically to user-defined types. Let us call these three functions the *universal generic functions*. Other functions that are commonly generic are READ, WRITE, and the arithmetic operators.

A generic function creates a semantic problem. In order for a process to be meaningful, the code that implements the process must be appropriate for the type of its arguments. In general, code that is meaningful for one type is not meaningful for other types. We must, therefore, ask how a function can meaningfully process data from a generic domain. In the older languages and their translators, this was done in an ad hoc manner. With a limited number of generic functions built into the language, as in Pascal and Ada, the translator can treat these functions as special cases, look at the types of the actual arguments, and generate specific code that is appropriate for them. On the other hand, if the user is permitted to define his or her own generic functions, the translator's type-checking algorithms must be extended to form some general mechanism for handling generic functions. Such mechanisms are the subject of this chapter.

Depending on the language, a user-defined generic function may be defined by one block of code whose parameter is from a generic domain, or by several independent blocks of code which have been declared to share a common name. When a function is defined by more than one body of code, each of the separately defined bodies is called a *method* for the function, and each method must be declared with arguments from a different combination of domains. We define the domain of such a function to be the union of the domains of all its methods.

There are three ways that a generic function may be defined by a single block of code: the processing method can be independent of the argument type (as in comparison for equality), the code can be polymorphic (see Chapter 18, Section 18.3), or the code can bypass the problem of processing a generic argument by passing the argument on in a call to some other generic function [Exhibit 17.4]. Functions that operate over ad hoc generic domains are either polymorphic or are defined as a collection of methods [Exhibit 17.2].

Dispatching a Function Method

It is more difficult for a translator to handle function names with multiple methods than names that represent one block of code. The process of deciding which method to use for a call is known as *dispatching the call*, and it is carried out by a part of the translator called the *dispatcher*. The dispatcher uses information about the function arguments to choose an appropriate method. Dispatching could be (and is, in some languages) done on the basis of the number of arguments, the types of one or all arguments, or the actual value of the arguments.

Exhibit 17.2.   A generic function as a collection of methods.

In this diagram a method is represented by a shield-shaped box, with its domain written across its top. A function is a set of methods with a common name. Note that the function "+" in FORTRAN 77 is much more extensive than the function of the same name in Pascal.

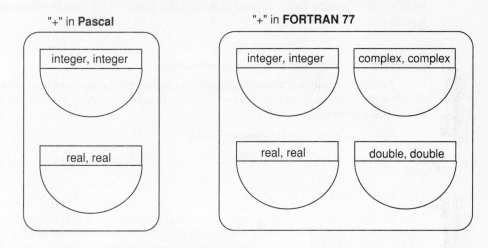

Some languages will try to coerce a function argument if the types of the actual arguments do not match any of the defined methods. Depending on the language, the dispatcher might use a subtype relationship (Pascal or Ada), possible type conversions (Pascal, FORTRAN), or hierarchical relationships among the domains (C++, Smalltalk). For example, if the function Square in Exhibit 17.3 were called with an integer argument, the hierarchical relationship between the domains integer and number could be used to dispatch the function call. If none of the defined methods is appropriate for the context, and no coercion is permitted that can make the arguments appropriate for some method, the function call contains a *type error*.

In Chapter 18 we consider several very different implementations of programmer-definable generic functions, with very different rules for dispatching. Some of these rules, such as those in Miranda, are quite general and require a sophisticated dispatcher. Others, such as the hierarchical dispatching rule in Simula and Smalltalk, are more limited and can be implemented simply.

Functions over Generic Domains

Some languages permit the programmer to define a generic function with an argument from a generic domain and only one defining method [Exhibit 17.4]. When such a function is called, the argument's type will be some specific type that is included in the generic domain. Such a method cannot operate directly on its parameters, but must either test its argument and take an appropriate branch (polymorphic behavior) or perform its process by calling other generic functions defined over the same domain. The lower-level function could, in turn, pass the argument on to another generic function. However, a chain of such generic calls must ultimately end with a call on a bottom-level polymorphic function or a generic function that is defined by a set of specific methods. This bottom-level function will include one body of code for each representation of the generic data type that the programmer is using. In the Prettyprint example of Exhibit 17.4, the chain of calls will end with a call on some body for print-node that is defined to format and print out the data from one specific type of node.

Exhibit 17.3.   A function with generic formal parameters.

Assume that number is a generic type which includes types integer and real. If we were to define the function Square on numbers (using a Pascal-like syntax), the function header would be similar to this:

    Function Square(a: number):number;

Assume that the integer variables k and m have been declared, and we call the function thus:

    k := Square(m);

We would like this call to be legal. The formal parameter, a, is generic, and the actual argument has a specific type which is a subtype of that generic. We would like the subtype integer to *inherit* the definition for Square that was supplied for its generic supertype.

Exhibit 17.4.   A generic function defined by a single method.

Assume that you are working with binary trees in a hypothetical language that permits definition of generic procedures. Prettyprint is a procedure that prints a generic data type called binary_tree.

Prettyprint calls the explicitly generic functions print-node, go-to-left-son, and go-to-right-son, but it does not do any operations that depend on how the tree is represented.

The programmer must define one method for each of these three functions for every kind of tree node being used. Once this is done, one method suffices to define prettyprint for the entire generic domain binary_tree, no matter how many ways that domain might be implemented.

Generic Functions in Ad Hoc Domains

An ad hoc generic domain has subdomains that are related by their semantics rather than by having some common structure. Definitions of a function over two specific domains with an ad hoc relationship may look quite different if they depend on the representation. The most that can be said is that they perform the same semantic action on objects of the different specific domains. For example, consider the ADT "Stack", which includes the two generic subdomains "array_stack" and "linked_list_stack". The type declarations that are appropriate for implementing an "array_stack" and a "linked_list_stack" are shown in Exhibits 17.5 and 17.6. These sets of definitions have little in common except the names. Specifically, the selector functions defined in one bear no systematic relationship to the selectors defined for the other.

Exhibit 17.5.   Pascal definition of push on an `array_stack`.

Here are type declarations and the function push for a stack of 100 reals:

```
CONST len = 100;
TYPE real_stack= RECORD
        store:   ARRAY [1..len] OF real;
        top:   0..len  END;
VAR rs:   real_stack;
    value:  real;
FUNCTION push (VAR rs:real_stack; r:real):  boolean;
BEGIN
    IF rs.top = len THEN push := false (* error flag *)
    ELSE BEGIN
        push := true;
        rs.top := rs.top + 1;
        rs.store [rs.top] := r
    END (* IF rs.top *)
END; (* push *)
```

The code for push on an array-represented stack [Exhibit 17.5] bears no easily described relationship to the code for push on a linked-list-represented stack [Exhibit 17.6], even though they carry out the same abstract operation. Representation-dependent functions such as push and pop *must* be defined by separate methods for the species of an ad hoc generic domain. However, the common intent of the subdomains is known to the programmer, and the common functionality can be expressed by providing appropriate definitions for the stack operations. Further functions can then be defined in a representation-independent way for the generic domain `stack`, in terms of these declared abstract functions.

When two species of a generic domain are related by their intent, it is possible to define conversion functions that map the elements of one onto the elements of the other and vice versa. This mapping is done in such a way that corresponding elements are alternative representations of the same external object. When such a mapping is applied, the physical form of the program object is changed but the semantic intent is preserved. These conversion functions are unlike other functions. They do not merely operate on elements of the generic domain; they actually define the semantics of the generic relationship.

Exhibit 17.6. Pascal definition of push for a list_stack.

Compare the code below for the function push on a linked-list implementation of a stack to the code in Exhibits 17.5 and 17.15 for the same generic operation on an array implementation of a stack.

```
TYPE list_stack = ↑stack_cell;
     stack_cell = RECORD
          val :  real;
          next:  list_stack END;
VAR rs:  list_stack;
    value:  real;
FUNCTION push (VAR rs:list_stack; r:real):  boolean;
VAR t:list_stack;
BEGIN
    push := true;                 (* stack cannot overflow *)
    t := rs;                      (* save current stack pointer *)
    NEW(rs);                      (* append new cell to top of stack *)
    rs↑.val := r;                 (* initialize new cell *)
    rs↑.next := t
END (* push *)
```

17.2 LIMITED GENERIC BEHAVIOR

Working with domains that have several natural representations becomes difficult in a strongly typed language when the representations must interact, unless the language permits some deviation from the one-type-one-semantics rule. For this reason, many older languages support some predefined generics and/or permit some flexibility in the types of array arguments. In this section we explore ways in which limited forms of nonhomogeneous domains can be and have traditionally been supported.

17.2.1 Union Data Types

Generic domains arise naturally in many algorithms. For example, consider the data structure called a "balanced tree", or "B-tree". This is a branching index structure in which internal nodes point to other nodes and leaf nodes point to potentially large data records. "Node", then, has two varieties, "internal" and "leaf", and the programmer working with these trees must mix the two representations in one structure. What is needed is the ability to define a type "node" that has two independent realizations, or a type "pointer-to-node" that can point at either a data record or another node.

Union data types have been used to implement balanced trees, but they are not a good solution for two reasons. First is the possible violation of the semantic intent unless the union is discriminated, in which case the translator guarantees that the discriminant tag is always correct, and the type checker always checks this tag. With fewer restrictions, a function could be applied to the wrong variant. Second, union data types are not a practical solution when the size of the more frequently used representation is much smaller than the size of the other, because of the excessive amount of storage that would be consumed by the allocated but unused portions of every record. B-trees are an example of a programmer-defined domain for which union data types are not a good implementation.

The C language is popular partly because it permits a direct implementation of this kind of pointer structure. Any C pointer type can be cast to any other pointer type, and such a cast can be used to make a pointer to a leaf node assignment-compatible with a pointer to an interior node. Since types are not checked when pointer assignments are done, there is no problem having pointers in the same tree point at two types of nodes. Programmers then become responsible for doing their own type checking on the nodes. This kind of flexibility is not available, though, in languages that provide the semantic protection of thorough type checking.

17.2.2   Overloaded Names

The several methods of a generic function implement a single external operation over different species of one generic domain. In an ideal language, we would have one name per generic function, whether the function was predefined (like "=") or defined by the programmer. For example, no matter how many instances of the stack ADT we make, we would like to be able to refer to the stack functions as "push" and "pop". It is evident that older languages such as Pascal are far from ideal! If we defined two kinds of stacks in a Pascal program, we would have to define the stack functions twice and give them different names. In modern languages, we are permitted to "overload" a function name by defining multiple methods for one function. An *overloaded name* is a name with two or more bindings in the same scope.

Overloaded names, unfortunately, are not restricted to use with generic functions. If a language supports name overloading, nothing can stop a programmer from overusing it. An overloaded name could be used to denote semantically unrelated processes on unrelated types as easily as to denote a true generic function.

Ada supports the traditional generic arithmetic operators and extensible name overloading.[2] The semantics of these operators can be extended by adding new methods to the existing predefined set. This is called "overloading" because each operator name denotes several specific methods: a "heavy load" for one name. However, no distinction is made in Ada between methods that carry out the semantics of arithmetic and those whose semantics are unrelated. Both kinds of methods may be added to the primitive functions. For example, we might use overloading to extend Ada's "+" function to include methods for "`integer + float`" and "`string concatenate string`", as suggested in Exhibit 17.7. The first method belongs in the same generic family as the primitive methods. The second one is semantically unrelated and does not. The language permits any existing arithmetic operator to be overloaded, but new ones may not be defined.

---

[2] A short clarification of terminology seems necessary here to avoid confusion. Two kinds of generic objects are supported in Ada. In Ada references, the term "generic" refers to parameterized source-code modules, which are covered later in this chapter, and the term "overloaded" refers to operator names which have ambiguous meanings.

Exhibit 17.7. An overloaded function, "+".

Many different abstract processes have been called "+", all of them dyadic, associative, and resembling addition in some way:

- Addition: Compute the arithmetic sum of two numbers.
- Logical OR: Result is "true" if either argument, or both arguments, are "true".
- Set union: Join two sets together and eliminate duplicates.
- String concatenation: Attach one string to the end of another.

"+" is an overloaded generic function because these processes do not have the same semantic intent, and their domains are unrelated. At the same time, ordinary addition is defined over the generic domain "number", which includes integers, reals, etc. This subset of "+" that deals with addition forms a pure generic function.

Using the arithmetic function name "+" to symbolize something unrelated to addition (such as concatenation) is a questionable practice. We want to make a clear distinction between generic functions that implement a single abstract function and those that include methods for a mishmash of abstract functions. Hereafter, we will use the term *generic function* to mean a function name that represents a single abstract function over a generic domain. The term *overloaded function* will refer to a single name used to represent any collection of function methods, possibly having unrelated meanings. Pure generic functions have clean semantics and obey the principle of distinct representation (see Chapter 2.3); overloaded functions do not.

17.2.3 Fixed Set of Generic Definitions, with Coercion

"Number" is the best-known and most-used generic domain. It was recognized early in the history of computing that integers and reals (and in COBOL, BCD strings) are all representations of numbers, and that the programmer must be able to work with all kinds of numbers without worrying about type conversions. Thus the generic domain "number" has been built into most older languages. To say that this generic mode is built-in, we mean that the programmer is permitted to use objects belonging to both primitive types as if they belonged to the same domain. More precisely:

- Two or more representations of the external domain "number" are defined in the language as primitive types.
- Conversion functions are predefined that allow one- or two-way compatibility between those primitive types.
- The language syntax allows objects of the two types to be used together in contexts that were defined only for homogeneous pairs.
- The compiler will coerce an argument of one type to make it appropriate for a context that requires the other.

In FORTRAN 77, C, and Pascal, the functions "+", "−", "*", and "/" are generic functions, defined over the implicit generic domain "number" [Exhibit 17.2]. However, languages designed before the mid-1970s rarely permit the programmer to define new generic functions or even to define new methods for existing generic functions.

When generic functions are built into a language, they often interact with rules for type coercion. In the diagrams of "+" for both Pascal and FORTRAN, note the absence of a method for adding an integer and a real. These languages permit the programmer to write arithmetic expressions that involve a mixture of real and integer operands. However, these computations are not implemented by separately defined methods. Rather, they are implemented by a combination of the method for real addition and a coercion function which converts an integer to a real. The conversion from integer to real is meaningful because both domains can be used to represent the same external objects (whole numbers). These conversion functions can thus be invoked, without a change in the semantics of the argument, when they are needed to carry out the computation.

In contrast, Ada also supports the implicit generic domain "number" but not mixed-type arithmetic. The arithmetic operators are generic, and predefined methods for "+" include:

```
function "+" (x,y: integer) return integer;
function "+" (x,y: float ) return float ;
```

However, Ada does not support representation coercion of any sort, so addition of an integer and a float is not predefined. It *is* possible for a programmer to define a limited number of mixed-type operations in Ada. This is explained more fully in Section 17.2.4.

A more elaborate built-in generic function is the COBOL assignment command, MOVE. Several definitions of MOVE exist which allow the large number of numeric and nonnumeric data types to be used together. MOVE is also invoked automatically in the process of performing arithmetic, input, and output.

17.2.4 Extending Predefined Operators

As in most languages, the arithmetic operators in Ada are generic, and the intended meaning of each operator is determined by looking at the types of its operands and selecting the method defined for those types. This very limited generic facility was included in Ada, as in most common languages, for convenience, so that the programmer could use more than one representation of numbers without needing to learn unfamiliar unique names for the operator methods.

Unlike many languages, however, Ada does not provide automatic type coercion to make a set of operands conform to the types declared in one of the available methods. Thus mixed-type operations are not predefined. To compensate for this lack, Ada permits more methods to be loaded onto the existing arithmetic operators[3] [Exhibit 17.8]. Each new method must involve a new combination of operand types. As a happy side effect, the overloading mechanism permits us to extend the basic arithmetic operators to work on programmer-defined types [Exhibit 17.9]. A separate function must be explicitly provided for every combination of operator and operand types that the programmer wishes to use. This can lead to quite a lot of definitions if more than one operator or more than two types of operands are involved. To write a large number of these would indeed be tedious!

---

[3]A similar facility was provided by the MAD compiler, Arden, Galler, and Graham [1963].

Exhibit 17.8. Definition of new methods for an Ada operator.

We can implement mixed-type addition by adding new methods to the predefined set. The new method works by explicitly converting one of the operands to be compatible with the type of the other, creating operands of the right types for a previously defined method. The first definition below defines the semantics for "3 + 5.2" but not for "5.2 + 3". The second definition is also required to permit "+" to be called with integer and float operands in either order.

```
function "+" (x:  integer, y:float) return float is
    begin return float(x) + y end "+";

function "+" (x:  float, y:integer) return float is
    begin return x + float(y) end "+";
```

Exhibit 17.9. Extensions of Ada operators for new types.

This exhibit further develops the material in Exhibit 17.8. We extend "*" to operate on the mapped domain float and extend "+" to add two vectors.

```
type mass is new float;
type vector is array (1..5) of integer;
function "*" (x:  integer; y:mass) return mass is
    begin return mass (float(x) * float(y)) end "*";
function "+" (x,y:  vector) return vector is
    z:  vector;
    begin
        for k in 1..5 loop z(k) := x(k) + y(k) end loop;
        return z;
    end "+";
```

Examples of new method definitions are given in Exhibit 17.9. The first declaration extends "*" to work on an integer and a new type represented by float. The domain structure built up here begins to be complicated, demonstrating a two-step relationship within a generic domain. To multiply a mass by an integer requires a demotion cast (mass-to-float) and a conversion (integer-to-float). Finally, a promotion cast (float-to-mass) is required to correctly label the type of the result.

The second function defined in Exhibit 17.9 extends the "+" operator to a compound type, vector.[4]

17.2.5 Flexible Arrays

It is not difficult to code a function that can process any length array of a given base type. Processing of "flexible arrays" is supported in some very old languages, for ex-

---

[4]This is possible because Ada supports coherent passage of compound objects as parameters. An explicit declaration of k is not required; the for loop implicitly declares the loop variable.

ample both FORTRAN [Exhibit 17.10] and C [Exhibit 17.11]. These functions work because the method for summing the elements of a vector involves a process that is repeated for each vector element. The length of the vector is passed as a separate argument and used to stop repetition.

Flexible array parameters are implemented very simply and very similarly in C and FORTRAN. Array arguments are passed by reference in both languages. This avoids the need to allocate storage space for the argument in the function's stack frame, and the need to copy the contents of the array into that stack frame. Neither language supports automatic run-time bounds checks for arrays. The lack of prior knowledge of the size of the array causes no problem for the compiler, since no compile-time decisions are based on it. To ensure correct processing, a flexible array argument must have a recognizable terminating value, or the array length must be passed as a separate argument.

In FORTRAN, the dimensions of an array parameter do not need to be declared, so long as they are also passed as parameters or declared in a COMMON statement as global variables. Processing can proceed correctly so long as the array length is known at run time. Exhibit 17.10 shows how a flexible array might be processed in FORTRAN. Following are the program notes:

a. SUMUP is defined as a function of two parameters that returns a real.

b. The parameter AR is defined as a real array of unknown length.

c. This line defines the scope of a loop (up to statement #10) and directs that it should be executed N times, with I taking on the values 1 to N.

d. This is not a recursive call. FORTRAN does not support recursion. Within a function, the function name serves as a local variable.

e. The final value assigned to SUMUP is returned at END.

Exhibit 17.10.   An implicit parameterized domain in FORTRAN.

The letters at the right refer to the notes in the text; they are not part of the program.

```
        REAL FUNCTION SUMUP (AR, N)      (a)
        REAL AR(N)                       (b)
        SUMUP=0.0
        DO 10 I=1,N                      (c)
        SUMUP = SUMUP + AR(I)            (d)
   10   CONTINUE
        END                              (e)
```

Similarly, in C, arrays are passed by reference and subscript bounds are not checked at all. With multidimensional arrays, all dimensions except the first must be known at compile time in order to translate subscript expressions. However, the first (left-hand) dimension is not used in subscript computations. Thus the first dimension of an array parameter does not need to be declared in the function.

In Exhibit 17.11 we define a C version of the FORTRAN function in Exhibit 17.10. The following notes are keyed to the comments in the code. Line a declares the types of the formal parameters. Note that the length of array ar is not specified. Line b declares a local floating-point variable, sum, to be used as an accumulator. Lines c and d comprise a for loop that will be repeated n times, with variable i taking on the subscripts 0 to n − 1. This loop adds the i-th array element to the sum. Line e returns from the function with the final value of sum.

Exhibit 17.11.   A parameterized domain in C: array of floats.

```
real sumup (float ar[], int n)          /* a */
{   int i;
    float sum;                          /* b */
    for ( sum=0.0, i=0; i<n; i++ )      /* c */
        sum = sum + ar[i];              /* d */
    return sum;                         /* e */
}
```

These are examples of implicit, not explicit, parameterized generic domains. However, they demonstrate that an implementation of integer-parameterized domains can be straightforward. A function with a "flexible array" parameter is, technically, generic, because it can accept arguments of many specific types. However, it does not cause the compilation and interpretation problems inherent in type-parameterized generics. The code for a flexible array argument can be compiled and type checked (but not bounds checked) because all the types involved are determined at compile time.[5]

Arrays with Explicitly Parameterized Bounds

The inclusion (or exclusion) of flexible array parameters in Pascal caused a great deal of dissension among the twenty members of the International Standards Organization committee that developed the standard for Pascal. In the end, array arguments with flexible bounds, called *conformant arrays*, were included in ISO Level 1 Standard Pascal, but not in the ANSI standard. American implementations of Pascal, therefore, generally lack this important facility.

One of the issues the committee argued about was run-time bounds checks, which are normally part of Pascal semantics. Rather than expecting the programmer to pass this information separately or implicitly, the syntax for a conformant array parameter indicates that the bounds are passed *as part of* the argument. These bounds are named in the formal parameter list and can be accessed within the code. Exhibit 17.12 shows how the function to sum a vector would be written in ISO Pascal. The conformant array parameter can be passed as either a value or a VAR parameter.

---

[5] Automatic bounds checks cannot be done in C since the array bounds are not specified at compile time and are not supplied at run time in a form that the run-time system can access.

Exhibit 17.12.   A Pascal function with a conformant array parameter.

Compare this ISO Pascal function definition to the C example in Exhibit 17.11. Note that the bounds of the Pascal array are automatically passed as parameters to the function; they are named and can be used in the code.

```
Function SumUp(VAR ar[ Lower..Upper ] of real):real;
Var i:  integer;
    Sum:  real;
Begin
    Sum := 0.0;
    For i:= Lower to Upper do
        Sum := Sum + Ar[i];
    SumUp := Sum
End;
```

Here are some data declarations and two appropriate calls on the SumUp function.

```
Var Scores:  array[1..3] of real;
    Charges:  array[1..1000] of real;
    Answer := SumUp(Scores);
    Answer := SumUp(Charges);
```

17.3 PARAMETERIZED GENERIC DOMAINS

Varying the bounds or base type of an array or the type of a field in a record creates a collection of closely related types. If we write a type expression with dummy parameters in place of one or more of its fields, the result is a *parameterized type expression*. Consider the domain which is the union of all the domains associated with a parameterized type, for all possible values of the parameters. We call this a *parameterized domain*. Exhibit 17.13 shows a parameterized type and two domains which have been derived from it by instantiation.

Exhibit 17.14 shows a mutually recursive pair of types which include a parameterized type and a pointer type which depends on it. The two domains formed by these types are both generic. Type cell has explicit parameters. Type cell_ptr is defined in terms of cell and thus "inherits" the generic nature of cell.

A parameterized type expression is not compilable code as it stands. Rather, it is a template from which code can be created by instantiation. In an instantiation call, the programmer supplies actual, specific arguments. When this call is processed, the arguments are substituted for the dummy parameters in the type expression, according to the lambda calculus substitution rule. The result is an ordinary type expression. Instantiation happens during an early phase of compilation, before parsing. To use a parameterized generic type, the programmer would create a parameterized source code module containing the parameterized type expression(s) and related function definitions.

With a type-parameterized generic, the processing method is not quite independent of the type of an argument. For example, the code for pop and push on a stack of reals is almost the same as the code for a stack of integers, except that a different number of bytes of information will need to be fetched, stored, or returned to the calling program. Similarly, matrix multiplication is the same process whether operating on a matrix of reals or integers, except that appropriate methods for the "*" and "+" functions must be used.

Exhibit 17.13.   A parameterized type.

We define a type with two parameters, an integer and a type, then instantiate it to produce two specific subtypes. (The syntax used is an extension of Pascal.)

Intent: A buffer for items of type TT.
Parameterized type expression:

```
TYPE BUF(m:integer, TT: type) = array [0..m] of TT
```

Specific instances derived by instantiation:

Call	Resulting specific type
`Buf(5, real)`	`array [0..5] of real`
`Buf(10, integer)`	`array [0..10] of integer`

Exhibit 17.14.   A parameterized linked list type.

Intent: A linked list cell.
Parameterized type expressions:

```
Type cell_ptr = ↑cell;
Type cell(DD:type) = record data:  DD; next:  cell_ptr end;
```

Specific instances:

Call	Resulting specific type
`cell(integer)`	`record data:integer; next:cell_ptr end`
`cell(mytype)`	`record data:mytype; next:cell_ptr  end`

If a function were defined for several species of one type-parameterized domain, the source code for the various definitions would very likely be identical except for the types of the parameters. (Compare the code for push in Exhibits 17.5 and 17.15.) The object code, however, is not identical, because the compiler uses the type declarations to compile appropriate methods for the built-in generic functions such as fetch, store, "=", "*", and "+". Thus the types of objects must be known before the code can be fully compiled.

Exhibit 17.15.   Pascal definition of push on a stack of characters.

Here are type declarations and the function push for a stack of 15 characters. Note that the code between BEGIN and END is the same as in Exhibit 17.5; only the type declarations have changed.

```
CONST len = 15;
TYPE char_stack = RECORD
        store:  ARRAY [1..len] OF char;
        top:  0..len  END;
VAR rs:  char_stack;
    value:  char;
FUNCTION push (VAR rs:char_stack; r:char):boolean;
BEGIN
    IF rs.top = len THEN push := false (* error flag *)
    ELSE BEGIN
        push := true;
        rs.top := rs.top + 1;
        rs.store [rs.top] := r
    END (* IF rs.top *)
END; (* push *)
```

When a programmer writes specific type declarations and code that uses them, we say that the data types are *bound at source time*. This is the only programming style supported by languages in the Pascal family, and it does not permit use of user-defined generic domains.

17.3.1   Domains with Type Parameters

We should distinguish between an integer-parameterized domain (a flexible array) and a type-parameterized domain, which has a type parameter like the type cell in Exhibit 17.14. Few existing languages permit component types to be parameterized, while several languages permit functions to be written with implicit or explicit flexible arrays.

An ADT is a collection of types, functions, and objects that express an abstract process on abstract data. When Pascal programmers wish to use an ADT such as "stack" or "linked list", they start by writing type declarations for their own data and for the ADT; they then write out definitions for the ADT functions, making adjustments to the function headers so that they are compatible with their own types. If two variants on the generic domain are needed, each part of the ADT must be written out twice.

Rewriting and re-debugging the functions for a common ADT is tedious but not difficult. The code for each new variety of stack is so similar to the code for other varieties that code can be copied out of a reference book with minimal modification. This leads us to ask whether it is possible to automate the process of coding up a new version of an ADT. We would like to keep the ADT code in a library, so that it does not need to be reentered manually each time it is used.

Many ADTs can be expressed as sets of parameterized type definitions and functions with parameters of those types. Definitions of this sort can easily be kept in a library, but we need a way to relate the type parameters in the library modules to the types in a user's program. Also, the function headers for the ADT must be made compatible with the user's own data types.

The easiest way to achieve these goals is by adding a preprocessor to the language translator. The ADT is coded as a parameterized module that contains type and function declarations written in terms of the generic parameters. These symbols will be bound to specific meanings at precompile time by appropriate preprocessor commands. A library of parameterized source code modules could be made available to programmers to include and instantiate, as needed. Before compiling, the preprocessor is used to supply specific meanings for the generic parameters. The source code package is then expanded, like a macro, using these symbol definitions. All parameterized type declarations, function definitions, and object declarations in the package are expanded to form normal nonparameterized instantiations.

17.3.2   Preprocessor Generics in C

Exhibit 17.16 shows how one might use C to write code for a generic sorted-linked-list type. Such a package would contain definitions for several linked-list functions, including insert_item, delete_item, and several others. For simplicity, only one of these functions is shown here. (The identifiers written in uppercase are symbols that will be defined and instantiated by the preprocessor.)

Exhibit 17.16.   Definition of a generic domain in C.

Below are type declarations for a generic type "sorted linked list" and one function whose domain is this type. Each list cell consists of one data item and a pointer to the next list cell. The generic symbols are written in uppercase letters and will be defined as macros by the programmer and expanded by the C preprocessor before actual compilation. Exhibit 17.18 shows the result of expanding this code with one set of symbol definitions shown in Exhibit 17.17.

```
typedef struct cell {ELEMENT data; struct cell *next;} CELL;
typedef CELL * LIST;
/*--------------------------------------------------------------*/
int find_item(ELEMENT find, LIST head, LIST *scan, LIST *prior)
{
    scan = head;
    prior = NULL;
    while ( GREATHAN( find, (*scan)->data))
    {   *prior = *scan;
        *scan = (*scan)->next;
    }
    return EQUALS( find, (*scan)->data );
}
```

The generic function find_item was written in terms of the generic type names and the generic functions GREATHAN and EQUALS, which must be defined before expansion. The functions of dereference (*), selection (->), and assignment (=) are also used, but these are defined by the nongeneric part of the type definition. Nothing in the function code depends on the particular type to which ELEMENT will be bound; an ELEMENT could be a single character or a lengthy record.

To use the generic list package in Exhibit 17.16, the user must include in the program definitions of ELEMENT and of the associated type-dependent operations. In all, this is several lines of routine and tedious code. A convenient way to automate the inclusion process is to put the code for several commonly useful types into a header file and use conditional compilation to include only the appropriate set of definitions.

A header file is given in Exhibit 17.17 that would permit the generic linked-list module to be used for linked lists of character strings or of integers. If some other type of data were to be used, a group of similar definitions would have to be written for it and included in another conditional clause. To use this header file, the programmer must type one of the following pairs of lines at the top of the code:

For lists of strings	For lists of integers
#include "lists.h" #define ALPHA 1	#include "lists.h" #define INTEGER 1

Exhibit 17.17.   Using a generic type in C.

This is a header file that would permit the generic linked-list module to be used for linked lists of character strings or of integers.

```
/* The function "strcmp" performs alphabetic comparison of two strings, */
/* "strcpy" copies a string value into a string variable.  */
/* '\377' is the octal code for the largest 1-byte character.  */
#if ALPHA
    #define ELEMENT char *
    #define LESSTHAN(x, y)   ( (strcmp((x),(y)) < 0 )
    #define GREATHAN(x, y)   ( (strcmp((x),(y)) > 0 )
    #define EQUALS(x, y)     ( (strcmp((x),(y)) == 0 ))
    #define ASSIGN(x, y)     ( strcpy((x),(y)) )
    #define MAXVAL           '\377'  /* Octal for char code 255.*/
#elif SHORT
    #define ELEMENT short int
    #define LESSTHAN(x, y)   ( (x) <(y) )
    #define GREATHAN(x, y)   ( (x) >(y) )
    #define EQUALS(x, y)     ( (x)==(y) )
    #define ASSIGN(x, y)     ( (x)=(y) )
    #define MAXVAL           0x7fff
#endif
```

The value of the #define symbol is tested by the preprocessor's #if command, which triggers inclusion or exclusion of the dependent definitions. During preprocessing, the generic package is converted to a set of ordinary declarations and definitions which define and process a specific type. Exhibit 17.18 shows the ordinary code that results from expanding these generic definitions for type argument char*.

Exhibit 17.18.   Specific code results from preprocessing.

This function is the result of including the header file in Exhibit 17.17 with the symbol ALPHA defined to be 1, and expanding the parameterized code in Exhibit 17.16.

```
typedef struct cell {char * data; struct cell *next;} CELL;
typedef CELL * LIST;
/*------------------------------------------------------------*/
int find_item(char * find, LIST head, LIST *scan, LIST *prior)
{
    scan = head;
    prior = NULL;
    while ( strcmp( (find),((*scan)->data) ) > 0 ) {
        prior = *scan;
        scan = (*scan)->next;
    }
    return (strcmp( (find), ((*scan)->data) ) == 0);
}
```

Ada *Generic Packages*

We can implement an ADT in Ada as a *generic package*. A package is a module that contains type, data, and/or function declarations.[6] An Ada *generic* is a parameterized template which can be instantiated to create a subprogram or a package. We will examine a simple generic subprogram first, then tackle the problem of combining a generic with a package.

Parameters to a generic subprogram can be types, array lengths, or function names. The generic parameters are used as follows:

- The integer parameters to the package are used as array bounds in parameterized type expressions within the package.
- The type parameters are also used in parameterized type expressions. If the data structure within the package uses two interdependent types, such as "cell" and "cell_pointer", both must be passed as parameters.
- A generic must have one functional parameter for each representation-dependent function or operation that is used in the body of the generic.

Exhibit 17.19 gives an Ada generic definition for addition on length-three numeric vectors. Such a definition might be part of a generic package and be included

---

[6]Ada packages were described in Chapter 16.

in a library. Let us examine each part of the generic code in Exhibit 17.19 so that we may see how these parts work together.

Exhibit 17.19.   A parameterized domain in Ada: vector of numbers.

Step 1 is definition of the generic template:

```
generic
    type NUMBER is private;                                   -- (a)
    type VECTOR is array (1 .. 3) of NUMBER;                  -- (b)
    with function PLUS (x,y:  NUMBER) return NUMBER;          -- (c)
    procedure vector_add (v1, v2:  in VECTOR; v3:  out VECTOR); -- (d)
procedure vector_add (v1, v2:  in VECTOR; v3:  out VECTOR) is   -- (e)
    begin
        for J in 1..3 loop v3(J) := PLUS( v1(J), v2(J) ) end loop;
end vector_add;
```

We begin definition of a generic subprogram by declaring the generic parameters (written here in capital letters). Line (a) declares a dummy type name, NUMBER. The predefined generic domain named private is used for any type parameter for which assignment and tests for equality are defined. Thus this generic definition can be instantiated with arrays of integer, float, or any other type which permits assignment and tests for equality.

Ada provides a very small collection of predefined generic domains. In addition to private, generic domains are defined for integer types, floating-point types, fixed-point types, finite types, and pointer types, and for the completely general type with no known properties. Ada programmers are not allowed to define their own generic domains; each generic type parameter must be declared to belong to one of the predefined domains. The programmer, therefore, selects one that comes closest to the properties of his or her own application's domains. We use the type NUMBER in this example, which is a superdomain of all the numeric generic domains that are predefined. We, therefore, declare NUMBER as private.

A second type parameter, VECTOR, is declared on line (b). Even though VECTOR is defined in terms of NUMBER, it must be passed as a separate parameter. This certainly makes the preprocessor easier to implement but is annoying for the programmer.

The code of the generic routine cannot "just use" any operations except assignment and equality-comparison, since these are the only functions that are "guaranteed" for the domain private. Often this is no problem, as the code of many functions relies only on these two basic operations. For example, only assignment is needed to define the "push" and "pop" functions for stacks. However, the code for vector_add uses both assignment and "+" for NUMBERs. To do so, "+" must be declared as a parameter (line c).

The generic procedure header must be declared before the actual definition is given. Line (d) uses the parameter names to declare the function named vector_add. There are three parameters, two vectors to add up, and one to receive the answer. On line (e) we finally begin definition of the actual procedure. The syntax is the same as an ordinary nongeneric procedure, except that it uses the generic type parameter(s).

A generic procedure or package must be instantiated before the code can be compiled. Prior to instantiation, the programmer must write a specific type definition for each type parameter and a specific function method for each of the package's functional parameters. Finally, the programmer must write an instantiation command using these predefined specific objects as arguments. The instantiation call is given as part of a declaration for the name that will be bound to the instantiated procedure or package. This name must be a new, unique name. To instantiate a generic procedure or package we write:

> **procedure** ⟨procedure name⟩ **is new** ⟨generic name⟩ (⟨specific argument list⟩);
> **package** ⟨package name⟩ **is new** ⟨generic name⟩ (⟨specific argument list⟩);

During the instantiation process, the compiler substitutes the actual arguments supplied by the programmer for the generic parameter names and expands the template into ordinary, fully specific, compilable source code. This is then compiled and bound to a unique function name supplied by the programmer. This name refers to exactly one procedure or package and is not generic or ambiguous at all. If the programmer wishes to instantiate the same package twice, she or he must supply two names for the results.

To instantiate the `vector_add` template we must first define any new specific types and functions needed for the parameters PLUS, NUMBER, and VECTOR. For example, to create a vector of floats, type `float` and floating-point addition are already defined, but we need to declare a new type consisting of an array of three floats. Then we write an `is new` declaration containing a call on the template with these actual arguments.

In Exhibit 17.20, we define two length-three numeric array types—`int_vec` and `real_vec`. We use each of these types to instantiate the generic from Exhibit 17.19. In line (g) we instantiate the `vector_add` template. We indicate that the type parameter NUMBER is to be replaced by the type `integer`, VECTOR is to become `int_vec`, and PLUS is the standard "+". The translator will make these substitutions and generate ordinary, compilable, nongeneric code for a procedure named `int_vector_add`.

Exhibit 17.20.   Instantiating a generic template in Ada.

```
type real_vec is array (1 .. 3) of float;                              -- (f)
type int_vec is array (1 .. 3) of integer;
procedure int_vector_add                                               -- (g)
   is new vector_add(NUMBER=>integer, VECTOR=>int_vec, PLUS =>"+");
procedure real_vector_add                                             -- (h)
   is new vector_add(NUMBER=>float, VECTOR=>real_vec, PLUS =>"+");
```

We repeat the instantiation process in line (h) with types `float` and `real_vec`, producing the nongeneric procedure named `real_vector_add`. Now we have two ordinary procedures that are alike except for their names and the types of their parameters. The object code will contain translations of both copies. Note that no definition of the function argument was given; when this is done it defaults to the definition (if any) for that symbol in the context surrounding the generic definition.

A Generic Package.

We have described both packages and generics in Ada. The normal way to use both generics and packages is by combining them—a package definition is placed inside a generic declaration, producing a generic package. Such a package has parameterized public and private parts that can be instantiated with various component types and array lengths to produce code tailored to an individual application. The elements that must be present in an Ada generic definition are:

1. The generic parameter declarations.
2. The package header, containing declarations of the public symbols.
3. The package body, containing definitions of public and private symbols.

As an example, we show in Exhibit 17.21 how the code for the stack package in Exhibit 16.6 can be generalized to a parameterized generic module. First, the entire package is nested within a generic declaration. Then all references to the base type of the stack and the length of the stack are replaced by references to the generic parameters.

We can instantiate this package, as shown in Exhibit 17.22, to create multiple stack packages, each with its own storage and its own copy of the code for each function. Within this code, calls on PUSH, POP, and TOP will be compiled with meanings for the fetch and store operations that are appropriate for the actual type of the type-argument. Note that we give a name to each specific package in the instantiation command. When we call the PUSH that belongs to a package, the name of the package is used, with ".PUSH", to denote the proper method for PUSH. The equivalent of the stack package in Exhibit 16.6 could be created by instantiating STACK with the parameters (10, INTEGER).

Evaluation

An abstract data type (ADT) is a collection of types, functions, and, possibly, objects that express a generic process on generic data. An ADT can be defined in C by using the preprocessor and in Ada by using a generic package. Ada's generic preprocessor is very much like the C macro preprocessor.[7] Thus the capabilities of Ada generics are very similar to those in C.

These preprocessor generics are relatively easy to implement and make real progress toward the goal of creating practical, flexible code libraries. However, they are far more limited than the support for generic types provided in various object-oriented languages. The primary limitation is that final binding of the type parameters happens at precompile time. Thus all type flexibility is lost before compilation begins. If a program deals with a domain that has two or more representations, there

---

[7]There is one major difference in name scoping. Unbound names in a C macro will be interpreted in the context of the macro call. In contrast, unbound names in an Ada generic function will be interpreted in the lexical context of the module in which the generic was defined, not the module containing the instantiation request.

must be two or more instantiations of the package, and two or more names for those instantiations.

Exhibit 17.21.   Declaration of a generic stack package in Ada.

```
generic
    MAX: POSITIVE;                   -- A positive integer.
    type ELEMENT is private;     -- Type of generic parameter.
package STACK is                   -- Declare functions in package.
    function PUSH(X: ELEMENT);
    function POP return ELEMENT;
    function TOP return ELEMENT;
package body STACK is           -- Functions, variables for package.
    stk:array(1..MAX) of ELEMENT;
    tos:  INTEGER range 0..MAX;
    function PUSH(X: ELEMENT) is
    begin
        if tos<MAX then
            tos:=tos+1;  stk(tos):= X;
            return true;
        else return false;
        end if
    end PUSH;
    function TOP return ELEMENT is
    begin
        if tos >0 then return stk(tos);
        else raise STK_FULL;
        end if;
    end TOP;
    function POP return ELEMENT is
        ans:  ELEMENT;
    begin
        ans:= TOP;  tos:=tos-1;
        return ans;
    end POP;
begin
    tos:=0;                          -- Initialization for this package.
end STACK;
```

It is much more difficult to support code with run-time generic flexibility. Most languages which do so are translated by interpreters, not compilers. To support run-time generics, the type of each object must be known at run time, and the translator must include a sophisticated method-dispatcher which examines those types at run time and selects an appropriate method. We will discuss run-time dispatching in Chapter 18.

Exhibit 17.22.   Instances of the stack package.

In writing a program to do a precedence parse and code generation for arithmetic expressions, one needs to use two stacks: a stack of tokens and a stack of expression trees. Here we instantiate the generic stack package from Exhibit 17.21 twice to create these two stacks. For simplicity here, assume that tokens are represented by single characters, and that the function named do_error is the programmer's own error handler and is defined previously.

```
type TOKEN is CHARACTER;
type TREE is access CELL;
type CELL is record
    data:   TOKEN data;
    lson:   TREE;
    rson:   TREE;
end record;
declare
    package tok_s is new STACK(20, TOKEN);
    package tree_s is new STACK(60, TREE);
begin
    if not tok_s.PUSH('#')        -- Push beginning-of-line symbol.
    then do_error("Stack full.") -- Check error return.
    endif;
    ...
```

EXERCISES

1. Contrast generic domains and specific domains.
2. Describe the four ways in which a domain may be considered generic.
3. What are the problems involved in the implementation of generics?
4. What is a virtual function? What is its role?
5. What are the universal generic functions? Explain.
6. What semantic problems are created by the generic function?
7. What is a method? What is dispatching the call?
8. Why must functions such as "push" and "pop" be defined by separate methods for the species of an ad hoc generic domain?
9. Why is generic behavior considered "limited" in older languages?
10. What is a union data type? What are its limitations?
11. What is an overloaded name? What are the dangers involved in overloading?
12. How do built-in generic functions interact with rules for type coercion?
13. How do Ada's predefined operators limit mixed-type operations? How does Ada compensate?
14. What is a flexible array? Why is a function with a flexible array parameter considered generic?

15. What is a parameterized domain? A parameterized type expression?

16. What is the difference between an integer-parameterized domain and a type-parameterized domain? Why do some languages support the former but not the latter?

17. What is the role of the preprocessor in relating the types in library definitions to the types in a user's program?

18. What is a generic package in Ada? How are generic packages related to ADTs?

18

Dispatching with Inheritance

Overview

Types have traditionally been used for the two disparate purposes of describing storage and describing semantics, and this dual use has led to compromises in the power of the language to express type relationships. One approach to the conflict generated by the two needs is to eliminate or subordinate one use. If type checking for function applicability is not done, the language never stands in the way of the programmer, never prevents programmers from doing things they know are sensible or exploiting relationships they know exist. This approach is taken in C. Types are used at the bottom level to allocate, access, and encode but are not used to describe the semantics of classes of objects.

On the other hand, we have languages such as Smalltalk where all objects are represented as pointers. In Smalltalk the type (class) is used primarily to control function application, and data representation is simplified into near uniformity.

Future languages will separate the storage mapping of an object and its domain membership, permitting them to be defined separately. Doing so will enable us to retain the safety of type checking within a language that can exploit domain relationships. A mode graph gives us a systematic way of representing domain relationships and type conversions.

The goal is a language in which the programmer can manipulate abstractions of both objects and functions. This requires that we be able to describe objects and related classes of objects, actions, and variants of those actions. Then the translator must use that information to dispatch functions and coerce arguments.

Implementation of these mechanisms opens up new problems and leads to the need to define parameter domains using type expressions with constraints, rather than simple type constants. The semantic basis of a generic language must include a general type-deduction or type-calculation system.

18.1 REPRESENTING DOMAIN RELATIONSHIPS

In the familiar strongly typed languages, each type declaration creates a new domain, and it is not possible to define two structurally dissimilar types to represent related external domains, then further declare and use the relationship between them. In these languages, types are used both to define the physical representation of an external domain and to define the semantic properties (function applicability) of program objects. Some domain relationships are built into programming languages. For example, most languages have a few conversion routines that can be used by the compiler, when needed, to make sense of the code. However, most languages do not provide a way to express relationships among user-defined domains.

Sometimes a programmer's newly defined domains are unrelated to other domains used in a program. In this case it is not a burden to define a new set of functions for each newly defined domain. However, a programmer's domains are often related and share common properties with each other. Some functions might operate correctly on objects from a variety of related external domains. In the traditional strongly typed language, the programmer must represent all related external domains as variants of one type if they are to be processed by the same set of functions. Generic functions and domains have been developed to solve this dilemma: they permit each variation of a domain to be defined as its own subdomain, and then the relationships among the subdomains are separately declared and used by the translator.

The class hierarchies in the common object-oriented languages (Smalltalk, C++) are tree-structured. The only class relationship supported is the one created by deriving one class from another, and each class can only be derived from one parent. Generalized graphs of classes are not possible in these languages because the objects of a derived class are represented by adding fields to the record type used to represent the parent class. But it is possible to use virtual functions, not class derivation, as the basis for declaring class relationships, and once we do this, we can build a generalized graph of classes.

18.1.1 The Mode Graph and the Dispatcher

In this discussion, we will use a structure called a *mode graph* to discuss how both domain relationships and dispatching can be generalized. We call one node in the graph a *mode*, and diagram it as a round-cornered box, like the box labeled "Number" in Exhibit 18.1. The contents of a mode box vary according to the type of the mode: generic mode boxes contain a list of virtual functions, specific mode boxes contain a type object. Methods defined for a mode are sometimes listed near it. We will consider typed modes, parameterized modes, subdomain modes (or submodes), generic modes, and representation modes. As we discuss modes, we will point out the aspects of this mode graph that have been incorporated into modern languages.

The *dispatcher* is a process built into a generic programming language that uses the information in the mode graph to dispatch methods for function calls. You may visualize it as a mouse that crawls along a maze of tunnels (the mode graph) looking for a method definition that will satisfy the call. Depending on the language, the dispatcher has more or less information available to it, and has more or less freedom to move from one domain in the graph to another, related domain.

Exhibit 18.1. Mode graph for the generic domain "Number".

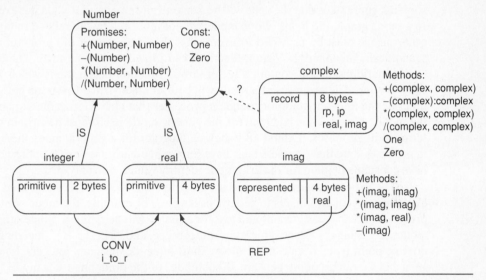

The job of dispatching potentially has two components: work that can be done at compile time because all relevant information is available then, and work that must be deferred until run time. We will distinguish these two job components by talking about the *compile-time dispatcher* and the *run-time dispatcher*. Traditional languages have only a primitive compile-time dispatcher. Modern languages, including object-oriented languages and functional languages, have an extensible compile-time dispatcher and a run-time dispatcher.

Typed Modes.

A typed mode is used in the mode graph to represent nonpolymorphic types, such as `integer` or a record type. Every typed mode has an associated type object.[1] Actual objects all belong to some typed mode, and all function translation and dispatching must start with the typed mode of the argument.[2]

Generic Modes and Promises.

A generic mode represents an abstract domain. Its meaning is defined by a set of virtual functions, rather than by a representation. A generic mode is similar to a C++ base class but differs in two important respects. First, a C++ class has an associated representation, from which other representations may be derived; further, derivation is the only way to create an additional representation of a class. In contrast, a generic mode has no representation when it is first created, but typed modes and other generic modes may be attached to it later. The typed modes are representations of the generic. They might be structurally related, like the instances of a parameterized domain, or might have an arbitrary, ad hoc relationship to each other, like `integer` has to `real`.

---

[1] Review Chapter 14 if necessary.
[2] Just as object-oriented dispatching starts with the class of the implied argument.

In an object-oriented class hierarchy, both the fields of the representation record and the functions that operate on the record are inherited. It is this inherited relationship that guarantees that the code will be semantically meaningful when it is executed. In a mode graph, the fields of one mode are not inherited by the related modes, and other means must be provided to assure that the operation of the program will be semantically meaningful. Virtual functions can provide this assurance. The box for each generic mode will contain a set of virtual function declarations which we will call *promises*. The promises of a mode will be used, like virtual functions in C++, to describe the implementation-dependent processes that characterize the semantics of the mode. Any functions defined for the generic mode itself must be written only in terms of its promises. Exhibit 18.1 shows a diagram for a generic mode Number. In it, promises state that numbers must have four defined arithmetic operations and also have constants defined for the arithmetic identity values, one and zero.

The generic facility in Ada has six predefined modes which can be used to declare the types of arguments to generic packages. For example, the mode "private" promises only that assignment and test for equality will be defined. Some other Ada modes are "range <>", meaning some integer type, and "digits <>", meaning some floating-point type. In our terminology, short integers, unsigned integers, long integers, and subranges of integers are all submodes of the predefined Ada mode "range <>". In turn, "range <>" is a submode of the mode "(<>)" (which includes any discrete type).

Ada would be a better language if it provided a way for programmers to declare new modes with different promises. Having only six modes available, as in Ada, is severely limiting. If the properties of a programmer's domain do not happen to match one of the predefined modes, the programmer must use some other mode with fewer promises, or limited private which has no promises at all. If a function is needed that should be defined for the desired abstract mode, that function must be passed as an argument in the call that instantiates the package. This is a nuisance, at best, and half defeats the purpose of having generics.

Submodes.

A mode graph can be used to represent a variety of domain relationships by introducing varied kinds of links from one mode to another. The links corresponding to Ada modes and to the "derived from" relationship in C++ are called *submode* links and are labeled by the word IS. A submode is one representation of its base mode and inherits function methods from it. In Exhibit 18.1, the modes integer and real are shown as submodes of Number.

An ad hoc generic domain includes two or more specific domains that are related by their meaning rather than by their structure. Physically, the two domains might be represented differently, but logically, they have a common intent and common functionality. An IS link expresses the subdomain relationship that exists between a generic domain and its representations.

In some languages, operations are defined only for specific domains, and the IS relationship is not exploited. In contrast, consider APL, whose designers expected programmers to have infrequent concern about the representation of numbers and frequent use for the semantic relationship among the representations in use. The generic domain "Number", not one of its specific representations, was made primitive. Further, the relationship between the generic domain and its subdomain was made explicit and flexible.[3] Many APL operations are defined for numbers, rather than for either integers or reals. Others, which require the semantics of a discrete type, are defined only for integers.

Declaring and Using Mode Relationships.

The set of promises on a mode provide a semantically sound criterion for being a submode. Thus if modes, promises, and links were all declarable, we could declare M' to be a submode of M as soon as all promised methods were defined for M'. In a generalized graph structure, a mode might have several supermodes, so these methods might be defined directly for M', or might be inherited by M' down some other submode link. In our example, there is no problem with declaring that `integer` and `real` are submodes of `Number`. But before the submode link for `complex` can be declared, the promised arithmetic functions and constants must be defined. Once this is done, we can declare that `complex IS Number`. Now the submode `complex` will inherit the functions defined for `Number`, just as the predefined submodes `integer` and `real` do.

The promises defined for a generic mode guarantee that the promised functions will be defined for every specific instance of the generic mode. This permits us to write representation-independent functions whose domain is the generic mode. When one of those functions must access a representation, it calls a promised function.

When we declare that a specific mode IS a submode of a generic, all functions defined on the generic mode are inherited by the submode. That means that a programmer can call a function F, defined for the generic mode G, on an argument from the submode, S. If F calls one of the promised functions, the dispatcher must find the appropriate method to carry out the promise. To do this, it must look for and dispatch the method that is applicable to the submode S. Often, this dispatching can be done at compile time, but in the most general case, the mode S is not known until run time, and dispatching must be done at the last minute.

Instantiation Modes.

Parameterized generic domains were discussed in Chapter 17, Section 17.3. The C and Ada implementations discussed there both require instantiation of the generic mode and its dependent functions at compile time. The result is that a set of specific types and functions are generated and compiled, and the fact that these were derived from a generic is forgotten. The mode graph can be used to represent the relationship between a parameterized generic domain and an instantiation of that domain. We will diagram this relationship as a BIND link, labeled by the bindings for the generic parameters that were specified in the instantiation call. A BIND link is illustrated in Exhibit 18.2. We will explore the question of delaying binding until run time and consider the advantages and problems caused by that delay.

---

[3]In APL, a number is an integer if and only if it differs from an integral value by no more than the currently defined comparison tolerance.

Exhibit 18.2.   Diagram of an instantiated mode.

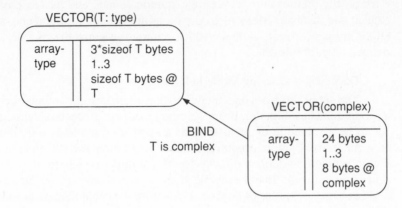

Conversions and Coercions.

Not every one-argument function is a conversion or a cast. Casts arise only from mapped domains and are simply part of the strong typing system of the language. Conversions are defined ad hoc, and only the programmer can know which of his or her functions are legitimate conversions. The important aspect of a conversion is that it must not change the meaning of an object. Defining a conversion can be done in any reasonable language, but most languages do not provide a way to tell the compiler that the function is, indeed, a conversion. C++ permits the programmer to define and declare conversion functions (called constructors), and languages that are now at the stage of research will incorporate more general provisions for declaring conversion functions. Once the compiler knows about the conversion, its dispatcher can use it to coerce arguments, just as the built-in conversions are used.

Without some provision for coercion, domains with multiple representations are unwieldy and almost impractical to use. We can demonstrate the problem in Ada. Ada permits the programmer to define new domains, then define new methods for the existing generic operators that operate on the new domains. The definitions of "+" and "*" for the new domain imag are an example [Exhibit 17.9]. But even though we can extend the intrinsic operators, it is a tedious job to achieve the ease of use of mixed-type arithmetic that is built into Pascal, FORTRAN, and C, because Ada lacks any provision for type coercion. To implement mixed-type arithmetic, the programmer must include definitions for every combination of operator and operand types desired [Exhibit 18.3]. Thus if F binary functions are to be defined over a generic domain with R representations, the number of method definitions needed would be $F \cdot R^2$!

FORTRAN actually supports these four numeric types and supports mixed-type arithmetic on all combinations of operands. However, FORTRAN does not have 64 method definitions for these functions. It has only 16 methods (four each for four operators), plus the conversion functions listed in Exhibit 18.4.

Exhibit 18.3.   Exponential explosion of method definitions.

Assume that a programmer is using four representations of the domain Number: integer, float, double, and complex. To implement full mixed-type arithmetic for these four types, without type coercion, 16 method definitions must exist for each operator. Thus for "+" we would need:

+(int, int)	+(float, int)	+(double, int)	+(complex, int)
+(int, float)	+(float, float)	+(double, float)	+(complex, float)
+(int, double)	+(float, double)	+(double, double)	+(complex, double)
+(int, complex)	+(float, complex)	+(double, complex)	+(complex, complex)

For four arithmetic operators, we would need 64 methods!

Exhibit 18.4.   Coercions built into FORTRAN.

Result Type	Functions Defined
integer	`INT(REAL), NINT(REAL), INT(DOUBLE)`
real	`REAL(INT), REAL(DOUBLE), ABS(CMPLX)`
double	`DBLE(INT), DBLE(REAL)`

Type coercion between alternate representations of the same external domain reduces the number of function method definitions necessary. That is why PL/1 provided coercions from any basic type to any other, directly or through a series of changes. This coercion facility was completely general. Unfortunately, it masked real type errors by changing the type of an erroneous argument to whatever would seem to work. Sometimes this was beneficial, but sometimes it made semantic hash out of the data. It is obviously impossible to create a fixed set of conversions that will handle all mode relationships for all time in a semantically valid manner. When PL/1 tried to anticipate all future conversion needs, and used these conversions to coerce arguments, it resulted, all too often, in converting an object to something else with an unrelated meaning. Worse, coercion errors were especially difficult to track down because the semantically erroneous action was not caused by anything explicitly written in the program, but by some subtle and poorly understood type conversion built into the system.

The only adequate solution is to permit programmers to define their own conversion functions and to declare them in such a way that the compiler can use them for coercion. It would then be the programmer's responsibility to define only semantically valid conversions. We will diagram a conversion function, F, that converts from mode $M1$ to mode $M2$, as a link from $M1$ to $M2$, labeled with "CONV" and the function name. In Exhibit 18.1, a conversion link is shown from integer to real, for a function named "i_to_r". This means that i_to_r can be used explicitly or through coercion to convert an integer to a real.

Represented Modes, Casts, and Coercions.

Both conversion functions and casting functions take a single argument from one domain and return a value from a different domain. When the argument and result are both representations of the same object in the same external domain, the function is a conversion.[4] When the argument type was defined by mapping it onto the result type, or vice versa, the function is a cast.

A cast represents the relationships between two domains. Casts are used, in some languages, by function dispatchers. Thus we want to represent them in our mode graph. A cast relationship is created when the programmer specifies that one mode is to be represented by another. We show it in the mode graph by noting that the type of a mode is a represented type. For example, there is a REP link from imag to real in Exhibit 18.1, because real numbers are being used to represent type imaginary.

Although definition and use of a conversion is often similar in syntax to a cast, the difference is very important: a conversion preserves semantics, a cast changes them. Therefore, a conversion is "safe" for coercion, a cast is not. A cast should never be applied unless the programmer explicitly directs it, and even then, the uses should be restricted to the private parts of classes or their equivalent.

Dispatching

We can view a function as a collection of methods, and dispatching as the problem of choosing the best method for each call. Simply put, the best method is the one whose parameter domains make the best match for the types of the actual arguments. In older languages, only a few predefined operators had more than one defining method, and the "best match" was easy to define; a method is best if:

- Its parameter types match the argument types exactly, or,
- No method matches the argument types exactly but for some method, every nonmatching argument can be coerced, by a built-in conversion function, to match exactly.

The dispatching problem is much more complex in a modern language. First, user-defined functions, as well as predefined operators, have multiple defining methods, so the dispatcher must be written in a more general way. Second, user domains have declarable relationships to other user domains; where a subdomain or an instantiation relationship exists, it should be used by the dispatcher to find methods that can be inherited. Third, user-defined conversion functions must be considered and integrated, as coercions, into the dispatching process.

A mode graph gives us a systematic way to represent domain relationships and type conversions and, thus, forms a framework in which we can look at the dispatching problem. We will use the concept of a mode graph to discuss dispatching in C++, Miranda, and Aleph, which is a newly developed language that provides full support for generics.

---

[4]Review Chapter 15, Section 15.5, if necessary.

18.2 SUBDOMAINS AND CLASS HIERARCHIES

18.2.1 Subrange Types

A domain D' is a *subdomain* of a *superdomain* D if all the elements of D' also belong to the domain D. Many programming languages allow the programmer to declare a new domain that is a subdomain. In Pascal and Ada, the domain corresponding to the subrange type is a subdomain of the domain formed by the base type [Exhibit 18.5].

Exhibit 18.5.   Defining a subdomain in Pascal.

```
TYPE fingers = 1..10;    { A subrange type declaration.}
VAR f1, f2:  fingers;
...
readln(f1);              { Integer functions are defined for fingers.  }
f2 := f1 + 5;            { A legal computation on subdomain fingers.  }
```

The type declaration for `finger` defines a subdomain of the integers; integer operations such as "+" and `readln` are defined over this subdomain.

The domain formed by a subrange type is the easiest kind of subdomain to implement because elements of the subrange type and the base type have the same representation. Values from the subrange type may be freely stored in base-type variables; base-type values may be stored in subrange variables if they are within the defined limits of the subrange. Subrange and base-type values may be compared directly for equality.

Functions defined for the superdomain are *inherited* by the subdomain; that is, any function defined for D is also applicable to objects of subdomain D'. In mathematics, the integers are a subdomain of the reals which are, in turn, a subdomain of the complex numbers. Thus complex operations are applicable to reals and real operations are applicable to integers. With Ada and Pascal subrange types, functions defined for the base type are inherited by (applicable to) objects in the subdomain, but not vice versa.

Any function defined for the base type could accept and process arguments from the subrange type. We say that the subrange type can *inherit* these functions from the base type. No special checking or conversion is needed to make a subrange-type argument appropriate for the base-type function. Conversely, functions defined for a subrange type can process any values from the base type that are within meaningful limits. Thus the base type can inherit functions from the subdomain, and those functions will be meaningful part of the time.

To make subdomains and these simple inheritance relationships work, a translator must include run-time range checks to ensure that every program object stored in a subrange variable or processed by a subrange function does actually belong to the subdomain.

18.2.2 Class Hierarchies

Smalltalk and the other object-oriented languages provide much broader support for subdomains. They allow the programmer to define a new subdomain whose representation is semantically related to the superdomain but is not structurally identical to it. These languages exploit the hierarchically related nature of many external domains. Start with a classification system, such as that shown in Exhibit 18.6. Lines connect each domain (above) to its subdomains (below). Less detail is known about or relevant to the broad class at the top of the hierarchy, but as we move down the subdomain links, more and more details can be specified. Each category in the diagram has its own specific characteristics and inherits characteristics from the categories above it. These domains and their relationships are described in Exhibit 18.7.

Exhibit 18.6.   Diagram of a domain hierarchy.

Domains are diagrammed above their subdomains. As we travel down the links, more and more specific information can be known about each subdomain.

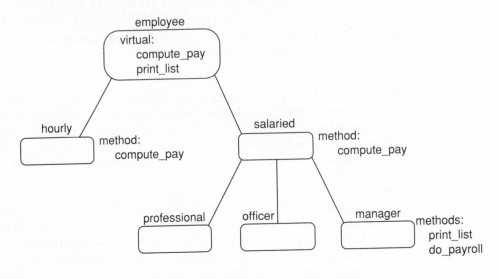

Altogether, we have defined five kinds of data records, where each one must contain all the information of the domain above it, plus more. For example, a "manager" record must contain fields for an annual salary, name, social security #, two codes, and a link, because a manager *is* a salaried employee and *is* an employee. However, a manager's record must also contain a pointer to the list of employees managed. Thus although the record types that might implement these domains are structurally different, they have semantic commonalities. A function that processes employee data could also process manager data correctly *if the data fields of the two types were represented in a compatible order.*

An object-oriented language, such as Smalltalk or C++, permits the programmer to declare and use this kind of domain/subdomain relationship to define a hierarchy of domains. C++ classes were introduced in Chapter 16 as an implementation of abstract data types. Classes are also used to implement generic domains with subdomains and function inheritance.

Exhibit 18.7. A group of related domains.

Here are descriptions of the fields in the records for two kinds of employees. (These records have a link field so that they can be organized into lists.) In a representation of these domains, the record describing the superdomain (employee) is a subrecord of that describing the subdomain.

Domain	Superdomain	Information to be recorded	Functions defined
Employee		Name, social security #, dept code, job code, pointer to next employee	Print employee list Print paycheck Enter new employee
Hourly_emp	Employee	Pay rate, hours worked, overtime, vacation days, group number	Compute pay Enter time card Change data
Salaried_emp	Employee	Annual salary, vacation days used	Compute pay Enter vacation
Manager	Salaried_emp	List of employees managed	Print list of people managed Do payroll Add new employee to list
Professional	Salaried_emp	Group number	
Officer	Salaried_emp	List of managers managed, sign checks: yes/no	Permission predicate

We will use C++ syntax and rules to explain how these class hierarchies work. Given a class, G, we can derive a subclass G' from G, such that G' has all the members (data and/or functions) of G, plus more. The C++ syntax for declaring a derived class is :

class	⟨new-class-name⟩ **: [public]** ⟨base-class-name⟩ {	(a)
	⟨new-private-members⟩	(b)
public:		
	⟨new-public-members⟩	(c)
};		

When we use a derived-class declaration, a new class, G', will be constructed that is a subclass of the specified base class, G. If the keyword **public** is used (line a), all the public parts of G will also be public parts in G'; if omitted, the public parts of G will become private parts of G'. If G has private members, an instance of G' will contain fields for these parts, but they are not visible to the functions defined for G' and can only be accessed by functions defined for G (unless a "friend" declaration is included in G). This visibility rule supports modular data-hiding, which is so important for achieving reliable systems.

In section (b), the private members of G' are listed. Included here are data fields that exist for the subclass G' but not for the superclass G, and functions (if any) that will be used only locally, by other functions defined for G'. Finally, additional public members of G' are listed in section (c). These must include all basic functions needed to operate on the subclass. Additional classes may be derived, similarly, from either G or G'.

Exhibit 18.8 shows the C++ declarations that would implement part of the domain hierarchy from Exhibit 18.7. To finish implementation of this hierarchy, we need to supply definitions for the remaining class, `officer`, and definitions for all the functions declared in all the classes. Definitions for these functions can be placed anywhere in the program, but good style dictates that they should be placed just after the class declaration. The functions that must be defined are:

`employee::employee`	`employee::print_paycheck`	`employee::print_list`
`employee::compute_pay`	`salaried::compute_pay`	`salaried::take_vacation`
`hourly::hourly`	`hourly::compute_pay`	`hourly::record_time_card`
`manager::manager`	`manager::add_employee`	`manager::print_list`
	`manager::do_payroll`	

Although these method *definitions* are outside the class declaration, the function methods themselves were *declared within the class*, and are class members with full access privileges. The placement of the function definition (before or after the end of the class declaration) makes no difference in the semantics—the only difference is practical; definitions inside the class are expanded in-line, like macros, those outside are compiled as subroutines. C++ functions can be overloaded, that is, a function name can have several defining methods, belonging to several classes. For this reason, the full name of a function method must be used when we define it outside its class. Thus we must write `hourly::compute_pay()` and `salaried::compute_pay`, not simply `compute_pay`.

Representation and Visibility.

A program object is created by instantiating a class and this action is triggered either by a declaration or a "`new`" command. The result is a record with one field for each of the variables (both public and private) within the class. A derived class will be represented by the same type of record with fields added on the end. The names of the class variables are like the names of the fields of a record, except that more complexity is involved because of information-hiding.

In a Pascal record, all the fields have the same *visibility*; that is, if one part is accessible in a given context, then all parts are accessible. But in a C++ class, the fields corresponding to private members have visibility restricted to the class functions, while public members have broader visibility. When we make a derived class, fields for private members of the parent class will be part of the record and take up space, but the names of those fields will not be known within the derived class, and those fields will be inaccessible to new functions. However, the public functions of the base class become members of the derived class and can be used to manipulate these fields.

Limiting Visibility.

It is possible to use a derived class to modify the visibility of members of an existing class. Let us say that class G has some private members and some public members. There is no way that deriving a class from G can affect the visibility of its

Exhibit 18.8.   Deriving classes in C++.

Below are declarations for some of the classes described in Exhibit 18.7. Exhibit 18.6 is a diagram of the relationships among these classes. This code is discussed throughout the rest of this chapter. We presume that card and pay_data are previously defined classes.

```
class employee {
    char name[], soc_sec[13], *dept_code, *job_code;
public:
    employee * link;
    employee(int)              // The constructor; argument is name length.
    void print_paycheck;
    virtual pay_data compute_pay;
    virtual void print_list;
    void employee::print_empl()
    {   cout << "Name:  " << name << "\n\t" << soc_sec
             << "\tDept:  " << dept_code << "\tJob:  " << job_code
             << "\n";
    }
};                             // End of class employee.
class salaried :  public employee {
    int annual_salary, vacation_used;
public:
    pay_data compute_pay();
    void take_vacation();
};                             // End of class salaried.
class manager :  salaried {
    employee* staff;
public:
    void add_employee();
    void print_list();
    void do_payroll();
    manager();                 //The constructor function.
};                             // End of class manager,
class hourly :  public employee {
    float pay_rate, hours_worked, overtime;
    int vacation_used;
public:
    pay_data compute_pay();
    void record_time_card(card*);
    hourly();
};                             // End of class hourly.
```

private members—they may be accessed only within G. But the public members of G may be made private in a class derived from G. To do this, omit the word "public" from the header of the derived class declaration. Public members of the base class then become private members of the derived class. We say that a derived module is "opaque" when it completely hides its base module. A half-and-half, or semi-opaque, situation may also be achieved. When the keyword public is omitted, you may list the names of selected members from the base class in the public part of the derived class. This does not create an additional field in the derived class; it simply controls the visibility of the base-class field. The syntax is:

class   ⟨new-class-name⟩ : ⟨base-class-name⟩ {
              ⟨new-private-members⟩

public:
              ⟨base_class_name⟩::⟨member_name⟩;
              ⟨new-public-members⟩
        };

Type Compatibility.

If G' has a public base class G, then an object of type pointer-to-G' can be stored in a pointer variable of type $G*$ (pointer-to-G) without use of explicit type conversion. For example, the class employee has a field named link of type employee*. Every instance of class manager and hourly also has this field, because manager and hourly were derived publicly from employee, and link is public in employee. The link field is able to store addresses of type hourly* and manager* because these classes were derived from employee. Thus we may make a linked list of hourly employees and store the head in a manager record.

This is a crucially important issue. The idea of a class hierarchy is that all variants of a base class are semantically related. Even more, an instance of a derived class *is* an instance of the base class, with some added information. Compatibility of pointer types throughout the levels of a hierarchy is essential to implement this underlying semantic notion.

18.2.3   *Virtual Functions in* C++

C++ contains a simple kind of support for virtual functions. A base class may contain a "virtual" declaration, such as the print_list function in Exhibit 18.8. The intent is that a virtual function should be used where the method for carrying out some abstract process is implementation-dependent. Let us use the term *virtual class* to mean a class that contains a virtual function or one that is derived from another virtual class. All the classes in the "employee" example are virtual classes because the base class contains one virtual function.

A virtual function *must be defined* for the base class in which it is declared, but it may be redefined for any derived classes that need a different method. In our example [Exhibit 18.9] the method for computing a paycheck is different for salaried and hourly people, and depends on data that is specific to these classes. The function compute_pay is, therefore, declared as a virtual function and defined separately for the two classes. Another application of virtual functions is to allow a method to do some actions specific to its local class, then call the general function from a higher class to complete the job. In our example, the `print_list` method for `employee` prints some headings, then calls the base method, using its full name, `employee::print_list`.

Exhibit 18.9. Calling a C++ function with two defining methods.

We define output function methods for the classes in the `employee` hierarchy established in Exhibit 18.6. The method in the derived class calls both of the methods in the base class.

```
void employee::print_list() // Does not print head of list.
{   employee * scan;
        for (scan=link; scan != NULL; scan=scan->link) print_empl();
}
void manager::print_list()
{   cout << "\n\nManager:  ";
    print_empl();
    cout << "\nEmployees Supervised:\n";
    employee::print_list();
}
```

If another class is derived from a derived class, the classes form a hierarchy. A virtual function may be defined at several levels of a hierarchy. In this case, several methods for a virtual function may all be applicable to instances of a class at the bottom of the hierarchy. In our "employee" example, two methods are defined for `print_list` (in class `manager` and the base class, `employee`). Both could be applied to an instance of class `manager`, but only the method in the base class could be applied to instances of the classes `salaried` and `employee`.

If a function is called using its full name (class_name::function_name) there is no ambiguity, and the call is translated in the ordinary manner. However, if a function is called without using its class name, the call is ambiguous and must be resolved by the dispatcher. The same dispatch rule can be used here as is used in the simple case: start at the bottom of the class hierarchy and look up the hierarchy tree until a method is found for the function. Thus if the programmer wishes to use a method that is not the closest one to its object's class, the full, qualified name of that method must be written.

It is up to the compiler and the linker to make the necessary connections between the virtual function and its methods, and to ensure that all those methods are consistently typed. Similarly, it is up to the translator to dispatch the correct method for a call on a virtual function. This is complicated because the method being called might not even exist when the call is compiled, and the actual dispatching must be done at link time or at run time.

To understand *why* dispatching must be delayed, consider the `do_payroll` function defined for class `manager` in our "employee" class hierarchy [Exhibit 18.7]. Assume that `do_payroll` calls `print_paycheck` to print out a paycheck for each employee on the manager's `staff` list. By inheritance, we can use this function to print a paycheck for any employee, and we can call it from the class `manager`. However, assume that `print_paycheck` calls upon the virtual function `compute_pay` to get the data needed for a check. Now, `compute_pay` is defined differently for hourly and salaried employees, and a manager's staff list will generally contain both kinds of employees. Thus at run time a single function call written in the `print_paycheck` function must sometimes dispatch `hourly::compute_pay` and sometimes `salaried::compute_pay`.

This decision cannot be made until each list element is processed. Thus the type of the argument to `print_paycheck` must be examined at run time. Happily, once this type is known, the simple dispatching rule *still works*. In traditional compilers (such as the typical C compiler) the type information from the declarations is put into the symbol table, used at compile time, then discarded. Little or no type information is carried over to run time. In order to dispatch a virtual function, though, it is necessary to have this information at run time. Some version of the translator's type objects must exist then, and each object must include a type pointer.

For this reason, objects belonging to virtual classes in C++ are compiled differently. A type field (a pointer to the type object for the object's class) is made part of every object in a virtual class. The dispatcher examines this type field and selects the right method for an object at run time. Thus we incur space overhead when we use a virtual class, and time overhead when we call a virtual function.[5] The benefits of virtual functions, however, outweigh these costs. Using function inheritance and virtual functions, we can:

- Avoid proliferation of nearly identical names for implementations of the same external process.
- Avoid writing duplicate copies of code for related classes.
- Write simple code with highly flexible run-time behavior.
- Extend the benefits of strong typing to nonhomogeneous domains.
- Create class hierarchies that are easy to extend when new, related data types must be defined.

18.2.4 Function Inheritance

The real importance of the class hierarchy is that it defines a system of classes with related semantics on which a system of function inheritance can operate. Briefly, functions defined in any class become members of every derived class and may be applied to instances of the derived class and called as if they were local. We say that the derived class *inherits* the function from its base class.

Every function call has an implied argument, which we will call the *object of the call*. To translate a call, the compiler must find and dispatch the correct method for that object. The dispatching rule is this:

- If a method is defined in the same class as the object of the call, the translator will dispatch that method.
- Otherwise, move up the class hierarchy, one level at a time, looking for function-members with the correct name. Dispatch the first method for the function that is encountered.

---

[5]This overhead is incurred only for virtual classes. It does not reduce the efficiency of operations on nonvirtual classes.

- Unless the function is declared to be "virtual" in the base class, there should be exactly one applicable method in the hierarchy. If no appropriate method is found, there is a type error.

Constructors in Derived Classes.

A constructor function is atypical, since we do not ordinarily call it explicitly. Whenever the translator allocates space for a new class instance, it calls the constructor function for that class to initialize the new storage. However, to instantiate a derived class which has a constructor, the translator must execute *two* constructor functions—first, the constructor for the base class, then the constructor for the derived class. Thus the derived class must "inherit" the constructor from its base class.

This leads to a real problem, since many constructor functions have parameters. The header line of each constructor definition specifies what parameters it needs, but how can the constructor for the derived class convey the right arguments to the base constructor? The solution is to expand the syntax of the language to allow the programmer to supply argument lists for a series of constructor functions. Arguments for the constructor of the derived class are given in the instantiation call. Arguments for the constructor of the base class (or classes) are given in the *definition* of the constructor for the derived class. The syntax is:

⟨derived_name⟩::⟨derived_name⟩ (⟨argument_list_for_derived_class⟩) :
  (⟨argument_list for base class constructor⟩)
  ⟨initializers for base class members⟩
  { ⟨body of derived constructor⟩ }

In the definition of the derived constructor, the programmer can use the base-class's argument list to pass on the derived-class arguments or to supply the base class constructor with constant arguments. If there are several nested derived classes which have constructors, a list of argument lists (separated by commas) is given, with the list for the most basic class first. The constructor for the base class will be executed *before* the constructor for each class derived from it. (If both classes have destructors, the destructor for the *derived* class will be executed before that of the base class.)

Strengths and Limitations.

The classes in C++ are immensely powerful and, when used well, can reduce both programming errors and tedious, repetitive coding work. This language is a giant step beyond standard Pascal. Several major semantic ideas are covered here that go beyond the traditional languages. They give C++ much of its power. These are:

- Controllable public/private data and functions.

- Declarable class relationships.

- Functions with multiple defining methods.

- Function inheritance.

By themselves, these semantic mechanisms are somewhat limited. We briefly list these limitations below and consider solutions in Section 18.4.

- These mechanisms do not address the problem of generic domains with representations that are related in an ad hoc manner. The only domain relationship that can be modeled is that between a record type and a longer record type with the same initial parts.
- All hierarchies and all function inheritance are totally tree structured; no class can have two parent-classes. However, some external generic domains naturally form graph-structured relationships in which a domain inherits properties from two different directions.
- During dispatching, the types of the arguments to a call are not considered. Only the class of the object of the call is used to select a method.
- C++ is still a superset of C, and, therefore, you can get around all the visibility rules of C++ by using pointers, which are semantically insecure types in C! The problem is that a pointer to any type can be cast to any other pointer type. This can be used to gain access to private data.

18.2.5   *Programmer-Defined Conversions in C++*

With some limitations, the C++ programmer is able to define conversions that the dispatcher can use. A class definition normally contains an ordinary constructor function, which is invoked automatically when a new storage object for the class is allocated. In addition, the class may contain one or more one-argument methods with the same name as the constructor. Each one is taken to be a conversion function and must create a value of the type of the class. As with any C++ constructor, the new value is returned by assigning values to some or all of the class members—an explicit return statement is not used in a constructor. The programmer must make sure that any constructor with one argument is a semantically valid conversion function from the type of the argument to the type of the class, because the compiler will use these methods, whenever needed, for coercion.

C++ can use constructor functions to coerce arguments in simple cases. In the class `complex` of Exhibit 18.10, four constructor methods are defined. The first one constructs the complex number zero and will be used to initialize every complex variable for which no other initializer is specified. In the example, the variable `cx` is initialized using this method.

The second method constructs a complex value from real and imaginary components [Exhibit 18.11]. This will be used primarily to define the member functions for the class; it defines the relationship between a complex number and its components. It can also be used to construct initializers for complex objects, as in line (b), and to create complex objects during execution, as in line (d).

The last two methods are semantically valid conversion functions from types `float` and `imag` to type `complex`. They can be called explicitly, but they will also be used by the translator to coerce arguments in calls on complex operations. Lines (a) and (d) illustrate contexts where an argument will be coerced. In line (a), the float number -1.6 is used as an initializer for an instance of class `imag` (from Exhibit 16.10). This triggers a call on the conversion from float to imag that was defined in class `imag`.

In line (d), the operator "+" is called to add a complex number and a float. This situation is somewhat more complex. The dispatcher looks at this call on "+" and must find an appropriate method for it. The dispatching rule in C++ is given in Exhibit 18.12. By this rule, the method `complex operator+(complex, complex)` is finally selected, and the second operand, `fl`, is coerced to type complex.

Exhibit 18.10.   Conversion functions in C++.

```
class complex
{   rp:  float;
    ip:  imag;
public:
    complex(){ rp=0.0; ip=imag(0.0); }
    complex(float f, imag i){rp=f; ip=i;}
    complex(float f){rp=f; ip=0;}
    complex(imag  i){rp=0; ip=i;}
    complex operator-() { return complex(-rp, -ip); }
    friend complex operator+( complex c1, complex c2 );
    friend complex operator*( complex c1, complex c2 );
    friend complex operator-( complex c1 );
}
complex operator+( complex c1, complex c2 )
{   return complex( c1.rp+c2.rp, c1.ip+c2.ip ); }
complex operator*( complex c1, complex c2 )
{   return complex( c1.rp*c2.rp + c1.ip*c2.ip, c1.rp*c2.ip + c1.ip*c2.rp ); }
```

Exhibit 18.11.   Coercion with a programmer-defined function.

```
main()
{   float fl=2.5;
    imag im=-1.6;                              //(a)
    complex cx;                                // Initialized to zero.
    complex dx = complex( 1.0, imag(1.0) );    //(b)
    cx = new complex( .1, im );                //(c)
    cx = cx + fl;                              //(d)
}
```

Exhibit 18.12.   Dispatch rules for C++ overloaded functions.

1. Look for a method whose operand types match the argument types exactly.

2. If none is found, look for a method such that the argument types can be made to match the parameter types by using no more than one predefined conversion function on each operand.

3. If none is found, and one or more operand belongs to a defined class, look for a method such that the argument types can be made to match the parameter types by using no more than one user-defined conversion function per operand.

4. If more than one possible way to do user-defined conversions is found, or if none is found, the dispatch fails.

Programmer-Defined Casts in C++.

In C++, as in C, no distinction is made between conversions and casts. We have seen that a C++ class can be used to implement a mapped domain with semantic protection against misuse. But casts are required to implement the basic functions for the new mapped domain, and casting is not automatically defined for such a class. In this situation, the facility for programmer-defined conversions can be used to define an upward cast. To specify the downward cast, from the class type to a representing type, an operator function may be used. This defines the target-type name as a conversion function that can be called explicitly using the normal syntax for casts. Both kinds of programmer-defined casts are illustrated in Exhibit 16.10, where their use is required to define the basic functions for the new mapped class.

It is important that the two casts were defined as private functions. This means that, within the class, the representation of a class object can be manipulated, as it must be, to make the necessary calculations. However, outside the class, the relationship between the two domains is completely unknown.

18.3 POLYMORPHIC DOMAINS AND FUNCTIONS

18.3.1   Polymorphic Functions

A *polymorphic type* is a single type definition that includes two or more alternative specific type declarations. A *polymorphic object* is the representation of one of these species along with some form of discriminant field that encodes *which* species is present.

It is important to understand the differences between polymorphic functions and the generic arithmetic operators in languages such as Pascal and Ada. The generic nature of the Pascal operator extends only until compile time; the compiler then chooses a specific method to implement the operator. Thereafter Pascal code is fully specific. A polymorphic function does run-time type checking, when necessary, and a language with good support for polymorphism will do this checking automatically. For example, APL is an array-oriented polymorphic language which tags each data object with a type field that describes the number and extent of its dimensions. The programmer may write an APL function, say Fun, to operate on a pair of numbers. The programmer may then call it with a simple pair of numbers or with two equal-length arrays of numbers. The shapes of the actual arguments are tested automatically, and the translator executes appropriate code. It will apply Fun once if given a simple pair of numbers, but apply it repeatedly to each corresponding pair of elements if given two arrays.

The Pascal variant record is an early attempt to implement limited polymorphic types. It permits the programmer to specify that objects of the type may have a variety of different sizes and structures. However, it is not a very satisfactory implementation of polymorphism for two reasons:

- When creating a polymorphic object, storage is allocated for the largest variant, even when the value stored there is much smaller.
- The theoretical semantics of variant records are not enforced by the translator, and run-time tests of the discriminant field must be coded manually.

More modern languages have extended this idea and addressed the problems.

A *polymorphic function* is a function that accepts arguments of a polymorphic type. It tests the argument at run time to determine which variant is present, then executes code appropriate for that argument. These run-time type tests might be automatically generated by the translator or explicitly written by the programmer.

Polymorphism becomes very important in functional languages because they support higher-order functions. A higher-order function, often called a *functional*, may take functions as parameters and/or produce a function as its result. Some familiar functionals are functional composition and `reduce` [Exhibit 12.15]. But, in a typed language, functionals are almost useless unless they are polymorphic. Thus higher-order functions have been a strong motivating force in the development of polymorphism in functional languages.

Even a language with little or no support for domain checking may be extended to perform polymorphic domain checking manually. To accomplish this the programmer would explicitly attach some type information to every data object, then explicitly include code in the function definitions to test this type field.

18.3.2 *Manual Domain Representation and Dispatching*

Before looking at a modern implementation of polymorphic domains, let us see how polymorphism might be implemented manually in an older language. An *ad hoc polymorphic domain* is the discriminated union of two or more specific types. If an object OB belongs to an ad hoc polymorphic domain, PD, then its value at run time may belong to any specific type included in PD. It is not possible to predict, at compile time, which specific type this will be. However, at run time, the specific type of any object is known.

In some languages, for example, Pascal, an ad hoc polymorphic domain may be implemented as a variant record with a tag field. Exhibits 14.25 and 14.24 show a polymorphic type declared in Ada. However, neither Ada nor Pascal supports the run-time type checking that is necessary to ensure valid use of such domains. To process polymorphic objects, we must write code, such as that in Exhibit 18.13, which explicitly tests the tag field and branches appropriately.

Exhibit 18.13.   Manual polymorphic dispatching in Ada.

In older languages, we use manual type-testing to write code to process a polymorphic type. The Ada procedure below might be written to print out an item belonging to the polymorphic type Person that was defined in Exhibit 14.25. In this type, the field named "Sex" is the discriminant tag. We explicitly test the contents of this field and dispatch one of three specific functions.

```
PROCEDURE Print_Person ( Who :  Person ) IS
BEGIN
    CASE Who↑.Sex IS
            WHEN Male =>      THEN Print_Male(Who);
            WHEN Female =>    THEN Print_Fem(Who);
            WHEN OTHERS =>    Sex_Error(Who);
    END CASE
END Print_Person;
```

Explicit Domain Testing versus Strong Typing.

Achieving semantic validity is the purpose of both strong typing and explicitly testing the discriminant tags on a polymorphic type. However, there are some major differences between the results achieved by the two systems.

On the practical side, explicit type testing can get to be cumbersome. It forces the programmer to write out, in every function definition, the instructions to check the discriminant tag of the argument and produce an error comment if there is a mismatch. A strongly typed language handles this kind of domain checking automatically for simple types; the programmer needs only to declare a domain name for each object and parameter.

Second, polymorphic type checking both permits and requires domain testing to be postponed until run time. On the one hand, simple strong-type-checking, which happens at compile time, is significantly more efficient if the program is ever used to process a lot of data. Run-time checking is time consuming. On the other hand, run-time domain checking is inherently more powerful and flexible. It permits the domain-checking system (or the programmer) to make finer distinctions between appropriate and inappropriate arguments. A run-time test can depend on the actual data values, not just on the declared type of the argument. For example, in Pascal, strong-typing ensures that a list-processing function will always get a list argument. In Miranda, automated polymorphic domain testing can distinguish lists from nonlists but can also be used to distinguish lists containing data from null lists.

18.3.3   Automating Ad Hoc Polymorphism

Polymorphic Domains

The modern functional languages have more advanced support for generics than any existing languages in the ALGOL family. This support comes at two levels:

- User-defined domains may be ad hoc polymorphic. A domain may have several alternative representations, like a discriminated union type. Functions can be written that test the discriminant automatically and dispatch the appropriate code.
- A generic type may be defined with a type parameter, and functions may be defined with generic parameters of this sort. (These are covered in Section 18.4.)

We use Miranda to illustrate these powerful general definition and dispatching methods. A type definition is written using the symbol "::=", which we read as "is type". A polymorphic type declaration consists of a series of clauses separated by the "or" symbol, "|", which correspond to the alternatives of a discriminated union type in Ada or Pascal. Each clause has a discriminant name followed by a tuple of type specifiers, much like a simple Pascal record declaration. The discriminant names can be used either as constructors, for making an object of that type out of appropriate components, or as type predicates, when defining a function for the type.

In Exhibit 18.14 we use Miranda to define `tree`, a polymorphic type. The notes for this example follow:

a. We define the type tree. A tree may be a leaf, which is an integer, or a node, which is a tuple of two trees. This declaration defines the discriminant tags `Leaf` and `Node`, which we use later as object constructors and as type predicates.

b. We construct a tree of the first form, using the constructor `Leaf`. Note that the tag name is part of the constructed object—the result of this line is that the name `leaf1` is bound to a two-tuple consisting of the tag `Leaf` and the number 3.

c. We construct two leaves, as in the line above, and use them immediately to construct one node. That node is, in turn, combined with the previously constructed leaf, `leaf1`, to make a tree named `tree1`. The structure of this tree is shown in Exhibit 18.15.

Exhibit 18.14.   A tree type in Miranda.

We define an ad hoc polymorphic type named "`tree`". This also defines the constructor/predicate names "`Leaf`" and "`Node`" for the two variants of type `tree`. The last two lines construct two trees named `leaf1` and `tree1`. The letters on the right key the code to the notes in the text.

```
tree ::= Leaf integer | Node tree tree         (a)
leaf1 = (Leaf 3)                               (b)
tree1 = (Node leaf1 (Node (Leaf 17) (Leaf 49))) (c)
```

Exhibit 18.15.   A tree with polymorphic nodes.

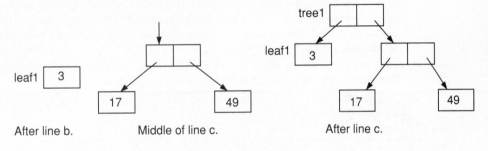

After line b.   Middle of line c.   After line c.

Unlike Pascal, part names for the fields of a tuple are not supplied in the type declaration, and the new type name may be referenced recursively in the declaration. The lack of defined part names requires explanation. In Miranda, the type of an object is not part of the object, as in APL, nor is it part of a name, as in Pascal. Types are deduced from the structure of objects. Field names, in turn, are not part of the type definition. When an object is passed as an argument, a sophisticated type-deduction algorithm[6] is used to check whether it belongs to the domain of the function. The tuple- or list-structure of the argument is checked, along with the types of its simple components. As part of this checking process, dummy parameter names, defined in the function header, are associated with each field of the argument. These are temporary and local, like parameter names in traditional languages, and are used to access the fields of the argument within that function. Thus the two parts of a pair may be called "`left`" and "`right`" within one function body and "`head`" and "`tail`" in another.

---

[6]This algorithm is derived from the work of Hindley and Milner. Cf. Milner [1978].

Miranda permits us to write functions over ad hoc polymorphic domains, like `tree`, that will be domain-checked and dispatched automatically. A function definition is written as a series of methods, each one defined for a different subdomain. The domain predicates are called *patterns* and are written on the left. A pattern can specify an argument type, a discriminant tag (called a *constructor* in Miranda), and/or data values. Following the pattern is an "=" and the appropriate computation method for that particular subdomain. In Exhibit 18.16, we define a simple function that processes the tree type defined in Exhibit 18.14. Following are line-by-line notes for the code in the exhibit:

a. On this line and the next, the discriminant tags defined by the type declaration are used as domain predicates (left), controlling the choice of computation methods (right). Line (a) defines the function `max-tree` for any argument which matches the type named "Leaf". Within the body of the method, the single component of a `Leaf` will be called "`ldata`". The value of the expression on the right will be returned as the value of the function. This code states that the maximum of a `Leaf` is the number stored in it.

b. The remaining code defines `max-tree` for arguments that are tuples with two fields. These fields are named "n1" and "n2" within the method body.

c. The "`where`" clause defines a local context for this method, containing local names "`max1`" and "`max2`". When the outside-in, lazy evaluation process reaches the first reference to `max1` or `max2`, the expression following the name in the "`where`" section is evaluated and the result is bound to the local name. This value remains bound to the name throughout evaluation of the block; subsequent references to the name refer to the value computed for the first reference.

d. The function `max-tree` is called, recursively, with the left field subtree as its argument. The maximum value in the left subtree is bound to the name "`max1`".

e. This guarded expression compares the two maxima of the left and right subtrees and returns the greater.

Exhibit 18.16.   Polymorphic dispatching in Miranda.

We define and call a polymorphic function named `max-tree` with methods to process both kinds of trees (nodes and leaves). The letters on the right key the example to the explanation in the text.

```
max-tree (Leaf ldata)   = ldata                    (a)
max-tree (Node n1 n2)   = max1, max1>max2          (b)
                        = max2, max2>max1          (e)
                        = max1, otherwise
                          where                     (c)
                          max1 = ( max-tree n1 )    (d)
                          max2 = ( max-tree n2 )
```

Evaluating (`max-tree leaf1`) yields 3, and evaluating (`max-tree tree1`) yields 49.

This automated run-time dispatching of function methods is implemented by a very general and powerful pattern-matcher. It is not limited to checking for subtypes of a polymorphic domain, but can also perform run-time checks involving the values of data objects. For instance, Exhibit 18.17 has one method defined for null lists and another method defined for lists with at least one component.

Exhibit 18.17.   Dispatching a Miranda call using data values.

```
sum-list []      = 0
sum-list (a:ls)  = a + sum-list ls
```

We recursively sum a list by adding the value of the first list item to the sum of the rest of the list. If list1 = [3, 4, 17, 9, 5] and we evaluate sum-list list1 the result is 38.

Exhibit 18.18 summarizes and gives examples of the kinds of patterns that the Miranda programmer may use to define methods. Dispatching a function call is done by a run-time case analysis, examining each pattern in turn, until one is found that matches the structure and/or value of the actual argument. When a match is found, the dummy names used to write the pattern are bound to the parts of the argument, and these bindings are used within the function body. Exhibit 18.19 shows the bindings that would happen for some calls on the functions sum-list [Exhibit 18.17], max-tree [Exhibit 18.16], and pow10 [Exhibit 12.20].

Exhibit 18.18.   Pattern construction in Miranda.

Pattern type	Example
constant	factorial 0 = 1
number greater than 0	factorial (n+1) = (n+1)*factorial n
null list	sum-list [] = 0
nonnull list	sum-list[a:x] = a + sum-list[x]
tuple	max-tree (Node n1 n2) = ...

The important principle here is that the dispatch is done at run time, distinguishing it from anything that can be done with nonunion types in languages such as Pascal and Ada. It is true that an Ada programmer can emulate run-time dispatching by using a discriminated union type and coding the dispatching process manually, as in Exhibit 18.13. However, manual type checking is never as convenient or as safe as checking that is built into the semantic basis of the language. The Miranda function definitions using pattern matching are far clearer and more elegant than corresponding Ada code.

18.3.4   Parameterized Domains

Miranda is a strongly typed language. Every object has a type, even though it is not declared. The type is deduced from the structure of the object. Functions, also, have types which are deduced from the function code. If a function is called with an argument whose type is inconsistent with the function definition, a compile-time error comment is generated. The programmer may also choose to declare the type of a function, in which case a compile-time error is produced if the declared type and the deduced type do not match.

Exhibit 18.19.   Binding during the pattern match.

Data object definitions:

type	name value
tuple	`leaf1 = (Leaf 3)`
tuple	`tree1 = (Node leaf1 (Node (Leaf 17) (Leaf 49))`
list	`list1 = [ 1, 3..11 ]`
list	`list2 = []`
integer	`numb1 = 17`

The functions below were defined in Exhibits 12.15, 12.20, 18.16, and 18.17.

Call	Bindings
`max-tree leaf1`	ldata is 3.
`max-tree tree1`	n1 is leaf1, n2 is (Node (Leaf 17) (Leaf 49)).
`max-tree numb1`	Pattern match fails.
`max-tree list1`	Pattern match fails.
`pow10 numb1`	n is 16.
`sum-list list1`	a is 1, ls is [3, 5..11].
`sum-list list2`	Pattern matches null list, no binding necessary.
`reduce '+' list1 0`	f is '+', a is 1, x is [3, 5..11], and n is 0.

Names may be defined for types and used as a notational convenience. The names carry no semantic meaning in themselves but are simply a shorthand for the structural description.[7] To define a type name, you use the "==" sign:

⟨typename⟩ == ⟨type expression⟩

Miranda supports domains with type parameters and provides a notation for talking about a type parameter. Ordinary types are expressed structurally, as shown in Exhibit 18.20. The type of a list is denoted by writing the type of its elements inside list brackets; the type of a tuple is written as a tuple of types. The type of a function is written in curried notation, starting with the type of the first argument and ending with the type of the result.

---

[7]See the discussion on type identity in Chapter 15, Section 15.4.

Type parameters are denoted by strings of asterisks. If a type expression has one type parameter, we write "*"; for an expression with three distinct types, we write "*", "**", and "***". If a type expression uses the same type parameter symbol twice, it means that both occurrences must be replaced by the same argument. For example, the type of the subscript function is:

```
!  ::  [*]  →  num  →  *
```

Exhibit 18.20.   Miranda type expressions.

Assume T, T1, etc. are types. Then we can write the following type expressions:

Expression	Interpretation
[T]	A list with elements of type T.
[[T]]	A list of lists of elements of type T.
(T, T1, T2)	A tuple of three elements of types T, T1, and T2.
T → T1	A function with argument type T and result type T1.
* → *	A function whose argument and result have the same type.
[*] → *	A function that returns an element of the same type as the base type of its list argument.
* → ** → **	A function of two arguments whose result is the same type as the second argument.

Abstract Data Types.

Miranda supports code modules analogous to the generic packages in Ada, except that Miranda's type parameters are not bound at compile time, so it is capable of true run-time generic behavior. A Miranda script may contain the directive to "%include" the script in some other file, or a directive to "%export" some locally defined symbols. Scripts may have parameters, just as in Ada, and a parameterized script must be instantiated by supplying arguments in the "%include" command.

An ADT, called an "abstype", is declared by specifying the ADT interface (public symbols) followed by the definitions of those symbols (private part). Exhibit 18.21 declares a stack ADT with a single type parameter for the base type of the stack. The stack itself will be represented by a list. The rules for type compatibility and access to private parts are very similar to those in C++ classes; within the scope of the declaration, the type "stack *" is considered to be just the same as the type "[*]", and the implementation equations may access it using the ordinary list operations. Outside the abstype declaration, though, a stack may only be accessed using the declared functions.

Exhibit 18.21. The ADT "stack" in Miranda.

```
abstype stack *
with empty::stack *
        isempty::stack * → bool
        push ::  * → stack *  → stack *
        pop ::  stack * → stack *
        top ::  stack * → *
stack * ==[*]        || A stack is a list of anything.
empty     = []       || A literal stack, to start things off.
isempty s = (s=[])   || A null list represents an empty stack.
push a s  = (a:s)    || Append the new item to the head of the list.
pop (a:s) = s        || Remove list head and discard; return changed stack.
top (a:s) = a        || Return the list head, don't change the stack.
```

18.4 CAN WE DO MORE WITH GENERICS?

We have looked at a variety of languages that support generic and/or polymorphic functions. It is appropriate, now, to look back and compare these facilities, to analyze strengths and weaknesses, and to ask whether a language could do more.

Binding Time, Flexibility, and Efficiency

The *binding time* for type variables is the first and biggest difference among the languages we have studied. Ada, C++, and Miranda all support some sort of generic behavior. However, Ada's generics are much simpler, more efficient, and less flexible. Ada does not need a dispatcher at all, because the programmer binds specific names to instantiations of generics, and uses those specific names when writing the code. The result can be fully compiled, and it is easy to compile, but it does not permit any run-time variability at all. For example, variable-length strings are quite clumsy to manage in Ada.

Contrast Ada to Miranda. Variable-length lists are used everywhere in Miranda programs, and polymorphic tuple types exist at run time. The idea of "type" is defined in Miranda so that a single type includes more than one specific representation. The Miranda compile-time dispatcher verifies that a function is defined for the type but does not worry about which representation of the type will be present later. The run-time dispatcher examines the actual arguments and dispatches the particular method that matches the argument. Many Miranda functions do repetitive processes on data structures built from polymorphic tuple types. The run-time dispatching is essential to support this, since the method selected will differ from one call to the next, depending on the shape of the data structure.

Miranda's run-time variability makes a language that is flexible and easy to use; strong typing ceases to be a barrier between the programmer and his or her work, and becomes a pure asset. The cost, however, is execution speed. Repeating the pattern match for every repetition of every function is a great deal slower than doing it once at compile time.

The C++ compiler takes a middle course. It makes a distinction between function calls for which complete information is known at compile time and those where some run-time variability can possibly exist. In the former case, fixed code is compiled, as it would be in C. In the latter case, the run-time dispatcher is called. (Review the discussion of virtual functions in Section 18.2.3.) Using a mixed strategy like this seems to be the best strategy, although it is also the most difficult to implement.

The real problem with a mixed strategy is deciding what can and what cannot be known or deduced at compile time. C++ solves this problem simply by deciding that any computation that involves a virtual function will be dispatched at run time. Ordinary functions will be dispatched at compile time. This works to achieve reasonable efficiency only if the use of virtual functions is relatively unusual.

Defining and Representing a Generic Function

In a traditional language, we know what a function is; it is one body of code, with one type. This situation becomes complicated when we deal with generic functions, and we need to decide what a function is and what can be done with functions.

We need to distinguish between the situation in which a function name is overloaded, that is, used for two unrelated methods, or truly generic. A function is truly generic if the translator knows about more than one method, knows the methods are related, and uses that relationship in the dispatching process.

In comparing generic languages, we see different approaches to the question of "what is a function?" In Miranda, a function can have several defining clauses, giving it polymorphic behavior, but everything relevant to one function is defined in one place. Miranda functions are first-class objects that can be passed to other functions and created dynamically. When we pass a functional argument, this entire polymorphic unit is passed.

In contrast, C++ virtual functions are defined in bits and pieces, with each method "inside" a different class. A constructor function, on the other hand, may have multiple definitions in the same class. Finally, built-in functions (casts, arithmetic operators) have several definitions and are not included in a class at all. Methods for these functions are defined piece by piece, as needed. It is not necessary to know about or edit prior definitions of a function in order to extend the function to handle a new submode type; the new method is simply included where it is needed.

Both constructors and virtual functions are true generic functions, not simply overloaded names. The constructors in a class all bear a semantic relationship to each other; they all return an object of the type of the class. The methods for a virtual function also are semantically related, even though they are defined at different times and may be written by different people and compiled in different code modules. In Miranda, this would not be possible; the methods for a virtual function would all have to be collected and written in one place. Thus the C++ approach for defining a generic function has a definite advantage for writing large systems.

A generic function is a collection of methods, each one defined over a different subdomain of a generic domain. Some languages (such as Miranda) require the

methods to be lexically grouped on the page, in other languages they are semantically grouped by the translator (like Ada's arithmetic operators), in yet others they
are tucked into classes and accessed through the class hierarchy so that the methods
are never connected together or treated as a unit (like virtual functions in an object-
oriented language).

Operations on Generic Functions

Let us consider a generic function to be a list (not ordered) of methods. You may
picture it as a linked list of code modules. There are three operations that we would
like to define for a generic function: passing it as an argument, dispatching it, and
executing one of its methods.

When passing a generic as an argument, do we pass the entire unit (including
all the methods), as in Miranda? Or do we pass a single method? Passing an entire
function is only meaningful if we have a run-time dispatcher. In Ada, we sometimes
pass a function as an argument when a package is instantiated. If we wish to send
"+" as an instantiation parameter, Ada permits us to name the entire function as the
argument; it does not require that we denote a single method for "+" [Exhibit 17.20].
An Ada instantiation argument is passed at precompile time and is substituted in the
package before Ada's compile-time dispatcher works on the code. This is not the same
as passing an entire function at run time. Functional parameters in C must be single
methods, because no run-time dispatcher exists to handle whole functions. Miranda
scripts can pass entire generic units at run time because all dispatching is done at run
time.

Then consider dispatching; the dispatcher selects one method for each generic
function call, if an appropriate method exists. The compiler must keep the methods
for a function in some sort of data structure so that it can search all possibilities during
dispatching.

A class hierarchy forms a convenient data structure for organizing the methods
of a function. The dispatching algorithm is easy to write if each method is attached to
a class and no class has more than one method for the same function. The algorithm
searches for a method starting at the class of the first (implied) argument and crawls
up the class hierarchy tree until it either finds a method or comes to the base class. In
C++, the base class is required to have a method for each virtual function, guaranteeing that the dispatch will never fail at run time. (This restriction is not necessary,
though.)

Handling methods that are not attached to classes is more difficult, as is handling
functions that have multiple definitions within one class. To make sense of this, the
dispatcher must examine a list of methods, looking at the type of each method. If the
type of each argument matches the declared type of the corresponding parameter,
the method may be dispatched. We need to define precisely what "match" means,
and what happens if no match is found, or if more than one is found.

18.4.1 Dispatching Using the Mode Graph

Consider a generalized dispatching algorithm in which generic functions are represented as lists of methods, and the dispatcher can move around the entire mode graph,

including submode links, binding links, and conversion links. This kind of dispatching algorithm is used in two current research languages, Haskell[8] and Aleph.[9] In the rest of this section, we will refer to this generalized algorithm as the *Dispatcher*, with a capital letter.

Dispatching starts with a particular function (a list of methods) and a particular context for the function call. The context is formed from the types of the actual arguments and (possibly) the type of object that the function must return. The Dispatcher examines each method for the function, in turn, and either eliminates it, selects it, or puts it on a *short list* for future consideration.

In an object-oriented dispatch, the only part of the context that is considered is the type of the implied argument. This is easy to implement, but it is limited and can handle only simple dispatches. Even in the examples we have seen, it is inadequate to handle the problem of two constructors in one class. A more general and symmetric dispatcher would consider the types of all the arguments, as C++ does with constructors, and as the Miranda dispatcher does with all functions. The Dispatcher will consider each argument, in turn, and select a method only if all arguments match or can be coerced to match. Functions such as constructors, which can have different methods for different combinations of arguments, will be dispatched correctly.

Matching.

Dispatching one argument reduces to the problem of finding a path through the graph from the mode containing the type of the argument to the declared mode of the parameter. The dispatcher will start at the argument mode, search up IS links and BIND links and across CONV links, trying to reach the target mode. Unlike C++ dispatching, the Dispatcher is not limited to using a single CONV link, and it can use CONV links in combination with the other links.

Using conversions freely brings up the question of semantic validity. What is there to prevent a string of conversions from distorting the meaning of the argument beyond recognition? This issue is the reason that we must distinguish carefully between casts and semantics-preserving conversions. A cast is a semantically invalid operation, done only to access the underlying representation for bootstrapping purposes. Casts should never be used freely and never to coerce arguments. Any chain of conversions that goes through two casts is almost certainly semantically invalid. This puts a burden on the programmer to distinguish which functions represent casts, and which are valid conversions, then leave the casts out of the mode graph. So long as all links in the mode graph are individually valid, the combination of those links should also be valid.

With a class hierarchy, there is only one way to travel from one class to another: up the tree toward the base class. In contrast, a mode graph is an arbitrary graph; one mode can have two or more IS links leading out of it and also have CONV links. We can consider CONV links to be more costly than the other links. The dispatcher must therefore consider more than one path from the starting point to the goal, and dispatching becomes a process of finding the shortest path through a weighted graph, not just traveling up a tree structure.

---

[8]Hudak et al. [1992].
[9]A. Fischer and M. Fischer [1973], A. Fischer [1985], and R. Fischer [1992].

Where the types of objects are fixed at compile time, all of this work can be done by the compile-time Dispatcher, which then replaces the ordinary type checker. The Dispatcher identifies a type error when the compile-time dispatch fails to find any applicable methods. Where the types of objects may retain some run-time variability, the Dispatcher can still identify total type mismatches and eliminate many methods as possibilities. Sometimes, though, more than one method is potentially applicable; in this case, the compile-time Dispatcher must return a short list of potential methods, to be further culled by the run-time Dispatcher.

Generics Make Some Problems Easy.

Let us define a sample generic mode and show how dispatching would work on it. Assume we are writing a graphics program, in which we are concerned with representing and manipulating points on the plane. There are two good methods for representing points: in Cartesian coordinates, as (x, y) pairs, or in polar coordinates, as (r, theta) pairs. Selector functions x and y are defined for type carts, and r and theta are defined for type polar. Note that selectors are ordinary functions and can be called using ordinary function syntax, even though they are defined as part of the type declaration. This program will need to do many operations on points, including rotation, translation, input, and output. Either representation can be converted to the other using trigonometric functions or square roots.

Translation, that is, moving the point up, down, or sideways, is easy in Cartesian coordinates but difficult in polar. Rotation, that is, moving a point in a circular arc around the origin, is easy in polar but not Cartesian. Output must be in Cartesian, because the terminal screen uses Cartesian coordinates. Some input is in polar, other in Cartesian. The program must use both representations, and the programmer would like to have both available but not worry about representation all the time.

The mode graph for these types is shown in Exhibit 18.22. The generic mode, point, promises the function read and has two typed submodes, carts and polar. Any "point" data structures and functions in the surrounding program are declared in terms of the generic mode, point.

Note that both submodes are represented by pairs of reals, but neither type must ever be cast to the other, because their semantics are totally different. A package for ADT point will contain private type declarations for the two point representations and public definitions for the ADT functions. There would also be two data objects (or constant functions) for each type, named Zero and One.

Exhibit 18.23 illustrates the power of this generic language to simplify the programmer's task.[10] Two variables are declared and data values are read for them. The Dispatcher examines the methods defined for Read and chooses the appropriate ones for the two Read commands. The If statement then applies the selector function theta to both points, causing the point c1 to be coerced before the selection can be done. One of the Write statements also coerces its argument.

Everything in this example can be dispatched at compile time. Even though Read is a virtual function, it is only used with arguments whose type is fixed and known at compile time, permitting the Dispatcher to identify the correct methods and necessary conversions.

---

[10]The syntax used here is Pascal-like, so that readers will understand it readily. However, you could certainly not write this code in Pascal!

Exhibit 18.22.   Mode graph for points on a plane.

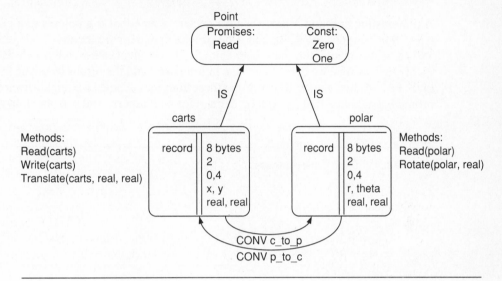

Exhibit 18.23.   Generic calls.

```
VAR p1:  polar;
    c1:  carts;

    Read(c1);         ~~ No problem: Read is defined for type carts,
    Read(p1);         ~~ and also for type polar.
    If theta(p1)      ~~ The selector theta returns a real.
       > theta(c1)    ~~ The Cartesian argument is coerced to polar.
    then Write(p1)    ~~ The polar argument is coerced to Cartesian.
    else Write(c1);   ~~ Write is defined for Cartesian.
```

Contrast this situation to the problem in Section 18.2 which illustrates the need for run-time dispatching. In that application, cells of differing specific types were linked together in one list by pointers with a generic base type. In that case we could do compile-time dispatching on pointer operations but we still needed run-time dispatching for operations on base-type objects.

This small example is a little artificial, but it illustrates that the programmer using a generic language is, indeed, freed from constant concern about which representation is being used at the moment. In a real program, there would be some reason why a particular point would be represented one way or another, and the time spent performing conversions would be useful. The gain, over traditional languages, is that the programmer can think in terms of the semantics of points, not the semantics of carts and polar. The resulting code denotes the job of computation more clearly, uncluttered by constant nuts-and-bolts conversion commands.

18.4.2   Generics Create Some Hard Problems

Dispatching Pointer Arguments

An interesting question arises when we declare a type that is a pointer to a generic type. For example, let P, Q, and R be of type "`pointer to Number`" (see Exhibit 18.1) and assume that they have been initialized to point at values as shown in Exhibit 18.24. Now assume we dereference the pointers and add the results by saying P↑ + Q↑ or Q↑ + R↑. At first glance, it seems that these additions should be straightforward; the promises guarantee that "+" will be defined for all `Numbers`, and P, Q, and R have the same type.

Exhibit 18.24.   Using generic pointers.

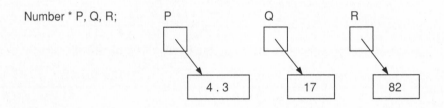

Looking again, though, we see that the things that P, Q, and R point to may or may not have the same type! Here is a situation in which dispatching must be delayed until run time. The compile-time Dispatcher must make a short list of all the methods for "+" defined on submodes of `Number`, and the particular method to be used must be selected at the last moment. In our example, the method "`+(real,real):real`" will be selected for the first addition and "`+(integer,integer):integer`" will be selected for the second.

A second problem involves possible run-time type incompatibilities. The promises for `Number` guarantee that every submode will have a definition for "+". However, "+" is a dyadic function, and these definitions all require that the two arguments to "+" have the same specific type. No methods at all are defined for mismatched operands, like P↑ + Q↑ in the example. These are supposed to be handled by the coercion mechanism, and in this case, they would be. The integer operand will be converted to real by the CONV function `i_to_r`. But without the conversion links between the submodes, the computation could not be done, and the dispatch would fail. To avoid run-time errors, the programmer *must* provide enough CONV links to define the relationships among all the submodes of a generic mode.

Using Generic Definitions

One of the attractions of generic dispatching is that functions defined "high" in the mode graph, for high-level generic modes, can be inherited by all the submodes below them. Inheritance works much as it does in a class hierarchy. But when we use a high-level generic method definition, there is a problem with knowing the type of the result. The method definition can only define the result type in terms of the generic mode to which it is attached. However, when this definition is used, it is used with a specific type object, and we would like to know the specific type of the result, not just its generic category.

If we lose track of the specific type that results from an operation, no more compile-time dispatching can be done with that result; all further dispatches for the entire expression must be done at run time if they involve the result of the generic. Unless there is a way to keep track of the specific types involved, generics become too impractical to use extensively, defeating their purpose.

Let us look at one example of this problem. Assume an object belongs to a typed mode, `Vector`, which was derived from a parameterized mode, `Array(N,T)`. `Vector` is connected to `Array` by a BIND link that gives the bindings `N=3`, `T=real` [Exhibit 18.25]. The generic function `Subscript` (written with the symbol "!") is defined for mode `Array` and has the type:

$$! \quad :: \quad \texttt{Array(N, Any)} \rightarrow \texttt{integer} \rightarrow \texttt{Any}$$

where mode `Any` is the predefined supermode of all modes.

Exhibit 18.25.   What type is returned?

```
k:  integer;
r:  real;
v:  vector;
...
r := v ! k ;
```

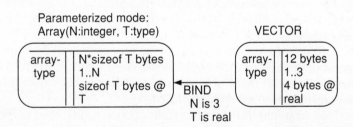

Parameterized mode:
Array(N:integer, T:type)

What type is returned when we call `Subscript` on a `Vector`? The `Subscript` function was defined to return mode `Any`. We know, though, that it will return a real in this case, and it is important for the compile-time Dispatcher to be able to use that fact to compile `Vector` expressions.

This is one instance of a very general and difficult problem that arises with parameterized generic modes. We must be able to keep and pass on the specific attributes of the submodes if generic functions defined for supermodes are to be useful. Of course, `Subscript` is predefined in all languages on all array types and is treated as a special case; the programmer does not have to define it. However, a powerful generic language should permit a programmer to redefine subscript or to define other functions of this general nature.

To address this specific/generic problem, a language and its translator must have three things:

1. A general type notation that lets the programmer specify type constraints when she or he uses generic modes to declare a function type. For example, the programmer must be able to state that one argument must be the same type as another, or must have a specific structural relationship to another argument's type.

2. Both the dispatcher and the programmer must have access to the information on the BIND links and in the type objects for typed submodes. Type operations such as "type of ", "value of binding", and "dimension of" must be supported.

3. The dispatcher must perform type calculations, using these type operations. The purpose of these calculations is twofold: to guarantee that any specified type constraints are obeyed, and to deduce the most specific information available about the return types.

In the discussion of Miranda, in Section 18.3, we saw the use of the symbols "$*$", "$**$", etc. to denote mode variables, and mode expressions such as "$[*]$" to denote a list of a generic type. These asterisk symbols and expressions serve purpose (1), above; they permit the programmer to specify constraints (for example, "is the same type as" and "is a list of base type the same as") in a generic function declaration.

Requirement (2), above, is partially met in Ada by providing many predefined type operations which, essentially, let the programmer (or the system) access most of the fields of a type object. Using this information, a programmer-defined function could do things that are built in and nonextensible in traditional languages, such as bounds checks, variations on the subscript function, and the like.

Miranda accomplishes part of goal (2) by permitting the programmer to specify patterns for use by the dispatcher. What seems to be missing is the ability to access the instantiation parameters for parameterized modes. (Ada does not have this problem because all instantiation is done before the program is compiled, and a program has full knowledge of the instantiation parameters used.)

Requirement (3) is invisible to the programmer; it does not affect the language syntax or the list of defined operations. However, it affects the semantics in a major way. A dispatcher that is able to do this will permit much more general use of generics and still be able to maintain strong typing.

Mechanisms like these form part of the semantic basis of Haskell and Aleph, and are sure to play a central role in languages of the future.

EXERCISES

1. Why can't we use two structurally dissimilar types to represent one external domain in a traditional strongly typed language?
2. How do generic functions solve this problem?
3. What is a generic mode? How is a generic mode different from a C++ base class?
4. How do Ada's predefined modes limit the programmer?
5. What are submode links? Promises? Supermodes?

6. Why are domains with multiple representations less practical to use than domains with a single representation?

7. What is the danger of providing a general coercion facility?

8. Why should the dispatcher's coercion facility care whether a function is a conversion or a cast?

9. What is a "best match" in dispatching in older languages?

10. Why is dispatching more complex in modern languages?

11. "A subrange type can inherit functions from a base type." Explain.

12. How does a class hierarchy provide broader support for subdomains? Be specific.

13. What is the difference between the handling of a C++ function definition placed inside a class and outside it?

14. When is a derived module considered opaque? How is this accomplished?

15. Why is the compatibility of pointer types throughout the levels of a hierarchy essential?

16. What is a virtual class? Why is it necessary?

17. Why must dispatching of virtual classes be delayed until link or run time? How is this accomplished in C++?

18. What are the benefits of virtual functions? The costs?

19. What is the dispatching rule for function inheritance in C++?

20. Why is the definition of a constructor function for a derived class more complicated than for a base class?

21. What is a polymorphic type? Object? Function?

22. How was polymorphism implemented in older languages?

23. What are the differences between explicit domain testing and strong typing?

24. How do modern functional languages support generics?

25. How are types of objects deduced in Miranda? Explain.

26. In Miranda, what is a pattern? A constructor?

Bibliography

ABELSON, H., ET AL. The revised revised report on Scheme or an UnCommon Lisp. AI Memo 848, MIT Artificial Intelligence Laboratory, Cambridge, Massachusetts, August 1985.

ABELSON, H., AND G. J. SUSSMAN. *Structure and Interpretation of Computer Programs*. The MIT Press, Cambridge, Massachusetts, 1985.

Adobe Systems Incorporated. *PostScript Language Reference Manual*. Addison-Wesley, Reading, Massachusetts, 2nd edition, 1990.

ALLEN, J. R., M. E. BURKE, AND J. F. JOHNSON. *Thinking About TLC-Logo*. CBS College Publishing, New York, 1983.

ARDEN, B., B. GALLER, AND R. GRAHAM. *The Michigan Algorithm Decoder*. Computing Center, University of Michigan, 1963.

BARNES, J. G. P. *Programming in Ada*. Addison-Wesley, Wokingham, England, 3rd edition, 1989.

BÖHM, C., AND G. JACOPINI. Flow diagrams, Turing machines, and languages with only two formation rules. *Communications of the ACM*, 9(5):366–371, May 1966.

BOOCH, GRADY. *Software Engineering with Ada*. Benjamin/Cummings, Menlo Park, California, 1987.

Borland International, Scotts Valley, California. *Turbo Pascal Reference Manual, Version 2.0*, 1984.

BRINCH HANSEN, P. The programming language concurrent Pascal. *IEEE Transactions on Software Engineering*, 1:199–206, 1975.

BRODIE, L. *Starting FORTH*. Prentice Hall, Englewood Cliffs, New Jersey, 2nd edition, 1987.

BROWN, J. A., S. PAKIN, AND R. P. POLIVKA. *APL2 at a Glance*. Prentice Hall, Englewood Cliffs, New Jersey, 1988.

CHURCH, A. The calculi of lambda conversion. *Annals of Mathematical Studies*, 6, 1941.

539

CLOCKSIN, W. F., AND C. S. MELLISH. *Programming in Prolog*. Springer-Verlag, Heidelberg, 1981.

COOPER, D. *Standard Pascal User Reference Manual*. W. W. Norton and Company, New York, 1983.

DALE, N., AND S. LILLY. *Pascal Plus Data Structures, Algorithms, and Advanced Programming*. D. C. Heath, Lexington, Massachusetts, 1985.

Dartmouth College Computation Center, Dartmouth, New Hampshire. *A Manual for BASIC*, 1965.

DIJKSTRA, E. W. Programming considered as a human activity. In *Proceedings of IFIP Congress*, pages 213–217, Amsterdam, Netherlands, 1965. North-Holland.

——. Go To statement considered harmful. *Communications of the ACM*, 11(3):147–148, 1968.

FASEL, J. H., AND P. HUDAK. A gentle introduction to Haskell. *ACM SIGPLAN Notices*, 27(5): T1–T53, May 1992.

FISCHER, A. E. *A Semantic Basis for a Programming Language with Declarable Mode Relationships*. PhD thesis, Harvard University, 1985.

FISCHER, A. E., AND M. J. FISCHER. Mode modules as representations of domains. In *Proceedings of the ACM SIGACT/SIGPLAN Symposium on Principles of Programming Languages*, pages 139–143, October 1973.

FISCHER, A. E., AND R. P. FISCHER. Aleph implementation, 1992. Work in progress.

FREGE, G. *Begriffsschrift: A Formula Language, Modeled upon That of Arithmetic, for Pure Thought*. Halle, 1879.

GALLER, B. A., AND M. J. FISCHER. The iteration element. *Communications of the ACM*, 8(6):349, 1965.

GOLDBERG, A., AND D. ROBSON. *Smalltalk-80: The Language and Its Implementation*. Addison-Wesley, Reading, Massachusetts, 1983.

GORSLINE, G. W. *Computer Organization*. Prentice Hall, Englewood Cliffs, New Jersey, 2nd edition, 1986.

GRISS, M. L., AND A. C. HEARN. A portable LISP compiler. *Software Practice and Experience*, 11:541–605, 1981.

GRISWOLD, R. E., AND M. T. GRISWOLD. *The Icon Programming Language*. Prentice Hall, Englewood Cliffs, New Jersey, 1983.

GRISWOLD, R. E., J. F. POAGE, AND I. P. POLONSKY. *The SNOBOL 4 Programming Language*. Prentice Hall, Englewood Cliffs, New Jersey, 2nd edition, 1971.

HARBISON, S. P., AND G. L. STEELE JR. *A C Reference Manual*. Prentice Hall, Englewood Cliffs, New Jersey, 3rd edition, 1991.

HINDLEY, J. R. The principal type-scheme of an object in combinatory logic. *Transactions of the AMS*, 146:29–60, 1969.

HOLT, R. C., P. A. MATTHEWS, J. A. ROSSELET, AND J. R. CORDY. *The Turing Programming Language*. Prentice Hall, Englewood Cliffs, New Jersey, 1988.

HOROWITZ, E. *Programming Languages: A Grand Tour*. Computer Science Press, Rockville, Maryland, 2nd edition, 1985.

HUDAK, P., ET AL. Report on the programming language Haskell: A non-strict, purely functional language, version 1.2. *ACM SIGPLAN Notices*, 27(5):R1–R164, May 1992.

INMOS Limited. *occam*® *2 Reference Manual*. Prentice Hall, Hempel Hempstead, England, 1988.

KEMENY, J. G. *True BASIC*. Addison Wesley, Reading, Massachusetts, 1985.

KERNIGHAN, B. W. Why Pascal is not my favorite programming language. In A. Feuer and N. Gehani, editors, *Comparing and Assessing Programming Languages: ADA, C, Pascal*, pages 170–186. Prentice Hall, Englewood Cliffs, New Jersey, 1984.

KERNIGHAN, B. W., AND D. M. RITCHIE. *The C Programming Language*. Prentice Hall, Englewood Cliffs, New Jersey, 2nd edition, 1988.

KESSLER, R. *LISP, Objects, and Symbolic Programming*. Scott, Foresman and Company, Glenview, Illinois, 1988.

LANDIN, P. J. The mechanical evaluation of expressions. *Computer Journal*, 6(4):308–320, 1964.

MCCARTHY, J., ET AL. *LISP 1.5 Programmer's Manual*. M.I.T. Press, Cambridge, Massachusetts, 2nd edition, 1962.

MEISSNER, L. P., AND E. I. ORGANICK. *FORTRAN 77 Featuring Structured Programming*. Addison-Wesley, Reading, Massachusetts, 1980.

MILNER, R. A theory of type polymorphism in programming. *Journal of Computer and System Sciences*, 17:348–375, 1978.

MORRIS, W., editor. *The American Heritage Dictionary of the English Language*. Houghton Mifflin Co., Boston, 1969.

NAUR, P. Report on the algorithmic language ALGOL 60. *Communications of the ACM*, 3:299–314, 1960.

NAUR, P., AND M. WOODGER. Revised report on the algorithmic language ALGOL 60. *Communications of the ACM*, 6:1–20, 1963.

NEWELL, A., editor. *Information Processing Language-V Manual*. The RAND Corporation. Prentice Hall, Englewood Cliffs, New Jersey, 1961.

Oracle Corporation, Belmont, California. *Introduction to SQL*, 1987.

PERLIS, A. J., AND S. RUGABER. The APL idiom list. Research Report 87, Yale University, Department of Computer Science, April 1977.

PEYTON JONES, S. L. *The Implementation of Functional Programming Languages*. Prentice-Hall, 1987.

POLIVKA, R. P., AND S. PAKIN. *APL: The Language and Its Usage*. Prentice Hall, Englewood Cliffs, New Jersey, 1975.

POUNTAIN, D., AND D. MAY. *A Tutorial Introduction to occam*® *Programming*. BSP Professional Books, London, 1988.

REYNOLDS, J. C. Gedanken—a simple typeless language based on the principle of completeness and the reference concept. *Communications of the ACM*, 13:308–319, May 1970.

ROBINSON, J. A. Logic and logic programming. *Communications of the ACM*, pages 40–65, March 1992.

ROCKEY, C. J. *Structured PL/1 Programming*. Wm. C. Brown, Dubuque, Iowa, 2nd edition, 1985.

SAMMET, J. E. *Programming Languages*: *History and Fundamentals*. Prentice Hall, Englewood Cliffs, New Jersey, 1969.

SETHI, R. *Programming Languages*: *Concepts and Constructs*. Addison-Wesley, Reading, Massachusetts, 1989.

SLADE, S. *The T Programming Language*. Prentice Hall, Englewood Cliffs, New Jersey, 1987.

STANDISH, T. PPL—an extensible language that failed. *ACM SIGPLAN Notices*, pages 144–145, December 1971.

STERN, N., AND R. STERN. *Structured COBOL Programming*. Wiley, New York, 1988.

STROUSTRUP, B. *The C++ Programming Language*. Addison-Wesley, Reading, Massachusetts, 1986.

TURNER, DAVID. An overview of Miranda. *ACM SIGPLAN Notices*, December 1986.

United States Department of Defense. *Reference Manual for the Ada Programming Language*: *Proposed Standard Document*, July 1980.

VAN WIJNGAARDEN, A., ET AL. Report on the algorithmic language ALGOL 68. *Numerische Mathematik*, 14:79–218, 1969.

WEGBREIT, B. *Studies in Extensible Programming Languages*. PhD thesis, Harvard University, 1970.

——. The treatment of data types in EL/1. *Communications of the ACM*, 17(5):251–264, May 1974.

WILENSKY, R. *LISPcraft*. W. W. Norton and Company, New York, 1984.

WIRTH, N. The design of a Pascal compiler. *Software Practice and Experience*, 1:309–333, 1971.

——. The programming language Pascal. *Acta Informatica*, 1:35–63, 1971.

——. Modula: A language for modular multiprogramming. Technical Report TR18, ETH Institute for Informatics, March 1976.

Index